Modern Banking
in Theory and Practice

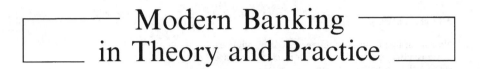

Modern Banking in Theory and Practice

Shelagh Heffernan

Professor of Banking and Finance
City University Business School, London

JOHN WILEY AND SONS
Chichester • New York • Brisbane • Toronto • Singapore

Published 1996 by John Wiley & Sons Ltd,
Baffins Lane, Chichester,
West Sussex PO19 1UD, England

National   01243 779777
International   (+44) 1243 779777

Reprinted December 1996, March 1998, October 2000, September 2001, September 2002

Other Wiley Editorial Offices

John Wiley & Sons, Inc., 605 Third Avenue,
New York, NY 10158-0012, USA

Jacaranda Wiley Ltd, 33 Park Road, Milton,
Queensland 4064, Australia

John Wiley & Sons (Canada) Ltd, 22 Worcester Road,
Rexdale, Ontario M9W 1L1, Canada

John Wiley & Sons (Asia) Pte Ltd, 2 Clementi Loop #02-01
Jin Xing Distripark, Singapore 129809

Library of Congress Cataloging-in-Publication Data

Heffernan, Shelagh A., 1956–
    Modern banking in theory and practice / by Shelagh Heffernan.
      p.   cm.
    Includes bibliographical references (p.   ) and index.
    ISBN 0-471-96208-2 (cloth : alk. paper). — ISBN 0-471-96209-0
    (pbk : alk. paper)
      1. Banks and banking.   I. Title.
    HG1601.H44   1996
    332.1–dc20   95-44830
                                                    CIP

British Library Cataloguing in Publication Data

A catalogue record for this book is available from the British Library

ISBN 0-471-96208-2 (Cloth)
ISBN 0-471-96209-0 (paperback)

Typeset in 10/12pt Times by Keyword Typesetting Services, Wallington, Surrey
Printed and bound in Great Britain by Antony Rowe Ltd., Chippenham, Wiltshire
This book is printed on acid-free paper responsibly manufactured from sustainable forestation,
for which at least two trees are planted for each one used for paper production.

To Peggy Heffernan, and in memory of John Heffernan

Contents

5 Management of Risks in Banking

Contents _____ xi

8 Strategic Issues for Banks

9 Case Studies

Acknowledgements

Many individuals have helped and/or commented on different parts of the book. Three anonymous referees made some useful suggestions, which were incorporated into the text. Stephen Funnell, a BSc Banking and International Finance graduate (1996), helped with the collection of data and the compilation of stylised facts at the end of Chapter 1. Kim Nam, a BSc Banking and International Finance graduate (1995), helped to update the case studies, chased up references, and compiled the author and subject indices. Thanks go to Mario Levis, Director of Research, who administers the CUBS Research Award System, which funded these two students during the summers of 1994 and 1995, respectively. I am also grateful to my colleagues in the Department of Banking and Finance, who provide the stimulating atmosphere which allows one to write papers and books. The banking undergraduates and the MBA Finance students at City University Business School acted (unknowingly!) as guinea pigs for much of the material that appears in the book. I am also grateful to Roy Batchelor, Alec Chrystal, Charles Goodhart, Alfred Kenyon, David Llewellyn, Shiv Mathur, Richard Taffler, and Peter Sinclair, who provided useful comments on different parts of the book.

Very special thanks to Ingo Walter (Charles Simon Professor of Applied Economics, Director of the New York University Salomon Center and Swiss Bank Corporation Professor of International Management at INSEAD), who, as Director of the NYU Salomon Center gave permission to use the 10 case studies that make up Chapter 9. Originally, these case studies appeared in the New York University Salomon Center Case Series in Banking and Finance. The authors of the original cases are Roy C. Smith (Clinical Professor of Finance and International Business at the Stern School of Business, New York University; Limited Partner of Goldman Sachs and Company), Anthony Morris (doctoral candidate at the Stern School of Business, New York University), Richard Freedman (Professor of Management at the Stern School of Business, New York University), Jill Vohr (doctoral candidate in Management at the Stern School of Business, New York University), Richard Herring (Professor of Finance at the Wharton School, University of Pennsylvania), Antony Sinclair (MBA Finance from the Stern School of Business, New York University, currently with an independent investment bank specialising in emerging market transactions in Budapest), and Ingo Walter. All of these cases were edited and updated by Shelagh Heffernan; the questions at the end of each case were set by Shelagh Heffernan.

All errors and omissions in the text, are, of course, my responsibility.

Introduction and Guide to the Book

This book is about the theory and practice of banking, and its prospects for the future, in the new millennium. The book is written for banking and finance undergraduates, MBA candidates choosing an option in banking, and banking professionals who wish to deepen and broaden their knowledge of the modern theory and practice of banking.

Unlike many other books in this area, this text is devoted to the *micro* issues of banking. There are many excellent texts that study the macroeconomics of banking, and the role of financial institutions in a monetary economy. However, there are very few books that provide readers with a systematic treatment of the key micro banking issues. This area of banking is important, and it is hoped this book goes some way to rectifying the deficiency.

Bank professionals require a thorough grounding in the micro foundations of banking, if they are to make important managerial decisions, or implement banking policies. Take the most radical question: Why do we have banks at all? Answering this question begins to show how banks should evolve and adapt— or fail.

There are a number of important themes running throughout the text.

- Information costs and the demand for liquidity explain why banks find it profitable to intermediate between borrower and lender.
- Like firms in other sectors, banks want to maximise profits. It is the way banks earn their profits, through the management of financial risks, that differentiates them from non-banking firms.
- The central intermediary role played by a bank is evolving through time, from the traditional intermediation between borrowers and lenders, through to more sophisticated intermediation as risk managers.
- In banking, mergers, acquisitions, or the formation of financial conglomerates do not necessarily result in scale economies and synergies, because there are numerous measurement problems, and the empirical evidence is mixed.
- In retail banking, banks can develop quite sophisticated pricing strategies, which take advantage of consumer inertia, and increase profitability. The global nature of wholesale banking means it is a far more competitive market.

and also the Euromarkets which transformed the way global capital moves from country to country. Foreign direct investment previously had been a main conduit for flows of capital flowed between countries; euromarkets provided large new channels for the global movement of capital.

Attention then turns to the relationship between multinational and wholesale banking. The Japanese and American banks that dominate global markets are singled out for special attention, and results of empirical studies which identify the factors that explain multinational banking activity are discussed. Chapter 2 goes on to consider the welfare costs and benefits of international banking. Though there are resource costs from globalisation, it is generally accepted there has been a net welfare gain. The next section takes a closer look at the performance of the major international banks in the 1980s. Using standard measures such as profitability, major international banks have performed relatively poorly, due largely to the deterioration of the quality of assets, beginning with developing country loans in the early 1980s and followed by non-performing corporate and property loans in the early 1990s. These banks have tried to improve their performance by cutting back on global lending and concentrating more on fee-earning businesses.

The main objective of Chapter 3 is to provide an overview of bank structures and related issues in industrialised countries, developing economies, and emerging markets in Eastern Europe. Recent trends show a relative decline for American banks and the rapid globalisation of the Japanese banks, though recent problems may mean this does not continue. Chapter 3 also reviews bank structure in the United States, Japan, and the European Union, with a special section on Britain. In the UK, the old specialised firms offering differentiated products have been subject to integration. Traditional boundaries have been eroded. The forces behind these changes are discussed, as is the UK's emphasis on self-regulation of non-banking financial firms.

The idiosyncrasies of the American banking structure are traced to numerous 20th-century banking regulations, ranging from controls on the offerings of bank and non-bank financial products, to the separation of investment and commercial banking, and limits on intra- and interstate banking. The US banking system is concentrated, even though there are over 27 000 deposit-taking firms. By contrast, banking systems in other industrialised countries normally have three to five key banks, offering a wide range of wholesale and retail banking services. There are some leading global money centre and investment banks, but they do not dominate the US banking system in the way that leading banks do elsewhere. The US banking structure is fragmented, inward-looking, and in some respects, outdated. Take, for example, the payments system. In 1994, this author sent a US dollar cheque (drawn on a US dollar account held in Toronto) to one of the Federal Reserve banks, in payment for an annual conference hosted by them. It was not possible to pay by credit card. The cheque was returned several weeks later with an "unable to clear" stamp on it, and an accompanying remark, "we are unable to process an International check"!

Reform of the US system is a long and slow process. It was not until July 1994 that new legislation removed key obstacles to interstate banking. Several attempts to eliminate the division between investment and commercial banking have been blocked by powerful lobbies. But there is some hope that Congress will succeed in implementing this reform before the end of the century.

The Japanese banking system is known for its high degree of segmentation along functional lines, and the close supervision of banks by the Ministry of Finance, in conjunction with the Bank of Japan. Deregulation of interest rates, a 1992 reform package aimed at reducing segmentation, the phasing out of fixed commissions on the stock market, and equal treatment of foreign banks should gradually remove many of the barriers that exist. The Japanese banking structure itself is under serious threat, because of large holdings of bad debt, now estimated at close to $500 billion. The largest Japanese banks will likely withstand the problem, but some smaller banks and credit institutions are quite vulnerable. To date, there has been no taxpayer-funded bail-out, though it is a possibility. The role of banks in *keiretsu* is also being undermined, as manufacturing firms seek out cheaper sources of finance in liberalised financial markets, at home and abroad.

In the European Union (EU), the integration of the different banking systems into a single banking market is quite a long way off, though much of the regulation to create a single market is in place. Chapter 3 considers some of the potential barriers to an integrated European banking market, such as differences in taxation, and regulatory, fiscal, cultural, structural, technical and legal barriers. The question of how banking prices would be affected in a single market is also discussed. Additionally, there is an important strategic issue for EU and third country banks: since most of the EU countries are already well supplied by domestic banks, is there any room for the entry of EU banks from other states in any segment of the banking market?

Issues related to developing country banking structures are also discussed in Chapter 3. Some developing economies exhibit a high degree of financial instability. Others do not. Foreign banks play an active role in a few developing countries. They are banned in others, even though there is fairly conclusive evidence that the exclusion of foreign banks makes domestic banks more profitable but less efficient. Oppressive regulation of financial markets often results in the growth of informal, unregulated financial markets, known as curb (or kerb) markets. Developing country banks share a number of common problems. Operating costs are high; unanticipated inflation can be responsible for windfall profits for the banks, which, in turn, mask inefficiencies in the system. Selective and named credit policies raise default rates among borrowers. Loan portfolio quality and asset management are often poor. Related problems include lack of accountability and training, political interference in management decisions, and regulations which limit banks to prescribed activities, and/or prohibit certain financial innovations. Using Indonesia as a case study of a country which embarked on a programme of rapid economic and banking reform, Chapter 3 gives the reader an opportunity to consider various developing country banking issues. One of the main problems experienced by Indonesia was the failure of bank risk evaluation systems to keep pace with the speed of financial reform.

funding), settlements (or payments), interest rate, market (or price), foreign exchange (or currency), gearing, sovereign, political, and operating risks. Global banking normally results in diversification of assets, but the business of risk management becomes more complex. Chapter 5 reviews important, growing, phenomena in banking, including asset securitisation, derivatives, and off-balance sheet banking. While these new methods and instruments offer banks alternative ways for managing risk, they also present a considerable challenge. For example, banks can use derivatives to hedge their own risks, to speculate on the proprietary trading account, and to advise (largely) corporate customers on the use of derivatives in corporate financial risk management. Bank management needs to have adequate internal controls, and to understand the uses of derivatives, the implications of customer advice on risk management, and how securitisation or an increase in off-balance sheet banking will affect the bank's bottom line. There are allegations of well-known banks giving poor advice to large corporations on the use of risk management tools.

Chapter 5 also examines how banks manage their financial risks. The key principles of credit risk management are reviewed. A case study on the sovereign debt problem exemplifies these. Chapter 7 picks up on this theme, when a poor-quality loan portfolio (usually caused by lack of diversification of loans and collateral) is shown to provide the main explanation for why a bank fails. Chapter 5 also describes the traditional asset-liability management methods for the management of interest rate and liquidity risks. Gap, Duration, and Duration Gap analyses are explained, and the chapter briefly considers currency risk management. The value added and the stress simulation approaches to the management of market risk are also described, and there is a brief look at the role of financial innovation in risk management. Chapter 5 also contains a general discussion of three principles of risk management for any bank: diversification, risk management systems, and the risk management process. It goes on to consider the organisational structure of "British Bank plc", based on one of the major clearing banks in the UK. Finally, Chapter 5 covers the political aspects of risk analysis, reviewing quantitative models used to identify political variables which affect bankers' perceptions of creditworthiness or the probability of a country having to reschedule its debt.

Chapter 6 turns to the regulation of banks by government authorities. It begins by explaining why banks are singled out for special regulation—their unique position in a national economy. They are a classic case for government intervention, because bank failures can create substantial external or social costs, especially when a failure threatens the safety of the financial system. There is a comprehensive review of prudential and related bank regulations in the UK and the USA. The comparison of these two, very different systems sets the framework for understanding bank regulation in any country. The UK review illustrates the evolution of a private bank into a central bank, which gradually assumed responsibility for prudential regulation of banks. But this objective can be at odds with a policy of achieving price stability through monetary control. This conflict is one reason why some countries, like

Germany, assign the two functions to separate, independent institutions. The UK is also characterised by comparatively little formal banking legislation, supervision through moral suasion or consensus management, and the use of private independent auditors to evaluate banks. For example, the 1979 Banking Act which introduced depositor protection, was the first specific banking law in the UK. It was revised in 1987. The Bank of England is responsible for granting bank status and for supervision.

The USA employs quite a different system of bank regulation and supervision. American banks are subject to an extensive range of statutes, which govern everything from bank examination and branch banking, to the functional separation of banks. There is no consensus approach to the supervision of banks. The USA was the first country to introduce deposit protection legislation. Many of the laws enacted, including the Federal Reserve, Glass-Steagall, McFadden, and Bank Merger Acts, reflect a commitment to discourage collusive behaviour, either between different private banks, or between the Federal Reserve and the banks it supervises. Recently, there have been attempts to reform the banking system, to bring the US bank structure closer into line with those of other industrialised economies.

Chapter 6 also looks at the regulations that accompany the creation of an European Union single banking market. EU banks, provided they are recognised as credit institutions in one state, have a banking passport which means they can operate in other EU states, without seeking host country permission to do so. The European Commission has implemented many directives (EU laws) which, it is hoped, will create a single banking market. These include the second Banking Directive, two directives which effectively require all EU banks to conform to the 8% risk assets ratio, and directives on deposit insurance and capital adequacy. The directives set minimum standards, and the programme hopes to achieve mutual recognition, as opposed to harmonisation, of banking laws. Large gaps exist in the area of EU prudential regulation. If the European Central Bank (ECB) eventually assumes responsibility for monetary control and price stability, there remains the question of the degree to which responsibility for prudential supervision passes to the ECB or remains in the hands of "state" central banks. Whatever the final arrangement, the ECB will have to, at some point, confront the conflict of objectives between price and financial system stability.

Chapter 6 goes on to review regulation of Japanese banks. The Ministry of Finance is the principal regulatory authority. There are six bureaux within the MoF; they are responsible for very close supervision of banks and other financial institutions, ranging from control of interest rates (phased out in late 1994) to the licensing of financial institutions, and ruling on acceptable activities these firms can engage in. As in Britain, moral suasion is an important part of supervision, but the interpretation of the term is different. In the UK, it is synonymous with consensus banking, whereas Japan's version has the MoF, under regulatory guidance, interpreting the relevant laws as they apply to banks and other financial institutions. In the post-war period, the MoF and Bank of Japan have coerced healthy banks into merging with weak ones, to

strategy. Strategies should be looking at the means by which the firm can create and sustain a competitive advantage in the banking market. This may range from the production of low-cost commodity products, such as standard deposit or loan accounts, which attract customers because of a competitive price, to sophisticated, differentiated, risk management products offered to finance directors of companies, which, if difficult to copy, can earn the firm a high return.

Chapter 8 concludes by considering the management challenges in banking. First, faced by a rising number of players, banks must formulate strategies to create and sustain competitive advantage in all existing and potential future markets. Operating costs should be reduced, and banks must choose from a glittering array of new technology. Global banking operations are increasingly subject to more regulation, in addition to greater competition. Finally, given that the human resource component is an important part of the success or failure of a bank, banks must adopt rigorous recruitment policies. There may be some low-priced commodity products where customer contact is of little importance, but for the vast majority of products and markets, the opposite is true—banks should focus on the introduction of successful products and services.

In Chapter 9, readers are given the opportunity to apply many of the concepts and ideas covered in the text to 10 different case studies. Each case introduces key themes, which should serve to enhance the reader's understanding of different parts of the text. The Goldman Sachs case covers the differences between relationship and transactional banking, how diversification into off-balance sheet banking may still leave a bank exposed to volatile interest rates, how a corporate culture is defined, and the role of architecture, as defined by Kay (1993). The case studies on American Express, Sakura, and Bancomer raise important issues related to economies of scale and scope. American Express teaches some strategy lessons, and the role of personalities in a large financial conglomerate. The Sakura and Nomura cases give readers a practical insight into the workings of financial firms within the tightly regulated Japanese financial structure. The Sakura case provides a good example of the effects on a bank of a speculative bubble; Nomura illustrates the role of *keiretsu* in the Japanese system.

The Bancomer case pinpoints the potential problems with banking in a developing or emerging economy, issues to consider in the event of privatisation, how a macroeconomic crisis can undermine the value of an otherwise healthy bank, and the effects of political risk on banking. The Kidder Peabody case raises the issue of how synergy might be achieved, and more generally, covers problems encountered by the financial subsidiary of a multinational corporation.

Causes of bank failure and issues relating to bank regulation are demonstrated in the Continental and Crédit Lyonnais (CL) cases. The CL case also touches on a difficult issue which the European Union will, eventually, have to confront—the extent to which EU states should be allowed to support failing banks. CL also shows how nationalised banks are subject to government interference—for example, CL was used to provide indirect subsidies to other, troubled, state enterprises. Both cases illustrate how management can be a critical factor in the failure of the bank.

The Schweizer Universal case highlights some potentially difficult problems for Swiss banks, as the country opts out of the EU's single financial market. It illustrates how a strategic plan (in this case, Plan 2001) can be affected by unanticipated events, and gives the reader an opportunity to judge the applicability of the various bank strategy models, explained in Chapter 8. The final case in the chapter is Bankers Trust. It portrays a bank which changed its strategy comprehensively, and how it went about implementing the strategic change. The case shows the problems a bank might encounter if customer focus takes a back seat to product focus. Readers can see how Bankers Trust increased its use of derivatives, and how risk management systems were revised to reflect this new off-balance sheet business. Finally, the case demonstrates why it is vital for a bank to understand how derivatives and other off-balance sheet instruments are being used, especially when advising large corporate customers.

The presentation of this book is organised to give the reader/instructor a flexible means of reading and/or teaching. The material is largely non-technical—it is the ideas and concepts that are challenging, not the statistics. It is advisable to cover Chapter 1 and, possibly, Chapter 2, first, but subsequent chapters can be taken in the order chosen by the reader/instructor. Chapters 5 and 6 should be covered in sequence. If the course is being taught to undergraduates with little or no relevant work experience, then Chapters 3 to 8 should be taught first, though the subject order can be varied. The case studies can be taught either concurrently, or as a separate set of exercises at the end of the subject lectures. MBA students taking an option in banking may be sufficiently experienced in the financial sector to embark on the case studies first, though the relevant chapters should be used to back up the cases, because on average an MBA group will tend to be long on experience but short on knowledge of the foundations of banking. The questions at the end of each case study are set to test not only the reader's command of the case, but also whether he/she is able to link these cases to the ideas covered in the text.* Students with background courses in introductory economics and quantitative methods will be able to progress more quickly than those without. It is possible to cover the material in the absence of an economics and/or quantitative course, by deviating to teach some basics, from time to time. For example, in Chapter 1, if a group has no economics, the instructor may find it useful to explain the basic ideas of supply, demand, and the market, before progressing to Figures 1 and 2. In Chapter 4, it may be necessary to give a brief talk about simple regression analysis before explaining structure-conduct-performance tests.

---

*A manual with answers to the case questions is available to instructors who adopt this book as their main text.

1
The Modern Banking Firm

INTRODUCTION

The purpose of this chapter is to examine the theoretical reasons for why banks exist, to consider modern banking in the context of the traditional model, and to review key statistics on banking activities in the industrialised economies. The chapter is organised as follows. First, there is a review of the traditional theory of banking, addressing the question of why banks exist. The role of banks as financial intermediaries is explored in the next section, which also discusses the banks' organisation, drawing on the theories used to explain the structure of profit maximising firms. There is then a review of the diversification of banking activities, which is followed by a consideration of whether banks will disappear in the next century. The chapter goes on to look at how bank performance is measured, and considers the results of relevant studies. Finally, this chapter presents a cocktail of stylised figures on banks in industrialised countries, with a view to providing readers with an overview of modern banks as the century draws to a close.

WHY DO BANKS EXIST? THE TRADITIONAL THEORY OF BANKING

To answer the question, "Why do banks exist?", it is useful to begin with a definition of a bank, using a very simple model of the traditional role banks have played in the economy, acting as *intermediaries* between depositors and borrowers.

Banks are normally distinguished from other types of financial firms in that they provide deposit and loan products. The deposit products pay out money on demand, or after some notice. Thus, banks are in the business of managing liabilities, and, in the process, banks also lend money, thereby creating bank assets. Alternatively, one can argue banks are in the business of managing assets, which are funded by deposits or other liabilities. As is demonstrated in the next section, the intermediation function normally results in banks offering a payments service to their customers.

In modern banking systems, there exists a whole range of specialist banks, which focus on niche markets, and generalist banks, which offer a wide range of banking and other financial products, as diverse as deposit accounts, loan products, real estate services, stockbroking, and life assurance. For example, there are firms which act as "private bankers", accepting deposits from high net worth individuals, and investing in a broad range of financial assets. Merchant banks in the UK and investment banks in the USA have a relatively small deposit base but access a wide range of funds, from the equity, bond, and syndicated loan markets. Commercial banking, an American term, consists of wholesale and retail banking activities, but not investment banking. Universal banks, the norm in Germany, combine investment, wholesale, and retail banking services, and offer non-banking financial products, such as insurance. However, the differences in the functions of banks do not alter the fundamental definition of banks, that they perform an intermediary role in an economy, by accepting deposits and making loans.

To illustrate the traditional intermediary function of a bank, consider Figure 1, a simple model of the credit market. On the vertical axis is the rate of interest; the volume of deposits/loans is on the horizontal axis. Assume the interest rate is *exogenously* given (for example, by government regulation, or a market rate is determined on the international markets, independent of the actions of individual banks). In this case, the bank faces an upward sloping supply of deposits curve (S_d). There is also the bank's supply of loans curve (S_l) showing that the bank will offer more loans as interest rates rise, though this curve may be discontinuous at one point because of adverse selection (as

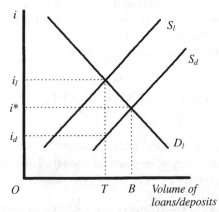

i_l - i_d: Bank interest differential between the loan rate (i_l) and the deposit rate (i_d), which covers the cost of the bank's intermediation.

S_d: Supply of deposits curve

S_l: Supply of loans curve

D_l: Demand for loans curve

OT: Volume of loans supplied by customers

I^*: Market-clearing interest rate in the absence of intermediation costs

Figure 1 Simple model of the banking firm

interest rates rise, riskier borrowers apply for loans)[†] and adverse incentives (higher interest rates encourage borrowers to undertake riskier activities). D_l represents the demand for loans, which falls as interest rates increase.

In equilibrium, the bank pays a deposit rate of i_d and charges a loan rate of i_l. The volume of deposits and loans is OT, and OT loans are supplied. The interest margin is equal to $i_l - i_d$ and must cover the institution's non-deposit costs, the cost of capital, the risk premium charged on loans, tax payments, and the institution's profits. Interest margins should narrow, the greater is the competition for loans.

In the absence of intermediation costs, i^* is the market-clearing interest rate; the interest rate that would prevail if there were no costs associated with bringing borrower and lender together. The volume of business would rise to OB. But there are intermediation costs; for example, in the absence of a bank, the lender would have to estimate the riskiness of the borrower and charge the premium plus the costs of the risk assessment. Provided a bank can offer the lowest cost of intermediation, its services will be sought after. However, a bank may lose traditional sources of business, such as lending to highly rated corporates, because these corporations find that they can raise funds by issuing bonds, and the cost of borrowing by bond issue is cheaper than borrowing from a bank.

Figure 1 does not allow for the other bank activities most modern banks undertake, such as off-balance sheet business and fee-earning business. However, the same principle applies. Provided the bank can offer these new services at a lower cost than that which two parties incur if they arrange the deal themselves, there is a reason for the existence of a bank. On the other hand, banks will not offer banking services unless they are profitable. Figure 2 illustrates how banks supply fee-based services. The demand and supply curves

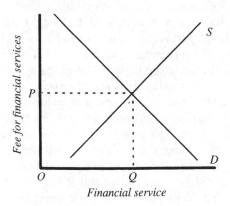

P: Price for fee-based service
Q: Quantity demanded and supplied in equilibrium

Figure 2 Fee-based financial services

[†]The problem of adverse selection is discussed in more detail below.

are for a fee-based product, which can be anything from deposit box facilities to arranging a syndicated loan. The demand and supply curves are like any other product, and the market-clearing price, P, is determined by the intersection of the demand and supply curves. The degree of competition in the market will determine how competitive the price is. The microeconomic aspects of competition in banking are discussed in Chapter 4.

To summarise, all modern banks act as intermediaries between borrowers and lenders, but they may do so in a variety of different ways, from the traditional function of taking deposits and lending a percentage of these deposits, to fee-based financial services. In the next section, the question of why firms play an intermediary role is considered.

BANKS AND FINANCIAL INTERMEDIATION

The Importance of the Intermediary Function

In the previous section, a definition of a bank was provided and the intermediary function of banks explained. However, there remains the question: why is it that we observe profit-maximising firms offering the intermediary function? Why can't borrowers and lenders come together, without an intermediary? The answer is twofold. First, the presence of information costs undermines the ability of a potential lender to find the most appropriate borrower, in the absence of intermediation. Second, borrowers and lenders have different liquidity preferences.

There are four types of information costs. *Search costs* will exist whenever there is a contract between two parties. Transactors and transactees have to search out, obtain information about, select, meet, and negotiate with other parties to a contract. When it comes to bringing borrowers and lenders together, the individual parties concerned would have to incur these *costs* if a bank did not. *Verification costs* also exist because before money is loaned out, lenders must verify the accuracy of information being provided by the borrower. Asymmetry of information between borrower and lender will give rise to a problem of *adverse selection*, which will cause inefficient allocation in markets. Suppose a borrower has more information than the lender on his/ her ability to repay a loan. The presence of adverse selection means a bank cannot just raise interest rates to compensate for the riskiness of a borrower, because borrowers who know they are likely to default on the loan will be content to negotiate a higher rate. Jaffee and Russell (1976), Leland and Pyle (1977), and Stiglitz and Weiss (1981) consider adverse selection as it applies to banking.*

Monitoring costs are also created because once a loan is negotiated, the activities of the borrower must be monitored, to ensure it is possible to

_____
*For a general treatment of adverse selection, see Akerloff (1970).

distinguish between legitimate and unsound reasons for a borrower missing, say, a payment date. Diamond (1984) elaborates on this theme.

In any contract, either of the parties to the contract may breach its conditions, and the injured party has to take action to either enforce the contract or seek compensation in the event of breach of contract. Thus, contracts carry *enforcement costs*. When money is loaned by one party to another, it is typically the borrower who is unable to meet the commitments as promised. For example, a borrower may refuse to adhere to an agreed schedule of debt repayments. If it is not possible to renegotiate the loan conditions, the lender will have to take action to recover the loan.

These four types of information costs will be incurred by any lender. If a bank can, through its intermediary function, allow lenders (depositors) to offer loans with lower associated information costs than they would incur if they tried to negotiate with a borrower directly, then individuals will choose to make deposits at a bank. Borrowers will seek out banks if the search (and possibly enforcement) costs associated with negotiating a loan are lower than if the borrower sought out an individual.

Unlike an individual lender, the bank may enjoy informational economies of scope. *Economies of scope* are said to exist when two or more products can be jointly produced at a lower cost than if the same products are produced individually.* *Informational economies of scope in lending* mean banks can pool a portfolio of assets which have a lower default risk but the same expected return than what would be possible if depositors had tried to lend funds directly. Banks may be able to gain informational economies of scope in lending decisions because they have access to privileged information when making a lending decision; banks can also obtain information on future borrowers because they hold accounts at the bank. It is often not possible to bundle up and sell this information, so banks use it internally, to increase the size of their loan portfolio.

Banks design and implement loan contracts to improve the prospects of the loan being repaid. For example, a bank might write restrictive covenants into the loan contract to give it some control over the firm's management. In addition, it will demand collateral as insurance for unforeseen developments after the loan contract is agreed.

Differences in liquidity preferences also explain why banks exist. Banks transform illiquid assets into liquid liabilities. It is typical for firms in the business sector to want to borrow funds and either repay them in line with the expected returns of an investment project, which may not be realised for several years after the investment. By lending funds, savers are actually agreeing to forgo present consumption in favour of consumption at some date in the future. Either the borrowing or the lending (depositor) parties may change their minds because of unexpected events. If banks are able to pool a large number of borrowers and savers, it is likely both parties are going to be

---

*In the business strategy literature, the term "synergy" is often used instead of "economies of scope". For a detailed discussion of this point, see Chapter 4.

satisfied, because the banks have the necessary liquidity. Thus, *liquidity* is an important service a bank offers to its customers, and if it can offer this service at a lower cost than what would be incurred in the absence of bank intermediation, borrowers and lenders alike will demand the services of the bank. It is this aspect of banking which differentiates banks from other financial firms offering near bank and non-bank financial services, such as unit trusts, insurance, and real estate services. It also explains why banks are singled out for prudential regulation; the claims on a bank function as money, hence there is a public goods element to the services banks offer.

There is a link between the payments (more generally, liquidity) service a bank offers and its lending, even though the latter activity means banks are holding what are largely illiquid assets in their portfolios. Depositors earn a rate of return on their deposits, but have access to liquidity. Loans give borrowers more liquidity. Most customers will hold deposits in surplus (unless offered full overdraft facilities) because the cost of maintaining a balance which just matches payments demands is too high. These transaction costs mean most customers will only demand a fraction of their deposits at a given point in time. For the bank, which pools these surplus funds, there is an opportunity for profit through *fractional reserve lending*, that is, lending out money at an interest rate which is higher than what the bank pays on the deposit, after allowing for the riskiness of the loan and the cost of intermediation. Therefore, bank intermediation and payments services are inextricably linked. Banks can profit by combining payment and intermediation services to their customers, since the payment function of money overlaps with the store of value function of money. Additionally, banks achieve a reduction in the riskiness of a loan portfolio through risk pooling.

Even potential borrowers are likely to keep deposits at a bank if they think they are less likely to be credit-rationed when they ask for a loan. Firms may also be attracted to bank debt finance over other types of finance because it signals to the market that the customer is creditworthy, enabling the firm to gain cheap sources of funds from other sources (Fama, 1985). A related contribution was made by Stiglitz and Weiss (1988), who argued that a loan made to a firm by a reputable bank was a signal to others that the firm is likely to stay in business, encouraging customers and suppliers to enter into long-term relationships with the firm.

Lewis (1991) argued that in financial markets, information and liquidity problems are overcome either by organised markets, where contracts and trading are relatively standardised, or by informal markets which are created by or exist within financial firms. For example, stockbroking firms operate in organised markets by making markets in certain stocks; banks as lenders operate in informal markets, because the loan decision-making process is internal to the bank organisation.

Thus, one may also think of bank products as a collection of contracts. Traditionally, banks offered contracts which differ from those which would be exchanged on organised markets. For example, because banks "borrow short and lend long", firms can negotiate loans for longer periods while savers can lend for shorter periods than would be available on organised markets. However, most modern banks are also active in organised markets, through, for example, off-balance sheet activity (see Chapter 5), or because they own a stockbroking subsidiary.

The Organisational Structure of a Bank

In the previous sections, the intermediary and payments functions identified the reasons why banks exist, but another question one needs to address is why a bank exhibits the organisational structure it does. Any profit-maximising bank shares the same objective as any other firm; so this question is best answered by drawing on the traditional models which explain firms' existence. Coase (1937), in his classic analysis, argued that the firm acted as an alternative to market transactions, as a way of organising economic activity, because some procedures are more efficiently organised by "command" (for example, assigning tasks to workers and coordinating the work) than reliance on market price. In these situations, it is more profitable to use a firm structure than to rely on market forces.

The existence of the "traditional" bank, which intermediates between borrower and lender, and which offers a payments service to its customers, fits in well with the Coase theory. The intermediary and liquidity functions of a bank are more efficiently carried out by a command organisational structure, because loans and deposits are internal to a bank. Such a structure is also efficient if banks are participating in organised markets. These ideas were developed and extended by Alchian and Demsetz (1972), who emphasised the monitoring role of the firm and its creation of incentive structures. Williamson (1980) argued that under conditions of uncertainty, a firm could economise on the costs of outside contracts.

A *principal–agent* problem exists within any firm because both internally and externally, its activities are a collection of contracts between principals and agents. The *principal–agent* problem arises if the principal (for example, the depositor) delegates some authority to the agent (for example, the bank) to act on his/her behalf. But the agent has more information about his/her own characteristics than the principal. So the principal may not get exactly what he/she wants because the task has been delegated to the bank. For depositors, customers purchasing fee-based services from the bank, and a bank's shareholders, there is the question of who monitors the bank. This is a classic problem between principal and agent; customers delegate some control over their financial affairs to an agent, who may lack the incentives to act in customers' best interests, and can plead bad luck when outcomes are poor. The principal–agent theory also explains the nature of contracts between shareholders of a bank (principal) and its management (agent), the bank (principal) and its officers (agent), and the bank (principal) and its debtors (agent).* Incentive problems are created because the principal cannot observe

---

*Readers are referred to Bhattacharya and Pfleiderer (1985), Diamond (1984), and Rees (1985).

the agent's actions (for example, bank shareholders and management) or the principal has inferior information compared to the agent (for example, the bank manager and the borrower).

Differences in information held by principal and agent can give rise to *adverse selection*, if an agent, the firm, borrows money from a bank, the principal. *Moral hazard* is another potential problem if the principal, the depositor, invests money in the agent, a bank. Moral hazard arises whenever, as a result of entering into a contract, the incentives of the two parties change, such that the riskiness of the contract is altered. There are several reasons why depositors do not monitor bank activities closely enough. First, the depositor's cost of monitoring the bank becomes very small, the larger and more diversified is the portfolio of loans. Though there will always be loan losses (they are inherent in the nature of the contract), the pooling of loans will mean the variability of losses approaches zero.* Second, deposit insurance schemes reduce the incentive of depositors to monitor the bank. If a bank can be reasonably certain a depositor either cannot or chooses not to monitor the bank's activities once the deposit is made, then the nature of the contract is altered, and the bank may undertake to invest in more risky assets than it would in the presence of close monitoring. Shareholders do have an incentive to monitor the bank's behaviour, to ensure an acceptable rate of return on the investment. Depositors may benefit from this monitoring. But shareholders also face agency problems if managerial utility functions are such that managerial action conflicts with shareholder interest.

Relationship banking can help to minimise the principal–agent and adverse selection problems arising between a lending bank and borrowers. Lender and borrower have a *relational contract*: an understanding between both parties that it might be some time before certain characteristics related to the contract can be observed. The customer establishes a relationship with a bank whereby, over an extended period of time, the customer uses the bank for its financial needs. For example, a corporate borrower may come up with a brand new production technique, the fruits of which may not be realised until some years later. The bank has to decide whether the plan is worth the credit risk. If the two have had a long-standing relationship where the individual or firm has never defaulted or run into serious financial difficulties, the bank is better able to assess the riskiness of the new venture, and therefore, more likely to enter into a loan agreement. Even though a clause in the loan agreement will mean the bank can recall the loan at any time, the borrower knows that would be highly unlikely, because of the nature of the relationship. A relational contract improves information flows between the parties, and allows the lender to gain specific knowledge about the borrower. It also allows for flexibility of response, should there be any unforeseen events.

An arm's-length *transactional* or *classical contract* is at the other extreme, and gives rise to *transactional banking*—where many banks compete for the customer's business, and the customer shops around for several banks. Little in

---

*See Diamond (1984) for more detail.

the way of relationship exists between the two parties—both sides stick to the terms of the contract. In banking, there is more scope for borrower opportunism in a relational contract, because of the information advantage the borrower normally has. The Jürgen Schneider/Deutsche Bank case* is a timely example of relationship banking gone wrong. A transactional contract deters opportunistic behaviour. Another advantage is that the contract is negotiated, so both parties can bargain over the terms. On the other hand, information flows will be significantly curtailed, and the detailed nature of the contract reduces the scope for flexibility.

Relationship banking is most evident in countries such as Japan and Germany where there are cross-shareholdings between banks and non-financial corporations. In other countries, such as the USA and the UK, classical contracts are more evident, though there is a high variance in the degree of relationship banking depending on whether it is in or out of vogue. In Japan and Germany, the close bank–corporate relationships were, in the 1970s and 1980s, praised as one of the key reasons for the success of these economies. But in the 1990s, global financial deregulation has undermined relationship banking, because it has increased the number of methods for raising corporate finance, and the number of players in the market. In Japan, the close relationship enjoyed by groups of firms (including a bank) is being undermined because Japanese banks suffered a drastic reduction in the market value of their equity portfolios due to the prolonged decline in the stock market after 1990.

DIVERSIFICATION OF BANKING ACTIVITIES

Modern banks are typically either highly specialised in a narrow range of activities, or they offer a broad range of financial services, some of which, at first sight, do not appear to conform to the principal reasons why banks exist, discussed above. It is this relatively recent development which has given rise to growing speculation that the future of banks is in jeopardy, as other types of financial firms increasingly engage in non-banking financial activities. A brief discussion of more recent financial activities of banks illustrates their consistency with the basic principles of banking, outlined earlier.

International and Multinational Banking

Many banks in OECD countries engage in international banking activities. To the extent that these activities are international extensions of the intermediary and payment functions discussed above, the presence of international banks does not contradict the basic model of banking. However, international bank-

---

*Mr Schneider was a long-standing corporate customer of Deutsche Bank, having built up a property development empire. He successfully hid growing problems in the firm and in 1994 suddenly absconded, leaving a mountain of debts. Mr Schneider and his wife are being held in a Miami jail, awaiting extradition to Germany on fraud charges.

ing is such an important aspect of modern banking that a separate chapter of this book, Chapter 2, is devoted to its principles and practice.

Financial Conglomerates

Increasingly, banks are part of financial conglomerates that are active in both informal markets and in organised financial markets. The existence of financial conglomerates does not alter the fundamental reasons of why banks exist. Like many profit-maximising organisations, banks may expand into other, non-banking financial activities as part of an overall strategy to maximise profits and shareholder value-added. (Readers can find a more extensive discussion of financial conglomerates in Chapter 6.)

Non-bank Financial Services

Banks don't just take loans and offer deposits; they typically offer a range of financial services to customers, including unit trusts, stockbroking facilities, insurance policies, pension funds, asset management, or real estate. Non-bank financial services are offered by banks for two reasons. First, a bank provides intermediary and liquidity services to its borrowers and depositors, thereby reducing the financing costs for these customers, compared to the costs if they were to do it themselves. If a bundle of services is demanded by the customer (because it is cheaper to obtain it in this way), then banks may be able to develop a competitive advantage, and profit from offering these services. Second, buying a basket of financial services from banks helps customers to overcome information asymmetries which can make it difficult to judge quality. For example, if a bank earns a reputation from its intermediary role, it can be used to market other financial services. In this way, banks become "marketing intermediaries" (Lewis, 1991).

Wholesale and Retail Banking

Wholesale banking typically involves a small number of very large customers such as large corporates and governments, whereas retail banking consists of a large number of small customers who consume personal banking and small business services. Wholesale banking is largely *interbank*: banks use the interbank markets to borrow from or lend to other banks, to participate in large bond issues, and to engage in syndicated lending. Retail banking is largely *intrabank*: the bank itself makes many small loans. Put another way, in retail banking, risk-pooling takes place within the bank, while in wholesale banking it occurs outside the firm. Improved information flows and global integration constitutes a major challenge to wholesale banking. Retail banking is threatened by new process technologies. These points are discussed in turn, below.

Even though the sophistication of some wholesale banking customers might lead one to think they do not need banking services, the reality is quite different. To see why banks profit from intermediary and payment functions offered to wholesale customers, it is important to understand why large corporate bank customers tend to concentrate their loans and deposits with one or two banks, and why depositors do not effectively insure themselves against liquidity needs by pooling them with other groups of depositors, through a wholesale market. The answer is twofold. First, correspondent banking and interbank relationships signal that banks trust each other, enabling them to transact with each other more cheaply, thereby reducing costs for customers. Second, it is cheaper for banks to delegate the task of evaluating and monitoring a borrowing firm to one or more group leaders than it is to have every bank conduct the monitoring. Loan syndicates make it possible for one bank to act as lead lender, specialising in one type of lending operation.

American *investment banks* and British *merchant banks* are good examples of financial institutions that engage in wholesale banking activities. US investment banks began as underwriters of corporate and government securities issues. The bank would purchase the securities and sell them on to final investors. Modern investment banks can be described as finance wholesalers, engaged in underwriting, market making, consultancy, mergers and acquisitions, and fund management. The traditional function of the merchant bank was to finance trade by charging a fee to guarantee (or "accept") merchants' bills of exchange. Over time, this function evolved into one of more general underwriting, and initiating or arranging financial transactions. Big Bang (in 1986) gave merchant banks the opportunity to expand into market making, mergers and acquisitions, and dealing in securities on behalf of investors. Today, many UK merchant banks perform functions similar to their US cousins, the investment banks, though they are not restricted to these activities by statutory regulations such as the Glass–Steagall Act (see Chapter 6). The terms "merchant" and "investment" banks are now used interchangeably.

Financial market reforms, the increasing ease with which financial instruments are traded, the use of derivatives to improve risk management, and communications technology which enhances global information flows, have contributed to the integration of global financial markets over the last two decades. The challenge for wholesale banks is to maintain a competitive advantage as intermediaries in global finance, though some might survive as financial boutiques. This point is supported by recent takeovers of relatively small British merchant banks. In 1995, Barings collapsed and was later purchased by ING Bank, S. G. Warburg was purchased by Swiss Bank Corporation, and Kleinwort Benson was taken over by Dresdner Bank. In 1989, Deutsche Bank bought Morgan Grenfell.

The retail banking sector has witnessed rapid *process innovation*, where new technology has altered the way key tasks are performed. Most of the jobs traditionally assigned to the bank cashier (teller) can now be done more cheaply by a machine. The cost of an ATM transaction is approximately one-quarter the cost of a cashier transaction. In the UK, the number of ATMs in service has risen from 568 in 1975 to 15 208 in 1995, a trend observed in all the industrialised countries. Likewise, telephone banking is growing in popularity. In the UK, First Direct (a wholly owned subsidiary of Midland

Bank) has captured about 700 000 customers from other banks. First Direct claim they handle 375 accounts per staff member, compared to roughly 100 per staff member in conventional British banks. Correspondingly, many of the clerical jobs in banking have disappeared. In Britain, it is estimated 70 000 banking jobs were lost between 1990 and 1995. Branches have also been closed at a rapid rate. More recent technological developments likely to prove popular are automated branches and home banking. Automatic branches permit the customer to choose when to go to the bank, making short banking hours a thing of the past. Compared to the ATM or even telephone banking, the customer has access to more services and can, via video-link, obtain a full banking service. Spain already has a network of automated branches; in the US, they are growing in popularity. Home banking, which has been slow to get off the ground, should experience a leap in demand once the majority of households are connected to the internet.

An even greater threat to branch banking is the development of electronic cash. An interim development is the advanced smart card. While debit card networks (retailers accept debit cards that allow transactions to be paid into and debited from a bank account) have replaced the need for cheques, smart cards mean customers will not need to carry cash for small transactions. Early smart cards, such as those widely available in France, had a computer chip which stored information about the customer. But current research is focused on a chip that will substitute for cash, and will dramatically alter the payments system for small cash transactions. National Westminster Bank, Midland Bank, and British Telecom jointly own Mondex, a card with units of value stored on it. Mondex is due to be operational across Britain in 1996. Mondex has sold rights of use to Hong Kong and Shanghai Bank in Asia, and has a deal with two large Canadian banks. Mastercard and Visa are about to introduce chip-based cards.

In the United States, some American regional banks have taken the first step to offering banking services on the internet. Regulators are to allow Security First Network Bank to offer *virtual banking* on the internet. Non-banks have also been making moves into internet financial services, but, to date, none has announced plans to offer the core banking products, intermediation and liquidity services.

Internet e-cash will replace many debit, credit, and smart card transactions. Initially, e-cash will permit instant credit or debiting of accounts for a transaction negotiated on the internet. It even has the potential of cutting out the intermediary. Before e-cash is introduced, however, the problem of verification on the internet must be resolved, because there is no way of distinguishing between real money and a digital forgery. One possible solution is a hidden signature to accompany each transaction. Two firms, Digicash in the Netherlands, and a US firm, Cyber-cash, are in the early stages of developing a system but in both cases, a third party, the intermediary, has to provide collateral and settlement for the e-cash. Thus, e-cash is ready to act as a medium of exchange, but not as a store of value. If e-cash has to be converted into traditional money to realise its value, the role of the intermediary changes, but does not disappear. While e-cash performs only an exchange function, there is still a role for banks, money markets, and currency markets. Ultimately, however, e-cash could become a global currency, issued by governments and private firms alike. These changes will, in time, render branches, ATM machines or smart cards obsolete, though past experience suggests customers are slow to accept new money transmission services. The disappearance of branches alone will transform retail banking, because the sector will lose one of its key entry barriers. If, as expected, governments impose sovereign control over the issue of money, be it sterling, US dollars, or e-cash, an intermediary function will remain. Banks with a competitive advantage in an e-cash world will continue to exist.

Universal Banking

The concept of *universal banking* refers to the provision of most or all financial services under a single, largely unified banking structure. Financial activities may include:

- intermediation;
- trading of financial instruments, foreign exchange, and their derivatives;
- underwriting new debt and equity issues;
- brokerage;
- corporate advisory services, including mergers and acquisitions advice;
- investment management;
- insurance;
- holding equity of non-financial firms in the bank's portfolio.

Saunders and Walters (1994) identified four different types of universal banking:

- *The fully integrated universal bank*: supplies the complete range of financial services from one institutional entity.
- *The partially integrated financial conglomerate*: able to supply the services listed above, but several of these (for example, mortgage banking, leasing, and insurance) are provided through wholly-owned or partially owned subsidiaries.
- *The bank subsidiary structure*: the bank focuses essentially on commercial banking and other functions, including investment banking and insurance, which are carried out through legally separate subsidiaries of the bank.
- *The bank holding company structure*: a financial holding company owns both banking (and in some countries, non-banking) subsidiaries that are legally separate and individually capitalised, in so far as financial activities other than "banking" are permitted by law. Internal or regulatory concerns about the institutional safety and soundness or conflicts of interest may give rise to Chinese walls and firewalls (see Chapter 6). The holding company often owns non-financial firms, or the holding company itself may be an industrial concern.

In some countries (Germany, Switzerland, the Netherlands, Sweden, Austria, Belgium, and Luxembourg), banks hold equity stakes in non-financial corporations. Not only does a bank provide these firms with commercial and investment banking services, it will also have board seats and perform a critical role in corporate governance. In Japan, the norm is a cluster (*keiretsu*) of banks, financial firms and non-financial firms, with cross-shareholdings, shared directorships, close supplier–customer relationships, and an emphasis on cooperation within the cluster. In both systems, the public holds shares in both industrial companies and banks. Markets for corporate equity and debt tend to be under-developed. Canada, France and the UK are examples of countries where certain features of universal banking prevail. The European Union banking laws (see Chapter 6) were drawn up on the assumption that universal banking would be the relevant model.

Off-Balance Sheet Banking and Securitisation

Off-balance sheet (OBS) instruments are contingent commitments or contracts which generate income for a bank but do not appear as assets or liabilities on the traditional bank balance sheet. They can range from stand-by letters of credit to complex derivatives, such as swaptions. For a detailed discussion of off-balance sheet activities, readers are referred to Chapter 5. Banks enter the OBS business because they believe it will enhance their profitability, for different reasons. First, OBS instruments generate fee income, and are therefore typical of the financial product illustrated in Figure 2. Second, these instruments may improve a bank's risk management techniques, thereby enhancing profitability and shareholder value added. For example, if a bank markets its own unit trust (mutual fund), it will sell shares in a diversified asset pool; the portfolio is managed by the bank, but the assets are not owned or backed by the bank. Or a bank can pool and sell mortgage assets, thereby moving the assets off-balance sheet. Third, to the extent that regulators focus on bank balance sheets, OBS instruments, in some cases, may make it easier for a bank to meet capital standards. These instruments may also assist the bank in avoiding regulatory taxes which stem from reserve requirements and deposit insurance levies.

Securitisation is the process whereby traditional bank assets (for example, mortgages) are sold by a bank to a trust or corporation, which in turn sells the assets as securities. Thus, while the process may commence in an informal market (usually with a bank locating borrowers), the traditional functions related to the loan asset are unbundled so that they can be marketed as securities on a formal market. Securitisation is discussed in detail in Chapter 5.

The growth of off-balance sheet and securitisation activities is not inconsistent with the basic principles of banking outlined earlier. The growth of the derivatives and securities markets has expanded the intermediary role of banks to one where they act as *intermediaries in risk management*.*

---

*This term is discussed in more detail in Chapter 5.

WILL BANKS DISAPPEAR?

A recent popular view is that the contribution of banks to the economy will diminish significantly, or even that banks will disappear by early in the next century, as the traditional intermediary and payment functions of the bank decline in the face of new financial instruments and technology, such as off-balance sheet products and securitisation, services which can be produced by non-bank financial firms. As noted in the previous section, it is just a matter of time before secure *e-cash* is available on the internet, enabling users to shop and purchase goods and services on e-mail. The critical question is whether the new technology will allow the global risk-pooling role played by the banks to be taken over by individuals. This scenario is only possible if agents are able to arrange loans, deposits, and payments facilities with each other more cheaply than the banks can. Even with the most advanced technology, the chances are slim, because of the time and cost of collecting the information to decide where the optimal place for a deposit is, to pool risks with other depositors, or to locate the most suitable loan(s). Provided banks can maintain a competitive advantage in the supply of intermediation services once the majority of house-holds and firms have access to the information superhighway, the traditional core product they offer is unlikely to disappear. Additionally, many banks will expand into non-bank financial services, again, because of competitive advan-tage. Bank functions will evolve over time, but this is a phenomenon common to firms in most sectors of the economy.

It is certainly true that non-banks have begun to offer financial services. For example, General Electric Capital (GE Capital), is the financial services sub-sidiary of General Electric. It has the largest issuance of commercial paper in the USA, supplies credit card facilities to department stores, is the largest insurer of private homes, and for nine years owned a securities firm, Kidder Peabody. In the UK, Marks & Spencer plc, well known for its retail clothes, food, and home furnishings, began in the 1980s to offer a selection of financial services, starting with an in-house credit card business and expanding into personal loans, unit trusts, personal equity plans, and, from 1995, insurance and pensions. Marks and Spencer is able to fund its asset requirements because it is top-rated by key rating agencies. However, it is noteworthy that these non-bank firms have chosen to enter niche markets, which do not threaten the intermediary/payments function offered by banks. Furthermore, there have been examples of failed entry into these markets. Sears Roebuck was one of the first large retail firms to offer financial services, but it has recently scaled back its activities. Westinghouse wound up its credit arm after it lost nearly $1 billion in property loans. In 1994, GE sold its investment bank, Kidder Peabody, after losses on the mortgage-backed securities portfolio, and dubious trading activities in government bonds. Under the terms of agreement to sell Kidder Peabody to PaineWebber, another investment bank, GE received $90 million for its investment bank; it had paid $600 million for it in 1986.

The survival of well-known banking firms will depend on whether they are able to adapt to offer the most efficient intermediary and payments service, newer non-bank financial services and functions, or both. While the structure of the financial firm may well change such that the traditional activities of the bank are only one of many services, the role of banking itself will evolve, rather than decline or disappear. To maintain a competitive advantage in the financial market place, banks will have to adapt to the changing nature of intermediation, new technology which has the potential of narrowing information asymmetries, reducing the need for an intermediary, and ever-changing consumer preferences, as computer-literate customers demand value for money and sophisticated intermediation, payments, and a wide range of financial services. Competition may heighten, which could threaten the viability of some banks, but banks themselves are here to stay unless they prove unable to maintain a competitive advantage in the products they offer.

THE PERFORMANCE OF BANKS

This section begins with a review of the methods used to measure bank profitability and then considers the issue of why banks appear to under-perform compared to other sectors of the economy. Aliber (1984) reported Q ratios for the national banks of the industrial countries and compared them with the performance of the industrial sector, for the period 1974–82. The Q ratio is defined as the ratio of the market value of a firm (as reflected in the value of its shares) to the book value of the firm. Increases in Q ratios may reflect increases in anticipated profitability or reductions in the cost of capital. Firms expand when their Q ratios exceed one and contract when they are less than unity. He showed the Q ratios for international banks had fallen relative to the Q ratios for all other firms listed. In Japan, Switzerland and Canada (for most years) bank Q ratios were higher for banks than industrial sector firms but they were lower for American and British banks.

McCormick (1987) compared bank Q ratios with those of other US industries in 1984. The banking ratio was the lowest at 0.6, the Q ratios of other industries ranging from 0.7–0.9 for steel, tyres, rubber, metals, mining, and railways to 2.5–2.7 for publishing and radio and television broadcasting. The measure is troublesome, for several reasons. The book value of a firm is *retrospective*, based on the historic value of physical assets, adjusted for depreciation and inflation. Market value is a *prospective* estimate of the firm's net present value, that is, its discounted dividend stream. Computing the Q ratio for banks is even more problematic because much of their book value is based on goodwill and the intangible assets they possess, meaning cross-industry Q ratios are not strictly comparable. Also, non-financial firms usually see the value of their assets rise with inflation (raising their market value) but financial firms see their asset values (loans) decline with inflation.

Return on assets (ROA) is the ratio of earnings to total assets and return on equity (ROE) is the ratio of earnings to total equity. *The Banker* has published data on the world's largest banks since 1969. It ranked the world's largest 300 banks from 1969–79, the world's largest 500 banks from 1980–88 and the world's largest 1000 banks from 1989. Currently, the annual rankings appear in the July issue. The current ranking is based on "strength", measured by "tier one" capital, defined as common stock, declared reserves, and perpetual, irredeemable, and non-cumulative preference shares, expressed in US dollars. Since July 1991, *The Banker* reports three other measures of bank performance; profit on capital (%), return on assets, and an FT composite credit rating: compiled by *The Financial Times Newsletters* using 12 international ratings. An arithmetical average of numerical scores is given to each agency's investment grade ratings. The highest score is 10, the lowest is 1. Prior to 1991, *The Banker* reported real profits growth and profits on capital as measures of performance. There is virtually no correlation between *The Banker's* different rankings; for example, there is no relation between asset size and profitability.

Goldberg and Hanweck (1991) identified the key measurement problems in *The Banker's* rankings. Data are difficult or impossible to obtain in certain countries, all mergers affect the relative rankings in the year they occur, and all data are converted to US dollars to ensure comparability but it is not clear if the appropriate exchange rate is used. Furthermore, most banks report data for 31 December but some countries report data for different dates.

Perhaps the best method for assessing the performance of any institution is *value added*, which is the amount by which a production process increases the value of a good or service. It is computed by sales revenue less the cost of inputs used to produce the good/service. In banking, the sales revenue will equal explicit charges plus the interest margin (what a bank charges to borrowers and pays out to depositors). Operating costs will include wages, materials and the cost of capital. Like any profit-maximising firm, a bank's cost of capital will consist of the capital required to maintain the bank's infrastructure, and "free capital", the capital set aside to protect depositors against losses.*

In a study of 25 European Community (EC) banks, LBS and First Consulting[†] attempted to measure the value added of these banks. Bank value added was computed as follows. Operating profits were adjusted to reflect changes in reserves not otherwise caught in reported profits. Then a notional charge for shareholder's equity (the home country's bond yield plus a 10% risk premium) was subtracted from the adjusted operating profits. The result was the bank's value added: the money it made above the amount needed to compensate shareholders. The value added figure was then divided by factor inputs used by the bank. Thus, *bank value added* =

$$\text{(adjusted operating profits} - \text{charge for shareholders' equity)}$$
$$\div \text{ bank factor inputs}$$

---

*Unlike other firms, banks are required to set aside capital because of prudential concerns. See Chapter 6 for a detailed discussion of the risk assets ratio—international banks must set aside a certain percentage of their capital to cover their assets, adjusted for risk.

[†]As reported in *The Economist* (8 August, 1992): p.77. LBS: London Business School.

The study used the measure to look at EC retail bank performance from 1987–90. Of the 25 banks studied, only five added value by this measure. For the other 20 banks, the value added measure was negative. Abbey National was the only British bank to add value. However, Kay (1993) showed that of 11 European retail banks, eight showed a positive value added in 1990, including, among the British "big four" banks, Barclays and Lloyds. Kay's definition of value added was adjusted operating profits less a charge for shareholders' equity.

Boyd and Gertler (1994) used US National Income Accounts (1947–87) to compute value added for commercial banks, Federal Reserve Banks, mutual saving banks, thrifts, credit unions, business credit institutions, mortgage banks, and rediscounting agencies. Here, value added was defined as the sum of payments to all factor inputs, that is, the sum of wages, salaries, profits, interest expense and depreciation. The value added was expressed as a percentage of the total value added of the financial intermediary sector. They found that over the long run, the banks' share of value added had remained constant, or had increased slightly over the period; in the 1980s, it was actually above trend. The authors also reported value added by the financial intermediary sector as a percentage of total national GDP—the measure more than doubled over the period. They concluded that banks have not lost market share over the period, and the financial intermediary sector, including banks, has been a growth industry, relative to the overall economy.

Value added has several advantages over other performance indicators. It provides a measure of the bank's competitive advantage, and is not affected by bank size, variable interest rates, or difference in regulatory regimes. Nor is it biased in favour of capital intensive banks. Value added is also less volatile than other measures, such as ROE. But the measure is not without its problems, especially in sectors where intangible assets are important. Unlike other measures, value added focuses on operating activities, rather than on returns to shareholders. For this reason, value added statements are usually computed for operating units within a firm, rather than for the firm as a whole. Thus, it is often not possible to obtain the required data from published accounts. Computing value added for banking services is so difficult that many countries with value added tax systems do not attempt to tax financial services.

Price–earnings (PE) ratios* can also be used to look at relative performance. A Federal Reserve Bank of New York study (1986) reported that in mid-1986, the PE ratio of US multinational banks was 10.2 and that of large regional bank holding companies was 12.2. This compared with a figure of 15.7 for the S&P 500. PE ratios for the investment banks were not available because they had only recently gone public. But for the five largest publicly quoted investment banks, the PE ratio for April 1986 was 14.9. These relatively poor PEs may be because banks are viewed as stodgy investments by the stock market

---

*The price–earnings ratio for a firm is the firm's market share price divided by the firm's earnings per share (most recently reported). It will vary with the market's assessment of the risks involved. If a company's PE ratio falls, it is an indication the market perceives it as a more risky investment.

and hence their PE ratios are lower. For example, the shrinking wholesale market affected the stock market assessment of earnings prospects. Additionally, adjusting earnings for inflation makes the PE ratios higher for the multinational banks than the S&P 500 in the period 1977–79. They were close to the 500 in 1981, and in 1984 above the 500.

Keehn (1994) used the Federal Reserve's flows of fund accounts and showed the commercial banks' share of total assets of all financial institutions fell from 48% in 1952 to 25% in 1993. Commercial bank loans as a percentage of total loans declined from 91% in 1950 to 59% in 1992. In the UK, the banks' share of total liabilities of intermediaries declined from 64% in 1913 to 27% in 1991. But as Keehn himself notes, these figures ignore off-balance sheet operations. Furthermore, assets as a measure of output in the financial sector is problematic.* Keehn also reported that employment in commercial banking kept pace with that in the finance, insurance and retail sectors from 1934–77. As a percentage of employment in the non-farm private economy, employment in banking increased through to 1983. Bank closures and consolidation in the 1980s and 1990s explains why employment has declined over the last decade, but it is too early to judge whether this is actually a trend.

Revell (1980) used interest margins as a measure of bank performance. He computed the ratios of interest margin (total reported interest income less interest expense) as a percentage of average total assets for US commercial banks. These rose over the period 1964–77, peaking in 1980. But pre-tax profits as a percentage of total average assets showed a flatter trend. This type of measurement is increasingly unhelpful as banks move away from traditional activities and offer non-banking financial services.

A number of studies have attempted to assess performance using either an index measure or multiple indicators. Arshadi and Lawrence (1987) looked at the performance of newly chartered banks in the USA. Since bank performance is a multidimensional concept, these authors used canonical correlation analysis (rather than the more common multiple regression analysis) to estimate the effect of internal and external variables on an index measure of performance. Performance of a new bank was defined as an index of profitability, pricing of bank services (average loan and deposit rates), and loan market share in the trade area. Fourteen endogenous and exogenous variables were selected in order to identify the external and internal factors influencing bank performance. A full list can be found in the paper. Data were taken from the period 1980–84 for a sample set of banks that gained their charters in 1977–79. Third and fifth-year financial data were used in the analysis.

The study by Arshardi and Lawrence reported a number of key findings. Performance measures found to be significant were market share, loan price, and return on assets. Average interest payments on deposit accounts did not appear to be a significant contributor to performance. Four explanatory variables turned out to be important to performance: wages and salaries, operating

---

*See Chapter 4 for more detail.

costs, size of the bank (the latter two show the importance of scale economies to the performance of a new bank) and two proxies for the structure of banking markets, the size of the trade area, and the presence or absence of a metropolitan area. The authors concluded that the performance of newly chartered banks is a function of endogenous factors under the control of bank management. Demand factors (demographics and effective income) appeared unimportant.

Hirtle (1991) devoted part of her paper to the assessment of the performance of 51 international banks and securities firms, using multiple indicators. Performance was assessed using four measures: profitability (return on assets and return on equity); size (the levels and growth rates of total assets and revenue); capitalisation (the shareholders' equity and price–earnings ratios); and productivity, the ratio of total revenue to non-interest expense. The data came from the financial statements of the 51 sample firms for the period 1985–89.

Hirtle found good performance among the Japanese, Swiss, German, British, Canadian, and American banks, though they did well by different measures. The Japanese banks performed well in terms of size, growth, and productivity; Swiss banks by capitalisation and profitability; German banks by real asset growth and productivity; Canadian banks by real revenue growth, productivity, and shareholders' equity ratio; UK banks showed some strength in size, productivity and shareholders' equity ratio. Banks in the US had a high score for total assets, but did less well using measures of productivity and capitalisation. For the German and Swiss banks, hidden reserves and unreported earnings will understate their profitability and capitalisation. Differences in national accounting practices and standards mean any cross-country comparisons must be treated with caution. This is especially the case for Japanese, German, and Swiss banks. Also, the performance measures were based on retrospective balance sheet data, which may not be good indicators of future performance.

Using a share price index measure, a Bank of England article (1992) on international bank performance showed that aggregate bank share price indices (1975–91) in Germany, the UK, and the US all under-performed their local stock market indices. But Levonian (1994) would argue that these findings only hold in the short run, at least for US banks. Levonian examined long-run bank profitability, using quarterly cross-section stock market data for 81 US banks in the period June 1986 to June 1992. Profitability was defined as the nominal rate of return on equity (R), assumed to converge to some long-run level (R^*). Based on his findings, Levonian argued recent poor profitability in the short-term does not reflect the true long-run condition of the industry because market pricing of stocks indicates that agents do not think the long-run profit spread (the difference between R and the cost of capital) is going to be negative, and profits in banking will cover the cost of capital. He concluded that either the market thinks the recent poor profitability is temporary and short-term, or it believes reported income of banks is lower than the true value.

The majority of studies referred to above suggest that the banking sector tends to perform poorly relative to other industrial sectors, independent of what measure is used. There are a number of possible explanations. First, interest rates. Bank share prices tend to rise (relatively more than in other sectors*) as interest rates fall because net interest margins (the difference between average loan rates and deposit rates) widen. Thus, the general upward trend in interest rates in the late 1970s had a more pronounced adverse effect on bank share prices. However, as banks diversify into fee-based financial products, their performance may be less sensitive to interest rate fluctuations.[†] Improved risk management techniques (see Chapter 5) should also mean banks are less sensitive to volatile interest rates. On the other hand, if banks are inexperienced in the risk associated with new financial products, these may be incorrectly priced, thereby adversely affecting performance. Another reason often cited to explain poor performance is the presence of oligopolistic banking structures which make the industry less efficient than other, more competitive industries. Increased international competition among banks and deregulation should make them more efficient, but at the expense of lower profitability.

Finally, a possibly very important explanation may be that the measures themselves are insufficiently accurate to give a true picture of bank performance. A study by Boyd and Gertler (1994) showed that US commercial bank performance is fairly steady, provided one adjusts the standard measurements for foreign bank lending and the growth in off-balance sheet business (fees, loan securitisation, bank guarantees on commercial paper, and derivatives). If foreign bank operations in the US are adjusted to include foreign loans booked offshore, the figures change quite dramatically. For example, in 1992, the unadjusted share of bank assets held by foreign banks was 11%; the adjusted share was 21%.

Boyd and Gertler used two indirect estimates of off-balance sheet activities. The first was the credit risk equivalents computed to satisfy the requirements of the Basle risk assets ratio (see Chapter 6); the second was the credit equivalent of off-balance sheet activities that would be required to generate the observed level of non-interest income. Boyd and Gertler then recomputed the banks' share in total intermediated assets and bank credit relative to GDP. Unadjusted, the shares of US bank assets as a percentage of total financial intermediaries assets declined from 46% in 1974 to 34% in 1992. If the figures are adjusted, the fall in the bank share that occurred

---

*Share prices rise as interest rates decline because the stream of profits is discounted at a higher rate, and therefore firms have a higher capital value.
[†] A note of caution should be sounded on this point. Financial intermediaries earned large revenues from fee-based activities such as the arrangement of bond issues by companies during falling interest rates, when these firms wish to refinance their debt. But in a period of rising interest rates, fee income will decline as firms issue fewer bonds, and households tend to transfer investments from the bond and equity markets back into high-interest deposit accounts.

after 1974 is halved. For over 40 years, the average bank share was just over 40%; in the late 1980s and 1990s, the share fell to slightly under 40%. Unadjusted, the ratio of commercial bank assets to GDP and commercial bank loans to GDP increased in the period 1957–92; these ratios remain unchanged between 1974 and 1992. But recomputed figures showed commercial banking increased in importance relative to economic activity. The value added figures reported by Boyd and Gertler (see p. 32) are consistent with these more positive trends, as were long-term profitability results reported by Levonian.

STYLISED FACTS ON BANKING*

Table 1 shows the average number of commercial and savings bank institutions over the period 1981–89, for most of the industrialised countries. There are relatively few commercial banks in North America, Japan, and the UK— approximately one per million habitants. But there are many more in Continental Europe, where one per 200 000 habitants is the norm. Germany leads the way in the number of savings banks, followed by the USA, Denmark and Spain. Germany also has an extensive cooperative movement, with nearly 3000 cooperative banks.

The annual average growth rate of banking assets is shown in Table 2, and Figure 3. There was a very rapid growth of assets in the 1970s, varying from 12.6% for the USA, to 33% for Luxembourg. In the 1980s, the growth rate of assets slowed to single figures for most industrialised countries, with the exception of Japan, Denmark, and the UK. The average ratio of total assets to nominal GDP for most industrialised countries in the period 1981–89 is illustrated in Figure 4. For most countries, banking assets are more than 100% of national income.

Figures 5 and 6 show the spread between, respectively, the money market rate and the deposit rate, and the loan rate and money market rate. The deposit rate is defined as the rate offered to resident depositors for demand, time, or savings deposits; the loan rate as an average rate quoted for short and medium-term loans. In Figure 5, one would expect to observe a positive margin, which is the case for most countries, with the margin widening in the period 1990–92. However, the margins are negative in both periods for Luxembourg and Portugal. It is likely these figures are too aggregated, producing somewhat unreliable results. For example, in the UK, the seven-day rate is reported, though most depositors choose deposit products with more competitive rates. Figure 6 shows loan rates typically exceed money market rates, but the gap varies widely—it is quite low in the UK, Japan, North America, and higher in much of Continental Europe. Again, the rates may to be too aggregated to

---

*I should like to thank Steven Funnell, a 1996 graduate of the BSc Banking and International Finance degree at City University Business School, for his assistance in compiling the figures in this section.

Table 1 Average number of commercial and savings bank institutions over the period 1981–1989

	Commercial[1]	Savings[2]
Belgium	85	30
Canada	10	NA
Denmark	217	216
France	403	NA
Germany	213	590
Italy	219	82
Japan	92	NA
Luxembourg	126	NA
Netherlands	87	NA
Portugal	23	NA
Spain	138	80
Switzerland	NA	217
UK	51	NA
USA	299	336

Source: OECD Paris (1991) *Bank Profitability Statistical Supplement.*

[1]*Commercial banks*

Canada – data relates to Canadian Bank groups reporting on a consolidated worldwide basis. The figures are for fiscal years ending 31 October.

Denmark – figures aggregated for commercial banks and savings banks.

France – figures aggregated for commercial banks and credit cooperatives. Data is for branches in France but excludes subsidiaries abroad.

Japan – Data related to fiscal year ending 31 March. Data is based on the annual publication of the Federation of Bankers Association of Japan "Analysis of Financial Statements of All Banks". The term Commercial Banks corresponds to the term All ordinary banks used in Japanese publications. As from 1988, the data includes Sogo banks.

Sogo banks are banks for small to medium sized industries.

Netherlands – As of 1986 the data includes the merged Postbank, one of the parties previously not recorded in the data.

Switzerland – Data is for large commercial banks: Data for 1988 and 1989 is not available.

UK – Data relate to London and Scottish banks groups ie: eight of the largest domestic banking groups reporting on a consolidated worldwide basis. The consolidated data include an unspecified number of branches and subsidiaries abroad as well as domestic non bank subsidiaries.

USA – The term Commercial banks is the same as insured commercial banks used in United States publications

[2]*Savings banks (NA for Canada, France, Japan, Italy (81 & 82) Luxembourg, Netherlands, Portugal, Switzerland, UK & USA (81–85)*

Denmark – data for Commercial and Savings Banks.

Switzerland – data for regional and savings banks.

USA – data for Mutual Savings Banks.

Table 2 Annual average growth rate of banking assets (%)

	Belgium	Canada	Denmark	France	Germany	Italy	Japan	Luxembourg	Netherlands	Portugal	Spain	Switzerland	UK	USA
1970 to 1979	21.3	15.4	15.5	27.2	15.7	18.7	19.3	37.1	21.5	14.0	19.8	12.4	20.6	11.7
1980 to 1989	8.8	7.7	16.6	6.6	6.4	5.4	16.9	9.3	7.1	7.8	9.3	9.1	15.1	8.4
1990 to 1993	NA	NA	6.2	NA	9.4	NA	NA	NA	5.5	18.9	6.30	0.9	-0.80	NA

Source: International Monetary Fund; (1994) *International Financial Statistics*.
The total assets of the banking system are calculated by summing section 20 "Deposit Money Banks" except for the liabilities.

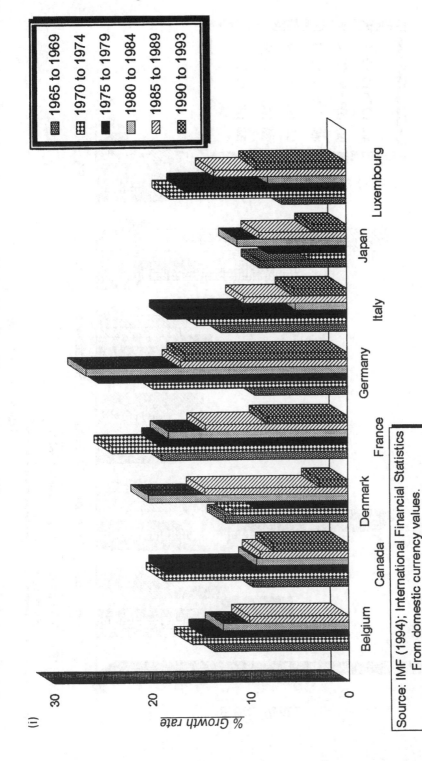

Figure 3(a) % Average annual growth rate of domestic bank assets

Source: IMF (1994); International Financial Statistics
From domestic currency values.

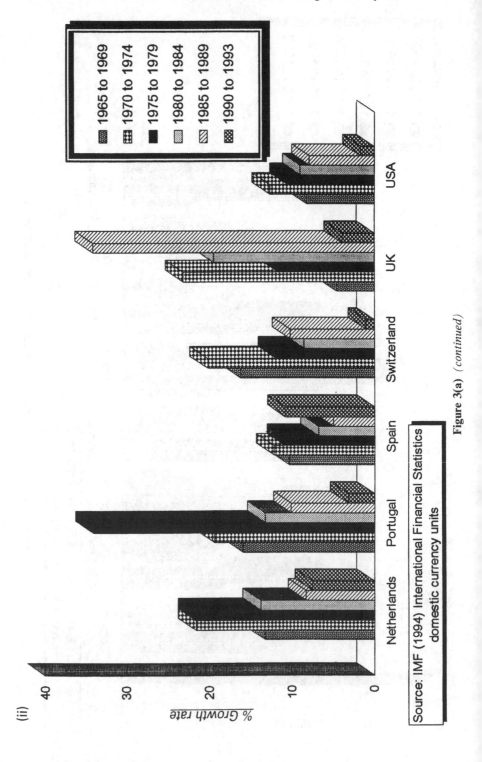

Source: IMF (1994) International Financial Statistics
domestic currency units

Figure 3(a) (continued)

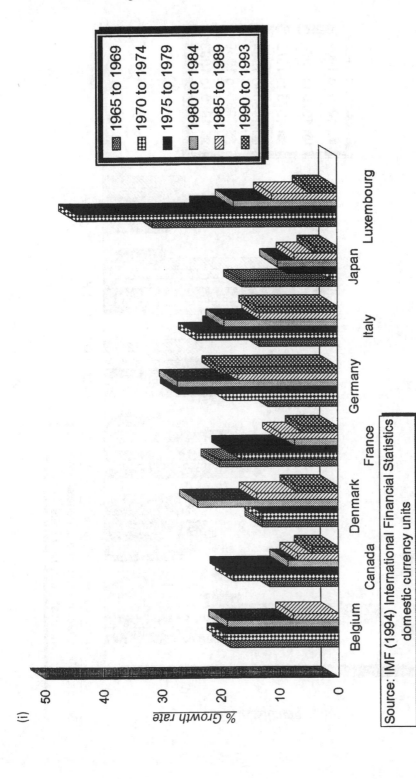

Figure 3(b) % Average annual growth rate of total bank assets (including foreign assets)

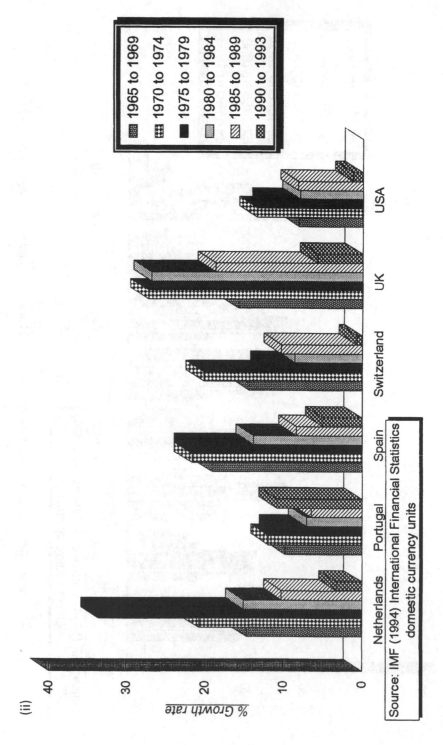

Figure 3(b) *(continued)*

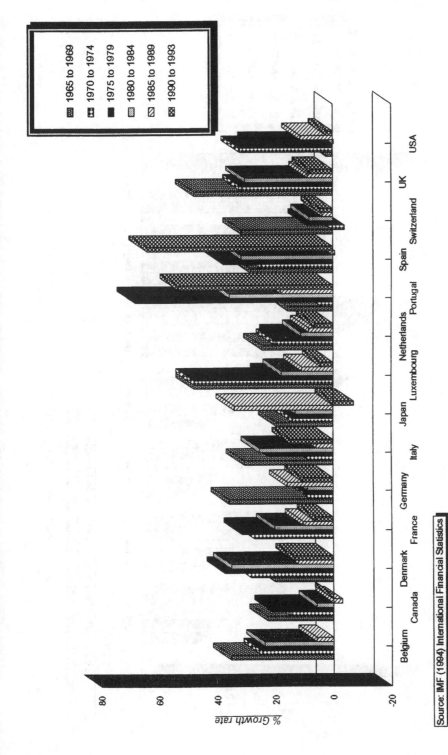

Figure 3(c) % Annual average growth rate of foreign assets

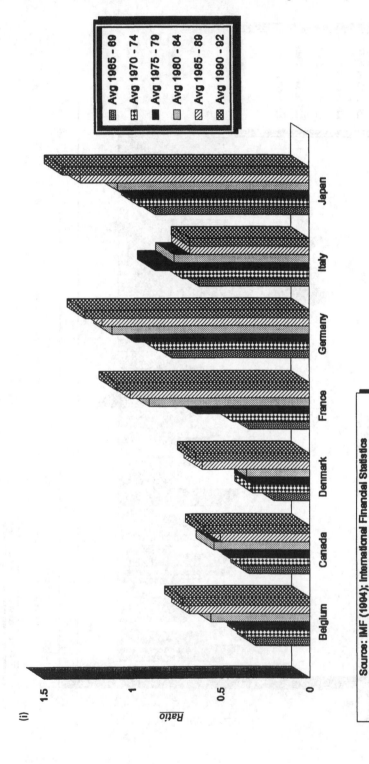

Figure 4(a) Ratio of total domestic bank assets to nominal GDP

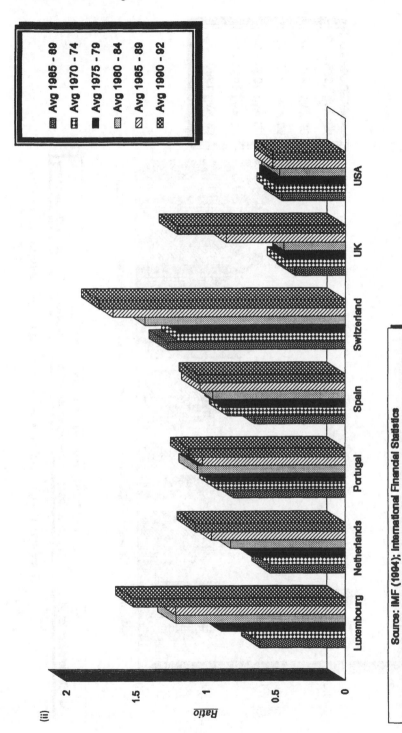

(ii)

Source: IMF (1994); International Financial Statistics
The ratio is calculated by dividing average total domestic bank assets by nominal GDP.

Figure 4(a) *(continued)*

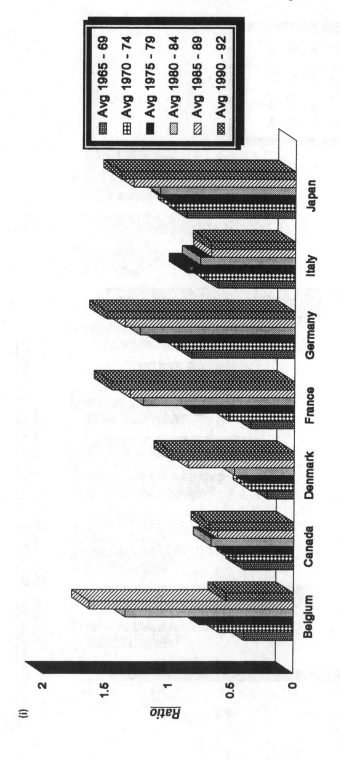

Source: IMF (1994) International Financial Statistics
The ratio is calculated by dividing total assets in domestic currency by nominal GDP in domestic currency

Figure 4(b) Ratio of total bank assets (including foreign assets) to nominal GDP

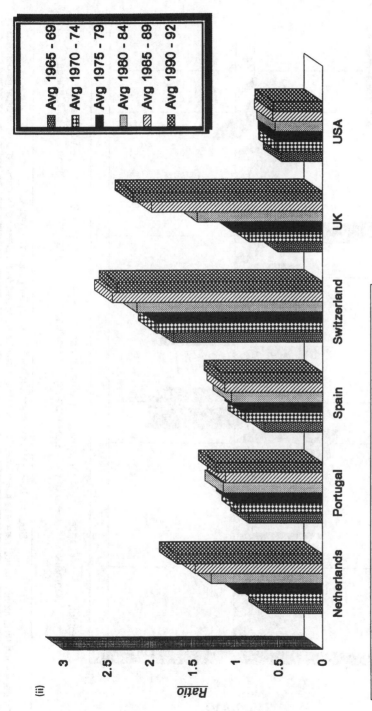

Source: IMF (1994) International Financial Statistics
The ratio is calculated by dividing total bank assets by the nominal GDP.

Figure 4(b) *(continued)*

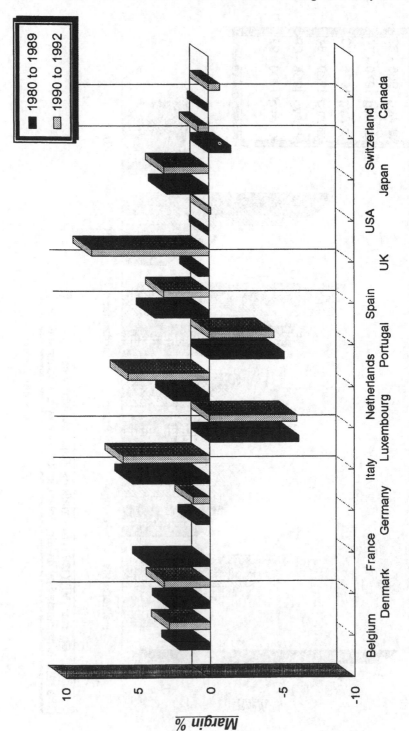

Figure 5 Average margins on deposits

Source: IMF. (1994); International Financial Statistics Yearbook.
Average short term money market rate less the average deposit rate (rate offered to resident customers for demand, time or savings deposits.)

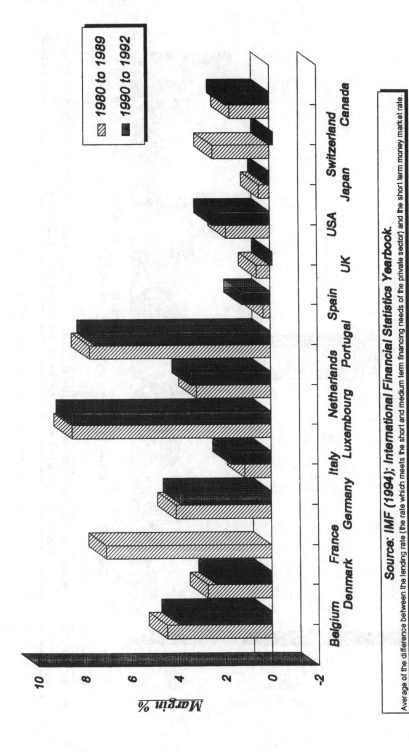

Figure 6 Average loan margin

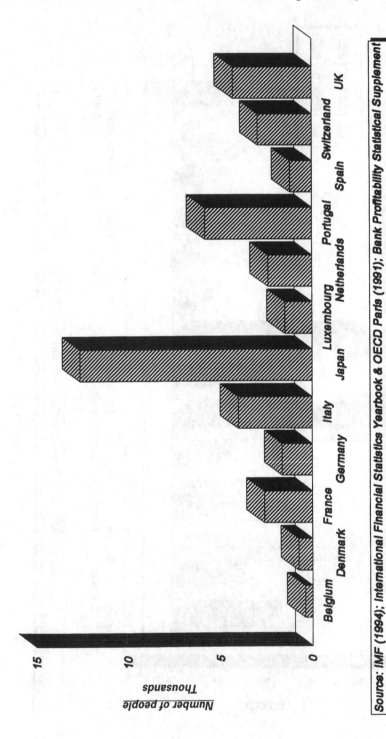

Figure 7 Average population per branch

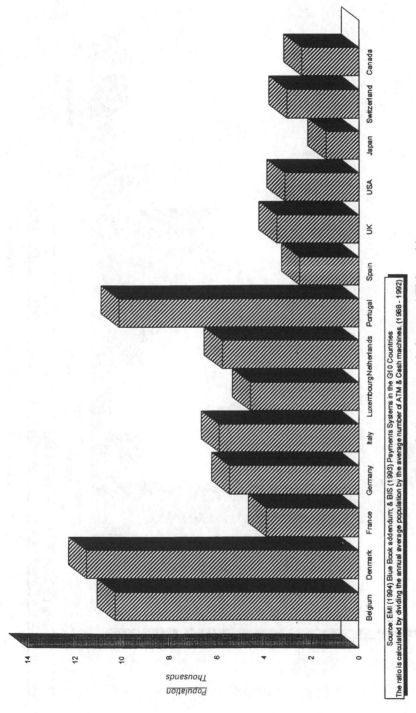

Figure 8 Average population per ATM machine

Source: EMI (1994) Blue Book addendum; & BIS (1993) Payments Systems in the G10 Countries
The ratio is calculated by dividing the annual average population by the average number of ATM & Cash machines. (1988 - 1992)

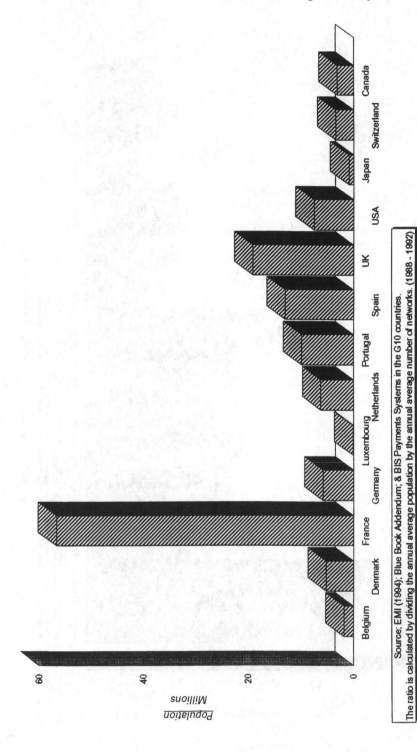

Source: EMI (1994); Blue Book Addendum; & BIS Payments Systems in the G10 countries.
The ratio is calculated by dividing the annual average population by the annual average number of networks. (1988 - 1992)

Figure 9 Average population per EFTPOS network

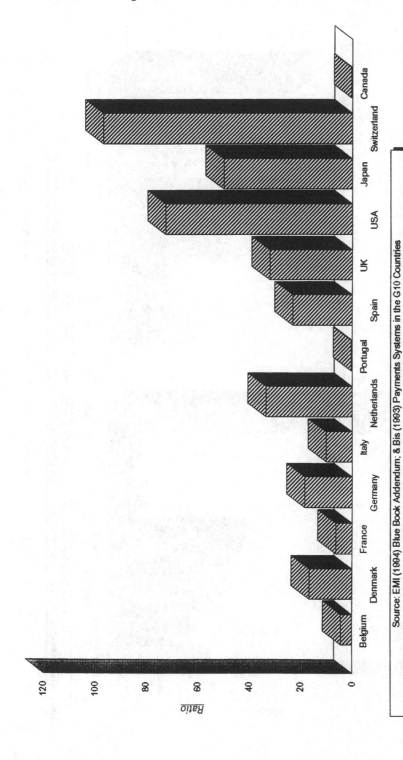

Source: EMI (1994) Blue Book Addendum; & Bis (1993) Payments Systems in the G10 Countries
The ratio is calculated by dividing the annual average value of paperless credit transfers by the annual average nominal GDP. (1988 - 1992)

Figure 10 Ratio of value of paperless credit transfers to nominal GDP

Figure 11 Ratio of value of payments by debit and credit cards to nominal GDP

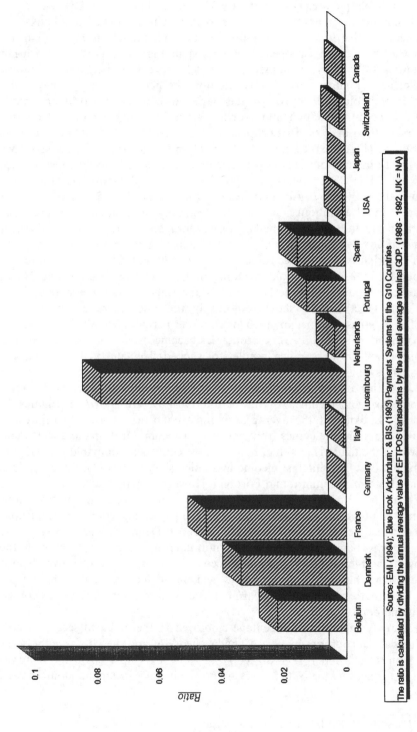

Source: EMI (1994); Blue Book Addendum; & BIS (1993) Payments Systems in the G10 Countries
The ratio is calculated by dividing the annual average value of EFTPOS transactions by the annual average nominal GDP. (1988 - 1992, UK = NA)

Figure 12 Ratio of value of EFTPOS transactions to nominal GDP

give a reliable picture. Heffernan (1993) showed that for the UK, an imperfectly competitive market causes rates to vary considerably among banks.

There are five times as many people per bank branch in Japan than, on average, in Western Europe, as illustrated in Figure 7. Western European countries differ widely, with extensive branch networks in Belgium, and fewest in Portugal. Figures 8 to 12 illustrate how the pace and form of payments-related technological innovation has varied widely between different industrialised countries. Japan and North America may have more inhabitants per bank than in Western Europe, but the spread of ATMs is much thinner in Europe (Figure 8). In Europe, Portugal and Denmark have fewest ATMs relative to population; Spain, Switzerland, and the UK have the most. France has one EFTPOS[†] network; the UK has three, and Japan has about 100. Figure 12 shows that EFTPOS transactions amount to 5–8% of GDP in France and Luxembourg; in the US, Germany, and Japan, less than one tenth of this. In Belgium, Canada, Luxembourg, and Portugal, nearly all credit transfers involve paper (Figure 8) but in Japan, Switzerland, and the USA, there is extensive use of electronic transfer. Credit and debit cards account for about 10–15% of household spending in Luxembourg, Britain, and North America (Figure 11). In the Netherlands and Italy, the figure is barely 1%.

Figure 13 (a) and (b) show, respectively, the ratio of pre-tax and post-tax profits to gross income for all banks for the period 1981–89. In the 1980s, Japanese banks, already very profitable, became even more so. But banks' profits elsewhere were either trendless or slipped. The late 1980s were marked by sharp swings in the profits of Anglo-American banks.

The ratios of net interest income to gross income and net non-interest income to gross income, for the period 1981–89, are shown in Figures 14 and 15. Looking at the averages, in most countries at least two-thirds of banks' gross income comes from net interest income. In Canada and Britain, however, the figure is less than half. In most countries, compared to 1981, the contribution of net interest income had fallen slightly by 1989, the exceptions being Belgium, Denmark, and Portugal. However, as illustrated by Figure 15, the trend is for banks to earn a larger proportion of gross income from non-interest sources; between 1981 and 1989, the percentage contribution of non-interest income to gross income rose, except in Denmark and Portugal. One reason why banks are moving into non-interest sources is because of the growth in interest-bearing current accounts and more competitive deposit rates, which have reduced the banks' *endowment* income, that is the income banks earn from non-interest earnings accounts and the difference between loan and deposit rates.

Figure 16 reports the percentage employed in the financial sectors of key industrialised countries in 1991. Canada, the USA, and the UK have the highest figures; just under 12% of people in work are employed in the financial sector. France and the Netherlands are not far behind. In Japan, about 8.5% of

---

[†]EFTPOS: Electric Funds Transfer at Point of Sale.

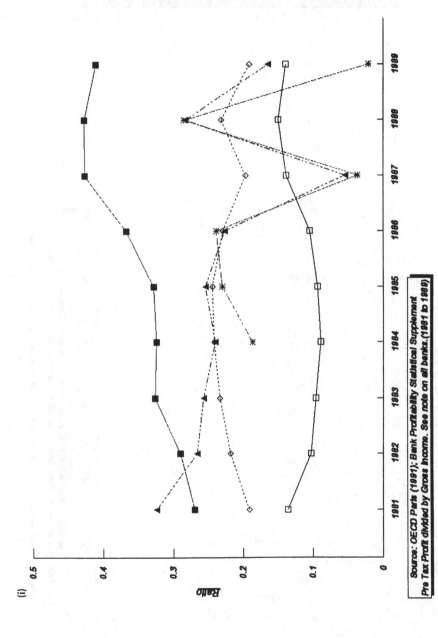

Source: OECD Paris (1991); Bank Profitability Statistical Supplement
Pre Tax Profit divided by Gross Income. See note on all banks.(1981 to 1989)

Figure 13(a) Ratio of pre-tax profits to gross income for all banks

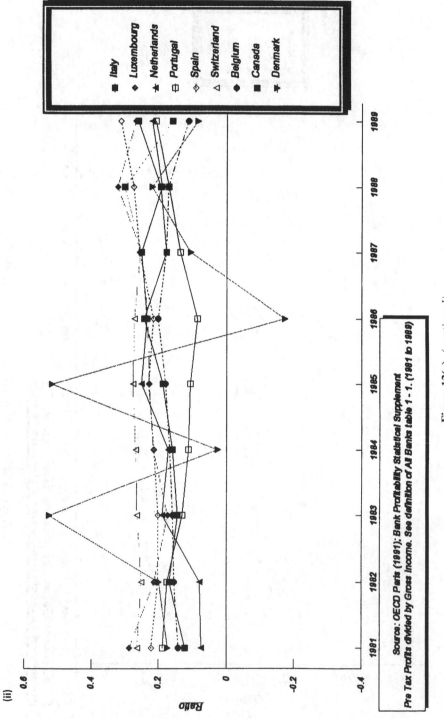

Source: OECD Paris (1991): Bank Profitability Statistical Supplement
Pre Tax Profits divided by Gross Income. See definition of All Banks table 1 - 1. (1981 to 1989)

Figure 13(a) *(continued)*

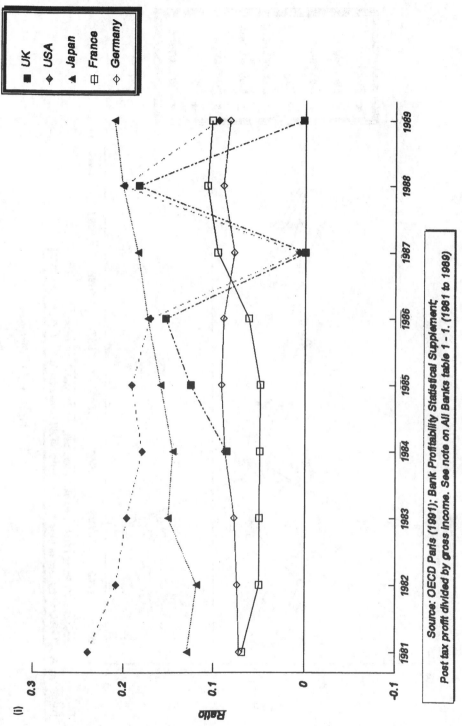

Figure 13(b) Ratio of post-tax profits to gross income for all banks

Source: OECD Paris (1991); Bank Profitability Statistical Supplement;
Post tax profit divided by gross income. See note on All Banks table 1 - 1. (1981 to 1989)

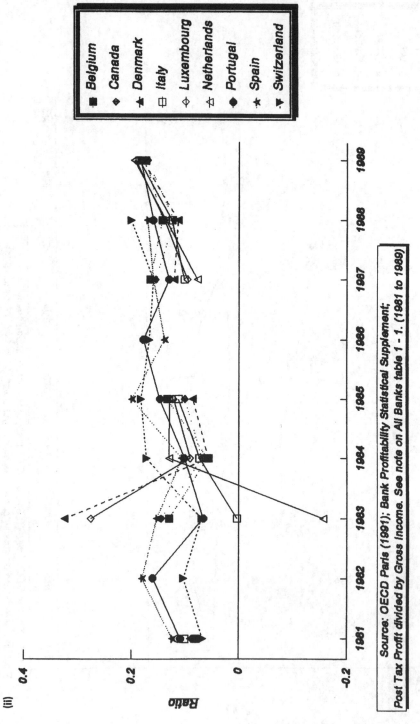

Figure 13(b) *(continued)*

Source: OECD Paris (1991); Bank Profitability Statistical Supplement;
Post Tax Profit divided by Gross Income. See note on All Banks table 1 - 1. (1981 to 1989)

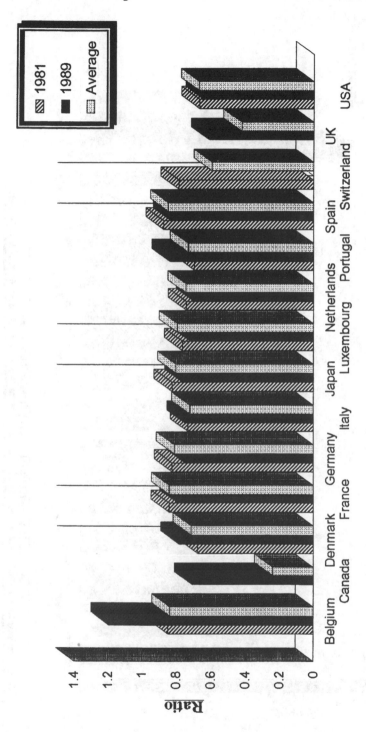

Figure 14 Ratio of net interest income to gross income for all banks

Source: OECD Paris (1991); Bank Profitability Statistical Supplement
Average Net Interest Income Divided by Gross Income. Average is for 1981 - 1989.

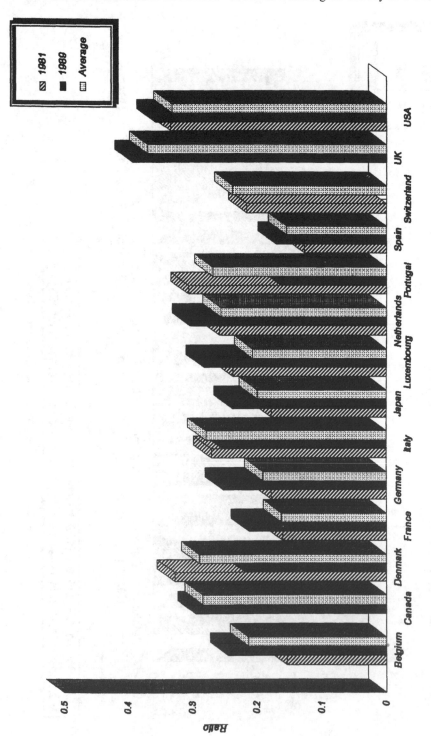

Figure 15 Ratio of net non-interest income to gross income

Figure 16 Financial sector share of total employment

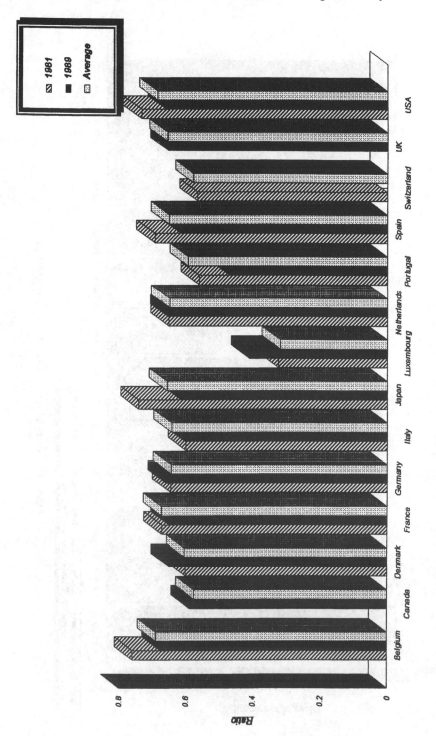

Figure 17 Ratio of operating expenses to gross income for all banks

Source: OECD Paris (1991): Bank Profitability Statistical Supplement
Average operating expenses divided by gross income. (1981 - 1989) See note on all banks. Average is 1981 - 1989

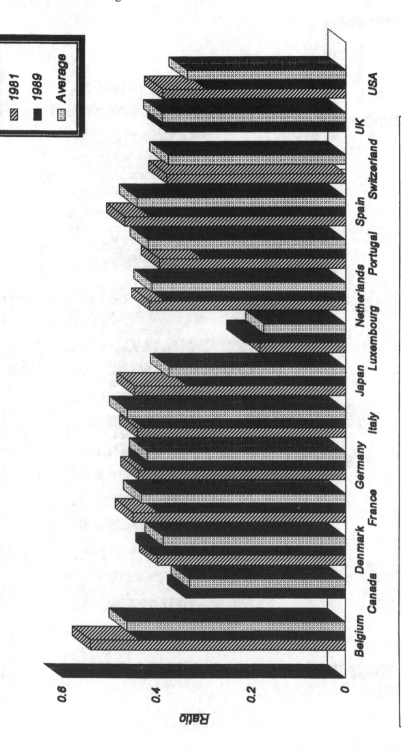

Source: OECD Paris (1991); Bank Profitability Statistical Supplement
Average Staff Costs divided by Average Gross Income for All Banks. See note on All Banks. Average is 1981 - 1989

Figure 18 Ratio of staff costs to gross income

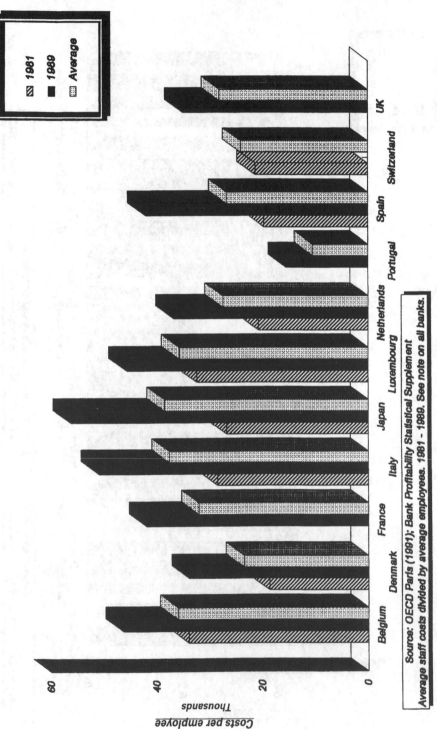

Figure 19 Average staff costs per employee

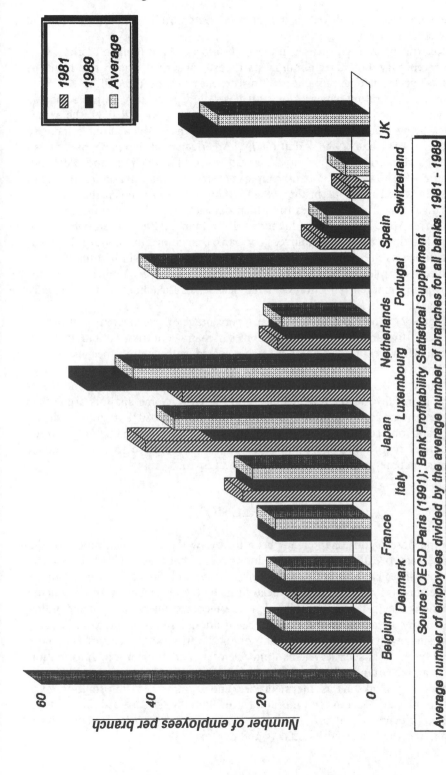

Figure 20 Number of employees per branch for all banks

the workforce is employed in the financial sector. Italy and Portugal are the lowest, at under 5%.

Relative operating expenses in the 1980s are shown in Figures 17 and 18. In every country but Luxembourg, staff costs absorbed about two-fifths of banks' gross income; total operating expenses about three-fifths. In most countries, operating expenses or staff costs as a percentage of gross income either remained unchanged or fell slightly between 1981 and 1989, the exceptions being Denmark and Luxembourg, where there was a notable increase between 1981 and 1989. Additionally, American and Japanese banks also showed a marked decline in these ratios; so did Belgium and Portugal. Figure 19 shows that a bank employee earned somewhat more in Japan than in western Europe in the 1980s. Labour costs were much the lowest in Portugal. In all the countries for which data are available, average costs per employee were substantially higher in 1989 than in 1981. There were more than five times as many employees per bank branch in Luxembourg, Portugal and Japan as in Spain or Switzerland (see Figure 20). Japan had managed to reduce its employees per branch by 1989 but most other countries have not shown any marked reduction over the decade. In Luxembourg, they actually increased.

Figure 21 shows loan provisions as a percentage of gross income represented between 10% and 20% of banks' incomes in many countries, but barely 2% in Japan. However, these figures must be treated with caution, because of the different tax treatment of loan provisions between countries. For example, Japanese banks are not normally permitted to write-off loan losses, and therefore, do no declare them as readily as in the USA. Some analysts argue that Japanese loan losses are underestimated by as much as 80%. Figure 22 shows the ratio on securities provisions to gross income for all banks. Only three countries report this figure, but they appear to be close to 3% of Italian banks' incomes, and much less in Japan and Spain.

CONCLUSION

The purpose of this chapter has been to review the traditional model of the bank, and to extend it to include more recent bank activities, such as off-balance sheet banking and the offering of non-bank financial services. Banks are distinguished from other financial firms by the intermediary and payments functions they perform, but this role is not incompatible with them expanding into newer areas of business. The organisational structure of banks is also consistent with Coase's classic analysis of the firm, and extensions of these ideas by authors such as Alchian and Demsetz and Williamson. Information plays an important role in banking; the presence of information costs helps to explain why banks act as intermediaries, and asymmetry of information gives rise to adverse selection and moral hazard. Banking, it is argued, illustrates a classic principal–agent problem between depositors and shareholders and a bank, and the bank and its officers and debtors.

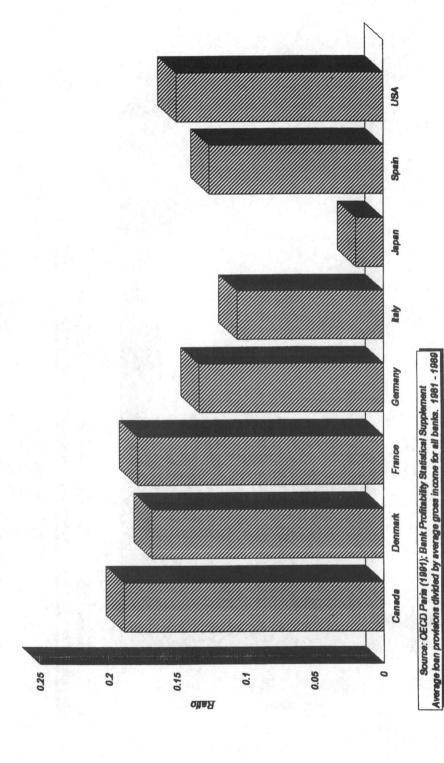

Figure 21 Ratio of loan provisions to gross income for all banks

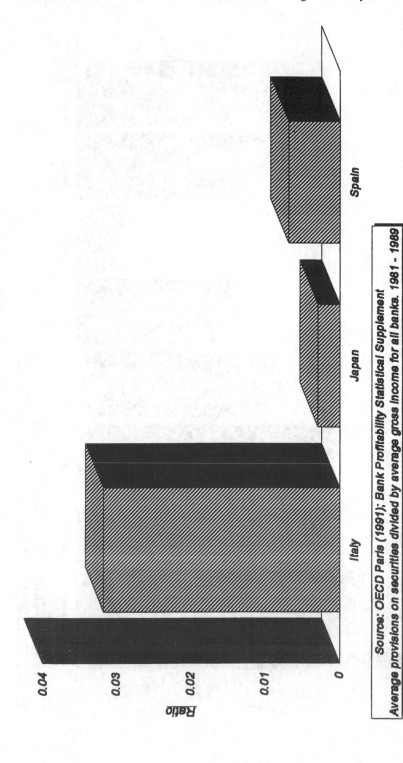

Figure 22 Ratio of provisions on securities to gross income for all banks

This chapter should have provided the reader with an overview of banking as the century comes to a close. The stylised facts on banking present a picture of a sector which has been largely stable over the 1980s, though, with the exception of Japanese banks, profits were largely trendless, and somewhat volatile for Anglo-American banks. There was no marked change in staff costs or operating expenses as a percentage of gross income, with the exception of American and Japanese banks, where the ratio fell. Average costs per employee were higher in 1989 than in 1981.

At first sight, it appears that the performance measures on banking are consistent with the view that the banking sector is in decline; that banks as we know them could disappear early in the next century. However, there is a question mark over the accuracy of most of these indicators. Furthermore, as was argued earlier in the chapter, based on the definition of banking there is no reason to think that banks will disappear, unless incumbent banks prove unable to maintain a competitive advantage in the provision of intermediary, payments, and other non-bank financial services. The next chapter considers what is arguably the most important trend in the financial markets as the century comes to a close: the globalisation of banking.

2

International Banking

INTRODUCTION

In Chapter 1, readers were introduced to the theory of banking, which considered the question of why banks exist and the reasons banks exhibit an organisational structure typical of most profit-maximising firms. It was stressed that the primary role of banks is direct intermediation between borrower and lender, though most banks are engaged in other financial activities, including fee-based services, off-balance sheet business and general risk management. In this chapter, the emphasis is on the theory and practice of international banking, because of its critical importance in the modern banking framework.

International banking is not a new phenomenon; international bank activity can be traced back to as early as the 13th century. What is new is the scale of international bank activity. For example, in the period 1989 to 1993, the stock of international bank lending averaged $7.7 trillion.*

This chapter is organised as follows. The following section looks at the theory of international banking; there is then a consideration of the trade in international banking services and of the growth of multinational banking. The theme is that banking is like any other sector made up of profit-maximising firms; it is important to consider both international trade in banking services, *and* foreign direct investment by banks. The chapter then reviews the welfare costs and benefits of international banking, and examines the performance of international banks in the 1980s.

THEORY OF INTERNATIONAL BANKING

Definition of an International Bank

According to Aliber (1984) there are at least three different definitions of an international bank. First, a bank may be said to be international if it uses branches or subsidiaries in foreign countries to conduct business. For example,

---

*Source: Bank of England (1994), Chart A.

the sale of US dollar-denominated deposits in Toronto by American banks with Canadian subsidiaries would constitute international banking; the sale of the same deposits by Canadian banks would be classified as domestic banking.

A second definition of international banking relates to the currency denomination of the loan or deposit, independent of the location of the bank. Any sterling transaction undertaken by a bank headquartered in the UK would be part of British domestic banking, irrespective of whether this transaction is carried out in a British branch or a subsidiary located outside the UK. But transactions in currencies other than sterling will be part of international banking, independent of the actual location of the British branch.

A third way of defining international banking is by the nationality of the customer and the bank. If the headquarters of the bank and customer have the same national identity, then any banking operation done for this customer is a domestic activity, independent of the location of the branch or the currency denomination of the transaction. For example, all Japanese banking carried out on behalf of Japanese corporate customers would be part of the domestic banking system in Japan, even if both the branch and the firm are subsidiaries located in Wales.

Noting these different definitions, Aliber (1984) opted for one close to the second definition, relating international banking activities to the association between national currency of the transaction and the country which has chartered the bank. A bank is said to be engaging in international banking when it sells deposits and buys loans in currencies other than the home currency—that is, the currency of the country in which it is chartered. Other authors have advocated the use of the other definitions.

The problem with all of the above definitions is that they are trying to give *one* answer to *two* separate questions in international banking. In formulating a definition, it is important to distinguish between the international activities of a home-based bank, and the establishment of cross-border branches and subsidiaries. The existence of *international bank service activity* is explained by the traditional theory of international trade, while *multinational banking* is consistent with the economic theory of the multinational enterprise. Thus, to gain a full understanding of the determinants of international banking, it is important to address two questions:

- Why do banks engage in international banking activities such as the trade in foreign currencies?
- What are the economic determinants of the multinational bank, that is, a bank with cross-border branches or subsidiaries?

International Trade in Banking Services

International trade theory may be used to address the issue of why banks engage in the *trade* of international bank services. Comparative advantage is the basic principle behind the international trade of goods and services. A country is said to have *comparative* advantage in the production of a good (or service) if it is produced more efficiently in this country than anywhere else in the world. The economic welfare of a country increases if the country exports the goods in which it has a comparative advantage and imports goods and services from countries which are relatively more efficient in their production. At firm level, firms engage in international trade because of *competitive* advantage. They exploit arbitrage opportunities. A firm will export a good or service from one country and sell it in another because there is an opportunity to profit from arbitrage.

The phenomenon of trade in international banking services is best explained by appealing to the theories of comparative and competitive advantage. In banking, the traditional core product is an intermediary service, accepting deposits from some customers and lending funds to others. The intermediary function involves portfolio diversification and asset evaluation. A bank which diversifies its assets can offer a risk/return combination of financial assets to individual investors/depositors at a lower transactions cost than would be possible if the individual investor were to attempt the same diversification. Banks also offer the evaluation of credit and other risks for the uninitiated depositor or investor. The bank acts as a filter to evaluate signals in a financial environment where the amount of information available is limited. If banks offer international portfolio diversification and/or credit evaluation services on a global basis, they are engaging in the international trade of their intermediary service. For example, a bank may possess a competitive advantage in the evaluation of the riskiness of international assets, and therefore, its optimal portfolio of assets will include foreign currency denominated assets.

As was noted in Chapter 1, a by-product of intermediation is bank participation in the payments system, including settlement, direct debit, and chequing facilities. If some of its corporate or retail customers engage in international trade activity, they will require global money transmission services. The simplest example is the provision of foreign exchange facilities for the international traveller. The use of credit card facilities across national frontiers is now well developed. In parts of Europe, it is possible to use a debit card from one state (for example, the UK) to obtain local currency in another state (for example, Spain).

To conclude, if a bank offers its intermediary or payments services across national boundaries, it is engaging in international trade activities and is like any other global firm which seeks to boost its profitability through international trade.

The Multinational Bank

To complete the theoretical picture of global banking, the second question should be addressed—that is, why do banks set up branches or subsidiaries and therefore become multinational banks? The question is best answered by drawing on the theory of the determinants of the multinational enterprise. A multinational enterprise (MNE) is normally defined as any firm with plants extending across national boundaries. Modifying this definition for banking, a bank with cross-border branches or subsidiaries* is a multi-national bank.

It is important to stress from the outset that *locational efficiency* conditions in a given country are necessary, but not sufficient to explain the existence of MNEs.[†] Locational efficiency refers to the choice of a plant location—comparatively, there is an advantage in being the lowest cost producer of a good or service. However, to explain the existence of the MNE, other factors are at work—otherwise, one would observe a domestically domiciled firm producing and exporting the good or service. Thus, one has to look beyond locational efficiency to explain why a plant is owned by non-resident shareholders.

There are two important reasons why an MNE rather than a domestic firm produces and exports a good or service. Barriers to free trade, due to government policy or monopoly power in supply markets, is the first explanation for the existence of MNEs. For example, Japanese manufacturers have set up European subsidiaries, hoping to escape some of the harsh European trade barriers on the import of Japanese manufactured goods. The second is imperfections in the market place, often in the form of a knowledge advantage possessed by a certain type of firm which cannot be easily traded. American fast food conglomerates have been very successful in global expansion through franchises, which profit from managerial and food know-how originally developed in the USA.

The same framework can be applied to explain the presence of multinational banks (MNBs). Banks may opt to set up branches or subsidiaries overseas because of barriers to free trade and/or market imperfections. For example, US regulations in the 1960s[‡] effectively stopped foreigners from issuing bonds in the USA and American companies from using dollars to finance foreign direct investment. US banks got round these restrictions by using their overseas branches, especially in London, because it was a key centre for global finance. Later, these banks used their London subsidiaries to offer clients investment banking services, prohibited under US law.

Additionally, the nature of banking means banks possess a number of intangible assets which cannot be traded in the market place. For example, a bank may wish to profit from the employment of superior management skills in a foreign country, provided locational efficiency conditions are met. Thus, US banks with management expertise in securitisation may transfer these experts to their London subsidiaries, as the securitisation business in Europe grows. Japanese banks have established subsidiaries in London and New York, where the markets are subject to fewer regulations than in Japan. This move was

---

*A bank branch is not legally independent from the parent, while a subsidiary is a separate legal entity.

[†]For a review of the literature on the economics of the multinational enterprise, see Heffernan and Sinclair (1990). Caves (1982) outlines the basic models used here. Empirical literature in this area includes Caves (1974), Dunning (1985), Maki and Meredith (1986), Meredith (1984), and Michalet and Chevalier (1985).

[‡]See p. 79 for more detail.

partly motivated by a belief that experience gained in other markets would give bankers a competitive edge in the event that Japanese financial markets are deregulated.

Reputation is an important intangible asset possessed by banks. Many of the London merchant banks have established offices in other countries, to exploit their reputation for expertise in corporate finance, and other investment banking services. It is not possible to sell reputation on an open market. Provided locational efficiency conditions are met, reputation may be a profitable reason for a bank expanding across national borders.

Many authors (for example, Coulbeck, 1984) have argued that MNBs exist because banks need to follow their corporate customers overseas. The theory outlined above is not inconsistent with this traditional explanation. Suppose the customer of a bank decides to set up a subsidiary in a foreign country. The lending bank may follow the customer to meet the service demands of the client. In the days of colonial trade, when banking systems were under-developed, this factor was more important than today, when firms are expanding into countries, which, in most cases, already have well developed banking systems. But even if the multinational has operations in a developed economy with an extensive banking system, it may wish to employ the services of a home country bank because the cost of local bank credit, with no local knowledge of the firm, is likely to be higher.

Additionally, the bank may follow the corporate customer overseas to protect its own assets. If the bank is going to lend funds to a multinational firm, it will require information on the foreign operations to properly assess the creditworthiness of the client. The optimal way of gathering information may be the establishment of a branch or subsidiary in the foreign country. Effectively, the bank internalises the implicit market for this information.

To summarise, the term international banking should be defined to include two different activities: trade in international banking services, consistent with the traditional theory of competitive advantage for why firms trade, and MNBs, consistent with the economic determinants of the multinational enterprise. Having classified international banking in this way, attention will now turn to developments in international banking services and multinational banking.

TRADE IN INTERNATIONAL BANKING SERVICES

This section reviews the post-war development of international banking services. With an international flow of funds, some banks will become important global financial intermediaries, if they possess a competitive advantage in offering this service. The international intermediary function lowers the costs and risks of international transactions, just as it does in the purely domestic case, discussed at length in Chapter 1. International financial intermediation has been enhanced by the development of the Euromarkets, the growth of the interbank markets, and an international payments system.

The International Payments System

A payments system is the system of instruments and rules which permits agents to meet payment obligations and to receive payments owed to them. As was noted in Chapter 1, banks, as intermediaries, are important players in the payments system because they are the source of the legal currency and they facilitate the transfer of funds between agents. Denial of access to payments can be used as an entry barrier in banking. If the payments system extends across national boundaries, it becomes a global concern. Typically, major banks act as clearing agents not only for individual customers but also for smaller banks. There is a high degree of automation in the international banking system. The key systems* are outlined below:

- *SWIFT*, the Society for Worldwide Interbank Financial Telecommunications, which was established in Belgium in 1973. A cooperative company, it is owned by roughly 2000 financial institutions, including banks,† worldwide. The objective of SWIFT is to meet the data communications and processing needs of the global financial community. It transmits financial messages, payment orders, foreign exchange confirmations, and securities deliveries to over 3500 financial institutions on the network, which are located in 88 countries. The network is available 24 hours a day, seven days a week throughout the year. The messages include a wide range of banking and securities transactions, including payment orders, foreign exchange transactions, and securities deliveries. In 1992, the system handled about 1.6 million messages per business day. Real time and on-line, SWIFT messages pass through the system instantaneously.
- *FEDWIRE and CHIPS*: both of these systems are for high value, dollar payments. *FEDWIRE*, the Federal Reserve's Fund Transfer System, is a *real-time gross settlement* transfer system for domestic funds, operated by the Federal Reserve. Deposit-taking institutions that keep reserves or a clearing account at the Federal Reserve use FEDWIRE to send or receive payments, which amounts to about 11 000 users. In 1992, there were 68 million FEDWIRE funds transfers, with a value of $199 trillion. The average size of a transaction is $3 million. *CHIPS*, the Clearing House Interbank Payments System, is a New York-based private payments system, operated by the New York Clearing House Association since 1971. CHIPS is an on-line electronic payments system for the transmission and processing of international dollars. Unlike FEDWIRE, there is *multilateral netting* of payments transactions, and net obligations are settled at the end of each day. At 1630 hours (eastern time), CHIPS informs each participant of their net

---

*For a comprehensive review of payment systems in developed economies, readers are referred to the annual edition of *Payments Systems in the Group of Ten Countries*, published by the Bank for International Settlements. The 1992 figures cited for SWIFT, CHIPS, and CHAPS are taken from the 1993 edition.
†In addition to banks, other co-owners of SWIFT are broker-dealers, investment managers, securities exchanges, central securities depositories, and clearing organisations.

position. Those in net deficit must settle by 1745 hours, so all net obligations are cleared by 1800. Most of the payments transferred over CHIPS are international interbank transactions, including dollar payments from foreign exchange transactions, and eurodollar placements and returns. It also makes payments associated with commercial transactions, bank loans, and securities. Obligations on other payment or clearing systems can be settled through CHIPS. In 1992, there were 40 million payments, valued at $240 trillion.

- *CHAPS*: London-based, the Clearing House Automated Payments System was established in 1984 and permits same-day sterling transfers. There are 14 CHAPS settlement banks, including the Bank of England, along with 400 other financial firms which, as sub-members, can engage in direct CHAP settlements. The 14 banks are responsible for the activities of sub-members, and settle on their behalf at the end of each day. The closing time is 1510 hours (GMT). The Bank of England conducts a daily check of the transfer figures submitted to them. In 1992, the total value of payments through CHAPS was £20 928 billion, equivalent to a turnover of British GDP every seven days. There are other payments systems in the UK;* CHAPS is for high-value, same-day sterling transfers. CHAPS accounts for just over half the transfers in the UK payments system; the average daily values transferred through the UK system was £161 billion in 1993. A framework for introducing real time gross settlement was drawn up in 1993. It will mean transactions across settlement accounts at the Bank of England will be settled in "real-time", rather than at the end of each day.

A number of the large global banks run their own electronic payments systems, primarily to facilitate internal global payments. These systems are run alongside SWIFT and other public systems. The internal systems are also used to attract corporate business. For example, Chase Manhattan and Citibank have offered a relatively cheap transfer service for their corporate clients.

SWIFT is the most popular electronic fund transfer system because it offers real-time gross settlement 24 hours a day and is a cooperative, non-profit-maximising system. CHIPS and CHAPs were criticised for their limited opening hours and excessive charges, especially for erroneous messages. Also, member banks (money centre banks in the US, clearing banks in the UK) effect transactions in CHIPS and CHAPS, so competitors must use these banks as their agents. All three systems have problems arising from complex and incompatible software, leading to high staff training costs. A potential competitor in the future will be a secure internet system which uses e-cash to settle transactions in real time.

---

*The other wholesale system was Town Clearing, which was paper-based, high-value, same-day settlement but confined to the City of London—it ceased operations in March 1995. There are three retail systems; Cheque Clearing and Credit Clearing, which are paper-based. BACS is the third system, offering electronic clearing for debt and credit items.

The Euromarkets

International banks operating in the Euromarkets play a critical role in international financial intermediation. Banks have been providing international trade finance for several centuries; but syndicated medium- to long-term loans, and the provision of brokerage and underwriting services in the international bond markets, are more recent developments. The growth of the Euromarkets has been well documented elsewhere, and will be summarised briefly here.* There are several factors which explain the emergence of the Euromarkets. First, the UK government had a long history (1939 – 79) of imposing exchange controls which restricted British banks in the external (that is, non-domestic) use of sterling. London was a centre for international trade finance and the controls posed a threat to the external operations of many British banks. However, in the absence of any restrictions on the use of foreign currencies to finance external operations, UK banks sought out dollar deposits for this purpose. Exchange controls were not removed until 1979.

Second, by the late 1950s there was a good supply of dollars because of large capital inflows into the US and increased foreign holdings of dollars. This increasing supply of offshore dollars, coupled with rising demand by London banks, led to the establishment of the "Eurodollar market", a European market in dollar deposits and loans. It was soon extended to the trade in the currencies of most of the industrial countries, hence the term Eurocurrency market, or Euromarkets.

Third, the interest equalisation tax and the foreign direct investment regulation imposed by the US government in the 1960s had the effect of discouraging foreigners from issuing bonds in the US and of deterring foreign direct investment by US firms, unless the funds to finance the foreign direct investment could be raised on overseas markets. The regulations did not cover foreign branches of American banks, so, foreign operations were shifted to overseas branches. These branches used the Eurodollar markets to meet the demand for international finance coming from US firms and bond issuers wanting to raise capital in US dollars via the Eurocurrency markets.

Fourth, non-residents of West Germany or Switzerland wishing to hold deposits in either Deutsche marks or Swiss francs could not do so in the respective countries, because banks were prohibited from paying interest on such deposits. Eurocurrency markets provided an alternative source for these currencies.

Fifth, there were a variety of domestic monetary regulations in the US and European countries during the post-war period until the 1980s, which effectively restricted the supply of credit. Examples of these policies include

---

*For a detailed account of the Euromarkets, readers are referred to Johnston (1983) and Melvin (1992).
†The "corset" was a series of interest rate taxes which discouraged banks from paying interest on deposits, and therefore limited the amount of funding they could use for lending. It was operative for 6 years.

Regulation Q in the US, and the "corset"[†] in the UK. Banks in these countries could turn to the Euromarkets for funds, which were more plentiful in the absence of interest rate ceilings and reserve requirements. Lastly, the sudden growth of OPEC revenues after 1974 and the severe deficit problems of the oil-importing countries gave the Euromarkets a new role: the recycling of the OPEC surpluses.

By the early 1980s, most domestic monetary and capital controls had been removed by the respective governments. The need for a market to recycle OPEC revenues had largely disappeared. However, by this time, the Euromarkets (Eurocurrency, Eurobond, Euroloan) had a competitive advantage in offering a variety of offshore services to customers. Hence, the demand for funds from the markets was sustained, even though domestic regulations had been eased. The size of the Euromarkets is enormous. For example, during the first six months of 1994, the top 25 lead managers of public Eurobonds were involved in 713 issues, with a total value of $213.6 billion.*

Prior to the emergence of the Euromarkets, international banking services were largely confined to offering foreign exchange facilities and other related services, to enhance either international trade or the foreign direct investment activities of multinationals. The importance of the Euromarkets cannot be overstated. Their growth enhanced the movement of global capital through the *flow* of international funds, as distinct from the flow of capital via foreign direct investment.

The Interbank Market

The interbank market is used by over 1000 banks in over 50 different countries. Interbank trading in the Euromarkets accounts for two-thirds of all the business transacted in these markets. The interbank market performs five basic functions. It enables banks to manage their assets and liabilities at the margin to meet daily fluctuations in liquidity requirements, thereby enhancing *liquidity smoothing*. *Global liquidity distribution* also takes place, because the market can be used to redistribute funds from excess liquidity regions to areas of liquidity shortage. The market also means deposits initially placed with certain banks can be on-lent to different banks, thereby facilitating the *international distribution of capital*. The *hedging of risks* by banks is made easier, because they can use the interbank markets to hedge their exposure in foreign currencies and foreign interest rates. *Regulatory avoidance* is the fifth function of the interbank market—bank costs are reduced if they can escape domestic regulation and taxation. Thus, the interbank market has enhanced the international banking system's role as an international financial intermediary by increasing international liquidity, which, in turn, reduces bank costs and increases the efficiency of global operations.

In 1993, interbank activity within the BIS (Bank for International Settlements) reporting area made up 68% of total international bank lending,

---

*Source: *Euromoney Bondware*, September 1994.

up slightly over what it was in the previous two years, but below the 1990 level of about 70% of the total. The proportion of lending to non-bank end users did not change in any significant way over the five-year period, 1989–93. Japanese banks continue to be the largest lender of funds within the BIS reporting area, with a share of just below 27%. However, their share has declined over the five years, after peaking at 38.3% in 1988.

MULTINATIONAL BANKING

Historical Background

Multinational banks (MNBs) are banks with subsidiaries, branches, or representative offices which spread across national boundaries. They are in no way unique to the post-war period. For example, from the 13th to 16th centuries, the merchant banks of the Medici and the Fugger families had branches located throughout Europe, to finance foreign trade. In the 19th centuries, MNBs were associated with the colonial powers, including Britain and, later on, Belgium, Germany and Japan. The well-known colonial MNBs include the Hong Kong and Shanghai Banking Corporation (HSBC), founded in 1865 by business interests in Hong Kong specialising in the "China trade" of tea, opium and silk. Silver was the medium of exchange. By the 1870s, branches of the bank had been established throughout the Pacific basin. In 1992, the colonial tables were turned when HSBC acquired one of Britain's major clearing banks, the Midland Bank.

The National Bank of India was founded in 1863, to finance India's export and import trade. Branches could be found in a number of countries trading with India. The Standard Bank was established in 1853 specialising in the South African wool trade. Headquartered in London, it soon expanded its activities to new developments in South Africa and Africa in general. Presently it is known as the Standard Chartered Bank, and though it has a London head office, the bank does virtually no domestic business in the UK. By 1914, the Deutsche Bank had outlets around the world, and German banks had 53 branches in Latin America. The Société Génerale de Belgique had branches in the Belgian African colonies, and the Mitsui Bank established branches in Japanese colonies such as Korea.

All of these banks were "colonial" commercial banks because their primary function was to finance trade between the colonies and the mother country. Branches were normally subject to tight control by head office. Their establishment is consistent with the economic determinants of the MNE, discussed earlier. Branches meant banks could be better informed about their borrowers engaged in colonial trade. Since most colonies lacked a banking system, the home country banks' foreign branches met the demand for banking services among their colonial customers.

A number of multinational merchant (or investment) banks were established in the 19th century—good examples are Barings (1762) and Rothschilds (1804). They specialised in raising funds for specific project finance. Rather than making loans, project finance was arranged and stock was sold to individual investors. The head office or branch in London used the sterling interbank and capital markets to fund the project finance these banks were engaged in. Capital importing countries included Turkey, Egypt, Italy, Spain, Sweden, Russia, and the Latin American countries. Development offices associated with the bank were located in the foreign country. Multinational merchant banks are also consistent with the economic determinants of the MNE. Their expertise lay in the finance of investment projects in capital-poor countries; this expertise was acquired through knowledge of the potential of the capital-importing country (hence the location of the development offices) and by being close to the source of supply, the London financial markets.

There was rapid expansion of American banks overseas after the First World War. In 1916 banks headquartered in the USA had 26 foreign branches and offices, rising to 121 by 1920, 81 of which belonged to five US banking corporations. These banks were established for the same purpose as the 19th century commercial banks, to finance the US international trade and foreign direct investment of US corporations, especially in Latin America. In the 1920s, these banks expanded to Europe, in particular Germany and Austria. By 1931, 40% of all US short-term claims on foreigners were German.

A few American and British banks established branches early in the 20th century, but the rapid growth of MNBs took place from the mid-1960s onward. Davis (1983) argued that in this period banks moved from a "passive" international role, where they operated foreign departments, to one where they became "truly international" by assuming overseas risks. However, such an argument makes ambiguous the distinction between the MNB aspect of international banks and trade in international banking services. As expected, the key OECD countries, including the USA, UK, Japan, France, and Germany, have a major presence in international banking. Table 3 summarises, by country, the number of banks that belong to *The Banker*'s "top 1000". Swiss banks occupied an important position in international banking because Switzerland

Table 3 Number of International Banks, by Country, in the "Top 1000"

Country	% of banks in the top 1000	Number of banks in top 1000, 1994
Canada	87.1	9
France	6.3	26
Germany	2.2	83
Italy	25.7	79
Japan	100	117
Switzerland	12.97	29
United Kingdom	67.33	34*
United States	19.05	178

Source: *The Banker*, July 1994. International banks are ranked by tier one capital—see Chapter 6 for full definition; OECD (1991), *Bank Profitability and Statistical Supplement*, Paris.
*16 of these "UK" banks are actually subsidiaries of banks headquartered in another country.

has three international financial centres (Zurich, Basle and Geneva), the Swiss franc is a leading currency, and they have a significant volume of international trust fund management and placement of bonds. Recently, however, some of the Swiss banks have experienced a decline in their global activities. The Canadian economy is relatively insignificant by most measures but some Canadian banks do have extensive branch networks overseas, including foreign retail banking; they are also active participants in the Euromarkets.

MNBs and Wholesale Banking Activities

Bank foreign direct investment in the form of MNBs primarily takes place to facilitate wholesale banking operations. It includes participation in the Euromarkets, offering investment advisory services to corporate clients, accepting corporate deposits, and making corporate loans. Some of these banks have specialised still further, concentrating on one of a few niche markets.

The reasons for concentration in wholesale banking are twofold. First, banks follow their corporate customers overseas, to offer them bank services and to gather information on the potential creditworthiness of the customer. Therefore it is not surprising that foreign branches of MNBs focus on wholesale banking activities. Second, the barriers to entry in the wholesale banking market are small in comparison to the retail banking system. In wholesale banking, the two crucial barriers are the confidence factor and regulation of banking activities. In the absence of regulatory restrictions on foreign bank entry, there are virtually no barriers to overcome because the MNB will have already gained the reputation needed among its corporate clients.

In retail banking, an additional critical barrier to entry is the requirement for an extensive branch network. The large capital outlay is not easily recovered should the venture fail. Wholesale banking activities are less dependent on branches; the bank's crucial asset will be its ability to offer expert corporate service to its clients. While new technology (e.g. electronic funds transfer and home banking) may ease the entry barriers to retail banking, its effects have been minor, to date. However, it is worth stressing that banks do offer international retail banking *services*, such as international investment facilities for the personal customer, foreign exchange facilities, and global automatic teller machines.

From the mid-1960s onward, MNBs were primarily engaged in the Euroloan and Eurobond market operations. In the early 1980s, banks began to enter new international capital markets, including the Euroequity market; Eurobonds with equity warrants (Eurobonds with an option to buy equity); currency and interest rate swaps; and the placement of Eurocommercial paper by banks for corporate clients.

International Banking Activity by American and Japanese Banks

The Japanese and American banks are the most important players in the global banking game, and for this reason, a sub-section is devoted to their activities. Darby (1986) outlined the growth of American MNBs from the 1960s onward. The 1960s saw the re-emergence of American banks on the international banking scene. The setting up of foreign subsidiaries was largely motivated by domestic banking regulations such as deposit interest ceilings, reserve requirements, various capital controls and restrictions on investment banking. The growth rate of foreign branches continued at an increasing rate, until the early 1980s. For example, the number of foreign branches of US banks rose from 124 in 1960 to 905 in 1984.

However, there was a decline in US MNB activity from the late 1980s onward, which, argued Darby, can be explained by a number of factors. In 1978, US banks were authorised to use international banking facilities (IBFs). An IBF allows a US bank to participate directly in the Eurocurrency market. Prior to this date, such participation could only take place through foreign branches or subsidiaries. The international competitiveness of US banks also declined and interest in foreign expansion waned as earnings from global sources contracted.

Foreign banks have increased their presence in the American banking market since the 1960s, and at an accelerating pace. They have established branches, agencies, subsidiary banks and non-banks and since 1978, Edge Act corporations. New restrictions placed on foreign banks by the International Banking Act (see Chapter 6) did not deter their growth. In 1972, there were approximately 46 branches/agencies/commercial bank subsidiaries, accounting for 3.6% of total US banking assets. In 1984, these figures had risen to 378 and 16.7%, respectively.*

Darby found several factors to be important in explaining foreign bank entry into the American market. First, there was a differential between US and Eurodollar interest rates; banks were able to fund their dollar-denominated assets more cheaply in the presence of a large differential. Second, the price–earnings ratios for American banks were relatively low (see Chapter 1), reflecting a low cost of entry by purchasing an existing US bank. Third, the size of net foreign direct investment was influential. Darby also found that branches, agencies and Edge Act corporations concentrated on wholesale banking, but subsidiary banks acted very much like US-owned banks with middle market and retail banking activities.

Between 1977 and 1987, the assets of Japanese banks in London increased from 8% to 25% of total assets (sterling plus foreign currency) of all foreign banks in the UK. From 1982 to the late 1980s, activities of Japanese banks in London grew at a faster rate than those of other nationality groups.[†] But since 1989, activity has declined. The growth of their international assets declined from $202 billion in 1989 to $153 billion in 1990. Excluding exchange rate effects, expansion was only one-third what it was in 1989. On the funding side, new borrowing from unaffiliated banks was scaled back by two-thirds. In 1991 and 1992, there was a marked withdrawal of Japanese banks from the interbank market, and the external lending of Japanese banks was actually negative between 1990 and 1992, turning positive again in 1993. London and

---

*Data on foreign banks were not collected by the Federal Reserve System until November 1972.
[†]Source: Bank of England (1987).

New York saw the main reductions, but activities expanded in continental Europe, especially in France and Belgium.

Burton and Saelens (1986) identified three stages of foreign direct investment by Japanese financial institutions. Up to the early 1970s, Japanese banks expanded abroad in response to the increasing importance of Japan in global financial markets and the derived demand for trade finance. Foreign direct investment was especially pronounced in the period 1970–74, and many banks followed their customers abroad. In stage two, the slowdown in the Japanese economy after the 1974 oil crisis, together with the increased competitive structure of domestic financial markets, caused banks and securities houses to aggressively expand foreign business. The authors suggested that branches operating in the unregulated supranational markets had an opportunity to achieve higher rates of return on equity.* During stage three, Japanese MNB activity expanded with a view to acquiring experience in the international markets that would be useful when the domestic financial market is deregulated.

The above factors are typical of the internationalisation of most banks, though the 1987 Bank of England study identified a characteristic somewhat unique to Japanese expansion—the growth in the surplus of Japan's external account in the 1980s. Since 1983, the Japanese government has introduced measures designed to increase the international use of the yen (there was a marked expansion in Euroyen activity and foreign currency borrowing by Japanese residents) and the opening up of the country's domestic financial markets, which put pressure on domestic banking markets and encouraged banks to expand internationally.

Japanese foreign branches are engaged in two types of loan business in the global markets. Credit is granted to Japanese wholesale distributors and securities firms, including trading houses, car importers, consumer electronics firms, stockbrokers, and the banks' own merchant banking subsidiaries. In addition, loans are made to non-Japanese institutions with a very low default risk. In the UK, these are building societies, governments, and utility companies. Both involve large volume simple loan instruments, so a bank must be able to provide the instruments at low cost. Japanese foreign branches and subsidiaries are not important players in foreign domestic markets. In the US and UK, they accounted for roughly 8% of loans to residents (1987 figures).

Empirical Studies on Multinational Bank Activity

Nigh, Cho, and Krishnan (1986) looked at foreign branching by US banks to identify the economic determinants of multinational banking. Drawing on data from the period 1976–82 in 30 countries, this study used cross-section and time series regression analyses to test three hypotheses: that US branch banking

---

*There is a flaw in the logic of this argument, because global markets are far more competitive than the home markets.

involvement in a foreign country is positively related to US business presence in that country, to local banking market opportunities in the host country, and to the openness of the country to the establishment of new foreign bank branches. There was strong evidence to support the first hypothesis. The expected positive relationship held not only for all countries but for subsets of countries; developed, less developed, Europe, Latin America, and Asia. No empirical evidence was found to support the hypothesis that MNB activity is positively related to local banking market opportunities.* The authors did find evidence to support the hypothesis that the openness of the foreign country is important. This effect was found to be more pronounced for developing nations, especially in Asia. This factor may involve a time dimension. By 1976–82, foreign branches would have achieved their desired presence in Europe and Latin America, so that local entry restrictions were no longer important.

Zimmer and McCauley (1991) observed the declining international competitiveness of US banks in the 1980s, which they attributed to capital costs. Capital costs were defined as the fee or net spread between bank borrowing and lending rates a financial product must generate to increase the market value of the bank. Their analysis showed Japanese banks enjoyed a low cost of capital, US, UK, and Canadian banks a high cost; and German and Swiss banks moderate capital costs.

Hirtle (1991) used a product-based approach to assess the competitive performance of internationally active banks and securities firms. Hirtle reviewed the competitive conditions in seven product markets to clarify which firms are successful competitors on an international scale. The Eurocredit market was cited as an example of a truly global financial market, with a high degree of segmentation. Different types of financial institution specialise in different sectors of the market. Commercial banks dominate the Euroloan market, while investment banks and universal banks tend to dominate Eurobonds. Nationality appears to be very important in the Eurobond market, but less important in the Euroloan sector. In the non-dollar bond sector, the nationality of the lead underwriter tends to be strongly correlated with the nationality of the currency. In the dollar bond market, there is a high correlation between the nationalities of the intermediary and the bond issuer.

In the Eurobond market, US securities firms were found to be among the most successful competitors, but the market share of US intermediaries has declined since 1983, in part reflecting the decline in issues by US borrowers. An increase in Japanese issues, especially in the equity-warrant sector, increased market share for Japanese firms. US and Japanese banks have the largest share of the Euroloan market.

Like the Eurocredit market, the swap market has an international focus. Interest rate and currency swaps are used by firms to reduce the cost of borrowing in foreign and domestic capital markets and to manage currency

---

*However, local manufacturing production was used as an indicator of local market opportunity, and may not be sensitive enough—the ratio of total assets to deposits may be a better indicator.

and interest rate risk exposures generated by economic and financial market activity. Swaps are denominated in a wide variety of currencies to meet the needs of a diverse, multinational customer base. The principal swap dealing teams are commercial banks and securities firms, which tend to deal in swaps denominated in their home country currency. Thus success in the swap market continues to be influenced by domestic market factors. The strongest competitors in the swap market are the large global financial institutions, including US money-centre banks, US diversified securities firms, and European universal banks.

The Hirtle study showed some of the large dealers (commercial banks) offered a wide range of foreign exchange services, while other dealers specialised in transactions involving particular currencies and instruments. The trading operations of US multinational banks appeared to be among the most profitable, relative to other international institutions, both in terms of absolute foreign exchange income and in terms of the share of total operating income derived from foreign exchange activities. Their position reflects the strength of the dollar as an international reserve currency. Swiss banks led, in terms of the profitability and income derived from their foreign exchange operations; British firms had a high rating for the quality of foreign exchange services they provide.

Hirtle identified four national markets for banking products: commercial lending, retail banking, government bonds and equities. There are significant differences in the way these markets function because of differences in regulation, sophistication, and traditions governing the relationship between the banks and their customers. National differences can act as a barrier to foreign firms trying to penetrate one of these domestic markets. To see this point, consider the national markets in the USA, Japan, Germany, and the UK. A number of factors affect the competitive position of banks in the US, UK, German, and Japanese commercial lending markets. The cost of capital will influence the ability of a bank to sustain a competitive advantage in loan pricing, and a firm's choice of lender depends on the ability of the bank to extend credit during tight credit periods. In the USA, aggressive pricing strategies have been an important influence on competitive success, whereas in Germany and Japan, customer relationships are important. This difference is probably explained by the relatively strong links between commerce and banks in Japan and Germany, whereas the USA is known for its weak links, consistent with anti-trust concerns.

In the USA, foreign banks (especially Japanese banks) have been quite successful in penetrating the US lending market. This is explained by the large volume of foreign trade, the presence of foreign-owned firms, and the ability of the Japanese banks to attract both American and foreign borrowers. There is also fairly extensive penetration of the UK commercial lending market, probably because of the foreign presence in the UK economy.

In Japan, Germany, the USA, and the UK, numerous regulatory reforms have been introduced to increase competition in retail banking markets. But domestic banks appear to have an advantage over foreign banks because of the large physical presence required to operate a large-scale deposit-taking operation. The main strategy of foreign banks has been to focus on niche markets, such as population niches (for example, foreign nationals) or product niches.

In Japan, Germany, the UK, and the USA, government bond markets are largely dominated by domestic financial institutions, which is partly explained by the historical tendency to limit participation in government bond underwriting to a specified group of domestic banks and securities firms. While regulations excluding foreign firms are no longer a major obstacle, penetration by foreign firms has been minor because of the need for large-scale operations with a large customer base and skills in a range of financial market activities.

Hirtle observed that the national equity markets in Japan, Germany, the UK, and the USA had distinctive market structures that affect the competitive environment facing both foreign and domestic financial firms. For example, in the UK and the USA, underwriting and brokerage fees were negotiated, while in Germany and Japan, they were still fixed. In each of these four markets, the demand for equity services is concentrated among domestic institutional investors, giving large and sophisticated financial institutions a competitive advantage. Additionally, Hirtle argued, scale and scope economies mean a handful of domestic firms dominate trading and underwriting in each of these four markets.

Faced with the problems of entry, foreign firms have adapted one of two strategies with a view to entering local equity markets. One is to establish product niches, normally by building on competitive strengths developed in the home market. A second strategy is to purchase a domestic firm that is active in the equity markets. Both strategies have met with limited success.

THE COSTS AND BENEFITS OF INTERNATIONAL BANKING*

The costs and benefits of the international banking system are reviewed with the objective of assessing the effect of the international banking developments on the welfare of the national economies. The key benefit from international banking is a rise in *bank consumer surplus*, the difference between what a consumer is willing to pay for a bank service and what the consumer (who in the case of international banking, is probably a corporate customer) does pay. For bank products, consumer surplus will increase if deposit rates rise, loan rates fall, and fees for bank services decline.

As the globalisation of banking increases, consumer surplus should rise, for several reasons. First, international banking should increase the *efficiency* of the international flow of capital. Prior to recent developments, the transfer of capital was achieved primarily through foreign direct investment and aid-related finance. The Eurocurrency markets have enhanced the efficient flow of capital by bringing together international lenders and borrowers. For

---

*This section is taken from Heffernan (1987).

example, the absence of regulation on the Euromarkets has permitted marginal pricing on loans and deposits—the unconstrained LIBOR* rates have eliminated credit squeezes which tend to arise under an administered rate. *New* capital movements will be observed if, prior to the emergence of the system, interest rates varied across countries. As was observed earlier, there is no doubt the Euromarkets enhanced the transfer of new capital between countries.

MNBs will increase the number of banks present in the country, thereby increasing competitive pressure by eroding the traditional oligopolies of the domestic banking system. Greater competition among the international banks should reduce the price of international bank products. Domestic banking systems will also be under greater competitive pressure if some of the country's consumers are able to purchase international bank products and by-pass higher prices in the domestic market. As a result, there should be more competitive pricing in domestic markets, for those customers who have the option of going offshore (mainly corporates).

International banking activities can also be responsible for a number of welfare costs. First, revenue for central government may be reduced. If a central bank imposes reserve requirements on deposits in the banking system, the introduction of international banking facilities will lead to the flow of funds out of the domestic banking system and into the international system where deposit rates are higher. A reserve ratio requirement is a form of taxation on the banking system because it requires idle funds to be held at the central bank. The reduced volume of domestic deposits as they move offshore will reduce government revenues accruing from this source. These will be reduced still further if the competition forces the central bank to abandon the reserve ratio requirement, or eliminate controls on deposit rates. To make good the loss from the implicit tax on bank reserves, the government may impose a new type of distortionary taxation.

Second, the international banking system is not truly global, because it is largely confined to the wholesale banking market. This means there is discrimination in loan and deposit rates, those having access to the offshore banks getting more favourable terms than their fellow nationals. Since only some of the customers in a national economy gain, it will not be possible to judge whether there is a net gain accruing to residents of a given country.

Third, the diversion of banking activity from onshore to offshore alters the real resource costs of banking. Whether they increase or decline is governed by the cost differential between inshore and offshore banking. The movement of the loan and deposit rates in the Euromarkets since their operation began suggests the real resource costs have been lower. But they may have been underestimated for several reasons. For example, the banks underestimated the cost of lending in the Eurocurrency markets, especially in the case of sovereign loans; banks thought this type of lending was almost risk-free, because a country could not be declared insolvent. More generally, banks

_____
*The London Interbank Offer Rate.

lack experience in setting the prices for newer financial products, commensurate with their risk.

Information asymmetries are normally more pronounced in international banking. In a domestic system a bank officer is able to assess creditworthiness on the basis of direct knowledge about the borrower. In the Euromarket only the final lender has certain knowledge of who the borrower is, the average deposit passing through several banks before being loaned to a non-bank borrower. Often, the exposure of other banks in the Euromarkets is unknown to each individual bank. If global banking aggravates information difficulties, confidence is undermined, making bank runs more likely.

In 1984, the Institute for International Finance (IIF) was established by banks to collate information on international bank activity. Its establishment suggests banks thought they may have underestimated the costs of information-gathering in international banking. But it may not be the optimal solution. Given increasing returns to the pooling of costly information, the IIF may not be the most cost-effective way of collecting information, because it consists of a small coalition of international banks. Also, it could encourage oligopolistic tendencies in international banking.

To conclude, there have been both welfare costs and benefits associated with the development of international banking. Though some of the resource costs associated with international banking are difficult to quantify, it is generally accepted that the net welfare effects have been positive because new flows of capital created by the system have increased global productivity.

THE PERFORMANCE OF MAJOR INTERNATIONAL BANKS IN THE 1980s*

During the 1980s, banking and financial markets grew rapidly, in some cases, bank assets grew faster than nominal GDP. But the performance of major international banks differed both between and within countries and by size and type of institution. While return on assets was fairly steady, return on equity was more volatile. Almost all banks experienced a decline in profit performance in the 1980s, mainly due to a deterioration in their asset quality. In the early 1980s, poor asset quality was explained by sovereign lending to lesser developed countries, particularly Latin American countries. After 1982, there was a sharp decrease in this type of lending (see Chapter 5) but it was not until 1987 and 1989 that large banks in the UK, USA, and Canada wrote off large amounts of developing country debt. In the early 1990s, the asset quality problems were due to non-performing corporate and property loan portfolios, especially in the USA, Canada, Australia, the Scandinavian countries and Japan. The poor quality of their loan portfolios, together with increased regulatory pressures (for example, the Basle capital adequacy ratio) have caused banks to reduce traditional international lending activities and concentrate

---

*This section is based on the Bank of England (1992).

more on fee-earning corporate and personal business, from securities under-writing, and trading.

Most OECD countries introduced reforms of financial markets during the 1980s. However, the *net* effect of these regulatory changes on performance is ambiguous. On the one hand, in most countries the changes in bank regula-tions meant they could expand into new markets. At the same time, an em-phasis was placed on policy changes to encourage greater competition in markets. In addition, there was a strengthening in the amount of prudential regulation to which banks were subjected.

As was noted in Chapter 1, international banks have not done very well in the reduction of their cost to income ratios in the 1980s. Operating costs still consume more than 60% of most banks' total non-interest and net interest income, and most of these costs arise from staff. These observations do not appear to apply to medium-sized banks in the major industrialised countries, especially when one looks at the quality of the loan portfolios. Most banks have introduced cost control measures, by reducing personnel and closing branches. The rapid development of information technology should improve bank productivity.

International banks have taken action to boost performance. They have improved capitalisation, improved the pricing of risks, and cut back on global lending. Banks have also sought out less capital-intensive ways of increasing earnings. For example, highly rated corporates have been able to issue their own paper, rather than relying on banks. Commercial paper issues have increased fee-earning business for banks because they usually provide letters of credit and/or act as arrangers and dealers. The phenomenon was most pronounced in the USA, but this type of market also grew in some European countries and Japan.

CONCLUSION

This chapter has explored the global dimensions of banking. It was argued that international banking is best understood in terms of international trade in banking services and the growth of multinational banks (MNBs). Like any other firm, a bank will seek to boost its profitability through trade if it has a competitive advantage in the provision of at least one banking service. The growth of an international payments system, the development of global inter-bank markets and the emergence of sophisticated Euromarkets demonstrate how banks rely on a global network to profit from trade in international banking services. Multinational banking activity, it was stressed, is consistent with the economic determinants of foreign direct investment and the multi-national enterprise. Colonial commercial banks financed colonial trade and the early multinational merchant banks raised funds on the London markets to finance projects overseas. Today, all the OECD countries have MNBs, which engage, principally, in wholesale banking activities. The review of empirical work on Japanese and American banking, MNB activity, and the performance of international banks in the 1980s lends support to the key message being conveyed in this chapter: that banks, like any other firms, use international trade and foreign direct investment to boost the profitability of their operations. The next chapter looks at banking structures around the world, including the USA, the UK, Japan, the European Union, developing countries and emerging markets.

3
Banking Structures Around the World

INTRODUCTION

This chapter reviews the key features of banking structures in developed economies and emerging markets, including eastern Europe. It is designed to give readers an insight into the structures and issues related to the different banking systems. Detailed accounts of the different systems are avoided; instead, the emphasis is placed on an overview of the key differences and concerns relevant to bankers. The chapter first considers banking structures in the industrial economies, with an emphasis on financial systems in the UK, the USA, Japan and Europe. The focus of attention then shifts to developing economies; the chapter which reviews the emergence of commercial banking, problems faced by banking systems in developing nations, Islamic banking, curb markets, and a case study of developing country banking, using Indonesia. The chapter then looks at banking in Eastern Europe, scrutinising the banking reforms in Hungary, and the special problems of the Russian banking system.

BANKING STRUCTURES IN INDUSTRIALISED COUNTRIES

In the 1980s, banking and financial markets in the developed economies grew rapidly. Between 1973 and 1988, assets of the top 300 banks grew at nearly twice the rate of growth of world GDP. Depreciation of the dollar in relation to other major country currencies explains a good deal of the growth in non-US banks in the mid to late 1980s. In 1969, Japan did not have any banks among the top 10; it had one by 1979, and by 1988, nine of the top 10 were Japanese. The US banks held seven of the top 10 positions in 1969, two in 1979, but none in 1988. Some European banks were in the top 10 in the interim period between the fall of the American banks and the rise of the Japanese banks. In 1994, one US bank, Citicorp, made it into the top 10, as did one UK bank, Hong Kong and Shanghai Banking Corporation Holdings. Apart from one Chinese bank (Industrial and Commercial Bank of China), and one French bank (Crédit Agricole), six of the top ten banks were Japanese.*

In an empirical study, Goldberg and Hanweck (1991) identified variables explaining the growth of the world's 300 largest banks between 1969 and 1986. The dependent variable is the change in the percentage of total assets of the 300 largest banks controlled by banks in each country for each year. To remove exchange rate effects, these shares are calculated as if the 1969 exchange rate relative to the US dollar persisted throughout the period.[†]

In Goldberg and Hanweck, the independent variables tested were:

D_j: initial period total country deposits in the jth country (negative sign);

$\dot{p}_j$: inflation rate per period in the jth country (pooled over five years— positive sign);

CFT_j: the rate of change in total foreign trade in the jth country;

$CGNP_j$: the rate of change in GNP in the jth country;

I_j: the rate of change in interest rates in the jth country, pooled over five years.

The authors carried out OLS regressions for annual and five-year periods. In the annual regressions, total deposits (D) was the only variable found to be statistically significant with a negative sign, that is, higher deposit levels in a country are associated with a decline in world shares. The negative sign is what would be expected if, as argued by the authors, larger economies are more mature and have a lower growth potential for their banking systems.

When the data were pooled over five years, inflation rates and the rate of change in interest rates are found to be significantly positive and negative, respectively. Like the one-year regressions, D was found to be significantly negative. Thus, a higher rate of inflation improves the country's position as a world banking centre—assets get inflated. No other domestic factors (for example, the rate of change in GNP, foreign trade) were found to be significant. The authors found that increases in interest rates worsen a country's position, which is consistent with a country trying to use higher interest rates to discourage capital outflows.

Banks have been plagued by a number of persistent problems in industrialised countries. Dubious asset quality is at the top of the list, first in developing country debt; more recently with property and corporate lending, and, in the UK, personal and small business lending. Banks also encountered difficulties in reducing the ratio of cost to income during the 1980s.

There is little evidence of a change in the concentration of international banks over the past 15 years. In 1974, the top 10 banks accounted for 23% of the activity of the top 100 banks, and 17% of the activity of the top 300 banks. These figures were, respectively, 26% and 20% in 1988. One gets the

---

*Source: *The Banker*, various issues. The ranking of the top 1000 banks by *The Banker* was changed from total assets to tier one capital on 1991. This means the figures are not strictly comparable.
[†]The authors qualitatively document the importance of exchange rates in the growth of shares of banking assets. For example, in the years of a strong yen (against the dollar) from 1975–78, Japanese banks increased their share.

same indication of relative stability if one looks at the top 20 banks. The single market in Europe after 1993 may lead to greater consolidation of banking within Europe.

Thus, since 1970, the evolution of the international banking structure has been characterised by the decline in the American banks, a rapid growth, followed by recent decline, in Japanese banking, and the stable position of the European banks. Each of these regions are considered in turn. Before doing so, it is helpful to begin with a general discussion of banking structure in the developed economies by reviewing the financial structure of the "G-10" countries (now 11): Belgium, Canada, France, West Germany, Italy, Japan, the Netherlands, Sweden, Switzerland, the UK and the USA. Cumming and Sweet (1988) used four criteria for comparison: the separation of banking and commerce, the separation of bank and non-bank financial services, official supervision of the banking system, and access to central bank and liquidity facilities.

There are differences in the degree of *separation between banking and commerce*.* Cumming and Sweet argued that it is the exception rather than the rule to find cases where major banks are owned and controlled by commercial concerns. Sometimes, one observes the ownership of commercial enterprises by banks through holding companies. The UK, Italy and Switzerland have virtually no integration of banking and commerce. Though not prohibited by law, it is discouraged by the authorities. Canada has specific legislation to discourage commercial links. In Germany, banks do have ownership control over commercial concerns, through equity share holdings. But the sum of a bank's equity investments (in excess of 10% of the commercial firm's capital) plus other fixed investments is not permitted to exceed a bank's capital. In Japan, there is no formal link between banking and commerce. A group of companies, *keiretsu*, usually including a bank, is loosely affiliated through shared directors, management relationships, and relatively minor equity ownership. In the USA, bank holding companies may have up to a 5% interest in a commercial concern, but most BHCs do not exercise this option. Until recently, some "non-bank" banks were owned by commercial concerns. But existing firms were "grandfathered", and new firms banned by new regulations (see Chapter 6). In France and Belgium, holding companies own both banks and commercial firms.

Turning to the *separation of financial services*, the issue is the extent to which bank and non-bank financial services should be separated. In most countries, they are closely linked. Cumming and Sweet defined banking financial services as deposit-based lending, though the definition should also include money transmission. Non-bank financial services consist of securities services (underwriting, trading, investing), insurance underwriting, trust activities and property services. The term "universal banking" originally referred to the German system, where banks offered bank and non-bank financial services, and were formally linked to commercial firms through equity holdings and

---

*For the extensive discussion on policy and performance issues related to the separation of the banking and commerce, readers are referred to the special issue on the separation of banking and commerce, published by the *Journal of Banking and Finance* (18,2,1994).

shared directorships. In Chapter 1 other, looser, definitions of universal banks were reviewed; these exist in France, Italy, the Netherlands and Switzerland. Separate insurance companies underwrite insurance, though insurance firms and banks are affiliated.

Countries with a "blended system" include the USA, UK, Canada, Japan, Belgium and Sweden. There is some overlap between banking and non-banking financial activities, but no complete system of universal banking. In all these countries except the USA, the integration occurs through bank ownership of non-bank financial subsidiaries. In the USA, a holding company enables banks to expand their activities through ownership of banks and non-banks. However, the USA, and, to a lesser extent, Japan, have a low degree of integration of bank and non-bank financial activities, due to, respectively, the Glass-Steagall Act and Article 65. These statutory restrictions are discussed at length in Chapter 6. Recent financial reforms in Canada, the UK and Sweden have accelerated the rate of integration. In Belgium, there has been a high degree of integration for many years.

Official supervision and access to central bank lending are discussed in detail in Chapter 6. With regard to official supervision, the key differences in the developed economies relate to consolidated supervision, functional rather than "type of firm" supervision, and separation of banks from their affiliates. The debate over access to central bank lending centres around the issue of whether non-bank financial affiliates should have access to lender of last resort facilities.

The British Banking System

According to Llewellyn (1991), until the 1980s, the UK financial system was characterised by specialist and differentiated financial systems, with clear, functional demarcations identified in following categories:

- commercial banking;
- investment and merchant banking;
- insurance;
- fund management;
- housing finance;
- securities trading.

Llewellyn argues that the central feature of the British financial system over the 1980s was an unprecedented combination of structural change and financial innovation. Structural change resulted in "institutional integration", whereby the traditional demarcations between different parts of the UK financial sector have been eroded. Financial innovation consisted of the creation of new financial instruments (*product* innovation), techniques (*process* innovation), and markets. It increased the range, number, and variety of instruments, and has permitted characteristics and risks of individual instruments to be unbundled, and possibly, reassembled in different combinations. Thus, financial innovation has led to "instrument integration", and has tended to erode the distinctions between bank and non-bank financial products. Hence, both structural change and financial innovation have been catalysts for a less specialised financial system.

Llewellyn argues that structural change and financial innovation have led to two discernable shifts in the focus of firms in the UK financial sector. The first trend has been a shift from wholesale to retail banking. In the early 1980s, UK banks transformed personal sector deposits into loans for the corporate sector. For example, in 1980, the net asset liability position of the UK financial sector against the personal sector (including small business) was −£19.6 billion (that is, outstanding liabilities exceeded outstanding assets), compared to a net position of the sector against industrial and commercial companies of £15.8 billion. In 1987, these figures, were, respectively, £15.11 billion and £20.7 billion. Table 4 summarises the lending patterns of UK banks, as a proportion of total assets.

Table 4 shows that *sector recycling* of 1980 had largely disappeared by 1987. There are a number of reasons why UK banks increased their focus on the retail sector in the 1980s. First, it was seen to be more profitable: domestic profits as a proportion of assets were approximately three times as great as profits on international business (Llewellyn, 1992: p.442). Second, the financial position of the corporate sector improved over the period: the rising rate of return on capital and profitability reduced the corporate sector's dependency on international finance, particularly bank finance. Third, there was a major stock adjustment in the personal sector, with a substantial and simultaneous rise in the proportion of financial assets and liabilities. Fourth, competitive pressures were far greater in the wholesale and international markets, thereby reducing margins in the corporate loan sector, mainly because corporate customers have more banks from which to choose, and also could access the capital markets directly as the facilities for securitisation improved.

The second trend identified by Llewellyn was the revolution in the UK securities industry during the 1980s. Restrictive practices, in place up until "Big Bang" (1986), had ensured a demarcation between firms operating on the Stock Exchange and other financial firms, such as banks. Under the 1908 London Stock Exchange single capacity rule, members of the Stock Exchange had to be either brokers or market makers ("jobbers") in securities, defined as bonds and equities but excluding Eurobonds. By tradition, Stock Exchange member firms had to be partnerships, but in 1969, the rule was changed to

Table 4 Lending Patterns of UK Banks

	1980	1987
Lending to:		
personal sector	18%	32%
other financial institutions	15%	24%
corporate sector[a]	53%	33%
unincorporated firms	14%	11%

[a]Industrial and commercial companies.
Source: Llewellyn (1991).

allow member firms to become limited companies and to have outside share-holders, up to a limit of 10% of the holding (raised to 29.9% in 1982). These limitations effectively excluded non-member financial firms from significant involvement in the UK securities industries. Note that the reasons for separation between banks and securities firms were not the same as in the US or Japan, where the division is enforced by statutory regulations.

Big Bang brought about important structural changes in the Stock Exchange. In March 1986, rules were changed to allow 100% outside ownership of stock-broking and jobbing firms. Fixed commissions for securities trading were abolished in October 1986, and the single capacity rule was relaxed. These changes resulted in a massive capital injection into the UK securities industry (with the rule changes, the new stockbroking firms required far more capital than was previously the case) by British and foreign banks, and very quickly, nearly all the securities firms became part of integrated financial institutions.

The Building Society reforms brought about by the 1986 Building Society Act, have the potential of altering the structure of the retail banking sector in the United Kingdom, because the Act allowed building societies to offer a full retail banking service and/or become fully-fledged banks. The details of these reforms are discussed in chapter six (pp. 229–31).

The US Banking System

The US banking system has over 27 000 deposit-taking institutions, compared to 500 (340 of which are branches or subsidiaries of foreign banks) banks and 83 building societies in the UK. Nonetheless, the US system is concentrated; commercial banks accounted for approximately 76% of the total assets held; thrift institutions held the remainder. One hundred and seven banks hold over half the commercial banking assets; 10 000 commercial banks, with assets of less than $300 million hold 20% of US commercial bank assets.*

In 1974, the American banks owned 41% of the total assets of the top 10 global banks, followed by France (25%), the UK (17%), West Germany (9%) and Japan (8%). By 1988, Japan held 92.25% of the total assets of the top 10, followed by France, with 7.75%. Nineteen seventy-four was the year the US banks were toppled from world dominance. The Bank of America showed the most significant decline: from 1968–83 it was either number one or two, but by 1988 it was only the 41st largest bank worldwide. Chase Manhattan also showed a big decline, falling to 33rd by 1987. Citicorp was the only US bank to stay in the top ten, but even it was relegated to 11th place in 1987: two Japanese banks took its place. De Carmoy (1990) argued that Citicorp had a well-defined global strategy: consumer banking worldwide, and computer-isation of its services which meant it could offer advanced technology products. It weakness was in commercial and merchant banking, with a high turnover of teams in Europe and Asia, making it difficult to secure a loyal set of commercial bank customers.

---

*These remarks are based on 1992 figures. Source: BIS (1993), various tables.

US banks exhibited a number of weaknesses. From 1979–85, there was a steady downward trend in profitability and market rate of return. In 1985 there was a slight recovery. In 1985–86, FDIC insured banks experienced a drop in the profitability rate on assets, to the lowest level in 15 years. At an international level, profits began to improve: for the 200 leading US banks in 1988, net earnings returned to $18.9 billion, compared with losses in 1986 ($13 billion) and in 1987 ($2.1 billion). However, of the top 1000 banks ranked by *The Banker* (July 1994), US banks took 178 of the positions, measured in terms of tier one capital.*

Most of the US money centre banks suffered because of developing country debt problems and a decline in agriculture, commodity, and real estate prices since 1980. Nineteen eighty-one marked the beginning of a large increase in US bank failures: there were 10 in 1981 and over 1000 by the end of the decade. Legislation which compartmentalises banking, securities, and insurance activities continues to hamper the evolution of the US banking system. The Federal Reserve Bank of New York report on market shares of multinational banks showed a declining presence in the credit market. In 1974, 43% of US commercial banks were active in wholesale banking, but by 1985 this figure had dropped to only 27%. Commercial banking declined because companies with abundant liquid funds could obtain rates that are more generous than those offered by the banks. On the other hand, as was noted in Chapter 1, performance improves if one takes foreign and off-balance sheet activity into account.

The failure of the Banking Reform Bill in 1991 means the US regulatory system is still outdated. For example, many of the successful regional banks (such as Wachovia and NationsBank) are prevented from becoming national banks because of regulation. However, in July, 1994 two banking bills were signed into law, the most important being the interstate banking bill to permit branching of banks across states. The more liberal treatment of branch banking should serve to make the US banking structure more like those in other industrialised economies. The second new reform, the Community Development Banking Bill, provides for subsidies to lenders in low income areas.

At the time of writing, three separate Bills were before Congress to repeal the Glass–Steagall Act, and a new Act could be in place by the close of the century, putting an end to the separation of investment and commercial banking. However, the apparent inability of Congress to pass new banking legislation should not be under-estimated. Powerful lobbies representing insurance firms, securities houses and even banks are actively discouraging reform. In the event of new legislation, commercial banks will face increased competition from some of the securities houses, which already have extensive, relatively low cost

---

*Tier one capital is defined in full in Chapter 6, but it consists mainly of common stock, declared reserves, and retained earnings. But as pointed out in *The Banker*, the US banks have been able to use cumulative preferred shares in the computation of tier one capital, thereby biasing the measure upward.

national branch networks. But securities houses want any reform to include a comprehensive requirement that banks have separately capitalised subsidiaries. A detailed review of the American regulatory regime may be found in Chapter 6. Chapter 4 considers some competitive issues related to US banking.

The Banking Structure in Japan

The Japanese banking system exhibits a number of distinctive characteristics. One is the high degree of supervision by the Ministry of Finance and the Bank of Japan. Their control extends over areas as diverse as the opening of new branches, opening hours, credit volume, interest rates, and accounting rules. Japanese banks play a pivotal role in financing and investing in international trade, investing in international projects, and providing funds for multinational firms. Many have a global presence; in 1994, the top six places in *The Banker*'s ranking of the top 1000 banks (measured by tier one capital) were occupied by Japanese banks.

The Japanese banking and financial system has a reputation for a high degree of segmentation, along *functional* lines. The structure is made up as follows:

- Commercial banks: 13 city banks and 130 regional banks, including Sumitomo, Fuji and Mitsubishi. One of the 13 city banks, the Bank of Tokyo is a specialised foreign exchange bank, though other City banks engage in foreign exchange related transactions. There used to be 64 regional banks but this number rose to 130 after 1989, when most of the mutual banks (see below) became regional banks. These domestically owned banks are prohibited from engaging in trust-related businesses (for example, management of pension funds or investment trusts) and cannot issue long-term debt, except convertible bonds and a limited amount of subordinated debt. These banks rely on deposits from the corporate and personal sectors for funding, although these deposits are restricted to a maturity of less than three years.
- Three long-term credit banks: the Industrial Bank of Japan, the Long Term Credit Bank of Japan, and the Nippon Credit Bank. Long-term credit banks are not permitted to use retail deposits as a source of funds, though they can hold deposits of client firms and government bodies. These banks can issue long-term debt with a maturity of up to five years.
- Seven trust banks, including Sumitomo, Mitsubishi, Yasuda, and Mitsui. These banks may conduct trust-related businesses and may raise funds through term deposits, for long-term financing through loan and money trusts.
- Mutual savings and loan banks, whose numbers have fallen from a peak of 64 after many of the banks converted to regional bank status. These *sogo* banks concentrate their activities in the smaller cities or a rural area. Additionally there are 450 *shinkin* banks, which are credit associations. These institutions exist largely to cater to the needs of small local businesses; clients must not exceed a certain size.

- Other specialised financial firms, including the Japan Development Bank and the Export-Import Bank. Their primary function is to allocate funds received from the Ministry of Finance Fiscal and Loan programme; they do not accept deposits. The funds for the MOF's Loan programme come from the postal savings and social insurance system. The postal savings system now takes about half the deposits in the Japanese banking system, making it an extremely large organisation. Until 1986, regulated interest rates made post office deposits attractive. Traditionally, the government has used the Post Office as a source of cheap funds through regulated deposit rates. The deregulation of all interest rates (completed in October 1994), should have raised the cost of funds for the Post Office and reduced their appeal to depositors. However, the Post Office is under no pressure to be profitable, and continues to attract depositors by offering a higher rate than banks. Furthermore, banks are still unable to compete directly with some of the Post Office's most popular retail deposit products and are required to seek approval from the MOF to open new branches. The Post Office has over 24,000 branches. By way of contrast, Sakura, with the most extensive branch network among national banks, has just over 570 branches.* These factors mean the Post Office can continue to maintain a competitive edge over banks.
- Eighty-one foreign banks operate in Japan (1987 figures), and they are permitted to offer almost the same range of services as domestic banks. They may also engage in securities business through partly owned affiliates, and in trust-related activities through a trust bank affiliate. However, they play a minor role in the Japanese financial system.
- Securities firms, which are prohibited from engaging in banking business.

Specialisation was a feature of the Japanese system before the Second World War and it was reinforced by US occupational influence, because of the view that specialisation would better utilise Japan's financial resources to rebuild the economy. For example, Article 65, passed in 1948, divided commercial and investment banking, and the 1949 Foreign Exchange Control law separated domestic and international finance. The 1973 OPEC-induced oil shock increased the need to finance Japanese deficits. A wide range of reforms was introduced in the 1980s to permit resident Japanese to participate in global markets. Firms were able to bypass Japanese regulations on interest rates, looking to offshore markets for intermediaries. Interest rates have been gradually deregulated since 1979.

The Japanese reform package of 1992 should reduce the amount of segmentation in the system. Different types of financial firms will be allowed to enter new financial activities through separate subsidiaries. For example, the City banks will be able to establish securities and trust bank subsidiaries and the securities firms will be able to engage in commercial banking activity. Financial

---

*Source: *The Economist*, 29 October, 1994: p.123.

market reforms will lead to an end of fixed commissions on Tokyo Stock Exchange, and the collapse of fixed commissions is likely to lead to increased entry and greater competition in stockbroking. The Japanese reforms are ahead of the American reforms, where attempts to end the restrictions imposed by the Glass-Steagall Act have, to date, come to nothing.

The internationalisation of the yen, stimulated by deregulation of Japan's financial markets, is the main reason behind the global expansion of Japanese banks. In 1982 the dollar accounted for 80% of the foreign currency positions of Japanese banks and the yen for only 3%. By 1988, these figures had changed to 63% and 17%, respectively. As is the case for other Japanese industries, the main strategy in global markets has been to target market share in markets which tend to be high volume and very price elastic.

Until late 1991, Japanese banks seemed well placed to meet the Basle Risk Assets ratio. But by early 1992, it was evident that many of Japan's large banks had serious problems because of financial mismanagement. The stock market decline over 1990–92 resulted in a drop in unrealised capital gains, causing a large fall in tier two capital, below the ceiling of 100% of tier one capital (see Chapter 6). For this reason, the authorities supported the issue of subordinated debt, to count as tier two capital, and perpetual preferred stock, to count as tier one capital. However, at the time of writing, Japan had not yet emerged from its most serious post-war banking crisis. It is accepted that Japanese banks under-report non-performing loans, possibly by more than 50%. Standard and Poor, the rating agency, estimates it will take five to 10 years for banks to clear their bad debts, with total bad debt estimates put at ¥30 trillion, about $250 billion; more recent estimates put the figure at nearly $500 billion. Thus, the size of the debt problem now exceeds that created by the thrift industry crisis in the USA.

There are several outstanding issues with respect to the long-term future of the Japanese banking and financial structure. The role of banks in *keiretsu* is under threat because the manufacturing sector is finding other methods of raising finance, apart from loans. In 1992, equity and reserves, bonds, and non-bank credit made up about 65% of capital for Japanese manufacturers, compared to about 55% in 1982. Financial liberalisation has given large corporates direct access to the international capital markets. Furthermore, there is a question mark over the affiliation of non-bank financial institutions to city banks. These non-bank firms acted as major creditors for firms engaging in speculative activities, and are now faced with a large portfolio of dud loans.

Structure in European Banking after 1993

The purpose of this discussion is to look at the implications of the single European financial market for the *competitive* structure of European financial markets, and more generally, for international banking. Most countries in the European Union (EU) have three to five large well-known banks, though in some countries such as Germany, Spain, Italy and France, regional banking is important because of the large number of mutual and cooperative banks. Continental Europe also has a large number of credit firms, specialised by either sector lending or the maturity structure of their assets (for example, Italy). Molyneux *et al.* (1994), using standard concentration measures,* reported the banking markets in Italy and France to be the most concentrated, followed by Belgium, the Netherlands and Spain. In Germany and the UK, the degree of concentration is comparatively low. Data on profitability (see Bisignano, 1992: Table 4.10) suggest that the UK, Spain, and Italy have the most profitable banking sectors. Highly concentrated banking countries (for example, the Netherlands) have not shown exceptional profitability. But there are problems with comparability of data on profits across EU states. France, Spain, and Italy have large state-owned banks, but all three countries embarked upon privatisation programmes in 1993.

In Germany, Spain and France, there is a close joint owner–creditor relationship of banks to non-financial firms through cross-shareholdings. In most EU countries, non-financial firms are not permitted to own banks, though in Italy it is not explicitly outlawed. France, Germany, Italy and the Netherlands have universal banking systems; Spain and the UK have a different form of universal banking. The EU laws will allow banks to offer a full range of financial services, in contrast to the US, where banks offer banking services, and, increasingly, securities services, but not other types of financial services.

Will a Single Financial Market be Achieved?

The answer to the question of how competitive a single market will be depends on whether the objective is actually achieved. There are a number of points worth considering. First, Butt Philip (1988) documented the dismal performance of European Community member countries in the adoption and implementation of EC[‡] directives. In the period 1982–86, the European Court of Justice received 325 references by the Commission in pursuit of member states which had failed to adopt an EC directive. Butt Philip also found a poor record for the implementation of EC law, especially in the case of laws involving liberalisation or competition policy. *The Economist* (1994) reported an increase in the rate at which directives are adopted, but not in the implementation rate.

The banking directives were supposed to become national law by January 1993,[†] though Belgium and Spain missed the deadline. In banking, mutual recognition will cover authorisation of parent banks and branches (not subsidiaries) in other EU countries. As is discussed in Chapter 6, the success of

---

*Concentration ratios measure the degree of concentration of a given market by a specified number of firms in the market. Chapter 4 discusses the various measures in more detail. In the Molyneux *et al.* (1994) paper, the concentration percentage of five firms and 10 firms is computed for the banking market, where the "market" is defined in terms of assets and deposits.

[†]For details of the relevant directives, readers are referred to Chapter 6.

[‡]The term EC, for European Community has gradually been replaced by the term EU, for European Union.

mutual recognition will depend on the degree of harmonisation in prudential regulation.

Even with all the directives in place, there are still limitations to entry into EU banking markets. During a transition period, new branches will be required to meet 50% of the host country's capital requirement. The host country may delay the establishment of a branch by the bank of another member country for three months, and notice must be given if cross-border services are offered and before a new service is introduced. These conditions give incumbent firms a chance to improve their strategic position before a new entrant is established or offers a new product.

There exists the potential for protection of host country banks because differences in regulation are allowed, provided they are no more stringent than that required for the "general good". But countries with such a wide variety of cultures will interpret "general good" differently, which could result in discrimination against out of state EU banks. For example, in some EU countries, interest-earning transactions (current) accounts are prohibited, for "general good" reasons. Banks from other EU states (such as the UK) possess expertise with these accounts, meaning the ban effectively discriminates against these financial firms.

Home country banks subject to more than the minimum regulation dictated by the EU directives could be placed at a competitive disadvantage. On the other hand, close regulation and supervision can give certain financial centres a reputation for quality, thereby attracting retail and wholesale customers.

The cross-border payments system is slow and under-developed. Domestic payments systems in the EU must be linked and a framework for cross-currency settlement created*. EU central banks should focus on the minimisation of payment risks, both within the EU and globally. As was noted in Chapter 2, the Bank of England is proposing *real time gross settlement*, with payments made in full throughout the day, rather than netted against each other at the end of the day. The Bank of France was to launch a similar system in 1994. At the moment, banks are able to run up large and unmonitored overdrafts during the day, exposing members of the system to the risk that a bank might fail before its payments are completed.

Differences in taxation may also affect the degree to which the banking market can be integrated. Reserve requirements, which act as a tax on banking activities, vary across EU states. When and if the European Central Bank (ECB) becomes operational, one would expect to see the imposition of a single reserve ratio. Other taxes will be more difficult to harmonise. In some countries, such as the UK, no withholding tax is charged on foreign deposits, but in

---

*In 1994, the European Commission reported that, for "urgent" transfers of funds between EU countries, the cost for the customer represented 25% fo the total transfer. The average time for the transfer was 4.15 working days, compared to 3.89 days for non-urgent transfer. Frequently the customer was subject to transaction charges by the sending and receiving bank, without being notified in advance.

others, a tax is levied. Unless a uniform tax is established, there is the possibility that countries like the UK will attract other EU deposits. At the same
time, UK resident taxpayers pay a composite rate tax on deposit interest
earned, and they could switch their deposits to countries with no withholding
tax such as Germany, Luxembourg and the Netherlands. Tax treatment on the
sale of financial products differs widely. EU banks from other states may also
discover that it is more costly for residents of the host country to do business
with them. For example, mortgage interest payments may qualify for a tax
deduction but only if the mortgage is negotiated with a "domestic" bank.
Another EU state taxes mortgages negotiated with finance houses but not
banks, effectively discriminating against building societies.

For the international banking community, there are two important issues.
First, subsidiaries (not branches) of non-EU banks *(third country banks)*
located in the EU will be eligible for the EU banking licence. In London, roughly
three-quarters of third country banks are branches. It is anticipated that third
country banking and securities houses will set up a "European" subsidiary in
one EU financial centre (such as London), and convert existing EU subsidiaries
into branches. Second, the plan is for the application of the principle of *equal
treatment* to third country banks, that is, banks headquartered outside the EU.
Under this principle, if EU banks are subject to the same regulations as domestic
banks in a third country, then third country banks will be allowed to engage in
the same activities as EU banks within the Union.

The Bank of England (1994) published the results of a small survey on the
progress of the single financial market. The survey consisted of informal discussions with about 25 firms, including banks and building societies. Four
types of barriers inhibiting the completion of a single market were identified.
Regulatory barriers included laws which discriminated against non-residents in
the sale of certain financial products (for example, higher-interest chequing
accounts), and on foreign participation in local business activities, such as
mortgage refinancing. Building societies, in particular, singled out housing
finance as an area with wide differences in laws among the member states in
relation to property, tax treatment and insolvency. *Fiscal* barriers were present
because of the complexities and differences in tax systems among the member
states. *Legal and technical* barriers, such as differences in labour laws and
insolvency laws raised the costs of operating in Europe. Most of the firms
surveyed thought *cultural and structural* barriers would be difficult to overcome. Examples included cross-shareholdings between industry and domestic
banks, consumer preferences for local firms and products, especially the choice
of home country suppliers by government, and a poor understanding of mutual

---

*The original study appears in Cecchini (1988) and Price Waterhouse (1988). The study covered the
key sectors of the EU economy, but the discussion here focuses on the banking market. For good
summaries, see Emerson *et al.* (1989: section 5.1) and Molyneux *et al.* (1994). Chakravarty *et al.*
(1995) consul caution in the interpretation of the Checchini study's predictions of gains for the
financial sector.

organisations, making it difficult for building societies to do business on the Continent.

Banking Prices in a Single Market

Price Waterhouse conducted a study of what would happen to prices in the event of a single European market.* The study estimated prices for a selection of financial products offered by banks, insurance firms and brokers. The banking products scrutinised were consumer credit, credit cards, mortgages, letters of credit, foreign exchange drafts, traveller's cheques, and commercial loans. The study compared prices before and after the achievement of a single internal market, including the removal of exchange controls. Current prices for each product were obtained through a survey of financial institutions on a given day at the end of 1985. The study made the simple assumption that post-1992, prices would be based on an average of the four lowest of the eight countries covered in the study. It also assumed only half of the disparities in prices across EU countries would be closed, recognising that even if all the directives were implemented, the market would not be fully integrated and perfectly competitive.

Table 5 The Average, Standard Deviation, Minimum and Maximum Percentage Differences for Financial Products in Eight EC Countries

Product	Average	Standard deviation	Minimum	Maximum
Consumer credit	45.6	63.6	−41.0 (Belgium)	136.0 (Germany)
Credit cards	33.9	39.4	−30.0 (France)	89.0 (Ireland)
Mortgages	36.8	41.6	−6.0 (Netherlands)	118.0 (Spain)
Traveller's Cheques	17.3	19.3	−7.0 (Germany -Luxembourg -United Kingdom)	39.0 (France)
Letters of Credit	15.6	20.4	−10 (Germany)	59.0 (Spain)
Foreign Exchange Drafts	39.4	65.3	−46.0 (Netherlands)	196.0 (Spain)
Commercial Loans	14.6	18.9	−7.0 (France)	46.0 (UK)

Source: Emerson *et al.* (1989) produced a table (5.1.4) showing the percentage differences of prices for these financial products, based on the average of the four lowest prices. In the table above, the raw figures were used to compute the average, standard deviation, minimum and maximum differences of these percentage differences. For example, consumer loans are 121% higher than the average in the UK, but in Belgium they are 41% below the average. The country with the minimum or maximum differences appear in the ( ) below the number.

Table 5 shows wide price differences in retail financial products, such as consumer credit. Thus, it is in retail banking where one would expect the largest price declines, though natural entry barriers (for example, economies of scale or the need for an extensive branch network) may inhibit competition. For products of interest to commercial banking clients, Germany, the Netherlands and France had the lowest prices on, respectively, letters of credit, foreign exchange drafts, and commercial loans. The UK had the highest price for commercial loans. This finding is surprising; as a key global financial centre, it is highly competitive in wholesale banking.

The study concluded there would be substantial welfare gains arising from the achievement of a single financial market, of about 1.5% of EU GDP. It was estimated that Germany and the UK would experience the largest gains, a puzzling finding because the UK and, to a lesser extent, Germany, have comparatively liberal financial markets.

Apart from the arbitrary assumptions about price declines, there are several problems with the Price Waterhouse study. First, the research is based on point data, so it is impossible to compute the statistical significance of the price differences. Second, non-price features are likely to differ, depending on the product and country, making it likely that there is a fair degree of product heterogeneity in each category. For example, the price of credit cards was measured by the annual cost to the consumer of assuming a 500 ECU debit, measured by the excess interest rate over money market rates. However, banks in some countries impose an annual fee in addition to charging an interest rate. The consumer loan rate was based on the annual cost to the consumer of a 500 ECU loan, ignoring the different risk profiles of consumers.

Furthermore, past experience has shown that EU incumbent firms that are threatened with new competition (as a result, say, of lowering trade barriers) try to restrict entry, through cartels. For example, banks might agree among themselves not to try and penetrate each other's territory and mergers, though the Commission is committed to taking action against anti-competitive behaviour.

Finally it will be difficult to distinguish the extent to which increased EU bank competition is due to an integrated market, financial innovation, new technology, or competitive pressures arising from the global financial community, because it is unclear how these respective factors have influenced prices.

Molyneux et al. (1994) used data from a sample of German, UK, French, Italian and Spanish banks for the period 1986–89 to conduct an empirical test of the degree of competition in the banking markets in these countries. They concluded that monopolistic competition best describes the markets of all of these countries but Italy, where there appears to be some degree of implicit collusion among the banks. In a related paper, Molyneux (1993) found that in the period 1983–86, collusive profits were present in the Belgian, French, Italian, Dutch, and Spanish banking markets. He argued that these results are consistent with the Price Waterhouse finding (1988) that these same markets would experience some of the largest price falls in financial services. However, the empirical methodology used is questionable, a point discussed at length in the next chapter.

There are a number of strategic questions faced by EU and third country banks planning to enter an enlarged European banking market. Assuming a single market is achieved, it is unclear whether it will offer more or fewer profitable opportunities for banks. For example, there may be little room for further entry into the safe borrower market consisting of banks, governments, and multinationals, and they may not need to be located anywhere other than London to gain access to this market. New banks may enter the middle market of corporate borrowers, where the credit risk is greater and spreads higher, but there is the question of how well they can compete if incumbent banks can better assess the risks. Finally, can banks from other EU states penetrate the retail financial markets, which, traditionally, are the exclusive territory of host country banks?

BANKING STRUCTURES IN DEVELOPING COUNTRIES

Introduction

The evolution of financial systems in developing countries and emerging markets reflects diverse political and economic histories. While some emerging markets, particularly in Asia, exhibit a relatively high degree of financial stability, others in Latin America and some former Soviet states experience frequent bouts of instability. This part of the section reviews banking in a selection of developing economies; the next section considers emerging markets in Eastern Europe.

Commercial banks are normally the first financial institutions to emerge in the process of economic development, providing the most basic intermediary and payment functions. Thailand is a good example. It is highly concentrated, with the Bangkok Bank holding about 40% of bank assets. The five largest commercial banks hold about four-fifths of total assets.

The role foreign banks are allowed to play is an important differentiating characteristic of banking systems in developing countries. In many of the very small lesser developing countries (LDCs) (for example, the Bahamas, Barbados, Fiji, the Maldives, St Lucia, Seychelles, the Solomon Islands, and Western Samoa) the banking system is dominated by branches or subsidiaries of foreign commercial banks. By contrast, in some of the large developing countries such as Thailand, foreign banks are prohibited from operating, or are restricted in their activities to certain types of business in specified parts of the country.

Terrell (1986), in a study of OECD countries, found that countries which exclude foreign banking earned higher gross margins and had higher pre-tax profits as a percentage of total assets, but exhibited higher operating costs than in countries where foreign banks are permitted to operate. He showed that excluding foreign bank participation reduces competition and makes domestic banks more profitable but less efficient.

Curb Markets

In many developing countries, economic regulation (for example, interest rate control) has led to the growth of an unregulated curb market, which is an important source of funds for both households and businesses. It becomes active under conditions of a heavily regulated market with interest rates that are held below market levels. In the Republic of Korea, it was estimated that in 1964, obligations in the curb market were about 70% of the volume of loans outstanding by commercial banks. By 1972, this ratio had fallen to about 30%, largely as a result of interest rate reforms in the mid-1960s. In the late 1970s, the market grew very rapidly after intervention by the monetary authorities. Recently, the market has declined, as business shifted from the curb market to non-bank financial institutions that are allowed to offer substantially higher returns. In Iran, there are money lenders in the bazaar, where the interest rate charged on a loan runs between 30% and 50%. In Argentina, the curb market grew after interest rate controls were reimposed. About 70–80% of small to medium-sized firm credit obtained from the curb market is extended without collateral, but most are reputed to use a sophisticated credit-rating system. The average annual interest rate on curb loans can be two to three times higher than the official rate.

The curb market is often closely integrated with the formal market. For example, an informal lender makes a savings deposit at a bank branch, which then extends a loan to the borrower who is designated by the depositor. The informal lender therefore earns the savings deposit rate plus about 1% a month from the borrower, without any risk of default.

Problems with Banking in Developing Countries

There are a number of problems related to banking structure which are common to all developing countries. Hanson and Rocha (1986) found high operating costs in developing countries, with high inflation rates and little or no competition. Financial repression, which rises with inflation, raises bank cost ratios because it reduces the real size of the banking system and encourages non-price competition. Take, for example, the case of Turkey. Fry (1988) looked at operating costs of the Turkish banks as a percentage of total assets. It was 6.6% in 1977 and by 1980 had risen to 9.5%. The causes of high operating costs were interest rate ceilings, an oligopolistic and cartelised banking sector, accelerating inflation, and high and rising reserve requirements.

Inflation, if unanticipated, is likely to be profitable for banks. The banks will hold deposits which decline in real value on a daily or even hourly basis. They also lend to government at high short-term interest rates. The outcome is high windfall profits, which, if prolonged, will mask inefficiencies in the banking system.

Reserve requirements tend to be higher in developing nations, which also raises bank operating costs. A reserve ratio is the percentage of total deposits a bank must place at the central bank. No interest is earned, so reserves are a tax on financial intermediation because the higher the reserve ratio, the lower the available deposits to fund revenue earning activities.

There is an ongoing problem with arrears and delinquent loans in developing countries, often because of selective credit policies. The World Bank (1989) reported that the following developing countries had experienced some form of financial distress recently: Argentina, Bangladesh, Bolivia, Chile, Colombia, Costa Rica, Egypt, Ghana, Greece, Guinea, Kenya, Korea, Kuwait, Madagascar, Malaysia, Nepal, Pakistan, Philippines, Sri Lanka, Tanzania, Thailand, Turkey, Uruguay, and members of the West African Monetary Union: Benin, Burkina Faso, Côte d'Ivoire, Mali, Niger, Senegal, and Togo.* Higher default rates reduces the net return to savers. They create a wedge between deposit and loan rates, thereby impairing financial inter-mediation.

The financial sectors of developing economies are inhibited by poor pay, political interference in management decisions and regulatory systems which limit banks to prescribed activities, and, in some cases, limit the rate of finan-cial innovation. In the absence of explicit documented lending policies, it is more difficult to manage risk and senior managers are less able to exercise close control over lending by junior managers. This can lead to an excessive con-centration of risk, poor selection of borrowers, and speculative lending. Improper lending practices usually reflect a more general problem with man-agement skills, which tends to be more pronounced in banking systems of developing countries. Lack of accountability is also a problem because of overly complicated organisational structures and poorly defined responsibil-ities. Training and motivating staff should be given top priority. Entry of foreign banks is a fast way of improving management expertise and intro-ducing the latest technology, but this option is often politically unacceptable.

Banking in Indonesia: A Case Study in Developing Country Banking

This case study is drawn largely from the paper by Schwartz (1991). By con-centrating on one country, the reader obtains a detailed insight into problems associated with developing country bank reform. Prompted by the mid-1980s crash of the international oil market, oil-rich Indonesia embarked on a number of economic reforms. The objectives were to reduce Indonesia's dependence on oil exports, and to strengthen the role of the private sector in the economy. This section considers the key reforms in the banking sector.

The banking sector reforms were introduced at the same time as other eco-nomic reforms. Indonesia chose not to follow one of the standard economic development models, which states that full financial sector liberalisation should not come about until after a country's manufacturing and industrial base is sufficiently developed. Rather, Indonesia's strategy has been to lead with finan-cial sector reform and let the rest of the economy follow.

---

*See Box 5.1 in World Bank (1989), *World Development Report*.

In 1967, Major General Suharto "pushed aside" President Sukarno. One aim of the "New Order" was to revive the deteriorating economy. It tried to create a more friendly environment for both domestic and foreign investors. Initially, the financial system was dominated by the state. Four out of the five very large banks had been local branches of Dutch banks, but had been nationalised in the late 1950s. Ten private banks were permitted to engage in foreign exchange transactions. Foreign banks had been gradually pushed out of Indonesia during the 1960s.

The "New Order" rewrote the banking laws, so that by 1968–69, 10 foreign banks had commenced operations in Jakarta. However, the foreign banks were limited in their activities, and state banks continued to dominate. The 1967 Banking Law gave the central bank, Bank Indonesia (BI), control over credit ceilings and put strict limits on licences for new private and foreign banks. Private banks were inhibited in their growth because of insufficient capital and reduced lending opportunities. All deposits from state enterprises had to be placed with state banks, giving them little incentive to compete. In the mid 1980s, the economy came under severe strain. The country's balance of payments was squeezed by the collapse of the oil market and the decline of the US dollar in mid-1985. Most of Indonesia's oil revenues were earned in dollars, while most of their external debt was denominated in non-dollar currencies, especially the Japanese yen.

The result was a shift away from the nationalistic economic policy to a "technocratic" model of economic development stressing growth led by a broad base of manufacturing exports and a liberal financial sector. There were numerous non-banking measures, but the focus of attention here is on the banking reforms, which were far-reaching. In June 1983, banks were allowed to set their own deposit and lending rates. Central bank credit ceilings were replaced by reserve money requirements. In 1984 and 1985, new money market instruments were introduced by Bank Indonesia (BI), to enable it to more effectively manage the money supply. BI also opened a re-discount window so it could be a more efficient lender of last resort.

In December 1987 and 1988, the stock market was reformed. A regulation limiting daily price swings to 4% of the price of the stock was abolished and foreigners were allowed to buy shares. Foreign securities houses were also allowed to form joint ventures and local partners. By June, 1990, eight joint ventures were operational; five more awaited approval from the Finance Ministry.

In October, 1988, the "Pakto" package was introduced. It removed restrictions on new private banks which had been in effect since 1971, eliminated all limits on domestic bank branching, and allowed foreign banks to form joint ventures with local partners. The foreign partner could hold a maximum of 85%, and the minimum paid-up capital requirement was $30 million. Foreign banks already present in Indonesia were allowed to branch out into six other cities besides Jakarta. State-owned firms could place up to 50% of their deposits outside state banks. The reserve requirement was lowered from 15% to 2% and Bank Indonesia (BI) extended the maturity of its currency swap facility from six months to three years. BI imposed lending limits which restricted a bank's aggregate amount of loans to 20% of bank capital for any one customer, and to 50% of bank capital to any one group of companies under common ownership.

In March 1989, Indonesia removed ceilings on foreign borrowings by banks with foreign exchange licences but banks could only hold up to 25% of bank capital in overnight foreign exchange positions. The measure limited the amount of currency speculation that could take place on the rupiah; it also provided strong encouragement for banks to increase capital. In January 1990, BI announced it would reduce its subsidised credit programmes by nearly one-half. All banks were required to lend 20% of their credit portfolios to small businesses, defined as firms with assets of less than $330 000.

Following Pakto, the Indonesian banking structure underwent a number of pronounced changes. Eighteen months after the October 1988 package, the number of banks increased from 108 to 147 and 1400 new state, private, and foreign bank branches were established. Deposits in the banking system increased from Rp30.8 trillion in December 1988 to Rp43.1 trillion ($24 billion) in March 1990. The biggest gain was in savings accounts, mainly in the form of new savings plans offered by the private banks. The Finance Ministry approved licences for 14 new joint venture banks, nine of them Japanese. Liquidity in the system rose sharply: the broad money to GDP ratio went from 24% in 1985 to 35% by the end of 1989—the equivalent ratio for neighbouring countries is 60%. However, interest rates have been kept high because of exploding loan demand and the growing stock market. A squeeze on the money supply in mid-1990 (because of inflation fears) caused a further rise in rates.

Many private banks rushed into consumer financing. The more aggressive private banks expanded their retail branch networks into the smaller urban areas (where the foreign banks are prohibited, thereby restricting the retail services they can offer) and increased the number of new consumer finance products. Foreign bank entry was encouraged, to counter the stagnant state-dominated system and to serve the increasing number of foreign investors. But the Finance Ministry requires all new joint venture banks to extend at least 50% of credit to export-related activities. The same rule applies to any wholly foreign-owned bank that operates a branch outside Jakarta.

There are risks associated with such rapid growth. The central bank is unlikely to have the resources to monitor the now very large banking system, and may fail to spot problems before they turn into crises. Like Bank Indonesia, private banks, especially those involved in the rapid expansion of the branch networks, are short of trained bankers and there is poaching of bank staff. Banks have moved into areas where they have little expertise and economies of scale do not exist. For example, in the USA, a viable credit card business requires about 500 000 cardholders but in Indonesia, the target is 10 000 customers. Collateral is of a lower quality because of competition among banks for borrowers. Vague laws mean many banks do not try to collect collateral on non-performing debts through the judicial system.

Indonesian companies increasingly look to equity issues to raise capital and pay down the high-cost local bank debt, which will put a downward trend on lending rates and encourage banks to seek out riskier borrowers.

Despite the expansion of the banking sector, there has been little progress in the way banks evaluate credit. Credit analysis is *named* rather than *analytical*— bankers depend too much on the name of the borrower, instead of considering the feasibility of the project. Auditing in Indonesia is of extremely low quality: there are no generally acceptable accounting principles for assessing the health of the banks, and there is a question mark over the expertise of the accounting and legal professions.

Anderson (1994) argued that Indonesia's reforms were too rapid, resulting in a rapid growth in banks and consequently, credit growth, forcing the central bank to intervene. The Philippines also suffered from financial reform which was too rapid. Based on his study of several developing nations, Anderson concluded that macroeconomic stabilisation should precede financial market reform, and when the reform takes place, banks must be capable of evaluating the riskiness of projects they finance, if they are to achieve the goal of allocating capital efficiently. However, as argued by the World Bank,* there are pros and cons with either a gradualist or rapid approach to economic reform.

Islamic Banking[†]

Several Islamic countries have introduced banking on Islamic principles. They include Iran, Malaysia, Pakistan and Saudi Arabia; Iran and Pakistan are the only countries to have adopted the system completely. The Koran forbids the charging of *riba*, defined as any interest, independent of the rate. Money, it is argued, is not a commodity, and must be used for productive pursuits. Thus, the main distinguishing characteristic of Islamic banking is the absence of fixed interest rates on deposits and loans. Returns from lending are usually earned through mark-up pricing or profit/loss-sharing.

The liabilities side of an Islamic bank's balance sheet is relatively straightforward. It consists of equity, raised through the sale of funds to the public, and investment deposit accounts, whereby customers share in the profits (or losses) of the bank but do not have any management control. The formula for profit-

---

*There are two issues on the question of how economic reform is implemented in developing economies and emerging markets. The first is whether the economic reform should consist of a gradualist or shock therapy approach. Readers are referred to the World Bank (1991), *World Development Report* (p.117), which summarises the key points. However, Sachs and Woo (1994), reviewing economic reforms in China and Eastern Europe, argued the methodology of reform is a non-issue. The second area for debate is whether financial reform should precede, be simultaneous with, or follow, macroeconomic reforms and the development of a manufacturing and industrial base. The qualitative studies of Indonesia and Hungary discussed here do not indicate that either approach is superior.

†For more detail on Islamic banking, readers are referred to Khan (1987) and Khan and Mirakhor (1987).

sharing is usually regulated by the central bank and agreed by both parties. Different weightings are applied, depending on the maturity and size of deposit. Savings deposits are held for precautionary and transactions purposes. Some banks offer no returns; others a profit/loss-sharing arrangement. Current deposits are for transactions, with no profit shared by depositors, though the bank can invest the funds. Often, prizes are offered to attract custom. A service charge is normally made, but depositors may approach the bank for short-term interest-free loans.

It is on the assets side of the balance sheet where notable differences are observed. The only form of loan permitted is the *qarz-e-hasna*, whereby a lender provides a short-term loan to a needy borrower at no charge, repayable when the borrower is able. Personal, health and education loans fall into this category. In mortgage financing, the bank buys a house and resells it at a far higher price to the borrower. Normally, the borrower is given 25 years to repay the price charged by the bank. Thus, the bank assumes some of the risk of volatile property prices. Or the borrower and bank buy the house, and the customer buys back the bank's share at cost price. The bank profits by leasing its share of the house to the householder for an annual fixed rate. For other consumer durables, instalment plans are encouraged. No interest is paid, but there is mark-up pricing to cover the cost of collecting and maintaining accounts related to the instalments. Firms selling the durables are financed on a profit-sharing basis.

Banks can enter into two types of partnership with firms to provide medium to long-term financing. Under the *musharaka*, the bank and firm make a joint contribution to the capital of the company or project. Both parties share an agreed proportion of the profits. A *mudaraba* involves the bank providing all the capital; and in return, a pre-arranged percentage of the profits is returned to the bank. The bank incurs any financial loss—the firm's time and labour are recognised as part of the contribution, so the firm does not have to meet any of the losses. Profit-sharing has its drawbacks, because there are problems with monitoring and control, especially when the lending is to small businesses. Double bookkeeping for tax evasion can be widespread, making it difficult for the bank to discover the actual profit made. The *hijara* substitutes for leasing arrangements. The bank leases out the good or service and demands a user fee, which is a fixed regular charge over a period of time. Usually it is possible for the lessee to gain title of the goods or assets at the end of the lease.

Trade finance is conducted through *murabaha* or *hijara*. *Murabaha* entails mark-up financing. The bank purchases the good/service, and sells it to the client at cost, plus an agreed mark-up charge for the bank. The mark-up covers the risk the bank incurs between buying the good and selling it to the firm. Other factors affecting the mark-up are the size of the transaction, the reputation of the buyer, and the type of good or service.

It is estimated that in pure Islamic banking systems, 80–95% of the banks' business is short-term *murabaha* finance. For this reason, risk management concentrates on the short term and attracting creditworthy clients. High reserve ratios, in the order of 30–40%, are maintained because of the short-term nature of the banks' liabilities. The risky nature of the ventures causes banks to confine their loans to well-established, valued clients. Also, a bank will monitor closely the employment of capital it has financed.

Iran nationalised its banks after the 1979 revolution; in 1983, the Usury-Free Banking Act limited the activities domestic banks could undertake. Savings and current accounts must be interest-free, though prizes and bonuses are allowed. There are short and long-term investment accounts, on which banks pay "interest". Banks charge fees for loans. Iran's overseas banking operations are exempt from the Act. Deposit "rates" and loan fees are determined by Iran's Supreme Council of Banks. To promote competition, the Supreme Council of Banks recently agreed to allow banks to earn different rates of return. Up to this time, all banks had the same rate of return.

Some Islamic banks have tried to expand into the global markets since the early 1980s, to capture a Muslim market overseas and diversify their portfolio. But they have faced a number of problems related to expansion. There are difficulties in being recognised as banks, because they cannot hold government securities,* and the profit/loss-sharing nature of their deposit and lending business is at odds with a western system which protects depositors and emphasises the importance of a transparent portfolio, where all assets can be valued. Furthermore, in cases where a bank lends money and shares in the profits, the borrower will have to repay the bank out of profits after tax. Those banks that do establish themselves in the west usually have to adapt their deposit-taking and lending rules to gain recognition. A few western institutions have also entered the Islamic banking market. For example, Kleinwort Benson, a London merchant bank, has a Middle East banking department, and a *shariah*† advisor. The bank and its clients engage in profit-sharing investment activity, and syndicated loans have been arranged. Kleinwort Benson have used *murabaha*, *mudaraba*, and *hijara* finance techniques. A large proportion of the resulting assets are short-term, so the bank is focusing on the development of long-term instruments that would be compatible with Islamic banking.

BANKING STRUCTURES IN EASTERN EUROPE

Introduction

Brainard (1991) raised two important questions with respect to the transformation of Eastern European states into market economies. First, how does financial market reform contribute to the transformation of Eastern Europe into a market-driven economy? Second, what is the current status of the reform process and what should be done to move closer to these goals? This section considers banking reforms in the wider context of emerging East European markets.

---

*Islamic banks may not hold interest-earning government bonds. Islamic states raise public funds through banks' profit-sharing loans to state enterprises; tax-exempt loan certificates are used to meet the demend for short-term funds.
†A *shariah* counsellor will advise on the moral obligations of muslims.

Brainard argued that the creation of a real capital market, where resources are allocated efficiently, is essential to achieving the transformation of the economies in Eastern Europe. Privatisation, improved financial discipline, and banking reform must be in place to achieve an efficient allocation of resources. Privatisation in the absence of banking reform will cause inefficient allocation within the private sector. Banks should be given not only independence, but the correct incentives to make sound banking decisions and protect their own capital positions against credit losses.

Banking reform in the absence of privatisation and financial discipline (imposed on all firms, including banks) would, Brainard suggested, aggravate the problem of banks accumulating a portfolio of bad loans. Transition to a market economy is only possible if there are combined policies of economic stabilisation (balancing the budget, freeing prices and increasing competitive forces in the economy) and comprehensive structural reforms. Under a socialist economy, banks accumulated the losses of state-owned firms for decades. Hence, the banks were responsible for misallocating resources on a massive scale. For example, in 1987, the Yugoslavian government's fiscal accounts showed a slight surplus, but losses incurred by the National Bank of Yugoslavia were 8.5% of GDP. In Poland, The World Bank (1988) estimated that interest rate subsidies provided to state enterprises through the banking system amounted to 10% of GDP. In both these countries, state-owned enterprises refused to service their existing debt, forcing banks to refinance loans and/or provide new loans, thereby allowing interest on the debt to be repaid. In Hungary, the three commercial banks set up by the National Bank in 1987 inherited a substantial portfolio of troubled loans. The banks have capitalised the interest due and accrued interest as income on non-performing loans, so that their published income statements differ greatly from generally accepted accounting procedures in the west.

Socialist Banking and Finance

The socialist banking model in Eastern Europe consisted of a central bank and several special purpose banks, which either managed personal savings and other banking needs, or focused on foreign financial activities. The former Soviet bloc states set up a *two tier* banking system by divorcing all of the commercial bank functions from the central bank. New commercial banks were organised along industry lines, except in Poland, where they were established on a regional basis. Table 6 summarises new bank creation.

Existing loans from the portfolio of the central bank were transferred to these commercial banks, hence, they commenced operations with an overhang of doubtful assets, highly concentrated by enterprise and industry. Banks were confined to doing business with enterprises assigned to them, stifling competition.

In their present form, these new banks have not been able to implement the structural reforms through the efficient allocation of capital. Many have negative capital. Nor do these banks put any of their own capital at risk, because

Table 6 New Banks Created in the Eastern European States

Country	Year	New commercial banks (state-owned)
Bulgaria	1987	7
Czechoslovakia	1990	2
GDR	1990	1
Hungary	1987	3
Poland	1988	9

Source: Brainard (1991: p.14).

either loan losses are disguised or the government injects new capital to cover the losses. Thus, the new banks have been acting as fiscal agents for the government; deposits held at these banks mean they collect a large part of the inflation tax and redistribute resources to enterprises, through a negative real interest rate. The misallocation of capital is exacerbated because banks have no leverage if firms refuse to pay up. They simply extend new loans to cover interest payments. Periodic devaluations in a country's currency mean the central banks also carry a large volume of losses on their balance sheets. Devaluation raises the local currency value of these liabilities; to balance this, a valuation adjustment occurs, by entering a corresponding asset entry. The sizes of these valuation losses carried by the central bank are very high. For example, in Hungary it is about 30% of GDP, or about $7 billion (1987 figures).

The stability of the banking systems is threatened by the stock of unprofitable enterprise loans. For example, in Hungary in 1989, non-performing loans amounted to between 28% and 44% of domestic credits to enterprises, with a small number of hard-core firms accounting for 30% of this. In Romania, three-quarters of commercial debts have been written off against government deposits. Neither bank management nor borrowing firms are accountable for poor outcomes.

The savings banks hold a stock of long-term housing loans at very low fixed interest rates. Involuntary saving has grown in recent years, thereby increasing the risk of excess demand, fuelling accelerating inflation. The highly segmented, concentrated nature of the banking systems means there is a low degree of risk diversification and little or no competition.

In some countries, the ownership structure of the banks is such that a large proportion of the bank's equity capital is held by non-financial enterprises, creating a high risk of insider lending. Staff skills are inadequate. The human resource problem might be alleviated by foreign banks if they were allowed to establish domestic franchises free of bad corporate debt.

There is insufficient monetary control due to large state deficits which could be dealt with by monetising the debt. Poland is the only country where the central bank is prohibited from financing government deficits or loss-making state enterprises. Adequate monetary control is also undermined by the presence of informal credit markets.

Banking in Hungary

Hungary has the longest history of reform in Eastern Europe, dating back to 1968, though reform of the financial structure was not evident until the 1980s. Prior to the banking reforms (1987), there were 14 financial institutions and the central bank, the National Bank of Hungary (NBH). The institutions included the Hungarian Foreign Trade Bank, the National Savings Bank (NSB), specialised financial institutions, deposit associations, and 260 savings co-operatives. There were also three joint venture banks (with foreign bank participation), one of them offshore. Capital formation at firm level was strictly regulated and so remained limited. Szoke (1991) described the reforms as gradual, with a number of advantages over other East European economies. There was limited scope for independent decision-making but some knowledge of financial management, because some attention was paid to firms' financial performance. Central credit control meant that training took place of experts at the macro-level, who learned something about how an economy is managed. The sometimes innovative borrowing of the central bank meant staff gained financial expertise. There was a also gradual but slow learning process by the population in the 1980s that helped the introduction of further reforms.

Related changes in the financial system included the introduction of bonds in 1982 and the issue of short-term treasury certificates and certificates of deposit in 1988. In an effort to break the banking monopoly, companies were allowed to grant commercial credits. A bills of exchange market was created, though it is still small and illiquid. In 1988, a short-term treasury certificate and one to three-year certificates of deposit were introduced. After a change in company law in 1989, firms were able to become joint stock companies, which has caused a steep rise in share issues. Individuals and firms have the right to buy shares. A Stock Exchange was created, to enhance property reform, privatisation, and to create a secondary market in securities. The central bank was made independent from the state by an Act passed in 1992.

Under the 1987 Banking reform, a two-tier banking system, consisting of the central bank, commercial banks, and specialised financial institutions (SFIs) was established. Three commercial banks became operational from 1 January 1987. Most of the National Bank of Hungary's (NBH) corporate banking business was transferred to these commercial banks, as was its entire loan portfolio. Thus, the burden of dealing with the weak industrial firms shifted to the commercial banking system. There is a potential for state interference in the three commercial banks, because the state holds about 42% of the shares; they can also call on the support of other state-owned shareholders. However, the 1987 reform granted these banks a fair degree of autonomy.

Hungary has a fairly well defined set of bank regulations. An institution is free to enter the banking sector provided it has a minimum paid-up capital of approximately $15 million, management is deemed to be "fit and proper", and computer systems are adequate. The Banking Act allowed commercial banks to be universal; special restrictions on foreign exchange transactions and on the taking of deposits from households were gradually lifted. Though the banks have holdings in industrial and commercial firms, the lack of skilled staff has discouraged activity in privatisation, merchant banking and in securities.

Like all the former socialist states in Eastern Europe, the commercial banks are burdened by problem loans made to state enterprises under the old regime. Based on a survey of the 1992 tax returns of 60 000 enterprises, 50% were reporting losses.* A strict bankruptcy law has led to a large increase in the rate of liquidation of firms. Initially, it was hoped the commercial banks could weather the bad debt problems, as the real value of debt was reduced through inflation, and lax accounting rules inflated banking profits. However, it became apparent that government intervention was necessary, and in 1991 a "bank consolidation" scheme was announced, to shore up the 10 key domestic banks. By the end of 1993, the first stage of the scheme was completed; the banks were recapitalised (at a cost of $3 billion, to date), but they are responsible for cleaning up their own balance sheets. The first stage brought all banks up to a capital adequacy of 0%. In 1994, further injections were aimed at raising capital adequacy to 4%; the plan is to raise the ratio to 8% through sub-ordinated capital granted to the banks. Reported real profitability in the Hungarian banking sector is quite high, due largely to continued high spreads. However, Vittas and Neal (1991) argued that if non-performing loans rise by even a small amount, profitability will be seriously affected.

Some special financial institutions (SFIs) were maintained to ease the financing of activities that would have been difficult for the new commercial banks. Other SFIs have converted into commercial banks. At the end of 1990, in addition to the original commercial banks, there were seven other commercial banks and nine SFIs. There were also two savings banks, 260 savings co-operatives, and the State Development Institute (Vittas and Neal, 1992). The National Savings Bank dominates the market for personal deposits, though there is some competition from the Postabank and the Bank for National Savings Cooperatives.

Foreign bank participation is permitted through joint venture banks; they are not allowed to have branches or to operate wholly owned subsidiaries. Vittas and Neal (1991) reported 14 joint venture banks, involving 22 foreign financial firms from Austria, Italy, Germany, France, the USA, Japan and Korea. Even though state-bank privatisation by 1997 is a stated objective, potential investors are reluctant to commit capital to such a troubled sector.

There are a number of issues to be resolved in Hungary, which highlight the problems most East European emerging financial markets face. First, the segmentation of corporate and household banking continues, as well as a division between old and new banks and small and larger banks. The structure is best described as a segmented oligopoly. Vittas and Neal (1991) suggested that this degree of segmentation is inhibiting competition in the banking field, though there is a fairly high degree of competition in corporate banking. Segmentation also forces commercial banks to rely on a narrow funding base. Ninety per cent

---

*"Budapest Sounds its Horn", *The Banker*, July, 1994: p.37.

of retail deposits are held at two savings institutions, which do not lend. Some commercial banks are trying to expand their highly limited retail business.

Managerial deficiencies also plague the banking system. Some 10% of bank problems are estimated to be due to fraud. Managerial problems are compounded by a system with little in the way of modern technology, and lacking in computing and general banking skills. As a result, credit and other forms of risk assessment are quite crude. There is political interference in senior appointments, and no way of stopping managers from making loans to friends. However, new legislation should improve managerial accountability. Laws passed at the end of 1991 require all companies (including banks) to adopt European standard accounting procedures, and banks must implement a stricter loan provision system. Provided banks conform to the new system, loan provisions are tax-deductible.

Vittas and Neal (1991) observed a collapse in long-term lending, because of conservative managers but lack of information on the creditworthiness of potential borrowers. The long-term financial needs of the Treasury tend to be financed by central bank loans and short-term treasury certificates, instead of long-term bonds.

Banking in Russia

Compared to Hungary, the Russian banking system has even more serious structural and other problems. Like other Eastern European economies, the USSR had a few highly specialised banks during Communist rule, whereby the banks allocated funds under state direction. With the creation of the Commonwealth of Independent States (CIS), separate banking systems emerged in each of the new CIS republics. There are roughly 2500 commercial banks in Russia, which have been created since 1990. One hundred banks make up two-thirds of the system. The Savings Bank has a branch network, but most other banks are unit banks. According to Shea (1993), all banks would be insolvent if western accounting measures were applied. Despite loan portfolios of extremely poor quality, banks are not required to identify losses or make provisions.

The position of foreign banks is uncertain. There is a law limiting foreign bank capital to 12% of all Russian banks, and there are restrictions on where they can operate. Though the central bank is in favour of encouraging foreign bank entry, a Yeltsin decree in November 1993 stipulated that any bank that is more than 50% foreign-owned (defined as more than 50% of share capital held by non-Russians) would not be permitted to do business with Russian residents, unless they have already exercised their licence to do so. The decree was to be in force until 1996, meaning only two foreign banks could commence operations. However, in 1994, an EU delegation persuaded Yeltsin to lift the decree. Russian banks immediately appealed to foreign banks to observe an unofficial moratorium on operations in Russia for an 18-month period.

Russia has a serious deficiency of trained and experienced banking staff, both in the private and state (central bank) sectors. Virtually none of the staff have experience in credit or other forms of risk analysis. Basic technology taken for granted in Western banking systems is absent. There are no cheques, few credit cards, and virtually no payments system. A large percentage of transactions involve cash, especially in hard currency. Counterfeiting dollars and roubles is a highly profitable activity. It is estimated that approximately 20% of American dollars in circulation in Russia are fake.* Fraud is rife. *Pyramid funds* advertising extremely high rates of return attract unsophisticated investors, and have proved extremely popular, even though they collapse as soon as some clients attempt to cash in on their investment.

There are signs that Russian banks, some of them only a few years old, may be trying to establish a cartel. In April, 1995, a group of Russian private banks offered to lend the Russian government about $1.8 billion, in exchange for being allowed to manage the sale of shares of state enterprises due to be privatised. Until privatisation, the shares would be kept as collateral by the banks. The longer-term implication could be extensive cross-shareholdings between banks and major Russian firms. However, the banks lack the managerial experience to advise these firms, and it is possible such an arrangement would encourage collusive behaviour by the banks.

CONCLUSION

This chapter has sought to provide readers with an overview of the structural aspects of different banking systems as the century draws to a close. In the developed economies, the banking structures vary considerably in terms of the separation between banking and commerce and the financial services banks offer. The British financial system has witnessed an erosion of the traditional demarcation between financial markets, and the emergence of a type of universal banking, but there is still a high degree of segmentation by function in the USA, and especially in Japan. Functional demarcation in Japan may be substantially reduced under recent reforms. In the USA, interstate branching has been made easier since July, 1994, and it is hoped the separation of commercial and investment banking will be repealed during the Clinton administration. The European single banking market, made possible by the Second Banking Directive and other directives, should result in greater integration, though national segmented markets (especially in the retail sector) continue to be a central feature. The problem of prudential regulation under the principle of mutual recognition and a single banking licence is discussed at length in Chapter 6.

Developing economies and emerging markets in Eastern Europe share similar structural problems, including inadequate monitoring by supervisory authorities, and poorly trained staff, which have compounded the general problem with credit analysis, questionable accounting procedures, and relatively high operating costs. Many developing countries exhibit signs of financial distress; the problem for banks in the emerging East European markets is

---

*Source: *The Economist*, 30 July, 1994: p.80.

debt overhang from the state enterprises. In some former Soviet bloc nations, such as Russia, there is little in the way of progress toward a stable financial structure. On the other hand, Hungary, which adopted a gradualist approach to financial reform, has created a workable structure, though its banks continue to be plagued by the state enterprises' bad debt. The "shock therapy" approach, adopted by Indonesia, caused an explosion in the number of banks operating there, and resulted in recent central bank intervention to stem rapid credit growth.

A review of structure immediately raises questions related to competition in banking, the subject of the next chapter.

4
Competitive Issues in Banking

INTRODUCTION

This chapter is concerned with a number of related competitive issues in banking, including productivity, efficiency, economies of scale and scope, and tests of competition in banking markets. These topics are not as straightforward in banking and finance as they are in other industries, because of the intangible nature of banking products, ranging from the non-price features associated with virtually all of a bank's services, to the maturity structure of bank assets and liabilities.

The chapter first looks at the definition and measurement of bank output and then reviews key productivity measures used in banking. There is then a selective review of empirical evidence on scale and scope economies in banking. This is followed by a review of the empirical models of competition in banking, including the structure-conduct-performance and relative efficiency models, contestability in banking, estimating interest equivalences for non-price features, and the use of qualitative tests for price discrimination and firm "survival". The results of estimating a generalised linear pricing model, which tested for competition in British and Canadian bank markets, are also reported in this chapter.

MEASURING BANK OUTPUT

Introduction

The definition of output and productivity is not straightforward for a bank. For example, should demand deposits be treated as an input or an output? Are bank services best measured by the number of accounts and transactions, or values of accounts? If it is shown that one bank is more productive than another, as measured by assets per employee, employees per branch, or assets per branch, is it also possible to conclude that the bank is more efficient?

The measurement of "output" of services produced by financial institutions has special difficulties because they are not physical quantities. Additionally, it is difficult to account for quality in a banking service. For example, the use of cash dispensing machines instead of a cashier at a bank branch is an improvement in the quality of payment services, because it increases the speed of transactions. ATM technology is also known to reduce bank operating costs, but if customers access the machine more frequently than they would otherwise visit the branch, the cost savings may be lower than expected.

Banks provide customers with many services, including intermediation, low risk assets, credit and payment services, and non-monetary services such as management of investment portfolios, accounting services, and protection of valuables. In some bank systems, direct payment for these services is the exception rather than the rule. For example, demand deposits may not earn interest, in exchange for other "free" services. Or "free retail banking" may be offered to all customers in credit, but those with an overdraft are charged very high fees and interest, effectively subsidising customers in credit. Corporate clients normally receive a package of banking services to accompany a loan or overdraft facility.

In aggregate, bank output, for the purposes of a country's national accounts, should be based on value added, the measurement of which was discussed in Chapter 1. However, in banking, reported profits normally exclude net interest receipts, because they represent transfers of earnings from activities in other sectors. The interest that a bank receives reflects a charge for the use of bank capital and for the services they provide to customers. Depositors can be paid a relatively low deposit rate, to compensate for non-price features associated with the account. While the capital charge item may be netted out, the exclusion of net interest leads means the operating profits of the bank will be understated, if there are implicit charges which are part of the net interest receipts. For this reason, if one looks at the financial sector as a share of GDP, net interest receipts are normally included in value added; in the US these are attributed to depositors, while in the UK, they are attributed to depositors and borrowers. However, empirical studies of banking do not normally use the national accounts definitions of bank output. Instead, a "production" or "intermediation" interpretation of bank output is employed.

The Production Approach

In the production approach to measuring bank output, banks are treated as firms which use capital and labour to produce different categories of deposit and loan accounts. Outputs are measured by the number of these accounts or the number of transactions per of account. Total costs are all operating costs used to produce these outputs. Output is treated as a *flow*, that is, the amount of "output" produced per unit of time, and inflation bias is absent. An example of the use of this type of measurement may be found in Benston (1965).

Several problems are associated with this approach. First, there is the question of how to weight each bank service in the computation of output. Second, the method ignores interest costs, which will be important if, for example, deposit rates fall as the number of branches increase. Furthermore, it is unlikely data from different banks are comparable, making accurate measures of relative efficiency difficult to obtain.

The Intermediation Approach

This approach recognises intermediation as the core activity—banks are *not* producers of loan and deposit services. Instead, output is measured by the value of loans and investments; total cost by operating costs (the cost of factor inputs such as labour and capital) plus interest costs. Deposits may be treated either as inputs or as outputs. The intermediation approach treats bank output as a *stock*, showing the given amount of output at one point in time.

However, if banks have a wide range of assets, such as trust operations or securities, the intermediation approach will make their unit costs appear higher than for banks which engage in traditional intermediation. The relative importance of different bank products may also be ignored in the computation, unless weighted indices are used. One way of obtaining weighted indices was shown by Greenbaum (1967), who used linear regressions to obtain average interest rate charges on various types of bank assets. However, non-credit output and the effects of inflation were excluded from the analysis.

Neither the intermediation nor the production approach take account of the multi-product nature of banking. For example, in Chapter 1, the monitoring role of the bank was identified as an important service offered by banks. Should the monitoring function be treated as a cost (to provide services) or as a service itself?

Most bank productivity studies use the intermediation approach because there are fewer data problems than with the production approach. But the empirical work suffers from a number of difficulties. First, the way output is measured varies considerably from study to study. Second, in the output measures, no account is taken of the different risks attached to each loan, or for example, the reputation of the bank in terms of the perceived probability of failure. Third, the maturity structure of loans and deposits, critical in banking, is ignored. Finally, any change in the structure of the banking market could distort output measures. For example, increased competition may narrow interest margins, which in turn will reduce output as reported in the national income accounts. In the production approach, the output measure is affected if the change in margins affects the volume of loans—a fall in margins could increase the volume of loans. An increase in the number of loan accounts will mean the intermediation approach records an increase in output; otherwise, the output will show a fall.

PRODUCTIVITY MEASURES

Productivity measures may be total, where all the factor inputs are used to compute total productivity. More typical are partial measures, such as output per man-hour. In banking, accounting ratios are typically used to obtain a partial measure of bank productivity. Revell (1980), in an assessment of cost trends among banks across 18 OECD countries (1964–77), used the ratio of operating costs to the balance sheet total (volume of business). Revell argued this ratio would be constant if productivity in banking was rising as fast as in manufacturing. However, the ratio was shown to rise, suggesting a lag behind manufacturing. Revell attempted to explain this finding by arguing that in banking, technological improvements are discrete events, but are more continuous in manufacturing.

Measures of partial productivity, though easier to obtain, are problematic because they will never include a measure of the cost of increasing, say, labour productivity by replacing people with machines. Labour productivity will rise, but the cost of the machines is not imputed in the measure.

Total Productivity

The *total factor productivity* (TFP) approach employs a single productivity ratio, using multiple outputs and multiple inputs. The most well used TFP measure is *data envelopment analysis* (DEA). DEA is "non-parametric", because it is not based on any explicit model of the frontier. The methodology was originally developed for non-profit-making organisations, because accounting profit measures are difficult to compute. DEA compares the observed outputs (Y_{jp}) and inputs (X_{ip}) of several organisations. It then identifies the relatively more efficient firms with the relatively less efficient, by identifying a "best practice" firm or firms. To do this, maximise the following:

$$Ep = \sum u_j Y_{jp} / \sum v_i X_{ip} \qquad (4.1)*$$

subject to $Ep \leq 1$ for all p and weights $v_i, u_j > 0$; where p represents several organisations. The model is run repetitively with each firm appearing in the objective function once to derive individual efficiency ratings. Each firm will have either a derived rating of $E = 1$ (implies relative efficiency) or $E < 1$, which implies relative inefficiency. $E = 1$ is the "best practice" unit—it is not necessarily efficient, but compared to other firms in the study, it is the most efficient.

DEA is advantageous because it produces a true frontier from which relative efficiencies can be computed. No functional form is imposed on the data and all outputs and inputs can be handled simultaneously. The DEA frontier is defined on the outliers rather than on the whole sample and, therefore, is susceptible to extreme observations and measurement error. Nor is it possible to draw statistical inferences from this approach, and the efficiency scores are not independent of market structure. Data problems also arise because it is necessary to obtain the same output and input measures for all the firms in the sample.

---

*This equation and some of the discussion is taken from Colwell and Davis (1992). Their working paper also provides a more complete review of related empirical studies.

Numerous studies have used DEA to measure the efficiency of banks. Here, only a selection of these studies is mentioned. Rangan *et al.* (1988,1990) tried to break down the efficiency of 215 US banks into that originating from *technical inefficiency* (arising from wasted resources) and *scale inefficiency* (operating at non-constant returns to scale). Bank output was measured using the intermediation approach. In the first study (1988) the results showed the average value of efficiency for the sample was 0.7, implying that, on average, the banks in the sample could have produced the same output using 70% of the inputs. Thus, a significant amount of inefficiency appeared to exist, almost all of it due to technical inefficiencies.

In Rangan *et al.* (1990), the study was extended to include a sample of banks from unit banking as well as branch banking states. The pooled sample was split into two sub-samples, and separate production frontiers calculated. No sizeable differences in efficiency as between the two types of banking were found.

Field (1990) applied the DEA method to a cross-section of 71 UK building societies in 1981. Eighty-one per cent were found to be inefficient, due to scale inefficiencies. Unlike the Rangan *et al.* studies, Field found technical efficiency to be positively correlated with firm size. Drake *et al.* (1991) applied DEA to building societies in 1988 after deregulation in 1987. Thirty-seven per cent were found to exhibit overall efficiency, an increase compared to the Field study.

Humphrey (1992) measured productivity and scale economies using flow and stock measures of banking output in identical models. He employed both a non-parametric growth accounting procedure and an econometric estimation of a cost function. A structural model of bank production was used, which incorporated both the production of intermediate deposit outputs as well as "final" loan outputs. Thus, both the input and output characteristics of deposits were simultaneously represented.

Humphrey obtained two measures of total factor productivity. He used data on 202 US banks from the Federal Reserves's 1989 *Functional Cost Analysis* survey. In the non-parametric growth accounting approach, a general production function was employed:

$$Q = Af(K, L, D, S, F)$$

where:

Q: bank output: Humphrey used three different measures of bank output;

QT: a transactions flow measure: the number of deposits and loan transactions processed;

QD: a stock measure: the real $ value of deposit and loan balances;

QA: a stock measure of output: the numbers of deposit and loan accounts serviced;

A: efficiency;

K,L: capital, labour;

D: demand deposits;

S: small time and savings deposits;

F: purchased funds.

The growth of production efficiency is a residual, obtained after subtracting the growth in inputs from the growth in outputs. The residual from the dual cost function also shows productivity growth: the shifts in the average cost curve after controlling for changes in input prices. Based on the cost equation, Humphrey's key findings were as follows:

- QT: banking productivity, was found to have been flat over 20 years, with an annual average rate of growth of only 0.4%;
- QD: total factor productivity (TFP) actually fell from 1968–80 but rose thereafter, though the overall average rate of TFP growth was 1.8% per annum;
- QTA: the real value of total assets: the average TFP rate was found to be −1.4% per year.

In Humphrey's econometric approach, expenditure share weights were estimated rather than being computed directly. He estimated a translog cost function.* TFP is derived from these equations, and can be decomposed into cost reductions arising from either technical change over time or scale economies. Humphrey specified scale economies of 0.9 (slight scale economies), 1.00 (constant costs), and 1.1 (slight diseconomies). The TFP results did not differ substantially as a result of the scale economies he imposed, so he reported the one for constant costs. He found the TFP results using the econometric approach virtually the same as for the growth accounting approach.

Humphrey found there was little difference in the predictive accuracy of the stock and flow measures of bank output. By the flow measure, productivity growth over the past 20 years was slightly positive; it was slightly negative when the stock measure was used. But for the last decade, both measures generated a small positive productivity growth. There are a number of possible reasons for the relatively low US bank productivity growth. First, banks lost low-cost deposit accounts as corporate and retail customers shifted to corporate cash management accounts and interest-earning cheque accounts. Second, quality differences in bank output were largely ignored. For example, the quality of bank services may have improved because lowcost bank services continued to be offered by banks, even though they had begun paying interest on most accounts.

SCALE AND SCOPE ECONOMIES

There is an extensive literature on the degree to which scale economies exist in banking.[†] The term, *economies of scale*, or *scale economies*, is a long-run concept, applicable when all the factor inputs which contribute to a firm's production process can be varied. Thus, if a firm is burdened with capital, property, or

---

*See equations (2) and (3) in Humphrey (1992).
[†]This section will report on only a selection of studies. For a full review of the literature, see Gilbert (1984), Clark (1988), and OECD (1992).

labour which are fixed, then economies of scale do not apply. Assuming all factor inputs are variable, a firm is said to exhibit *scale economies* when equi-proportionate increases in factor inputs yield a greater than equiproportionate increase in output. Firms are operating on the falling part of their average cost curves.* Consider the case of a simple bank, which has three factor inputs: capital from deposits, labour—the bank's employees, and property, in the form of a branch network. The bank produces one output, loans. Then economies of scale are said to exist if, as a result of doubling each of the three factor inputs, the bank is able to more than double its loan portfolio. Even in this simple example, the concept is fraught with difficulties when applied to a financial institution. First, of course, not all of the bank's inputs will be completely variable. It is difficult to imagine a bank being able to double the number of deposits at short notice. Second, there is the issue of risk. If indeed a bank can more than double its loan portfolio by doubling the three factor inputs, the risk profile is bound to change, a critically important consideration for any bank wanting to maximise shareholder value-added. Additionally, in banking, there is the question of what constitutes output. Some authors, including this one, have argued that deposits, in addition to loans, must be treated as bank pro-ducts, because deposits provide customers with a liquidity and saving service. Furthermore, most banks produce multiple outputs, namely, a fairly broad range of financial services. These observations mean it is difficult to apply the term economies of scale in the financial sector, a point confirmed by the widely varying empirical evidence on the degree to which economies of scale exist. Yet they are normally cited as one of the key reasons why a merger between financial institutions will be a profitable one for shareholders.

The concept of *economies of scope* is another one that, employed loosely, can lead to unrealistic expectations of the benefits of a merger or acquisition. Economies of scope exist if the joint production cost of producing two or more outputs is lower than if the products are produced separately. For exam-ple, suppose a bank offers three services to its customers: deposit, loans, and a payments service. Then if a bank can supply these services more cheaply through a joint production process than producing and supplying them independently, it is said to enjoy economies of scope. The core banking busi-ness, where the bank intermediates between borrowers and lenders by lending out a percentage of its deposits, is an obvious example of economies of scope. Though the payments service offered by banks is a by-product of intermedia-tion, it is not obvious that lower costs result from the joint production of this service with intermediation.

The business policy term for economies of scope is *synergy*, though synergy usually embraces broader ideas such as the newly formed, larger firm having a more powerful influence on suppliers, thereby enhancing profitability. Again, among financial firms, where skills and innovation may be the difference

---

*Constant returns to scale: equiproportionate increases in factor inputs lead to equiproportionate increases in output; decreasing returns to scale: equiproportionate increases in factor inputs lead to less than equiproportionate increases in output.

between success and failure, synergy may be costly to achieve if it requires a merger of different cultures, or stifles the entrepreneurial spirit typical of small, successful financial firms.

From the strategic standpoint of managers, the question of whether or not economies of scale and scope or synergy are present in the banking is important. Evidence of economies of scale will mean large banks have a cost advantage over small ones. If cost complementarities are present, multi-product banks will be more efficient than the financial boutique.

However, empirical studies of economies of scale and scope in financial institutions throw up mixed results, even if one looks at evidence from the UK and USA, two very different financial systems. Humphrey (1992) obtained estimates of scale economies using different measures of output: QT, QD, QA, and QTA. If InQ was used as the proxy, only QT (a flow measure of output) yielded scale economy results that were significantly different from constant costs—suggesting diseconomies. The other output measures (QD, QA, QTA) indicated constant costs. But when (InQ^2) was used, Humphrey found significant scale economies for small banks ($10–$25 million), constant costs for medium-sized banks ($200–$300 million), and scale diseconomies for all but QT in large banks ($2–$5 billion). The findings held for all four measures of bank output. To gain further insight into the question of which output measure is most appropriate for measuring scale economies, Humphrey looked at goodness of fit for the estimated cost functions. Using the weighted R^2s, he concluded QT (the number of loans and deposits processed) had the worst fit, with an $R^2 = 0.59$ and QD (the real dollar value of deposit and loan balances, or QTA, the real value of total assets) had a better fit, with an $R^2 = 0.95$. When Humphrey looked at the predictive accuracy of the different output measures, the findings were similar; QT was quite poor and QD much better. He concluded that the stock measure was more accurate than the flow measure of output. The findings suggest there are slight economies of scale for small US banks, but slight diseconomies for larger US banks.

Shaffer and David (1991) re-examined the question of economies of scale for very large US multinational banks. They observed that most empirical work found diseconomies of scale for large banks (for example, assets in excess of $25–$50 million, depending on the study). But these results are inconsistent with the observation that very large banks (with assets 1000 times greater) are financially viable over long periods of time. The authors also wanted to investigate the question of whether banks would take advantage of reforms to allow interstate banking if diseconomies of scale were present.

Shaffer and David used data from the 100 largest commercial banks in the USA in 1984, with assets ranging from $2.5 billion to $120.6 billion. They relied on the Federal Reserve's *Call Report* data. Though the *Functional Cost Analysis* data are more disaggregated and preferred by investigators, they are obtained from a voluntary survey of mainly small banks. Hence, the use of FCA survey data makes it difficult to draw any conclusions about the presence or otherwise of scale economies among large banks.

The aggregated nature of the *Call Report* data may obscure some of the factors which are different between the banks, such as output mix, input mix, strategy, regulatory environment and so on. All of these factors will influence the bank's level of costs. Thus, if one is going to estimate cost functions, it is important to correct for this problem. The *hedonic* cost function* allows for such corrections to be made. The conventional cost function expresses total cost as a function of a measure of scale (for example, total assets) plus a vector of input prices, since any change in an input price will change costs. The scale variable can be augmented with a vector of variables chosen to reflect qualitative differences (therefore, "hedonic" terms), to reduce heterogeneity among firms in the sample.

In Shaffer and David, the qualitative (hedonic) terms were used to take account of funding strategy, off-balance sheet activities, asset quality, the regulatory environment (unit versus branch banking), and target clientele. They estimated a translog cost function (InC) with the following independent variables:

y: assets;
w_1: price of labour;
w_2: price of physical capital;
C: total operating expenses;
q_j: the vector of hedonic terms;
$DMIX$: see below: used as a third factor, so both a two factor and three factor version of the cost function was estimated.

A two and three factor translog cost function was estimated, with and without the hedonic terms. In the absence of hedonic terms, they found evidence of economies of scale which were exhausted in the region of $21 billion–$25 billion of assets. F statistics rejected the hypothesis of constant returns to scale at the 1% level. In the translog cost equation with the hedonic terms, only one was included at a time, and each term was constrained to a linear form. A full model was also estimated, which included all the terms simultaneously. Efficient scale in the two factor and three factor full models was found to be slightly below that for the non-hedonic models, at $18.9 and $23.6 billion, respectively.

The explicit hedonic variables were:

- $DMIX$: the ratio of uninsured deposits to fully insured deposits. $DMIX$ was also used as a proxy for the price of funds and when it was, it was excluded as a hedonic term. It was found to be significant, and reduced efficient scale by 25%.
- OBS: the relative volume of off-balance sheet activity: the sum of loan commitments, foreign currency contracts, and stand-by letters of credit, expressed as a fraction of total assets. The OBS coefficient is expected to be positive because of the cost of providing them. Its inclusion should reduce the estimated efficient bank scale if larger banks have, on average,

---

*The hedonic cost function was developed by Spady and Friedlander (1978).

higher *OBS* ratios, because it will cause the average cost curve to turn up at a smaller size range. They found the *OBS* coefficient to be significantly negative, though when expressed as a quadratic, it was positive. However, *OBS* did reduce the apparent efficient scale by about 25%, to the range of $15–$20 billion of total assets.

- *BAD*: the volume of problem loans: the ratio of past due, non-accrual, renegotiated loans and lease financing receivables to total loans. The variable should exhibit a positive coefficient on the cost function. It was not found to be statistically significant.
- *UNIT*: a dummy variable; 1 for banks operating in states which forbid branch banking, 0 for unit banking. A positive coefficient was expected because such a restriction limits the profit-maximising choice of branches. The inclusion of *UNIT* should result in a larger estimated efficient scale, since the optimal number of branches should be a monotonic increasing function of overall bank scale. Though *UNIT* did increase estimated efficient scale, its coefficient was significantly negative.
- *CIL*: the ratio of commercial and industrial loans to total loans. The variable is a proxy for target clientele, asset mix and average loan size. It should display a negative coefficient in the cost equation if the production cost per dollar (net of average credit losses) is lower for commercial and industrial loans than for smaller and/or personal loans. The coefficient was found to be significantly negative. It increased the efficient bank scale by about 50%, to $35 billion of total assets.

Hardwick (1990) tested for scale and scope economies using UK building society* data. The author employed multi-product statistical cost analysis. Building societies were assumed to supply one type of financial service to borrowers (mortgages) and another type to lenders (personal sector savers). Hardwick argued that for a firm producing m outputs, the cost function may be written as:

$$TC = TC(y, p)^{\dagger}$$

where:

   TC: total cost
   y: vector of m output
   p: vector of n input prices.

Hardwick's definition of overall economies of scale (OES) was $\sum(\delta \ln TC/\delta \ln y_i)$. Thus, OES were measured by the elasticity of total cost with respect to a given composite input. If OES < 1 (> 1), there are overall economies (diseconomies) of scale. To identify the main sources of economies

---

*UK building societies are similar to US thrifts. They are mutual organisations. See Chapter 6 for a full definition.
†If it is assumed that the cost function is linearly homogeneous, monotonically increasing, and concave in input prices, then it is dual to the transformation function, $T(x, y)$, where x is a vector of n inputs.

or diseconomies of scale, it was necessary to estimate the cost saving attributable to the jth input as the firm expands. Hardwick employed the following equation:

$$\ln C_j = \ln S_j + \ln TC$$

where S_j is the jth input's cost share.

The OES_j (input specific overall economies of scale) is given by $OES_j = \sum(\delta \ln S_j / \delta \ln y_i) + OES$.

Hardwick also tested for *product specific* economies of scale. These measure the effect on the ith product's incremental cost of a change in the quantity of product i, with the quantities of the other products unchanged. It is captured by the elasticity of the ith product's incremental cost with respect to the output of the ith product. He used a marginal cost approach; a negative gradient of the marginal cost $(\delta TC / \delta y_i^2)$ confirms product specific economies while a positive gradient is indicative of diseconomies.

Economies of scope are said to exist if the total cost of the joint production function is less than the sum of the costs of separate production. If a firm is producing two goods, then the appropriate test is for $\delta^2 TC / \delta y_i \delta y^2$ to be significantly negative. If less than zero, the marginal cost of producing one good decreases with increases in the output of another good, implying cost complementarities and economies of scope.

Hardwick's data came from the 1985 annual returns of a sample of 97 building societies. The variables included in the model were:

TC: total operating cost; the dependent variable, measured by the sum of management expenses and depreciation, where management expenses include all staff expenses, auditors' remuneration, office expenses, advertising and various commission and agency fees;

y_1: the average number of outstanding mortgage accounts;

y_2: the number of outstanding share and deposit accounts;

p_1: effective wage rate;

p_2: effective price of capital; the rental rate on capital, measured as the [(annual expenditure on office accommodation and equipment + depreciation)/mean assets] $\times$ 100;

B: number of branch offices;

M: the average size of all outstanding mortgages and deposit accounts (D), to control for the heterogeneity of accounts;

S_1: labour's cost share, the dependent variable in the derived share equations;

S_2: capital's cost share, the dependent variable in the derived share equations.

Hardwick used a maximum likelihood procedure to estimate the full cost equation jointly with one of the share equations. Behind these equations is the assumption that the technology of the building society industry can be represented by a translog multi-product cost function, where the natural log of total cost is approximated by a quadratic in the natural logs of the two outputs, the two input prices, and the other explanatory variables.

To test for overall economies of scale (OES), the 97 building societies were put in one of eight groups, by value of mean assets:

A1: > £5.5 billion;
A2: £1.5 billion to < £5.5 billion;
B1: £450 million to < £1.5 billion;
B2: £280 million to < £450 million;
C1: £140 million to < £280 million;
C2: £60 million to £140 million;
D1: £15 million to < £60 million;
D2: £ < 15 million.

OES were found to be significantly less than unity for all eight size groups except A1. Hence, economies of scale were present for all but A1. In the case of A1, economies of scale could not be established (OES > 1 but was not statistically significant), due to the presence of significant diseconomies in the employment of capital. For the other groups, the cost savings attributable to the employment of labour were found to be greater than those from the employment of capital.

In an earlier study where the same methodology and database were employed, Hardwick (1989) reported a finding of significant diseconomies of scale for societies with assets in excess of £1.5 billion if an augmented economies of scale measure was used. The formula was augmented to account for the direct effect on TC of a change in output, and an indirect effect, arising from the induced change in the number of branches.

Hardwick tested for product economies of scale by looking at the gradient of each product's marginal cost. For output supplied to mortgage borrowers, the marginal cost gradients were negative for all size groups, indicating the presence of product specific economies of scale, though the findings were not significant for groups A1 and A2. For the output supplied to depositors and shareholders (y_2), none of the marginal cost gradients were significantly different from zero, so it was not possible to conclude whether there were economies or diseconomies of scale.

Looking at the derivative of each product's marginal cost with respect to changes in output of the other product, Hardwick did not find evidence either for or against economies of scope for A1 and A2 firms. But for building societies with assets of up to £1.5 billion, Hardwick found significant diseconomies of scope, suggesting diversification could actually raise the average operating costs of the society. Thus, there appeared to be virtually no case for diversification of building societies into the broader banking market.

Drake (1992), using a multi-product translog cost function, found evidence for economies of scale in the asset value range of £120–£500 million. He could find no evidence to support the earlier Hardwick (1989) finding of diseconomies of scale for building societies with assets in excess £1.5 billion. Nor did Drake find economies or diseconomies of scope for the building society industry or sub-categories of building societies, except for the second largest group (assets in the range of £500 million–£5 billion), which demonstrated significant diseconomies of scope. Drake was also able to test for product economies of scope. Mortgage lending showed significant diseconomies of scope, but scope economies were found for unsecured consumer lending and secured commercial lending.

Numerous US studies have tested for economies of scope in banking, with mixed results. Gilligan and Smirlock (1984) used balance sheet data from 2700 unit state banks in the period 1973–78. Two definitions of output were used, the dollar amount of demand and time deposits, and the dollar amount of securities and loans outstanding. Their test results supported the hypothesis of economies of scope because they found the structure of bank costs to be characterised by jointness, that is, the cost of production of one output depended on the level of other outputs. Lawrence (1989) used a generalised functional form to test for economies of scope in a multiproduct production function. He employed the Federal Reserve's *Functional Cost* data for the period 1979–82. The deposit size for banks in the sample ranged between $6 million and $2.6 billion—the largest banks in the US were not included in this dataset. Lawrence used three output measures: deposits, investments and loans; and three factor inputs: interest costs, wages and computer rental costs. He found cost complementarities to be present in the joint production of the three outputs.

Hunter, Timme and Yang (1990) used a sample of 311 out of 400 of the largest US banks at the end of 1986. Bank production was analysed using an intermediation approach and multicost production function. Deposits were treated as an output and as an input. The authors found no evidence to support the presence of sub-additive cost functions, meaning cost complementarities were not present. Mester (1987) reviewed eight US multiproduct studies published between 1983 and 1986. Based on this review, Mester concluded there was no strong evidence to either support or refute the presence of economies of scope.

Altunbas and Molyneux (1993), using a translog cost function, examined the 1988 cost structure in four European countries—France, Germany, Italy and Spain. The authors employed an intermediation approach, where output was defined as loans plus securities. They found overall scale economies to exist in all four countries, but in most cases the coefficients were not statistically significant. Italy showed significant scale economies over all levels of output; in Spain, they were present only for the smallest banks, with an asset size of $100 million; France showed significant scale economies over a range of bank sizes, up to an asset size of $3 billion. In Germany, diseconomies of scale were found at all asset levels, but the coefficients were insignificant.

When the equations were re-estimated to take account of the joint expansion of output and branches, Italian banks showed significant economies of scale for assets up to $600 million. Spain showed significant diseconomies of scale across all asset groups, suggesting Spanish banks would achieve a more cost effective outcome if they expanded output in existing branches, rather than creating more branches. Diseconomies of scale existed for German banks, though the coefficient was significant only for small banks. Small French banks (assets of less than $3 billion) showed significant diseconomies but with significant economies for larger banks.

In Altunbas and Molyneux (1993), the presence of economies of scope means the joint production of loans and securities is less costly than their production at separate banks. The findings were mixed. In Spain, significant economies of scope were evident for banks with assets of less than $1 billion; in France, it is the middle-sized banks which showed economies of scope. Diseconomies of scope were found for all Italian banks, independent of size. German banks with assets of less than $1 billion showed scope diseconomies; the largest banks showed scope economies.

EMPIRICAL MODELS OF COMPETITION IN BANKING

This section considers a number of empirical studies which have attempted to test for the degree of competition in different banking markets. It reviews evidence on the structure-conduct-performance model, the relative efficiency model, and contestability in banking markets. The section goes on to explores the measurement of non-price features of bank products, and reports on the use of a generalised linear pricing model to test for competition in Canadian and British retail banking.

The Structure-Conduct-Performance Model

Since the Second World War, a popular model in industrial economics has been the structure-conduct-performance (SCP) paradigm, which is largely empirical, that is, it relies on empirical data but for the most part, lacks a theoretical model behind it. Applied to the financial sector, SCP says a change in the market structure or concentration of banking firms affects the way banks behave and perform. There is well-defined link between structure, conduct, and performance. *Market structure* is determined by the interaction of cost (supply) and demand in a particular industry; *conduct* is a function of the numbers of sellers and buyers, barriers to entry, and the cost structure; *performance* will depend on pricing behaviour. *Conduct* in a market is determined by *market structure*, that is, the number and size distribution of firms in the market and the condition of entry. The conduct, in turn, results in a firm taking decisions about prices, advertising, and so on. The outcome is market *performance*, normally measured by profitability. Thus, conduct links market structure and performance, as illustrated below:

$$\text{Structure} \leftrightarrow \text{Conduct} \leftrightarrow \text{Performance}$$

The SCP is largely empirical. There are theories where, as concentration in a market increases, profitability will rise because firms with greater monopoly power can charge more for the good or service they supply. However, one normally thinks of market structure as being endogenous, not exogenous, as in the SCP model. In banking, the SCP model has been used extensively to analyse the state of the banking market in a given country or countries. The studies are industry based, and lack any explicit model of the banking firm.*

The "Efficient Markets" or "Relative Efficiency" Model

This model challenges the SCP approach. It argues that some firms earn super-normal profits because they are more efficient than others. This firm-specific efficiency is exogenous and reflected in high market share. Therefore, it is market share, rather than concentration, which should be correlated with profit. The relative efficiency model predicts the same (positive) profits-concentration relationship as the SCP model. However, the positive relationship is explained by collusive behaviour in the SCP case, but greater efficiency and higher market share (and concentration) in the relative efficiency model. According to SCP, concentration is exogenous, resulting in higher prices for consumers and higher firm profitability. In the relative efficiency model, exogenous firm-specific efficiencies result in more concentrated markets because of the market dominance of these relatively efficient firms. Prices and concentration are inversely related. The policy implications are different in the two cases. A confirmation of the SCP hypothesis provides a case for reducing monopoly power and concentration via anti-trust laws; if the relative efficiency model is found to hold, it would suggest the markets are best left alone.

Empirical Tests of Structure-Conduct-Performance and Relative Efficiency in Banking

There are many studies testing the SCP and/or relative efficiency models in banking, especially for the USA. It would be impossible to do justice to them all. This section does not attempt a comprehensive survey of the published work.[†] Instead, it provides a summary of the findings reported in Berger and Hannan (1989), Jackson (1992), and the Berger and Hannan reply to Jackson (1992). It also reports the key results from Molyneux and Forbes (1993).

Berger and Hannan (1989) conducted direct tests of the SCP and relative efficiency models using the estimating equation:

$$r_{ijt} = \alpha + \beta CONC_{jt} + \delta x_{jit} + \epsilon_{ijt} \tag{4.2}$$

where:

r_{ijt}: the interest paid at time t on one category of retail deposits by bank i located in the local banking market, j;

$CONC_{jt}$: a measure of concentration in local market j at time t;

x_{ijt}: vector of control variables that may differ across banks, markets, or time periods;

ϵ_{ijt}: error term.

---

*Hannan (1991) tried to rectify this deficiency by developing a theoretical model of the banking firm, from which the SCP relationship can be derived.
[†]For a survey article on SCP, see Gilbert (1984). See Brozen (1982), Smirlock (1985), and Evanoff and Fortier (1988) for articles which find evidence to support the relative efficiency model.

By the SCP hypothesis, β should be less than 0; that is, there is a negative relationship between concentration and deposit rates, the "price" of the banking service. If the relative efficiency model held, $\beta \geq 0$. Berger and Hannan collected quarterly data from 470 banks in 195 local banking markets over a 2½ year period, from 1983–85, resulting in 3500–4000 observations in each of the six deposit categories. The dependent variables were retail deposit rates paid by commercial banks, as reported in the Federal Reserve's monthly survey of selected deposits and other accounts. The six rates were:

MMDA: money market deposit account, 10 quarters: September 1983–December 1985;

SNOW: super now* account, 10 quarters: September 1983–December 1985;

CD rates: certificate of deposit rates for three, six, 12 and 30 months: nine quarters from January 1983–December 1985 (CD rates had not been deregulated in September 1983).

Banks in the sample were assigned to local markets, which were defined as metropolitan statistical areas (MSAs) or non-MSA counties. Banks with less than 75% of their deposits in one local market were deleted from the sample.

Berger and Hannan used two concentration ratios to measure the degree of firm concentration in the banking market. The "three firm" concentration ratio, CR_3, was defined as the proportion of output attributed to the top three firms in the industry. More generally, one can write this ratio as CR_n, where n is the output share produced by the top n firms in the industry. The Herfindahl index was also used, defined as $H = \sum s_i^2$, where s_i is the market share of the ith firm.[†] These measures were constructed both with and without the inclusion of saving and loans firms. The vector x included a number of additional explanatory variables:

- the growth rate of deposits in the bank's market, which may reflect local supply and demand conditions, and could have either sign;
- the number of bank branches divided by total bank branches plus savings and loan branches in the local market—it should have a negative coefficient if costs rise with the number of branches. Local per capita income was included to control for factors affecting the supply of funds to banks—in a non-competitive market, it may reflect a greater or lesser elasticity of deposit supply. The local bank wage, reflecting a cost factor, was another explanatory variable. Its sign is not predicted, because bank wages could also reflect local income differences;

---

*The negotiable order of withdrawal account (NOW). See footnote in Chapter 6 for more detail.
[†] The general formula is $H = \sum s_i^{\alpha}$, where:
s_i: the market share of the ith firm
α: is an elasticity parameter, the value of which determines the weight given to large firms relative to small firms. As α gets large, the weight given to small firms is negligible: as α approaches zero, the index is the number of firms. If $\alpha = 2$, the result is the Herfindahl index. For example, n firms of equal size would give an H value of $1/n$, which diminishes with n.

- whether a state in which a given bank operates prohibits (*UNIT*) or limits (*LIM*) branch banking. To the extent that such regulations limit entry, and therefore, raise cost, one would expect to observe a negative coefficient.

All four concentration measures* yielded similar results, so only the results using CR_3 were reported. The concentration variable was found to be negative and significant at the 1% level—that is, the more concentrated the market, the lower the deposit rate, a finding which is consistent with the SCP hypothesis but not the relative efficiency model. For example, *ceteris paribus*, banks in the most concentrated markets were found to pay MMDA rates which were 25–100 basis points less than what was paid on the less concentrated markets.

Similar findings were obtained for all but some CD rates. For the regressions using the short-term CD rates, there were some large and significantly negative rates; a few of the coefficients were insignificant. But for the longer-term CD rates (12, 30 months), the CR_3 coefficient was mostly negative but insignificant. The finding is not surprising because the longer the maturity attached to the CD, the greater will be the competition from other financial markets, not just the local deposit market.

The authors argued that the results were robust with respect to the use of separate OLS cross-section estimates in place of pooled time-series cross-section data, the choice of concentration measure, and the inclusion of firm specific variables such as market share, bank branches, or bank size. The treatment of concentration under different state branching laws, modelling the deposit rate as a premium (the difference between the deposit rate and the money market mutual fund rate), and the inclusion of savings and loans in the measures of concentration did not affect the results.

Jackson's (1992) key finding was that though a linear regression over the entire (Berger and Hannan) sample did produce a significant relationship between price and market share using MMDA rates, sub-sample regressions did not. The sub-sample consisted of:

- a low concentration group: relatively low market concentration: here the β coefficient was negative, large and significant at the 1% level;
- a middle concentration group: β was negative but insignificant;
- a high concentration group: β was positive and significant.

Over a certain initial range, Jackson found a negative relationship but it was insignificant over some middle range, and then turned positive and significant. These results suggest price is non-linear over the relevant range and, possibly, a U-shaped relationship. They support the relative efficiency type model; where high levels of market concentration signal the gaining of market share by the most efficient firms, but low levels of concentration signal entry of efficient new firms.

---

*Four measures were used because the equations were estimated with and without savings and loans.

In their reply, Berger and Hannan (1991) noted Jackson used monthly rather than quarterly observations, but did not correct the standard errors for serial correlation, thereby making some of his results questionable. Berger and Hannan repeated their earlier work, but allowed for the three levels of concentration. They found a negative β for the low concentration group; a negative and insignificant β for the middle concentration group; and a positive and insignificant β for the high concentration group for the summary equation, though it was significant for seven out of 10 of the individual periods. Changing the control variables in the high concentration group reversed the sign, which raises the question of how robust the model actually is. Berger and Hannan concluded that the price–concentration relationship is negative for some ranges of concentration, though it does vary across time periods. It is unclear that at high concentration levels, it turns positive.

Molyneux and Forbes (1993) tested the SCP and relative efficiency hypotheses using annual, pooled European banking* data for the period 1986–89. The competing hypotheses were tested using profitability (return on assets) as the dependent variable.[†] A 10-firm asset concentration ratio and firm-specific market-share were the key explanatory variables. A number of control variables are also included on the right-hand side of the equation. The main finding was a significantly positive concentration ratio, but the market share variable was negative and not statistically different from zero. The authors concluded that the SCP hypothesis is supported by this European banking sample.

Contestable Banking Markets

Some empirical studies have considered the question of whether banking markets are contestable. A *contestable market* is one in which existing firms are vulnerable to "hit and run" entry. For this type of market to exist, sunk costs must be largely absent. *Sunk costs* are fixed costs which cannot be recovered when a firm leaves a market/industry. Not all fixed costs are sunk costs. For example, if machinery has a secondary market value, it can be sold, making the costs fixed but not sunk. In the banking industry, some experts argue that most of the costs are fixed but not sunk, making it contestable. That is, firms can "hit and run" in banking markets by entering the market if incumbent firms are exhibiting price-making behaviour, hit the market and capture market share with lower prices, and then, because most of their costs are not sunk, exit the market when increased competition narrows profit margins. There are important policy implications if a market is found to be contestable. It will not matter if there are only a few firms in the industry, for example, a banking oligopoly. The mere threat of entry will mean incumbent banks price their

---

*The 18 European countries were Austria, Belgium, Denmark, Finland, France, Germany, Greece, Ireland, Italy, Luxembourg, Netherlands, Norway, Portugal, Spain, Sweden, Switzerland, Turkey, and the UK.
[†] The authors argued that using price as the dependent variable creates problems because of the multi-product nature of banking.

products at marginal cost, so consumer surplus will be maximised. Hence, there is no need for governments to implement policies to encourage greater entry into the market.

Shaffer (1982) and Nathan and Neave (1989) used the Rosse–Panzer (1977)* statistic (RPS) to test for contestability in, respectively, the US and Canadian banking markets. The technique involved quantifying the firms' total revenue reaction to a change in factor input prices. Input prices consisted of the unit price of labour, the unit price of premises, and the ratio of interest expenses to total deposits for banks. RPS, the Rosse–Panzer statistic, is defined as the numerical value of the elasticity of total revenue with respect to a chosen vector of input prices.

Shaffer (1982) used data for unit banks in New York, and estimated the RPS to be 0.318. He concluded that banks in the sample behave neither as monopolists (their conduct was inconsistent with joint monopoly) nor as perfect competitors in the long run. In Nathan and Neave (1989) a similar methodology was applied, using cross-section data (1982–84) from the Canadian banking system. RPS values for 1983 and 1984 were found to be positive but significantly different from both zero and unity. These RPS values, they argued, confirmed the absence of monopoly power among Canadian banks and trust companies. Nathan and Neave concluded their results were consistent with a banking structure exhibiting features of monopolistic, contestable competition.

Molyneux, Lloyd-Williams and Thornton (1994) tested for contestability in German, British, French, Italian and Spanish markets, using a sample of banks from these countries, for the period 1985–89. The authors found the RPS for Germany,[†] the UK, France, and Spain, to be positive and significantly different from zero and unity. Their conclusion was that in these markets, commercial bank revenues behaved as if they were earned under monopolistic competition. However, the authors cautioned that the result is different from the type of contestable market implied by the theory because incumbent banks were not undertaking perfectly competitive pricing. For Italy, the authors could not reject a hypothesis of monopoly or a conjectural variation short-run oligopoly for the years 1987 and 1989 because the RPSs were found to be negative, and both were significantly different from zero and unity.

Perrakis (1991) criticised Nathan and Neave and argued the RPS may be inadequate as a test for contestability.[‡] However, there are more fundamental problems with the use of RPS to infer contestability than those raised by Perrakis. There is a potential problem with the timing of the firms' entry and exit decisions. The computations by Shaffer (1982) and Nathan and Neave (1989) implicitly assumed there were no lags in interest rate adjustments, so interest rates were contemporary with the change in total revenue, and entry and exit by other firms was very rapid and in the same period.

---

*Rosse and Panzer (1977) used the RP statistics to test for competition in the newspaper industry.
[†] Except 1987.
[‡] Their reply to Perrakis' criticism is found in Nathan and Neave (1991).

Additional problems arise from the authors' argument that RPS should be positive for contestability. If firms have flat-bottomed average costs in a perfectly contestable market, the elasticity of total revenue to the input price vector is $1 - e$, where e is the price elasticity of demand if no firm actually enters or quits the market. e could be greater or less than unity, and therefore, RPS could be negative, even under conditions of perfect contestability. On the other hand, in a classic, incontestable Cournot oligopoly* with linear demand and horizontal marginal cost, RPS will be positive if the given number of firms is large and marginal cost is low. These examples suggest one cannot interpret a positive value of H as evidence of contestability.

Pricing Non-price Characteristics in Banking

An important feature of banking and other financial services is non-price characteristics associated with these products. In stockbroking, services such as analysts' advice and soft commissions feature prominently, in addition to commission rates. In banking, characteristics such as branch size, ATM access, and service charges are, among others, an integral part of the retail product offered to customers. The purpose of this section is to describe a methodology for "pricing" the non-price features of bank products, so interest rates can be adjusted for these non-price features.

The focus of attention is the UK retail banking market, where it was possible to obtain cross-section, time-series data for the period 1985–89. The data consisted of a monthly series on rates for different deposits and loans, and a biannual summary of the non-price features of these bank products.[†] Four retail banking products were examined, the higher interest deposit account (HID), the higher interest chequing account (HIC), repayment mortgages (RM), and personal loans (PL).

For these products, explicit interest and non-price characteristics are not mutually exclusive. To compute interest equivalences for the non-price features of bank products, the product interest rate is regressed on market interest rates (current and lagged) and the non-price characteristics of bank products. Such a regression makes it possible to identify the explanatory variables (non-price features) that are statistically significant. The equation, estimated by OLS, took the following form:

$$r = a + b_i \sum x_i + c_0 LIBOR + c_i LIBOR_{-i} + eTT + u_i \qquad (4.3)$$

where:

r: the rate of interest offered/levied by a bank on the product

x_i: the non-price characteristic $x, i = 1, .., n$

$LIBOR$: the three-month £ London Interbank Offer Rate, a proxy for the market interest rate

---

*In a Cournot oligopoly, as the number of firms increases, the price of the good or service falls. If a market is contestable, prices should not be sensitive to firm entry.

[†]For a more detailed account of the ideas presented in this sub-section, see Heffernan (1992).

LIBOR$_{-i}$: *LIBOR* lagged by $i, i = 1, 2$

TT: time trend

u_i: error term.

This equation was estimated for the cross-section, time-series database for the two deposit products, HID and HIC, and pooled interest rates for the products for HIC and HID (HICD), repayment mortgages and personal loans (RMPL). Coefficients on correctly signed, statistically significant explanatory variables were used to compute an interest equivalence for each non-price characteristic. The observation period ran from 01.08.85 to 01.11.89, depending on the bank product. Deposit rates were annual rates, unless otherwise stated.

Interest rates and other characteristics for higher interest chequing (HIC) and higher interest deposit (HID) accounts varied according to deposit levels, which ranged from £0 to over £53 000. Initially a series was created for 11 deposit levels, ranging from £96 to £53 500 and deflated by a quarterly money GDP deflator. Here, empirical findings for two of the deposit levels, £765 and £4590, are reported. These two amounts correspond closely to the average deposit levels for, respectively, current accounts and deposit accounts in the late 1980s. For mortgages and personal loans, it was not necessary to specify a loan amount, because banks and building societies tend to quote one interest rate that does not vary with the size of the loan. They do set minimum and maximum amounts, and these were included as non-price features of bank loans.

Information on the non-price "characteristics" of these products was compiled once or twice a year. There are a number of characteristics common to all firms. For example, the way bank statements are provided did not vary among banks. Non-price features of bank products common to all the firms in the sample were dropped from the database. The series created was based on characteristics which showed substantial variance among firms.

For the higher interest chequing account (HIC) the characteristics included:

- *MI*: a minimum investment requirement;
- *MD*: a minimum deposit requirement;
- *MC*: a minimum cheque constraint, where the customer is constrained to write cheques for values in excess of some minimum amount;
- *BRAN*: the number of branches for the firm offering the product;
- *INTPAID*: the number of times interest is paid in a given year;
- *ATM*: the number of automatic teller machines available.

The branch variable was included as a proxy for other non-price and near-bank features a bank may offer, such as convenience of location, retail stock-broking services, and foreign exchange facilities. In the UK, it is the larger branch banks (especially the big four clearing banks) that offer these sorts of services.

For the higher interest deposit account (HID) the non-price characteristics included: *MI, BRAN, INTPAID*, a maximum withdrawal (*MW*) constraint (a customer may only withdraw a specified maximum amount in a given day or week), and *NOTICE*, whether or not notice of withdrawal is required.

Data from HIC and HID were pooled at the two deposit levels, with the objective of establishing an interest equivalence for chequing facilities, the key feature which differentiates these two products. The aggregated product was called HICD (at £765 and £4590) and includes the following characteristics: a cheque dummy (*CHQ*), *MI, MW, BRAN, INTPAID, NOTICE* and *ATM*.

Data for repayment mortgages and personal loans (*RMPL*) were pooled and a security dummy inserted. Security is required for mortgages (the bank holds the title deeds to the house) but not for personal loans, so the dummy allows one to estimate an interest equivalence for security. Similarly for insurance (the borrower is required to take out insurance to cover the mortgage repayments in the event of death), though a 0.5 dummy is inserted to allow for optional insurance, where applicable. In addition, the minimum and maximum amount available for loans (*MIN, MAX*), minimum and maximum terms (*MINT, MAXT*), and number of branches were considered.

The list of non-price characteristics was not exhaustive. For example, at least two banks offered some form of home banking, but this feature was excluded from the list. The author was limited by the data because only selection of non-price features was reported. However, the information was gathered by a major clearing bank, and one would expect it was interested in non-price features thought to be the most important from the standpoint of its competitive strategy. In addition, it is only possible to include characteristics that showed a high degree of variance between banks. Omitted non-price characteristics must weaken the outcomes of the test. On the other hand, given that our sample probably includes the most important characteristics, they should not be ignored.

Equation 4.3 was estimated using OLS. The R^2s ranged from 0.6871 to 0.9599 and these are acceptable, given that the data are pooled cross-section time-series. The adjusted R^2s were not very different from R^2s. Serial correlation and heteroscedasticity were largely absent.*

For the higher interest chequing account (HIC765), the variables found with right-signed, statistically significant coefficients were: *LIBOR*, Minimum Investment (*MI*), and the number of branches (*BRAN*). The *t*-ratio for

---

*The interest rate changes only when there is a change in the central bank rate, creating the possibility of serial correlation. The Durbin Watson (DW) tests showed the null hypothesis of no autocorrelation could not be rejected for most of the products while for the other products, a Lagrange Multiplier test for higher autocorrelation allowed acceptance of the null hypothesis at the 1% and 5% significance levels.

The presence of heteroscedasticity is another concern, given the cross-section nature of the data. The Lagrange Multiplier test for heteroscedasticity was used, where the null hypothesis is that the disturbances have a constant variance. It was tested for significance at the 1% and 5% levels using the *F* distribution. For the deposit products, the null hypothesis of homoscedasticity cannot be rejected at the 1% and 5% significance levels but for loan products, heteroscedasticity problems meant only the estimates from one subset of the 1988 pooled RMPL product could be used with any confidence.

minimum deposit (*MD*) was nearly significant with the right sign. At deposit level £4590, *LIBOR*, *LIBOR2*, *MD*, and branches were statistically significant with the expected sign. The constant term (*CON*) was insignificant for HIC765 but negative and significant for HIC4590. The *ATM* coefficient (number of ATMs) was statistically significant for HIC765 and HIC4590 but the sign is positive at £765.00 and negative at £4590.00.

The coefficients on the following explanatory variables were found to be correctly signed and statistically significant for HID765: *LIBOR*, *LIBOR2*, *MI*, branches (*BRAN*), maximum withdrawal (*MW*), and the number of times interest is paid in a given year (*INTPAID*). Required notice of withdrawal (*NOTICE*) was significant but wrong-signed. The time trend (*TT*) was negative and significant, suggesting that interest rates were falling over time. The constant term was positive and significant. Similar results were obtained for HID4590, except that *MW* and the number of branches were no longer significant.

The *ATM* variable was difficult to interpret. On the one hand, it is a characteristic that eases consumer access to deposit funds, and using this reasoning, it should have a negative sign: the provision of ATM facilities lowers the interest rate offered on the product, as it appears to do for HIC4590. But it is also a piece of technology which if used instead of a cheque or withdrawal from a cashier-manned counter, reduces the cost of money transmission for banks. It was recently reported that in the USA, the average cost of a teller (or bank cashier) function is over $1.00. The same transaction cost 27¢ using an ATM; 35¢ by telephone.* For this reason, a positive coefficient would be anticipated, as was observed for HIC765, HID765, and HID4590. Van der Velde (1985) of the Bank Administration Institute, using US data, found ATMs to have a largely neutral effect on bank costs, because although costs per transaction were lower when compared to a full teller service, customers use an ATM more often, thereby raising overall costs. This point is supported by a survey of large US banks, which found that automation technology is offered to provide a better service, rather than to reduce costs.[†] Unfortunately, similar information on British ATM costs does not exist.

Turning to the aggregated product, *HICD*, the cheque dummy coefficient (1 for HIC, 0 for HID) was statistically significant with a negative sign—that is, if a chequing facility is offered, the interest rate falls.[‡]

For the pooled data on repayment mortgages and personal loans (*RMPL*), the results were only robust for the 1988 coefficients. The insurance and security dummies (*INSURANCE*, *SEC*) and the number of branches were statistically significant with the expected sign.

---

*Source: A study by John Karr, consultant, Ernst and Young, as reported in *The Economist*, 20 May, 1995: p.107.
[†] See *The American Banker*, 6 October, 1990.
[‡] For *HICD*, all the variables tested were significant with the expected sign with the exception of *LIBOR-1*, *NOTICE*, *ATM* and the HIC time trend (*TT2*) at £765.00 and *LIBOR-1*, *MW*, Interest Paid, *NOTICE*, and *TT2* at £4590. These results do not mean very much, since it is a synthetic product.

For most deposit products, *LIBOR* and *LIBOR* lagged by two months were statistically significant, suggesting that in general, there is a substantial lag in the responsiveness of deposit rates to a change in the market rate of interest. Many of the constant terms had large, significant coefficients. These findings are suggestive of "smoothing" by the banks, that is, they adjust interest rates slowly and in discrete jumps. There are several possible explanations for smoothing, including the presence of menu and/or switching costs or price-making behaviour, a topic discussed in the next section.

The coefficients from the OLS regressions were used to compute the interest equivalences for the non-price features of bank products. These are reported in Table 7 for HIC and HID at deposit levels £765 and £4590. Results for the 1988 pooled repayment mortgage and personal loan set are reported in Table 8. The coefficients on the non-price features give a direct measure of the *interest equivalence*, defined as the interest earned (forgone) because of a non-price feature in a product that is, from the standpoint of a consumer, negative (positive). The results are best interpreted by considering some examples. The coefficients on the branch variable show that as the number of branches increase, the interest offered on the deposit falls. In 1989, the average branch size for the big four clearing banks was 2477. Table 7 tells the consumer that for HID, up to 3.2% interest could be forgone at the lower deposit level because of the choice of a bank with an extensive branch network. On the other hand, the customer who could deposit £4590 would lose only 0.003% in interest if the no-branch bank is chosen. On average, the interest forgone is 0.75% at £765 and 0.01% at £4590. For the higher interest chequing account, the average interest sacrificed is between 0.1% and 0.3%, depending on the deposit level.

The number of times interest is paid on an HID account (one, two or four times a year) was found to be significant, and the interest sacrificed ranged between 0.09% and 1.7%. ATMs add to interest for HID but at the higher deposit level for HIC, the consumer actually loses interest because of the ATM facility.

The summation lines in Table 7 provide the reader with an idea of the overall interest lost/gained as a result of the presence of non-price features. For HID, the consumer loses an average of 1.1% at £765.00 and 0.7% at £4590. On average, the consumer gains 1.8% from non-price features associated with the higher interest chequing account at the lower deposit level and loses 0.3% at £4590. However, the provision of chequing facilities will increase the amount of interest forgone on this type of account.

Table 8, for loan products, is based on pooled 1988 data. The presence of security on the loan will reduce the interest rate charged by 7.8%. Insurance will lower it by 2.1%, and the option of insurance (under the heading 0.5) reduces it by just over 1%. Note that the interest contribution made by branch size is much smaller than was true for deposit products.

To conclude, based on this UK dataset and methodology, the non-price features found to be important were the levels of minimum investment, minimum deposit, and maximum withdrawal. The number of branches, ATM outlets, frequency with which interest is paid, and the provision of a chequing facility were also correctly signed and statistically significant. By

Table 7 Interest Equivalences[a] for Deposit Products

	Higher interest deposit account		
	Minimum interest equivalence (%)	Maximum interest equivalence (%)	Average interest equivalence (%)
Minimum Investment			
£765.00	0.02	1.12	0.54
£4590.00	0.006	0.6	0.15
Maximum Withdrawal			
£765.00	−0.75	−0.45	−0.66
£4590.00	na	na	na
Number of Branches			
£765.00	−3.2	−0.2	−0.75
£4590.00	−0.04	−0.0003	−0.01
Interest Paid			
£765.00	−1.7	−0.14	−0.28
£4590.00	−1.1	−0.09	−0.23
Number of ATMs			
£765.00	0	0.6	0.05
£4590.00	0	0.3	0.02
SUM			
£765	−5.6	0.9	−1.1
£4590	−1.1	0.5	−0.0

	Higher interest chequing account		
Minimum Investment			
£765.00	0	2.4	1.71
£4590.00	na	na	na
Minimum Deposit			
£765.00	0	0.3	0.07
£4590.00	0	0.46	0.09
Number of Branches			
£765.00	−0.2	0	−0.1
£4590.00	−0.5	−0.01	−0.3
Number of ATMs			
£765.00	0	0.6	0.09
£4590.00	−0.6	0	−0.1
SUM			
£765.00	−0.2	3.3	1.8
£4590.00	−1.1	0.5	−0.3
Chequing Facility	**No Cheque**	**Cheque**	
£765	0	−1.2	
£4590	0	−0.4	

[a]An interest equivalence is the interest earned (forgone) because of the presence of non-price feature in product that is, from the standpoint of the consumer, negative (positive). It is obtained from the statistically significant right-signed coefficients obtained from the estimation of equation 4.2. Minimum interest equivalence (MIN) is the smallest amount of interest gained or forgone because of the non-price feature; maximum interest equivalence is the greatest amount gained or lost; AVG is the average interest equivalence.

Table 8   Interest Equivalences for Loan Products

Number of branches				
0–104	0–829	0–1546	0–3086	0–210 171
0.055%	0.15%	0.20%	0.29%	0.75%

Insurance		
No Insurance	Compulsory Insurance	Optional Insurance
0	−2.09%	−1.05%

Security	
No Security	Security Required
0	−7.8%

computing interest equivalences in this way, a more accurate measure of price behaviour in retail banking markets can be obtained because the quoted deposit and loan rates have been adjusted for non-price features, translated into interest equivalences. A similar methodology could be applied to financial products in other markets, such as stockbroking services.

Testing for Competition Using A Generalised Linear Pricing Model*

Between 1971 and 1985, a number of regulations were passed in Britain, to encourage greater competition in banking. These included a break up of the clearing bank cartel under the 1971 Competition and Control Measures, permission for regional Trustee Savings Banks to offer a full set of retail banking services under the 1976 Trustee Savings Bank Act, several tax reform measures that encouraged increased banking activity,[†] the 1986 Building Societies Act which meant societies could, for the first time, offer a complete retail banking service,[‡] and the creation of a new Association for Payments Clearing Services in 1985, which eased access to the payments clearing system.

This section reports on a study of the competitive behaviour of British retail banks in the period 1985–89. Readers are referred to the previous section for details on the database. During this time, the national retail banking market consisted of four large clearing banks, a number of smaller banks, and large (in terms of asset size and branch networks) building societies (see Table 9). The main motivation for this study lies in the question of whether retail customers actually benefited from more competitive pricing policies. Is it

---

*For a more detailed version of this section, see Heffernan (1993).
[†]The tax reforms were the abolition of two taxes on bank deposits (the "Corset" in 1980 and a required reserve assets ratio in 1981) and, in 1982, of hire purchase controls, which had limited the growth of retail credit.
[‡]The Building Societies Act was preceded by the demise of the Building Society Cartel in 1983, and had the tacit support of the government.

Table 9   List of Banks and Building Societies included in the Database[a]

Banks	Asset size[b]	Branches
Barclays	92.8	2768
Lloyds	49.2	2183
Midland	55.6	2156
National Westminster	91.6	3098
Bank of Scotland	9.8	543
Royal Bank of Scotland	19.8	846
National Girobank	1.8	21 256
Co-op Bank	1.9	94
Trustee Savings Bank	18.0	1565
Yorkshire	2.7	242
Building Societies		
Abbey National[c]	29.3	676
Halifax	34.9	736
Leeds	7.8	384
Nationwide Anglia	15.4	759
Woolwich	10.5	466
National & Provincial	6.8	328
Britannia	4.8	246

[a]Unlike the United States but similar to Canada, the British retail banking market is a national (as opposed to local) market, where the deposit and loan rates associated with a given bank or building society are the same throughout the country. For example, the deposit rates quoted by the Royal Bank of Scotland branches in Inverness are exactly the same as those for the London branches of the Bank.
[b]Average total gross assets, 1985–89; average number of branches, 1985–89.
[c]Abbey National Bank converted from mutual status to PLC bank status in late 1989. In March 1995, the High Court cleared the way for the Halifax and Leeds building societies to merge. The new Halifax will seek plc bank status, and issue shares to its members. A merger between Lloyds Bank plc and Trustee Savings Bank is also going ahead.

Sources: For banks: Statistical Unit, Committee of London and Scottish Bankers, *Abstract of Banking Statistics*, various years. For Building Societies: Building Societies Association, *Building Society Fact Book*, various years.

possible to say that, by the late 1980s, the *law of one price* applied in British retail banking?

To answer these questions, this section reports the results of three tests, two qualitative and one quantitative. First, a *survival test* for deposit and loan products looks for the existence of dominated products which survive in the market place. Second, a measure of price discrimination is developed to assess whether some firms practise price discrimination in retail banking. Third, a generalised linear pricing model is used to test for competition in British retail banking.

The Survivor Test: Do Some Firms offer Superior Products?

In this sub-section, a qualitative "survivor test" is used to identify whether products offered by some firms in a given category are superior to others. A firm's product offering is said to be "superior" if it meets the survivor test criteria. In this test, a pairwise comparison of price and non-price characteristics was employed. Product offerings in each of the four categories (HID, HIC, RM and PL) were ranked in descending order by the deposit or loan rate associated with them and by each non-price characteristic.

For example, suppose three firms quote deposit rates for products A, B and C in the category HID765, together with a list of the non-price features offered with A, B, and C. Then pairwise comparisons are made:

- *In how many characteristics (price and non-price) is A ranked better than B? AND*
- *In how many characteristics is B ranked better than A?*

A is eliminated from the survivor set if it is dominated by B, that is, B is strictly greater in at least one of the characteristics and worse in none. But A remains in the survivor subset if B is dominated by A, A and B get equal rankings, or it is not possible to rank A and B because A > B in at least one characteristic and B > A in at least one characteristic. All characteristics were weighted equally in the test.

If product offering A stays in the survivor subset, then one goes on to compare product offerings A and C, and so on. If A is eliminated at any stage, one goes to the product that beat A, and all products beaten by A are also eliminated. The result is an objective, strict partitioning of the product set into a subset of dominated product offerings (empty under conditions of perfect competition) and a subset of *survivor product* offerings. The partition allows one to compute the percentage of retail bank products that are superior (that is, that pass the survivor test) and to identify the firms that offer superior products.

To conduct the test, it is necessary to have information on the interest rate and non-price features in the four bank product categories. The detail on deposit rates, loan rates, and non-price features for these products was described in the previous section. The "survivor test" was conducted on four product categories, that is, two types of deposit accounts, personal loans, and repayment mortgages. A 100% survival rate means all the products in a given category are in the survivor subset and the dominated set is empty, a situation which would arise under perfect competition. The detailed results are not reported here.* But they showed substantial variation over time and product. For the HIC accounts, a high percentage of firms survived. This was also the case for personal loans in the later part of the period. The percentage of product offerings in the repayment mortgage category that were in the survivor subset ranged from as low as 25% to just over 50%.

It was also possible to look at survival by individual banks. A survivor rate of 100% means the firm's product offering was in the survivor subset throughout the period, that is, from August 1985 to December 1989. Again, there was a wide variation across firms and products. For HID765, HID4590, HIC765, and HIC4590, about half the firms offered superior products throughout the

_____
*See Heffernan (1991), Tables 1 and 2, for detailed results.

period. Included in this group were the large banks, the smaller banks and a building society. For repayment mortgages, only a quarter of the sample ended up in the survivor subset all of the time—none of the building societies were survivors. For personal loans, half the banks were survivors all of the time, but most of the building societies were in the dominated subset for the whole period.

Price Discrimination

When a firm practises price discrimination, it offers the same product at different prices to different consumers. Price discrimination is successful if a firm can effectively separate consumers according to their different price elasticities of demand. Using the database outlined earlier, it is possible to test for the presence of price discrimination in retail banking.

On the deposit side, there are the traditional "seven day" and "basic rate" accounts offered by, respectively, banks and building societies. In addition, there are more recent higher interest chequing (HIC) and deposit (HID) accounts. All of these products offer the customer one basic feature: a means of saving. However, unlike the traditional accounts, the newer HIC and HID are characterised by a large number of non-price characteristics, which, as was discussed earlier, from the standpoint of the consumer, can be either positive or negative.

The previous section reported computed interest equivalences for each of these non-price characteristics. If one adjusts the HIC and HID deposit rates for the non-price features associated with them, it is possible to compare the interest rates paid on all the accounts, which should be the same in the absence of price discrimination. Thus, the measure of price discrimination for deposit products is:

$$PD_j = ADJINT_j - 7DAY/BASIC_i \qquad (4.4)$$

where:

PD_j: price discrimination by bank/building society j

$ADJINT_j$: the net (of tax) interest paid by a bank/building society on a higher interest deposit or higher interest chequing account, adjusted, using interest equivalences, for non-price features.

$7DAY/BASIC_i$: the average seven-day or basic rate paid to customers by, respectively, banks or building societies.

If PD is found to be anything but a number close to zero, price discrimination is present. For example, if PD is positive, then consumers holding a seven-day account are being paid a lower deposit rate than consumers who deposit their funds in one of the newer products. Based on the results, which are not reported in detail here,* one may make a number of observations. First, the average price discrimination for HID765 was much lower than for

_____

*See — Heffernan (1993).

the other three deposit products. With the possible exception of HID765, the consumer is discriminated against if a seven-day account was held in lieu of higher rate accounts, with or without chequing facilities. Second, between 1985–89, the amount of price discrimination, had, on average, increased. Thus, at a time when competition should have been increasing among banks and building societies, price discrimination was rising. The computations also revealed that firms differ significantly in the degree of discrimination they practise. Consider the product HIC765. At least one bank as not discriminating at all (a negative PD), while for another bank, PD was as high as 6.55%.

It was also possible to report on price discrimination for at least one loan product. In 1986, some banks began to offer "equity loans". These were directed at customers who had paid off their mortgage but wished to borrow money, using their property as security. One can compare average spreads[†] for equity loans and repayment mortgages. One would expect them to be similar or slightly lower for equity loans, given the relatively secure nature of the borrower. Over the observation period (31.01.86–01.12.89), the average spread for repayment mortgages was 1.78%. For equity loans, it was 4.06%, indicating price discrimination in equity loans.

These findings should be treated with caution for two reasons. First, to the extent that important non-price characteristics are excluded from the dataset, the price discrimination measure must be diminished in accuracy. Second, there is no information on the cost of administering these accounts, though anecdotal remarks by practising bankers suggests the seven-day account costs virtually nothing to administer. Price differences could be explained by cost variation between banks, but if true, it would indicate a departure from the competitive paradigm.

A Generalised Linear Pricing Model

The results of the two qualitative tests showed some banks/building societies offer dominated products which appear to survive over time and some banks/building societies practise price discrimination on certain products. These findings are suggestive of an imperfectly competitive market where individual banks are influential in the interest rates they set. However, one needs to be more specific in identifying the degree of imperfect competition. In this subsection, regression analysis is used to address two questions: by how much does British retail banking deviate from a perfectly competitive market, and to what extent is individual bank behaviour important?

To answer these questions, a generalised linear pricing model can be employed. The following multiple regression was run for HID and HIC, at deposit levels £765 and £4590:

[†]The spread is defined as The (equity loan or mortgage rate)—(LIBOR).

$$INT_j = A + a_j D_j + \sum b_k [LIBOR\text{-}k] + cFIRMS + dMOS + eTT \qquad (4.5)$$

where:

INT_j: the net (of tax) rate of interest paid on the account by bank j;*

A: a constant term;

D_j: a dummy variable for bank j;

$LIBOR$: three-month £ London Interbank Offer Rate;

$LIBOR\text{-}k$: $LIBOR$ lagged by 0,1,2, months;

$FIRMS$: the number of banks/building societies offering the product;

MOS: the number of months since the product was introduced;

TT: time trend.

The $LIBOR$ variables allow for a direct, quantitative test of the extent to which the interest rate is competitive. This is the "marginal cost pricing" aspect of the model.[†] In a fully competitive market with no time lags, one would expect the coefficients on the $LIBOR$ terms to sum to unity. In the presence of competition with a lagged response of one or two months, the sum of the coefficients on the $LIBOR$ terms should be unity. However, given the findings in the previous two sections, other explanatory variables should be considered. The inclusion of bank dummy variables modifies the model by capturing the competitive behaviour of the individual bank. A comparison of the coefficients on these bank dummies allow one to rank banks according to the relative degree of rip-off or bargain offered to consumers. To conduct this exercise, one bank dummy, BK3 (a large clearing bank) was excluded from the estimation. Thus, BK3 is a benchmark for comparison, with its coefficient constrained to 0. The coefficients of the other banks are compared. For deposit products, a negative sign on a bank dummy indicates a *relatively* bad deal; a positively signed coefficient is a relative bargain. A negative (positive) sign on a bank dummy coefficient on a loan product is indicative of a relative bargain (rip-off). Salop and Stiglitz (1977) presented the theoretical treatment of a bargain/rip-off model. The use of bank dummies in equation 4.5 is an empirical application of their theory.

Three other independent variables were included in equation 4.5 to permit further assessment of the factors influencing individual bank behaviour in the setting of retail deposit and loan rates. The number of months since the product was introduced (MOS) measures the extent to which the date of the product innovation influences price-setting behaviour. A bank could introduce a new product, with attractive terms, to catch customers with good information and high demand elasticity, and then let the terms gradually deteriorate as time proceeds. A positive significant coefficient on the MOS term would be indicative of this phenomenon. A negative sign on the MOS coefficient points

---

*Readers will note that the net of tax interest rate (INT_j) was used as the dependent variable, unadjusted for the non-price features of these accounts. An adjusted interest rate was tried but the diagnostics were poor, suggesting the unadjusted interest rate is a better indicator of price-setting behaviour. This finding is probably because non-price features of bank products tend to be fixed over relatively long periods of time.

[†]See Heffernan (1993) for an explanation of why this lag structure was chosen.

to the presence of price or production learning curves. The time trend, *TT*, allows a test of whether there is a significant upward (or downward) trend in deposit and loan rates over the estimating period.

The variable *FIRMS* is the number of firms offering the product and reporting their deposit and loan rates in the database. The argument for expecting the coefficient on *FIRMS* to be significant (positive for deposit products; negative for loan products) is based on the *Cournot model* of oligopoly. In that market form, the extent of competitiveness in a market is directly related to the number of competitors. This variable also provides an indirect measure of the impact of regulatory changes; at least eight reforms have increased the ease with which firms can enter the retail banking market. Hence, the *FIRMS* coefficient may provide some indication of the impact of these reforms on the setting of the interest rate for these products.

The detailed results from the estimation of equation 4.5 for the two deposit products, HID and HIC, are not reported here.* Instead, the key findings are reviewed. The diagnostics were acceptable: the adjusted R^2s were high, and the null hypothesis of homoscedasticity was accepted. The adjusted R^2 was lower for PL than for RM and the deposit products. In the PL estimation, the constant term and the time trend were dropped because they were the source of unacceptably high heteroscedasticity.

The coefficients on *LIBOR* and *LIBOR2* (*LIBOR* lagged by two months) were statistically significant and positive. The coefficient on *LIBOR1* (*LIBOR* lagged by one month) had the correct sign but is significant for HIC4590 only. The sum of the statistically significant *LIBOR* coefficients is well below unity, as illustrated in Table 10.

For deposit products, a coefficient of unity on the *LIBOR* variables would be indicative of a highly competitive market. However, the results from Table 10 indicate the rate of interest paid on these deposit products ranges from 43.5% to 61% of the competitive rate. Turning to the loan products (PL and RM in Table 10), all of the statistically significant *LIBOR* coefficients on PL sum to 1.70. This figure indicates that personal loan rates were about 70% higher than one would expect if the market for personal loans was perfectly competitive.

Table 10 Statistically Significant *LIBOR* Coefficients

Banking product	Sum of the statistically significant *LIBOR* coefficients
HIC765	0.56
HIC4590	0.61
HID765	0.57
HID4590	0.44
PL	1.70
RM	0.75

*See Heffernan (1993) for detailed results.

All the *LIBOR* coefficients were correctly signed and significant in the repayment mortgages regression, and sum to 0.75, which at first sight makes the market appear highly competitive because the mortgage rate is below a perfectly competitive rate. However, the significant and large constant term (with a coefficient of 8.97) is indicative of smoothing by banks, that is, absorbing some of the change in the market interest rate, without passing it on to the customer. Smoothing by banks may be explained by the presence of menu costs, such as an increase in default rates if mortgage rates are increased in line with the market rate. The positive and significant time trend means mortgage rates were rising over the period.

The coefficients for the number of firms offering the product (*FIRMS*) was significant with the expected sign for HIC4590 and RM, and correctly signed and nearly significant for HIC765. It was correctly signed and insignificant for HID765 but wrong-signed and significant for HID4590 and PL. Thus, regulatory changes which have eased market entry for banks and building societies appear to influence deposit and loan pricing behaviour in the cases of deposit accounts with chequing facilities and mortgages. However, one cannot draw similar conclusions for the HID or PL products. The failure of the *FIRMS* variable in the HID estimations may be because banks and building societies were permitted to offer this type of product throughout the estimation period. Hence the firm entry variable would be insignificant.*

The coefficient on the *MOS* variable was significant and positive for HIC4590 but significant and negatively signed for HID765. The variable was insignificant in HIC765 and HID4590. A negative sign means the deposit rate falls with the length of time the product is in existence, and is consistent with the idea that financial firms offer a high interest rate when the product is launched to attract new accounts, but over time allow the deposit rate to decline. But the HIC4590 result is consistent with a price or production learning curve phenomenon. Therefore, the econometric results do not shed any light on the question of bank deposit pricing policy after a new product is launched.

On the lending side, repayment mortgages are not a new product—they have been offered by building societies throughout the post-war period; by banks since the early 1970s. For this reason, *MOS* was not included as a variable in the estimation of the RM equation. It was possible to include a *MOS* variable for personal loans but it was defined to mean the number of months since the building societies began to offer personal loans, after the Building Societies Act came into effect in January 1987. In the PL estimation, the *MOS* variable is significantly negative, meaning that as the number of months since building societies began to offer personal loans increased, rates declined. This observation confirms the existence of an increasingly competitive personal loan market.

The time trend (*TT*) coefficient was significantly negative at HIC4590 and significantly positive for RM, suggesting that over the period, mortgage rates

---

*The *FIRMS* variable was negatively signed and nearly significant in the estimation of (2) for PL which included the constant and time trend.

increased over time while one of the HIC deposit rates has declined. Such a finding is not indicative of increasingly competitive behaviour by banks, though it holds for only two of the six products tested.

Turning to the individual bank dummy variables, recall that BK3 was removed from the estimation, effectively constraining this bank's coefficient to zero. BK3 was used as a benchmark for ranking products according to whether they are, in relative terms, good or bad deals. Table 11 ranks the deposit products in descending order of bargain for deposit and loan products. For HID765, BS5 offers, in relative terms, the best deal for the customer, and BK2 offers the worst deal. The numbers in parentheses are the coefficients for the best and worst bank dummies. They provide the reader with an idea of the range of relative bargains. Thus, for HID765, there is a difference in deposit rates of about 3.64% between the best relative bargain for the consumer, offered by BS5, and the worst rip-off, offered by BK2. At the other extreme, the interest differential for the best and worst HID4590 products is 1.32%. Similarly, there is a large rate differential between the best and worst products at HIC765, but less of a difference at HIC4590.

For personal loans, the higher the negative coefficient on a bank dummy, the greater the relative bargain. BK6 offered the best deal, but the customer gets the worst product if he/she takes out a personal loan from BS7. Here, the

Table 11 Ranking of Banks in Descending Order of Relative Bargain Deposit and Loan Products

Deposit products				Loan products	
HID765	HID4590	HIC765	HIC4590	PL	RM
BS5(1.14)	BK7(0.99)	BK5(2.34)	BK5(0.82)	BK6(−1.7)	BK15(−0.71)
BK1	BS4	BK6	BK9	BK7	BK8
BS4	BS3	BK11	BK6	BS2	BK1
BK6	BS5	BK10A	BK11	BS5	BK2
BS2	BS2	BK1	BK1	BK8	BK4
BS3	BS1	BK1	BK4	BK2	BK8
BK8	BK6	BK10B	BK10B	BK1	BS5
BK3(0)	BK8	BK9	BS1	BK3(0)	BS1
BK7	BK1	BK4	BK10A	BS4	BS2
BK2(−2.5)	BK4	BK2	BK3(0)	BK4	BK3(0)
	BK3(0)	BK8	BK2	BK9	BK5
	BK2(−0.33)	BK3(0)	BK8(−0.83)	BS1	BK9(0.61)
		BS1(−0.52)		BS6	
				BS7(3.25)	

Abbreviations:
HID765, HID4590: Higher interest deposit accounts at deposit levels £765.00 and £4590.00, respectively.
HIC765, HIC4590: Higher interest chequing accounts at deposit levels £765.00 and £4590.00, respectively.
PL: personal loans.
RM: repayment mortgage (no endowment policy attached).
(): figures in parentheses are the coefficients for the relatively best bargain and the relatively worst deal.

interest differential between the best bargain and the worst rip-off is just under 5%. There is also a substantial difference between the bargain repayment mortgage offered by BK15 and the relative rip-off offered by BK9. The rankings fail to reveal any one bank or building society dominating the market.

To conclude, this study of competition in British retail banking found wide variation in the percentage of survivor firms and products, the degree of price discrimination practised by each firm, the extent of competition, the influence of individual firms in the setting of prices, and in the number of relative bargains and rip-offs for a given product. If banks are ranked in their descending order by survival rates, average price discrimination, average spreads, and by bargain/rip-off products, there is little correlation between the rankings, illustrating the complexity of bank pricing behaviour.

The question raised in the introduction to this sub-section was: are consumers better off as a result of regulatory reforms aimed at increasing competition? The answer is equivocal. The competitive behaviour of banking firms now is very different from the pre-reform 1970s,* but this study finds no evidence to support a *law of one price* in the British retail banking market. Banks and building societies were found to be price-makers in a market where the more inert customers have inelastic deposit supply or loan demand curves. A consumer willing to shift to a new product when it is launched, and therefore switch products, and possibly banks, frequently, may be better off. However, gathering the information needed to find a bargain product may be difficult, and there are transactions costs associated with the frequent switching of accounts. Such constraints must contribute to consumer inertia; the results of this section suggest bank managers should be able to devise a pricing strategy that allows them to profit from its presence.

Competition in the Canadian Personal Finance Sector[†]

Historically, the Canadian financial sector consisted of five financial groups. Federally chartered banks focused on commercial lending, and since the late 1950s, personal lending and mortgages. Trust and mortgage loan companies originally offered trust and estate administration services and later, mortgages and long-term deposits. In the 1980s, trust companies expanded into the personal financial sector by offering demand deposit, short-term deposit, and personal lending products. Trust companies are normally in possession of a federal charter, though some are chartered by provincial governments and operate in local markets. There is also a cooperative credit movement, consisting of credit unions and *caisses populaires*. Provincial governments grant charters to the credit unions which service provincial markets, but they

---

*In the pre-reform 1970s, banks and building societies operated segmented cartels with uniform rates for well-defined products. For example, banks agreed to pay a deposit rate that was 2% below the base rate. No interest was paid on current accounts. The loan rate was fixed at 1–3% above the base rate. See Griffiths (1970) for a discussion of the banking system up to 1970.
[†]For a more detailed account of this section, readers are referred to Heffernan (1994).

do not have national branch networks. Life insurance firms, subject to federal and provincial regulations, have expanded from offering traditional life insurance products into the administration of pension funds and some savings instruments. The securities industry offers the usual products related to underwriting, brokerage, market making, and securities investment advice.

From the 1960s through to the 1980s, a number of federal and provincial legislative revisions* set the stage for greater competition in the Canadian financial system.[†] Much has been written about the dissolution of the traditional "four pillars" financial system.[‡] The section briefly reports on the results of a study of competition in Canadian banking which used a methodology similar to the one described earlier in this chapter. The study looked at pricing behaviour for four products: mortgages, term deposits, fixed rate registered retirement savings plans (RSPs) and registered retirement income funds (RIFs).[§] These products (with the exception of RIFs) are offered by more than one type of financial institution, making it possible to use the data in a test of competitive behaviour among different financial groups in the personal finance sector. There were five financial groups in the database: domestic banks, trust companies, foreign banks, savings and loan firms, and life insurance companies. The data were pooled, cross-section, time-series, for the period 1987–90.

The equation estimated was very similar to equation 4.5. The main findings may be summarised as follows.

- When the sample was split between "major" and "minor" firms,[¶] heteroscedasticity, present when the equation was estimated using the full sample, disappeared, and the adjusted R^2 are, in virtually every case, substantially higher in the major firm sample. These findings suggest the presence of systematic pricing differences between the major firms and the minor firms. Only one trust company offered RIFs; the rest were life insurance firms. Thus, though the "four pillars" may well have been eroded *de jure* in the sense that different types of financial firms may enter a given market, the regression results for mortgages, term deposits, and RSPs suggest that *de facto*, a fifth column consisting of the 12 major banks and trust companies has emerged, at least in the personal finance sector. Life insurance firms continue to be the major players in the RIF market.

---

*The first change in regulations appeared in the 1954 Bank Act but the key reforms were contained in the 1967 Bank Act, the 1980 Bank Act, 1990 legislation, the 1982 revised Quebec Securities Act, and the 1987 "Big Bang" in Ontario. See Heffernan (1994) for a detailed account of these reforms.
[†]For an extensive review of the Canadian banking structure, readers are referred to Kryzanowski and Roberts (1992).
[‡]The four pillars of the Canadian financial system are the chartered banks, trust and mortgage loan companies, life insurance dealers, and securities firms. For a discussion of the erosion of the four pillars, see Department of Finance (1985), Freedman (1987), and Fordyce and Nickerson (1991).
[§]Interest income from RSPs and RIFs is non-taxable if it is reinvested.
[¶]The major firm sample consisted of the 12 large bank and trust companies—national firms, with an extensive branch network. The minor firm sample consisted of firms operating in local markets.

- The finding of a significant, right-signed coefficient number of firms variable in most of the estimations supported the presence of Cournot-type behaviour, that is, the greater the number of sellers in a market, the lower the "price".
- There were notable, significant differences in the relative pricing behaviour of the different groups. For mortgages, trust companies were price-makers, setting above-average interest rates on mortgages, but also on term deposits. The chartered banks were shown to exert a strongly negative influence on term deposit rates in 1987 and 1988, that is, they offer customers significantly poor rates. Trust companies had a significantly (or nearly significantly) positive influence on deposit rates in all four years. For RSPs, domestic banks exert a negative influence on RSP rates. Foreign banks offered relative rip-off RSPs and mortgages but, in most cases, bargain term deposits. Life insurance companies did not offer significantly different terms when it came to the setting of fixed-rate RIFs.
- The dummy variable coefficients permitted a ranking of the different financial groups according to the degree of bargain/rip-off product on offer. In the case of mortgages, no one group offered a particularly good or bad rate. For term deposits, trust companies offered a relatively good deal, followed by saving and loans, foreign banks, and domestic banks. For RSPs, trusts and foreign banks offered the best deal, followed by life insurance firms and banks. Life insurance firms offered a relatively bad deal on RIFs in 1987 and 1990 but a better rate in 1989.

In comparison to the earlier studies of Canadian banking by Nathan and Neave (1989), Nathan (1991) and Shaffer (1990), this investigation finds no evidence to support a contestable markets model for the Canadian banking market, or one which exhibits features of traditional monopolistic competition. Rather, the findings here are consistent with Cournot-type behaviour of financial firms, where the gap between price and marginal cost is negatively related to the number of firms in the market. The significant coefficients on the financial group dummy variables mean different financial groups exhibit price-making behaviour for some personal finance products, offering relative bargains for some products, relative rip-offs for others. The presence of systematic pricing differences between the "fifth column" and minor firms operating in local markets is also inconsistent with the predictions from models of contestability and monopolistic competition.

There are some qualifications to the procedures used in the generalised pricing model. First, it is often argued that financial institutions produce financial products jointly, and hence looking at the rates associated with a single deposit or loan product may be misleading. While it is correct to recognise the joint production of deposit and loans, one would have to have detailed data on the relevant cost functions to model it empirically, and they are not available. Furthermore, there is nothing to stop a customer from using a different financial firm for each of the deposit and loan products. Just as one may shop at different food stores depending on the product one is seeking to buy, one can also shop around the different banks. The presence of transactions or switching costs may mean customers maximise their utilities by purchasing personal finance products at one firm but if true, such behaviour creates the opportunity for the financial firm to discriminate in prices. Furthermore, practitioners in the field report that when deciding upon, say, a deposit rate for a particular retail product, their primary consideration is the range of prices of similar products on the market.

A second caveat concerns risk characteristics. If one bank is considered by depositors to have a probability of failure that is higher than another bank or financial firm, then the funding costs for the bank will be higher because the bank will have to pay higher rates to attract deposits. Obviously, a difference in bank riskiness would affect the deposit pricing structure. In the case of assets, banks may charge different rates to reflect differences in risk among a class of borrowers. But there is no evidence to suggest banks/trusts in the sample would attract more risky mortgagees than any other firm.

CONCLUSION

This chapter has explored key competitive issues, as they relate to banking markets. It began by reviewing the complications that arise when one attempts to define and measure "bank output", with special attention paid to the production and intermediation approaches. Bank productivity measures were also discussed. Based on US and UK studies, it appears that bank/building society productivity growth tends to lag behind that of other sectors, though measurement difficulties may obscure these results.

There was an extensive discussion of scale and scope economies in banking. Scale economies imply the firm is operating on the falling segment of its average cost curve, and clearly, it is in the interest of bank management to be of a size (measured by size of bank assets) that ensures operations achieve economies of scale. The empirical results are quite mixed, a finding which is not surprising given that economies of scale are a long-run concept, risk issues are ignored, and the problem of measuring bank output is ever-present. Most US studies find economies of scale for relatively small banks, with assets in the range of $25–$50 million. However, Shaffer and David (1991), employing a different database, found economies of scale for very large commercial banks, with assets in the region of $21–$25 billion. Hardwick (1989) found evidence of diseconomies of scale for the bigger societies (with assets in excess of £1.5 billion); Hardwick (1990), using the same database but a slightly different technique, established the presence of scale economies for all but the largest building societies (assets in excess of £5.5 billion). Drake (1992) reported evidence for economies of scale among middle-sized building societies, with assets in the range of £120 to £500 million. Unlike Hardwick, Drake was unable to establish the existence of diseconomies of scale for large societies. Altunbas and Molyneux (1993) found scale economies for Italian banks, small Spanish banks, and most French banks, up to an asset size of

$100 million. Economies of scale and bank size are important for managers for two reasons. First, merger or organic growth options should be discouraged if the result is scale diseconomies. Second, economies of scale can be used by incumbent firms as an entry barrier, so deterring new competition. But managers may be the target of policy reforms designed to curb uncompetitive behaviour.

Whether or not economies of scope exist is important for bankers, because it indicates the extent to which synergy may be achieved through the joint production of different bank products, and diversification into non-bank financial activities. However, Hardwick (1990) and Drake (1992) found little evidence to support the presence of economies of scope among UK building societies; the Altunbas and Molyneux (1993) study reported mixed findings on tests for economies of scope for banks in Spain, France, Italy and Germany. The issue for managers is whether, given these mixed findings, synergies will be achieved through diversification.

The final section of this chapter looked at studies which attempted to measure the degree of competition in banking. Though the structure-conduct-performance model suffers from the implicit assumption that market structure is exogenous, most of the empirical tests tend to confirm the hypothesis, except, possibly, for very highly concentrated banking markets. The evidence is largely against the relative efficiency model. If the SCP hypothesis is accepted by policy-makers, bankers can expect their pricing behaviour to be the subject of intense scrutiny. However, the absence of any sound theoretical foundation for this model means the results of the empirical studies should be treated with extreme caution.

If banking markets were shown to be contestable, marginal cost pricing is the strategy for incumbent bank managers, and policy-makers need not concern themselves too much with the relatively high degree of concentration in the banking sector. However, what little empirical evidence there is to support contestable banking markets is questionable because of the formula used to test for contestability.

In any financial market, practitioners require a method for pricing the non-price characteristics associated with their financial products. A methodology for such pricing was described, and though it reported on deposit and loan products, similar techniques could be applied to other financial products. One can employ a generalised linear pricing model to test for the degree of competition in a banking market. The model was illustrated using data from the UK and Canada. Unlike most work in this area, it was possible to conduct a direct test of the degree of competition in banking markets, by measuring the extent to which deposit and loan rates deviate from competitive rates, the degree of price-making behaviour, and whether relative bargain and rip-off products can coexist in banking markets. For managers, the findings suggest that one profit-maximising strategy for a bank might be to set highly competitive deposit and loan products alongside uncompetitive products, thereby benefiting from the consumer inertia present in these markets. Since this type of behaviour is likely to be unpopular with customers and policy-makers, bankers can expect to be the target of efforts to make the sector more competitive, though policies aimed at reducing consumer inertia would be more effective.

The first four chapters of this book have laid the foundation for an understanding of the micro-structure of banking markets. The next two chapters turn to more precise management issues. Chapter 5 reviews the objectives and methodologies for managing risk, and Chapter 6 considers the role of regulation in banking markets.

5
Management of Risks in Banking

INTRODUCTION

Any profit-maximising business, including banking, confronts macroeconomic risks (for example, the effects of recession) and microeconomic risks (for example, new competitive threats). Breakdowns in technology, commercial failure of a supplier or customer, political interference, or a natural disaster, are additional potential risks all firms must face. However, banks also face a number of risks atypical of non-financial firms, and it is these risks which are the subject of this chapter.

In Chapter 1, it was argued that banks perform intermediary and payment functions that distinguish them from other businesses. The core product is intermediation, that is, to intermediate between those with a surplus liquidity, who make deposits, and those with a deficit of liquidity, who borrow from the bank. The payments system facilitates the intermediary role of banks. For banks, the core business is managing the risks arising from on- and off-balance sheet business.

Credit risk, the risk that a borrower defaults on a bank loan, is the risk most people think of in the context of banks, because of the lending side of the intermediary function. However, as banks become more complex organisations, offering fee-based financial services and relatively new financial instruments, other types of financial risk have been unbundled and made more transparent. The purpose of this chapter is to outline the key financial risks modern banks are exposed to, and to consider how these risks should be managed.

Throughout this chapter, readers should bear in mind that for all banks, from the traditional bank that concentrates on intermediation, to the complex financial conglomerate offering a range of bank and non-bank financial services, the objective is to maximise profits and shareholder value added, and risk management is central to the achievement of this goal. To quote Walter Wriston of Citibank: "The fact is that bankers are in the business of managing risk. Pure and simple, that is the business of banking", (*The Economist*, 10 April, 1993).

Shareholder value added is defined as earnings in excess of a "minimum return" on economic capital. The minimum return is the risk-free rate plus the risk premium for the profit-maximising firm, in this case a bank. The risk premium associated with a given bank will vary, depending on the perceived riskiness of the bank's activities in the market place. In the USA, the average risk premium is 7%; for banks in other OECD countries, it ranges between 7% and 10%. The risk-free rate refers to the rate of return on a safe asset, that is, a rate of return which is guaranteed. The nominal rate of return on government bonds is normally treated as a risk-free rate, provided there is a low probability of the government defaulting on its obligation. There is a possibility that a positive inflation rate will reduce the real return, but investors normally have the option of purchasing index-linked bonds, where the return on the bond is linked to the rate of inflation.

There is a connection between "shareholder value added" and better-known performance measures, such as return on assets or return on equity. ROA, ROE, and profitability are widely reported for publicly quoted firms, including banks, and are known to influence share prices. Thus, if bank shareholders use these measures as indicators of performance, they can affect shareholder value.

If the bank is organised in such a way that different units are designated profit centres, then the *return on economic capital* of the unit is important. The return on economic capital (ROEC) is the earnings of the bank or a unit of a bank divided by the capital allocated to it. Provided capital allocation reflects the risks undertaken, ROEC recognises the risk attributes of the activity. It is only when each shows a positive shareholder value added that the bank is compensated for the risks it undertakes, which in turn ensures shareholders earn a compensating return.

This chapter is organised as follows. First there is a review of the different financial risks that banks face. Derivatives and asset securitisation are then discussed, together with approaches to the management of financial risk within a bank. The organisation of risk management of a global bank is then reviewed, followed by the lessons of the sovereign debt case together with quantitative approaches to estimating the probability of default. Finally, the political aspects of risk analysis are considered.

DEFINITIONS OF THE RISKS BANKS FACE

Risk

As any student who has taken introductory courses in finance or economics knows, risk is defined as the volatility or standard deviation (the square root of the variance) of net cash flows of the firm, or, if the company is very large, a unit within it. In a profit-maximising bank, a unit could be a whole bank, a branch, or a division. The risk may also be measured in terms of different financial products. But the objective of the bank as a whole will be to add value to the bank's equity by maximising the risk-adjusted return to shareholders. In this sense, a bank is like any other business, but for banks, profitability (and shareholder value added) is going to depend on the management of risks. In the extreme, inadequate risk management* may threaten the solvency of a bank, where *insolvency* is defined as a negative net worth, that is, liabilities in excess of assets.

Credit Risk

Credit risk is the risk that an asset or a loan becomes irrecoverable in the case of outright default, or the risk of delay in the servicing of the loan. In either case, the present value of the asset declines, thereby undermining the solvency of a bank. If the agreement is a financial contract between two parties, *counterparty risk* is the risk that the counterparty reneges on the terms of the contract. The term counterparty risk is normally used in the context of traded financial instruments, whereas credit risk refers to the probability of default on a loan agreement.

Liquidity and Funding Risk

This is the risk of insufficient liquidity for normal operating requirements, that is, the ability of the bank to meet its liabilities when they fall due. The problem arises because of a shortage of liquid assets or because the bank is unable to raise cash on the retail or wholesale markets. Funding risk is the risk that a bank is unable to fund its day-to-day operations.

Liquidity is an important service offered by a bank. Customers place their deposits with a bank, confident they can withdraw the deposit when they wish. If the ability of the bank to pay out on demand is questioned, all its business may be lost overnight. Since the bank can do nothing to reduce its overhead costs during such a short period, it will incur losses and could become insolvent.

Maturity matching will guarantee liquidity and eliminate funding risk because all deposits are invested in assets of identical maturities: then every deposit can be met from the cash inflow of maturing assets. But such a policy will never be adopted because intermediation in the form of asset transformation is a key source of bank profit. In macroeconomic terms, provided there is no change in the liquidity preference of the economy as a whole, then the withdrawal of a deposit by one customer will eventually end up as a deposit in another account somewhere in the banking system. If banks kept to a strict maturity match, then competition would see to it that the bank which invested in assets rather than keeping idle deposits could offer a higher return than banks that just held idle deposits. Furthermore, the maturity profile of a bank's liabilities understates actual liquidity; deposits are normally not demanded at the end of a term, or "on demand", because customers tend to roll them over. Only a small percentage of a bank's deposits will be withdrawn on a given day,

---

*Corporate treasurers of non-financial firms may incur large losses as a result of poor financial risk management. But it rarely leads to insolvency of the firm, assuming its main business operations are sound. By contrast, for banks, risk management is the core business of the bank.

and maturity matching to reduce liquidity risk to zero will reduce shareholder valued added. Therefore, if the objective of a bank is to maximise shareholder value added, all banks will have some acceptable degree of maturity mismatch.

Settlement/Payments Risk*

Settlements or payments risk is created if one party to a deal pays money or delivers assets before receiving its own cash or assets, thereby exposing it to potential loss. A more specialised term for settlements risk is *Herstatt risk*, named after the German bank which collapsed in 1974 as a result of large foreign exchange losses. Settlement of foreign exchange transactions requires a cash transfer from the account of one bank to that of another through the central banks of the currencies involved. But the existence of different time zones may mean the settlement is delayed. When Herstatt was shut in the morning (German time), dollar payments to American banks which had been agreed over the previous two days were not delivered. The exposed US banks were faced with a liquidity crisis, which came close to triggering a collapse of the US payments system.

The risk is pronounced in the interbank markets because the volume of interbank payments is extremely high. For example, it can take just 1 ½ days to turn over the annual value of the GNP of a major OECD country. With such large volumes, banks settle amounts far in excess of their capital. Since the payments are interbank, a problem with one bank can have a domino effect.

Netting is one way of reducing payments system risk, by allowing a bank to make a single net payment to a regulated counterparty, instead of a series of gross payments partly offset by payments in the other direction. It results in much lower volumes (because less money flows through the payments and settlements systems), thereby reducing the absolute level of risk in the banking system. Some private netting systems have been established. For example, ECHO is an exchange rate clearing house organisation set up by 14 European banks; Multinet serves a similar purpose for a group of North American banks. Both commenced operations in 1994 to facilitate multilateral netting of spot and forward foreign exchange contracts. The clearing house is the counterparty to the transactions they handle, centralising and offsetting the payments of all members in a particular currency. Some central bank regulators are concerned the clearing houses lack the capital to cover a member's default on an obligation.

Netting is common among *domestic* payments systems in industrialised countries. At the end of each day, the central bank requires each bank to settle its net obligations, after cancelling credits and debits due on a given day. Not having to settle until the end of each day is an attractive feature. However, settlements risk arises because the netting is multilateral. If one bank fails to meet its obligations,

---

*Some practitioners use the term systemic risk to refer to payments risk. However, use of this term in this context can be confusing because systemic risk also refers to the risk of the financial system failing. In this book, the term systemic risk is restricted to the latter definition. See the discussion on organisational structure later in this chapter.

other banks along the line are affected, even though they have an indirect connection with the failing bank, the counter party to the exchange. Given the large volume of transactions in relation to the capital set aside by each bank, the central bank will be concerned about systemic risk, as the failure to meet obligations by one bank triggers other failures. Most central banks/regulators deal with this problem through a variety of measures including a voluntary agreement to conform to bilateral limits on credit exposures, capping of multilateral exposures, requiring collateral, passing the necessary legislation to make bilateral and multilateral netting legally enforceable, or imposing penalty rates on banks which approach the central bank late in the day.

Increasingly, there is pressure to move from netting to real time gross settlement. *Real time gross settlement (RTGS)*, defined earlier in Chapter 2, allows transactions across settlement accounts at the central bank to be settled, gross, in real time, rather than at the end of the day. By the mid to late 1990s, most EU countries, Japan, the USA, and Switzerland will have real time gross settlement systems in place for domestic large value payments. In the EU, the plan is for the domestic payments systems to be harmonised, commencing with RTGS in all countries for large value payments, with cross-border participation in the payments systems. Under a single currency, it is likely there will be an EU-wide RTGS.

Interest Rate Risk

Interest rate risk arises from interest rate mismatches in both the volume **and** maturity of interest-sensitive assets, liabilities, and off-balance sheet items. An unanticipated movement in interest rates can seriously affect the profitability of the bank, and therefore, shareholder value added. The traditional focus of an asset liability management group within a bank is the management of interest rate risk.

Banks can lend at either fixed or variable rates, where the variable rate is linked to some central base or bank rate. Banks will always have some interest mismatch, such as a mismatch between fixed and variable rate assets and liabilities. If they have excess fixed rate assets, they are vulnerable to rising interest rates; if excess fixed rate liabilities, they are vulnerable to falling rates. Banks may be either asset sensitive, meaning their interest sensitive assets reprice faster than their interest sensitive liabilities, or liability sensitive, where the opposite is the case. Typically, the former is the norm, meaning a fall in interest rates will reduce net interest income by increasing the bank's cost of funds relative to its yield on assets. If a bank is liability sensitive, a rise in rates will reduce net income.

Market or Price Risk

Banks incur market (or price) risk on instruments traded in well-defined markets. The value of any instrument will be a function of price, coupon, coupon frequency, time, interest rate, and other factors. If a bank is holding instruments on account (for example, equities, bonds), then it is exposed to price or market risk, the risk that the price of the instrument will be volatile. General or *systematic** market risk is caused by a movement in the prices of all market instruments because of, for example, a change in economic policy. *Unsystematic* or specific market risk arises in situations where the price of one instrument moves out of line with other similar instruments, because of an event (or events) related to the issuer of the instrument. Thus the announcement of an unexpectedly large government fiscal deficit might cause a drop in a general share price index, while the announcement of an environmental law suit against a firm will reduce its share price, but is unlikely to cause a general decline in the index.

A bank can be exposed to market risk (general and specific) in relation to debt securities (fixed and floating rate debt instruments, such as bonds) debt derivatives (forward rate agreements, futures and options on debt instruments, interest rate and cross currency swaps, and forward foreign exchange positions) equities, equity derivatives (equity swaps, futures and options on equity indices, options on futures, warrants), and currency transactions.

Foreign Exchange or Currency Risk

Under flexible exchange rates, any net short or long open position in a given currency will expose the bank to **foreign exchange risk**, a special type of market risk. A bank with global operations experiences multiple currency exposures. The currency risk arises from adverse exchange rate fluctuations, which affect the bank's foreign exchange positions taken on its own account, or on behalf of its customers. Banks engage in spot, forward and swap dealing. These banks have large positions that change dramatically every minute. Mismatch by currency and by maturity is an essential feature of the business—successful mismatch judgements may reflect successful risk management.

Gearing or Leverage Risk

Banks are more highly geared (leveraged) than other businesses—individuals feel safe placing their deposits at a bank with a reputation for soundness. There are normally no sudden or random changes in the amount people wish to save or borrow, hence the banking system as a whole tends to be stable, unless depositors are given reason to believe the system is unsound.

Thus, for banks, the gearing (or leverage) limit is more critical than it is for other businesses because their relatively high gearing means the threshold of tolerable risk is lower in relation to their balance sheet. For example, suppose banks conform to a risk assets ratio of 8%. An 8% capital ratio translates into a 1250% ratio of "debt" (liabilities) to equity,[†] in contrast to a 60–70% debt–equity ratio for commercial firms.

---

*Portfolio diversification will reduce unsystematic risk, but not systematic risk.
[†]For a risk assets ratio of 8%, the ratio of debt to equity, expressed in percentage terms is computed as follows: $(1/0.08) \times 100\% = 1250\%$. The regulatory aspects of the Basle risk assets ratio is discussed in Chapter 6.

Sovereign and Political Risks*

Sovereign risk normally refers to the risk that a government will default on debt owed to a private bank. In this sense, it is a special form of credit risk, but the bank may not have the usual tools for recovering the debt at its disposal. For example, if a private debtor defaults, the bank will normally take possession of assets pledged as collateral. But if the defaulter is a sovereign government, the bank is unlikely to be able to recover the debt by taking over some of the country's assets.

Political risk is the risk of political interference in the operations of a private sector bank. It can range from banks being subjected to interest rate or exchange control regulations, to nationalisation of a bank. For example, since the Second World War, France has vacillated between nationalisation and privatisation of its banking sector. All businesses are exposed to political risk but banks are particularly vulnerable because of their critical position in the financial system. Further discussion of sovereign and political risk is found later in this chapter.

Operating Risk

Operating risk is the risk associated with losses arising from fraud or unexpected expenses such as for litigation. A good illustration of this form of risk is the Hammersmith and Fulham Council case. This London borough had taken out interest rate swaps in the period December 1983 to Febrauary 1989. The swaps fell into two categories, one for hedging and one for speculation. With local taxpayers facing a bill of tens of millions of pounds, the House of Lords (in 1991) declared all the contracts null and void, overturning an earlier decision by the appeal court. Barclays, Chemical, the Midland, Mitsubishi Finance International and Security Pacific were the key banks left facing £400 million in losses and 15 million in legal fees.

Risks of Global Banking

Global diversification of assets often allows a bank to improve upon its risk management, thereby raising profitability and shareholder value added. However, global exposure makes the business of risk management more complex, for a number of reasons. First, banks with branches or subsidiaries in other countries have part of their infrastructure exposed to currency, exchange control, and political risk. Second, evaluating credit risks in foreign countries requires additional research and intelligence. Third, the interbank and Euromarkets are vulnerable to any unexpected financial shocks arising from key players in these markets, such as Japan or the USA. Fourth, sovereign risk may be a greater threat in the international arena, if political default in foreign

---

*Often, the term "country risk" is used in the literature. Sometimes country risk is defined the way sovereign risk is defined here; in other cases, it refers to the risk of political interference. To avoid confusion, this book adopts the terms "sovereign" and "political" risk.

countries is more common than in the home country. Finally, fraud or financial mismanagement is harder to detect in international operations, thereby increasing operating risk.

ASSET SECURITISATION AND RISK MANAGEMENT

Asset securitisation involves turning traditional, non-marketed balance sheet assets (such as loans) into marketable securities, and moving them off-balance sheet.* It has included the securitisation of residential mortgages, commercial mortgages, credit card receivables, commercial loans, student loans, trade receivables and loans to insurance policy holders. Asset backed securities were first issued in the USA during the 1970s; the first issue in the UK was in 1985. After the USA, the UK has the second largest market, but it is still a tiny proportion of total lending. At the end of December 1993, there were 94 issues with a principal value of £16 billion, compared with £640 billion worth of lending by banks and building societies.†

When a bank asset is securitised, the different functions traditionally played by the bank are unbundled, a structure known as "pass through". The unbundled functions include:

- *origination*: the borrower is located usually through the bank marketing the availability of the loan;
- *credit analysis*: the likelihood of the loan being paid off by the borrower is evaluated;
- *loan servicing*: ensuring the loan is serviced;
- *credit support*: an evaluation is made of the feasibility of supporting the borrower should there be a change in a borrower's creditworthiness at any time during the duration of the loan;
- *funding function*: funding of the loan is secured through creation of deposit products that are attractive to retail and wholesale customers;
- *servicing function*: the administration and enforcement of the loan contract;
- *warehousing function*: the loan is one of many largely homogeneous loans held in a portfolio.

For example, the traditional retail bank uses depositors' funds from savings accounts to fund a "portfolio" of mortgages. If mortgage assets are securitised, the bank may perform the origination function only. After the mortgages are originated by a bank, they are sold to a "special service vehicle" (trust or corporation), the sole function of which is to hold this type of security. Using an investment/merchant banker, the trust sells the securities, backed by the pooled cash flows of the individual mortgages. These securities are

---

*Securitisation can also refer to the way in which firms can borrow funds, i.e. investment grade firms rely on securities sold in financial markets rather than bank loans. In this chapter, the term is discussed using the definition outlined in the text.
†Source: Twinn (1994).

usually backed by a guarantee by a bank or insurance company, so they can be awarded an investment grade rating from a public rating agency. The collection and distribution of the cash flows from the underlying mortgage loans may be performed by some type of bank or a non-bank processing specialist.

New technology made it relatively cheap to unbundle the traditional credit product, with the responsibility for the bundle going to the agent with the greatest competitive advantage. The unbundling of functions implicit in securitisation has considerably altered the traditional intermediation role of a bank.

There are several reasons why a bank might find asset securitisation attractive. Unbundling will increase shareholder value added if it improves the quality of a bank's risk management procedures. For example, volatile interest rates forced bankers to manage interest rate risk more effectively. Securitisation allows the interest rate risk to be unbundled from credit risk, and the originating bank, which is good at assessing the credit risk, can pass on the interest rate risk to another institution which has a competitive advantage in managing the interest rate risk. Thus, securitisation can be used to pass on maturity mismatch to investors.

Securitisation may also improve credit risk management, because if a bank finds its lending to be too concentrated in a given sector, it can securitise some of its lending to reduce exposure. In exceptional circumstances, a bank may resort to securitisation to raise funds to improve liquidity. For example, the Bank of New England, after suffering heavy losses, found it could not raise funds to head off a growing liquidity crisis. Senior management decided to sell its credit card portfolio, to improve its funding position. However, the bank failed in 1991.

New prudential regulations have increased the incentive for managers to consider securitisation of a bank's assets, because it is a means of reducing these assets, from an accounting standpoint. The Basle risk assets ratio requires international banks to set aside £8.00 of capital for every £100 of risk weighted assets. By moving assets off the balance sheet, capital regulatory requirements can be more easily satisfied, thereby reducing regulatory costs. For example, if the mortgage portfolio of a bank is securitised, these assets are removed from bank's balance sheet. The denominator of the Basle ratio (risk weighted assets) falls and the ratio itself increases. But unless a third party assumes responsibility for credit support after the securitisation, there will not be any decrease in the cost of funds for the issuing bank, even though the securitised issue often has a better credit rating than the bank itself. Supervisory authorities in the USA and the UK allow securitised assets to be disregarded for capital adequacy purposes only if the bank is relieved of significant risk.

Securitisation, under certain circumstances, may have an impact on a bank's cost of funds. It will depend on whether any benefit from the securitisation of one class of assets is offset by the higher financing costs if the average quality of the loans which remain on the balance sheet is reduced.

There are a number of risks arising from securitised assets for investors, prepayment risk being the most notable, in addition to interest rate risk, maturity mismatch, and liquidity risk if the market is thin. For example, consider the recent American experience with mortgage-backed securities. Collateralised mortgage obligations (CMOs) were introduced in 1983. A CMO is a multi-tranche bond, backed by a pool of fixed rate mortgages. The original idea was to reallocate the interest and principal repayments associated with mortgages, and to unbundle them in such a way that different investors were attracted to the different bundles. But *prepayment risk* is an added risk with these securities—a mortgagee can decide to pay off a mortgage early, thereby stopping all interest payments associated with a mortgage. For example, if US interest rates fall quite sharply, some borrowers will decide to refinance the mortgage. Conversely, there is the risk of a slow-down in repayments during a period of rising interest rates. In both cases, the percentage of borrowers who opt to pre-pay/slow repay is uncertain. For this reason, mortgage-backed securities have a higher yield than government bonds.

It is worth concluding this section by noting the relationship between derivatives and securitisation. A derivative is an asset or security the value of which is a function of a more basic commodity or instrument, usually with a contractual link. Securitisation often involves the introduction of derivative products. For example, mortgage payments or loans with receivables (e.g. credit card payments) have been collaterised to act as a basic instrument for derivative products. Derivatives are discussed in the next section.

DERIVATIVES AND RISK MANAGEMENT

A derivative is a contract which gives one party a claim on an underlying asset, or cash value of the asset, at some fixed date in the future. The other party is bound by the contract to meet the corresponding liability. A **derivative** is a *contingent* instrument because it consists of a version of well-established financial instruments (for example, currencies) or commodities (for example, wheat). Derivatives give both parties more flexibility than the exchange of the underlying asset or commodity, because they are sold in well established markets.

Consider the case of the pig farmer who knows that in six months' time he/she will have a quantity of pork bellies to sell. The farmer wishes to hedge against the fluctuation in pork belly prices over this period. He/she can do so by selling (*going short*) a six month "future" in pork bellies. The future will consist of a standard amount of pork bellies, to be exchanged in six months' time, at an agreed fixed price on the day the future is sold. The agent buying the pork belly future *goes long*, and is contractually bound to purchase the pork bellies in six months' time. The price of the future will reflect the premium charged by the buyer for assuming the risk of fluctuating pork belly prices. The underlying or "basic" commodity is pork bellies; the futures contract is the contingent claim. If the actual pork bellies had been sold, the farmer would face uncertainty about price fluctuations and might also incur some cost from seeking out a buyer for an arm's-length contract. The future increases the flexibility of the market because it is sold on an established market.

Similarly, in the currency markets, futures makes it unnecessary for the actual currency (the underlying instrument) to be traded.

The key derivatives are futures, forwards, forward rate agreements, options and swaps. Table 12 summarises the growth of the market since 1987. Exchange traded instruments grew from $1.31 trillion in 1988 to $7.84 trillion in 1993. The main organised exchanges are the London International Financial and Futures and Options Exchange (LIFFE), the Chicago Board Options Exchange and the Chicago Mercantile Exchange. Smaller exchanges include France's Matif and Germany's Deutsche Terminbörse.

Additionally, there are the *over the counter (OTC)* market instruments, tailor-made for individual clients, consisting of interest rate and currency swaps, caps, collars, and floors, and other swap-related instruments. As can be seen from Table 12, in 1992 OTC instruments amounted to $5.4 trillion, accounting for 54% of total derivatives, though Folkerts-Landau and Steinherr (1994), using General Accounting Office data, put this figure at two-thirds. OTC derivatives are attractive because they can be tailor-made to suit the requirements of an organisation. However, the OTC markets have been the principal source of concern for regulators, because of the added risks

Table 12 The Size of the Derivative Markets
(Notional Principal Outstanding, US$ billions)

	1988	1989	1990	1991	1992	1993
Exchange Traded Instruments	1306.0	1768.3	2291.7	3523.4	4640.5	7839.3
of which: interest rate futures			1454.1	2157.1	2902.2	4960.4
interest rate options			599.5	1072.6	1385.4	2362.4
currency futures			16.3	17.8	24.5	29.8
currency options			56.1	61.2	80.1	81.1
stock market index futures			69.7	77.3	80.7	119.2
stock market index options			96	137.4	167.6	286.4
Over the Counter Instruments	na	na	3450.3	4449.4	5345.7	na
of which: interest rate swaps	1010.2	1502.6	2311.5	3065.1	3850.8	
currency swaps	319.6	449.1	577.5	807.2	860.4	
caps, collars, floors, swaptions	na	na	561.3	577.2	634.5	

na: not available
Source: BIS (1994), Sixty-fourth Annual Report: p.112.

inherent in this type of market. This point is discussed in greater detail in Chapter 6.

Though Table 12 indicates a rapid growth in the derivatives markets, their use by banks is concentrated among a few of the world's largest banks. For example, Bennett (1993) identified six US banks, Bankers Trust, Bank of America, Chase Manhattan, Chemical Bank, Citicorp and JP Morgan, as dominating the world of derivatives. She refers to a Federal Reserve finding that six US commercial banks account for 90% of the derivatives business, as measured by the percentage of total outstanding derivatives held by different bank groups. With reference to the USA, Sinkey and Carter (1994) observed that at year-end 1991, just over 600 banks used derivatives; over 11 000 banks did not. Within this users' group, derivatives activities were highly concentrated—13 members of the International Swaps and Derivatives Association accounted for 81.7% of derivatives activities undertaken by US commercial banks. In an updated version of the paper (1995), these figures had not changed by much. The authors argued that in view of information and scale economies offered by derivatives, correspondent banking could be an efficient way of giving the 11 000 other banks access to the risk management opportunities offered by derivatives'. Applied to this case, *correspondent banking* would involve a relationship between the 13 big derivatives banks and the other, smaller banks, whereby the smaller banks purchased derivatives services from the big bank.*

For banks, derivatives are off-balance sheet (OBS) commitments. The term "OBS" has been coined because they do not appear on the balance sheet of the bank. Hence, the capital needed to finance the instrument is lower than it would be if the bank were financing the instrument itself. It is worth stressing that not all OBS items are derivatives. Stand-by letters of credit or guarantees for commercial paper are OBS items and are as much a part of traditional banking as taking deposits and making loans. In London, merchant banks used to be known as "acceptance houses" because for a fee, they provided guarantees on behalf of merchants, thereby "accepting" the merchants' bills of exchange. Pooled and securitised mortgages will not appear on banks' balance sheets, but are not derivatives. But in this section, the attention is on derivatives as OBS instruments.

The main difference between the risk associated with derivatives and traditional bank risk management is that prior to these financial innovations, banks were concerned mainly with the assessment of credit risk, and after the third world debt crisis, a more specialised form of credit risk, sovereign risk. Banks continue to lend to countries, corporations, small businesses, and individuals, but banks can use derivatives to generate business related to *transferring* various risks between different parties. In other words, banks have been able

---

*Other examples of correspondent banking involve small banks selling part of their loan portfolio to bigger banks (usually to comply with regulations), or larger banks inviting small banks to participate in a loan syndicate.

to expand their traditional intermediary function between depositor and borrower (and therefore, credit risk management) to one where derivatives allow them to act as *intermediaries in risk management*.

In view of the above points, it is simplistic to argue that banks were attracted to derivatives to avoid capital requirements related to on-balance sheet items. In an empirical study of 91 US banks and the growth in the use of off-balance sheet instruments during the period 1984–91,* Jagatine, Saunders and Udell (1993) could find no empirical link between the growth of OBS activities and increased on-balance sheet requirements. Examining OBS adoption by product and across banks, the authors did find that adoption of individual OBS products varied in response to changing capital requirements; in 1990–91, the number of banks using options increased dramatically, while those using forwards and futures decreased, suggesting a switch by banks in the derivatives they use. The authors argued the switch occurred because in the computation of the weighted risk assets ratio, exchange-traded contracts were zero weighted but OTC derivatives had positive risk weights. However, the authors concluded that technological and learning factors were the key determinants behind the explosive growth of derivatives in the 1980s, a conclusion consistent with the idea that banks are attracted to derivatives because these instruments permit them to broaden the type of intermediation they undertake.

The growth in the use of derivatives by banks has meant management must consider a wider picture, that is, not just on-balance sheet asset-liability management (ALM), but the management of risks arising from derivatives. These OBS commitments improve the transparency of risks, so risk management should be a broad-based exercise within any bank. To illustrate this point, the well-known, relatively new financial instruments are briefly discussed.[†]

Futures

A future is a standardised contract traded on an exchange and is delivered at some future, specified date. The contract can involve commodities or financial instruments, such as currencies. Unlike forwards (see below), the contract for futures is homogeneous, it specifies quantity and quality, time and place of delivery, and method of payment. The credit risk is much lower than that associated with a forward or swap because the contract is marked to market on a daily basis, and both parties must post margin as collateral for settlement of any changes in value. An exchange clearing house is involved. The

---

*In June 1985, the Federal Reserve increased capital adequacy requirements for the largest 17 US multinational and regional banks; they were reduced for small banks. The switch to a risk-based capital requirement was announced in July 1988, to be partially implemented by the end of 1990 and fully satisfied by January 1993.

[†] Readers should refer to Group of Thirty (1993) and Kolb (1993) for a more detailed discussion of derivative products.

homogeneous and anonymous nature of futures means relatively small players (for example, retail customers) have access to them in an active and liquid market.

The use of futures to hedge against, say interest rate risk can give rise to *basics risk*, the risk that fluctuations in futures prices will differ from movements in the price of the item being hedged. Basis risk arises because of volatile interest rates, illiquidity and/or market inefficiency.

Forwards

A forward is an agreement to buy (or sell) an asset (for example, currencies, equities, interest rates and commodities such as wheat and oil), at a future date for a price determined at the time of the agreement. For example, an agreement may involve one side buying an equity forward, that is, purchasing the equity at a specified date in the future, for a price agreed at the time the forward contract is entered into. Unlike futures, forwards are not standardised—they are customised to suit the risk management objectives of the counterparties. The values of these contracts are large, and both parties to a contract are exposed to credit risk because the value of the contract is not conveyed until maturity. For this reason, forwards are largely confined to creditworthy corporates, financial firms, institutional investors, and governments.

Forward Rate Agreements (FRAs)

An FRA is a contract in which two parties agree on the exchange rate or interest rate to be paid on the notional deposit or specified maturity at the settlement date. Principal amounts are agreed but never exchanged, and the contracts are settled in cash. FRAs cater to the specific needs of the parties in question and are limited to the participation of large firms. In the terms of the FRA contract, the parties agree that they will indemnify each other against the impact of any change in exchange rates or interest rates on the notional deposit. If the forward agreement involves interest rates, the FRA technique allows the seller of a contract the opportunity to hedge against a future fall in interest rates, whereas the buyer gets protection from a future rise in interest rates. Currency forwards permit the buyer to hedge against the risk of future fluctuations in currencies.

Options

Options contracts are unilateral contracts which are only binding on the seller of an option. The holder of a *European option** has the right, but not the obligation, to buy or sell an agreed quantity of a particular currency, financial

---

*The holder of an *American option* can exercise the option during a specified period, up to an expiration date. The option is worthless after this date.

instrument, futures contract, etc. at an agreed (*strike*) price, before or at a certain date. The buyer loses no more than the premium he/she pays plus any brokerage or commission fees. The buyer has the potential to gain from any favourable net movements between the underlying market and the strike price. The seller of the option obtains any fees but is exposed to unlimited loss should the option move so that the strike price is below the current spot price. The interest rate option is a common instrument.

Options can be bundled together to create option-based contracts such as caps, floors and collars. Suppose a borrower issues a long-term floating rate note. Then he/she is exposed to the possibility that rates will rise. To hedge against this possibility, the buyer may purchase a *cap* (for a premium), which means the interest paid will never be more that the pre-specified cap rate. A *floor* permits the lender to hedge against a fall in the lending rate below a certain level. *Collars*, where the buyer of a cap simultaneously sells a floor (or vice versa) allow the parties to reduce the premium or initial outlay.

Currency options are like forward contracts except that as options, they can be used to hedge against currency fluctuations during the *bidding* stage of a contract. Purchasers of options see them as insurance against adverse interest or exchange rate movements, especially if they are bidding for a foreign contract or a contract during a period of volatile interest rates.

Swaps

These are contracts to exchange a cash flow related to the debt obligation of two counterparties. The main instruments are interest rate, currency, commodity, and equity swaps. Like forwards, swaps are bilateral agreements, designed to achieve specified risk management objectives. Negotiated privately between two parties, they expose both parties to credit risk.

The basis for an interest rate swap is an underlying principal of a loan and deposit between two counterparties, whereby one party agrees to pay the other agreed sums referred to as "interest payments". These sums are computed as though they were interest on the principal amount of the loan or deposit in a specified currency during the life of a contract.

A cross-currency interest rate swap is a swap of fixed rate cash flow in one currency to floating rate cash flow in another currency. The contract is written as an exchange of net cash flows which exclude principal payments. A basis interest rate swap is a swap between two floating rate indices, in the same currency. Coupon swaps entail a swap of fixed to floating rate in a given currency.

A currency swap is a contract between two parties to exchange both the principal amounts and interest rate payments on their respective debt obligations in different currencies. There is an initial exchange of principal of the two different currencies, interest payments are exchanged over the life of the contract, and the principal amounts are repaid either at maturity or according to a predetermined amortisation schedule.

Like forwards and options, hedging is one reason why a bank's customers use swaps. In a currency swap or interest rate swap market, a customer can restructure and therefore hedge existing exposures generated from normal business. In some cases, a swap is attractive because it does not affect the customer's credit line in the same way as a bank loan. Currency swaps are often motivated by the objective to obtain low-cost financing. For governments and firms with good credit ratings, swaps may reduce borrowing costs.

Hybrid Derivatives

These are relatively recent financial innovations, which are hybrids of the financial instruments discussed above. Floating rate notes, note issuance facilities, and swaptions fall into this category. For example, a swaption is an option on a swap: the holder has the right, but not the obligation, to enter into a swap contract at some specified future date. A lender (such as a bank) could buy an option on an interest rate swap which would protect the bank against a general decline in interest rates.

All of these financial instruments have a form of credit risk associated with them, but one normally refers to it as *counterparty risk*, because it is a risk that one party will fail to meet its contractual obligations, rather than a default on a loan agreement.* The bank will carry out a careful analysis of the counterparty risk before purchasing an option from a customer, or entering into a swap agreement. The counterparty risk of an FRA depends on the movements of interest rates or exchange rates and on the possible default of a counterparty. Normally, the credit exposure on FRAs is measured by setting a certain percentage limit (for example, 3%) of the principal against the counterparty's credit limit.

Any bank dealing in derivatives is exposed to market risk, either because they are traded on established exchanges, or, for OTC instruments, there is an adverse movement in the price of the underlying asset. For example, in the case of options, a bank has to manage a theoretically unlimited market risk, which arises from changing prices of the underlying item. Banks will usually try to match out option market risks, by keeping options "delta neutral", where the delta of an option indicates the absolute amount by which the option will increase or decrease in price if the underlying instrument moves by one point. The delta is used as a guide to hedging. In swap contracts, market risk arises because the interest rates or exchange rates can change from the date on which the swap is arranged. A bank may carry an open swap position, within a pre-set limit if the length of time and size of an open position depends on the total position in the currency concerned. The liquidity of the US and UK futures markets means that futures are used to hedge FRA positions in the high-volume traded currencies.

Derivatives also expose the banks to liquidity risk. For example, with currency options, a bank will focus on the relative liquidities of all the individual currency markets in writing them, especially if the currency options have a maturity of less than one month. Swap transactions in multiple currency markets will also expose

---

*In the literature, the terms "credit risk" and "counterparty risk" are often used interchangeably.

banks to liquidity risk. Additional risks associated with derivatives include operational risk (such as system failure or fraud) and legal risk, where a court or recognised financial authority rules a financial contract invalid.

Banks now confront a range of risks apart from credit risk when dealing in derivatives, but most have always been present for banks operating in global markets, where there was a risk of volatile interest or exchange rates. What these instruments have done is unbundle the risks and make each of them more transparent. Prior to the emergence of these instruments these risks were captured in the "pricing" of the loan. Now there is individual pricing for each unbundled risk. In the marketing of these new instruments, banks stress the risk management aspect of them for their customers. Essentially, the bank is assuming the risk related to a given transaction, for a price, and the bank, in turn, may use instruments to hedge against these risks. The pricing of each option, swap, or FRA is based on the individual characteristics of each transaction and each customer relationship. Some banks use business profit models to ensure that the cost of capital required for these transactions is adequately covered. In a highly competitive environment, a profitable outcome may be difficult to achieve, in which case the customer relationship becomes even more important.

Banks offer these products to customers as a fee-based service, but it is important to be clear on the different uses of these instruments by the banking sector. Banks can advise their clients as to the most suitable instrument for hedging against a particular type of risk, and buy or sell the instrument on their clients' behalf. Additionally, banks employ these instruments for hedging out their own positions, with a view to improving the quality of their risk management. But banks may also use derivatives for speculative purposes and/or *proprietary trading*, defined as trading on the banks' own account, with the objective of improving profitability. It is the speculative use of derivatives by banks which regulators have expressed concern about, because of the potential threat posed to the financial system. Chapter 6 will return to this issue.

Non-financial corporations are attracted to derivatives because they improve the management of financial risk. For example, a corporation can use derivatives to hedge against interest rate or currency risks. The cost of corporate borrowing can often be reduced by using interest rate swaps (swapping floating rate obligations for fixed rate). However, increasingly, some corporations, whether they know it or not, are using derivatives to engage in speculative activity in the financial markets. There have been many instances where corporate clients have used these derivative products for what turned out to be speculative purposes. In 1994, the chairman of Procter and Gamble announced large losses on two interest rate swaps. The corporate treasurer at Procter and Gamble had, in 1993, purchased the swaps from Bankers Trust. The swaps would have yielded a substantial capital gain for Procter and Gamble had German and US interest rates converged more slowly than the market thought they would. In fact, the reverse happened, costing the firm close to $200 million. The question is why these instruments were being used for speculative purposes by a consumer goods conglomerate, and whether the firm was correctly advised by Bankers Trust. Procter and Gamble is refusing to pay Bankers Trust the $195 million it lost on the two leveraged swap contracts. The firm alleges it should never have been sold these swaps, because the bank did not fully explain the potential risks, nor did the bank disclose pricing methods that would have allowed Procter and Gamble to price the product themselves. At the time of writing, the matter was before the courts. The bank will not be helped by the publication of internal tapes relating to the P and G case. In one video instruction tape shown to new employees at the bank, a BT salesman mentions how a swap works: BT can "get in the middle and rip them (the customers) off", though the instructor does apologise.*

Another customer of Bankers Trust, Gibson Greetings, sustained losses of $3 million from interest rate swaps that more than offset business profits in 1993, thereby undermining the solvency of the firm. The case was settled out of court in January 1995, after a tape revealed a managing director at Bankers had misled the company about the size of its financial losses. In December 1994, Bankers Trust agreed to pay a $10 million fine to US authorities, and was forced to sign an "agreement" with the Federal Reserve Bank of New York, which means the leveraged-derivatives business at Bankers Trust is subject to very close scrutiny by the regulator. Bankers Trust is also bound by the terms of the agreement to be certain that clients using these complex derivatives understand the associated risks.

Other well-known US banks, namely Merrill Lynch and Credit Suisse First Boston (CSFB) are being sued for similar reasons. Merrill's problems are linked to the $2 billion in losses from Orange County's investment fund, which forced Orange County into bankruptcy. The investors argue they were misled by Merrill because the firm failed to disclose the county's precarious financial position. The investment fund borrowed heavily to buy securities, the price of which fell, rather than rising as expected. Merrill Lynch loaned the county money and also helped it to raise cash by underwriting and distributing its securities. It sold many of the loss-making securities to the investment fund. Investors are suing Merrill for Orange County securities that the bank underwrote and distributed. The investment fund itself may also sue, because some of the securities sold to the fund were complex derivatives. The Securities and Exchange Commission is investigating the role of Merrill Lynch in these dealings. CSFB is being sued for underwriting an $110 Orange County bond issue by investors who allege the bank made false statements and did not disclose the county's financial problems.

In Japan, the currency dealers of an oil refining company, Kashima Oil, entered into binding forward currency contracts, buying dollars forward in the 1980s (in anticipation of future purchases of oil), which led to losses of $1.5 billion. Metallgesellschaft, a German commodities conglomerate, lost $1.4 billion on oil derivatives because they sold long-dated futures, hedging

---

*Source: The Economist, "Bankers Trust—Shamed Again", 7 October 1995, p 135.

the exposure with short-dated futures. It left the firm exposed to yield curve repricing risk*—the price of the long-dated futures increased but that of the short-dated ones declined.

Other examples of non-financial firms reporting significant losses because of trading on the financial markets include: Volkswagen, which lost $259 million from trades in the currency markets in the early 1980s, Nippon Steel Chemical, which lost $128 million in 1993 because of unauthorised trading in foreign exchange contracts; and Showa Shell Seikiyu, which lost $1.05 billion on forward exchange contracts. Allied-Lyons plc lost $273 million by taking options positions, and Lufthansa lost $150 million through a forward contract on the DM/US$ exchange rate. Barings plc, the oldest merchant bank in the UK, collapsed after losing over £800 million after a trader's dealings in relatively simple futures contracts went wrong (see Chapter 7).

The above cases clearly demonstrate that it is important for managers to ask why an instrument is being used—that is, is it for hedging or speculative purposes? Additionally, as illustrated by the Metallgesellschaft case, all parties to a hedging arrangement must ask whether an instrument used to hedge out one position has exposed a party to new risks.

APPROACHES TO THE MANAGEMENT OF FINANCIAL RISKS

The traditional focus of risk management in banking was the management of interest rate risk and liquidity risk, with a bank's credit risk usually managed by a separate department or division. "Asset-liability" management (ALM) is proactive management of both sides of the balance sheet,[†] with a special emphasis on the management of interest rate and liquidity risks. In the 1980s, risk management was expanded to include the bank's off-balance sheet operations, and the risks arising therein.

In this section, the traditional ALM function is reviewed but, in addition, it explores how new instruments have changed the risk management organisational structure within banks, to accommodate all the risks a modern bank incurs. In particular, it should be emphasised that while the traditional risk management focused on a bank's banking book (that is, on-balance sheet assets and liabilities), modern risk management is concerned not only with the banking book, but the trading book, which consists mainly of off-balance sheet financial instruments. The financial instruments of a bank's trading book are taken on either with a view to profiting from arbitrage or for the purpose of hedging. Financial instruments may also be held to execute a trade with a customer. The bank and trading books can be affected differently for a

---

*See below for a full definition.

[†]In the 1960s, the main focus of attention was on the efficient employment of funds for liabilities management.

given change, say, in interest rates. A rise in interest rates may cause a reduction in the market value of off-balance sheet items, but a gain (in terms of economic value) in the banking book. While the market value loss on the trading book has an immediate effect on profits and capital, the gain on the banking book will not be realised immediately.

Credit Risk Analysis

Increases in credit risk will raise the marginal cost of debt and equity, which in turn increases the cost of funds for the bank. Thus credit officers are required to follow some basic guidelines in formulating lending decisions. Techniques for credit risk management are well known because the banking sector has had a long history of experience in this area. Nonetheless, loan quality problems are an important cause of bank failure, a point discussed in Chapter 7. For this reason, all bankers, not just those in a credit risk department, should keep in sight the key factors affecting the quality of a loan portfolio.

Essentially, there are four ways a bank can minimise credit risk: through accurate loan pricing, credit rationing, use of collateral, and loan diversification.

- Pricing the loan: any bank will wish to ensure the "price" of a loan (loan rate) exceeds a risk adjusted rate, and includes any loan administration costs. Thus, the loan rate should consist of a "market" rate,* a risk premium, and administration costs. The riskier the borrower, the higher the premium. Should the risk profile of the loan be altered, the rate must be changed. However, this strategy must be balanced by the possibility of adverse selection, that is, a borrower may agree to pay a higher loan rate because he/she knows the probability of default is high. Indeed, high loan rates may actually increase the probability of loan default. The guidelines may also be difficult to implement in highly competitive markets.
- Credit limits: given the potential for adverse selection, most banks do not rely solely on loan rates when taking a lending decision. Instead, the availability of a certain type of loan may be restricted to a selected class of borrowers, bank managers are normally set well-defined credit constraints; borrowers find themselves subject to loan limits. In retail markets, banks normally quote one loan rate (or a very narrow range of rates) and then restrict the amount individuals or small firms can borrow according to some criterion, such as wealth. For large, established firms, where the bank has access to independent auditors' reports on a company's financial performance, a risk premium will be applied, so the rate paid by each firm will vary.

---

*The market rate may be determined in global markets (for example, LIBOR, the London Interbank Offer Rate), and/or may be set by monetary authorities as part of monetary policy. For example, a central bank will announce a base or prime lending rate; the banks in that country adjust their loan and deposit rates to reflect this central bank base rate.

- Collateral or security: banks also use collateral to reduce credit risk. However, if the price of the collateral (for example, houses, stock market prices) becomes more volatile, then for an unchanged loan rate, banks will have to demand more collateral to offset the increased probability of loss on the credit.
- Diversification: additional volatility created from an increase in the number of risky loans can be offset either by new injections of capital into the bank or by diversification. New lending markets should allow the bank to diversify and so reduce the overall riskiness of its lending portfolio, provided it seeks out assets which yield returns that are negatively correlated. In this way, banks are able to diversify away all non-systematic risk. Banks should use correlation analysis to decide how a portfolio should be diversified. An example of a lack of lending diversification was the US savings and loan débâcle, estimated to have cost the taxpayer up to $300 billion. Regulations required a high percentage of their assets to be invested in home mortgage loans and mortgage-related securities. The thrifts engaged in commercial real estate financing but this form of diversification was inadequate.

Most banks have a separate credit risk analysis department, the objective of which is the maximisation of shareholder value added through credit risk management. Managerial judgement always plays a critical role, but a good credit risk team will use qualitative and quantitative methods to assess credit risk. If a bank is unable to access information on a potential borrower (using, for example, annual reports), it is likely to employ a qualitative approach to evaluating credit risk, using a checklist to take into account factors specific to the borrower, such as the past credit history (usually kept by credit rating agencies), the borrower's gearing (or leverage) ratio, wealth of the borrower, the extent to which borrower earnings are volatile, and whether or not collateral or security is part of the loan agreement. The extent to which the future macroeconomic climate will affect a borrower will also be important. For example, a highly geared flexible rate borrower will be hit hard by rising interest rates. Thus, the credit risk group will have to consider forecasts of macroeconomic indicators such as the interest rate, inflation rate, and future economic growth rates.

Quantitative methods of credit risk analysis require the use of financial data to measure and predict the probability of default by the borrower. Normally, the analyst employs discriminant analysis, logit, or probit models. Taking data from past defaulters and healthy borrowers, the technique allows the analyst to identify the explanatory variables which are statistically significant in explaining why an individual or firm defaults on a loan. It is then possible to predict the probability of a potential borrower defaulting at a later date, and, over time, to measure the performance of the predictive ability of the model. The method is outlined in detail later in this chapter, where approaches to sovereign risk analysis are discussed. The same models are used to credit score individuals or corporations, though the variables used to determine the score will differ. For example, an individual might be scored on the basis of age, sex, income, employment and past repayment records. Different financial ratios (such as debt to equity) are used to score corporations.

Interest Rate Risk and Asset-Liability Management

Traditionally, the ALM group within a bank has been concerned with control of *on balance sheet* interest rate risk. To provide an example of the complexities of interest rate risk management, consider a highly simplified case where a bank, newly licensed by the relevant regulatory authority, commences operations as follows.

1. Liabilities consisting of one deposit product of £1000 and equity equal to £100. Thus, its total capital is £1100. It plans to lend money to an unsecured borrower. The amount it can lend, given a risk assets ratio of 8%, is £1012.*
2. The loan has a maturity of six months, when all interest and principal is payable (a "bullet" loan). It will be priced at the current market rate of interest, 7%, plus a spread of 3%. So the annual loan rate is 10% on 1 January 1994. The loan is assumed to be rolled over every six months at whatever the new market rate is, plus an unchanged risk premium of 3%.
3. A customer wishes to purchase the deposit product, a certificate of deposit (CD) on 1 January. The market rate is 7%, and because of highly competitive market conditions it is this rate which is paid on the CD. The bank has to decide what the maturity of the CD is going to be and once the maturity is set, the bank is committed to rolling over the CD at the same maturity.
4. The yield curve for the CD is assumed to be flat, that is, the same rate of 7% applies, independent of the maturity. But on 1 February 1994 there is an unexpected one-off shift in the yield curve, to a new flat value of 9%, because the market interest rate rises, suddenly, to 9%. There are no further shifts during the year.
5. Ignore all issues related to dividends and operating costs, with the exception of the requirement to conform to a risk assets ratio of 8%.

The ALM group may measure their performance in terms of net interest income (loan income less cost of deposit), the market value of equity (the market price of bank stock) or the economic equity ratio (new equity value ÷ new loan value), for an unexpected change in interest rates. To the extent

---

*The risk assets ratio (defined in full in Chapter 6) is the ratio of bank capital (defined as equity plus disclosed reserves) to risk weighted assets. Suppose the risk weight for this loan is 100%. Thus, if total capital = £1100.00, this bank can lend out a maximum of £1012.00, because it must set aside 8% of £1100.00, or £88.00.

that changes in net interest income affect bank stock market valuations, the three measures will be very closely linked.

As was noted earlier, there is a 2% increase in market rates on 1 February 1994. To examine what happens to a number of bank performance measures, it is necessary to use a compounding formula to compute the monthly interest rate from the annual rates, because of the potential mismatch in the *timing* of cash flows for the six month loan and the CD, the maturity of which is not determined.* Thus, for the six month loan, the monthly interest rate is 0.79741% when the annual rate is 10%, and 0.94888% when the annual rate is 12%. If interest rates rise by 2% on 1 February, the borrower pays monthly interest of £8.07 until 30 June (remember, the loan rate is fixed for six months), and £9.60 from 1 July.

For the deposit product, once the bank decides on the maturity of the deposit, it incurs interest rate risk. The only time there will be no risk is if the *volumes* of liabilities and assets are roughly equal, and the bank matches the maturity of the loan with the deposit. In our simple example, the size of the deposit (£1000) and loan (£1012) are almost equal, so if the bank offers a six-month deposit product, its losses as a result of the interest rate change on 1 February are considered using two maturities for the deposit product. In Case A, the bank opts for a three-month CD. Then the monthly interest rate on the deposit product is 0.56541 when the annual rate is 7%, rising to 0.72073% after the market rate rises to 9%. A three-month maturity on the deposit product will mean the monthly interest paid until the end of March will be £5.65, and, from 1 April, £7.21. These points are summarised in Table 13 for Case A. Here, there is a drop in the net interest margin per month (compare the first and second quarters) because of the sudden rise in interest rates. The fall in the net value of equity is calculated using the new market value for assets and liabilities, which is obtained by discounting the value of the asset and liability. The original loan rate of 10% is assumed to be the discount rate for the purposes of equity valuation.

Loan:
(no change in interest rate)

The value of the loan on 1 July = £1012.00 + 49.39, given the half-yearly interest rate of 4.88088%. Future payments are ignored. So the value of the asset discounted back to 1 February is: $[1012 + 49.39/(1.1)^{5/12}] = £1020.07$.
Deposit:
(no change in interest rate)

If the deposit is of three-months duration, then an interest income of £16.12 is payable at the end of each quarter (e.g. end March, end June, ignore future payments on 30/09, 31/12). So the value of the liability, discounted back to 1 February, is: $[1000 + 16.92 + 16.92(1.1)^{3/12}] \div (1.1)^{5/12} = £994.38$.

---

*To compute a monthly interest rate from an annual rate, a compounding formula is used: $[(y^{(x/12)} - 1]$, where $y = 1 + i$, i=interest rate, x=number of months. In the example in the text, when the annual loan rate is 10%, the monthly interest rate is $(1.1^{(1/12)} - 1) = 0.79741\%$.

Table 13   The Effects of an Unexpected Increase in Interest Rates
Case A: An unexpected 2% rise in rates, with a three-month deposit product and a
six-month loan

	Q1	Q2	Q3	Q4
Loan rate (per annum)	10%	10%	12%	12%
Monthly loan Income	£8.07	£8.07	£9.60	£9.60
Deposit rate (per annum)	7%	9%	9%	9%
Monthly interest cost of deposit	£5.65	£7.21	£7.21	£7.21
Monthly net interest income	£2.42	£0.86	£2.39	£2.39
Net interest margin[a] per month	2.42%	0.86%	2.39%	2.39%

[a]The net interest margin = (net interest income ÷ equity) × 100%.

Case B: An unexpected 2% rise in rates, with a six-month deposit product and a six-
month loan

	Q1	Q2	Q3	Q4
Loan rate (per annum)	10%	10%	12%	12%
Monthly loan income	£8.07	£8.07	£9.60	£9.60
Deposit rate (per annum)	7%	7%	9%	9%
Monthly interest cost of deposit	£5.65	£5.65	£7.21	£7.21
Net monthly interest income	£2.42	£2.42	£2.39	£2.39
Net interest margin per month	2.42%	2.42%	2.39%	2.39%

Therefore, the net value of the equity (with no change in interest rates) is:
1020.066 + 88.00 (the reserve asset) −994.3819 = £113.6841.

If the loan rate rises to 12% , because of a rise in the market rate of 2%,
then:

Loan:

(loan rate rises by 2% to 12%)

$[1012 + 49.39] \div (1.12)^{5/12} = £1012.44$

New total assets = 1012.44 + 88 = £1100.44

Deposit:

(three-month deposit product)

$[1000.00 + 21.78 + 16.92(1.12)^{3/12}] \div (1.12)^{5/12} = £991.26$

New total liabilities = £991.26
Net value of equity: 1100.44 − 991.26 = £109.18

Change in net value of equity: 109.18 − 113.68 = −4.5 or −3.96% (4.5 ÷ 113.68) (100%).

With a six-month deposit product, the bank does not experience the sudden drop in net interest income or the net value of equity in the second quarter, as in Case A. The table is reworked assuming a six-month maturity. If the deposit product had the same maturity as the loan (six months), then the six-month deposit liability would be £986.62 after the interest rate jump. Hence the net value of equity would be 1100.44 − 986.62 = £113.82. The change in the net value of equity is (113.82 − 113.68) = 13p, or 0.11%.

In Cases A and B, the economic equity ratio, defined as new equity value ÷ new loan value is, for case A: 109.18/1100.44 = 9.92%. For case B with a six-month deposit product, it is 113.82/1100.44 = 10.34%.

As the reader will observe, the longer the maturity of the deposit, the higher the net interest income the bank earns, and the higher the net value of the equity will be, should interest rates rise. On the other hand, had the interest rate declined by 2% on 1 February, the opposite would have been the case. Thus, if senior management, shareholders, and regulators want to maximise, respectively, net interest income, the market value of equity, or the economic equity ratio, then choice of maturity will depend on forecasts of interest rate changes.

However, the above result is obtained because the *volume* of this bank's loans and deposits is roughly equal, which makes the case for matching the maturity of the deposit with that of the loan, if the objective is to minimise interest rate risk. In reality, most banks have a loan portfolio which is a fraction of their deposit base. In this situation, matching maturities will lead to sizeable net effects, depending on the direction of the interest rate change. To see this point, suppose that the deposit product is £1000, equity is £1000 and there are no regulations (for example, no risk assets ratio). The bank decides to lend out all of its capital, i.e. £2000. The six-month loan is now £2000, and the deposit product is £1000. If the maturity on the deposit is three months, and market interest rates rise by 2%, then the outcome is as summarised in Table 14.

As can be seen from Case C, there is a sharp drop in the net interest margin per month, compared with the earlier case where the size of the deposit and loan were very similar. A three-month deposit will cut the discounted present value of the net assets by 1.15%. A six-month deposit would reduce the discounted present value of net assets by 0.76%, assuming the loan rate rises from 10% to 12% on 1 February. This is an example of a "liability" sensitive strategy, where liabilities reprice faster than assets, so net interest earnings fall with an increase in interest rates. If an asset sensitive strategy had been adopted, interest earnings would rise.

It should be stressed that interest rate changes can affect the "economic value" of a bank in a way that is different from the short-term profit and loss accounts. The current earnings perspective will focus on the sensitivity

Table 14 An Unexpected Rise in Interest Rates
Case C: three-month deposit product; six-month loan of £2000.00

	Q1	Q2	Q3	Q4
Loan rate (per annum)	10%	10%	12%	12%
Monthly loan income	£15.95	£15.95	£18.98	£18.98
Deposit rate (per annum)	7%	9%	9%	9%
Monthly interest cost of deposit	£5.65	£7.21	£7.21	£7.21
Monthly net interest income	£10.30	£8.74	£11.77	£11.77
Net interest margin per month	1.03%	0.87%	1.18%	1.18%

of the profit and loss account in the short term (for example, a year) to a change in interest rates. The effect on net economic value might be considered over the longer term, defined as the difference between the change in the present value of the bank's assets and the present value of its liabilities, plus the net change in the present value of its off-balance sheet positions, for a given change in market interest rates.* The difference between the two will be pronounced if marking to market instruments are not a major part of the bank's portfolio. It may be that while regulators focus on economic value, the principal concern of bank management is short-term profit and loss, because of the effect changes in net profitability have on stock market valuation.

The above cases refer to the interest rate risk caused by a shift in the yield curve, that is, *yield curve repricing risk*. However, there are other types of interest rate risk related to bank products. The interest rate on bank products is not necessarily linked to a market yield curve. For example, prime based loans and money market accounts may be linked to central bank or interbank rates, but it may not be a one-for-one relationship. Competition in the market and monetary policy will determine the extent to which this relationship is one-for-one. However, even if it is not one-for-one, provided it is not volatile, there will be little in the way of additional risk. Also, banks will find the balance of their liabilities change in a period of fluctuating interest rates. For example, as interest rates rise, customers will be reluctant to hold cash in non-interest-bearing deposit accounts because of the rising opportunity cost of holding money in these accounts. In a period of falling rates, customers may shift deposits into other assets that yield a higher rate of return.

---

*This definition of "net economic value" is taken from the Basle Committee's consultative document on The Prudential Supervision of Netting, Market Risks, and Interest Rate Risks, April, 1993.

There can also be one-sided interest rate risk associated with bank products that have options attached to them, which gives rise to different types of customer behaviour depending upon whether interest rates rise or fall. For example, *prepayment risk* arises with fixed rate mortgages. A prepayment* option will result in different outcomes; if interest rates rise, mortgage prepayments decline and the expected average life of the portfolio increases. On the other hand, if rates fall, prepayment increases (because the fixed payments are less attractive) and the average life of the portfolio declines.

Gap Analysis

Gap analysis is the most well-known ALM technique, normally used to manage interest rate risk, though it can also be used in liquidity risk management. The "gap" is the difference between interest-sensitive assets and liabilities for a given time interval, say six months. In gap analysis, each of the bank's asset and liability categories is classified according to the date the asset or liability is repriced, and "time buckets": groupings of assets or liabilities are placed in the buckets; normally overnight–3 months, > 3–6 months, > 6–12 months, and so on.

Analysts compute incremental and cumulative gap results. An incremental gap is defined as earning assets − funding sources in each time bucket; cumulative gaps are the cumulative subtotals of the incremental gaps. If total earning assets must equal total funding sources, then by definition, the incremental gaps must always total zero and therefore, the last cumulative gap must be zero. Analysts focus on the cumulative gaps for the different time frames. The above points are demonstrated in a simplified interest rate ladder, in Table 15.

Table 15 separates the assets and liabilities of a bank's balance sheet into groups with cash flows that are either sensitive or insensitive to changes in interest rates. An asset or liability is said to be *interest rate sensitive* if cash flows from the asset or liability change in the same direction as a change in interest rates. The "gap" (see Table 15) is the sterling amount by which sensitive assets > sensitive liabilities. A *negative gap* means sensitive liabilities > sensitive assets; a *positive gap* means sensitive assets > sensitive liabilities. The *gap ratio* is defined as sensitive assets ÷ sensitive liabilities — if the gap ratio = 1, then the rate sensitivity of assets and liabilities is matched, and the sterling gap will be zero. Suppose a bank has a positive gap, then a rise in interest rates will cause a bank to have assets returns rising faster than liabilities costs. If interest rates fall, liabilities costs will rise faster than asset returns.

Gap analysis provides the ALM group with a picture of overall balance sheet mismatches. While this type of analysis still takes place in most banks, it is used

---

*Prepayment refers to the payment of the principal of a loan before the scheduled payment date. For example, mortgages may be prepaid because of the changed conditions of the mortgagee: he or she sells the property or refinances the loan. In Canada and the United States, mortgages are attached to houses (rather than individuals) to minimise prepayment risk and to simplify transactions in the asset.

Table 15 Gap Analysis for Interest Rate Risk

	overnight–3 months	>3–6 months	>6–12 months	>1–2 years	>2–5 years	5 years or not stated[a]
Earning assets:						
Notes and coin	£100					
3-month bills		£20				
interbank loans	£20					
5-year bonds						
overdrafts	£20					
5-year loan					£20	
Property						£30
Funding sources:						
Retail deposits[b]	(£100)		(£50)	(£45)		
3-month wholesale deposits	(£5)					
Capital				(£10)		
Net mismatch gap	£35	£20	(£50)	(£55)	£20	£30
Cumulative mismatch[c] gap	0	(£35)	(£55)	(£5)	£50	£30

[a]Not stated normally includes a bank's equity because there is no maturity associated with the bank stock.
[b]Interest-earning.
[c]Cumulative mismatch: cumulated (that is, summed) from long to short.

in conjunction with other risk management tools, for two reasons. First, it ignores mismatches that fall within each time bucket. Returning to the case study examples, suppose the deposit product was given a maturity of 3.5 months, so that it was repriced after this time. The loan will not be re-priced until after six months, making the >3–6 month time bucket liability sensitive, though in the gap analysis it would appear to be asset sensitive, because the loan was £1012, funded by a £1000 deposit and £100 in equity; equity is in the "not stated" time bucket because it has no stated maturity. Second, some bank products, such as non-maturity accounts, non-market rate accounts, and off-balance sheet items cannot be handled in a gap analysis framework, though part of this problem has been overcome through duration gap analysis (see below).

Though no longer used in isolation, gap analysis is still an important method for monitoring interest rate risk. For example, the Basle Committee proposals of April 1993 recommended the use of a maturity ladder. It recommended all interest sensitive asset, liability, and off-balance sheet positions be placed in one of 13 time bands, based on the instrument's maturity or repricing characteristics. The positions in each time band would be netted, and the net position weighted by an estimate of its duration (see below). The net balance of the individual weighted positions would form the main basis for evaluating a bank's interest rate risk.

Duration Analysis

Duration analysis, another risk management technique, measures the impact on shareholders' equity if a risk-free rate, for all maturities, rises or falls. Duration analysis allows for the possibility that the average life (*duration*) of an asset or liability differs from their respective maturities. Suppose the maturity of a loan is six months and the bank opts to match this asset with a six-month CD. If part of the loan is repaid each month, then the duration of the loan will differ from its *maturity*. For the CD, duration will equal maturity if depositors are paid a lump sum at the end of the six months. A *duration gap* is created, exposing the bank to interest rate risk.

Duration is the present value weighted average term to repricing, and was originally applied to bonds with coupons, correcting for the *impurity* of a bond: true duration is less than the bond's term to maturity. The duration of an "impure" bond (that is, one with a coupon) is expressed as follows:

$$\text{Duration} = \text{Time to redemption}\{1 - [\text{coupon size}/(MPV.r)]\} \\ + (1+r)/r)[1 - (DPV \ of \ redemption/MPV)] \qquad (5.1)$$

where:
r: market (nominal) interest rate;
MPV: market present value;
DPV: discounted present value.

For example, suppose one wants to compute the duration of a 10-year £100.00 bond with a fixed £5.00 coupon. The coupon is paid annually, the first one at the end of the first year of the investment, and the last one at the time the bond is redeemed. The *current market price* for the bond is obtained by computing the present value, using the formula:

$$(c/r)[1 - (1+r)^{-T}] + R_T(1+r)^{-T} \qquad (5.2)$$

where:
c: coupon value (£5.00);
r: market interest rate, with a horizontal term structure, assumed to be 10%;
T: date of redemption;
R_T: the amount redeemed (£100.00).
In the example, the current market price of the bond is:

$$£100(1.1)^{-10} + £50[1 - (1.1)^{-10}] = £50[1 + (1.1)^{-10}] = £69.277.$$

There is a cash flow associated with the bond, and the idea is to discount each cash flow to the present value. To compute the duration, the formula from equation (5.1) is used:

$$D = 10[1 - (£5/£6.9277)] + (1.1/0.1)\{1 - [£100(1.1)^{-10}/£69.277]\} \\ = 7.661 \ \text{years.}^*$$

———————————

*As opposed to a 10-year maturity.

As can be seen from the example, duration analysis emphasises market value, as opposed to book value in gap analysis. All cash flows are included in the computation, and there is no need to choose a time frame, as in gap analysis.

Duration analysis has been widened to include other assets and liabilities on a bank's balance sheet with flexible interest rates, and paid by borrowers or to depositors at some point in the future. In these cases, the duration of the equity is computed as:

$$D_E = [(MPV_A \times D_A) - (MPV_L \times D_L)] \div (MPV_A - MPV_L) \qquad (5.3)$$

where:

D_E: duration of equity;

D_A: duration of rate sensitive assets;

D_L: duration of rate sensitive liabilities;

MPV_A: market present value of asset;

MPV_L: market present value of liability.

The computed duration of equity is used to analyse the effect of a change in interest rates on the value of the bank, because it will approximate a zero coupon bond with the given duration. Clearly, the greater a bank's duration mismatch, the greater the exposure of the bank to unexpected changes in interest rates.

Duration Gap Analysis

This form of analysis mixes both gap and duration analysis. The duration of the assets and liabilities are matched, instead of matching time until repricing, as in standard gap analysis. The on- and off-balance sheet interest sensitive positions of the bank are placed in time bands, based on the maturity of the instrument. The position in each time band is netted, and the net position is weighted by an estimate of its duration, where duration measures the price sensitivity of fixed rate instruments with different maturities to changes in interest rates. If the duration of designated deposits and liabilities are matched, then the "duration gap" on that part of the balance sheet is zero. This part of the balance sheet is "said to be *immunised* against unexpected changes in the interest rate. In this way, *immunisation* can be used to obtain a fixed yield for a certain period of time because both sides of the balance sheet are protected from interest rate risk. Note however, that the protection is less than 100%, because market yields can change in the middle of an investment period, and other risks are still present, such as credit risk. Furthermore, it is important to realise that the duration measure used assumes a linear relationship between interest rates and asset value. In fact the relationship is normally convex. The greater the *convexity* of the interest rate-asset value relationship, the less useful is the simple duration measure. Hence, the use of duration to measure interest rate sensitivity should be limited to small changes in the interest rate.

Under the Federal Deposit Insurance Corporation Improvement Act (1991), US regulators are required to revise their method for measuring the interest rate exposure of banks. The new method, likely to be in place sometime in 1995, uses a duration gap analysis approach.* The Basle 1993 consultative document recommended the use of duration gap analysis by regulators to monitor interest rate risk exposure of banks. It proposed 13 time bands, with a risk weight for each band computed as follows:

Risk weight (for a given time band) = duration weight
× assumed change in yields.

Liquidity Risk and Asset-Liability Management (ALM)

Management of liquidity risk is the other traditional focus of an ALM group. As defined earlier, it is the risk that a bank is unable to meet its liabilities when they fall due. Assuming the liquidity preferences of a bank's customers are roughly constant, the problem usually arises if there is a run on the bank as depositors try and withdraw their cash. A bank liquidity crisis is normally triggered either by a loss of confidence in the bank or because of poor management practices, or the bank is a victim of a loss of confidence in the financial system, caused, possibly, by the failure of another bank. Contagion and systemic risk are discussed in detail in the next chapter.

The objective of liquidity risk management should be to avoid a situation where the net liquid assets are negative. Gap analysis can be used to manage this type of risk. The gap is defined in terms of net liquid assets: the difference between net liquid assets and volatile liabilities. Liquidity gap analysis is similar to the maturity ladder for interest rate risk but items from the balance sheet are placed on a ladder according to the expected time the cash flow (which may be an outflow or an inflow) is generated. Net mismatched positions are accumulated through time to produce a cumulative net mismatch position. The bank can monitor the amount of cash which will become available over time, without having to liquidate assets early, at penal rates.

The ALM group in a bank is not normally responsible for risk management in other areas, though how risk management is organised does vary from bank to bank. In some banks, the ALM group has been replaced by a division with overall responsibility for risk management, but credit risk continues to be managed separately. In modern banking, the absence of a division with overall responsibility for coordinating risk management may prove problematic.

Currency Risk Management

Foreign exchange risk or currency risk arises from exposure in foreign currencies. In the foreign exchange markets, duration analysis is used to compute the change in the value of a foreign currency bond in relation to foreign currency

---

*See Saunders (1994: pp.143–151) for more detail.

interest rates, or domestic currency interest rates, or the spot exchange rate. Gap analysis may also be employed in the foreign exchange markets, where gaps that exist in individual currencies are identified.

Some global banks reduce currency risk through *multicurrency based share capital*, that is, denominating their share capital in multiple currencies. For example, the Scandinavian Bank Group* reconstituted its sterling share capital in four currencies: the US dollar, Swiss franc, Deutsche mark, and sterling. If share capital is denominated in a mixture of currencies to match the volume of business assets and liabilities, then capital ratios will not change by much during exchange rate fluctuations and currency risk is reduced without using hedging instruments.

To cover the topic of currency risk management in any detail requires a separate book, and, indeed, there are many books on the market which serve this purpose. Readers are referred to, among others, Kenyon (1981, 1990). Most international finance texts will consider the topic in some depth; for example, Aliber (1989), Heffernan and Sinclair (1990) and Madura (1992).

Market Risk and the VaR Approach

For banks, market risk arises if financial instruments are held on the trading book. It also exists if banks hold equity as some form of collateral or, in Germany and Japan, as part of their overall investment strategy. The value at risk (VaR) approach is, increasingly, becoming the industry standard by which market risk is measured. For example, in the G-30 (1993) report, VaR was identified as the best measure of market risk for OTC instruments. *Value at risk* is the total value of a potential risk a customer stands to lose while holding a market position. The exact computation of VaR will depend on assumptions about:

- The distribution of price changes—for example, do they follow a normal distribution?
- The extent to which today's change in the price of an asset is correlated to past changes in the price—can it be assumed these price changes are serially uncorrelated?
- The extent to which the characteristics of mean and standard deviation (volatility) are stable over time.
- The interrelationship between two or more different price moves.
- The data series to which these assumptions apply.

Most researchers use historical market data on different financial assets when computing a measure of market risk. A good example is the approach taken by

---

*The Scandinavian Bank Group, SBG, was established in 1969 by the major Nordic banks in Sweden, Norway, Iceland, Denmark and Finland and is headquartered in London.

JP Morgan.* JP Morgan begin by refining the meaning of types of market risk. First, there is market risk as it applies to traders. Normally, traders think of market risk in terms of the amount that can be lost until a given position can be sold or neutralised, through, for example, a hedge. The time horizon is short, normally a day or days, and is the time it takes to sell or hedge out a position. Second, market risk is associated with an investment portfolio. The time horizon is longer (months as opposed to days), and is the time over which a chosen investment strategy is expected to succeed, or the interval over which an investment manager's performance is measured. For a given position, the market risk will be the amount by which a strategy under-performs some benchmark, such as expected return over a period.

In view of the difference between trading market risk, and investment market risk, JP Morgan's general definition for value at risk is the maximum estimated losses in the market value of a given position that can be incurred until the position is neutralized or reassessed. Thus,

$$VaR_x = V_x \times dV/dP \times \Delta P_i$$

V_x: the market value of position x;

dV/dP: the sensitivity to price move per \$ market value;

ΔP_i: adverse price movement over time i; for example, if the time horizon is a day, then VaR becomes daily earnings at risk: $DEaR = V_x{}^*dV/dP \times \Delta P_{day}$.

JP Morgan specify the following assumptions in their measure of VaR:

- Prices of financial instruments are assumed to follow a stable random walk. Therefore, price changes are normally distributed.
- Price changes are serially uncorrelated; there is no correlation between the change today and changes in the past.
- The standard deviation (volatility) of the price or rate changes is stable over time, that is past movements can be used to characterise future movements.
- The interrelationships between two different price movements follow a joint normal distribution.

JP Morgan admit the assumptions of a normal distribution and no serial correlation are controversial, because of evidence that financial markets do not follow a random walk and the presence of autocorrelation. However, they justify the assumptions on the grounds that other distributions are un-suitable; for example, if another type of distribution was assumed, it might not be possible to measure risk in terms of standard deviation. Also, the measure is not being used for estimation purposes.

It is worth emphasising that value at risk is a measure of variance, using the second moment of the distribution. However, shareholders and regulators of banks will be concerned with worst case/ catastrophic scenarios, the lower tail

---

*The author is grateful to JP Morgan for permission to quote their documentation on Riskmetrics, the methodology developed by JP Morgan to assess and quantify market risk. For more detail, readers are referred to JP Morgan (1994), *Riskmetrics*, technical document, second edition.

of the distribution, or skewness. To take skewness into account, the third moment of the distribution must be looked at. Value at risk excludes the skewness, making "stress simulations" (see below) all the more important.

The G-30 (1993) recommended that for OTC instruments, VaR be calculated using a common confidence interval of two standard deviations. This would give rise to a more conservative estimate of risk than that used by JP Morgan, 1.65 standard deviations—there is a probability of 90% that an individual outcome will fall within 1.65 standard deviations either side of the mean (thus, the confidence interval is 95%). A time horizon of one day over which VaR is computed was also recommended by the G-30.

The market risks of derivatives can be managed by dealers using a *portfolio approach*, by considering the net or residual exposure of the overall portfolio. This is because a portfolio will normally contain many offsetting positions, which reduce the overall risk of the portfolio, so that hedging concerns are focused on a much smaller residual risk.

To determine the net position of the portfolio,* the overall portfolio is broken up into underlying fundamental risk factors, to be quantified and managed. They include the following:

- Absolute price/rate or *delta risk*: the exposure to a change in the value of a transaction/portfolio arising from a given change in the price of an underlying instrument.
- Convexity or *gamma risk*: the risk arising from situations where there is a non-linear relationship between the price of the underlying instrument and the value of the transaction/portfolio.
- *Volatility risk*: the exposure to a change in the value of a transaction/portfolio which arises because of a change in the expected volatility of the price of the underlying instrument. The term used to describe volatility in the G-30 publication is vega risk (see Group of Thirty 1993: p. 44). A vega is a Cuban tobacco field or a low, moist tract in Spain or Cuba. Apparently, this term crept into the options literature because players had trouble writing the lower case Greek letter lambda, which looks, it is said, like an upside down v. This author thinks it is high time to discard the use of the term "vega" risk to mean volatility—a whole generation of bankers is beginning to think it is a Greek letter! If an abbreviation is necessary, "vol risk" is more suitable.
- Time decay or *theta risk*: the exposure to a change in the value of a transaction/portfolio because of the passage of time.
- Basis or *correlation risk*: the exposure of a transaction/portfolio to the differences in the price performance of the instruments in the portfolio.
- Discount rate or *rho risk*: the exposure to a change in the value of a transaction/portfolio arising because of a change in the rate used to discount future cash flows.

---

*The discussion of the underlying fundamental risks is taken from Group of Thirty (1993: pp.43–44.)

Once a portfolio has been disaggregated into parts according to the above classifications, it will be possible to aggregate each of these risks and manage them on a net basis. These fundamental risks underlie market risk, and are measured across the term structure of the instruments in the portfolio.

Market Risk and Stress Simulations

The value at risk measure includes volatility, the second moment of the distribution, but if one is concerned about skewness (which would include worst case outcomes), the third moment of the distribution, then value at risk will not be of any help. Stress simulations (along with scenario analysis and safety first portfolio strategies) means skewness can be taken into account.

Stress simulations involve identification of possible events or changes in market behaviour that could have an unfavourable effect on portfolios, and the ability of the bank in question to withstand them. With respect to these worst case scenarios, the risk management team should consider the following:

- The unfavourable events to be included in the stress tests. Examples include non-parallel shifts in the forward curve, decreases in liquidity, failure of a counterparty, failure of a group of counter parties concentrated in a certain region or industry, unexpected market interruptions, and unexpected collateral obligations or cash margin calls.
- The frequency with which stress simulations should be performed—daily, weekly, monthly, quarterly, semi-annually, annually, or on an "as needed" basis.
- How will the firm use the results? Examples include guidance in adjusting positions, guidance in adjusting capital against positions, or to form contingency plans.

The analysis would involve computing the probability of each event and worst case scenarios. The Bank for International Settlements (July, 1994) recognised scenario analysis as the preferred method of market risk management. It is consistent with the *building block* or *additive risk* approach to risk management that has begun to be associated with the Basle Committee. Readers are referred to Chapter 6 for a more detailed discussion.

Financial Innovation and Risk Management

The financial products discussed above are examples of recent financial innovations. Like the manufacturing sector, financial innovation can take the form of *process* innovation, whereby an existing product or service can be offered more cheaply because of a technological innovation. *Product* innovation involves the introduction of a new good or service. The new financial instruments discussed above are examples of where technological changes resulted in product innovations.

Silber (1975, 1983) argued that product innovation arises because of constraints placed on a bank—namely, regulation, competition, and risk. Kane (1984) thought it important to observe the regulatory and technological factors behind any financial innovation. However, it is more useful to think of financial innovation, regulation, and risk management as being interdependent. For example, regulations (such as exchange controls) can be a catalyst for financial innovation which allows bankers to bypass the rules. The Eurocurrency markets developed in just this way—US interest rate restrictions and limits placed on foreign direct investment by US multinationals, together with UK exchange controls, created a demand for and supply of an offshore dollar market, the Eurodollar market. As technology advanced, this became the Eurocurrency market, allowing bankers to trade in all the key currencies outside any domestic regulations. Even though most of the offending regulations have since been relaxed, the market continues to thrive.

Risk management and financial innovation are also interdependent. Financial innovation makes it possible to unbundle the different types of risks which, in turn, has led to direct pricing of the different types of risks. At the same time, financial innovation has forced banks to re-examine their risk management systems, because banks are increasingly exposed to new forms of risk, which are quite different in nature from the traditional credit risk. For example, Bankhaus Herstatt collapsed in 1974 because of inexperience in dealing with foreign exchange risk. However, to date, very few bank collapses can be said to have been caused by a failure to understand risk exposure associated with a new instrument.

BANK ORGANISATIONAL STRUCTURE AND RISK MANAGEMENT

General Principles of Risk Management in Modern Banking

In modern banking, three aspects of risk management should be stressed. First, if a bank has the objective of maximising shareholder value added, *diversification* of its portfolio will be critical because large reductions in unsystematic risk can be obtained. Models should take account of the covariances across the bank's entire portfolio of risky positions. Second, there is a need for *risk management systems* which integrate head office, divisions, and branches for the purposes of risk management. It needs to be an on-line, real-time global risk management system, able to provide the bank with a single source of data. Third, the *risk management process* is important. Many banks now employ a "risk points" system. A common denominator for risk is used, and exposure targets for different activities are set. The organisation of risk management within a bank is of paramount importance, in view of the revised Basle 1995 proposals on market risk management and the emphasis placed on self-regulation by the Group of Thirty (1993). Readers are referred to Chapter 6 for more detail on these proposed regulatory changes.

A review of how risk is managed in the 1990s in a multinational bank should improve the understanding of the issues and problems faced by bankers today. To conduct this review, the next sub-section considers a major bank, A Bank plc, headquartered in London.

The Organisational Structure of A Bank plc

A Bank plc is one of the four major clearing banks in the UK, engaged in retail, commercial and investment banking business. It has over 2500 branches in the UK and operates in 76 other countries. It is divided into three main operating divisions. The Banking division covers global retail and corporate banking activities and the group's insurance, trust and stockbroking services, and credit/debit card business. IBS is the investment banking subsidiary of the bank, conducting business in corporate finance, structured finance, foreign exchange, money markets, equities, and investment management. The Services business division is responsible for the group's transactions processing, information technology, traveller's cheques, custody business, and servicing the other businesses. There are a number of non-operating groups, the most important being UK Group Finance, made up of the corporate secretariat, treasury management, risk management, financial control and planning, economics, and taxation.

The Group Treasury is largely responsible for risk management, excluding credit risk. It has five main sections:

- Capital Management: services and manages existing domestic and international capital, and has responsibility for raising new capital.
- Treasury Risk Management: the main function is to set limits for interest rate and foreign exchange risk, and to monitor adherence to these limits. It is also responsible for the management of liquidity risk (apart from US dollars) on a country-by-country basis.
- Systemic Risk Management: responsibility for controlling risks related to the failure of the infrastructure, such as the payments system and/or the futures exchange. It has a brief to look at netting schemes.
- Financial Risk Management: engages in two main activities. It is responsible for traditional balance sheet management—measurement and control of all of the group's structural positions outside the trading room. The key tasks are looking at the fixed interest versus floating interest cash flows, non-interest bearing cheque accounts, and techniques for hedging the bank's capital. This involves centralising the gross exposure, setting up a pricing system to determine the marginal cost of funds, and covering the net position through this centralised pricing system. In addition, it is responsible for risk research and development, which involves undertaking research into the technical framework for new risk management systems. The risk research group created the risk points system (see below) for the measurement and control of trading risks.

- Treasury Management (UK Operations section): looks after the day-to-day treasury functions pertaining to the UK. For example, this section will maintain balances with the Bank of England and set UK liquidity limits.

The Group Treasury sets the guidelines for liquidity risk, which are followed across all centres. Within the framework of these guidelines, the actual management of liquidity is carried out by local management and money market traders. The liquidity is then "transfer-priced" to the various operating units in a given country.*

Credit risk is managed at the local country level, subject to head office guidelines. To monitor risk, bank borrowers are divided into two categories. For other financial institutions and multinational corporates limits are set at head office by the credit department. These limits are based on credit ratings, and the risk is managed from London, separate from the Group Treasury. If a centre wants to exceed these limits, they will have to refer the case to head office. Local credit committees set the limits for local corporates but there is a limit on overall country exposure which is designed to cover any political risk; this is set by the credit department at head office.

A Bank has a category of risk it calls "structural risk", defined as the risk that arises from non-trading operations, especially the risk generated by its retail activities in overseas countries. For A Bank, the key structural risk arises in the UK, USA, France, Spain and Portugal, where the bank has an extensive branch network. It is managed on a country basis. For example, in the case of fixed rate loans, the local treasuries in each country give a fixed rate to the branches, which are covered against any interest rate movements. The branches then price the loan based on this rate plus a spread. The local treasury hedges out the interest rate risk and the net positions (using techniques like duration or gap analysis, and simulation). For non-interest bearing accounts, a rolling average account is used to accrue a constant stream of income. In other countries without much retail activity (for example, Japan and Singapore, where the main business is corporate loans) structural risk is managed by a single team, with the additional responsibility of managing trading risks.

The A Group also has a category of risk it calls "trading risk", the risk that arises from the trading activities of the bank, in its various trading centres. It is composed of two risks: interest rate risk and foreign exchange risk. Trading risks are monitored and controlled from head office, using a system of risk points, developed by the financial risk management section of the Group Treasury. One risk point is equal to a given amount of risk, expressed in US dollar terms. The risk points for a position are computed by multiplying the size of the position by the risk point weight for the position. The risk point weight is determined by looking at the maturity and an estimate of the relative

---

*The objective of transfer pricing is to find a risk-adjusted net interest income value for every unit, product, or customer relationship (Uyemura and Van Deventer, 1993: p.292). Its main purpose is to risk-adjust an income flow for the purpose of profitability analysis. For more detail see Uyemura and Van Deventer (1993: ch. 14).

volatility of rates for different periods. Longer maturity transactions will receive a heavier risk weight than shorter transactions. Correlation analysis takes into account the likelihood of two positions offsetting each other. Thus, the total risk of a combined position at any moment is the difference between the two risk point weighted positions plus a percentage of a smaller figure.

Group Treasury allocates the total number of risk points to each trading centre or product line. The chief dealer is responsible for the management of the risk points per centre, constrained by the overall allocation of risk points to it. Thus, head office has overall control over gross position risk the bank is exposed to, but each centre can manage its positions according to market movements, without having to secure head or regional office approval. Profitability of each centre is the key performance measure, subject to the allocation of risk points.

The risk points system allows a common standard to be employed when measuring the risk arising from all types of positions. Assigning points provides Treasury management with a tool for measuring risk in terms of the amount of money that could be lost by taking a particular position, because of an adverse movement in interest rates or currency values. The loss is calculated in present value or market value terms. Thus, though the loss may not be reflected immediately in the bank's books, it would be the loss that arises if the position was closed out.

As of 1993, risk points were not being computed for options or equities but they were applicable to other instruments such as bonds, swaps, and FRAs. However, there was ongoing research to collate data on historic volatilities for options or equites, to bring these under the domain of risk points.

It is notable that within A Bank's organisation, risks are not necessarily defined in line with the definitions which appeared in the first section of this chapter. The terms trading risks and structural risks are made up of a number of different risks defined earlier. Also, the Systemic Risk Management section is concerned with the management of settlements or payments risk. Of course, it would be quite wrong for bank organisational structures to define and manage every risk as separate categories.

For the A Bank Group, the system of risk management could be improved in a number of ways. First, risk points could be computed for credit risks, though the calculations would not be straightforward unless loans are traded on a secondary market. Second, the Group should consider netting off the risk points used for compensating positions rather than having them grossed up. Third, a centralised "risk management unit" should be created. At the moment, Group Treasury is responsible for trading, systemic, and liquidity risks but the central credit department is responsible for credit risk. Such an arrangement reduces the scope for coordination of management of the different risks. For example, it may explain why netting is so underdeveloped. Fourth, the Group could benefit from a risk adjusted return on capital (RAROC)* system, which could be used to identify an optimal risk–return

---

*Bankers Trust was the first to develop a RAROC system.

trade off. RAROC would measure the risk inherent in each activity or product and charge it accordingly for the capital required to support it. Thus profitability of the product would be measured by looking at returns against capital employed. At A Bank, it is expected a RAROC system will be operational by 1996.

A Bank has dispensed with the traditional asset liability management group within the bank. However, organisational structures vary, depending on the bank. For example, another major clearer has an Asset and Liability Committee (ALCO), made up of the representatives of the major divisions within the bank. The committee sets the overall limits of operation for the entire banking group, but risk management is the responsibility of the divisions. The committee is operated as a value added centre, rather than safeguarding profitability *per se*. This bank has a Strategic Planning group upon which the director of the ALCO sits, thereby ensuring that risk management issues are an integral part of strategic formulation.

THE SOVEREIGN DEBT CASE

What Lessons does it Teach Bank Managers?

In August, 1982, Mexico announced it could no longer meet its debt servicing obligations on its sovereign external debt. Other developing countries quickly followed suit. The world financial community was forced to confront problems arising from sovereign external debt owed by developing nations. Sixty-four developing countries negotiated multilateral debt relief agreements between 1980 and 1993, amounting to a total of $6.2 billion. Total external debt amounted to $658 billion in 1980, rising to $1.2 trillion in 1986, with a projected 1993 figure of $1.8 trillion.* The total stock of arrears in 1992 was $116 billion, up from $112 billion in 1990, and $71.7 billion in 1988. Much of the debt in the early period was in the form of *sovereign* debt, defined as loans guaranteed or directly owed by the nation's government to the western private banking system.

The focus of this discussion here is on the supply bank side of sovereign lending. Many banks in the USA (Citicorp, Bank of America, Manufacturers Hanover, and Chase Manhattan Bank, the UK (especially the Midland Bank), and Japan heavily exposed in sovereign debt were forced to accept that a large number of sovereign loans on their books were unlikely to be repaid, or would be rescheduled over a long period in the future. Most banks responded by increasing provisions for bad debt or moving the loans off their balance sheets, and selling them on the secondary markets at a substantial discount. In the secondary external debt market, loans to the Philippines, Mexico, Venezuela, Brazil, Ivory Coast, Nigeria, and Argentina were, in November 1988, valued at less than 50% of their face value. From 1992, there was a steady upward trend,

---

*Source: World Bank (1994), *World Debt Tables*, 1993–94.
†For a discussion of the causes of bank failure, see Chapter 7.

to about 65% of face value, for Argentina, Costa Rica, the Philippines, Mexico, and Uruguay, the so called "Brady" countries (see below). But for other severely indebted countries, debt traded at just under 30% of face value in 1993.

In this section, the sovereign debt problem is used as a case study on how not to manage risk. It will be shown that the key mistakes related to credit risk assessment. It continues to be true that most bank failures are caused by failure to assess credit risk properly, rather than to manage to other forms of risk discussed in previous sections.[†]

To gain an insight into the how the sovereign debt problem was created, three questions are addressed in the next few sub-sections; namely, Why do third world countries demand external finance?; What factors determine the composition of the external finance?; and, If the external finance is in the form of a syndicated loan, why was most of the debt in the form of sovereign loans?

The Demand for External Finance by Developing Nations

Capital importing developing nations demand capital in excess of their own domestic capital base. The demand for external finance is explained by the "development cycle" hypothesis. Countries demand capital based on expectations of higher future income streams. By borrowing capital, the country is able to finance a more rapid rate of economic growth and to smooth consumption and investment paths over time. Provided the country's domestic capital base is insufficient to meet its growth rate targets and the expected marginal productivity of the domestic endowment of capital exceeds the rate of interest charged for the borrowed capital, it will borrow capital from the international capital markets, that is, it will import capital.

An analysis of how the problem emerged should begin with a look at the composition of a developing nation's external finance. A country's *foreign gearing* (or leverage) ratio (FGR or FLR) is defined as the ratio of foreign debt to foreign equity of a capital importing nation. Foreign debt consists of loans made plus bonds purchased by non-residents; foreign equity of direct and portfolio investment by non-residents.

In the 1960s, foreign direct investment as a percentage of external finance was, on average, 39%. Official finance and commercial loans each contributed about 30% to external finance in developing countries. But from the late 1960s onward, the growth rate in the real value of foreign direct investment was close to zero. Commercial medium and long-term lending increased at an annual average real rate of just under 10% per annum, most of it in the form of sovereign loans. Thus, by the late 1970s, foreign direct investment had fallen to less than 15% of the total external finance component; sovereign loans peaked at 75%, falling after 1982. External finance from official sources fell steadily until 1982, and then from 1982–88 it increased to over 50% of the total. Issues of foreign bonds and foreign equity were negligible until the late 1980s.

The increased sovereign lending corresponded with, on the supply side, a rise in syndicated lending (where a lead bank arranges the loan, and involving a syndicate of other banks). The syndicated loan market peaked in 1982, with the majority of the loans arranged for sovereign borrowers. After a decline of several years, 1987 saw a rapid increase in the volume of syndicated loans arranged but these are largely confined to the private sector. Normally, the loans were in US dollars and subject to a variable rate of interest.

It is important to explore the reasons behind the dramatic rise in developing country FGRs (FLRs) through the 1970s, and the emergence of sovereign credit as the predominant form of lending. Three parameters play a crucial part in the determination of a country's optimal foreign gearing (leverage) ratio. These are risk attitudes, moral hazard, and interference costs.*

Risk Attitudes

Suppose borrower and lender are risk neutral, that is, the agents are indifferent to a fair bet with even odds. In this case, foreign debt and equity are perfect substitutes, and neither party has preference for one instrument over another. If one of the parties is risk averse, the agent will refuse a fair bet with even odds. To isolate the importance of risk attitudes in international debt, assume there are no costs associated with moral hazard or interference, borrower and lender treat foreign equity as a risky asset, (the returns on foreign equity are proportionate to domestic output) and foreign debt is treated as a safe asset (the returns to debt are guaranteed, payable at a fixed rate, and independent of what happens to domestic output). Under these assumptions, the composition of external finance will be 100% equity if the borrower is risk averse and the lender risk neutral; 100% debt if the lender is risk averse and the borrower is risk neutral, and a combination of debt and equity if both parties are risk averse.

Risk attitudes provide a partial explanation for the rise in developing country external debt through the 1970s. Lenders treated sovereign loans as safe assets, because banks, drawing from their experience of credit analysis for individual and corporate borrowers, focused the probability of a debtor remaining solvent. Bankers correctly assumed the probability of default on a sovereign loan was very low because a country could not go bankrupt. However, the subsequent debt crisis taught them that when it comes to sovereign loans, the solvency issue is not enough. If a nation encounters a long period of illiquidity (that is, it has a positive net worth but lacks the means to meet its maturing liabilities when they fall due), the true book value of the lender's assets will be undermined. Banks made the mistake of assuming sovereign loans had zero or little risk, but risk of illiquidity turned out to be as serious as risk of default.

Interaction Between Moral Hazard and Interference Costs

Moral hazard arises whenever an agreement between two parties alters the incentive structure for either party. In the case of the loan, the borrower may choose a more risky production technique should the bank fail to closely

---

*For a technical version of the points outlined below, readers are referred to Heffernan (1986).

monitor the use of the funds. The problem is aggravated if the borrower thinks the loan agreement may be altered when the country encounters debt servicing problems. The lender usually reacts to borrower moral hazard by demanding a higher risk premium on a loan and/or a higher yield in the equity. A moral hazard problem can also arise on the lending side if there is a "too big to fail" policy or a lender of last resort. For the moment, ignore this aspect of moral hazard and assume it is exhibited only by the borrower.

Asymmetry of information explains why moral hazard may affect the foreign gearing ratio. The lender should know how borrower incentives have been affected by looking at choice of production technique or for signs of reduced effort. But often, these cannot be observed, and the bank is unable to penalise the behaviour. One remedy is for the bank to choose a premium to cover the estimated cost of borrower moral hazard. Alternatively, the investor may use *sighted* investment to minimise asymmetry in information. Here, managers are sent to the country to discourage under-performance of the local workforce. Project finance is a type of sighted investment, as is monitoring the developing country more closely, in the event of repayment problems.

However, "sighted" investment by a lender may be treated as an *interference cost* by the capital-importing country. The country may be concerned about the degree to which the sighted investment impinges upon the *microeconomic sovereignty* of the country. Interference costs are difficult to measure because of the value judgements associated with them. However, during the 1970s, many Latin American countries placed a heavy weight on what they perceived as a loss of microeconomic sovereignty if they allowed foreign direct investment; countries in the Far East were less concerned. External loans did not seem to involve any loss of sovereignty, because virtually no conditions were attached to the loans, and bankers did not monitor the use of these loans very closely. However, developing nations failed to impute the existence of hidden costs arising from International Monetary Fund *macroeconomic* stabilisation conditions imposed when debt was rescheduled. It was not until after the Mexican rescheduling package had been agreed that developing countries realised the full consequences of being unable to service this type of debt.

The attraction of sovereign lending over other forms of investment is exacerbated if there is a moral hazard problem on the lending side of the banks. The argument here is that banks will engage in riskier investments than they otherwise would if they think they are going to be bailed out by a lender of last resort. But banks were attracted to sovereign loans because they genuinely thought they were low-risk assets. Subsequent intervention by the IMF did not give bankers an easy time of it. Hence, the moral hazard problems created by the sovereign debt crisis were probably minimal.

To summarise, to understand why developing countries allowed themselves to become highly geared by sovereign borrowing, it is important to recognise the interaction between the three factors discussed above. First, western banks were willing to make sovereign loans because they thought the asset was low-risk; risk premiums and monitoring were kept to a minimum. Developing countries were willing to borrow from private banks to finance development and because interference costs were thought to be comparatively small. Both parties ignored the impact of random economic shocks on their borrowing and lending decisions. For example, many countries borrowed on the strength of wildly optimistic forecasts about future commodity prices. In the cases where commodity prices did rise as forecast (e.g. oil), they were far more volatile than had been anticipated. Subsequent oil price declines prompted serious debt servicing problems for these countries. By definition, it is not possible to forecast random shocks, but in this situation scenario analysis might have helped the banks better assess the impact of possible changes in the global macroeconomic situation.

Rescheduling and Debt Conversion Schemes

Since the Mexican announcement in August 1982, many indebted countries have entered into or completed renegotiations for the repayment of their loans. The International Monetary Fund (and, to a lesser extent, the World Bank) has played a critical intermediary role.* Virtually all of the rescheduling agreements reached between the debtor, the borrowing bank and IMF involve the postponement of debt repayments, leaving the foreign gearing (leverage) ratio largely unchanged. The rescheduling agreements share a number of common features. First, the debtor country is required to implement an IMF macroeconomic adjustment programme. Since the IMF insists on the adoption of stabilisation policies (including a removal of subsidies which distort domestic markets, strict inflation and budget deficit targets, and reduction of trade barriers), the country loses *macroeconomic sovereignty* because its government no longer has control over the choice of macroeconomic policy. Thus, *ex post*,

---

*Both the IMF and World Bank were created under the 1944 Bretton Woods Agreement. The IMF Articles of Agreement assign to the "Fund" the responsibility of assisting members with balance of payments difficulties, including the monitoring of exchange rates and policies of member countries. In its 1986 *World Economic Outlook*, the Fund emphasised its function as a neutral third party between first world lenders and third world borrowers, to further promote private external finance. It stressed that direct participation in commercial financing arrangements (such as the provision of guarantees on private debt) was not possible under its Articles of agreement. The World Bank was created to encourage the economic growth of third world countries. In the post-war period, the bank emerged as the key lender to developing countries, with an emphasis on both project finance and lending conditional on structural adjustment programmes that promote growth. Conditionality substitutes for the more traditional collateral normally demanded by private lending agents. The World Bank also grants loans conditional on structural adjustment programmes (a substitute for the more standard collateral), encourages private foreign direct investment through the provision of non-commercial risk insurance through MIGA (Multilateral Investment Guarantee Agency), and acts in an advisory capacity to investors.
†For a theoretical treatment of debt–equity swaps, readers are referred to Blake and Pradhan (1991).

it can be argued that sovereign borrowing exposed these countries to very high interference costs.

The agreement typically involves a rescheduling of the total value of the outstanding external debt. Banks are required to provide "new money", to allow the debtor country to keep up its interest payments. Therefore, the total amount of the outstanding debt is increased. The IMF insisted on this increased exposure by the private banks in exchange for IMF intervention and loans. The agreement also included bridging loans and a guarantee of inter-bank and trade facilities, sometimes suspended when a country announced that it was unable to service its external debt.

Debt–equity swaps are another means of dealing with a sovereign debt problem, though this form of refinancing has not been on the same scale as IMF rescheduling packages.[1] A debt–equity swap involves the sale of the debt by a bank to a corporation at the secondary market price for the debt. The corporation exchanges the debt for domestic currency through the central bank of the developing country, usually at a preferential exchange rate. It is used to purchase equity in a domestic firm. This method reduces a country's foreign gearing (leverage) ratio. However, it has proved unpopular with most countries (except Chile) because it can be inflationary, and the country loses some micro-economic sovereignty. Similar debt conversion schemes in the private sector have allowed firms to reduce their external debt obligations.

Other types of swaps have consisted of debt–currency swaps, where foreign currency denominated debt is exchanged for the local currency debt of the debtor government, thereby increasing the domestic currency debt and redu-cing its FGR (FLR). A *debt–debt* swap consists of the exchange of LDC debt by one bank for the debt of another LDC by another bank. It has no implica-tions for the foreign leverage (gearing) ratio of these countries, but is likely to improve the portfolios of the banks. Debt for trade swaps emerged between developing countries as a means of settling debt obligations between them. They are a form of counter-trade because the borrower gives the lending country (or firm) home-produced commodities. Alternatively, a country could buy imports if the seller agrees to buy some of the country's external debt on the secondary markets.

Debt–bond swaps or *"exit" bonds* allow lenders to swap the original loan for long-term fixed rate bonds. The FGR (FLR) is unchanged in the short term, but the developing country is less exposed to interest rate risk. In a period of sustained rising interest rates, the fixed rate bonds will lower debt servicing costs for the borrowing country. The Mexican restructuring agreement of March 1990 is a good example of the new options offered to lenders. In addi-tion to the new money options, banks could participate in two debt reduction schemes; either an exchange of discount bonds against outstanding debt or a par bond, that is, an exchange of bonds against outstanding debt without any discount, but with a fixed rate of interest (6.25%). There is to be a one-off repayment of the bonds in 2019; the principal is secured by US Treasury zero-coupon bonds. Participating banks could also take part in a debt–equity swap programme linked to the privatisation of state firms. Thirteen per cent chose the new money; 40% the discount bond (at 65% of par), and 47% the par bond.

Exit bonds are commonly referred to as Brady bonds, because they were an integral part of the Brady Plan introduced in 1989. This plan superseded the earlier Baker Plan (1985), which had identified the "Baker 15", the most heavily indebted LDCs as the key focus of action.* The Baker Plan also called for improved collaboration between the IMF and World Bank, stressed the importance of IMF stabilisation policies to promote growth, and encouraged private commercial lenders to increase their exposure. The Brady Plan reiterated the Baker plan but explicitly acknowledged the need for banks to reduce their sovereign debt exposure. The IMF and World Bank were asked to encourage debt reduction schemes, either by guaranteeing interest payments on exit bonds or by providing new loans. The plan called for a change in regulations (e.g. tax rules) to increase the incentive of the private banks to write-off the debt.

Figure 23 summarises the debt reduction schemes for the period 1985–92, excluding rescheduling agreements. Debt–equity swaps peaked in value in 1990, amounting to about $10 billion. Debt buyback and exchange schemes became popular in the same year; in the first 10 months of 1992 they formed by far the greatest proportion of debt reduction. In the period 1980–93, total multilateral debt relief agreements amounted to $6.2 billion.

In the 1990s, the external debt problems of developing countries are no longer a central policy concern. They are not considered a threat to the stability of the international financial system because the most heavily exposed American, Japanese, and British banks have removed these assets from their books by selling them on the well-developed secondary market. There has been some decline in LDC foreign gearing (leverage) ratios because of debt reduction and repatriation of capital, and there has been more foreign direct investment as countries relaxed their regulations. As of 1992, the ratio of external debt service to exports of goods and services (DSR) was for the following respective countries: Mexico, 44.4% (after peaking at 54.2% in 1986); Brazil, 24.4% (peaked at 63.1% in 1980); Chile, 20.9% (peaked at 48.4% in 1985); and Argentina, 37.6% (peaked at 76.2% in 1986). There has been a noticeable improvement in the ability of some countries to repay their debt because IMF macro-stabilisation programmes have contributed to increases in economic growth rates in these countries. Mexico is the only country sticking to its debt service schedule, but its DSR has crept up from a low of 26.3% in 1990.

As Table 16 illustrates, the private lending of the 1970s was replaced by official finance from the late 1980s on. This trend is not surprising, as private banks began to realise that sovereign lending meant they were subsidising the economic development of the countries, without getting full compensation for it.

---

*Richard Baker and Tom Brady were both Treasury Secretaries in the Reagan administration. They had no formal powers to resolve the LDC debt problem, but their ideas carried a great deal of influence.

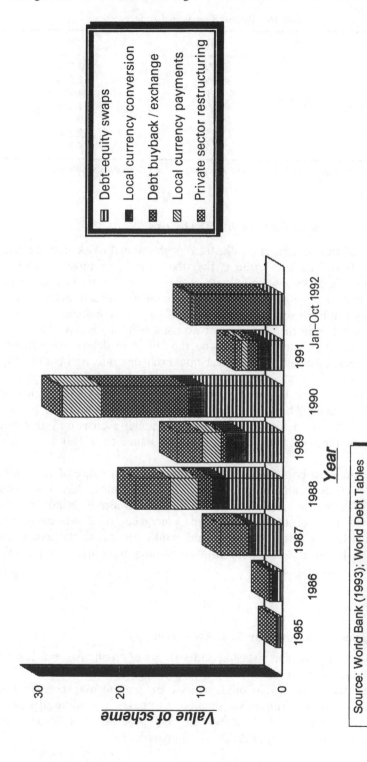

Figure 23 Debt reduction schemes (US $ billions)

Source: World Bank (1993); World Debt Tables
Total multilateral debt relief agreements, 1980–93

Table 16   Recent Trends in Lending

	1981	1991
Portfolio	0.1%	3.7%
FDI	8.3%	16.5%
Bonds	1.2%	4.8%
Commercial loans	46.1%	17.4%
Official loans	26.0%	30.8%
Export credits	11.0%	12.3%
Grants	7.3%	14.5%

Source: World Bank (1993), *Global Economic Prospects and the Developing Countries.*

Lessons for Bankers from the Sovereign Debt Crisis

The purpose of this section is to illustrate problems with risk management that bankers face. The key lesson is that bank managers must be able to properly assess the risks associated with a given set of assets. The sovereign lending boom of the 1970s demonstrates that bankers failed to acknowledge that illiquidity can be as serious as insolvency if there is no collateral attached to the loan, and this in turn led to poor assessment of credit risk. They also ignored the impact of random shocks on the ability of debtor countries to repay their loans, especially, the interest rate, exchange rate, and commodity price risk most debt countries were exposed to. Though by definition, random economic shocks cannot be forecast, scenario analysis could have improved their risk assessment. The refusal of central banks to bailout the private banks serves as a lesson to bankers that even though a crisis may threaten the stability of the world financial system, assistance or a bail-out is not guaranteed.

There continues to be a nagging doubt that the main cause of the crisis, that is, excessively high foreign leverage/gearing ratios, has not been addressed, because the rescheduling agreements and Brady bonds merely postpone repayment of the debt. But the emergence of a well-developed secondary market in this debt has meant banks can move the assets off their balance sheets, and for those with continuing exposure, it is possible to price these assets.

Banker Judgement and Sovereign Risk Assessment

The assessment of sovereign risk, like other forms of credit risk, can consist of either the use of formal forecasting methods, that is, the estimation of an econometric model based on fundamentals or judgemental assessments, when bankers rely on subjective opinion to make a lending decision. Continuing with the use of the sovereign debt problem as a "case", the performance of these two approaches is compared.

One paper which reports the results of such a comparison is Somerville and Taffler (1993).* In this paper, a problem country is one with a creditworthiness problem, signalled by the emergence of debt-service arrears. In most of the published literature, a country that reschedules its debt is defined as a problem country. However, the authors argue that the emergence of arrears can be used as the dependent variable because it is almost always followed by the negotiation of a rescheduling package.

The data for the sample run from 1979–89; 1979–90 for the dependent variable. With a view to looking at true *ex ante* predictive ability of the quantitative and judgemental models, the data are split into an estimation period (1979–86) and a forecast period (1987–1990). The data from the estimation period are used to obtain estimates of the cut-off values, based on the banker rating, and to estimate the probability of a country going into arrears, derived from the forecasting models.

To measure banker judgement, Somerville and Taffler used the rankings of countries reported in the Institutional Investor (II). The ratings are published twice a year; but the study chose to employ the September ratings because they measured the forecasting performance formed in year t for debt-servicing status in year $t + 1$. The *II* ratings come from a survey of 75–100 international banks, which were asked to grade each country on a scale of 0 to 100. The responses are weighted, to reflect the fact that some banks have greater exposure and more sophisticated country risk analysis systems.

The forecasting models used by these authors are typical of the literature: multiple linear discriminant analysis and logit analysis. In both these approaches, the objective is to identify statistically significant explanatory variables which affect the probability of bankruptcy, or in this case, the probability of a country going into arrears. A stepwise procedure allows a test of a whole range of explanatory variables.

Discriminant analysis, used in the context of sovereign risk analysis, assumes that a country will come from one of two populations: the countries which go into arrears (or reschedule) are in one population (P1) and countries that do not reschedule are placed in population 2 (P2). Data from past economic performance are used to derive a function that will discriminate between countries by placing them in one of two populations. Thus, if Z is a linear discriminant function of a number of independent explanatory variables, then, $Z = \sum a_i X_i, i = 1, .. n$, where X_i: the independent explanatory variables. Sample data are used to test whether the discriminant function places countries in one of the two populations, with an acceptable error rate.

Logit analysis differs from discriminant analysis in that it does not force countries into separate populations but instead assumes that the combined

---

*The discussion in this section is drawn from a paper by A. Somerville and R. Taffler (1993) "Banker Judgement versus Formal Forecasting Models: The Case of Country Risk Assessment", City University Business School Working Paper Series # 93/4-Centre for Empirical Research in Finance and Accounting.

effect of certain economic variables will serve to push a country over a given threshold. In this case, it would be from the non-arrears group into the arrears group. Note that in logit analysis, the dependent variable is a binary event, and the objective is to identify explanatory variables which influence the event. The logit model may be written as follows:

$$P(y_{it} = 1 = 1|x_{it}) = [e^{b+c'x_{it}}]/[1 + e^{b+c'x_{it}}]$$

where

x_t: the value of explanatory variable i at time t;

$P(y_{it+1})$: the probability of a country being in arrears at time $t + 1$; $y = 0$ implies the country is not in arrears.

The results of the best discriminant function and the best logit model are reported in Table 17.

Somerville and Taffler used these estimates to forecast which countries will or will not go into arrears. These are compared to the forecasting errors implied by the II ratings. They find the II ratings give rise to 0 type-I errors, that is, there were no errors where a country is not forecast to go into arrears but does. However, there was a high type-II rate (that is, a country is forecast to go into arrears but does not) of 62%. The predictions of the type-I and type-II error rates are, respectively, 11% and 17% for the discriminant model; 10% and 14% for the logit model.

However, the average costs of the two types of errors will differ. A type-I error means the value of the lender's assets will fall, whereas with a type-II error the profitable lending opportunity is missed—the bank loses in terms of opportunity cost. For this reason, it is normally assumed that a type-I error has

Table 17 Key Results from the Somerville and Taffler Study

	Statistically significant variables	Definition of variables	Sign[a]
Discriminant model	NARY	[foreign exchange reserves (end period) + reserve position with IMF − public and private disbursed debt] ÷ GDP	+
	DCPI	inflation rate	−
	INPS	interest payments ÷ external debt service (annual)	−
	DGDP	real annual GDP growth rate	+
	INVR	gross fixed capital formation ÷ GDP	+
Logit model	NARY,DCPI, INPS,DGDP	defined as above	(−),(+), (−),(+)

[a]: a + sign implies that an increase in the variable raises the probability of the country going into arrears; a negative sign means an increase in the variable reduces the probability of the country going into arrears. NARY (+) in the discriminant model is the only variable which is incorrectly signed.

a higher average cost for creditors than a type-II error. However, it is necessary to decide where the cut-off is going to be, that is, at what point the *II* rating will lead to a prediction of a country going into arrears, or the cut-off given an estimated probability of default from a logit model. The optimal cut-off will depend on the value of the cost ratio, defined as:

$$C = \text{average costs of type-I error} \div \text{average cost of type-II error.}$$

For example, if enough weight is placed on type-I errors, that is, type-I errors are given a high average cost $(C > 2.5)$, then the *II* ratings do achieve a lower misclassification cost than the forecasting models.

Somerville and Taffler's main conclusion was that the *Institutional Investor* country credit ratings, translated into a measure of banker judgement of the probability of a country going into arrears, is biased towards an adverse view of the creditworthiness of LDCs during 1987–89. There are a number of possible reasons for bias; bankers may be backward-looking rather than forward-looking in their expectations formation;* sentiment rather than economic fundamentals may cloud their judgement about some countries, and a "herd instinct" behaviour may be present.

THE POLITICAL ASPECTS OF RISK ANALYSIS

The political risk aspect of banking in a foreign country (or even the home country) has long been a source of concern to bankers. A bank will want to analyse the risk of takeover of foreign firms, if it has made loans to finance the foreign direct investment. More important, if the bank is exposed in lending to a foreign country, then it will want to assess the effects of the political situation on the ability or willingness of the country to repay its debt. Much has been written on the methods for assessing the risk of expropriation of foreign firms with branches or subsidiaries located in foreign countries.† This section reviews the quantitative models which have been developed to test the influence of politics on the probability of a debtor country going into arrears or rescheduling.

Brewer and Rivoli (1990) tested for the effects of political instability on banker perceptions of the creditworthiness of the country in question. They expected to find negative relationships between political stability and a country's capacity to service its debt or perceived creditworthiness. They also

---

*If agents use "backward-looking rules", they are said to be relying on different forms of technical analysis, such as extrapolation or regression, based on past data. If expectations are formed using forward-looking rules, rational expectation is said to apply, that is, agents do not make systematic forecasting errors.

†Detailed discussion of the literature on expropriation and other forms of political interference lies outside the scope of this chapter and only has an indirect impact on banks because of their loan exposure in foreign branches or subsidiaries of a multinational firm. For further discussion of the approaches taken to assess political risk in this context, readers are referred to Shapiro (1988) and Calverley (1990).

wanted to identify the types of political stability which affect creditworthiness perceptions.

These authors considered three types of political instability, including government regime change (that is, the frequency of regime change, which is assumed to be inversely related to political stability); political legitimacy (as measured by the degree to which a country's political system is democratic as opposed to authoritarian, arguing that while authoritarian regimes may be stable in the short run, they are unstable in the long run) and internal (civil wars) or external armed conflict.

The authors used a least squares regression technique to test for the effects of proximate instability and chronic instability on perceived creditworthiness. The study employed 1986 data for the 30 most heavily indebted countries. The dependent variable, perceived creditworthiness of a country, was taken from the 1987 *Institutional Investor (II)* and *Euromoney (EM)*. For details of how the *II* scores were compiled, readers are referred to the previous section. The *Euromoney* ranking is based on the weighted average spread borrowers are able to obtain from the Euromarket.* Thus, the *II* scores represent banker assessments of the countries' creditworthiness and the *EM* scores reflect the actual market conditions. The scores of *II* and *EM* were interpreted as probabilities, which allows logistic transformation of the credit rating.

The independent variables tested were:

- PHI or CHI: the number of changes in the head of government between 1982–86 (proximate head instability) or, for CHI, 1967–86 (chronic head instability);
- PGI, CGI: the number of changes in the governing group between 1982–86 (proximate group instability) or, for CGI, (1967–86) (chronic group instability);
- PPL, CPL: political rights scores for 1986 (for proximate instability) and 1975–86 (chronic instability). These variables are the proxy for political legitimacy and are taken from the annual reports on human rights.[†]
- PAC, CAC: armed conflict scores indicating, proximate armed conflict at the end of 1986 (0,1) and chronic armed conflict: the number of years the country had been involved in armed conflict;
- CAB: the 1986 current account balance (CAB) expressed as a percentage of GNP;
- TED: total external debt as a percentage of GNP in 1986.

Brewer and Rivoli found perceptions of creditworthiness had a greater sensitivity to proximate head instability as measured by regime change, suggesting lenders focus on short-term recent changes rather than considering a country's

---

*The weighted average spread for country $i = \sum$ (vol × spread × maturity) ÷ $\sum$ (vol × maturity), where vol: is the volume of loans signed by country i during a given year, spread is the margin over LIBOR, and maturity is the length of the loan to repayment.
[†]As reported in R. Gasktil (1987), *Freedom in the World*, Westport, Conn.

experience from a longer-term perspective. Regime change was a better measure of political instability than either armed conflict or political legitimacy. But the authors argued it was important to use several measures of political instability, because it is not a single phenomenon that can be measured by a single variable. The findings should be treated with caution, for two reasons. Compared to related published studies, the economic variables were not given much attention. Furthermore, perceptions of political risk may already be included in the *II* and *EM* scores.

Balkan (1992) used a probit* model of rescheduling to examine the role of political (in addition to economic) factors in explaining a developing country's probability of rescheduling. He included two political variables in the model. A "political instability" variable was an index which measured the amount of social unrest which occurred in a given year. The "democracy" variable reflected the level of democracy, measured by an index, which in turn, was captured by two components of the political system: participation (the extent to which the executive and legislative branches of government reflect popular will) and competitiveness, the degree of exclusion of political parties from the system and the ability of the largest party to dominate national elections. Balkan also included some standard economic variables in his model, such as debt service ÷ exports, interest payments ÷ exports, and so on. To minimise simultaneity problems, all the explanatory variables were lagged by one year. The sample period ran from 1970–84 and used annual data from 33 developing nations. Balkan found an inverse relationship between a country's level of democracy and the probability of rescheduling, a direct relationship between the probability of rescheduling and the level of political instability, and a reduction in type-I and type-II errors when the political variables were included in the model.

CONCLUSION

This chapter has considered the various aspects of bank risk management, in theory and practice. It began by noting that banks differ from other firms in the range of financial risks they assume. The management of these risks will be a crucial determinant of their profitability and shareholder value added. The traditional intermediary function of banks entailed management of credit, interest rate, and liquidity risks. Increasingly, however, banks act as intermediaries in risk management; a central objective of the modern bank is the management of a whole range of unbundled risks including credit/counterparty, sovereign, liquidity, settlements/payment, interest rate, market, currency, gearing, operating, and global banking risks.

The sections on asset securitisation and derivatives explained how their growth transformed risk management for banks. Asset securitisation allows

---

*Probit differs from logit in that it assumes the error terms follow a normal distribution, whereas in logit, the cumulative distribution of error terms is logistic.

different functions normally assumed by a bank to be unbundled, from origination to warehousing, so that the institution with the competitive advantage in performing a certain function assumes responsibility for that function. The growth of exchange traded and customised over-the-counter derivatives has meant banks can broaden the type of intermediation they undertake. Banks can use derivatives for proprietary trading and speculation, to hedge, or as part of fee-based risk management services offered to customers. It was argued that banks and customers alike must understand the purpose for which a given instrument is being used. There have been many cases where large corporations have lost enormous sums and have claimed, in some cases correctly, that they were ill-advised by their banks.

The section on the approaches to the management of financial risks began with a review of the well-known guidelines used for credit risk assessment. Next, asset-liability management was discussed; it was stressed that ALM was developed to manage on-balance sheet interest rate and liquidity risks. Gap analysis was identified as a method for managing interest rate and liquidity risks. The Basle 1993 proposals suggest gap analysis has a role to play in the monitoring of interest rate risk. Duration and duration gap analysis techniques were also explained. Value at risk and stress simulation were identified as important methods for assessing market risk. The section was concluded with a brief exploration of the relationship between financial innovation, risk management, and regulation.

The next section considered how one bank organises its risk management function. If the objective is to maximise profits and shareholder value added, then the organisation of risk management within a bank is as important as the development of risk management tools and techniques. This message assumes even greater importance now that the Basle Committee apparently accepts the benefits of self-regulation, with capital requirements for market risk being calculated using models that are internal to a given bank.

The section on sovereign debt case illustrated the lessons it could teach bank managers. It provides a good example of where managers can go wrong in their assessment and management of risks. The case illustrates the need for good internal controls. The political element of risk analysis is also important, especially for banks with cross-border exposure, either through direct loans or through loans to firms engaging in foreign direct investment.

In this chapter, it has been stressed that bank risk management has undergone a profound change with the advent of securitisation and derivatives, though banks should not ignore the importance of good management of more traditional forms of risk, such as credit risk. In the next chapter, risk is again the central topic, but here the principal concerns of regulators are identified. The objectives of regulators, to ensure the operation of an efficient but stable financial system, contrasts sharply with the goal of any bank, to maximise profit and shareholder value added. Thus, it is important for managers to understand how and why governments tend to single out banks for special attention, and how the regulations will impact on bank activities. These issues are reviewed in Chapter 6.

6
Regulation of Banks

INTRODUCTION

This chapter considers the issues related to the prudential supervision of banks by government authorities. In most countries, the national banking systems are singled out for special regulation, which is more comprehensive than for other sectors of the economy, for a number of reasons.

To the extent that banks offer fairly homogeneous products to customers, they are collectively exposed to the same risk. At the micro level, a marginal borrower will seek out all the banks until a bank makes the loan. At the macro level, banks are rapidly affected by events such as changes in monetary policy. *Financial fragility*,* a heightened probability of default by households, businesses, or the bank itself, can lead to a loss of confidence in a bank or banks and provoke a bank run, preventing the bank from offering one of its important products, *liquidity* (see Chapter 5). Illiquidity, in turn, can erode the net worth of the bank because not only is it unable to offer one of its profitable services, but it is costly for the bank to unwind relatively illiquid assets.

Lack of transparency of bank balance sheets, the intermediary function of banks, and the cost of acquiring information mean the reputation of a bank is extremely important; any market rumour will undermine depositor confidence. It is argued the banking system is particularly vulnerable to *contagion* effects, when lack of confidence associated with one poorly performing bank spreads to other, healthy banks. It arises because if customers know that once a run on a bank begins, liquidated bank assets will decline in value very quickly, they will want to withdraw their deposits before a run. Thus, even healthy banks may be subject to a bank run.[†] If most banks are affected, the financial system may well collapse.

Economists of a monetarist persuasion use fractional reserve banking to explain why bank runs occur. The failure of a key financial firm prompts the

---

*The term "financial fragility" was introduced by Minsky (1977, 1982), though a similar version of financial crises is discussed by Fisher (1932, 1933). Kindelberger (1978) argued that in an economic upturn, banks do not make sufficient provision for risk, and there is heightened speculative activity by investors on financial markets, because of the "euphoria" of the upturn.

[†]For a rigorous treatment of bank runs, see Diamond and Dybvig (1983).

run, as depositors panic and try to withdraw deposits. The fractional reserve system will mean that as depositors try to withdraw their deposits, there is a multiple contraction of deposits. If there is no central bank intervention (or suspension of convertibility), healthy banks are also threatened as the value of their assets declines. Thus, a run may be the cause of a financial crisis. Inflation is viewed as the root cause of the crisis because it creates uncertainty and therefore increases credit and interest rate risk. The monetarist school assert a crisis normally occurs after the upturn in the business cycle; the financial fragility school argue it is the crisis itself which initiates the downturn in the cycle. The monetarists stress that provided a financial safety net is in place, no crisis will arise from an important bank failure. For example, Schwartz (1986) argued that recent "crises" should not be labelled in this way, because the financial system would not have collapsed, even in the absence of central bank intervention. According to Schwartz, the last genuine crises were in 1866 in the UK, and in 1933 in the US. For a detailed discussion of these points, readers are referred to Cagan (1965), Friedman and Schwartz (1963), and Schwartz (1986).*

Most countries offer some form of deposit protection scheme to bolster confidence and counter bank runs, but in return demand that banks subject themselves to close regulatory scrutiny by the authorities, to ensure a minimum standard of quality. However, 100% deposit insurance is normally required to be fully effective but such a scheme escalates moral hazard problems. The deposit insurance debate is discussed later in this chapter and in Chapter 7.

The vulnerability of banking to contagion creates *systemic risk*; the risk that disturbances in a financial institution or market will spread across the financial system, leading to widespread bank runs by wholesale and retail depositors, and possibly, collapse of the system. The breakdown in the financial system will, in turn, severely hamper money transmission; in the extreme, the economy could revert to barter exchange.

For these reasons, it is widely accepted that the banking system has a unique position in a national economy. A widespread collapse of the banking system can lead to the decline of intermediation, money transmission, and liquidity services offered by banks which, in turn, will cause an inefficient allocation of resources in the economy. The problem is compounded by the macroeconomic role played by banks; they help to implement government monetary policy. For example, the government may use the banks (changing a reserve ratio or setting a base rate) to achieve certain monetary growth targets. If the financial system collapses, there may be a dramatic reduction in the money supply, with the usual macroeconomic implications.

Thus, bank failures can carry a substantial external or *social* cost, in addition to the obvious private costs of failure.† Losses to a bank's creditors, or damage

---

*For a more detailed review of the various theories, see chapter 5 of Davis (1992).

†In economics, "social cost" means the total costs of an activity, including private costs borne by the main party and all "external" costs borne by others. The collapse of a financial firm will involve a private cost for investors, depositors, and employees of the firm, but a collapse of the banking system creates social costs because the economy no longer has a method of intermediation and money transmission.

to other sectors of the economy are external to the individual banks and therefore will not be considered in bank management decisions. Nonetheless, bank management should be aware of the reasons behind government intervention in the financial sector and also have an understanding of the regulatory framework a bank is likely to be subject to.

Systemic banking risks are compounded by the Euro and interbank markets, which, as was noted in Chapters 2 and 5, play a crucial role in global banking scene. The interbank market acts as a risk absorber and risk spreader but at the same time makes the global banking system vulnerable to certain exogenous shocks.

An alternative school of thought advocates *free banking*. In the 19th century, free banking described a system where it was possible to enter the banking market without first obtaining a charter or licence to operate. The Scottish banking system between 1716 and 1844 is considered a model of 19th century free banking. The banks operated with virtually no restrictions imposed by government authorities. Cameron (1972) argued that Scottish free banking helped to promote economic growth because of the intense competition between the banks, which forced them to innovate. He credits the banks as being the first to introduce branch banking, interest paid on deposits, and overdraft facilities.

Modern-day usage of the term free banking refers to a highly competitive system operating without a central bank or regulations. Free banking proponents view a central bank as a body with the potential to encourage collusive behaviour among banks, thereby increasing their monopoly power. The system would not be threatened by runs or collapse because the private banks will have a collective interest in devising a framework to prevent runs. It could take the form of private deposit insurance or a private clearing house which acts as lender of last resort. See, among others, White (1986). However, if there are several banks, there will be a free rider problem. Furthermore, private deposit insurance and/or lender of last resort institutions merely replicate what a central bank does, so the same monitoring problem will exist. Though the free banking idea is interesting in theory, it is very unlikely that the regulatory systems of western countries will be dismantled to allow an experiment. The issue is not explored any further, because the principal objective of the chapter is to consider the managerial implications of modern regulatory regimes.

This chapter explores different aspects of bank regulation which emerged in the light of the points discussed above. It first considers bank regulation in the UK, and then looks at US bank regulatory practices. By comparing and contrasting these two systems, one gains an insight into the key issues related to prudential regulation, for any country. There then follows a discussion of the proposals for prudential regulation of banks in Europe. This is followed by a consideration of the regulation of banks in Japan. The emphasis of this chapter is on regulation of banking activities, as opposed to other financial products (for example, life insurance, pensions) a bank might offer. Once one moves away from the core banking products, the issue of financial malpractice is central, rather than concerns about the health of the system as a whole. These points are discussed in the context of financial conglomerates. Finally, the chapter looks at the international coordination of prudential regulation.

PRUDENTIAL REGULATION IN THE UNITED KINGDOM

The growth of central banking activities in England laid the foundation for the development of central banks in other countries. For this reason, analysing the evolution of the Bank of England (which was founded in 1694) as a central bank is useful in any study of prudential regulation.

The role of the central bank, as it has evolved in the UK, is threefold. **Monetary control**, has, as its central objective, the stabilisation of the price level through control of the money supply. It was the principal function assigned to the Bank by the Bank of England Act, 1844. This Act called for strict adherence to the quantity theory of money, that is, a strict money supply growth rule, where the growth rate in the money supply was equal to the growth rate in the economy's real output. Since the mid-1980s most monetary authorities have used interest rates to implement monetary policy, for the purpose of achieving price stability.

Prudential control, the minimisation of financial crises, is the second key function of the Bank of England, because of the social costs incurred in the event of such a crisis. The 1914 Bank Charter Act allowed it to adopt a discretionary monetary policy, meaning the Bank could supply liquidity in the event of speculative manias. The change from a strict to a discretionary rule was a consequence of a number of crises (1847, 1857, 1866), when the 1844 Act had had to be suspended (and more money printed) as reserves dwindled to nothing. The term "lender of last resort" originated with Baring (1797), but the idea was further developed by Thornton (1802), and Bagehot (1873). From 1844 to the close of the century, the Bank of England offered LLR facilities, following the Thornton–Bagehot model. The 1914 Act formalised the Bank's role as a *lender of last resort* in times of financial crisis, meaning the Bank is the ultimate supplier of liquidity to bank(s) threatened by a liquidity crisis. In more recent times, the Bank has led *lifeboat* rescues, whereby healthy banks assist in the rescue of a troubled bank.

The placement of **government debt** on the most favourable terms possible is the third function of the Bank of England. In times of rising national fiscal deficit, it is tempting for governments to *monetise the debt*, entailing an excessive growth rate in the money supply,* causing inflation, which, in turn, reduces the real value of government debt. Additionally, governments may seek to raise *seigniorage* income. For example, a reserve ratio acts as an implicit

---

*An "excessive" growth rate in the money supply is normally defined as a money supply growth rate which exceeds the growth rate of real national income. The result is a positive growth rate in the price level, that is, inflation.

form of tax and a source of revenue for the state, because it requires banks to place non-interest-bearing deposits at the central bank.

There is an inherent conflict between these three functions. It is not possible to adhere to a strict quantity theory of money if the central bank has to print more money, in its capacity as lender of last resort. A modern version of the same story is the conflict between a high interest rate policy to achieve a goal of price stability, and the effect of this policy on the economic health of the banking system. For example, a period of rising interest rates usually raises personal and corporate default rates, leading to lower bank profitability or, in the extreme, bank failures.

A key policy issue is the extent to which the three functions should be the responsibility of different institutions. Goodhart and Schoenmaker (1995) conducted an exhaustive review of the arguments for and against the separation of monetary policy from banking supervision. They could find no overwhelming argument for either model, consistent with their finding that of the 27 countries examined, half separate the two functions, the other half integrate them.

The focus of this section is on the prudential regulation of the banking system, though the other functions of the Bank of England should be kept in mind. In other countries, the three functions have been divided up among different government agencies, with the central bank being given the responsibility for price stability. Before looking at modern prudential regulation in the UK, consider a statement made in 1985 by Mr W.P. Cooke, an associate director of the Bank of England:

> It has long been the perceived wisdom of the Bank of England that the interests of the bank supervisory authorities and good commercial bank management are one.*

Another quote from Mr Eugene Ludwig, US Comptroller of the Currency, is also worth citing:

> Three questions should be asked of any new activity for banks. Can the risk of the new activity be adequately monitored? Can monitoring be verified, by supervisors, by management, by directors, by shareholders, by creditors? Can the risk be managed? If the answer to any question is "no", we should take a hard look at any banking organisation that engages in the activity.†

One of the objectives of this chapter is to persuade readers that the above messages are, at the very least, questionable. The role of a central bank (or the government agency with responsibility for prudential supervision) is to minimise the possibility of financial collapse in a system, because the social costs of bank risk-taking exceed the private costs. Private banks, on the other hand, have the objective of maximising profits and shareholder value added by taking risks. There is no reason why bank management should be concerned with the social costs of bank failure. Furthermore, if managers demanded that the riskiness of every new product be properly measured from the outset,

---

*Cooke (1985: p.219).
†Ludwig (1994), p11.

financial innovation would be non-existent, and the profitability of banks undermined.

The 1979 Banking Act (amended, 1987)

Until the 1979 Banking Act, there was no specific banking law in the UK. Private banks were treated like other commercial concerns, though they were not required to disclose profits. Individual agents or firms could accept deposits without a licence. The 1979 Banking Act[*] formed the basis for the current prudential regulation of the UK banking system. It was amended in 1987.

The 1979 Act identified two classes of financial institution, recognised banks and licensed deposit-takers.[†] The financial institutions governed by the Act are the clearing banks, the merchant banks, the finance houses, and the discount houses.[‡] The 1987 Act eliminated the distinction between banks and licensed deposit-takers. Any institution authorised by the Bank of England and with paid-up capital and reserves of at least £5 million[§] may call itself a bank.

The Act extends to foreign banks operating in London. These banks must seek recognised status and report statistics to the Bank, but if there is a problem with solvency, they are governed by their home central bank, in line with the 1983 Basle Concordat.

Any firm seeking recognised bank status from the Bank of England must offer a broad range of services, including current (chequing) deposit accounts, overdraft and loan facilities, and at least one of foreign exchange facilities, foreign trade documentation and finance (through the issue of bills of exchange and promissory notes), investment management services, alternatively a bank can offer a highly specialised service, though the Act does not elaborate on what constitutes a highy specialised service, though discount houses are recognised as banks using this criterion.

---

[*]The 1979 Banking Act was a product of a review of regulatory policy following the secondary banking crisis of 1972–73. It also conformed to the requirements of the EC's First Banking Coordination Directive, which defined a "credit" institution.

[†]Licensed deposit-takers had a lower paid-up capital requirement (£250,000.00), and included branches of foreign banks which have a sound reputation, but have not been operating in the UK for long enough to provide the full range of sevices typical of an established bank. The Bank of Credit and Commerce International was a licensed deposit-taker until the 1987 Amendment, when it became a fully fledged bank.

[‡]In the UK, discount houses are wholesale bankers for the Bank of England and private banks, offering a place for banks' deposits on an overnight or short-term basis and making a market in Treasury bills and bank bills. The Bank of England uses the discount houses to pursue monetary policy. The primary function of finance houses is in the provision of medium-term credit facilities (mainly in the form of hire purchase) retail and corporate customers; many are now subsidiaries of clearing banks. The clearing banks, with extensive branch networks, are universal banks in all but name, offering retail, commercial, and investment banking services, but do not have extensive shareholdings in non-bank firms. Since "Big Bang" (1986), UK merchant banks, have become more like US investment banks (see Chapter 1). Merchant banks have no branch network, and many are now wholly-owned subsidiaries of one of the clearing banks, US commercial banks, or European universal banks.

[§]now ECU 5 million by the Second Banking Directive (see p. 244)

Additionally, the Bank of England must be satisfied that a firm applying for bank status has an excellent reputation in the financial community, its affairs are conducted with "integrity and prudence", and it is able to manage its financial affairs. Since 1987, the Bank has applied "fit and proper" criteria to all directors, controllers, and managers.

The 1987 Amendment to the 1979 Banking Act was in response to concerns raised by the Johnson Matthey Bank collapse.* A new supervisory board was created, chaired by the Governor of the Bank of England, with most of its members drawn from outside the Bank. The 1987 Act "encouraged" auditors to warn supervisors of bank fraud: auditors were to be given greater access to Bank of England information. While it did not impose a statutory limit on lending, any exposure to a single borrower which exceeds 10% of a bank's capital is supposed to be reported to the Bank of England, and supervisors should be consulted before more than 25% of a bank's capital is lent to a single borrower. The amendment also specified Bank of England control over foreign bank entry; the Bank may block a purchase of more than 15% of a British bank by a foreign entity. Investors with more than a 5% stake in a British bank must declare themselves.

The 1979 Act created a **Depositors Protection Fund**, to which all recognised banks must contribute. The fund compensates for 75% of any one deposit, the maximum insurable deposit being £20 000, (raised from the original £10 000.00 set in 1979). The presence of *co-insurance* means the maximum insurance pay-out is £15 000.00.

Once bank status is granted, the Bank of England is responsible for ensuring that the firm continues to be justified in calling itself a bank. It therefore has an important supervisory function. Unlike many supervisory authorities in other countries, the Bank does not conduct an official audit of banks. The audit role is left to private auditing firms which carry out the main inspections on banks. This point is considered in more detail later in the chapter.

The Bank of England acts as a prudential regulator by supervising the risks in which banks engage. The assets side of a bank's balance sheet is regulated through measures of capital adequacy, and the liabilities side through measures of liquidity adequacy.

The Bank of England and Capital Adequacy

To supervise risk on the assets side of the balance sheet of a bank, the Bank of England employs two measures of capital adequacy: the gearing ratio and the risk assets ratio. The gearing ratio is defined as:

$$\frac{\text{a bank's deposits} + \text{external liabilities}}{\text{a bank's capital} + \text{reserves}}$$

---

*Johnson Matthey Bankers collapsed in 1984, and was rescued by a Bank of England-led lifeboat. The rescue of JMB prompted the establishment of a committee of Bank of England and Treasury officials, with a remit to look at bank supervisory practices, and the relationship between the Bank of England and the independent auditors. The 1987 Act resulted from the findings of this committee. Readers are referred to Chapter 7 for a full review of the JMB affair.

In the UK, capital plus reserves of a bank consist of:

- share capital;
- loan capital;
- minority interests;
- reserves and general provisions.

However, the following items are deducted:

- investments in subsidiaries and associates;
- goodwill;
- equipment;
- premises and other fixed assets.

Deposits plus external liabilities include:

- all deposits;
- non-capital liabilities, excluding contingent liabilities.

To see why the Bank of England uses the gearing (leverage) ratio as one measure of capital adequacy, consider two examples.

Example 1

Suppose a bank's balance sheet is such that:

$$\text{bank's deposits} + \text{liabilities} = \text{£1 million}$$
$$\text{bank's capital} + \text{reserves} = \text{£1 million}$$

Then the gearing ratio is = 1. If the bank lends £2 million and 50% of the bank's borrowers default, the bank will lose all of its capital, but all depositors will be repaid.

Example 2

In this example, the balance sheet is:

bank's deposits + liabilities = £2 million
bank's capital + reserves = £1 million

Then the gearing ratio = 2. If the bank lends £3 million and there is a 50% default rate, the bank loses £1.5 million, £0.5 million more than its capital base. Therefore, 25% of total deposits will be lost.

There is a difference between a bank gearing ratio and the well-known concept of gearing or leverage as applied to a non-bank's commercial operations. The gearing of a firm is the ratio of debt to equity; if this ratio rises, a firm is said to be more highly geared or leveraged. Since a bank obtains some of its capital from its depositors, who may be individuals, firms, or other banks, the denominator will include loan capital, in addition to share capital.

The above examples demonstrate that the lower the gearing ratio, the lower the risk that the bank will lose its capital, therefore, the lower the risk of insolvency. But if a bank borrows funds (for example, by accepting deposits) and on-lends these funds, it is said to be "gearing up" the risks to its own solvency. The problem for policy-makers is that a profit-maximising bank will arrive at a private gearing ratio that is higher than the public gearing ratio, because its sole concern is with the rates of return for its shareholders.

No private bank considers the wider social costs of bank failure when formulating its optimal gearing ratio. A bank will recognise the trade-off between a low gearing ratio that will give investors and depositors confidence, and a high gearing ratio, which maximises shareholder value added. However, the optimum ratio will be where the marginal private advantage of the additional capital is just offset by the marginal private disadvantage. The divergence between private and social costs or benefits is a classic case for government intervention. Here, it is in the form of a central bank (the Bank of England) intervening to impose minimum gearing ratios on banks.

The precise gearing ratio considered acceptable will vary according to the nature of a bank's business and its assets. The Bank of England admits that qualitative factors enter into the assessment of the capital adequacy; hence a range of ratios are regarded as adequate. A bilateral agreement is reached between bank management and the Bank of England, known the *consensus* approach to bank supervision. Agreements are reached through meetings that are held several times a year between these two parties. While the Bank of England lays down a methodology to assess the various categories of risk, it does not attempt to impose specific ratios. The success of a consensus approach depends on having only a few banks in the system; a large number of banks would aggravate monitoring problems for the Bank. Bank functions must also be well defined. The Bank is also dependent on accurate reports of private auditors. If the structure of the UK banking system were to undergo a major change, supervisory problems could arise if these conditions were no longer satisfied. However, the Bank of England does act as final arbiter because it is empowered with the authority to revoke bank status if a bank fails to meet all the conditions outlined in the previous section.

The risk assets ratio is the second measure of capital adequacy used by the Bank of England. In the UK, the risk assets ratio was introduced after several years of consultation with the banking community, culminating in the publication of the Bank of England's "Measurement of Capital" (1980). A risk assets ratio explicitly recognises that different assets on a bank's balance sheet carry different degrees of risk, unlike the gearing ratio, where risk weights are not used. Formally, the risk assets ratio is the ratio of capital to weighted risk assets. Weighting allows a heterogeneous set of assets to be valued. The higher the risk associated with an asset, the greater the weight the asset receives.

The Bank of England and US authorities were the first to recognise the importance of such a ratio but the accepted measure is now the *Basle risk assets ratio*, following the Basle Capital Adequacy Agreement (July 1988).*

---

*The 1988 Basle Accord is one of several agreements (see later in this chapter) reached by the Basle Committee on Banking Supervision, a committee of banking supervisory authorities established by the central bank governors of Belgium, Canada, France, Germany, Italy, Japan, Luxembourg, the Netherlands, Sweden, Switzerland, the UK and the USA. The Committee was established in 1975. For more detail on the Accord, see Basle Committee (1988) and Norton (1991).

All international banks supervised in member countries were expected to implement the ratio by January, 1993. It was hoped the accord would bring about international convergence of the measurement of capital ratios, with explicit recognition of the different risks associated with different types of assets, including off-balance sheet risk.

The *Basle risk assets ratio* (capital/weighted risk assets) is computed as follows. A bank's capital is divided into tier one and tier two capital. *Tier one or core capital* consists of equity capital plus disclosed reserves. Equity capital includes permanent shareholders' equity (issued and fully paid ordinary shares/common stock and perpetual non-cumulative preference shares). Disclosed reserves include share premiums, retained profits, general reserves and legal reserves. The definition excludes revaluation reserves and cumulative preference shares. Not all assets on the balance sheet of a bank are weighted for riskiness, because plant and equipment, intangible assets and investments in subsidiary and associated companies are deducted from the capital side of the ratio. *Tier two or supplementary capital* comprises all other capital; revaluation and loan loss reserves such as cumulative perpetual preferred stock and subordinated long-term debt. National regulators have some discretion over what constitutes tier two capital, though the accord did set binding limits. For example, there is a 55% discount on unrealised gains on holdings of securities, and subordinated debt may only be included up to a limit of 50% of tier one capital.

Risk weights are assigned to assets. Five rates are used: 0%, 10%, 20%, 50%, and 100%. The higher the risk, the greater the weight. For example, the risk weighting for commercial loans, mortgages, and treasury bills are, respectively, 100%, 50%, and 0%. Off-balance sheet instruments are converted into "credit risk" equivalents in five categories. For example, stand-by letters of credit are converted into assets at 100%, commercial letters of credit at 20%. Foreign exchange and interest rate contracts are also converted.

The Basle risk assets ratio is set at a *minimum* of 8% for each bank, and 4% for core capital. In other words, by 1993, banks had to back each £100.00 of assets with £8.00 of capital, and could afford to lose 8% of these assets without there being any threat to deposits. A bank can lose up to £4.00 of core capital for every £100.00 of assets.

For example, suppose Simple Bank has the following set of on-balance sheet assets:

Cash	£500
Government bills (all maturities)	£2000
Mortgages	£15 000
Commercial loans	£10 000

Unadjusted for risk, the value of these assets is £27 500. Adjusted for the Basle risk weights, the value of these assets falls to:

$$£500(0) + (£2000)(0) + (£15\ 000)(0.5) + (£10\ 000)(1.0) = £17\ 000.$$

The risk assets ratio would then be equal to:

(tier one capital + tier two capital)/(£17 500 + the credit risk equivalents for OBS items).

Suppose tier one capital + tier two capital = £1500. Credit risk equivalence for OBS items = 0. Then the risk assets ratio = £1500/£17 500 = 8.6%

A number of problems have been raised in relation to the Basle ratio. In the computation of tier one capital, the emphasis is on book value of equity rather than market value. The inclusion of equity fails to recognise that different countries allow their banks varying degrees of access to the stock market. For example, in France, nationalised banks did not have access to the stock market and had to find other ways of raising capital if the government would not supply them with funds.

Tier two capital is split into two sections, known as upper and lower case, depending on the extent to which the capital may be used as a source of funds when a bank gets into trouble. A percentage of loan loss reserves and categories of subordinated and convertible debt are included in tier two. The ambiguity about the constituents of tier two capital has encouraged agents to innovate to get round the regulations. Also, different standards apply in each country. For example, Japanese banks, until recently, were prohibited from issuing subordinated debt, but US money centre banks could. On the other hand Japanese city banks have substantial revaluation reserves (to the extent that these are unrealised gains in their cross-shareholdings in other companies), while US banks do not.

The Basle ratio attempts to measure risk associated with off-balance sheet instruments by calculating credit risk "equivalents". However, interest rate, liquidity, currency, and operating risks are almost completely ignored. Consider two government bonds with different maturities (for example, five years and 30 years). Both are given a 0% risk weighting, which is acceptable in terms of credit risk. But the assets carry different interest rate risks, which the risk assets ratio ignores.

There is no reward for banks which reduce their systematic risk, because the Basle ratio does not acknowledge risk diversification of a bank loan portfolio through covariance analysis. While concentration of risk among individual customers is picked up by the ratio, over-exposure in particular industries is ignored. Nor does the ratio recognise that banks undertake different financial activities. A merchant bank in the UK or an investment bank in the US will have quite different risk profiles from universal banks engaged in wholesale and retail banking activities. Yet both are expected to conform to the same risk assets ratio requirements.

The regulations may give banks a false sense of security, or cause them to make sub-optimal decisions. Since industry concentration is implicitly ignored by the ratio, banks may become complacent about the lack of portfolio diversification across sectors. They may also place too much emphasis on meeting the Basle ratio, at the expense of other types of risk management such as interest rate or funding risk.

Scott and Iwahara (1994) criticised the Basle accord on two counts. First, they argued, differences in tax and accounting rules mean that the measurement of capital continues to vary widely among countries. Thus, the risk assets ratios quoted by banks in different countries are not comparable. Second, the accord has failed to achieve the objective of a level playing field among international banks, because the degree of competition in a system is determined by other factors, such as the structure of the banking system and the degree to which a government is prepared to support its banks. Until very recently, Japan's well-known "safety net" meant Japanese banks could borrow capital more cheaply from wholesale markets than banks from countries where failures have been allowed.

The Basle Committee tried to address the treatment of interest rate, market, and currency risks in a 1993 Consultative document, and a follow-up 1995 proposal. The proposals are discussed later in this chapter. Also, it is worth stressing that banks are subject to additional supervision in their own countries. For example, the Bank of England monitors other forms of risk-taking, including liquidity risk and currency risk. The US regulators insist on higher standards if a bank is to be classified as "well capitalised". However, different supervisory approaches to the management of other risks somewhat defeats the purpose of the Basle ratio, which is to improve the soundness of international banks and, at the same time, ensure prudential regulation does not create an uneven playing field for international banks.

The Bank of England and Liquidity Adequacy

The Bank of England's monitoring of liquidity adequacy recognises that the liabilities side of a bank's balance sheet can also contribute to instability of the financial system, because illiquidity can quickly undermine a bank's net worth. Here, the Bank's objective is to minimise the social costs arising from illiquidity.

The Bank of England employs liquidity gap analysis to ensure that liquidity or funding risk incurred by a bank is within reasonable limits. The assets and liabilities are inserted in a ladder and the net positions of each time period are accumulated. Thus, the liquidity ladder provides a measure of a series of accumulating net mismatch positions in successive time bands. The first maturity bands on the ladder permit comparison of the sight and near sight liabilities with cash and assets capable of generating cash immediately, and therefore is similar to a liquidity ratio. Marketable assets are placed on the ladder at the start of the maturity date, rather than according to their maturity date. The Bank takes into account any limitations on their marketability or their susceptibility to price fluctuations. The Bank of England also uses gap analysis to monitor interest rate risk, focusing on the average net cumulative position for a specified time period.

The Bank of England divides the foreign currency exposure of a bank into two parts. A bank's dealing position consists of foreign currency exposures that arise from a bank's day-to-day banking operations. The longer-term foreign currency exposure makes up a bank's structural position. Examples include exposures arising from a bank's fixed long-term assets and liabilities such as loan capital, premises and investment in subsidiaries and associates. The structural position is excluded from its measurement and control of currency exposure. However, the Basle ratio includes an aggregate foreign currency position, which takes account of dealing and structural positions.

The Bank of England sets guidelines for dealing positions. A net open position in any one currency may not be more than 10% of the adjusted capital base, as defined earlier. Net short open dealing positions may not exceed more than 15% of the adjusted capital base. More conservative guidelines are used for banks inexperienced in foreign exchange dealings. Again, the Bank relies on a consensus approach to set the exposure for individual banks.

Banks' currency positions are monitored by the Bank of England through a system of monthly returns. These returns give the net spot long or short position and the net forward long or short position in each currency at the close of business on the reporting day. Banks are also expected to report any position which has exceeded the guidelines for the previous reporting period.

The Bank of England does not issue any specific guidelines for dealing with counterparty risk arising from foreign exchange instruments, such as futures and forwards. However, together with the Federal Reserve Board and Bank for International Settlements, it monitors the Euromarkets in terms of size and maturity mismatching.

Other Relevant UK Financial Market Regulations

It is unwise to treat prudential regulation in isolation, because other regulations affect the competitive environment in which a bank operates, which in turn can influence the way banks behave and the risks they take. In the UK, a number of changes in regulations of financial firms, not necessarily prudential, have affected the competitive environment in which banks operate. These include, in addition to the Banking Act (already discussed), competition and credit control (1971); the special supplementary deposit scheme (the "corset"— December 1973–74, 1976–77, 1978–80); the end of exchange controls, 1979; the collapse of the building society interest rate cartel, 1983; the Stock Exchange reforms, 1986; the Financial Services Act,1986; and the Building Societies Act, 1986.

These changes in the regulatory environment affected the structure of the UK banking system in a number of ways. The deregulation of bank and building society interest rates changed the pricing behaviour of financial firms. Entry of new players was encouraged by the Stock Exchange reforms and the Building Societies Act. The British banking structure was discussed in Chapter 3, but three cases related to prudential regulation are worth noting. The Building Societies Act (1986; effective January 1987) specified what functions a building society might undertake. The key reforms allowed building societies to offer a full retail banking service, and to convert from mutual* to public limited company (bank) status.

Unless a building society actually becomes a bank recognised by the Bank of England, the prudential regulator is the Building Societies Commission. Compared to banks, societies are subject to more stringent requirements on assets and liabilities. At least 90% of the assets of a building society must be in the form of residential mortgages, termed "Class 1" assets. Class 2 assets make up the other 10%, and can consist of other types of mortgage asset, but may not exceed 10% of commercial assets. Class 3 assets (for example, equity holdings in estate agencies, land, and unsecured loans) may not exceed 5% of total assets. The Class 3 limit is part of the overall Class 2 limit of 10%.

The Act allowed building societies to use the wholesale markets for funding, but in a very limited way. Wholesale money plus wholesale deposits cannot exceed 20% of total liabilities (later raised to 40%; now 50%). Thus, while the majority of societies are now permitted to offer full retail banking, compared to banks they are far more limited in their access to wholesale markets. However, access to wholesale markets can be a two-edged sword—funding tends to be more volatile than in retail markets, but the added degree of freedom for the banks must work in their favour.

The Building Societies Commission (BSC) was created by the 1986 Act.[†] The remit of the BSC is to protect investors, ensure financial stability, and administer the regulations set out in the Act. The Commission authorises societies, may revoke authorisation, can request a change in business practice, and inspect societies. While the Act does not specify capital requirements, the Commission does. Assets are weighted according to risk, but the method is different from that used by the Bank of England. Mortgages with a maturity of more than five years on owner-occupied dwellings require a capital backing of 1% of assets. Mortgages with a shorter maturity have a 2% weight; riskier mortgages are subject to a 4–6% weight. New activities permitted under the Act (for example, unsecured lending) attract an even higher weight. Individual capital requirements are summed to produce a "desired level of capital", on which societies are expected to base their business plans, and the "minimum acceptable level of capital", below which the capital of the building society may not fall. Under the EU directive, building societies will have to conform to an 8% risk assets ratio—most have ratios in the range 13–18%.

While there is no stated liquid assets ratio in the Act, the Commission has defined what counts as liquid assets: cash, bank deposits, central government paper, deposits at the Bank of England or National Savings Bank, treasury bills, some eligible commercial bills, certificates of deposits from banks and large corporates, and local authority loans and bills. The Commission

---

*All building societies in the UK are mutual organisations, meaning most of the funds in the building society are in the form of "share" accounts, which allocates one vote to the investor, independent of the value of the account. No dividends need be paid to shareholders. Operational changes in the building society require a two-thirds majority vote (not just of those who cast a vote) by shareholders.

[†]Prior to the 1986 Act, the main regulator of the society was the Registrar of Friendly Societies.

encourages societies to maintain liquidity levels above 15% of assets, though the Act stipulates the ratio is not to exceed 33.3%. The 1986 Act created an investor protection scheme, which gives 90% deposit insurance up to a limit of £20 000.00, so the element of co-insurance is smaller.

The Stock Exchange reforms, in place by 1986,* meant banks could purchase stockbroking firms because of the change in ownership rules, to allow non-members to own up to 100% of a member firm. Banks could participate directly in Stock Exchange activities, and other new Stock Exchange rules implied, for the first time, that firms could operate in a dual capacity, that is, act as market makers and broker dealers. Since the Banking Act did not restrict banks to either commercial or investment banking activities, the changes gave London a comparative advantage over New York and Tokyo.

The Financial Services Act (1986) was concerned primarily with putting in place adequate safeguards to protect investors. The Act set up a system such that non-banking financial activities (for example, stockbroking, insurance) would be regulated by *self-regulatory organisations* (SROs). The Securities and Investment Board (SIB), as the umbrella regulatory agency, has the responsibility for certifying SROs. Any firm which carries on financial activities designated by the Financial Services Act (dealing, managing, or advising on investments) must be a member of an SRO; in a few cases, the SIB grants direct authorisation.

The original SROs were FIMBRA (Financial Intermediaries, Managers, and Brokers Regulatory Association), AFBD (Association of Future Brokers and Dealers), TSA (The Securities Association), IMRO (Investment Managers Regulatory Association), and the PIA (Personal Investment Authority). The PIA was established in 1993, though in its early days it encountered difficulties attracting members. LAUTRO (Life Assurance and Unit Trust Regulatory Association) was dissolved after the PIA was formed. The Securities and futures Association (SFA) has absorbed FIMBRA, TSA and the AFBD. To qualify for membership a firm must be considered fit and proper, have adequate capital, and conform to set standards in the conduct of business. A compensation scheme operates for firms which are members of SROs and default. Claims up to £30 000 are met in full; for claims over this amount, there is a 10% co-insurance: up to a ceiling of £50 000, 90% of any claim is paid, thus giving a maximum protection of £48 000.

The question of *self-regulation* versus *external or public regulation* is important in financial markets, where customers often lack the information to properly assess the quality of the product on offer. The warning *caveat emptor*[†] does

---

*Reforms in the structure of the London Stock Exchange (now called the International Stock Exchange), began in 1982, when non-member ownership of member firms was increased to a limit of 29.9%, up from 10%. Dual capacity dealing in non-UK stocks was permitted after April, 1984; in 1986, it was permitted in domestic markets as well. In 1986, this rule was relaxed to allow non-members of the Stock Exchange to own up to 100% of a member firm. Later in 1986, new member firms were permitted, without having to buy into a member firm. Minimum commissions were abolished in March 1986.

[†]"Buyer beware".

not work very well in financial markets, especially in personal banking and finance. Those in favour of self-regulatory bodies argue self-regulators have an information advantage over public regulators and thus are the best judges of proper standards and rules of conduct for their members. A workable system of self-regulation which fails will cause a decline in the market's reputation and/ or government intervention. On the other hand, while self-regulators may draw up an impressive set of rules, they often lack the incentive to enforce them. Regulation by an external body is unlikely to experience serious enforcement problems, but they will suffer from a lack of information and could react by imposing excessively restrictive rules. Also, a public authority can exhibit signs of *regulatory forbearance* or *regulatory capture*, as demonstrated in the management of the US thrift crisis (see Chapter 7) and in the Bank of England's behaviour during the County NatWest scandal (see below). The UK is the best example of self-regulation of a major financial market, but it is still too early to judge the degree of success the system enjoys. The issue is an important one for modern British banks engaging in a wide range of financial activities, because in addition to having to meet Bank of England requirements, they are also required to belong to and satisfy the regulations of several SROs. In other countries, such as the USA, multi-function bank holding companies must satisfy several prudential regulators, and conform to standards and rules of conduct imposed by other public bodies.

PRUDENTIAL REGULATION IN THE UNITED STATES

As in the UK, the central bank and bank supervisory functions in the USA have evolved through time. However, there are four important differences between the two systems. First, US regulators have been far more inclined to seek statutory remedies in the event of a new problem, resulting in many more pieces of legislation. Second, protection of small depositors is of greater historical importance and has received more formal attention in the USA. Third, concern about potential collusion among banks has received as much weight in the USA as anxiety over the stability of the banking system. Fourth, the consensus approach to prudential regulation typical of the UK banking system has no US equivalent.

To gain an understanding of the current system of regulation, it is useful to consider the historical background on US banking legislation. However, given the numerous different statutory changes relevant to bank regulation, the review is best approached by considering the legislation under the following subject headings:

- creation of a central bank and bank supervision;
- deposit insurance;
- separation of commercial and investment banking;
- regulation of bank holding companies;
- regulation of branch banking;
- regulation of foreign banks;
- non-bank banks and bank products.

Creation of a Central Bank and Bank Supervision

The National Bank Act was passed in 1863 and amended in 1864. It outlined the power, duties and regulations covering national banks, which are federally chartered by the Comptroller of the Currency (an official in the US Treasury Department). *The Federal Reserve Act,* 1913, created a central bank for the US banking system, following panics over a number of banks and trust companies, which originated in New York, in October 1907. Concerns about other banks spread to different parts of the USA, causing banks to restrict payments in New York and in other states. The 1913 Act allowed the Federal Reserve Bank to provide an "elastic" currency, that is, to supply liquidity in the event of crises. In 1934, the Federal Reserve Bank (The Fed) was granted the authority to adjust its reserve requirements, independent of the legislators.*

In contrast to the UK, there has always been a great deal of concern that a central bank with a lender of last resort function could add to and/or encourage oligopolistic banking behaviour, going against the American philosophy of free competition in all industries, including banking. As a result, the Federal Reserve System (FRS) had a number of checks and balances built into it to discourage the development of cartel-like tendencies. The emphasis was on decentralisation; it is made up of 12 regional Federal Reserve Banks and a Board of Governors. The primary function of the Federal Reserve Bank is to pool the reserves of each of these banks.

The Federal Reserve System is one of several regulators in the US banking system. To operate as a bank, a firm must obtain a national or state charter, granted by either the Comptroller of the Currency or by a state official, usually called the Superintendent of Banks. The regulations that a bank is subject to depend on the origin of the charter. If it is a national charter, then the bank must join the Federal Reserve System and be subject to its regulations; membership is optional for state chartered banks. The regulations that apply to state chartered banks are historically less stringent than those that apply to national banks. In the 1980s, about 40% of banks were national banks but they held more than 75% of total deposits.

There are costs and benefits arising from membership of the Federal Reserve System (FRS). The costs are bank examination, conducted by officers from the Comptroller of the Currency at least three times every two years. Bank examiners use the CAMEL system to evaluate banks. Banks are scored on a scale of 1 (the best) to 5 (the worst) using five criteria: capital adequacy, asset quality, management quality, earnings' performance, and liquidity. A composite score is also produced. Banks with scores of 1 or 2 are considered satisfactory, but additional supervision is indicated if the score falls between 3 and 5. Banks with scores of 4 or 5 are closely monitored, and a composite score of 5 is a signal that examiners think the bank is likely to fail. The examinations are meant to prevent fraud and to ensure a bank is complying with the various

---

*This authority was part of The Glass-Steagall Banking Act, 1934, which is discussed in section 6.3.3, below. Friedman and Schwartz (1963) dispute the inelasticity of currency (p.168-173) during the panic.

rules and regulations related to its balance sheet and off-balance sheet holdings. For example, banks can be ordered to sell securities if they are considered to be too risky, or to write off dud loans. Bank examiners may declare a bank a "problem bank" if it is deemed to have insufficient capital, has too many weak loans, has an inefficient management, or is dishonest. Since the 1991 Federal Deposit Insurance Corporation Act (see below), regulators are obliged to take a well-defined set of actions if banks are deemed to be under-capitalised, or significantly or critically under-capitalised.

The Federal Reserve also has the authority to examine member banks, and the Federal Deposit Insurance Corporation has the right to examine insured banks. To avoid duplication, the Fed normally examines state member banks, the Comptroller of the Currency examines the national member banks, and the FDIC examines the non-member (of the FRS) insured banks.

Banks which are members of the Federal Reserve System must meet a *tier one capital assets or leverage* ratio of at least 5%.* The tier one capital assets or leverage ratio is different from the UK gearing ratio discussed earlier. It is defined as:

$$\frac{\text{a bank's core (tier one) capital (equity capital } + \text{ long-term funds)}}{\text{a bank's assets}}$$

The higher the ratio of capital to assets, the more secure is the bank. If a bank's capital ratio = 5% of its assets, then the bank can afford to lose 5% of these assets (for example, unsound loans) without undermining the bank's ability to repay its depositors. Only shareholders will lose.

For small banks, the main benefit derived from Federal Reserve membership used to be the ability to borrow from the Federal Reserve Bank, though this right has recently been extended to non-members and depository institutions that hold reserves at the Fed. Federal Reserve membership for larger banks means they can attract deposits from smaller banks, in a correspondent relationship. For all members, it confers an image of quality and reputation, because of the requirements to which all members must conform.

Over the years, piecemeal legislation has resulted in complex bank supervision in the USA, with a great deal of overlap between supervisory authorities. Table 18 summarises the various supervisory responsibilities.

In November 1993, the US Treasury Secretary, Lloyd Bentsen, proposed a reform of the law to create one federal agency responsible for the supervision of banks. The supervisory responsibilities of the Comptroller of the Currency, the Federal Reserve Board, the FDIC, and the Office of Thrift Supervision would be merged. The FDIC would focus solely on deposit insurance; the Federal Reserve Bank on monetary policy. State charters would be permitted but state banks would be subject to supervision by the state and national authorities. Alan Greenspan, the Fed Chairman, objected to the reform, mainly because he believe problems arising from financial instability cannot be divorced from monetary policy. The proposal died but the Treasury and the

---

*See pp. 234 for more detail.

Table 18 Bank Supervisory Responsibilities in the USA

Supervisors (year established)	Financial Institutions	Number	Assets ($ billions)
Office of Comptroller of the Currency (1863)	Federally Chartered Commercial Banks	3387	2060
Federal Reserve Board (1913)	Bank Holding Companies	6348	3261
	State chartered commercial banks which are members of the FED	957	638
Federal Deposit Insurance Corporation (1933)	State chartered commercial banks which are not FED members	6732	862
	Some state-chartered savings banks	578	221
Office of Thrift Supervision (1989)	Thrifts whose deposits are insured by the Savings Association Insurance Fund	1719	785
National Credit Union Administration (1970)	Federally insured credit unions	12 421	277

Source: *The Economist*, 5 March 1994: p.107.

Federal Reserve have been working together on a plan to consolidate banking regulation into two agencies.

Deposit Insurance

Deposit insurance has been an important component of the US system since the Federal Deposit Insurance Corporation (FDIC) was created after the *US Banking Act* (1933),* following losses arising from the massive bank failures that occurred in the years 1929–33. All member banks of the Federal Reserve System are required join the FDIC; non-members may join if they meet the FDIC admission criteria. Membership is important for any new bank, if it is to attract depositors, effectively giving the FDIC veto power over the formation of almost any new bank. Ninety-seven per cent of US banks, representing 99.8% of deposits, are insured by the FDIC.

FDIC member banks pay an insurance premium to the FDIC; the FDIC uses the premia to purchase securities, which provide it with a stream of revenue. With these funds, the FDIC insures deposits of up to $100 000. Initially, the FDIC was allowed to borrow up to $3 billion from the Treasury, but in the 1980s FDIC resources were seriously threatened because of the increase in bank failures, and for this reason the limit was raised by Congress (see below).

---

*Four sections of this Act were given the title the Glass–Steagall Banking Act.

From 1933 until very recently there was little in the way of debate in the USA about the need for deposit insurance. The US insurance scheme was devised with a view to protecting small depositors and preventing widespread runs by depositors on banks. It is argued that small depositors and middle-sized businesses are most inclined to initiate runs, because of the absence of detailed information about the quality of the bank, which is too costly for small depositors to obtain, even if the information is available. Unlike the UK, small depositors do not bear some of the cost of failure through co-insurance. Large depositors are expected to have the information necessary to make an informed judgement and to impose market discipline on the banks. However, runs are still possible; in the case of Continental Illinois, it was the very large depositors who withdrew their money first—they may have learned from the Penn Square failure in 1982, when they lost out because the FDIC allowed it to fail.*

Looking at US commercial bank failures as a percentage of healthy banks in the period 1934–91, the annual average was 0.38% from 1934–39 and did not rise above 0.08% between 1940 and 1981. In 1981 it jumped to 0.29%, rising steadily to peak at 1.68% in 1988.[†] The FDIC has tried to reduce demands on its insurance funds by merging problem banks with healthy banks; thus, *all* depositors turned out to be protected.

The Federal Savings and Loan Insurance Corporation (FSLIC), the insurance fund for the thrift industry, came under an even more serious threat and was declared insolvent in early 1987, because of the large number of thrift failures during the 1980s. Under the 1989 Financial Institutions Reform, Recovery, and Enforcement Act (FIRREA), the FSLIC was dissolved, as was its regulator, the Federal Home Loan Bank Board.[‡] Two new deposit funds were created, the Bank Insurance Fund and the Savings Association Insurance Fund (SAIF), to replace the dissolved FSLIC. These funds are supervised by the FDIC. The law also imposed higher deposit premiums for commercial banks and thrifts, to raise the reserves for the respective insurance funds. Under the Act, regulation of thrifts was tightened by creating the Office of Thrift Supervision, modelled after the Comptroller of the Currency. The Act also authorised $50 billion of government-backed bonds, to help pay off depositors at insolvent thrifts.

---

*Readers are referred to Chapter 7 and case study 7 (in Chapter 9) for detailed accounts of the collapse of Penn Square and Continental Illinois.
[†] See White (1992), Table 1.
[‡] In 1932, Congress passed the Federal Home Loan Bank Act. The Act created 12 Federal Home Loan Banks and the Federal Home Loan Bank Board (FHLBB) as their supervisory agent. The aim was to provide thrifts with an alternative source of funding for home mortgage lending. In 1933, the government became involved in the chartered savings and loans firms. The Home Owner's Loan Act was passed, and it authorised the Federal Home Loan Bank Board to charter and regulate the savings and loan associations. The National Housing Act, 1934, created a deposit insurance fund for savings and loan associations, the FSLIC. Unlike the FDIC, which was established as a separate organisation from the Federal Reserve System, the FSLIC was placed under the auspices of the FHLBB. Basic insurance coverage for S&L depositors is $100 000.00

The argument against a system of 100% deposit insurance is based on the moral hazard problem. Bank management will undertake greater risks than they otherwise would have, thus undermining the soundness of the bank, if they believe the bank will be bailed out with taxpayers' funds. Protected depositors have no incentive to monitor a bank's activities. The experience of widespread bank and thrift failures in the 1980s increased the pressure for reform of deposit insurance schemes.

In 1991, the *Federal Deposit Insurance Corporation Improvement Act* (FDICIA) was passed by Congress to reform the role of the FDIC. The Act requires the FDIC to use a "least cost" approach for resolving bank failures. Riskier banks are required to pay higher insurance premiums to the FDIC. The FDIC was to establish a system of risk-based deposit insurance premia, to be implemented not later than January 1994. There is also a requirement for regulators to take specific action if a bank falls out of the "well capitalised" group, defined below.

well capitalised
total risk assets ratio $\geq$ 10%
AND tier one risk assets ratio: $\geq$ 6%
AND tier one leverage: $\geq$ 5%

adequately capitalised
total risk assets ratio: $\geq$ 9%
AND tier one risk assets ratio: $\geq$ 4%
AND tier one leverage: $\geq$ 4%

under-capitalised
total risk assets ratio < 6%
OR tier one risk assets ratio < 4%
OR tier one leverage < 4%

significantly under-capitalised
total risk assets ratio < 6%
OR tier one risk assets ratio < 3%
OR tier one leverage < 3%

critically under-capitalised
equity: assets < 2%

Basis points are assigned to determine the premium rates, with eight points between the highest and lowest ratings. Risk classifications are kept confidential and based on supervisory evaluations, rather than credit ratings from private agencies. It is notable that banks wishing to be in one of the first two categories will have to conform to more stringent requirements than the 8% risk assets ratio laid down in the Basle accord. Under the Act, it is mandatory to appoint a receiver if the tier one leverage ratio is $\leq$2%. There is also a list of mandatory and discretionary actions which must be taken if any bank falls into a group below well capitalised. For example, brokered deposits* may only be taken by well capitalised banks, and, subject to FDIC approval, by adequately capitalised banks.

These reforms are designed to reduce moral hazard problems by computing deposit insurance premia on a risk-related basis, thereby effectively curbing bank risk-taking. It is hoped that the "least cost" requirement will expose depositors to greater risks than was true in the past, which, in turn, should increase their incentive to monitor bank activities. However, explicit co-insurance continues to be absent.

Another proposal to combat the problems created by deposit insurance is to limit coverage to *narrow banking* activities. Insurance, with no upper limit, would be available only if deposits are used for transactions purposes; a minimum level of non-transactions deposits, of about $25 000. Banks would have to invest these liabilities in safe government bills and top-rated commercial paper. Any other activities undertaken by banks would not be covered by deposit insurance. Effectively, this would mean banks could become financial conglomerates, but without the special protection of insurance, except for their transactions-related deposit business.

Separation of Commercial and Investment Banking

The *Glass-Steagall Banking Act* (1933)[†] separated commercial banking from investment banking, thus limiting the number of financial products these types of banks could offer. Under the Act, commercial banks had their securities functions severely curtailed; they were limited to underwriting and dealing in municipal government debt. Investment banks can engage in securities and underwriting, but are prohibited from taking deposits. The objective was to reduce the degree of collusion in the banking sector. It was argued that if a bank could hold a firm's equity and underwrite its securities, there would be great potential for collusion between bank and customer. There was also a belief that separation of commercial and investment banking would prevent another financial crisis arising from the large number of bank failures between 1929 and 1933.[‡]

---

*Brokered deposits are deposits of wealthy individuals (or even institutional investors) which are spread among banks by deposit brokers, to take advantage of the deposit insurance scheme, which operates per bank. In the 1980s, relatively weak banks used relatively high deposit rates to attract these deposits as a means of raising funds, because of their inability to attract funds from the wholesale markets.

[†]The formal title for this Act is the US Banking Act (1933); the four sections of the Act (16,20,21,and 22) dealing with the separation of commercial and investment banking are known as the Glass-Steagall Act.

[‡]The latter point is controversial. Recent evidence suggests the absence of a division between commercial and investment banking had little to do with widespread US bank failures in this period. White (1986) was able to show that banks engaged in securities activities actually had a lower rate of failure than banks without a securities arm. Benston (1990) suggests that there is no evidence of securities being mishandled by banks in this period.

There is pressure to repeal the Glass-Steagall Banking Act. In June 1991 a key House of Representatives Committee (considering a Banking Reform Bill) voted in favour of breaking down barriers between banking and commerce. But most aspects of this legislation collapsed in November 1991. In October 1993 Lloyd Bentsen, the Treasury Secretary, set out an agenda for banking reform. The plan was far less comprehensive than what had been proposed in 1991. The Clinton administration would support the Fair Trade in Financial Services Bill, which like the European Community's second banking directive, will limit foreign bank operations in the US to the extent that their own system is closed to American banks. The Bentsen agenda did not call for a repeal of Glass-Steagall (in contrast to 1991), but did support reforms for interstate banking (see below).

However, at the mid-term elections held in November 1994, Republicans took control of the House and Senate Committees responsible for legislation to reform the banking and securities sector. The Chairman of the House banking committee (Mr Leach) has stated that his top priority is to repeal Glass-Steagall, to allow banks to engage in investment and commercial banking. In March 1995 Robin Rubin, the Treasury Secretary in the Clinton cabinet, put forward a plan for repealing Glass-Steagall. There are three different proposals for reform. Mr Leach suggested bank holding companies be allowed to own separate banking and securities subsidiaries, but insurance firms would not be allowed to own banks. Mr Rubin would allow banks direct ownership of securities firms; insurance firms could own or be owned by banks. Senator Alfonse D'Amato of New York supports the Rubin proposals but thinks banks should be allowed to own non-financial firms. A repeal of Glass-Steagall is implicit in all three of the proposals. At the time of writing, it appears that this Act will finally be repealed, though similar circumstances have prevailed in the past, only to see the reform bills die in Congress.

Technology and other pressures mean the boundary between commercial and investment banking is gradually being eroded. Investment banks have been able to enter retail banking through money market funds, cash management accounts, and through non-bank banks, though the latter have been terminated through new legislation (see below). Commercial banks have moved into the private placement, corporate finance, and commercial paper markets, through bank holding company subsidiaries which are investment banks in all but name. The Federal Reserve permitted commercial bank subsidiaries to underwrite commercial paper, municipal bonds, and securities (backed by consumer debt or mortgages) and sell stocks and bonds, provided the affiliate earns no more than 10% of its gross revenue from these activities. The Supreme Court (1988) ruled this was not a violation of Glass-Steagall because the underwriting firms affiliated to banks do not engage in it as their "principal" activity. Furthermore, the option of using London subsidiaries for investment banking purposes is still available. Banks have also expanded into the insurance business. Perhaps the greatest pressure will be competitive, from universal banks in Europe.

Regulation of Bank Holding Companies (BHCs)

Until the 1960s, bank holding companies were a minor part of the US banking scene, controlling about 15% of total bank deposits. By the 1990s, 92% of banks were owned by BHCs. They became popular in the 1950s as banks found they could establish a bank holding company to circumvent the regulations: only wholly owned banking subsidiaries were required to conform to banking regulations.

The *Bank Holding Company Act*, 1956, defined a BHC as any firm holding at least 25% of the voting stock of a bank subsidiary. It required BHCs to be registered with the Federal Reserve Board. The purpose of the Act was to restrict BHC activity that had not been subject to the usual regulations. However, it actually enhanced the growth of BHCs, because it gave them legal status.

There were several reasons for BHC growth. One was to circumvent the interstate branching laws, via "multi-bank" holding companies. The BHC organisational framework also meant banks could diversify into non-bank financial activities such as credit card operations, mortgage lending, data processing, investment management advice and discount brokerage. However, they have not been permitted to engage in certain financial businesses (for example, securities) excluded by Glass-Steagall, or in businesses not closely related to banking, as specified in the regulations. Tax avoidance is another reason why BHCs are attractive; interest paid on BHC debt is a tax deductible expense, dividends from subsidiaries are a tax exempt source of revenue for BHCs, and non-banking subsidiaries may avoid local taxes.

The Amendment (1970) to the 1956 Act increased control of the Federal Reserve over BHCs, which in turn tried to limit BHC activity to banking products, rather than non-banking financial activities. However, the bank holding company structure continued to expand, with BHCs seeking acquisition of other domestic and overseas banks. In 1989, the Federal Reserve began to require that state banks which are part of a BHC to obtain approval to operate any business which is a subsidiary of the bank. It imposed this rule because in a BHC structure, there are two alternatives for business subsidiaries: a BHC with state bank subsidiaries, which in turn have separately incorporated subsidiaries or a BHC with business subsidiaries. If a business was a subsidiary of a state bank, as opposed to the BHC, the affiliated business was implicitly protected by the Deposit Protection Scheme and more generally, the federal safety net (for example, the practice of selling off, rather than liquidating a failing bank to the highest bidder, with FDIC support). Such protection gave the business subsidiary an edge over its competitors. Under the new requirement, the Federal Reserve can be sure the federal safety net does not apply to the non-bank activities.

Branch Banking Regulations

To discourage concentration, the USA has always imposed restrictions on branch banking, unlike most of the other banking systems in the industrialised world. This was seen as one means of offsetting the oligopolistic tendencies arising from a regulated sector. The *McFadden Act* (1927) permitted branching for national banks but required them to obey state branching regulations, hence the proliferation of different rules with regard to interstate and intrastate banking. The *Douglas Amendment of the Bank Holding Company Act* (1956) gave each state the ultimate authority to approve entry by out-of-state banks. Under the *Bank Merger Act* (1960), which set out guidelines for mergers between federally insured banks, individual states were given the final say on expansion of out-of-state banks.

Interstate branching has always been permitted in the USA, subject to an important qualification—banks were not allowed to open branches in other states to collect retail deposits. By the late 1980s, many states had either passed legislation, or were about to, to permit some form of interstate branching. For example, in the 1980s and 1990s most states agreed to allow out-of-state bank entry through the merger of healthy BHCs with unsound local banks and thrifts. Guidelines for mergers were set out in the *Bank Merger Act* (1960), an example of where concern for soundness of the banking system received priority over anxiety about concentration of economic power. The Banking Reform Bill, which died in Congress in 1991, had proposed allowing banks to branch across state borders to promote a sounder industry. However, as of December 1993, all states (plus the District of Columbia) except Hawaii permitted their banks to be acquired by out-of-state bank holding companies, though a few continue to allow it only on a reciprocal basis. Some states permit banks to branch across state lines. In Arizona, Nevada, and Washington, 80–90% of banking assets are controlled by non-local BHCs.

The 1993 Bentsen agenda for banking reform proposed allowing banks to convert their existing multi-bank or multi-state operations into a single bank with branches. The *Riegle-Neal Interstate Banking and Branching Efficiency Act*, 1994* changed the Bank Holding Company Act to allow adequately capitalised and well managed BHCs to acquire banks in other states. From 1995, BHCs can acquire or establish a bank anywhere in the country, regardless of state law. From June 1997, federal banking agencies may approve applications from BHCs to consolidate their multi-state operations and branch interstate. States wishing to opt out of the new interstate branching must pass legislation to this effect by 1 June 1997, and the clause must apply to both state and national banks. States opting in must pass legislation to allow interstate branching for their state banks. State laws requiring out-of-state BHCs to enter by acquisition only will continue to apply, though banks may acquire just a branch rather than a whole bank. Also, states can pass a law to prevent *de novo* branching (that is, the setting up of new branches from scratch) by out-of-state banks. To discourage excessive bank concentration, the Act limits a BHC to 10% of national insured deposits, and 30% of insured deposits within the state, though states can waive the 30% limit. In the case of a failing or failed bank,

---

*This interpretation of the Act was taken from a special edition of the *CSBS Examiner*, a weekly report from the Conference of State Bank Examiners—EC Lamb, editor, September, 1994.

the FDIC may arrange for acquisition without regard to these restrictions. BHCs will continue to be subject to all federal and state anti-trust laws. The Federal Reserve will have a final say over interstate bank acquisitions. Banks within a BHC can act as agents for each other, receiving deposits, renewing time deposits, accepting payments, closing and servicing loans, and providing services to customers of affiliate banks. The limited reforms appeal to the insurance companies, threatened by the proliferation of bank branches. The insurance lobby was largely responsible for the failure of the 1991 Bill.

Prior to these recent reforms, banks could effectively escape some of the interstate banking restrictions. "Loan production" offices were established, to arrange business loans; deposits by borrowing firms were also permitted. Banks set up "Edge Act" branches located in other states. The *Edge Act* (1919) allowed banks to establish out-of-state subsidiaries, provided deposits accepted and loans made by these subsidiaries were related to international finance. These banks are regulated by the Federal Reserve Board. Financial innovation and technology also eroded the ability of states to control the entry of out-of-state banks. For example, ATM networks meant branching restrictions could be bypassed.

A status report by the Federal Reserve (1993) concluded that while interstate banking increased the concentration of deposits at national level, local banking markets had not become more concentrated. A study of the response of bank holding company stock returns to changes in interstate banking laws over the period 1964–89 concluded that interstate banking tends to enhance actual or potential competition in state banking markets.*

Intrastate branching has, historically, been restricted in some states, but the interstate branching reform has made them redundant. It has been argued that at the local level, these restrictions added to the monopoly power of banks located in small cities. However, empirical evidence suggests that the easing of branch banking laws does not necessarily erode local monopoly power since banks frequently enter a new market by merging with an existing bank rather than starting up rival branches. On the other hand, in the absence on branching restrictions in California, small banks have been able to coexist alongside major branch systems.

Regulation of Foreign Banks

The main objective of The *International Banking Act* (1978) was to level the playing field between domestic banks and foreign banks operating in the US market. Prior to the Act, foreign banks had been subject to a patchwork of different regulations, which in certain areas gave them a competitive advantage over domestic banks. Foreign banks were not required to meet Federal Reserve reserve requirements on liabilities. Nor were they covered by the 1927 McFadden Act, so they could establish branches across state boundaries. They were also exempt from the Glass-Steagall and Bank Holding Company

*See Laderman and Pozdena (1991).

Acts (including the 1970 amendments) and could engage in activities closed to domestic banks, such as the sale of equities and underwriting. However, foreign banks were ineligible for FDIC insurance and denied access to FRS facilities such as cheque collection and the discount window, thereby inhibiting entry into the retail banking markets.

Under the 1978 Act each foreign bank is required to designate one state as its home state; deposits from outside the state were restricted to international banking and finance. Foreign banks are prohibited from acquiring banking offices outside their home state. The 1994 Riegle-Neal Interstate Banking and Branching Efficiency Act allowed foreign banks to engage in interstate branching but by acquisition only, unless a state has passed a law to allow all out-of-state banks to open *de novo* branches within the state.

Reserve requirements were imposed on all federal and state licensed foreign bank branches and agencies whose parent had more than $1 billion in international assets, thereby covering virtually all foreign banks in the USA. FDIC insurance was made mandatory for all foreign banks that accepted deposits. However, the Act allows foreign banks to apply for a federal charter, thereby gaining access to federal services such as cheque collection and clearing. Investment and non-banking activities of the foreign banks were made subject to the Bank Holding Company Act and the Glass-Steagall Acts. Finally, the Act introduced a reciprocity principle for foreign bank entry; foreign banks are only permitted to enter US banking markets to the degree that US banks are allowed entry into the foreign market.

In 1991, the *Foreign Bank Enforcement Supervision Act* was passed to establish uniform federal standards for entry and expansion of foreign banks in the USA. The Act was designed to expand the supervisory powers of the Federal Reserve over foreign banks, in response to their rapid growth. When the International Banking Act was passed in 1978, there were 122 foreign banks with US offices, accounting for $90 billion in assets. Japanese and British banks are the key foreign operators in both wholesale and retail banking. By 1991, there were 280 foreign banks, with assets amounting to $626 billion, 18% of total banking assets. These banks had 565 offices, the majority of which were state-licensed. Essentially, the Act ensures that foreign bank operations are regulated, supervised, and examined in the same way as home country banks. For example, foreign banks wanting to set up state licensed branches or agencies must obtain approval from the Federal Reserve Board, and are subject to examination and supervision by the Board.*

US banking activities overseas are regulated by the Federal Reserve. US banks are required to seek permission to open foreign branches, and may only invest in foreign banks through bank holding companies. Edge Act corporations can invest in financial activities such as leasing, trust businesses, insurance, data processing, securities, and dealing in money market funds.

In the 1970s, the Federal Reserve began to allow establishment of *International Banking Facilities* (IBFs) by US banks. IBFs may accept foreign

_____

*For more detail, see *Federal Reserve Bulletin* (1993).

deposits and make foreign loans without being subject to reserve requirements or interest ceilings, provided the transactions exceed $100 000. The objective of introducing IBFs was to bring offshore business back to the US. However, a minimum term of 48 hours for IBF deposits has discouraged their growth.

Regulation of Non-Bank Banks and Bank Products

Non-bank banks were financial firms that accepted deposits and which required notice of withdrawal. Since a bank was defined as an institution that accepted deposits payable on demand and made loans, these firms could escape banking regulations and interstate branching restrictions. The *Competitive Equality Banking Act* (1987) prohibited the formation of non-bank banks. Non-bank banks in existence prior to the Act are permitted to continue, though their activities have been curtailed.

The US also has a history of regulating the type of retail deposits that banks can offer their customers. However, with rapid financial innovation from the late 1970s onward, the authorities recognised it would be difficult to continue such restrictions. The *Depository Institutions Deregulation and Monetary Control Acts*, 1980 (DIDMCA) were only partly concerned with prudential regulation. The DID committee (consisting of the secretary of the Treasury and heads of the federal agencies regulating depository institutions) was instructed to phase out Regulation Q* by 1986. It allowed banks to offer NOW[†] accounts, set aside a court decision that had invalidated automatic transfer accounts and remote terminals of savings and loan associations, eased restrictions on mortgage loans of thrifts (these firms were given permission to invest up to 20% of their assets in consumer loans, commercial loans and corporate securities) and eliminated state usury law ceilings on mortgage loans. For a three-year period, other usury ceilings were allowed to fluctuate with the Federal discount rate.

The Act also lowered reserve requirements, though they were extended to cover all transactions accounts (demand credit balance accounts) and non-personal time deposits. The Fed was given authority over reserve requirements of all deposit-taking institutions, even if they are not part of the Federal

---

*Under Regulation Q, the Federal Reserve Bank could set ceilings on interest rates offered on savings and time deposits. No interest could be paid on demand deposits. This gave thrifts a competitive edge over commercial banks because they were allowed to pay 0.25% more interest than commercial banks. It was responsible for the growth of new financial products, such as NOW accounts, money market mutual funds, and sweep accounts. By the time of this Act, Regulation Q had become ineffective. The prohibition of interest on demand deposits dates from the Glass-Steagall Banking Act, 1933.

[†]NOW accounts are negotiable order of withdrawal accounts. They were first introduced by savings banks in Massachusetts and New Hampshire in 1972, but their legal status was uncertain because they paid interest on demand deposits, which violated the Federal Reserve Regulation Q. DIDMCA also authorised banks to continue with automatic transfer services for shifting funds from savings to chequing accounts. For a detailed account of DIDMCA, see Federal Reserve Bank of Chicago (1980).

Reserve System. The Federal Reserve must charge for its services, but can extend its lending facilities to all depository institutions holding reserves. DIDMCA also raised the deposit insurance ceiling to $100 000, from $40 000.

Under the (*Garn-St.Germain*) *Depository Institutions Act* (1982), depository institutions were allowed to offer money market accounts at an interest rate competitive with money market funds. From the beginning of 1984, Regulation Q was to be the same for depository institutions as for banks. The FDIC and FSLIC were given expanded powers to merge failing savings and loans with sound ones, across state lines or with banks. The Act allowed troubled savings and loans to obtain interest-free loans from the FSLIC, unless they had positive net earnings. These new powers proved to be temporary, and disappeared with two new Acts already discussed, FIRREA (1989) and FDICA (1991). With the benefit of hindsight, it is now acknowledged that giving the insurance corporations these powers contributed to the problem of *regulatory forbearance*, which is discussed in more detail in Chapter 7.

PRUDENTIAL REGULATION IN THE EUROPEAN UNION

January 1993 was an important date in the European calendar because completion of the internal market was to be achieved through the removal of all impediments to free trade in goods, services, labour and capital across European frontiers, including free trade in financial services and equal access to financial markets. In Chapter 3, the structural implications of a single, integrated European banking and financial markets were discussed. Here, the objective is to consider the key regulatory and prudential issues for an EU financial market, with special emphasis on the banking market. There are several differences in the prudential regulation of banks across European countries. Minimum capital requirements are highly variable, ranging from ECU 1.18 million in Belgium, to ECU 16.28 million in Italy.* Equally, deposit protection schemes vary considerably. Luxembourg offers coverage equivalent to ECU 11520, while Italy's is as high as ECU 662 000. Some countries, such as the UK and Italy, have an element of co-insurance. Germany operates a completely different system, whereby depositors receive 30% of a bank's liable capital. There is a wide safety net in some EU countries because the authorities have not permitted any bank failures, which raises the question of whether a deposit insurance scheme is necessary. French and German banks are required to satisfy explicit liquidity requirements; in other states, liquidity is monitored.

The degree to which EU banks are universal varies widely. In France, Germany and Spain they are universal. In Italy, banks are not permitted to hold shares, while France, Germany and Spain do permit some equity participation, which is substantial in Germany. The Bank of England strongly discourages British banks from taking equity holdings in non-financial firms and the securities arm of a bank is a separate subsidiary. Non-financial firms

---

*Source: OECD (1987).

are allowed to own banks in Belgium, France, and Germany, but not in Italy, and only up to 20% of a bank's equity in Spain.

The move to monetary union with a European central bank would largely resolve the issue of monetary control. A European central bank and single market set the stage for an integrated European banking system.* However, though many directives have been passed, there are still gaps and inconsistencies in proposals for prudential regulation. Below, the various key directives are outlined, followed by a discussion of the potential for problems arising from the current arrangements.

The main directive applicable to the banking industry is the *Second Banking Directive* (1989), which was to be implemented by member countries by January 1993. It follows the *First Banking Directive* (1977), which defined a "credit institution" as any firm making loans and accepting deposits. The First Directive also set up a Bank Advisory Committee, and called for harmonisation of bank regulation, without specifying how it was to be achieved. The Second Banking Directive, like all directives passed since the Single European Act (1986), attempts to bring about a single banking market through mutual recognition rather than harmonisation.[†]

The Second Banking Directive gave EU credit institutions a "passport"[‡] to offer the same service anywhere in the EU, without having to seek authority from the host state, but subject to the constraint that it offers the service in the home state. The financial services covered by the directive include:

- deposit-taking;
- other forms of funding;
- lending;
- money transmission services;
- financial leasing;
- securities issues;
- traveller's cheques, credit cards, other means of payments;
- securities, derivatives, and foreign exchange trading;
- money broking;
- portfolio management and advice;

---

*The single market extended to the European Free Trade Association countries which joined the European Economic Area in May 1992, that is, Austria, Finland, Iceland, Liechtenstein, Norway, and Sweden. Switzerland is the only EFTA country which did not join the EEA. In 1995, Austria, Finland and Sweden became full members of the EU.

[†] By the principle of "mutual recognition" the European Commission devises minimum standards in the formulation of directives (EU laws); if a firm operating in one EU state meets these standards, it has a right to operate in any other EU state. Harmonisation was an attempt to have the same rules of operation for all EU states, but it was abandoned (because it proved extremely difficult to pass directives) with the Single European Act. The SEA also introduced qualified majority voting for directives. All directives, with the exception of those related to fiscal matters, are passed by the European Council of Ministers, using a system of qualified majority voting.

[‡] The term 'EC passport' was first coined by the Bank of England (1993).

- safekeeping and administration of securities;
- credit reference services;
- safe custody services.

Prior to the Second Directive, entry of banks into other member states was hampered because the bank supervisors in the host country had to approve the operation, and it was subject to host country supervision and laws. Some countries required foreign branches to provide extra capital as a condition of entry. These constraints have been removed. The directive also specifies that the home country where a bank is headquartered is responsible for solvency of that bank and any branches located elsewhere in the Community. It is the home country which decides whether or not a bank should be liquidated, but there is some provision for the host country to intervene. Branches are not required to publish separate accounts, in line with the emphasis on consolidated supervision. Host country regulations will apply to risk management and implementation of monetary policy, though the latter will shift to the European central bank when and if it becomes operational.

The Second Banking Directive imposes a minimum capital (equity) requirement of ECU 5 million on all credit institutions. Supervisory authorities must be notified of any major shareholders with equity in excess of 10% of a bank's equity. If a bank has equity holdings in a non-financial firm exceeding 10% of the firm's value and 60% of the bank's capital, it is required to deduct the holding from the bank's capital.

The Second Banking Directive also contains articles to deal with third country banks, that is, banks headquartered in a country outside the EU. Essentially, the principle of *equal treatment* is to apply: the EU has the right to either suspend new banking licences or negotiate with the third country if EU financial firms find themselves at a competitive disadvantage because foreign and domestic banks are treated differently (for example, two sets of banking regulations apply) by the host country government. In 1992, a European Commission report acknowledged inferior treatment of EU banks in some countries, but seemed to favour using the World Trade Organisation to sort out disputes, rather than exercising the powers of suspension.

The *Own Funds Directive* (1989), which defines what is to count as capital, and the *Solvency Ratio Directive* (1989), which requires a risk assets ratio of 8%, came into effect in 1993. These directives are consistent with the Basle capital adequacy requirements but are legally enforceable in the EU, and apply to all credit institutions in the EU, not just international banks.

The *Large Exposures Directive* (1992) came into effect in January 1994. Regulations covering exposure of financial firms to individual borrowers or groups of connected clients are to be harmonised. The directive applies on a consolidated basis for credit institutions in the EU. Exposures of 10% or more of a bank's funds must be reported and no bank may have an exposure to one borrower or related group of more than 25%. Exposure to one borrower or group of borrowers is limited to 40% of a bank's funds. The total of a bank's large exposures may not exceed eight times the size of its own funds.

Exceptions include exposures to other banks and exposures accompanied by certain types of collateral. Transitional arrangements may mean that full implementation is unlikely to occur until 2001.

The *Money Laundering Directive* (1991) came into effect in 1993. Money laundering is defined to include either handling or aiding the handling of assets, knowing they are the result of a serious crime, such as terrorism or illegal drug activities. It applies to credit and financial institutions in the EU—they are obliged to disclose suspicions of such activities, and to introduce the relevant internal controls and staff training to detect money laundering.

The *Deposit Insurance Directive* (1993) is an attempt to impose a minimum level of deposit insurance of 20 000 ECU for all EU member states. The objective is to protect depositors and discourage bank runs. Branch depositors are to be protected by the home member state, but branches will have the option of joining the host country scheme, if it is more generous than that of the home country. However, if home country insurance is larger than a host country scheme, the branch in the host country will not be allowed to exceed the limit of insurance for host country banks. For non-EU branches, the host country will decide whether or not they may join the insurance scheme. The directive will apply to foreign exchange deposits. Individual EU states will determine how the scheme is to be run. Some alternative schemes offered by, for example, savings banks, will be considered equivalent to that required by this directive. The draft was accepted by the Council of Ministers in September, 1993, by qualified majority—Germany voted against. Apart from an optional 10% co-insurance, no attempt has been made to deal with the potential for moral hazard arising from the scheme.

There is also a proposed *Credit Institution Winding Up Directive*, whereby the home country supervisor will have the authority to close a credit institution, and the host country will accept the decision.

The *Capital Adequacy Directive* (1993), is to come into effect in January 1996, and will mean that trading exposures (for example, market risk) arising from investment business will be subject to separate minimum capital requirements. To ensure a level playing field, securities firms and banks will have to conform to the same capital requirements. Banks with securities arms must classify their assets as belonging to either a trading book or a banking book. Firms will be required to set aside 2% of the gross value of the portfolio, plus 8% of the net value. However, banks will have to conform to the risk assets ratio as well, which means more capital will have to held against bank loans than securities with equivalent risk. For example, mortgage-backed securities will have a lower capital requirement than mortgages appearing on a bank's balance sheet. Thus, banks will have an incentive to increase their securities operations at the expense of traditional lending, creating a potential for distortion in the market place.

There have been two Consolidated Supervision Directives (1983, 1992). The original directive was passed in 1983 but this was replaced by a new directive in 1992, to take effect in January, 1993. It applies to the EU parents of a financial institution and the financial subsidiaries of parents where the group undertakes what are largely financial activities. The threshold for consolidation is 20% of capital, that is, the EU parent or credit institution owns 20% or more of the capital of the subsidiaries.

The *Investment Services Directive* (1993) is to take effect by January 1996. The objective was to prevent regulatory differences giving a competitive edge to banks or securities firms. It is to apply to all firms providing professional investment services. The core investment products covered include transferable securities, unit trusts, money market instruments, financial futures contracts, forwards, swaps, and options. The directive also ensures cross-border access to trading systems. A number of clauses do not apply if a firm holds a banking passport but also meets the definition of an investment firm.

Three other directives are relevant to the operations of some EU banks. The *UCITS (Undertakings for the Collective Investment of Transferable Securities) Directive* (1985) took effect in all EU states in 1989, except for Greece and Portugal, where it was to be implemented by April 1992. Unit trust schemes authorised in one member state may be marketed in other member states. Under UCITS, 90% of a fund must be invested in publicly traded firms and the fund cannot own more than 5% of the outstanding shares of a company. *Insurance directives* for life assurance and non-life insurance have been drafted three times. These directives will create an EU passport for insurance firms, by July 1994.* The first *Pension Funds Directive* is under negotiation, but should allow a pension fund in one member state to choose an investment manager from any EU state; it will be possible to invest funds anywhere in the Union.

This review of the current state of prudential regulation in the EU reveals that, as in the USA, many statutes have been enacted. However, unlike the USA, the legislation has not been introduced on an *ad hoc* basis to deal with problems as they arise. Instead, the objective of the directives is to bring about a single competitive banking and financial market in the EU. It is too early to say whether or not the goal of competition will actually be achieved, though it is worth noting that the wholesale banking markets are already highly competitive because of the global operations in London.

The European Commission's *micro* objective of achieving a single financial market, and its *macro* goal of a single currency and a European central bank, have left gaps in the area of EU prudential regulation. If greater competition is created by a single market and intra-marginal banks fail, the failures could pose a threat to the stability of the EU financial system via the usual contagion effects. On the other hand, the easing up of capital flows and the directives on unit trusts and pension funds should give all EU banks a greater opportunity to diversify their systematic risks, thereby reducing the probability of failure.

As the situation currently stands, it is the regulators in the home country who have responsibility for ensuring bank solvency. However if a decision is taken to bail out a failing bank or to use lender of last resort facilities, the liquidity implications mean the ECB will have to be involved. To date, there is no proposal that the ECB should have a lender of last resort function; its sole

---

*For more detail on the Insurance directives, see the Bank of England (1993: p.96).

concern is with ensuring price stability within the EU. Thus, there is a real potential for conflict between the state central banks and the ECB. If the ECB does end up with LLR responsibilities, it is likely to insist on a role in the supervision of EU banks. A proliferation of supervisory bodies within the EU could ensue, as happened in the USA.

As in the USA, EU deposit insurance is aimed at the protection of small depositors. However, as the next chapter demonstrates, there are many cases where large depositors have contributed to a bank run. Furthermore, the potential for moral hazard is great because there is no requirement that EU states impose risk-adjusted premiums on banks to fund their respective schemes. Optional co-insurance will mean depositors have little incentive to monitor banks' activities. It is also questionable whether any scheme is necessary, when some EU states are known to intervene before a bank fails, so that depositors never lose out.

REGULATION OF BANKS IN JAPAN

In Japan, the Ministry of Finance (MOF) is the principal supervisory authority over the financial system, and the Bank of Japan (BJ) fills the other functions of a central bank, that is, the implementation of monetary policy and acting as a banker for commercial banks and the government. The MOF regulates the financial markets through a Banking Bureau, a Securities Bureau, and the International Finance Bureau. Through these bureaux the MOF controls interest rates* on deposit accounts (unless these are held in postal savings[†]), examines financial institutions, supervises the deposit insurance scheme, licenses financial institutions, rules on acceptable international and domestic financial activities for financial firms, and formulates financial policy. Similar to the Bank of England's "moral suasion", the MOF does not depend exclusively on statutes to enforce regulations but instead uses "regulatory guidance", a MOF interpretation of the laws, conveyed to practitioners.

The Bank of Japan engages in financial transactions with all types of financial institutions, not just banks, is the primary regulator of the interbank market, and implements monetary policy. It is consulted on most regulatory decisions taken by the MOF. The MOF and BJ conduct on-site examinations of all financial institutions every other year, meaning all firms are subject to external scrutiny once a year.

After the Second World War, some components of the Glass-Steagall Act were exported to Japan. Japan's Article 65 of the 1948 Securities and Exchange Law restricts banks from engaging in the securities business, defined as the buying and selling of securities or acting as an intermediary, broker or agent

---

*The long history of interest rate controls in Japan ended in October 1994, when the last of the deposit rates was fully deregulated.
[†]Postal savings rates are set by the Ministry of Posts and Telecommunications. Usually these rates are higher than those set by private banks.

with respect to the trading of securities, underwriting securities, the secondary distribution of securities, and handling the public offering of new or outstanding securities. Articles 10 and 11 of the 1981 (revised) Banking Law confirmed that banks could underwrite and trade in government (including local government) bonds and debentures. Since 1987, banks have been permitted to be fully active in the government bond market.

Unlike Glass-Steagall, Article 65 has not been effective in excluding banks from operating in the securities business, in three important respects. First, securities firms do underwrite bond issues in the Japanese system, but banks are also involved because of the system of "commissioned underwriting", which means banks may act as financial advisors on an issue, be responsible for the preparatory groundwork, receive and deliver proceeds, and act as trustee with a responsibility for ensuring any security is kept safe until the bond is redeemed. Second, Japanese banks are permitted to purchase corporate stocks and shares for their investment account. Thus, unlike their US counterparts, Japanese banks may have unlimited holdings of equities in corporations and are able to purchase new issues of firms with close business connections. Third, in Article 65, there is no equivalent of the Glass-Steagall Act which prevents US banks from being associated, in any way, with securities firms. The Anti-Monopoly Law in Japan does restrict Japanese bank holdings to no more than 5% in another company, including securities firms, but banks have circumvented this law through cross-shareholdings in other companies, which effectively gives them control in securities firms. For example, Fuji Bank is affiliated with Daito Securities, Sumitomo Bank with Meiko Securities, and Tokai Bank with Maruman Securities. However, banks continue to be excluded from market making and distribution of corporate securities.

In 1988, the MOF instructed Japanese banks to limit their ownership of securities firms to less than 50%, and to ensure separate management of the parent bank and securities affiliates. Foreign banks have been permitted to own 50% of a securities branch in Japan since June 1986. Since December 1986, American commercial banks have been allowed to apply for securities dealing licences: the number of foreign-held licences stands at 46, including four US commercial banks.

In 1995, there were some early indications that the Ministry of Finance and Bank of Japan might be reversing their long-standing policy of preventing any failures by forcing healthy and troubled banks to merge. The Bank of Japan in particular has suggested that some banks should be allowed to fail, at the taxpayers' expense. However, it is unclear whether the reversal of policy is permanent—it has been met with hostility by the public.

INTERNATIONAL COORDINATION OF PRUDENTIAL REGULATION

The growth of international banking, especially the spread of multinational banks, has brought the issue of prudential regulation across borders to the fore. It is important not only for regulators and policy-makers, but for bank managers, because of potential threats to the stability of the international financial system, and therefore the environment in which all banks operate. It is sometimes argued that international banking is largely wholesale, making prudential regulation less important from the standpoint of consumer protection, depending as it does on interbank and corporate business. However, the performance of a global bank will affect the confidence of depositors and investors located in the home country. Unprotected wholesale depositors are capable of starting bank runs, and the enormous size of the interbank market means the potential for a rapid domino effect is great.

If a branch of a bank is located in another country, there is the important question of which supervisory authority should have jurisdiction over the branch. Home country regulators will want to ensure a bank's overseas operations meet their supervisory standards because foreign operations will affect the performance of the parent. But any home country supervisory effort might be hampered by the absence of any physical presence in the foreign country. Host country authorities are concerned with the effect the failure of a foreign bank could have on the confidence in its banking system. They will want to see the foreign branch operating under adequate supervision, but will lack information about the parent operations. For these reasons, effective international coordination will only be achieved if there is good communication between the supervisory authorities.

The Basle Committee

Two major international bank failures in 1974 (Bankhaus Herstatt and Franklin National Bank*) resulted in the formation of a standing committee of bank supervisory authorities, consisting of the central bank governors of the G-10 countries plus Luxembourg and Switzerland. The main purpose of the Basle Committee is to consider regulatory issues related to activities of international banks in member countries. Their objective is to prevent any international banking operation from escaping effective supervision. Several concordats and agreements have been reached by the members.

The *1975 Basle Concordat* was the first agreement. The supervision of foreign branches or subsidiaries of banks was to be the joint responsibility of the authorities in the parent and host countries. The supervision of liquidity would be the primary responsibility of the host country. Solvency of bank branches was to be the responsibility of the home country supervisory authorities, because a branch has no legal independence, and is considered to be an integral part of the parent company. The solvency of foreign subsidiaries was a matter for the host country supervisory authority. It was stressed that consolidated data should be used to supervise the activities of a global bank, to provide an accurate picture of performance. While offshore banking centres are not party to this agreement, the Committee did not consider them to pose a

---

*See Chapter 7 for details of these two bank failures.

major threat to international financial stability because their operations are relatively minor.*

In 1983, a revised Basle Concordat was agreed upon, largely in response to the gaps in supervision of foreign branches and subsidiaries which came to light after the Banco Ambrosiano affair.† The revised agreement assigned joint supervisory responsibility to home and host countries for solvency problems arising from subsidiaries, and liquidity problems arising from either a subsidiary or a branch. The central bank in the parent country was to assume responsibility for solvency problems associated with a branch.

A number of issues were not addressed in either Concordat. First, no reference was made to lender of last resort (LLR) responsibilities. A lender of last resort normally aids a bank in the event of a liquidity crisis. Lifeboat operations serve a similar purpose, where the central bank persuades other healthy, private banks that it is in their interest to inject liquidity into the ailing bank. The argument in favour of LLR and lifeboat operations is that they prevent widespread bank failures and a collapse of the banking system. On the other hand, if banks are confident they will be rescued, serious moral hazard problems are created.

At the time, the Basle committee did not feel able to offer guidelines because the LLR function is often assumed by institutions other than central banks in many countries. However, as is demonstrated in Chapter 7, LLR intervention has been quite frequent in most westernised countries in the post-war period. There will be problems with achieving satisfactory international coordination if a run on foreign branches or subsidiaries occurs because the parent has run into difficulties. Guttenhag and Herring (1983) identified three types of banks that are vulnerable under the current arrangements: banks headquartered in countries with no LLR facilities (such as Luxembourg); banks headquartered in countries with non-convertible currencies or a shortage of foreign exchange reserves; and subsidiary banks with ambiguous access to the parent bank facilities.

Second, the Concordats said nothing about the extension of deposit insurance to all deposit liabilities. Wholesale, foreign currency, and interbank deposits are not normally covered in deposit insurance schemes. Foreign

---

*Offshore banking is defined as the part of a country's banking business that is denominated in foreign currencies and transacted between foreigners. They include the traditional banking centres of London, Zurich, and Luxembourg, but they are also to be found in a number of developing or newly industrialising countries including the Bahamas (Cayman Islands), Bahrain, Hong Kong, Singapore, and the Philippines. The threat to international financial stability posed by these operations is thought to be minor. To quote W.P. Cooke, Director of Banking Supervision at the Bank of England:

It is true that there are a few, but now only a very few, territories around the world where banking companies are licensed and allowed to operate without any serious effort to accompany a license with effective supervision. But such institutions are minuscule in relation to the market as a whole, widely known and recognised for what they are, and generally regarded as unacceptable counterparties by the banking community at large, and in no position to undermine the strength of the system as a whole. (W.P. Cooke, 1983.)

†See Chapter 7 for details of the collapse of Banco Ambrosiano.

currency deposits tend to be excluded because of the concern that deposits might be shifted between the foreign bank and its parent, to the detriment of the former.

The recent activities of the Basle Committee have continued to focus on supervision rather than financial stability. The *Basle Accord* (1988) tried to establish a single set of capital adequacy standards. The agreement led to the adoption of a risk assets ratio by international banks in participating countries from January 1993, the details of which were discussed above.

In April 1993 the Basle Committee published a consultative document which it was hoped would form the basis for a new agreement on the treatment of market risk, interest rate risk and netting arrangements by the supervisory authorities of international banks. Like the 1988 accord, the main objective is to ensure that international banks meet certain capital adequacy requirements. The proposals represent an attempt to treat off-balance sheet exposure more directly, rather than converting them into credit risk equivalents, as is done in the computation of the existing risk assets ratio.

On **market risk**, the Basle Committee has proposed that open positions in debt, equity (held in the bank's trading portfolio), foreign exchange, and derivatives be subject to a specific capital charge. Securities held in banks' investment accounts would continue to be treated the way they have been since the 1988 Accord, but interest rate risk is to be monitored. The Committee stated it prefers capital requirements to limits because the former give banks an incentive to use hedging techniques. However, the Committee acknowledged that some national supervisors may wish to impose limits as well.

The Committee recognised that foreign exchange, traded debt, and equity trades have different characteristics underlying their market risks. For securities and equities, a distinction is made between specific (or unsystematic) risk and general (or systematic) market risk in the computation of the requirements, to allow the offsetting of matched positions. Capital charges for debt securities and equities would apply to the current market value of items in the trading books of banks. Derivative products taken on to hedge positions in the banking books would be excluded. All other items would be subject to the present capital requirements, using credit risk equivalents, as set out in the 1988 Accord.

To see how the computations would be done, two cases are considered in detail here: debt securities and equities.* For debt securities, a capital charge will be levied against specific risk to protect against an adverse movement in the price of a security. Offsetting would only be permitted for matched (long and short) positions in an identical issue. The weighting for specific risks is to be in five categories, as follows:

- government: 0%;
- qualifying—residual maturity $\leq$ 6 months: 0.25%;

---

*The consultative paper also provides detail on how exposure in debt derivatives and equity derivatives would be estimated, but these are not discussed here.

- qualifying—residual maturity of 6–24 months: 1%;
- qualifying—residual maturity of 24 months: 1.6%;
- other: 8%.

The government category includes all government paper, though paper issued by foreign governments could have a specific risk weight applied to it by national supervisors. Qualifying items will include securities issued by public sector entities and multilateral development banks. Additionally, this category would include securities that are rated investment grade by at least two recognised credit rating agencies.* The different weights in the qualifying category reflect the view that uncertainty about creditworthiness increases with maturity. The "other" category has a specific risk charge of 8%, which is the same as that for a private-sector borrower under the Basle risk assets ratio.

A capital requirement will also be specified for general market risk, designed to capture the risk of loss arising from changes in the market interest rate. Banks would be permitted to use one or two measurement methods. First, they could use a ladder with 13 maturity bands for long and short positions of debt securities and debt-related derivatives. Fixed rate instruments would be allocated according to the residual term to maturity; floating rate instruments according to the next repricing date. Opposite positions in the same amount of the same issues will not incur interest rate risk, so banks may exclude them.

Net long and short positions[†] in each time band would be weighted by a factor designed to reflect the price sensitivity of the securities to interest rate movements. The weights would consist of a modified duration of a bond with a maturity set equal to the mid-point of the respective time band, and an assumed change in yield, designed to cover about two standard deviations of one month's yield volatility in most major markets. The two numbers would be multiplied to give a weighting factor for each time band.

In addition, there would be *vertical offsetting*, whereby the weighted longs and shorts in each time band are offset. Full offsetting will not be allowed because there are different maturities within each time bucket. Instead, a vertical disallowance factor of 10% will be applied to the smaller of the offsetting positions. For example, suppose, in a given time bucket, the sum of the weighted shorts is £200 million and that of the weighted longs is £100 million. Then the first weighted position is £100 million and the second position is the vertical disallowance for the time bucket, £10 million.

There would also be an allowance made for *horizontal offsetting*, recognising that there is room for some offset for long and short positions across time

---

*Securities rated investment grade by one investment grading agency, with another agency (specified by the supervisor) not rating the security less than investment grade would also be included as qualifying items. So will unrated securities considered to be of comparable investment quality by the bank/securities firm, where the issuer has securities listed on a recognised Stock Exchange.

[†] A long position in a financial instrument means the position rises in value with a rise in the price of the instrument, a short position means there is an inverse relationship between value and price.

bands because interest rates for securities with different maturities may move together. With these vertical and horizontal disallowances, it is possible to compute the market risk charge for the portfolio, together with the specific risk charge. An alternative method for computing the general risk aspect would be for banks to use their own in-house method for computing duration, subject to national supervisory approval, and provided the results were shown to be equivalent to the standard method.

Like debt securities, the proposal for equities involves computing the overall capital requirement, made up of a charge based on specific and general market risk. The minimum standard is expressed by the formula $X + Y$, where X denotes specific risk, as applied to a bank's sum of all long and all short equity positions, and Y denotes the general market risk, to apply to the overall net position in a given equity market, that is, the difference between the sum of the shorts and the sum of the longs. The charge for Y is to be 8% of the net open position. The charge for X would also be 8%; 4% if it could be demonstrated that the portfolio is both liquid and well-diversified, at the discretion of national regulators.

Levonian (1994) provided a helpful summary of how the minimum capital ratio would be calculated for, in this case, an equity portfolio. A bank would compute a weighted aggregate position, using the formula

$WAP = w_g GAP + w_n NAP$,

where:

WAP: the weighted aggregate position;

NAP: the net aggregate position, the net $ value of the portfolio, netting shorts against longs;

GAP: the gross aggregate position, the sum of the absolute values of the long and short positions. The weights w_g and w_n are selected by the Basle Committee. The amount of capital that must be set aside is determined by the formula $k \geq cWAP$, where c is the minimum capital ratio (for example, 4% or 8%).

An implicit assumption is that WAP is proportional to the portfolio volatility. The proposed minimum capital ratio, c, and weights will vary depending on the type of risk being assessed. For example, if an equity portfolio is to qualify for a lower weight on GAP, it must be well diversified and liquid. For traded debt securities, the positions are premultiplied by capital ratios before WAP is computed, using the capital ratios for interest rate risk. Thus, higher capital will be required against bands with more volatile returns. This account provides a good demonstration of why the approach taken by the Basle Committee has been called an *additive risk* or *building block* method.

Turning to **foreign exchange risk**, it is proposed that capital charges be imposed for open currency positions. A bank's net open position in a single currency would be computed by summing:

- the net spot position, defined as all assets less liabilities, including accrued interest in a given currency;
- the net forward position in a given currency;

- guarantees (and similar instruments) which will be called and are likely to be irrecoverable;
- net future income/expenses not accrued but fully hedged;
- net delta equivalent of the total book for currency options.

For the foreign exchange risk arising from a portfolio of foreign currency positions, the Basle Committee proposes use of either a simple method or a more complex simulation procedure. The simple method would consist of converting the nominal amount of the net position in each currency and the net position of each precious metal at spot rates into the reporting currency; the net open position would be measured by aggregating the sum of the short positions and the sum of the long positions, whichever is greater, plus the total of each net position in each precious metal. The capital charge would be 8% of the higher of the longs and shorts, plus gross positions in the precious metals.

Alternatively, some banks could employ a simulation method where exchange rate movements over a past period are used to revalue the bank's present foreign exchange positions. The revaluations are, in turn, used to calculate simulated profits/losses if the positions had been fixed for a given period. However, national supervisors would have to be satisfied that the simulation technique was adequate for the purposes of computing capital requirements.

It was the Committee's view that *interest rate risk* be measured and monitored, rather than used in the computation of an explicit capital charge, because current capital adequacy requirements cover interest rate risk. The measurement system would be able to identify institutions that are incurring excessive amounts of interest rate risk and national supervisory authorities would then be expected to remedy the situation, using, for example, explicit capital charges in certain cases.

The *netting proposal* outlines the conditions under which banks will be allowed to net credit risks arising from trades in financial instruments. The 1988 Capital Adequacy Agreement provided for risk weighting of net (rather than gross) claims arising out of swaps and other OBS instruments in the computation of credit risk equivalents. However, it only allowed for bilateral netting by novation* for the same currency and same value date. The 1993 proposals are in line with the Lamfalussy Report,[†] that is, bilateral netting schemes would be extended to interbank payment orders and forward value contractual commitments such as foreign exchange contracts. Counterparty risk exposure on bilaterally netted forward transactions would be computed as the sum of the net marked to market replacement cost plus an add-on based on the notional underlying principal. National supervisors would have to be mutually satisfied that the agreed minimum national requirements are met. No concrete multilateral netting arrangements were put forward, the Committee arguing that it requires further analysis.

---

*Bilateral netting by novation occurs when foreign exchange transactions are netted out.
[†]The Lamfalussy Report by the BIS Committee on Interbank Netting Schemes, 1990.

To summarise, if the Basle 1993 proposals were to be implemented, the overall minimum capital requirement for a bank will be:

- the existing capital requirements to cover credit risk from loans and investments, and counterparty risk from derivatives;
- specific capital charges for market risk arising from open positions in debt securities and equity, of the sort outlined above;
- capital charges for foreign exchange risk, as outlined above;
- interest rate risk is to be measured and monitored;
- netting arrangements have been expanded; banks may reduce the amount of capital they have to set aside if they have netting arrangements with other banks.

In short, the market risk capital charges for debt securities and equities on a bank's trading book will substitute for the credit risk weights currently used. The capital charge for a bank may be higher or lower, depending on the profile of its trading book. If positions are well hedged or debt securities, on average, have a high investment grade, the capital requirement could actually be lower.

Since the publication of the proposals, international banks have expressed some disquiet over the approach taken by the Committee. One concern is with the Basle *building block or additive risk approach* which, increasingly, draws a sharp distinction between each type of risk and then tries to compute a capital charge for it. The use of risk weights and explicit charges does not address the riskiness of a bank's overall position. Excessive disaggregation of risk will not allow for the potential counterbalance between different types of risk, arising because of negative correlations between instruments in a portfolio. A second objection has been raised because the treatment of equity differs from the Capital Adequacy Directive of the European Union. This directive means the capital charge imposed on a bank's equity portfolio could be as low as 2% of the gross value of the portfolio (not 4%, as in Basle), provided it is well diversified. International banks subject to Basle will therefore be placed at an unfair advantage, because securities firms in Europe will have to conform to the directive but not any Basle standard.*

A study by Dimson and Marsh (1993) compared the American, proposed EU, and British regulatory requirements for the equity portfolios of securities firms. The US Securities and Exchange Commission employs a comprehensive approach, where the firm is required to set aside 15% of the value of long positions plus 15% of short positions, for all short holdings with a value in excess of one-quarter of the value of the long positions.[†] Like the Basle proposal, the EU capital adequacy directive uses a less complicated building block

---

*In its press release (30 April 1993), the Basle Committee noted, with regret, that the International Organisation of Securities Commissions (IOSCO) has not been able to reach an agreement on capital charges for securities firms in relation to market risk. Therefore, it was not possible to come to a collaborative arrangement prior to the publication of the Basle proposal.
[†]Assuming the value of long positions exceeds that of short positions.

approach. Securities firms will, by 1996, be required to set aside 2% of the gross value of the portfolio; 8% of the net value. In the UK, the amount of capital which must be set aside depends on the net position of the portfolio, and riskiness, defined as the extent to which a portfolio is likely to fluctuate in a given week, based on past values.

To look at the effectiveness of these measures, Dimson and Marsh considered whether the amount of capital required increases with the riskiness of a portfolio. Specifically, they used a sample of 58 trading books from UK securities firms and studied the extent to which the position risk requirements of the three approaches are related to the risks of the trading books. The American approach showed no correlation between the riskiness of the trading book and the position risk requirement. The EU approach did better because it allows for the reduction of market risk in situations where long and short positions are offsetting. The UK portfolio approach showed the best correlation, because it takes account of risk reduced through diversification, in addition to offsetting positions.

Banks are also concerned that the costs of meeting the requirements of the Basle proposals will be high. For example, as was noted above, banks may measure general market risk using their own duration techniques, but these will have to be shown to give equivalent results to the standard approach. Furthermore, risk management systems within each bank would have to be adapted to meet both Basle and, possibly, the national requirements of different countries. If the Basle 1993 proposals are implemented in the absence of broad consensus, the international coordination objective of this Committee could be severely undermined.

On 12 April 1995, the Basle Committee announced amended proposals for the treatment of market risk, in response to the many objections received after the publication of the original framework. Banks will be given a choice in the computation of market risk; either they can employ the Basle building block method, or they can use their own models. If in-house models are used, *value at risk*, the maximum amount a bank can be expected to lose by holding a portfolio of positions for a certain period of time must be calculated, on the assumption that positions are held for 14 days, and that any movements in the market would not give rise to a financial loss for the bank which exceeds that predicted by the models in 99% of cases. The capital requirement will be reduced for banks that perform well in terms of model forecasting and internal controls. Some negative correlations between different instruments in a portfolio will also be taken into account when computing the precise capital requirement for a bank. These amended proposals are now at odds with the EU Directive on Capital Adequacy, which, as was noted earlier, uses a similar building block method, but does not permit banks (or securities firms, also covered by the directive) to employ their own models.

In view of the Basle proposal to allow banks to opt to use their own models to compute capital requirements for market risk, the G-30 report (1993) on derivatives is important—its key recommendations are discussed below.

The Group of Thirty (G-30) Report on Derivatives

The Group of Thirty (1993) published a detailed report on the nature and management of over the counter derivatives. As was noted in Chapter 5, derivatives are either exchange traded or over the counter. OTC instruments have been singled out for attention by the regulatory authorities, for a number of reasons. The customised nature of OTC instruments makes them less liquid and less transparent. Each organised exchange has a clearing house, which consists of all the major market participants. It acts as counterparty in all trades for listed contracts. Credit or counterparty risk is managed by the clearing house, which marks positions to market on a frequent basis, and imposes initial margins (based on the volatility of the contract price) and maintenance margins. The clearing house also regulates membership—all members are subject to minimum capital requirements, and maximum net position limits. Most exchanges have a reserve fund. OTC instruments are bilateral agreements and the presence of credit risk is heightened because an agreement is not subject to daily settlements or margin calls. The absence of multilateral netting and marking to market increases payments risk.

The key recommendation of the G-30 was self-regulation, with bank management adhering to certain guidelines.

The Role of Senior Management

Senior managers in both financial and non-financial firms should be directly involved in the formulation of risk management policies if the firm is active in derivatives markets. Overall risk management and capital policies and controls should be approved by the senior management. The policies and controls should be enforced by management at all levels.

Valuation and Market Risk Management

- For risk management purposes, dealers should mark their derivatives positions to market at least once a day.
- The derivatives portfolios of dealers should be valued at mid-market levels or on appropriate bid and offer levels. If mid-market valuations are used, adjustments should be made for expected future costs such as unearned credit spread, future administrative costs, investment and funding costs, close-out of net open positions, and hedging costs.
- Dealers should measure the components of revenue regularly by:
  —identifying derivative revenue by customer origination, credit spread, and other trading revenue;
  —measuring derivatives trading revenue by type of market risk factor, such as directional rate moves, volatility, and basis;
  —measuring derivative revenue by underlying source, such as interest rates, commodity, equity, and currency.
- Daily market risk of the derivatives positions should be calculated using a consistent measure, and compared to market risk limits. A *value at risk*

approach, discussed in Chapter 5, should be adopted, which includes probability analysis based upon a consistent confidence interval and time horizon.
- Several fundamental components underlying market risk should be considered across the term structure. These include: delta (absolute price or rate of change), gamma (convexity), volatility, basis or correlation, and rho (discount rate).*
- *Stress simulations* should be conducted regularly, to determine how portfolios will perform over a certain length of time under certain stress conditions, such as a severe decrease in liquidity, non-parallel shifts in the forward curve, decreases in liquidity, failure of a significant counterparty, unexpected interruptions in the market, and unexpected collateral obligations or cash margin calls. Stress simulations allow for the effects of skewness, effectively ignored by value at risk measures.
- From time to time, dealers should forecast the cash investing and funding requirements arising from their derivatives portfolios.
- There should be an independent market risk management group, with authority and independence from the trading function. The risk management system should measure all risks incurred in their derivatives, including market and credit risks.

Credit Risk Management and Measurement
- Dealers should measure current and potential risk exposure.
- Credit exposures on derivatives and all other credit exposures to a counterparty should be aggregated, taking into account any enforceable netting arrangements. Credit exposures should be calculated on a regular basis, and compared to other credit limits.
- Firms should have an independent credit risk management group, capable of analysing credit risk related to derivatives, and with clear independence and authority.
- Where possible, one master agreement with counterparties should be used to document existing and future derivatives transactions. The master agreement should provide for payments netting and close-out netting.
- The costs and benefits of credit enhancement and related risk-reduction arrangements should be assessed. For example, if a credit downgrade is proposed that will trigger early termination or collateral requirements, firms must consider the consequent funding demands placed not only on their counterparties, but themselves as well.

Systems, Operations, and Controls
- There must be a high degree of professional expertise in all derivatives activities.

---

*Readers are referred to Chapter 5 for more detail on these underlying risks.

- There must be adequate systems in place for data capture, processing, settlement, and management reporting.

Accounting and Disclosure

- Derivatives transactions should be accounted for by marking them to market.
- The disclosure of financial statements on derivatives should provide information on the reason why a derivatives transaction is undertaken, the degree of risk involved, and how each transaction has been accounted.

Additional Recommendations

- All firms involved in derivatives should employ well recognised valuation procedures.
- Management information systems should be implemented.
- Accounting procedures and satisfactory disclosure rules should be developed for firms involved in derivatives, because current accounting methods are inadequate, and reduce the transparency of a firm's exposures. Additionally, international coordination of accounting and disclosure standards should be encouraged.

Ongoing Issues Related to International Bank Supervision

On the international front, bank supervisors face three related problems: lack of harmonisation, rapid financial innovation, and the growth of financial conglomerates. Each of these issues is discussed in turn, below.

Lack of Harmonisation of National Supervisory Arrangements

Differences in capital adequacy standards have, to a degree, been overcome by the Basle risk assets ratio, though, as was discussed earlier, this is not without its problems. However, there are still pronounced differences in examination systems. As was discussed in earlier sections, in the UK and Japan, a consensus approach is used; in the USA there are several supervisory bodies which carry out formal examinations and inspections in banks. In the single banking market in Europe, it appears that bank inspection will remain the responsibility of individual states, but there are no plans to harmonise the system. Since neither the US nor the UK regulatory regimes has been able to prevent banks from collapsing, it is not clear that either system is superior. However, the British system would be unworkable in countries where there are a large number of banks. On the other hand, during the 1980s the number and rate of bank failures was higher in the US than in any other OECD country.

There continues to be a poor standardisation of accounting principles and differences in the treatment of loan loss provisions, hidden reserves, consolidation, and valuation of assets. In June 1992 the Basle Committee reinforced its

1975 agreement by pointing out to members that a strong emphasis should be placed on consolidated supervision of international banks, including subsidiaries. However, to date, few countries have enforced this requirement. The International Accounting Standards Committee (IASC) is attempting to harmonise accounting rules, and hopes to have a system in place by the end of the century. However, there is a fair degree of tension between the USA and Europe on this issue, because of differences in objectives. For example, Europeans look upon American methods as burdensome, designed as they are to provide a "true and fair view" to shareholders. In some EU countries, especially Germany, accounts are drawn up with tax issues in mind, because firms consider their principal obligation is to creditors and employees.

Finally, the objective of international harmonisation is difficult to achieve for the same reason as it will be in the EU, because of the conflicting goals of price stability and financial stability (through the provision of liquidity). This problem may explain why the Basle Committee has always given priority to international supervisory issues, rather than prudential regulation.

Rapid Financial Innovation

Rapid financial innovation has led to the introduction of new products which are not immediately covered under existing capital adequacy and liquidity rules, especially derivatives and securitised assets. International coordination is made more difficult because there is a lag in the rate of recognition of new instruments by different supervisors and the different treatment the new instruments receive. For example, the Bank of England and the Federal Reserve introduced a risk assets ratio long before the Basle Accord became operational. In the USA, there is pressure to regulate the derivatives market more closely, independent of recent Basle Proposals. In April 1994, the chairman of the Banking Committee of the US House of Representatives introduced a bill to increase supervision of banks involved in derivatives. The US was the first country to introduce risk-related deposit insurance premia for banks and thrifts.

Financial Conglomerates

Financial conglomerates, of which banks are a part, can create additional regulatory problems. Deregulation in many countries has increased the tendency for banks to form financial conglomerates. For example, "Big Bang" (1987) in the UK and other countries in the late 1980s allowed banks to buy stockbroking firms. Banks have also purchased insurance firms and real estate companies.

Some regulatory authorities use the concept of *dedicated capital* to enforce the capital adequacy of financial conglomerates. Capital is identified and allocated to back different parts of the business. *Firewalls* (to divide the different firms in the conglomerate legally, financially, and managerially) are often erected to prevent a securities affiliate/subsidiary of a bank/subsidiary exposing the bank as a result of problems with the affiliate/subsidiary.

Under the 1986 UK Financial Services Act, conglomerates are subject to functional supervision, that is, different parts of the conglomerate are supervised by different authorities, with a strong emphasis on self-regulatory organisations (SROs). However, functional supervision means the conglomerate is having to answer to a number of authorities, and despite firewalls, damage to the reputation of one part of the firm could cause a loss of confidence for other parts of the firms, including its banking arm. Two contrasting examples of this problem are the Johnson Matthey Bank case (1984) and the collapse of British Commonwealth Holdings (BCH), a financial services group, in 1990. When Johnson Matthey Bank collapsed, the Bank of England deemed it necessary to intervene to protect the gold bullion subsidiary of Johnson Matthey. After news of serious financial problems in the computer leasing subsidiary of BCH (Atlantic Computers) in April 1990, there was a run on British and Commonwealth Merchant Bank. Two months later, the Securities and Investment Board removed the merchant bank from its approved list, and to prevent a further run, depositors' funds were frozen by the courts and an administrator appointed. The subsequent report by the administrators found the merchant bank to be sound.

Dale (1992) discussed the advantages and disadvantages of financial conglomerates. The main advantage from conglomerates that combine financial and securities activities is economies of scope (synergy) and, therefore, the more efficient operation of the financial system. However, it is worth pointing out that following Big Bang (1986), banks in London which tried to integrate these businesses have found it to be much more costly than expected. For example, the acquisition of Hill Samuel by the Trustees Saving Bank achieved the exact opposite to achieving synergy, and caused large losses for the former savings bank. Also, if economies of scale and scope are realised, they can actually reduce competition in the financial sector, and may result in greater inefficiency.

According to Dale, the key disadvantage arising from financial conglomerates is that the risk to the financial system as a whole increases if banking and securities activities are combined, even though most banks use their securities arm to reduce overall risk. This is because a conglomerate determined to operate a high risk/return strategy has more opportunities to undertake risky activities if they so choose. Thus, systemic risk increases, which has implications for the lender of last resort function. However, to date, there have been no cases where the banking arm of a conglomerate has been subject to a run as a result of problems with the securities part of the business.

The case of *County National Westminster Bank* (September 1987) provides a good example of the regulatory issues raised, in relation to financial conglomerates. County National Westminster Bank (County NatWest, CNW) was a merchant bank located in London, and a wholly owned subsidiary of one of the big four clearing banks, National Westminster Bank. The market maker for the merchant bank was County National Westminster Securities (CNWS), the securities subsidiary of the bank, which had been acquired in anticipation of Big Bang.

CNW was handling a rights issue for Blue Arrow, an employment agency. The rights issue expired on 27 September 1987 but Blue Arrow's shareholders had, by 28 September, taken up only 49% of it. CNWS's story was that it was pressurised into taking up 4.6% of BA in exchange for an indemnity with County NatWest, whereby CNWS would be reimbursed for any losses on the shares. Additionally, County NatWest would meet the financing costs and take only 30% of any profits made. Under this arrangement the profitability of CNWS would not be affected, nor would the profit-related bonuses of its staff. However, County NatWest claimed CNWS took the shares willingly, there was no specific deal of the sort outlined above, and no indemnity.

Under section 209 of the Companies Act, shares held by the market maker do not have to be disclosed if held in the normal course of business. There was no disclosure. The shares did not appear on CNWS normal trading books nor on the back book. None of the firm's dealers at the securities firm were aware the stock was being held.

Phillips and Drew, the London stockbroker for Blue Arrow, was a subsidiary of Union Bank of Switzerland (UBS). Both firms took some of the shares, as did some corporate clients of County NatWest. It is estimated that in total, 60% of the issue was taken onto the books of CNW-related firms. UBS insisted on a written indemnity that CNW would meet any losses borne by UBS on its shares. In the indemnity it was made clear that CNW had no control over the timing of the share sales, or over their voting rights. Though the indemnity was kept secret within CNW, the Bank of England was informed about it.

On 19 October 1987 the London stock market crashed; shares in Blue Arrow dropped from 166p to 80p. Pressure was put on CNW to disclose its stake, but it was reluctant to do so until it had unwound the UBS indemnity. National Westminster Bank negotiated with UBS on CNW's behalf and after several weeks the matter was settled at a cost of about £30 million to the bank. On 17 December 1987, County Nat West disclosed its 9.5% stake in Blue Arrow and announced a £49 million provision for loss in the shares, and reported a loss of £116 million for the year. National Westminster Bank had to inject £80 million into its merchant bank subsidiary.

CNW's two top executives resigned in February 1988. Initially the Bank of England persuaded the Department of Trade and Industry to allow National Westminster Bank to launch an internal investigation. After a year-long trial (ending in February 1992), four defendants were found guilty of conspiracy to defraud, though some of these convictions were overturned on appeal.

Several regulatory concerns arise from the Blue Arrow affair. First, the 1986 Financial Services Act in the UK called for the erection of *Chinese walls* to restrict the flow of information between related firms in a conglomerate, thereby preventing conflicts of interest from arising. However, in this case, the Chinese wall was too flimsy to prevent the information from flowing between the corporate finance arm of County NatWest and market makers at CNWS. Second, if private client portfolio holdings of Blue Arrow shares (arranged by County NatWest Securities), had been added to the National Westminster group exposure in Blue Arrow, it would have risen above 5%, necessitating disclosure by the group, under the UK Companies Act. But no such disclosure was made.

Third, it is clear that the parent bank, National Westminster, participated in a cover-up of financial malpractice in one of its subsidiaries. *Regulatory forbearance* (or *regulatory capture*) was also a problem because the Bank of England was aware of the UBS indemnity from an early date but failed to query it, and was prepared to allow National Westminster to conduct its own internal investigation of the affair.

CONCLUSION

This chapter has explored the state of bank regulation, and the ongoing issues related to it. It was argued that even though prudential regulation is very much in the government policy domain, bank management should understand why and how banks are singled out for special regulation. After a brief discussion of the reasons why the financial sector, especially banks, are subject to more comprehensive regulation than firms in other sectors, prudential regulation in the UK, the USA, Japan, and the European Union was reviewed. Quite different systems have evolved in the USA and the UK. In the USA, the small depositor has been singled out for special protection since 1933. Concerns about possible collusion between private banks and regulators, and excessive concentration of the banking sector, have had a profound influence on the banking statutes passed by Congress. Though many features of Japanese regulation are borrowed from the USA, Article 65 has not been as effective as Glass-Steagall in keeping investment and commercial banking separate. Also, the principle of "regulatory guidance" used by the Japanese Ministry of Finance is not unlike the UK consensus approach. It is notable that although there are marked differences in all three systems of prudential regulation, problem banks are a feature of each of these countries.

The EU has chosen to implement a set of well-defined directives to shape the single banking market, but the responsibility of the European Central Bank for prudential regulation in a one-currency Europe remains unclear. Supervision is likely to be the responsibility of "state" central banks (for example, the Bank of England), but it is hard to imagine the ECB accepting a passive role if it is expected to act as lender of last resort in the event of a threat to the stability of the EU banking system.

The chapter also reviewed attempts at international coordination of prudential regulation, which, given the growth of global banking, is a feature of modern bank regulation. The Basle Committee, established after two international bank failures in 1974, has been responsible for a number of concordats and agreements which focus on supervision rather than financial stability. Of course, it is hoped that effective supervision of banks with significant international activities will prevent failures among these banks, and so avoid a global domino effect which threatens international financial stability. The Basle accord (1988) tried to set a single set of capital adequacy standards, though it is too early to judge whether compliance with the risk assets ratio will improve the soundness of global banks. Scott and Iwahara (1994) questioned whether the ratio can be compared across countries, and disputed any suggestion that it creates a level global playing field.

Recently, the Basle Committee has turned its attention to the treatment of market risk, interest rate risk, and netting arrangements by supervisory authorities. The 1993 consultative document attempted to establish a more direct method of measuring and managing these risks. If the proposal is accepted, the current risk assets ratio would continue to cover loan credit risk and derivative counterparty risk, but explicit capital charges would be introduced for market risks associated with traded debt securities and equity and for currency risk. International bankers have expressed concern with the building block or additive risk approach taken by the Basle Committee, and the different treatment of capital adequacy by the EU. The revised Basle proposals (April 1995) addressed one of these issues, because banks are to be permitted to compute their capital requirements for market risk based on in-house models or the building block method. However, EU banks will find themselves having to meet two sets of capital adequacy standards, and EU securities firms will be subject to more stringent control than their counterparts in other parts of the world. The G-30 recommendations on derivatives were received more warmly by the banking community, because of the stress placed on self-regulation by senior management within banks.

There are still large gaps in the coordination of international bank supervision. National supervisory arrangements are quite diverse when it comes to bank examinations, standardisation of accounting principles and differences in the treatment of loan loss provisions, hidden reserves, consolidation, and the valuation of assets. Rapid financial innovation can impair international coordination because of the different response rates by supervisors. Finally, the emergence of financial conglomerates, a trend in part encouraged by regulatory reforms of the 1980s, has created new supervisory headaches for bank regulators, as illustrated by the County NatWest case.

This chapter has demonstrated that managers should expect the prudential regulation of banks to remain at the forefront of policy concerns, and is an issue that is fraught with difficulties. It is probably fair to say that to date, no country has struck an optimal balance between government supervision of banks and allowing banks to conduct business like any other firm in other sectors. International coordination of bank regulation and supervision remains, at best, patchy. It will always be difficult to find an ideal method of regulation and supervision, because of the potential for conflict between the objectives of financial and price stability. Certainly, despite the development of different but nonetheless comprehensive bank regulations in key countries, bank failures and consequent concerns about financial stability have not been eliminated. These failures are the subject of the next chapter.

7

The Determinants of
Bank Failure

INTRODUCTION

Bank managers, investors, policy-makers and regulators share a keen interest in knowing what causes banks to fail and in being able to predict which banks will get into difficulty. Managers normally lose their jobs if their bank fails. The issue is also important for policy because failing banks may prove costly for the taxpayer; depositors and investors want to be able to identify potentially weak banks. In this chapter, the reasons why banks fail are explored, using both a qualitative approach and quantitative analysis.

Usually, a firm is said to have failed if it is insolvent, that is, has a negative net worth. In some countries, banks do fail and are liquidated, but in others, such as Japan* and some European states, no bank has been declared insolvent in the post-war period, because of real or imagined concerns about the systemic aspects of bank failure. Thus, most practitioners and policy-makers adopt a broader definition; a bank is deemed to have "failed" if it is liquidated, merged with a healthy bank under government supervision, or rescued with state financial support.

This chapter is organised as follows. First it looks at individual cases of bank failure. Based on these studies, some qualitative lessons on the causes of bank failure are then drawn. Empirical tests on a model of bank failure, with a view to quantifying the determinants of bank failure, conclude the chapter.

CASE STUDIES ON BANK FAILURE

Bank failures, broadly defined, have occurred in virtually every country throughout history. In the 14th century the Bardi family of Florentine bankers was ruined by the failure of Edward III to meet outstanding loan obligations—

---

*In Japan, five banks (broadly defined) were allowed to fail in 1995, the first failures since the end of World War II.

the only time in history, to date, that a British government has failed to honour its debts. Some failures seriously undermine the stability of the financial system (as happened, for example, in the UK in 1866 and the USA in 1933). Others do not. In some cases, state support of problem banks proves costly. For example, the taxpayer's bill for the US thrift bail-out is put at around $300 billion, while recent problems with the Japanese banking system may cost the taxpayer there as much as $500 billion. In this section of the chapter, bank failures are examined on a case-by-case basis, the objective being to identify the qualitative causes of bank failure, beginning with a historical review, and continuing with modern bank failures, commencing with the failure of Bankhaus Herstatt in 1974.

Historical Overview

This sub-section is a selective, brief review of well-known bank failures in Victorian England and between 1930 and 1933 in the USA. In England, there were two major bank failures in the 19th century: Overend, Gurney, and Company Ltd in 1866, and Baring Brothers in 1890.* Until the 1850s, Overend Gurney was a prosperous financial firm, involved in banking and bill broking. After changes in management in 1856 and 1857 it began to take on bills of dubious quality, and lending with poor collateral to back the loans. By 1865 the firm was reporting losses of £3–4 million and was floated as a limited company in the summer of 1865. By 1866, a number of speculative firms and associated contracting firms, linked to Gurney through finance bills, failed. London-based depositors began to suspect Gurney's was bankrupt; the consequence was a drawing down of deposits and a fall in Gurney's stock market price. On 10 May 1866 the firm sought assistance from the Bank of England, which was refused; Gurney's was declared insolvent the same afternoon. The Gurney failure precipitated the collapse of a number of country banks and firms associated with it, and country banks initiated a run on London banks and finance houses, which in turn, led to a run on the Bank of England. Several banks and finance houses, both unsound and healthy, failed. The Bank Charter Act was suspended to enable the Bank of England to augment a note supply, which was enough to allow the panic to subside. Gurney's was liquidated, and though the Bank Act was not amended, the episode made it clear the Bank of England would act as lender of last resort in situations of extreme panic.

Baring Brothers and Company was a large international merchant bank which failed in 1890. Barings had been founded in 1762, largely to finance the textile trade in Europe. After the Napoleonic wars, Barings began to move into the area of finance for public projects in foreign countries; initially the long-term lending to foreign governments was concentrated in Europe and North America, but in 1821–22 the loan portfolio was expanded to include Mexico and Latin America, notably Chile, Colombia and Brazil. Though these loans were non-performing, between 1888 and 1890 Barings granted

*The detail on these bank failures is taken from Batchelor (1986).

additional, large loans to the governments of Argentina and Uruguay. By the end of 1890, these loans made up three-quarters of Baring's total loan portfolio. Problems with key banks in Argentina and Uruguay led to suspended payments and bank runs. Barings' Argentine securities dropped in value by one-third; the firm also faced a drop in income from loan repayments, and liabilities arising from a failed utility. Despite borrowing heavily from London banks, Barings, reported the crisis to the Bank of England in November 1890. The Governor of the Bank of England organised subscriptions to a fund (contributions were made by London's key merchant banks) to guarantee Barings liabilities for three years. Eight days after Barings reported its problems to the Bank, its illiquidity had become public knowledge. But there was nothing in the way of a significant run, and no other banks failed. Barings was put into liquidation but was refloated as a limited liability company, with capital from the Baring family and friends.

Both banks underwent notable changes in bank management in the years leading up to the failures. The collapse of the banks was due largely to mismanagement of assets, leading to a weak loan portfolio in the case of Barings, and, for Gurney's, the issue of poor-quality finance bills. Batchelor (1986: pp.68–69) argued that, unlike Barings, the Gurney failure caused a serious bank run because the public lacked crucial information about the state of the bank's financial affairs. The Latin American exposure of Barings was well known but there was no run because of its historical reputation for financial health in the banking world.

One of the most important series of bank failures occurred in the USA between 1930 and 1933.* The stock market crash of October 1929 precipitated a serious depression and created a general climate of uncertainty. The first US banking crisis began in November 1930, when 256 banks failed; contagion spread throughout the US, with 352 more bank failures in December. The Bank of the USA was the most notable bank failure, because it was the largest commercial bank, measured by volume of deposits. It was a member of the Federal Reserve System, but an attempt by the Federal Reserve Bank of New York to organise a "lifeboat" rescue with the support of clearing house banks failed. It was followed by a second round of failures in March 1931. Other countries also suffered bank failures, largely because the depression in the US had wide-reaching global effects. The largest private bank in Austria, Kreditanstalt, failed in May 1931, and in other European states, particularly Germany, banks were closed. Another relapse followed a temporary recovery, and in the last quarter of 1932 there were widespread bank failures in the Midwest and Far West of the USA. By January 1933 bank failures had spread to other areas; by 3 March, half the states were required to declare bank holidays to halt the withdrawals of deposits. On 6 March 1933, President Roosevelt declared a nationwide bank holiday, which closed all banks until 13–15 March, depending on their location. Prior to the bank holiday period,

---

*The details of the US bank failures reported in this section is taken from Friedman and Schwartz (1963: pp.332–49, 351–53).

there were 17 800 commercial banks, but fewer than 12 000 were allowed to open, under new federal/state authority licensing requirements. About 3000 of the unlicensed banks were eventually allowed to remain open but another 2000 were either liquidated or merged with other banks. The suspended operations and failures caused losses of $2.5 billion for stockholders, depositors, and other creditors. Friedman and Schwartz argued a poor quality loan book and other bad investments may have been the principal cause of some bank failures in 1930,* but in the later period, the bank failures were caused largely because of bank runs, which forced banks to divest of their assets at a large discount.

Bankhaus Herstatt

This West German bank collapsed in June 1974, because of losses in the foreign exchange market. The losses were originally estimated at £83 million but final estimates put the figure at £200 million. At the time it was unclear how the bank had managed to run up such losses. Foreign banks which had engaged in deals with the bank the day it closed also suffered losses if they were caught in the middle of a transaction. The US payments system was put under severe strain. The risk associated with the failure to meet interbank payment obligations has since become known as *Herstatt risk*. In February 1984, the chairman of the bank was convicted of fraudulently concealing foreign exchange losses of DM 100 million in the bank's 1973 accounts.

Franklin National Bank (FNB)

In May 1974, FNB, the 20th largest bank in the USA (deposits close to $3 billion) faced a crisis. The authorities were aware of the problem; at the beginning of May, the Federal Reserve refused FNB's request to take over another financial institution and instructed the bank to retrench its operations because it had expanded too quickly. A few days later, FNB announced it had suffered very large foreign exchange losses and could not pay its quarterly dividend. It transpired that in addition to these losses, the bank had made a large volume of unsound loans, as part of a rapid growth strategy.

These revelations caused large depositors to withdraw their deposits and other banks refused to lend to the bank. FNB offset the deposit outflows by borrowing $1.75 billion from the Federal Reserve. Small depositors, protected by the FDIC, did not withdraw their deposits, otherwise, the run would have been more serious. In October 1974, its remains were taken over by a consortium of seven European banks, European American.

---

*Friedman and Schwartz (1963: pp.354–55) argue there is a difference between the *ex ante* quality of bank assets and the *ex post* quality of assets. They suggest that *ex ante*, the loan and other investment decisions of banks in the late 1920s were not very different from the early 1920s, the main difference being that the loans and investments had to be repaid or matured in the middle of the Great Depression. Thus, the number of bank failures caused by inferior investment decisions is debatable, with the exception of foreign lending.

FNB had been used by its biggest shareholder, Michele Sindona, to channel funds illegally around the world. In March 1985 he died from poisoning, a few days after being sentenced to life imprisonment in Italy for arranging the murder of an investigator of his banking empire.

Banco Ambrosiano (BA)

BA was a commercial bank based in Milan and quoted on the Milan stock exchange. It had a number of foreign subsidiaries and companies located overseas, in Luxembourg, Nassau, Nicaragua, and Peru. The Luxembourg subsidiary was called Banco Ambrosiano Holdings (BAH); 69% of BAH was owned by BA in Milan. BAH was active on the interbank market, taking Eurocurrency deposits from international banks which were on-lent to other non-Italian companies in the BA group.

The parent bank, BA, collapsed in June 1982, following a crisis of confidence among depositors after its Chairman, Roberto Calvi, was found hanging from Blackfriars bridge in London, 10 days after he had disappeared from Milan. The Bank of Italy launched a lifeboat rescue operation; seven Italian banks provided around $325 million in funds to fill the gap left by the flight of deposits, BA was declared bankrupt by a Milan court in late August 1982. A new bank, Nouvo Banco Ambrosiano (NBA) was created to take over the bank's Italian operations. The Luxembourg subsidiary, BAH, also suffered from a loss of deposits but the Bank of Italy refused to launch a similar lifeboat rescue operation, causing BAH to default on its loans and deposits.

The main cause of the insolvency appears to have been fraud on a massive scale, though there were other factors, whose contribution is unclear. The BA affair revealed a number of gaps in the supervision of international banks. The Bank of Italy authorities had weak supervisory powers, lacking the statutory power to supervise Italian banks. Nor was a close relationship enjoyed between senior management and the central bank, the way it is in the UK. It appears that Sig. Calvi's abrupt departure may have been precipitated by a letter sent to him by the surveillance department of the Bank of Italy seeking explanations for the extensive overseas exposure, asking for it to be reduced, and requesting that the contents of the letter be shown to other directors of the bank. This activity suggests the regulatory authorities were aware of the problem. The Bank of Italy refused to protect depositors of the subsidiary in Luxembourg because BA was not held responsible for BAH debts; it owned 69% of the subsidiary. The Bank of Italy also pointed out that neither it nor the Luxembourg authorities could be responsible for loans made from one offshore centre (Luxembourg) to another (Panama) via a third (Latin America).

In 1981, the Luxembourg Banking Commission revised some of its rules to relax bank secrecy and allow the items on the asset side of a bank's balance sheet to be freely passed through the parent bank on to the parent authority, though bank secrecy is still upheld for non-bank customers holding deposits at Luxembourg banks. The authorities in Luxembourg also obtained guarantees from the six Italian banks with branches in Luxembourg that they would be responsible for the debts of their branches. The Basle Concordat was revised in 1983 (see Chapter 6), to cover gaps in the supervision of foreign branches and subsidiaries. In July 1994 the former Prime Minister of Italy, Bernard Craxi, was convicted of fraud in relation to the collapse of Banco Ambrosiano.

Continental Illinois and Penn Square

Several factors led to a run on Continental Illinois (CI). In the summer of 1982, a number of CI customers were having trouble repaying their loans because of the drop in oil prices. The decline in oil prices also undermined the value of the collateral securing these loans. On 5 July 1982, the Penn Square Bank, located in Oklahoma City, with $465 million in deposits, collapsed. The banks were closely connected because Penn Square passed many of its energy loans to CI. Shortly after the collapse of Penn Square, CI announced a second-quarter loss of $63.1 million and revealed its non-performing loans had more than doubled to $1.3 billion. In subsequent quarters, the bank was slow to recover and its non-performing loans held steady at approximately $2 billion, even though the non-performing loans related to the Penn square connection were down.

The first-quarter results of 1984 (17 April) revealed the bank's non-performing loans had risen to $2.3 billion, representing 7.7% of its loans. Increasingly, CI had been relying on the overseas markets to fund its domestic loan portfolio. On the eve of the crisis, 60% of its funds were being raised in the form of short-term deposits from overseas. This reliance on uninsured short-term deposits, along with its financial troubles, made it especially vulnerable to a run.

Rumours about the solvency of the bank were rife in the early days of May 1984, thereby undermining the ability of the bank to fund itself. On 10 May the rumours were so serious that the office of the US Comptroller of Currency took the unusual step of rebutting the rumours, though normal procedure is a "no comment" approach. The statement merely served to fuel more anxiety and the next day, CI was forced to approach the Chicago Reserve Bank for emergency support, borrowing approximately $44.5 billion. Over the weekend, the Chairman of Morgan Guaranty organised US bank support for CI: by Monday 14 May, 16 banks put in place a $4.5 billion facility under which CI could purchase federal funds on an overnight basis. However, the private lifeboat facility was not enough. The run on the bank continued and the bank saw $6 billion disappear, equivalent to 75% of its overnight funding needs.

On 17 May the Comptroller, the Federal Deposit Insurance Corporation (FDIC), and the Federal Reserve Bank announced a financial assistance programme. The package had four features. First, there was a $2 billion injection of capital by the FDIC and seven US banks, with $1.5 billion of this coming from the FDIC. The capital injection took the form of a subordinated demand loan and was made available to CI for the period necessary to enhance the bank's permanent capital, by merger or otherwise. The rate of interest was 100 basis points above the one-year treasury bill rate. Second, 28 US banks provided a $5.5 billion federal funds back-up line to meet CI's immediate liquidity requirements, to be in place until a permanent solution was found. It had a spread of 0.25% above the Federal funds rate. Third, the Federal Reserve gave an assurance that it was prepared to meet any extraordinary liquidity requirements of CI. Finally, the FDIC guaranteed all depositors and other general creditors of the bank full protection, with no interruption in the service to the bank's customers.

In return for the package, all directors of CI were asked to resign and the FDIC took direct management control of the bank. In October 1986 it was revealed that in 1984 the FDIC had assumed $3.5 billion of CI's debt. The Federal Reserve injected about $1 billion in new capital. The FDIC received 32 million preference shares that convert on sale into 160 million common shares in the bank's parent CI Corporation and $320 million in interest-bearing preferred stock. It also obtained an option on another 40.3 million shares in 1989, if losses on doubtful loans exceeded $800 million. It was estimated they exceeded $1 billion.

Continental Illinois got into problems for a number of reasons. First, it lacked a rigorous procedure for vetting new loans, resulting in poor-quality loans to the US corporate sector, the energy sector, and the real estate sector. Second, CI failed to quickly classify bad loans as non-performing; the delay caused depositors to be suspicious of what the bank was hiding. Third, the restricted deposit base of a single branch system forced the bank to rely on wholesale funds as it fought to expand. Fourth, supervisors should have been paying closer attention to liability management, in addition to internal credit control procedures. Fifth, the global nature of CI's funding base made it imperative that the FED and FDIC act as LLR to avoid the risk of a run by foreign depositors in other US banks—one of the first applications of the *too big to fail doctrine*.

Johnson Matthey Bankers (JMB)

JMB is the banking arm of Johnson Matthey, dealers in gold bullion and precious metals. JMB had to be rescued in October 1984, following an approach to the Bank of England by the directors of JM, who believed the problems with JMB might threaten the whole group. The original lifeboat rescue package consisted of the purchase of JMB and its subsidiaries by the Bank of England, for a nominal sum (£1.00) and wrote off a large proportion of their assets. The bullion dealer, Johnson Matthey, was required to put up £50 million to allow JMB to continue trading. Charter Consolidated, a substantial investor in JM, contributed £25 million. Other contributors were the clearing banks (£35 million), the other four members of the gold ring (£30 million), the accepting houses which were not members of the gold ring (£10 million) and the Bank of England (£75 million).

On 7 November 1984 an agreed package of indemnities was announced to cover the possibility that JMB's loan losses might eventually exceed its capital base of £170 million. In May 1985 the Bank of England declared that provisions of £245 million were necessary to cover the loan losses. With this increase in loan provisions, all lifeboat contributions were raised to make up the short-fall; the Bank of England and other members of the lifeboat contributing half the amount of the shortfall each. On 22 November 1984, the Bank of England made a deposit of £100 million to provide additional working funds.

JMB got into trouble because it managed to acquire loan losses of £245 million on a loan portfolio of only £450 million, so it had to write off over half of its original loan portfolio. Compare this to the case of Continental Illinois, where non-performing loans were only 7.4% of its total loans. Press reports noted that most of these bad loans were made to traders involved with third world countries, especially Nigeria, suggesting a high concentration of risks. The Bank of England's guideline on loan concentration (banks should limit loans to a single borrower or connected group of borrowers to 10% of the capital base) appears to have been ignored. The Bank of England was aware of the problems in 1983 but did not act until the full extent of the problems emerged after a special audit in 1984.

The auditors also appeared to be at fault. Under the UK Companies Act, their ultimate responsibility lies with the shareholders and they are required to report whether the accounts prepared by the bank's directors represent a "true and fair view". In assessing the bank, the auditor reviews the internal audit and inspections systems, and on a random basis examines the record of transactions to verify that they are authentic, and discusses with the directors decisions made in highly sensitive areas such as making provisions against bad and doubtful debts. Auditors are not permitted to discuss the audit with bank supervisors, without the permission of the clients. The auditors can either agree with the directors that the accounts represent a true and fair view, or they can disagree with the directors, in which case they must either resign or qualify the accounts. The auditors at JMB signed unqualified reports, implying all was well. On the other hand, if the auditors had sig-nalled problems by signing a qualified report or resigning, it might have precipitated a bank run, and the authorities may not have had enough time to put together a lifeboat operation.

As was noted in Chapter 6, the Bank of England's system of supervision is a flexible one. However, the JMB affair revealed two gaps in the reporting system. First, auditors had no formal contact with the Bank of England and were unable to register their concerns, unless they either resigned or qualified their reports. Second, the statistical returns prepared for the Bank of England, based on management interviews, are not subject to an independent audit. The 1987 amendment to the Banking Act addressed these problems partially; auditors were encouraged to warn supervisors of suspected fraud, and were given greater access to Bank of England information.

The JMB affair prompted the establishment of a committee involving the Treasury, Bank of England officials and an external expert, to review the bank supervisory procedures, especially the relationship between the auditor and supervisor. The result of the review of the affair was an amendment of the Banking Act (1987). However, the effectiveness of private auditing was again questioned after the BCCI closure (see below).

The JMB case illustrated the use of a lifeboat rescue by the Bank of England, and is a rare example of where the too big to fail doctrine was extended to protect non-banking arms of a financial firm. The main point of a rescue is to prevent the spread of the contagion effect arising from a collapsed bank. Johnson Matthey was one of the five London gold price fixers. Obviously, the Bank of England was concerned that the failure of the banking arm would spread to JM, thereby damaging London's reputation as a major international gold bullion dealer. The episode suggests the Bank is prepared to engage in a lifeboat rescue effort to protect an entire conglomerate, provided it is an important enough operator on global financial markets.

US Thrift Institutions

Between 1980 and 1993 there were about 1300 thrift failures in the USA.* Thrifts are savings and loan (S&L) mutual banks. Until recently, they were backed by deposit insurance provided by the Federal Savings and Loan Insurance Corporation (FSLIC). The FSLIC was in turn regulated by the Federal Home Loan Bank Board. Both institutions were dissolved by statute in 1989.

In 1932, Congress passed the Federal Home Loan Bank Act. The Act created 12 Federal Home Loan Banks, with the Federal Home Loan Bank Board (FHLBB) as their supervisory agent. The aim was to provide thrifts with an alternative source of funding for home mortgage lending. In 1933, the government became involved in the chartered savings and loans firms. The Home Owner's Loan Act was passed, authorising the Federal Home Loan Bank Board (FHLBB) to charter and regulate the savings and loan associations. The National Housing Act, 1934, created a deposit insurance fund for savings and loan associations, the Federal Savings and Loan Insurance Corporation (FSLIC). Unlike the FDIC, which was established as a separate organisation from the Federal Reserve System, the FSLIC was placed under the auspices of the FHLBB. Insurance coverage for S&L depositors is $100 000.00.

The first signs of trouble came in the mid-1960s, when inflation and high interest rates created funding problems. Regulations prohibited the federally insured savings and loans from diversifying their portfolios, which were concentrated in long-term fixed-rate mortgages. Deposit rates began to rise above the rates of return on their home loans. In 1966, Congress tried to address the problem by imposing a maximum ceiling on deposit rates paid by thrifts, though they were authorised to pay 0.25% more on deposits than commercial banks (Regulation Q), thereby giving them a distorted comparative advantage. Unfortunately, the difference was not enough because market interest rates rose well above the deposit rate ceilings. The system of interest rate controls became unworkable and aggravated the thrifts' maturity mismatch problems. The 1980 Depository Institutions Deregulation and Monetary Control Act

---

*This figure comes from Ludwig (1994). For a detailed account of the crisis, see White (1991).

(DIDMCA) took the first significant step toward deregulating the industry. The DIDMCA allowed interest rate regulations to be phased out, and permitted thrifts to diversify their asset portfolios to include consumer loans other than mortgage loans, loans based on commercial real estate, commercial paper, and corporate debt securities. But lack of experience meant diversification contributed to a widespread loan quality crisis by the end of the 1980s.

DIDMCA came too late for thrifts facing the steep rise in interest rates that began in 1981 and continued in 1982. Federally chartered S&Ls had not been given the legal authority to make variable rate mortgage loans until 1979 and then only under severe restrictions. Variable rate mortgages could not be freely negotiated with borrowers until 1981. By that time, deposit rates had risen well above the rates most thrifts were earning on their outstanding fixed rate mortgage loans. Accounting practices disguised the problem because thrifts could report their net worth based on historic asset value, rather than the true market value of their assets.

Policies of regulatory forbearance aggravated the difficulties. Kane and Yu (1994) defined *forbearance* as "a policy of leniency or indulgence in enforcing a collectable claim against another party" (p. 241). *Regulatory forbearance* refers to the situation where supervisory authorities adopt lenient policies in the enforcement of claims against thrifts, because the regulators have a vested interest in prolonging their survival. In 1981 and 1982, the FHLBB authorised adjustments in the Regulatory Accounting Principles, thereby allowing thrift net worth to be reported more leniently than would have been the case had Generally Accepted Accounting Principles been applied. In 1980 and 1982, the FHLBB lowered minimum net worth requirements. These changes reduced the solvency threshold and meant thrifts could record inflated net worth values. Fewer thrift failures meant fewer demands on the FSLIC's fund.

The FSLIC also introduced an income-capital certificates programme, to counter any crisis of confidence. Thrifts could obtain income certificates to supplement their net worth because they were reported as a part of equity. Since the FSLIC did not have the money to cover the certificates, it usually exchanged its own promissory notes for them. Firms included these notes as assets on their balance sheets. Thus, the programme amounted to the purchase of equity in an insolvent firm by the FSLIC, using its own credit. The certificates reduced the number of thrift failures, but heightened the FSLIC's financial interest in preventing troubled thrifts from failing.

The Garn-St Germain Depository Institution Act of 1982 created a net worth certificate programme, a derivative of the income capital certificates. The net worth certificates differed from the income capital certificates in that they did not constitute a permanent equity investment but were issued only for a set time period, authorised by the legislation. These certificates could not be used to reorganise insolvent thrifts or to arrange mergers, because they were not transferable. The Act also liberalised the investment powers of federally chartered thrifts. Additionally, some states (for example, California) took the initiative to deregulate savings and loans even further.

In late 1982, interest rates were lower and less volatile but failed to curtail difficulties because credit quality had become a serious problem. For example, by 1984 it was reported that asset quality problems explained 80% of the "problem" thrifts. In 1985, the FHLBB introduced a "Management Consignment Program". This was designed to stem the growing losses of insolvent thrifts. Usually, it resulted in a thrift's management being replaced by a conservator selected by the Bank Board. It was to be a temporary measure, until the FSLIC could sell or liquidate the thrifts. It became increasingly apparent to financial market participants that the FSLIC lacked the resources to deal with the heavy losses accumulated by the troubled savings and loan industry. They became reluctant to accept the promissory notes which backed the income capital certificates. By 1985, the deteriorating condition of the insolvent thrifts strained the resources of the FSLIC to the point that it needed outside funding. Despite efforts to recapitalise it, the FSLIC was declared insolvent in early 1987, with its deficit estimated to exceed $3 billion at the end of 1986. This raised more concern about the creditworthiness of the FSLIC's promissory notes. The 1987 Competitive Equality Banking Act (CEBA) authorised the issue of $10.8 billion in bonds to recapitalise the FSLIC. But the possibility of a taxpayer-funded bail-out of the FSLIC appeared in the financial press, heightening concern about the riskiness of FSLIC notes.

In 1988, the General Accounting Office (GAO) warned of the costs of dealing with more than 300 insolvent thrifts that the FSLIC had yet to place under receivership, estimated to reach as high as $19 billion. By the end of 1988, the estimate was raised to over $100 billion, as the GAO recognised the problem was far more extensive than had first been thought. The final bill was approximately $300 billion.

To deal with the crisis, the Bush Plan was unveiled on 6 February 1989. It became the model for the Financial Institutions Reform, Recovery, and Enforcement Act (FIRREA), 1989. Several components of the Act were relevant to the thrift crisis. It restricted the investment powers of savings and loans, requiring them to specialise more in mortgage lending, thereby reversing earlier policy; it also put an end to the regulatory forbearance policies of the 1980s. Under the Act, Savings and Loans are required to meet capital requirements at least as stringent as those imposed on commercial banks. The Act dissolved the FSLIC and established the Savings Association Insurance Fund (SAIF) under the auspices of the FDIC. It also created the Resolution Trust Corporation (RTC) to take over the case-load of insolvent thrifts, and disbanded the Federal Home Loan Bank Board, replacing it with the Office of Thrift Supervision, (OTS) under the direction of the Secretary of the Treasury. The RTC was allocated funds to pay off the obligations incurred by the FSLIC, and subsequently received $50 billion in additional funding, to be used by the Corporation to take over the 350 insolvent thrifts, and either liquidate or merge them. Four hundred thrifts thought to be on the threshold of insolvency were not covered by the plan. FIRREA also allowed commercial banks to acquire healthy thrifts—prior to this Act, they could only take over failing savings and loans.

The Financial Recovery, Reform, and Enforcement Act (FIRREA) left a number of problems unresolved. Requiring savings and loans to specialise more in mortgage lending limits opportunities for diversification. Though capital requirements are more stringent, risks will be concentrated in home loans. However, greater diversification would only be successful if staff had the experience and training to manage a more diversified portfolio. No measures have been introduced to prevent the massive fraud that occurred throughout the industry from happening again. FIRREA set new rules for a higher minimum net worth but there is no statutory provision for ensuring that insolvent institutions will be closed more promptly in the future than they have in the past. FIRREA had nothing to say about the problem of insolvent deposit insurance funds, but the Federal Deposit Insurance Corporation Act (1991) requires a least cost approach to failure and risk-based deposit insurance premia. FIRREA did reduce some of the conflicts of interest that gave rise to regulatory forbearance and exacerbated the crisis.

To summarise, the thrift industry suffered as a result of concentration of credit risk in the real estate market and exposure to interest rate risk through long-term fixed interest loans and mortgage backed securities, valued on their books at the original purchase price. Rising interest rates reduced the value of these securities and forced the thrifts to bear the burden of fixed interest loans. The problem was compounded by policies of regulatory forbearance: the FSLIC and the Bank Board had a vested interest in keeping them afloat.

US Commercial Bank Failures

In the period 1980–93 there were approximately 1500 commercial bank failures in addition to the collapse of 1300 thrifts.* Below, some of the more notable failures are discussed.[†] First RepublicBank was the biggest bank in Texas, and called in the FDIC for restructuring talks in March 1988. First Republic forecast a loss in 1988, due to a fall in the value of its property loan book. In August 1988 North Carolina National Bank took over First Republic, but the FDIC filled a negative equity gap of $1.1 billion, with a buy-out option for NCNB. The FDIC was to cover all losses arising from First RepublicBank's $5 billion property loan book.

Other Texas state banks also required large amounts of federal support, namely First City (1988) and MCorp (1989). Over 25% of the US bank failures in the late 1980s occurred in the state of Texas. Problems arose largely because of a concentration of lending in the energy sector, using real estate as collateral. When the price of oil collapsed, so did the value of Texas real estate. Uninsured wholesale depositors switched to safer banks, further restricting growth. The funding problem was aggravated by bank regulations, which prohibited Texan banks from having branches and out-of-state banks from purchasing Texan

---

*Figures from Ludwig (1994).
[†]For more detail, see White (1992).

banks. The former limited expansion into the retail sector and the latter discouraged mergers in the early days of the problem loans.

At one point, the Bank of New England was the 15th largest in the US, but it failed in 1991 due to a large number of non-performing loans. The FDIC bailed out depositors, but shareholders and bondholders suffered heavy losses. Joint bidders took over some of the Bank of New England's operations, with assets worth $15 billion, approximately half the bank's total assets. The FDIC did not take over the bank's problem loans, but provided nearly $1 billion in working capital. At takeover, the FDIC received $100 million in preferred stock and $25 million in cash.

Freedom National Bank, was a small community bank based in Harlem. The FDIC liquidated the bank, but only 50¢ in the dollar was paid to account holders with deposits in excess of $100 000.00, prompting accusations of racism.

Bank of Credit and Commerce International (BCCI)

On Friday, 5 July 1991, the Bank of England, together with the Luxembourg and Cayman Islands authorities, closed all branches of BCCI and froze all deposits. Though BCCI was not incorporated in the UK, once the winding-up order was made, sterling deposits in branches of the UK were eligible for compensation from the Deposit Protection Fund, which covers 75% of a deposit, up to a maximum of £15 000.00, prompting accusations of racism.

In 1972 BCCI was founded by the Pakistani financier Agha Hasan Abedi and incorporated in Luxembourg, with a small amount of capital, $2.5 million (below the Bank of England's £5 million requirement). The Bank of America took a 25% stake. By the time it was closed in 1991, BCCI is estimated to have had a negative net worth of about £7 billion. Losses are estimated at about £12 billion.

BCCI, which has come to be known as the "Bank of Cocaine and Criminals International", had a long history of fraud and illegal dealings. In 1975 the US authorities blocked BCCI's attempt to take over two New York banks, criticising Abedi for failing to disclose details about his company. In 1977, Abedi and BCCI joined forces with a Saudi billionaire, Ghaith Pharon. BCCI launched a hostile takeover bid for Washington's largest bank, Financial General Bankshares. The bid was blocked by the US Securities and Exchange Commission. In 1981, Bankshares was taken over by Middle East investors closely associated with BCCI, though the authorities were assured there was no connection between the banks. In 1983, BCCI bought a Colombian bank, with branches in Medellin and Cali, centres for the cocaine trade and money-laundering. Manuel Noriega, the Panamanian dictator, was a customer of the bank from 1985–87. It later transpired the bank had laundered $32 million of drug money. BCCI was indicted in Florida for laundering drug money in 1988. In London, one of the branches was raided by British customs, who seized evidence of Noriega's deposits, and by 1989 BCCI was announcing losses from bad loans amounting to nearly $500 million. In 1990 five bank executives were imprisoned in Florida after BCCI pleaded guilty to laundering money. The bank was fined $15 million and taken over by Sheikh Zayed Bib Sultan al-Nahyan, ruler of Abu Dhabi. An audit showed large financial irregularities. Bankshares reported a loss of $182 million—it had come to light that BCCI was the secret owner of Bankshares in 1989. In January 1991, John Bartlett of the Bank of England was sent a copy of the "Project Q" interim report. The report identified a core group of 11 customers and 42 accounts linked to the international terrorist, Abu Nidal, but no immediate action was taken, though in March the Bank ordered a section 41 investigation by the auditors.

A number of regulatory gaps and problems came to light as a result of the BCCI scandal. In 1979, the Bank of England restricted BCCI to licensed deposit-taking status, preventing it from having a branch network in England. But after the Banking Act was amended in 1987, it obtained full banking status, because the distinction between banks and LDTs was eliminated. The change gave BCCI the opportunity to extend the branch network, which meant unsophisticated personal and small business customers used the bank for making deposits and to obtain loans. A year later, senior BCCI executives were charged and later convicted of laundering drug money. Top managers were shown to have known about and approved of the money laundering. It was clear that BCCI management failed the "fit and proper" test. But the Bank of England did not suspend management, even though it had the discretionary power so to do.

The Florida drug case prompted the establishment of a College of Regulators because of concern about BCCI. The original group consisted of regulators from the UK, Switzerland, Spain and Luxembourg. Hong Kong, the Cayman Islands, France and the United Arab Emirates joined later. However, it was largely ineffective. In July 1989 Manhattan District Attorney staff attended an international conference on money laundering, held in Cambridge, UK. They discovered BCCI had an international reputation for capital flight, tax fraud, and money laundering. Assuming the Bank of England also knew about it, there is the question of why BCCI was allowed to stay open. Furthermore, it is alleged the Bank of England and Price Waterhouse failed to cooperate with the US authorities. For example, investigators from the New York District Attorney's office claim they were refused access to BCCI London documents in July 1989. Also, the Manhattan District Attorney and the Federal Reserve were unsuccessful when they tried to get a copy of the Price Waterhouse special audit report. In the autumn of 1990, the Federal Reserve demanded a copy of the audit.

Price Waterhouse had been BCCI's sole auditor since 1988, and submitted 10 reports to the Bank of England. Two Price Waterhouse reports were published in April and October 1990, indicating large-scale fraud. The Price Waterhouse evidence to the British House of Commons (February 1992) confirmed Price Waterhouse had informed the Bank of England as early as April 1990 that at BCCI, "certain transactions have either been false or deceitful". In October 1990 it reported fictitious loans and deposits to the Bank of England. By December, the auditors told the Bank the main shareholders in Abu Dhabi were aware of the fraud. The Bank of England admits that it received its first indication of fraud in January 1991 but it did not activate section 41 of The Banking Act until March, 1991. The section 41 investigation carried out by Price Waterhouse confirmed large-scale fraud, but it was a further four months before BCCI was closed.

At the time of writing, two people have appeared in a UK court, charged with conspiring to mislead BCCI's auditors. Mohammed Abdul Baqi is a former managing director of a London-based trading group and was convicted in April 1994 and given a custodial sentence. In the US, two Washington "super lawyers", Clark Clifford and Robert Altman, were accused of concealing BCCI's ownership of Bankshares, fraud, conspiracy, and accepting $40 million in bribes, but the charges were dropped in early 1993. In Abu Dhabi, 14 ex-BCCI managers were convicted in 1994 and one was extradited to the USA in 1994 to face further charges.

The Bingham Report (October 1992) criticised the Bank of England for failing to act after receiving a series of warnings, over many years, of fraud and other illegal activities at BCCI. Price Waterhouse was criticised for failing to fully brief the Bank of England about the extent of the fraud it had found in early 1991. A US Senate report (from a Senate foreign operations subcommittee, October 1992) criticised the Bank of England for wholly inadequate supervision. Price Waterhouse was also criticised for failing to cooperate with the US authorities, and is being sued by the liquidators of BCCI.

The UK government announced a number of measures to be implemented following the Bingham Report. The Bank of England had to set up a special investigations unit to look into suspected cases of fraud or financial malpractice. A legal unit was established to advise the Bank on its legal obligations under the Banking Act. The Banking Act is to be amended to give the Bank of England the right to close down the UK operations of an international bank if it feels the overseas operations of the bank are not being conducted properly.

As a result of the Bingham recommendations, auditors now have a legal duty to pass on information related to suspected fraud to the Bank of England.* Auditing firms in the UK objected to the change, claiming it would no longer be profitable for them to conduct bank audits, though no accounting firm, has, to date, withdrawn from this market.

With respect to international supervision, the Bingham enquiry recommended a method for international monitoring of supervisory standards and an international database of individuals who have failed to pass a "fit and proper" criterion. If a financial centre permits a high degree of bank secrecy, regulators in other countries should be able to close down foreign branches or subsidiaries.

Barings

On Sunday, 26 February 1995, the oldest merchant bank in the UK, Barings (founded in 1762) ceased trading and was put into administration.† It owed over £800 million on financial derivatives contracts, but had a capital base of just £540 million. The Bank of England, which had spent the last weekend in February 1995 trying to put together a lifeboat rescue package involving other

---

*Building society and insurance company auditors will be subject to similar requirements.
†Administration is a procedure introduced under the 1986 Insolvency Act. An administrator (usually an accountant) is assigned the task of trying to save the business instead of having it liquidated. While a receiver has as his/her main objective the protection of creditors' interests, the administrator is appointed to try and maintain the firm as a going concern. While a firm is in administration, there is a statutory freeze on enforcement of creditors' rights and remedies.

banks, conceded defeat late on Sunday night. It could not persuade a bank or banks (both domestic and foreign) to close futures contracts entered by a trader, Mr Nick Leeson, in Barings' Singapore offices. A syndicate of commercial and investment banks was ready to recapitalise Barings (at an estimated cost of £700 million), but none would accept a fixed fee in exchange for closing these trading positions. The Bank of England announced it was ready to provide liquidity to the markets if necessary, but refused to use public funds to bail out Barings. As it turned out, global market disruptions following the collapse proved to be minimal, confirming the Bank of England's judgement that the collapse was unlikely to provoke systemic failure.

The Chancellor of the Exchequer, Mr Kenneth Clarke, announced that the Barings collapse would be investigated by the Bank of England's Board of Banking Supervision, but ruled out a public or independent inquiry. This Board is chaired by the Governor of the Bank of England and consists of six outside members, in addition to Bank of England representatives. In March 1995 Mr George revealed that six external members had been asked to make an independent assessment of the Bank of England's supervision of Barings. The Board of Banking Supervision's Report ("The Report") was made public on 18 July 1995.

Before its collapse, Barings was well known in the City of London for mergers and acquisitions and its strength in emerging markets. About one-third of the bank's employees were based in Asia, and about one half outside the UK. The broking and market making arm of the bank, Barings Securities, was a leading equity broker in Asia and Latin America. The fund management operation had a reputation for its expertise in eastern Europe. Just as exposure in Latin America had led to near ruin in 1890, so exposure in the Far East was the cause of Baring's downfall in 1995.

On 6 March 1995, Internationale Nederlanden Group (ING Bank) a Dutch bancassurance concern, purchased Barings' banking, securities, and asset management businesses for one pound. *Bancassurance* is the combination of banking and insurance into one group. ING had been formed as a result of the merger, in 1991, of Nationale Nederlanden (the largest Dutch insurer) with the Netherland's third largest Dutch bank, NMB Postbank, known for its lending to small and medium-sized Dutch companies. Bank branches sell insurance and the group has been able to offer new financing schemes to corporations by pooling the short and long-term funds from, respectively, the banking and insurance arms of the company. ING took responsibility for Barings' existing liabilities (estimated at £860 million) but any future liabilities will be borne by Barings plc, the holding company, which ING did not buy. The administrators, Ernst and Young, are expected to liquidate Barings plc. ING has little experience in third party fund management, corporate finance or brokerage, but has expanded its insurance activities into emerging markets, selling insurance in Argentina and Peru. ING has a minority holding in Poland's third largest bank, Bank Slaski, and has obtained foreign bank licences in Romania and Bulgaria. Barings' expertise in this area should prove beneficial. The chairman of ING announced that all senior executives of Barings would be kept on until the publication of the Bank of England report. Staff bonuses of close to £100 million were to be paid, though executive directors of Barings had waived them and senior employees directly involved in the losses did not benefit from the bonuses.

Though the downfall of Barings was due to unlimited exposure in the derivatives market, there was nothing very complicated about the derivatives that got the bank into trouble. Mr Leeson was an arbitrageur, whose job was to spot differences in the prices of futures contracts and profit from buying futures contracts on one market and simultaneously selling them on another. The margins are small, and the volumes traded large. The procedure does not entail much risk, because one establishes a long position in one market (speculating on a rise), and a short position in another market (betting on a fall), making a profit from the price differences.

Mr Leeson was supposed to have been trying to profit by spotting differences in the prices of the Nikkei-225 futures contracts listed on the Osaka Securities Exchange (OSE) and the Singapore Monetary Exchange (SIMEX). SIMEX attracts Japanese stock market futures because the Osaka exchange is subject to more regulation and hence is more costly.* The Report claimed that rather than hedging his positions, Leeson seems to have decided to bet on the future direction of the Nikkei index. By 23 February, when his actions came to light, Leeson had purchased $7 billion in stock index futures and sold $20 billion worth of bond and interest rate futures contracts. Most of the losses came from the stock index futures. Meanwhile, the senior management at Barings were under the impression that the extraordinary profits Leeson was claiming came from the relatively risk-free arbitrage, hence they remained unconcerned. The Report criticised the former chairman and deputy chairman of Barings, respectively, Mr Peter Baring, and Mr Tuckey, for failing to ensure they were properly informed of Mr Leeson's activities, and the source of his apparent (extraordinary) profits. Mr Peter Norris, chief executive of Barings was cited as being responsible for inaccurate reports being submitted to the Bank of England, the Securities and Futures Authority, and Coopers and Lybrand, the external auditors. Mr Ron Baker, the former head of the financial products group, was criticised for not knowing what Mr Leeson was really doing, and for his general lack of understanding of Singapore's operations.

Though early reports suggested Mr Leeson had acted on his own, it has since become apparent that "rogue trading" is an insufficient explanation for the events leading up to the collapse. The *Financial Times*[†] reported that an internal audit at Barings Futures in Singapore had been initiated by Barings' management because of the subsidiary's exceptional profitability. The purpose of the audit was to investigate whether rules were being broken and/or exceptional risks being taken. The audit report was submitted in August 1994 and concluded the profits had been made by legitimate means—it appeared

---

*Investors taking a position on the OSE market must deposit 30% of the initial value of the contract with the exchange. In Singapore, the position is a fraction of this.
[†] *Financial Times*, 4 March, 1995: p.1,18.

to accept that the Singapore office had found a method to make exceptional profits through derivatives arbitrage, without assuming much risk.

However, the audit noted Mr Leeson held the position of General Manager, head of both trading (front office) and settlements (back office), thereby making it possible for him to circumvent the controls in place, because he could intitiate transactions in the front office and use the back office to ensure they were recorded and settled as per his instructions. The report accepted that Barings Futures was a relatively small operation (25 employees) which, in the absence of more experienced staff, would mean Leeson would continue to play an active role in both offices. Instead of appointing a full-time risk manager, it was agreed the risk manager in Hong Kong would conduct quarterly reviews of the Singapore operations. The internal auditors did suggest Mr Leeson should no longer supervise the back office team, cheque-signing, signing off on the reconciliations of activities at SIMEX, and signing off bank reconciliations. However, it is unclear whether Mr Leeson relinquished any of these duties.

The *Financial Times** was the first to report that Mr Leeson had used a secret error account 88888 to hide trading losses. In the report by the Board of Banking Supervision, it appears the secret account 88888 was opened much earlier by Mr Leeson, in July 1992, a few months after he had arrived in Singapore. Initially the account was included in reports to Barings, London, but at some point Mr Leeson was able to persuade a computer expert to confine information about this account to just one report. He used the account to hide losses and exaggerate his earnings, which in turn increased the size of his bonus. By year-end 1992, the account had a cumulative loss of £2 million, and it remained at about this level through to October 1993. By the end of 1993, losses had risen to £23 million, and by 1994, to £208 million.

The problems began in January 1994,[†] when Mr Leeson sold put options (conferring a right to buy) and simultaneously, sold call options (conferring a right to sell) on the Nikkei 225 index. Up to 40 000 contracts were sold. The deals would have been profitable if the Japanese market had proved less volatile than that predicted by the option prices. But Kobe was hit by a devastating earthquake on 17 January, and the Nikkei fell slightly. Mr Leeson needed the Nikkei to stay in the range of 18 500 to 19 500 to stay in profit. In an attempt to bolster the Nikkei, Leeson bought Nikkei futures on an enormous scale but on 23 January the index lost 1000 points, falling to under 17 800. He continued to buy futures, in the hope that he could influence the market, keeping in mind that bonuses were due to be fixed on 24 February. His attempts failed, leaving Barings with £827 million in losses.

Financial Times, 3 March, 1995: p.2.
[†]This version of events was first reported by *The Economist*, 4 March, 1995: pp.19–21. Most of the key points have since been confirmed by the official report.

Throughout this time, Barings London was deceived into thinking Mr Leeson had made profits from arbitrage. But losses were accumulating in the 88888 account. For example, Leeson earned a £130 000 bonus in 1993, and in 1994, it was reported Leeson had earned £28.5 million in revenues, more than three-quarters the profits of the Barings Group. It transpires that the London head office had transferred large amounts of funds to Singapore, under the impression it was being used for clients' business, when in fact it was being used for margins, to cover Leeson's options positions.

This account was used again when Mr Leeson went long on the Nikkei 225 index. In a memorandum written by Mr Tony Hawes, Barings Group Treasurer on 24 February 1995, the account had over 61 000 long positions on SIMEX, in the form of futures contracts. It also had 26 079 short positions in Japanese government bonds, and 6485 positions in Euroyen. The total loss on the account came to £384 million. But the writer of the memorandum did not appear to know about further losses on options contracts. Auditors failed to notice its significance, because, it was claimed, it had been disguised as a receivable.

Since the collapse, it has been widely acknowledged that internal controls at Barings were lacking, especially in the area of risk management. On paper, the controls appeared satisfactory. At the end of 1994 a new unit in Barings called Group Treasury and Risk was formed to oversee risks. It reported to an Asset Liability Committee, which was supposed to meet daily to oversee risk, trading limits, and capital funding. This new unit was created as part of the effort to integrate the merchant bank, Barings Brothers, with Barings Securities, the broking arm, into a single investment bank. But Barings, it was rumoured, faced the usual problems of trying to merge traditional merchant banking with trading cultures. Barings may have expanded into derivatives trading too quickly, before internal checks were in place. For example, Barings appears to have had no gross position limits on proprietary trading operations in Singapore. The deals undertaken by Mr Leeson aroused little suspicion until it was too late, even though traders at rival firms and regulators at the Bank for International Settlements (BIS) were amazed at the growth of Barings' positions.

Regulatory authorities are also open to criticism. The SIMEX and Osaka exchanges failed to act, despite the rapid growth of contracts at Barings. Mr John Sander, Chairman of the Chicago Mercantile Exchange noted that such a build-up of contracts would not happen on the CME. A CME trader buying or selling more contracts than allowed by the regulations would be barred from the exchange within an hour. Participants on this exchange are required to have a surveillance team to conduct regular and independent monitoring.* SIMEX blamed Barings' management in London, claiming the group had continuously assured SIMEX it could meet any obligations, throughout January and February.

Financial Times, 3 March, 1995.

According to the Bank of England's Board of Banking Supervision, the Bank of England was deficient in its supervision of Barings, in a number of respects. Barings had been granted *solo consolidation* status, meaning the parent bank and its subsidiary, Barings Securities were required to meet a single set of capital and exposure standards. This meant the Bank of England had sole responsibility for the supervision of all of Barings, even though the Securities and Futures Association (SFA) is much more experienced in the supervision of securities activities. Solo consolidation also meant Barings depositors were exposed to trading losses. The alternative, more common method of supervision is known as *solo plus*, whereby the bank and the securities subsidiary are separated for the purposes of regulation, meaning different capital standards may be applied. Effectively, a firewall is erected between the two parts of the business, so the bank does not have to fund trading losses from the parent bank. These points raise broader questions about the best way to supervise financial conglomerates, an issue that was discussed in Chapter 6.

The Bank of England will also have to address the question of why a breach of European Union rules by Barings was not detected. Under EU regulations, banks are not allowed to put more than 25% of their equity capital into a single investment without Bank of England approval. The capital for Barings' investment banking operations was £440 million, limiting it to a single exposure of no more than £100 million. Yet in the first two months of 1995, Barings transferred a total of £569 million to Barings Futures, Singapore. The losses accumulated in Mr Leeson's account amounted to £384 million. Barings did not report the exposure to the Bank of England. However, the Bank of England should have been able to detect the substantial increase in credit exposure through the monthly liquidity report, supplied by a bank's treasury to supervisors. Though some other banks, including the BIS, noted Barings' increased borrowings on the money market by the end of January 1995, the Bank of England apparently did not. Mr Chris Thomson, the supervisor for merchant banks, resigned from the Bank of England in the week before the Report was published. He had agreed to allow Barings to exceed exposure limits on the Osaka Securities Exchange. This informal concession was granted without any consultation with more senior Bank of England officials. Once discovered, the Bank of England took over a year before it rescinded this concession, in January 1995.

One gets a sense of *déjà vu* when reading the Report's criticism of Barings' external auditors, Coopers and Lybrand. Coopers and Lybrand London was criticised for failing to conduct sufficiently comprehensive tests that would have detected the large funding requests from Singapore, which were inconsistent with the claim that Leeson's profits were coming from arbitrage. Coopers and Lybrand Singapore had audited Barings Futures Singapore in 1994, and had been satisfied that proper internal controls were in place. Coopers London has responded that it did find and report a £50 million discrepancy (the documentation for a £50 million receivable was insufficient). The firm also argues it cannot be criticised, because Barings collapsed before it had conducted its 1994 audit. But the Board of Banking Supervision has called for improved communication between internal and external auditors, and regulators—recall that similar conclusions were reached after the JMB and BCCI investigations.

Mr Leeson fled to Germany (enroute to London) after the losses came to light. He was arrested by the German authorities after Singapore filed an extradition request. In late November 1995, Mr Leeson gave up his fight against extradition, and, as this book goes to press, is in Singapore, awaiting trial on multiple fraud and forgery charges.

In September, 1995, it was reported that a senior trader, Mr Toshihide Iguchi, lost just over $1 billion while working for the New York branch of **Daiwa Bank**. He is now in a U.S. prison awaiting trial on charges of fraud and forgery. It was revealed that the money had been lost over a ten year period. The trading losses were covered up through the sale of securities stolen from customer accounts, which were replaced by forged securities. The losses remained undetected until Mr Iguchi confessed to Daiwa in July. Mr Iguchi was allowed to audit his own accounts. The Ministry of Finance in Japan had given the New York branch a clean bill of health in 1994. The branch had also been subject to joint regulatory scrutiny by the Federal Reserve Bank of New York and state banking authorities since 1991. The auditors in Japan (part of Ernst and Young International) did not conduct a separate audit of the New York branch, and failed to spot any problems. While the parent bank has sufficient capital to absorb the loss, American regulators have prohibited Daiwa from conducting any banking business in the United States.

Scandinavian Bank Failures

In Denmark, there have been five problem banks since 1985, the key difficulty being excessive exposure to certain clients. For example, Kronenbanken, the seventh largest bank in Denmark, exceeded its lending limits to an engineering firm. A small bank, C + G Banken, exceeded lending limits to a construction firm which went bankrupt. A niche bank, Juli Banken, incurred large losses after excessive lending to a group of developers.

In Finland, there have been three problem banks since 1991, caused by bad loans and poor stock market investments. There was state intervention in 22 Norwegian banks in the period 1988–91, caused by problem loans, principally in the shipping sector (at least three banks), but also in the shipyards, petroleum and fishing. There were asset quality problems in the mortgage business and also losses from export finance. In Sweden, three banks were rescued between 1991 and 1993, because of heavy credit losses, especially in the property and construction sectors. By the end of 1994, the future of Swedbank, a group of saving banks which had to be bailed out in 1991 was looking promising, after a major reorganisation which increased central management control, closed branches, and led to 3500 redundancies (out of a staff of 13,500). These changes enabled the Swedbank to cut its operating costs by 20%. The bank has also weathered the worst of dud property loans, after the collapse of the property market in 1992.

Canadian Bank Failures

During the autumn of 1985, five out of 14 Canadian domestic banks found themselves in difficulty. Two banks (Canadian Commercial and Northland) had to close. The problems of Canadian Commercial Bank (CCB), based in Edmonton, originated with its loan portfolio, which was concentrated in the real estate and energy sectors. An inspection in early 1982 revealed two-thirds of uncollected interest was on property loans and another 16% on energy-related loans. In the summer of 1985 (after CCB had approached the authorities), government investigations revealed that 40% of the loan portfolio was marginal or unsatisfactory. To attract deposits, CCB had to pay above-average rates, as did other regional banks.

In March 1985, CCB informed the authorities it was in danger of collapse. Despite indications of trouble, the inspection system failed to identify the serious problems. A rescue package (CDN $225 million) was put together, the six largest banks contributing $60 million. This action failed to restore the confidence of depositors and a contagion effect spread to other smaller regional banks in Canada; depositors (for example, municipal treasurers) who had been attracted by their higher interest rates began to withdraw their deposits on a large scale, as did the big banks that had participated in the rescue package. The Bank of Canada responded by granting short-term loans to cover these deposit withdrawals but soon had to extend this facility to the Calgary-based Northland Bank, because of contagion runs on this bank. The Northland Bank had been receiving liquidity support from the major private banks since 1983, but the agreement ran out and the bank turned to the Bank of Canada for support at the same time as CCB asked for help. The two banks were forced to close in September 1985, after the Bank of Canada withdrew its support because of a supervisory report (by the Inspector General of Banks) which indicated insolvency at both banks because of weak loan portfolios.

Two other banks, Mercantile and Morguard, were merged with larger institutions. Mercantile Bank was a Montreal-based bank, in which Citicorp had a 24% interest. This bank was involved in wholesale bank business. The bank began to experience trouble attracting deposits. The Bank of Canada did not intervene but persuaded the six large banks to provide short-term loans to Mercantile. A few weeks later, it was purchased by the Montreal-based National Bank. In November 1985, Morguard Bank was taken over by California's Security Pacific Bank.

Continental Bank experienced a serious run on deposits. Although this bank had a healthy loan portfolio, it had suffered from low rates of profitability: the return on assets was 0.29% in the 12 months to 31 October 1985. The Bank of Canada and the six largest banks granted Continental CDN $2.9 billion in standby credit lines when it experienced a run, which proved to be short-lived. Some depositors returned after the bank launched a campaign to restore confidence, which included an examination of its loan portfolio by 25 officials from the big six banks.

Japanese Bank Problems

Toyo Sogo Bank ran into problems in 1991 because of excessive exposure to a local shipbuilder and other bad loans, and was taken over by another bank. Another bank, Toyo Shinkin Bank, ran into problems in 1991 because of forged certificates of deposit (CDs) issued in its name, and bad debts. Though Toyo Shinkin is part of the Sanwa Bank group, the Industrial Bank of Japan (IBJ) has had to bear most of the burden because it was viewed as the main bank of a restaurant entrepreneur, Ms Nui Onoue. IBJ was required to forgive 70% of its loans to Toyo Shinkin, because it had allowed Ms Onoue to take back some collateral (its own debentures), which she used to borrow somewhere else. Fuji Bank had to write off a similar amount, and so did two non-banks. The Deposit Insurance Corporation assisted by loaning the bank money at favourable rates.

There was a series of financial scandals in 1991, the most notable being bad loans to Nui Onoue. She borrowed about ¥14 billion from 12 of Japan's largest banks, including the Industrial Bank of Japan, which has a reputation for applying strict credit criteria. In October 1992 the senior officials of IBJ, including the chairman, resigned. Onoue was the largest individual stockholder of IBJ, Dai-Ichi Kangyo (the world's largest bank) and Nippon Telephone and Telegraph. She is being held in prison on fraud charges, in particular forgeries of ¥1.5 billion certificates of deposit.

There have also been a large number of company failures, leaving about US $29 billion in bad debts by September 1991, excluding companies not servicing their debts. Banks have encouraged debtors not to dump collateral (especially property), fearing a collapse of property prices. Unlike regulations in the USA and UK, Japanese banks are not required to disclose non-performing loans and can report income from a problem loan a year after it has stopped receiving interest. There is no monitoring of the adequacy of reserves against bad debts. Thus, in the year ending 31 March, 1991, banks reduced the new reserves they set against bad debts even though non-performing loans were rising.

The seriousness of the Japanese banking problems has been highlighted by the establishment of the Cooperative Credit Purchasing Corporation (CPCC), a body similar to the Resolution Trust Corporation in the US, which helps to bail out troubled banks. Unlike the RTC, the CPCC is privately (bank) owned and buys distressed loans from banks. Provided a bank sells a loan to the CPCC at a discount to face value, losses can be deducted from taxable income. The CPCC liquidates the loans by selling underlying collateral to investors. No taxpayer's money has been committed, to date. However, sale of collateral has provided the CPCC with less than 1% of what it has paid for the loans. Initially, the banks transferred loans to the CPCC at two-thirds the face value of the loan, but by May 1995, this figure had declined to just over a third (38%). The problem is the collateral attached to these loans, property. In the early days, it was thought the CPCC could use collateral to cover the two-thirds value of the loans. But property prices are now 80% below their 1989 bubble levels, forcing down the discount.

The Ministry of Finance has agreed to let banks subtract from taxable income the difference between interest received on concessionary loans to troubled firms and the cost of funding the loans. The interest rate concessions have to be deemed essential to the survival of the firm or to be "socially relevant". Since 1992, the MOF has also allowed banks to make tax-free contributions to reserves for loans to borrowers that are insolvent for a minimum of one year. Both these policies discourage banks from declaring bad loans and writing them off. In Japan, unless bankruptcy can be proved, neither bad debt provisions nor loan write-offs are tax deductible. However, between March and September 1994, 11 of the city banks provided for or wrote off about $5.8 billion worth of problem loans.

By mid-1995, it was apparent that large Japanese banks could ride out the storm, but the very small banks were threatened. Banks are plagued by additional problems. From 1994–95, the Nikkei stock market index fell still further, which will mean banks will have to report losses on their equity portfolios. New bad loans continue to be a problem, and the write-offs are expected to continue until 1998. The top 21 banks had write-offs in 1994 that were one-third higher than in 1993. This threatens weaker banks because they loaned money to the same borrowers. In October 1994, under pressure from the Ministry of Finance, Mitsubishi Bank, a healthy bank, announced its rescue of Nippon Trust, with a bad loan portfolio estimated at ¥500 billion ($5 billion). Nippon's net asset value is estimated to be about ¥180 billion, meaning the Trust has a negative net worth, even if half the bad loans are actually repaid. But Mitsubishi, which already owned shares in the Trust, paid ¥200 billion for it, raising its shareholding to 69%. The MOF was of the view that Mitsubishi was obliged to bail out the Trust because of its shareholding. Additionally, Mitsubishi was offered a carrot: it will, through the Trust, be allowed to manage pension funds, because it has acquired an existing trust; other City banks will not be allowed to manage pension funds if they set up trust subsidiaries.

Faced with the collapse of weak banks (for example, Norinchukin, housing loan banks, and Hyogo Bank), the Ministry of Finance is expected to use public funds to rescue these banks. In December 1994, the Bank of Japan announced its first lifeboat rescue. Two troubled credit associations, Tokyo Kyowa and Anzen, were taken over by a new bank, with a ¥20 billion injection from the central bank, and another ¥20 billion from private banks. The rescue, which prompted a public outcry, is a departure from the standard solution, when healthy banks have been coerced into absorbing insolvent banks. As this book goes to press, the official figure for bad debt is ¥40 trillion, or just under $500 billion—unofficial estimates put the figure at double this amount. The debate over the use of public funds to bail out banks is just beginning, and it is unclear what the final bill for the taxpayer will be.

COMMON LESSONS FROM BANK FAILURES

The previous section reviewed, on a case-by-case basis, the well-known bank failures which have occurred over the last 20 years. The case review allows one to draw a number of qualitative conclusions about what causes bank failure. First, weak asset management, as reflected in a weak loan book, appears to be the principal reason why banks get into difficulty. A poor-quality loan book characterised by excessive exposure to one sector (or in a few cases, a single firm) was the main cause of bank failure in the UK (Johnson Matthey Bankers), Italy (Banco Ambrosiano), Canada (two regional banks), the US thrift and commercial bank sectors, Denmark, Norway, Finland, Sweden and Japan. It is noteworthy that in most of the cases cited above, the exposure was overlooked by the supervisory authorities, even though it exceeded well-defined regulations.

Poor asset management frequently extends to choice of collateral. Its value is often highly correlated to the performance of the sector where the excessive exposure occurs. The Texan state banks were heavily exposed in the oil sector, and Texan real estate was the main security for their loans. When the oil price collapsed, real estate prices plummeted. Recently, major banks in Japan have been disinclined to call in bad loans because of the effects it will have on the value of collateral, if property prices were to go into free fall.

Some banks encountered difficulties because of inexperience with new products. The foreign exchange losses incurred by FNB and Bankhaus Herstatt are suggestive of inexperience in dealing with what was then a relatively new product—foreign exchange services. In Denmark certain problem banks experienced heavy losses in securities trading. In Norway, some banks ran into difficulty because of losses related to export finance. A poor understanding of the effects of volatile interest rates on the price of mortgage-backed securities aggravated an already difficult situation for many US thrifts. Not only did bank management misjudge the riskiness associated with these products, but bank supervisors also missed the signals of trouble. However, in all these cases, a poor quality loan book was at least as important as the problems created by "non-bank" financial products.

General managerial deficiency was also a contributory factor. This point is clear from the case studies, and was also the main reason for state intervention and support of Crédit Lyonnais in France and Banesto in Spain, in 1994. Poor internal controls at Barings was acknowledged as a contributory factor in its collapse in 1995. If managers of problem banks (with a negative current net worth), want to save their banks, only highly risky undertakings stand any chance of reversing insolvency. Promotion criteria for bank employees may compound the problem. If individuals are associated with what appear at the time to be innovative techniques, they are more likely to be promoted than those who concentrate on traditional banking products, because it may not be known for years that the innovation results in losses for the bank or financial firm. Most businesses experience this problem, but in banking the maturity structure of a given bank's assets is such that unprofitable investments may not be realised until long after the employee who took the investment decision has been promoted to some other activity within the bank, or hired by a rival institution. It is worth stressing that all of the above remarks should be read in the context of *failing* banks—many of the highly successful banks are on the leading edge of product differentiation, behaviour which is consistent with good management in other types of business.

Often, an indicator of sub-standard management is the well known "herd instinct", or "copycat externality" (Gowland, 1994), which aggravates the tendencies of unsound lending and inexperience in new products. Bankers tend to copy the activities of their competitors, rather than trying to differentiate their products. Asymmetric information, a problem that is particularly acute in banking, may help to explain mimicry, as bankers undertake what they think is a profitable activity when they see other banks engaged in it. For example, suppose one bank grants a loan to a firm undertaking what is viewed as a profitable activity—say property development. Other banks treat this as a signal that such an investment is a good one, and lend to other property development firms which are undertaking similar activities. As a result, the number of players in the property market increases, thereby reducing market share and profitability. Default can occur not only on the second and third loans, but the first loan as well. Prudential regulation may actually encourage herd instinct behaviour, to the extent that banks are expected to conform to a single set of rules. A good example of mimicry is in Japan, where small banks followed the large banks, and ended up with a similar set of borrowers. But market players do not always follow blindly. When Mr Leeson attempted to create herd-like behaviour in the Nikkei index futures market, he failed.

Bank fraud or dishonesty were common to a number of the case failures: Banco Ambrosiano, Bankhaus Herstatt, Franklin National Bank, BCCI, and the US thrift industry. At the time of writing, Mr Nick Leeson, the Barings trader is wanted in Singapore on fraud charges. There were allegations of fraud in the Johnson Matthey Bank case, though no charges were laid. Illegal activities could become more problematic as off-balance sheet activity grows; fraud becomes more difficult to detect because unlike on-balance sheet assets and liabilities, there is not necessarily a cash flow associated with these items. But bank fraud as a *primary* cause of bank failure is rare. The Bank of Credit and Commerce International (BCCI) is the only clear-cut example of a spectacular collapse because of fraud; in the other cases, there were asset management problems which were just as serious.

More typically, outright fraud and managerial incompetence can be hard to tell apart, a point demonstrated by the US thrift industry experience. Akerlof and Romer (1993) took this line of argument even further, using a "looting" hypothesis to explain the magnitude of the US thrift débâcle. Thrift managers, aware an institution would go bankrupt, took advantage of regulatory changes to steal as much as they could from a thrift, before it went under. For example, accounting rules which were relaxed in the early 1980s to encourage wider diversification allowed thrift managers to boost short-term profitability (thereby raising dividends) through loans which added to their long-term liabilities. Similarly, thrifts could buy risky debt (such as junk bonds) and profit from very high interest rates, even though default was highly likely. This hypothesis is a rational explanation for why bank managers, faced with a high probability of a negative net worth, go for broke, and is a more satisfactory interpretation than the traditional view that bankers act in this way because of the moral hazard associated with deposit insurance and "too big to fail" attitudes.

Gowland (1994) raised the possibility that ownership structure affects the probability of bank failure. He suggested that the decline in mutual ownership of thrifts is a partial explanation for the thrift industry crisis. In a mutual organisation, profits are not paid out to shareholders but are accumulated as reserves. When a mutual firm is sold to shareholders, the reserves become the property of the new shareholders. Since the reserves form part of the funds used to finance risky ventures (in addition to the equity), investment in risky loans offered an attractive risk reward combination. Gowland noted that over 60% of "soon to fail" thrifts were shareholder-owned, but only 25% of mutually owned thrifts were in this category.

The case studies demonstrate that supervisors, bank inspectors, and auditors missed important signals of problem banks. For example, even though most have upper limits on the concentration of loans and exposure, there was evidence of concentrated loans or over-exposure in the Johnson Matthey Bank and Banco Ambrosiano cases, and in a number of recent Canadian regional bank failures (Canadian Commercial Bank and Northland—these banks closed in late 1985), the US thrift industry, and other US problem commercial banks. The Bank of England apparently failed to detect signals in the money markets and the monthly liquidity reports that Barings was transferring large amounts of capital to their Singapore operation, which exceeded the 25% of equity capital that banks are allowed to put into one investment. The role of private external auditors has been criticised in the official investigations into the failure of JMCB, BCCI and Barings. It seems reasonable to ask whether it is time for the auditing of banks by private firms to be replaced with a government body with direct responsibility for bank examination and auditing, as is the case in most countries.

The BCCI failure illustrates that problems arise if there is confusion over which regulators are in charge. As a Luxembourg holding company, BCCI was not classified as a bank and therefore was not subject to Luxembourg banking regulations. BCCI also split its banking operations between Luxembourg and the Cayman Islands, making it difficult for regulators to follow what was going on. The Bank of England did not provide comprehensive supervision of BCCI, even though it had a branch network, because it was headquartered in Luxembourg. The case shows how easy it is to avoid the Basle principle (1983) of consolidated supervision. Banco Ambrosiano escaped regulation in the same way. It is clear there are gaps in the coordination of regulating international banks, despite the numerous Basle Agreements aimed at improving it.

Johnson Matthey Bank and Continental Illinois were provided with liquidity by a lender of last report. The Luxembourg subsidiary of Banco Ambrosiano, as well as Bankhaus Herstatt, BCCI and Barings, were all allowed to fail. Franklin National Bank was initially given some support from the Federal Reserve, but in the end was taken over by European American. In the case of the five Canadian banks (all of them second tier), two banks closed (despite a Bank of Canada led rescue package), two banks were merged with larger institutions, and a bank run was stopped after the Bank of Canada and the six largest banks extended their credit lines. The Texan First City Bancorp was bailed out, but many of the smaller bankrupt Texan banks were allowed to go under. In the US thrift industry, rescues in the form of mergers (banks permitted to buy up troubled thrifts) have been the norm. There have also been government-influenced rescues of Scandinavian and Japanese banks. It continues to be the norm to rescue or merge failing banks in Spain and France, as the Banesto and Crédit Lyonnais cases illustrate.

The pattern suggests that banks are likely to be rescued if they are deemed to be "too big to fail", that is, if regulators believe a bank to be of such national or international importance that a collapse could provoke a major run or be the cause of lost business in a major international financial centre. The principle effectively extends to every bank in some countries, such as in France, Spain, and Japan, where the safety net encompasses all banks. The policy is problematic, for three reasons. First, moral hazard is heightened because the too big to fail banks have an incentive to take on greater risks, in the knowledge that their importance will mean they are bailed out. Second, bank supervisors may not monitor the activities of the smaller banks as closely as they otherwise would, if the principle is used selectively. Finally, the doctrine gives large banks a competitive advantage over small banks. Hughes and Mester (1992), employing 1990 US data on 304 banks, showed that for banks in the largest size category* an increase in size (holding default risk and asset quality constant) significantly lowered the uninsured deposit rate[†] these banks have to pay. Likewise, banks in countries which employ a wide safety net should find it less costly to raise global capital than those located in countries with a reputation for selective support.

In several countries, notably the USA and Japan, there is a tendency to rescue banks through merger, which can create additional problems. Smaller banks may undertake greater risks, knowing the worst outcome is merger. If the state assumes responsibility for dud assets of the problem bank, part of the banking system ends up being subsidised by the state. Mergers also increase concentration in the banking system.

The review of bank failures also illustrates a problem of *regulatory forbearance*, whereby regulators put the interests of the regulatory body ahead of that

---

*Banks with assets in excess of $6.5 billion.

[†]Defined as the interest paid on certificates of deposit over $100 000.00 ÷ the average volume of deposits in 1990.

of the taxpayer, by not closing insolvent banks. The US thrift industry experience is the obvious example, though recent policy by the Japanese Ministry of Finance is also suggestive of regulatory forbearance. To overcome the problem, the agency responsible for declaring a bank insolvent must be identified, and should be divested of other potentially conflicting interests.

One of the main reasons for the introduction of the Basle Risk Weighted Capital Assets ratio was to try and ensure banks have adequate capital and so help to prevent bank failure. But one study of thrift failures in the US shows little in the way of a correlation between capital adequacy and bank failure (see Simons, 1992). However, the capital adequacy measure was simplistic compared to the risk assets ratio.

In the USA, an unbalanced deposit base has also been a contributory factor because regulations have limited access to funding. For example, the savings and loans industry was prohibited from accessing the wholesale markets; Continental Illinois had to rely on relatively high-cost short-term wholesale funding because of branch banking restrictions in Illinois. First RepublicBank in Texas suffered the same problem but to a lesser degree, because 20% of its deposits came from the wholesale markets and 40% from regional companies. Other US banks faced similar branching restrictions, but did not use the CI route to overcome the problem, relying instead on more innovative methods of funding though bank holding companies, Edge Act banks, and non-bank banks.

Deposit protection schemes normally cover the small depositor with a view to preventing bank runs. Several of the cases demonstrate the necessity of 100% deposit insurance, if the objective is to eliminate bank runs. However, such a scheme creates moral hazard problems because banks have an incentive to assume greater risks than they would in the absence of deposit insurance, and depositors have little reason to monitor banks. Eliminating or "privatising" deposit insurance would force a bank with a portfolio of assets showing a comparatively high variance in rate of return to pay higher interest on deposits, or to pay higher deposit insurance premia than banks with less risky portfolios. The recent introduction of risk-based deposit insurance premia by the FDIC in the US is an attempt to reduce the moral hazard problems created by deposit insurance. Co-insurance encourages depositors to scrutinise bank activities more closely.

Finally, though it is not obvious from the individual case studies, bank failures in a country tend to be clustered around a few years, rather than being spread evenly through time. Looking at US commercial bank failures as a percentage of healthy banks in the period 1934–91, the annual average was 0.38% from 1934–39 but did not rise above 0.08% between 1940 and 1981. In 1981, it jumped to 0.29%, rising steadily to peak at 1.68% in 1988.* Other nations have experienced these clusters, though comparable figures are not

_____
*Source: White (1992), Table 1.

available. In Spain, the period 1978–83 saw a total of 48 out of 109 banks "fail"; the central bank rescued three, 10 banks were taken over, and 35 entered the Deposit Guarantee Fund. In Norway, 22 banks were the subject of state intervention between 1988 and 1991, after a post-war period free of bank failures. State support of problem banks has also occurred in Canada (1985) and in Japan (1991,1994). At first glance, the UK appears to be the exception to this rule—well-known but isolated bank failures were Johnson Matthey Bankers (1984), BCCI (1991) and Barings (1995). However, the secondary banking crisis (1973–74),* the provision of liquidity by the Bank of England to a number of smaller banks in late 1991, and the closure of four banks in 1991 lends support to the clustering hypothesis. The presence of clusters suggests the state of the macroeconomy is a contributory factor in bank failures.

QUANTIFYING THE CAUSES OF BANK FAILURE

Introduction

The observations in the previous sections provide the reader with an impression of many aspects of recent bank failures. However, practitioners and policy-makers require precise identification of the determinants of bank failure and a means of forecasting future problem banks. This section develops a model to quantify the causes of bank failure.

A bank is deemed to have failed if it is liquidated, taken over under government supervision, or rescued with a package which includes state financial support.[†] This definition differs from the standard one for bankrupt firms, that is, a negative net worth. It is used because regulatory authorities often intervene before a bank reaches this point, because of the systemic aspects of bank failure.

The Data

To conduct an econometric investigation of the causes of bank failure, the first requirement is to have a sufficiently large sample of healthy banks and failed

---

*The secondary banking crisis arose because several small banks located in the UK used the wholesale money markets to fund long-term loans, mainly to property and construction companies. A tightening of monetary and fiscal policy in 1973 raised interest rates, and caused share and property prices to fall. The first OPEC oil price hike aggravated the situation. The Bank of England arranged a lifeboat operation; the secondary banks were supported by 1.3 billion in loans, 90% of which came from the large UK clearing banks. Shareholders and creditors were persuaded by the Bank not to take action which might precipitate a failure. Some of these banks were eventually taken over by other banks or the Bank of England. For more detail, readers are referred to the Bank of England (1978), Davis (1992) and Reid (1982).

[†]Martin (1977) provides a detailed discussion of the relative merits of different definitions of bank failure, in the context of US banking regulation.

banks, for which comparable financial ratio data are available. If one limits the study to one country, the sample will not be large enough, unless the investigation is confined to the USA.* The data for this study come from two main sources. Bank financial ratio data were obtained from a bank rating agency (IBCA Ltd),[†] with offices in New York and London. IBCA divides its financial ratio data into several categories and collects them for most OECD country banks. It reports annual data on internal capital generation, capital adequacy, liquidity, loan loss coverage and performance measures for banks, including return on assets or return on equity. All of these measures are termed "micro-management" variables because bank management is influential in their determination.

IBCA does not report financial ratio data for every bank in a country, nor do they publish data or ratings deemed to be unreliable. Thus, in some countries, there are no financial ratio data for banks which have failed, or for some of the minor (but healthy) players. Lack of data limits the countries which can be included in the pooled sample to Australia, Finland, France, Sweden, Norway and the USA. Table 18 lists the 27 healthy and 12 failed banks, by country, which were included in the dataset. Countries which experienced bank failures in the 1980s but were excluded from this study because of data deficiencies include Austria, Belgium, Canada, Denmark, Germany, Ireland, Italy, Japan, Luxembourg (BCCI), the Netherlands, Spain and Switzerland. Furthermore, IBCA only began to report some ratios quite recently; a good example is the tier one risk assets ratio. If a ratio was not available for the entire period, it was not possible to include it in the econometric tests.

There is no pairwise grouping of data (that is, one healthy bank matched with one failed bank), for two reasons. First, pairwise grouping will give rise to sample bias because of the relatively low frequency of bank failures. Second, it would have meant the sample was too small. Here, all of a given country's banks are included in the sample, provided the bank has had financial ratio data compiled and reported by IBCA.

Some banks in different countries vary in the financial ratios they report. For example, while banks in most countries report operating profit/total assets, US banks do not—they report net income/total assets. Table 19 summarises the explanatory variables used in this study and the countries which report them.

Another data problem arises because in most countries, bank failures tend to be clustered around a few years, rather than being spread over a long period of time, thereby making it difficult to rely solely on time series data for one country, or to test the influence of macroeconomic variables. However, the

---

*In the USA, during the 1980s there were over 1000 bank failures and over 1000 failures of saving and loans. As a result, virtually all the published studies use US bank data. See later sections of this chapter for citation of the key studies on US bank failure.

[†]The author is grateful to the London office of IBCA Ltd for their help in providing bank spreadsheet data, especially David Andrews (director).

Table 18 Banks Included in the International Pool

Country	Healthy banks	Failed banks
Australia	Australia & New Zealand Banking Group (ANZ) National Australia Bank Commonwealth Bank of Australia State Bank of NSW Westpac	State Bank of Victoria (1990)
Finland	Postipankki Okobank	Skopbank (1991) Kansallis-Osake Pankki (1992) Union Bank of Finland (1992)
Norway	Union Bank of Norway Bergen Bank	Christiania Bank OG Kreditkasse (1991) Fokus Bank (1991) Den Norske Bank (1991)
Sweden	Scandinaviska Enskilda Banken Svenska Handelsbanken Swedbank	Gota Bank (1991) Nordbanken (1992)
France	Caisse Nationale de Crédit Agricole Compagnie Bancaire Banque Paribas Crédit Commercial de France Société Générale Banque Worms Banque Indosuez Banque Nationale de Paris Banque Française du Commerce Extérieur	Banque Arabe et Internationale D'Investissement (1989) Union de Banques Arabes Françaises (1989)
USA	Bank of Boston[a] Barnett Banks Inc Continental Bank First Fidelity Marine Midland	Bank of New England (1991)

[a]IBCA reports financial ratios for US banks but classifies them by peer group. There are seven peer groups in the IBCA classification, and banks are assigned to a peer group according to their asset size, measured in US dollars. The Bank of New England, which failed in 1991, was in peer group 2. Thus, comparable financial ratios for healthy banks classified in the same peer group were used. Therefore, use of the IBCA data severely constrains the US failed banks one may include in the sample; on the other hand, its data set is international.

clustering of bank failures around a given year or years suggests the state of the macroeconomy may be a contributory factor. In this pooled international sample, macroeconomic indicators in one country will differ from those in other countries, depending on the stage of the economic cycle a given country is at. This study includes annual country data on real and nominal interest rates, the consumer price index, the rate of inflation, the real and nominal exchange rates, and the annual growth rate in real GDP. The sources of these data were Datastream and/or the IMF's *International Financial Statistics*.

In addition to the management and macroeconomic explanatory variables, the dataset also includes the annual IBCA rating of a bank and three "size" variables: US dollar (USD) assets for bank i/total USD assets for reporting banks in a given country, bank i's assets in US dollars, and USD assets for bank i/US nominal GDP. Once a bank has failed, IBCA usually stops reporting financial ratio data. In the estimations, the fifth period is the last year IBCA cites data for a failed bank; four years of annual data were entered as the earlier periods.*

The micro-management, macroeconomic, rating, and size variables are pooled across banks and countries to test for their statistical significance in a logit model of bank failure. Multicollinearity means not all the variables listed in Table 19 can be tested simultaneously. In addition, not all the financial ratios are available for each bank in the pooled cross-country sample. For these reasons, a stepwise estimating procedure was used, that is, variables were added to or deleted from the model, depending on their overall contribution to the McFadden R^2. Financial ratios in a given category were tested separately, and all banks reporting a given ratio were included in the pooled sample. Macroeconomic variables which are not independent of each other were also tested using a stepwise procedure. Finally, the IBCA rating variable was estimated in a separate regression, with and without one of the size variables.

The Model

The model for bank failure is borrowed and modified from the corporate bankruptcy literature. Empirical tests of the determinants of company failures are conducted using multiple discriminant analysis, probit or logit models, where the dependent variable is whether or not a firm goes bankrupt, and the explanatory variables are financial ratio data.[†] There is also a fairly extensive empirical literature on the causes of bank failure, which incorporates statistical techniques drawn from the corporate bankruptcy literature. However, the relatively low frequency of bank failures has meant that all the published literature have relied on US data. Rather than provide an exhaustive review of the literature, published articles are cited only if directly relevant to the results reported here.

Logit analysis is a common method used to identify the determinants of bank failure. The logit model was discussed in Chapter 4 but to understand

_____

*In the LIMDEP software program, the logit for panel data model restricts the number of periods one can use in the estimation to five.
[†]Readers are referred to the original work by Altman (1968, 1983) and Beaver (1966). For a UK application, see Taffler (1984); Barnes (1978) provides a critical review.

Table 19 Explanatory Variables and Countries for Which they are Available

	Explanatory variables[a]	Common to
IKG	Internal capital generation (increase in bank equity due to retained profit)	Australia, Finland, France, Sweden, Norway
PR1	Operating profit/total assets (avg)	Finland, France, Sweden
PR2	Net interest revenue/total assets (avg)	Australia, Finland, France, Norway, Sweden
PR3	Net income/equity (avg)	Australia, Finland, France, Norway, Sweden
PR4	Net income/total assets (avg)	All countries
PR5	Total non-interest expenses/(net interest revenue + other op. income)	Australia, Finland, France, Norway, Sweden
PR6	Pre-tax profits/total assets (avg)	Australia, Norway
PR7	Earning asset yield (avg)	USA
PR8	Net interest income/avg earnings asset	USA
PR9	Non-interest income/avg assets	USA
PR10	Non-interest expense/avg assets	USA
KA1	Equity/total assets	all countries
KA2	Capital/risks	Finland, France, Norway, Sweden
KA3	Tier one capital/risks	Finland, France, Norway, Sweden
KA4	Dividends/net income	USA
L1	Liquid asset/customer and short-term funding	Australia, Finland, France, Norway, Sweden
L2	Loans/customer and short-term funding	France
L3	Avg liquid assets/avg assets	USA
L4	Avg loans/avg assets	USA
L5	Avg deposits/avg assets	USA
LC1	Loan loss reserves/loans	Australia, France, Norway, Sweden
LC2	Net charge-offs/loans	Australia, France
LC3	Non-performing assets/total loans & OREO	USA
LC4	Reserves/non-performing loans	USA
LC5	Reserves/total loans	USA
LC6	Net charge-offs/avg loans	USA
LC7	Recoveries/gross charge-offs	USA
LC8	Net income before loan loss provisions & taxes/net charge-offs	France
$SIZE_i$	USD assets for bank i/total USD assets	All countries
US_i	USD assets for bank i	All countries
ASSGDP	USD assets for bank i/US nominal GDP	All countries
LNAG	Log ASSGDP	All countries
INT, RINT	Average annual nominal (INT) or real (RINT) interest rate: annual average computed from monthly money market rate	All countries
REU	Average real effective exchange rate for year	All countries
NEU	Average nominal effective exchange rate for year	All countries
INF	Annual inflation rate	All countries
IND	Annual consumer price index	All countries
RGDPG	Annual real GDP growth rate	All countries
R	IBCA rating for bank	All countries; a small number of banks in the sample not rated

[a]All financial ratio data are year-end, unless otherwise stated in the table.

how logit analysis works in the context of bank failure, consider a simple example, where only one variable, capital adequacy, is said to be the cause bank failure. The relationship is negative—that is, as capital adequacy rises, the probability of bank failure falls. Here, the logit function can be illustrated in a two-dimensional diagram, as shown in Figure 24. The explanatory variable, capital adequacy (KA), is on the horizontal axis; on the vertical axis is the probability of bank failure. Since bank failure is a binary event, the logit function must fall between 0 (the bank does not fail) and 1 (the bank fails). The sigmoid-shaped curve is the logistic transformation; it is steep near the intercept unity as KA approaches zero and the probability of failure increases, but is flatter close to zero, as KA rises. If a variable (e.g. loan losses) positively influenced the probability of failure, the logit transformation would be shaped like a flat S.

Of course, several variables are likely to influence the probability of bank failure, in which case it is no longer possible to use a diagram to illustrate the logit transformation. However, a software program capable of estimating a logit model* with many explanatory variables is used, where the dependent variable is whether or not the bank fails. An extensive range of explanatory variables can be tested for their ability to explain bank failure, and it is also possible to measure the explanatory power of the model as a whole, by looking at statistics on the overall fit of the equation.

In the logit models estimated by Espahbodi (1991), Martin (1977) and Thomson (1992),[†] the dependent variable is a binary outcome, where $p = 0$ for no bank failure and $p = 1$ for bank failure. On the right-hand side of the equation are the explanatory variables, usually financial ratio data. One of the distinctive features of this study is to test the extent to which macroeconomic circumstances also contribute to bank failure.[‡] In addition, the cross-country data on bank failure permits one test for the causes of bank failure in countries

---

*The logit model is based on a logistic transformation function, where the cumulative distribution of the error terms is logistic, as opposed to a probit model, where the error terms follow a normal distribution.

[†]Some of the earlier work employed multiple discriminant analysis. See, for example, Altman (1977) and Meyer and Pifer (1970). Espahbodi (1991) uses both logit and discriminant models. However, as argued by Martin (1977), the linear discriminant function is just a special case of the logit model. Other studies have employed a probit model; for applications to general bankruptcy predictions, see Pastena and Rutland (1986). Bovenzi, Marino and McFadden (1983) applied both probit and discriminant analysis to US commercial bank failures. Espahbodi (1991) favours the logit model over probit because the latter is based on the cumulative normal probability function (but the normality assumption is not normally met), while logit is based on the cumulative logistic probability function.

[‡]None of the key studies in this area provides systematic treatment of the state of the macro-economy as a contributing factor explaining bank failure. In the published literature, the only exception is Thomson (1992) who, in a study of US failures, considers state-level gross domestic product, county-level employment data, state level personal income, and small business failure rates.

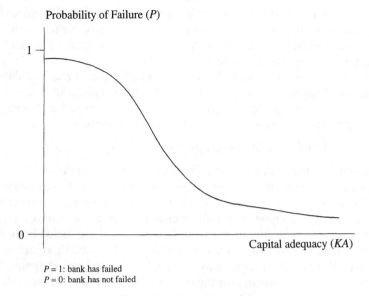

Probability of Failure (P)

$P = 1$: bank has failed
$P = 0$: bank has not failed

Figure 24 The logit model

other than the USA; virtually all of the published bank failure studies rely exclusively on US data.

The articles cited above employed a standard logit regression on cross-section US data for a sample of failed and healthy banks, but this methodology may give rise to inconsistent estimates. Consider the standard logit model,

$$z = \beta x + \epsilon$$

$$p = 1 \text{ if } z > 0 \text{ and } p = 0 \text{ if } z \leq 0$$

Time series data should be used in the estimation of this model. In the case of banks, one should estimate the equation for one bank, based on data collected over many years. However, severe data limitations will be encountered because in most industrialised countries, bank failures are quite rare. Thus, as discussed in the previous section, it is necessary to pool the data across banks and countries, with a view to developing a reasonably large dataset.

However, pooling in this way produces a panel dataset, requiring modification of the standard logit form. A logit specification for panel data was described by Chamberlain (1980). He showed that a standard logit regression on panel data will result in inconsistent estimators, if there are only a small number of observations per group. Suppose the sample consists of grouped data that could be estimated by the linear regression:

$$E(y_{it}|\mathbf{x}, \boldsymbol{\beta}, \boldsymbol{\alpha}) = \boldsymbol{\beta}'\mathbf{x}_{it} + \alpha_i (i = 1, \ldots N; t = 1, \ldots T) \tag{7.1}$$

where there are T observations in each of the N groups. The α_i controls for group specific effects, that is, for group-specific variables that are constant within the group. The standard logit function does not make allowances for the group, and if the function does not condition for the group, then it will not, in general, be possible to identify β, and there will be omitted variable bias, resulting in inconsistent estimators.

This problem will arise with the bank panel data used here. The data have been grouped according to whether or not a bank fails, and therefore, it is necessary to condition for the group. Chamberlain devised a "conditional" logit model, with a separate intercept for each observation:

$$\text{Prob}[y = 0, 1] = \exp(d_i)/[1 + \exp(d_i)], d_i = \alpha_i + \beta' x_i \qquad (7.2)$$

In equation 7.2, the likelihood function is based on the conditional distribution of the data, where the distribution of the α_i is not considered to be independent of x. The Chamberlain specification allows one to obtain estimators that converge to β as the number of groups increases, even if the number of observations per group (e.g. the number of observations in the failed bank group) is small. Here, the α_i will capture individual bank effects if equation 7.2 is estimated. If a standard logit model is used, these effects are ignored, with the implication of inconsistent estimators arising from omitted variable bias.

Results

Logit regressions, based on equation 7.2, were run on an international pool and Scandinavian pool (Finland, Norway, and Sweden).

The detailed empirical results are found in Heffernan (1995). Only the key findings are reported in this sub-section. Turning to the explanatory variables in Table 19, consider first the micro/management or financial ratio variables. *PR4* (net income/total assets) was the profitability measure available for most of the banks in the pooled sample. The coefficient was correctly signed (as this ratio rises, the probability of failure falls) and significant (or nearly significant) in 11 of the 15 regressions which tested this variable. In two other regressions, it was correctly signed but insignificant. For the other profitability measures, the number of data points was much smaller because not all the banks report these ratios. *PR2* (net interest revenue/total assets) is correctly signed and significant (or nearly significant) in the two regressions where it was included, but these regressions exclude the US banks because they do not report this ratio. *PR3*, the ratio of net income to equity, had the expected sign but was insignificant.

The second category of management variables to be tested is capital adequacy. Unfortunately, more sophisticated measures of capital adequacy, such as a risk-weighted capital assets ratio (*KA2*, *KA3*) only began to be reported recently, so it is difficult to make any definitive statements about them. However, *KA1*, the ratio of equity to total assets, has been reported widely. One would expect *KA1* to have a negative sign, that is, as the ratio of equity to assets rises, the probability of failure falls. The coefficient on *KA1* was correctly signed in 21 regressions; eight of these were statistically significant or nearly significant.

For the other management variables, the findings are quite limited. Internal capital generation (*IKG*) is any increase in bank equity from retained profit, and one would expect the probability of bank failure to fall as *IKG* rises. The sign on this coefficient changes from negative to positive, but is never significant. *L1*, a measure of liquidity, is the ratio of liquid assets to customer and short-term funding. It should be negatively signed—that is, as *L1* rises, the probability of bank failure falls. In the regressions which tested this variable, the coefficient was correctly signed, but only (nearly) significant in one regression. Unfortunately, the measurement of loan loss coverage varied too much from country to country to generate a sample large enough to test for the significance of this important indicator.

A number of variations of a bank size variable was tested, including $SIZE_i$, US_i, *ASSGDP* and *LNAG*. Of these, only the log of (bank i's assets in USD/US nominal GDP) (*LNAG*) was found to be significant, or nearly so; in these cases, it has a negative sign, that is, the probability of bank failure falls as the size of the bank increases. Thus, either larger banks (in terms of assets) are inherently safer, or they are less likely to fail because of the consequences of "too big to fail" policies (for example, closer regulation) operating in most of these countries.

Macroeconomic variables were included in the model to test whether the state of the macroeconomy had any effect on bank failures. The real GDP growth rate (*RGDP*) was, as one would expect, negatively signed, but was not significant. In some regressions, nominal and real interest rate variables were positively signed (as interest rates increase, the probability of failure rises) and significant at the 5% level. The nominal and real effective exchange rates (*NEU, REU*) were significant (at the 2.5% and 10% levels) in two of the equations which included these variables. The negative signs mean that as the domestic currency appreciates in value, the probability of bank failure falls, a finding consistent with the use of high interest rates to control inflation, under a flexible exchange rate regime. The price index (*IND*), was found to be positive and significant, suggesting that the probability of bank failure rises with the index; the opposite was true for the inflation rate (*INF*). The different signs are explained by a falling inflation rate in all of the countries over the estimating period, even though the price index was rising. Thus, a falling inflation rate is associated with an increase in bank failure. This finding may be consistent with interest rate-led inflation control policies typical of these OECD countries in the late 1980s.

The final variable tested was the IBCA rating given to each bank. Each year, IBCA provides two bank ratings. Banks are rated individually on a scale from A (excellent, a consistent rating of above-average profitability) to E (a bank with very serious problems which is likely to require external support). In this database, banks given an A rating were assigned a number of 5, descending to 1 for those with an E rating.* The individual rating must be tested by itself,

---

*For non-US banks, IBCA also assigns a legal rating, which is an IBCA estimate of how likely it is a bank will be bailed out by the state, should it encounter serious financial difficulties. This rating was not used here.

because it will not be independent of either the management ratios or the macroeconomic variables. The results, using 155 observations, showed a strongly significant negative coefficient, suggesting that as the IBCA rating on a bank increases, the probability of bank failure falls. The McFadden R^2 (0.564) was slightly lower but similar to those values obtained for equations which test management and/or macroeconomic variables.

For the Scandinavian pool, the findings are similar. When the *IKG* variable is included, it has a negative sign and is nearly significant. In other words, as the amount of a rise in bank equity due to retained profit increases, the probability of bank failure falls. Similarly for the three profitability ratios, *PR2* (net interest revenue/total assets), *PR3* (net income/equity) and *PR4* (net income/total assets), and the two capital adequacy ratios, equity/total assets (*KA1*) and dividends/net income (*KA4*). The coefficient on the liquidity measure, *L1*, was also negative and significant; as liquidity rises, the probability of bank failure declines. The size variable (*LNAG*) was insignificant and changed sign. Of the macroeconomic variables, the coefficient on the real interest rate was positive and significant; the coefficient on the real GDP growth rate was significantly negative in one equation. As with the international pool, the IBCA rating was significantly negative, with a McFadden R^2 of 0.586.

Standard logit regressions were also run for the international and Scandinavian pools. Due to space constraints, the detailed results are not reported here, but the performance of the equations was quite poor, compared to their counterparts estimated using the logit for panel data program. For example, in the case of the international pool, the MR^2 ranged from 0.16 to 0.32, though the *t*-ratios for the explanatory variables were similar and the constant term was significant or nearly significant at the 1% level. However, the estimates may be inconsistent because of omitted variable bias.

This study confirms the importance of bank financial ratios as determinants of why banks fail, especially the profitability ratios (*PR4* and *PR2*) and one measure of capital adequacy (*KA1*). There is also some indication that liquidity is an important explanatory variable. The findings are largely consistent with Martin (1977), who used a logistic approach on US bank data for 1974. His best estimation had four variables which were statistically significant with the right sign, and were measures of profitability (net income/total assets and expenses/operating revenues), asset quality (commercial loans/total loans and gross charge-offs/net operating income + loan loss provision), and capital adequacy (gross capital/adjusted risk assets). Other studies using standard logit models on US data also identify the importance of financial ratios. See, among others, Avery and Hanweck (1984), Barth *et al.* (1985) and Benston (1985).*

---

*Studies which used discriminant analysis identify certain financial ratios as being statistically significant in bank failure models. For example, Altman (1977), in a study of savings and loans failures (1966–73), found different measures of capital adequacy, asset quality, and earnings to be important. See Sinkey (1975) for a discriminant analysis of failed US commercial banks.

More recent studies which have employed US bank data report somewhat different results. Espahbodi (1991) failed to find various measures of liquidity, capital adequacy, efficiency, loan quality, loan volume or profitability to be significant explanatory variables. He does find two sources of fund measures, a use of funds variable and a deposit composition measure to be significant. Thomson (1992), in a two-step logit model using a sample of failed and healthy US FDIC insured banks, found the following variables to be significant with the correct sign: a proxy for net worth or solvency,* non-deposit liabilities/cash + investment securities, overheads/total assets, net income after taxes/total assets, loans to insiders/total assets, and unit banking state and bank holding company dummies, the log of total assets, and the log of average deposits per banking office.

Prediction and Performance

The discussion in this section is confined to the best-performing equations. For the international pool, one of the best regressions was the equations where $PR4$, the ratio of net income/total assets, was strongly significant at the 5% level; the size variable ($LNAG$) and the nominal interest rate (INT) were significant at the 10% level. The McFadden R^2 was 0.708. Also considered is the regression with a significant coefficient on $PR4$ (at the 1% level) and nearly significant REU (at the 10% level), with an MR^2 of 0.719. The equation with the IBCA bank rating variable was strongly significant, with a good fit. For the Scandinavian pool, the equations chosen for further discussion include one with a significant coefficient on $PR4$, and another with the IBCA variable.

The superior performance of the panel logit regressions over standard logit was noted earlier, suggesting bank-specific effects are an important explanatory variable. Unfortunately, the LIMDEP software program does not report the α_i estimates in the logit for panel data program, so the magnitude of the individual bank effects is unclear. To identify the α_i, the subset of the best equations from the international and Scandinavian pool were re-estimated using the standard logit program but with individual bank dummies; the coefficients on the bank dummies should be equivalent to the α_i in the panel logit model. In the modified regressions, the McFadden R^2s were found to be higher than for the same regression using panel logit. The dummy variables for the failed banks are significant or nearly significant at the 1% level—that is, bank-specific effects are a significantly positive contributor to bank failure. Again, the equations using the IBCA rating variable did best, and in these regressions all the banks that failed had significant coefficients on the dummy variables.

Thus, allowing for bank-specific effects improves the fit of the equation and should be an important consideration in any prediction exercise. The published literature[†] which employs out-of-sample data to test the predictive ability of a

---

*(Book-equity capital + the reserve of loan losses net of non-performing loans)/total assets.
[†] See, for example, Espahbodi (1991) and Korobow and Stuhr (1985).

model assumes bank specific effects are zero, using standard logit estimation, without bank dummies. However, the nature of bank-specific effects means they cannot be modelled *ex ante*; at best, out-of-sample prediction would be based on arbitrary values for the α_i. For this reason, an out-of-sample test of performance is not used here.

Nonetheless, it is important to verify stability of the coefficients in the model through a sample-reusing test. A very general test was employed; the significance of coefficient deviations were assessed when regression equations were subjected to sequential censoring.* Based on these tests, one can reject the hypothesis that sample shrinkage by rotating country deletion significantly affects the coefficients for some of the best performing equations.

CONCLUSIONS

This chapter has conducted both qualitative and quantitative analyses of troubled banks, with a view to identifying the chief determinants of bank failure, defined as any bank which is liquidated, merged with a healthy bank under government supervision, or rescued with state financial support. The case studies reveal that bank failures have a long history, and one of the principal causes of failure is sub-standard asset management, as reflected in a poor-quality loan portfolio. Managerial deficiencies were also important, highlighted by the herd instinct (and, possibly, aggravated by prudential regulation), though it is often difficult to distinguish between incompetence and fraud. The clustering phenomenon is suggestive of contributory macroeconomic factors. Problems were exacerbated by incomplete deposit insurance, regulatory forbearance, and the apparent inability of supervisors and auditors to pick up important signals of problem banks.

The quantitative section of the chapter used a logit for panel data model to identify what variables are significant in explaining bank failure. Unlike much of the published work in this field, the study employed a pooled international dataset and tested for the significance of macroeconomic indicators, in addition to the more typical financial ratio data one finds in virtually all studies. It also tested the performance of an agency's rating of each bank in the sample.

The results showed macroeconomic indicators to be important explanatory variables which should be tested in any model of bank failure, in addition to financial ratios. Nominal interest rates, the real exchange rate and inflation were found to be the best-performing macroeconomic variables in the international pool; real interest rates and real GDP growth in the Scandinavian pool. The micro/management variable, net income:total assets, is the best-performing financial ratio; it is notable that it does better than capital adequacy measures.

---

*See Heffernan (1995), Table 5, for detailed results.

The IBCA bank rating was strongly significant, with an overall fit similar to the best-performing equations which included financial ratios and/or macro-economic variables. Practitioners usually employ rating agency information in their investment decisions, but bank regulators (for example, the FDIC) have shied away from using their services. Clearly, not all rating agencies will neces-sarily add value the way IBCA apparently does, but regulators should be eval-uating whether private ratings can help them in their assessment of individual banks.

The empirical work has revealed that bank-specific effects played a significant role in explaining bank failure. Many of the published articles in this field have produced inconsistent estimates because fixed effects are constrained to zero in the standard logit estimation. Furthermore, superiority of a logit for panel data model over standard logit must question the accuracy of tests for bank failure prediction which rely on out-of-sample data, because the nature of bank-specific effects means that, at best, only arbitrary values can be attached to them.

The estimation of the panel logit model is not without its limitations. A cross-country dataset is beneficial because it permits a broader study of bank failure than that which is possible if one focuses on just one country. But country accounting differences narrows the range of financial ratios which can be tested. In particular, the lack of comparable loan loss measures means it is not possible to test for the significance of a poor quality loan book. But inferior asset management should be reflected in the ratio of net income to total assets. Clearly, however, there is a need for consistent inter-national measures of the on and off-balance sheet activities of banks. Finally, the inability of the software program to quantify bank-specific effects meant an indirect method had to be employed.

To summarise, the empirical results of the quantitative approach are con-sistent with the findings from the case studies, and provides the reader with a precise quantification of the causes of failure, namely:

- falling profitability, as measured by the ratio of net income to total assets. This ratio was found to be a more significant indicator than capital adequacy measures. Based on the case studies, falling profitability that results in bank failure is most likely caused by the deterioration in the quality of a bank's loan portfolio;
- the state of the macroeconomy, as measured by the performance of nominal interest rates. As nominal interest rates rise, the probability of bank failure rises;
- bank-specific effects: failing banks are characterised by unique characteris-tics which cannot be quantified ahead of the event. It may be that this variable is picking up problems related to managerial deficiencies and/or fraud, but in the absence of any explicit measures, the presence of these effects will undermine the accuracy of bank failure forecasts.

8

Strategic Issues for Banks

INTRODUCTION

The purpose of this chapter is to explore strategy in the context of the banking world. One of the key questions bank managers need to ask themselves is this: is there a coherent strategy a bank can adopt which will achieve the joint objectives of maximising profitability, shareholder value added, and survival in the market place? To answer this question, it is first necessary to review the literature on business strategy, and then to look at studies of strategy in banking. First, this chapter considers definitions of strategy and related literature. It goes on to review contributions to the bank strategy literature, research conducted by MBA groups on the strategies of individual banks located in London and Toronto, and the work by Davis (1985, 1989) on what makes an "excellent bank".

THE MEANING OF STRATEGY

In this chapter, it would be impossible to do justice to the entire discipline which centres around strategy. Rather, a brief review is undertaken, with the objective of linking fundamental ideas to the strategic issues faced by banks.

In a review essay which examined the relationship between strategy and economics, Rumelt, Schendel and Teece (1991) considered the development of strategic management as a discipline. According to Rumelt *et al.*, interchangeable terms, such as strategic management, business policy or strategy is "about the direction of organisations, and most often, business firms" (p. 6). These authors argued that for a firm operating in a competitive environment, strategic choices will include:

- the selection of goals;
- the positioning of the firm in the market place;
- deciding on the degree of diversity in the goods and/or services on offer;
- the administrative systems and policies used to ensure the workplace actually achieves the stated goals.

Most proponents of strategic management or business policy agree that the above choices are critical in determining the success or failure of a firm. Porter, in *The Competitive Advantage of Nations* (1990), outlined a strategy for firms seeking an international competitive advantage. Porter argued:

- competitive advantage grows out of, and is sustained by, *improvement, innovation, and change*;
- competitive advantage is based on a complete value system, where the value system is the entire array of activities involved in a product's creation and use, encompassing value chains of the firm, suppliers, channels and buyers;
- competitive advantage is sustained by a firm upgrading its sources of competitive advantage.
- sustaining the advantage often requires a global approach to strategy, including selling worldwide, locating activities in other nations to capture local advantages, offset particular disadvantages, or to facilitate local market penetration, and coordinating and integrating activities on a worldwide basis to gain economies of scale, enjoy the benefits of brand reputation, and serve international buyers.

Essential to understanding Porter is his *diamond*, which allows a firm to identify competitive advantages and disadvantages.* The diamond can be used by a firm to consider the interaction between factor conditions, demand conditions, related and supporting industries, and firm strategy, structure and rivalry. Nations will achieve comparative advantage if the national diamond favours certain industries or industry segments. In Porter (1990), the diamond is expanded to allow for questions posed in terms of global competition.† A global strategy will consist of the analysis of foreign competitors, including national characteristics and probable host country firm competitive behaviour.

Mathur (1992) defined *strategy* as a major business plan to improve future business performance, and competitive strategy as "a plan about the future positioning of the business's offering, relative to those of competitors, in the eyes of customers" (pp. 201–202).

Mathur defined an offering as what customers buy. A firmlet is a business with a discrete offering in a single competitive market (p. 207). Firmlets, not organisational units (such as strategic business units or companies), have competitive strategies. Though competitive strategies are dynamic, they are not spontaneous and must be planned. In the Mathur model, the key competitive strategy questions are:

- How does a firmlet compete for customers now?
- How should it compete in the future?
- Why should a particular method of competing be adopted?
- How can it be adopted?

---

*See Figure 3-1 in Porter (1990: p. 71).
†Readers are referred to Table 11-2 of Porter (1990: p. 603) for more detail on the components of the diamond.

According to Mathur, corporate strategy is concerned with achieving financial success, that is, ensuring the firm earns extra returns on capital invested. Thus, an excellent corporate strategy would be one where firmlet "winners" are chosen, and losers are divested.

Kay (1993) argued the strategy of a firm is the match between its internal capabilities and its external relationships. He described how a firm responds to its suppliers, customers, competitors, and the social and economic environment in which it operates. Kay's definitions of corporate and competitive strategy are similar to Mathur's. Corporate strategy consists of a firm's choice of business, markets, and activities. Competitive or business strategy is concerned with the firm's position relative to its competitors in the markets where it operates.

Kay reviewed the different definitions of a "successful" firm. For example, success may refer to size and market share, or profitability and returns to shareholders. He argued that though definitions of success differ, experts tend to come up with a list of the same companies when identifying the successful ones. Chapter 1 reviewed bank performance based on different measures. Kay's own view is that a successful firm is one that adds value, that is, creating an output which is worth more than the cost of the inputs which it uses.

Kay argued that a firm's competitive advantage will depend upon its distinctive capabilities, strategic assets, and market structure. Kay identified three primary sources of *"distinctive capability"*, which, depending on the market, can be applied to create and sustain competitive advantage. The first is *architecture*, defined as a "network of relational contracts within or around the firm" (p. 66). In banking, external and internal architecture is related to the establishment of long-term relationships between the bank and its customers and the bank and its officers (p. 299). Architecture varies considerably among countries. In Germany and Japan, shared directorships and cross-holdings of shares give rise to strong relational contracts between banks and non-financial firms, whereas British and American banks tend to rely on transactional or classical contracts, making lending decisions on the basis of security of assets and project feasibility.

Kay used architecture to explain a clustering phenomenon identified by Porter. Porter had argued that the interactive diamond promoted a clustering of a nation's competitive industries, with the successful industries of a nation linked through vertical or horizontal relationships (pp. 148–49). However, Kay thinks it is due to architecture, citing the clustering of investment banks on Wall Street as an example.

Architecture can also be easily destroyed. In the case of retail banking, relational contracts between the bank and its employees, and the bank and its borrowers, became less important in the 1970s and 1980s, with an emphasis on a more performance-based internal structure and aggressive marketing of new customers. Classical contracts became more important than relational contracts; transactions banking replaced relationship banking. The result, Kay suggested, was a decline in the average quality of bank loan portfolios.

Relational contracts in banking are important, Kay argued, because of the time lapse between when a loan is agreed and the long-term effect of the asset on the quality of the bank's loan portfolio. But recent revelations about the seriousness of dud loan problems in Japan demonstrate that relational contracts are no guarantee of success in banking.

Reputation is the second distinctive capability identified by Kay. It is the market's method of dealing with the attributes of goods and services where it is difficult for customers to obtain independent information. Clearly, for banks, reputation is extremely important, because if depositors lose confidence in the ability of the bank to provide liquidity on demand, the bank will soon lose all of its business, moving rapidly from a problem of illiquidity to one of insolvency. Borrowers might be reluctant to negotiate a bank loan if a bank has a reputation for calling in loans. Kay argued that neither strategic assets (such as customer base and branch network) nor reputation are easily transferable across national boundaries, limiting the extent to which some aspects of banking can be globalised. The same is true of architecture—relationships and information flows tend to be local. A good example of the problem was the attempt by Citibank to become a global wholesale and retail bank. It has been successful in its global expansion of wholesale business, but has encountered problems in most of its attempts to expand retail operations outside the USA. Thus, banking reputation may be confined to one aspect of the business, and may not be transferable to other areas of banking.

Innovation is the third distinctive capability. But often, firms do not succeed in using innovation to create and sustain competitive advantage, for at least one of three reasons. First, high costs are associated with innovation, and success is often uncertain. Second, the process of innovation is difficult to manage. Finally, if easily copied, innovation is not appropriable. Kay cited the case of Midland Bank's attempt to enter the US retail market as an example of problematic innovation. The Bank had hoped to employ new technology to overcome branching costs and offer new products, but it was unable to do so because of managerial deficiencies and weak competitive positioning. On the other hand, First Direct, a telephone banking subsidiary of Midland, is a good example of how most aspects of branch banking can be successively replaced through the application of new technology in the retail sector. In wholesale and investment banking it is difficult to plan a strategy of innovation to gain competitive advantage, because innovations are easily copied.

In addition to distinct capabilities, Kay argued that some firms may dominate a market because they possess *strategic assets*, which arise because of natural monopoly, relatively high sunk costs, or because of market regulation. Unlike distinctive capabilities, strategic assets are available to any firm which succeeds in entering the market. In retail banking, examples of strategic assets are the branch network and a loyal customer base.

Unlike most business policy analysts, Kay emphasised there are *no* generic strategies for corporate success. If there were, their adoption would eliminate any competitive advantage that might exist. A firm is successful because of features which are *unique* to the company. Successful strategy, Kay argued, is rarely a copycat strategy: it is based on differentiation, or offering a particular good or service on better terms than most rivals. He suggested that instead of allocating resources to the creation of distinctive capabilities, firms should focus on identifying what distinctive features they have which other firms lack, and take steps to ensure they are appropriable—of exclusive or principal benefit to the company. It is necessary to identify markets where it is possible not only to use features to create competitive advantage, but to sustain it. For example, financial innovation might be a distinctive capability, but if it can be copied, is not appropriable. Reputation is another distinctive capability that is important to banking; but though sustainable, reputation is difficult to create and establish. However, the argument is not as straightforward as Kay suggests: some distinctive capabilities derived from, for example, innovation, may assist in the creation of a reputation, which, in turn, can be used to establish competitive advantage.

In addition, Kay observed that market structure will help determine the competitive advantage of a firm. At the two extremes of market structure are perfect competition (with many firms in the market, which, combined with other conditions, makes firms price-takers in the market place) and pure monopoly, where only one firm supplies a product, has no competitors, and is a price-maker. In most markets, there is some degree of imperfect competition, whereby output and pricing decisions of firms in a particular market are interdependent. In the financial services sector, oligopolistic behaviour is typical, particularly in domestic markets where a few well-established banks tend to dominate the market. There is more competition at the global level. In addition to the formulation of strategy based on the identification of distinctive capabilities, firms must be able to define the type of market structure in which they operate. The precise market structure is determined by the interaction between cost and demand. For a given market demand curve, U-shaped average cost curves will support many firms, while economies of scale (firms operating on the falling part of the average cost curve) will mean the market can only support one or two firms.

To summarise Kay's position, corporate success comes from creating a competitive advantage, which, in turn, depends on a firm having distinctive capabilities which are sustainable and appropriable. In banking and other financial services, attributes might be reputation and product innovation. Strategic assets and market structure are also important; all three are interdependent. For example, the firm may use a distinct capability to differentiate itself which, in turn, alters market structure.

Hamel and Prahalad (1993) argued the real function of a company's strategy is not to match resources with opportunities or establish elaborate plans, but rather, to set goals that stretch the company beyond what most managers believe is possible. They argue in favour of *strategy as stretch*, stretching ambition to the limit, even if a particular firm is already the market leader. Firms must aspire to market leadership, even though leadership itself cannot be planned for. Their opinion is consistent with the growing body of business people who believe that systematic development of strategy does not necessarily translate into more profitable outcomes or increased shareholder value added.

STRATEGY AS IT APPLIES TO BANKING

Davis

In *Managing Change in the Excellent Banks* (1989) Davis had a chapter on strategy and one on strategic positioning, but said little about strategy *per se*. Davis reminded readers that strategy had not been a key priority among the excellent banks in 1984. The banks seemed to know what they were about and where they were going. But by 1988, strategic direction had become very important, with the emphasis on getting their priorities right in an overcrowded market. He quoted George Davis of Citibank:

> Our problem is identical to that of other major US banks: we are no longer bankers—we're financial intermediaries of some sort. We know we are not in the same business we were five years ago, but we're not sure what we'll be in the future (Davis, 1989: pp. 62–3).

Walter Wriston of Citibank had a focused view about what banking in the 1990s is all about: "The fact is that bankers are in the business of managing risk. Pure and simple, that is the business of banking" (*The Economist*, 10 April, 1993).

In chapter 10, Davis (1989) defined strategy as long-term competitive positioning, that is, establishing and maintaining a competitive advantage in one or more businesses which can be used to earn an acceptable rate of return on shareholder funds. The question is, what constitutes a competitive advantage? Davis argued the answer is easy for a bank with a nationwide consumer franchise, or for others with an acknowledged product advantage. However, he doesn't discuss how competitive advantage might be identified or, indeed, how it is maintained, even for a bank with an extensive branch network or product superiority.

Based on Davis' second survey of the excellent banks, some bankers stressed the importance of the niche market; low-cost production was identified by others. Identification of strengths and building on them was also important, as was disciplined entrepreneurship, that is, thinking change, avoiding lemming-like behaviour, launching a product ahead of competitors, or differentiating by quality. It was also important to accept the possibility of a trade-off between strategic direction and entrepreneurial drive.

Herve de Carmoy

Herve de Carmoy (1990) considered strategy for global banks, based on his experience as an international banker. He argued that principal global players in banking follow three roads. First, there is *strategy of conquest*, which can only be adopted by a limited number of institutions and requires a will to succeed. An offensive strategy may have the following targets:

- the personal sector: to provide the bank with stable deposits, market for new services, and investment products;
- corporate sector;
- trading activities: the only area of banking which is essentially global.

The second strategy is a *strategy of change*. It is multidimensional and to be successful, requires a change in mentality. The bank should refocus on activities where the bank traditionally excels by looking at its personal, corporate, and trading activities. De Carmoy seems to imply that this strategy is often associated with a crisis in the bank, but does not discuss how such a crisis might arise, or how it might be avoided.

Third, there is an intermediate *strategy of consolidation*. It may precede a strategy of conquest, involve a phase of assimilation right after an offensive period, or a phase of conservation after a period of major setback.

The global strategies put forward by de Carmoy seem to be interdependent, because they are used at different stages of the bank's development. Like Porter, de Carmoy stressed the importance of the home base. However, in international banking, an obvious question is, this: is the "home base" retail, corporate, or trading activities, or all three?

Kenyon and Mathur

Kenyon and Mathur (1987) surveyed the strategic responses of 14 international commercial banks to growing international competition in the 1980s. Their article was based on the outcome of their interviews, conducted between December 1983 and September 1984. The banks had operations outside their own countries and were headquartered in the USA, UK, Germany, France and Japan. In addition, two other banks were interviewed.

The main question put to the banks concerned how they responded to the increasingly competitive climate in international banking. The answers revealed two major changes in attitude. First, managers no longer assumed banks were in some way unique—they were now thought to be no different from any other businesses. Second, banks expressed concern about profits. Profitability ratios were being used, with performance monitored against them. The emphasis was on what Kenyon and Mathur referred to as the "financial model": trying to maximise ratios of return on assets. It represented a move away from the traditional focus on balance sheet growth and asset size typical of the 1960s and 1970s. This financial model, they argued, differed from the "Porter Business Policy Model", with its emphasis on market share, customers, suppliers, competitors and entry barriers. However, the move to an emphasis on profitability should mean the banks are approximating a Porter-type model because the focus on profitability will lead to a greater concern about the role of these factors, given the market structure in which they operate.

Kenyon and Mathur found the banks responded to the new challenge of greater competition in international banking by employing one of at least five strategies. A number of banks had adopted a *global* strategy: offering a wide range of banking products to a wide range of customers in different parts of the world. The focus was on undifferentiated products, marketed at competitive prices. Thus, in contrast to Porter (1990), who stressed the importance of a global strategy for all firms, Kenyon and Mathur suggested only a selection of the banks surveyed adopted this approach.

Some banks were implementing a *product focus* strategy—one bank had shifted its attention away from the core banking products (intermediation) to a selection of innovative products. The emphasis was on product differentiation and profitability of individual products. Other banks had adopted a *customer focus* strategy, choosing to gain competitive advantage by focusing on the needs of a selective group of customers. Two types of customers were targeted, those requiring a package of banking services and those with special banking needs. An *expansionist focus* strategy involved some banks expanding into global markets, for example, Japanese banks were looking for new customers and products not available to them in Japan. A *geographical focus* strategy was also observed—that is, some banks had a historical focus on certain parts of the world. *Tactical responses* were also observed, though Kenyon and Mathur questioned whether these could be labelled strategic responses. For example, some German banks had suffered a sharp setback in the period leading up to 1981, but they were responding to technical banking problems rather than to strategic or competitive setbacks, therefore it would be unwise to classify this behaviour as a strategic response. Certain French banks also appeared to be employing tactical responses. As publicly owned institutions, independent strategies were less important because of the role of the state. Compared to the banks headquartered in other countries, less priority was placed on profits. The banks accepted that key lending and other banking decisions were dictated by public policy.

MBA Studies of Bank Strategies

In 1992, MBA student groups in London and Toronto* completed projects on global strategy, looking at the following banks:

---

*The Toronto project groups consisted of Michael Hunck, Christain Jasserand, Sabine Kress, Brian Sokoliuk, Philip Woolff (Bank of Montreal); Robert Calderan, Dennis da Silva, Rossanna Delieto, Dan MacDonald (Toronto Dominion); Andrew Cheng, Gary Ivany, Brook Riggins, Marco Salvanti, Steve Trotter (Royal Bank of Canada); Aaron Feldman; and Andrew Keith, Peter Reich, and Martin Sillich (Bank of Nova Scotia). The London project groups consisted of Shahin Shojai and T Zimmerman (Swiss Bank Corporation); Richard Burton, Ugo Formenton, and Vittoria Szego (National Westminster Bank); Chee Lai, Nita Hiranandani, Pradipto Mazumdar, Vijay Lee (Standard Chartered Bank); and Antonio Galanta, Bernard McGuire, Ian Wilson (Citibank).

Bank of Montreal
National Westminster
Citibank
Royal Bank of Canada
Scotiabank
Standard Chartered Bank
Swiss Bank Corporation
Toronto Dominion Bank.

The groups were asked to compare and contrast the strategic policy approaches outlined by Porter (1990), de Carmoy (1990), and Kenyon and Mathur (1987). The groups encountered difficulties trying to apply models developed to describe "industry". The project group looking at Standard Chartered Bank (SCB) summarised the differences between international banks and other businesses. First, they argued supplier power is largely irrelevant, limiting the applicability of the Porter model. Second, products are basically similar and innovations easily copied, limiting the use of product differentiation. Differentiation normally occurs in the area of service and support. This group argued that there was a case for segmentation of a global bank into independent strategic business units based on geography. Product segmentation is not always suitable because products are interdependent (for example, advances and deposits), or complementary (trade finance and foreign exchange), or there is a high degree of cross-subsidisation. On the other hand, certain product segments are international by nature and cannot be associated with a particular country. Some customer segments, like multinational companies, require services in numerous countries, making advanced matrix structures necessary. The SCB group did identify a use for Porter's model, if applied to the different strategic business units within the bank. Each unit would have to focus attention on the widespread generic strategies to be adopted, to gain a broad comparative advantage. But, the group argued, the Kenyon-Mathur model is more applicable in situations where the objective is to consider the general positioning of offerings. The Standard Chartered project group concluded that de Carmoy's model takes too broad a perspective to be of any practical use. Several other project groups based in London reached the same conclusion. The National Westminster Bank group found all three models to be helpful, to some degree, in describing NatWest's strategy. But they found the Kenyon-Mathur model to be the most applicable, because it set out the logical steps of decision making and focused on the relative strength of "firmlets" in the market.

The Swiss Bank Corporation (SBC) project group identified the achievement of competitive advantage as important, but criticised the Porter model. They disputed the claim that the possibility for new ways of competing grows out of some discontinuity or change in industry structure such as new technologies (for example, the introduction of better accounting or trading systems), new or shifting buyer needs (for example, institutional buyers requiring better rates), the emergence of new industry segments, shifting input costs, or changes in government regulations. Based on their study, the group concluded these advantages were difficult to identify because most differentiated products quickly become commodities.

The Citibank student group argued that all three models provide a framework on which to start building a successful strategy but criticised them for being too general. The group concluded that the Kenyon and Mathur model is more applicable to banks because it was based on a survey of banks; they also claimed Citibank does not fit into just one of the four well-defined categories, but three.

Among the Canadian banks, all the groups found the de Carmoy model applicable because of the emphasis on strategies of consolidation and change. Each of the respective bank groups adopted this strategy, following extensive exposure of these banks to third world country debt in the early 1980s. At the Bank of Montreal, the move was a switch from a strategy of conquest, as it cut back on foreign operations and began to focus on the North American "domestic" market, not only because of its earlier over-exposure to sovereign loans, but because of an unsuccessful attempt to expand its corporate business overseas. The change in strategic direction was reflected in the appointment of a new chairman, Matthew Barrett, to replace William Mulholland, who had become chairman in 1981, and largely responsible for the attempt to develop the bank's expertise in global corporate business. In his address to shareholders in 1990, Matthew Barrett emphasised the role of the Bank of Montreal as a North American bank focusing on small business and retail markets. The geographical and customer focus is consistent with the Kenyon–Mathur description of possible generic strategies.

The groups working on the four Canadian banks found it difficult to apply the Porter model to the strategies being undertaken by these banks. In particular, all four banks, having suffered large losses arising from developing country debt exposure, were retrenching into a regional market, North America, a strategy which is somewhat at odds with Porter's emphasis on global expansion to sustain competitive advantage. In the case of Toronto Dominion, it was recognised that the bank was at a competitive *dis*advantage in global markets because other players were based in countries with comparatively low capital costs (for example, Japan). For this reason, the bank switched from a universal banking strategy to one which focused on Canadian retail and wholesale banking, and wholesale banking in other developed economies, especially the USA. For Scotiabank, the group concluded the strategy was very much one of the "opportunistic follower", that is, seeking business opportunities in market niches. The group found a top-down management style, with the strategy largely decided by the President. The pursuit of this strategy was deemed to be of low intensity, with inadequate resource support.

WHAT MAKES AN EXCELLENT BANK?

This section considers the work by Davis, who attempted, in two books (1985, 1989), to explore the criteria for an excellent bank. The approach was a banking application of Tom Peter's *In Search of Excellence* (1982).

The Excellent Banks in 1984

Davis (1985) reviewed the management characteristics of 16 "excellent" banking institutions. Davis was not able to use bank evaluation criteria such as return on assets and return on investment, because he was looking at bank performance on a global basis and, he argued, there are significant differences in disclosure, accounting principles, and tax practices.

Davis used a panel of independent professional observers with a global knowledge of banks. Bankers were excluded from the panel to prevent obvious problems with bias. The selection panel of 15 included financial journalists, management consultants, regulators, senior rating agency officers, and experienced bank and credit analysts based in the UK, the USA, and western Europe. The panel was asked to select the top 10 commercial banks they considered to be the best-managed in the world. Small regional and community banks were excluded, because, Davis argued, the competitive pressures they face are less pronounced. Only financial firms engaged in commercial bank business offering a core intermediary product were considered, thereby excluding British merchant banks.

The panel was asked for their views in 1984. Banks had to receive a certain number of votes in order to rank as an excellent bank. The list of excellent banks included:

Bank of Tokyo
Bankers Trust New York
Barclays Bank PLC
Bayerische Vereinsbank AG
Citicorp
Deutsche Bank AG
HongKong Bank
Morgan Guaranty Trust Company of New York
Security Pacific Corporation
Scandanaviska Enskilda Banken (SE Banken)
Sumitomo Bank
Swiss Bank Corporation
Texas Commerce Bancshares, Inc.
Toronto Dominion Bank
Union Bank of Switzerland
Wachovia Bank and Trust Company

Another bank received the minimum number of votes, but would not be interviewed. Davis compared these banks to the top 100 banks listed in the June 1984 edition of *The Banker*. He found 15 of the 16 banks to be in the top 100, measured by asset size. Three of the world's 10 largest banks were on Davis's "excellent" list. Texas Commerce and Wachovia were the only regional banks in the middle-sized category. Six of the 16 banks were American, there were two banks each from Japan, Switzerland, and Germany, and one bank, respectively, from Hong Kong, Sweden, Canada and the UK. Classified by product range, there were three strictly commercial banks, offering retail/wholesale banking services but not investment banking products. The rest were universal (offering a complete product range), some of these offering commercial services in their domestic markets and universal services in foreign markets.

According to Davis, three characteristics did *not* appear to be central to excellence. First, organisational structure. Banks had found different ways of resolving the trade-off between geography and client, decentralisation of decision-making and collective versus individual decision-making. Second, environmental factors, such as regulatory constraints, the nature of home markets, and extent of local competition, did not seem to be determining factors of excellence. In favourable environments, there are many examples of unsuccessful banks alongside the excellent banks, suggesting good management is the key to overcoming environmental factors. Finally, management style was not considered by Davis to be central to excellence, because among the 16 banks there were examples of both a democratic style of management and a "top down" management style.

Davis's view about the irrelevance of environmental factors is debatable. The discussion of the economic determinants of international banking in Chapter 2 noted that environmental factors (for example, market failure, lack of equal access, trade barriers) explains why banks set up foreign subsidiaries overseas. Other factors explain the growth of international trade in banking services. Furthermore, all of the excellent banks operate in oligopolistic banking structures. Additionally, in Chapter 6, it was noted that the effect of regulation on the competitive environment is one important explanation for certain management decisions. For example, the US commercial banks set up foreign investment banking subsidiaries because of constraints such as the investment equalisation tax and foreign direct investment regulations imposed by the US government, also they are prohibited from offering these services at home. The comparatively low capital costs of Japanese banks is largely due to the 100% safety net extended by the Ministry of Finance and the Bank of Japan, which, in turn, affects risk-taking behaviour.

Other characteristics, argued Davis, were central to excellence. One was an *open culture*, defined as extensive horizontal and vertical communications in the day-to-day running of the bank. Davis found among the excellent banks a large number of firms that had an open culture with a relatively slow decision-making process. In a top-down type of management, it would be difficult to achieve a high degree of vertical and horizontal communication. Certain dynamic excellent banks were the exception, including Citibank and Hong Kong and Shanghai Bank. However, this observation appears to be inconsistent with the earlier point that management style does not matter.

A second feature central to excellence was strong shared values among the managerial staff, consisting of an open culture, a positive heritage, and emphasis on quality staff, who were performance-oriented and who identified with the objectives of the bank. It was achieved by the banks "growing their own talent", that is, recruiting potential management at a relatively young age and establishing in-house training programmes. However, Davis noted, parochial attitudes may develop that affect the ability of the bank to respond to a changing competitive environment.

Profit objectives were also identified as an essential feature of excellence—a satisfactory earnings trend was the central focus of a majority of the excellent banks. Like Kenyon and Mathur, Davis argued there has been a change in the attitudes of bankers: in the past they tended to focus on asset growth (a measure of physical size) and market share. Customer-driven orientation was another feature of excellent banks. These focused on the customer, segmenting their markets and restructuring their organisation and delivery systems to deal with the needs of the segments. This finding is consistent with the Kenyon–Mathur customer focus strategy.

The excellent banks also showed a willingness to invest in new products. All the excellent banks had adopted successful electronic delivery systems, innovative credit card/cheque facilities, and interest rate swap techniques. This reflects an acceptance of the need for product innovation, though some banks were leaders in the field (for example, Citicorp) while other players copied the innovation, once it had proved successful.

A matrix-based management information system was another feature of the excellent banks—they had developed a product and client-based management information system. A pre-condition for a client-oriented strategy and the effective cross-selling of products is the development of data that will measure the attractiveness of different business segments and the performance of those responsible for them. The banks which measure performance on a branch or geographic basis will find it very difficult to motivate these units to cross-sell products or execute a target-marketing programme unless they have the necessary profit and performance information. Davis noted Citibank and Bankers Trust had progressed furthest along these lines. On the other hand, some of the European banks had not yet arrived at this point.

The final feature of excellent banking identified by Davis was a strong and balanced credit process. Davis noted that the holding of excessively risky loan portfolios was due to a misuse or circumvention of a programme of credit evaluation that would otherwise yield good loan decisions. He argued that lack of enforcement of a good credit evaluation system was the source of the problem, including poor documentation, lack of follow-up, and unanticipated concentration of lending.

The Excellent Banks in 1988 and 1992

How have Davis's excellent banks fared since the publication of his book in 1985? Davis compared these banks to *The Banker*'s top 100. A similar exercise may be conducted based on *The Banker*'s "Top 100" in 1988 and 1992.

Table 22 lists the ranking of each of the excellent banks as reported in *The Banker* (July 1988). Table 23 considers the ranking in 1992. It will be observed that in 1988, with the exception of three banks, all the excellent banks appear in the top 100 ranked by size of capital and reserves. The exceptions are Wachovia, which appears as First Wachovia (having merged with First

Table 22 The Excellent Banks in 1988

Bank	Size[a]	Profit[b]	Performance[c]
Bank of Tokyo	25/100	30/100	
Bankers Trust	52/100	72/100	
Barclays	1/100	32/100	
Bayerische Vereinsbank	32/100*	54/100	
Citicorp	3/100		
Deutsche Bank	8/100	9/100	
Hongkong Bank	24/100		
JP Morgan	18/100	59/100	
Security Pacific	37/100		
SE Banken	54/100	25/100	35/50*
Sumitomo Bank	6/100	14/100	
Swiss Bank Corporation	9/100	24/100	
Chemical Bank	49/100		18/50***
Toronto Dominion Bank	57/100	67/100	
Union Bank of Switzerland	7/100	17/100	
Wachovia	98/100		

[a]Size (top 100): capital and reserves, capital/asset ratio, deposits,* deposits.
[b]Profits (top100): pre-tax profits.
[c]Performance (top 50): real growth in assets (see ***), real growth in pre-tax profits (not in this table), pre-tax profits per employee (see **).
Source: *The Banker*, various tables, July, 1988.

American and First National Atlanta in 1987), and Texas Commerce (purchased by Chemical Bank in 1987). Only two of these banks rank in the top 50 when measured by performance.

Though the majority of banks identified earnings as their key objective, most of the excellent banks do not show outstanding profitability in terms of the top 100. The exceptions are Deutsche Bank, Sumitomo Bank and Wachovia (given that it is not in the top 100 by asset size). In 1992, all but the bottom two banks appear in the top 100 banks when measured by capital strength. However, none of these banks do very well using any of the performance measures. The majority of banks get a ranking in excess of 500, that is, they are in the bottom half of the sample when one looks at performance. A similar comment may be used with respect to the soundness ratio. Some of the banks' credit ratings are very good, others very poor. There is no correlation between the top banks measured by capital, and the top 10 measured by soundness or performance. In 1991, there were a number of US bank mergers. Wachovia bought South Carolina National: it reported a $40 million loss in the first quarter of 1992, largely because of a $207 million charge it had taken against South Carolina's bad debts. Manufacturers Hanover merged with Chemical Bank; Bank America with Security Pacific.

Table 23 Davis's Excellent Banks in 1992

Bank	Out of 1000 (Capital)[d]	Performance 1[e]	Performance 2[f]	Performance 3[g]	Credit rating[h]	Soundness
Sumitomo	1	576	547	608	2.8	756
Union Bank of Switzerland[a]	7	146	593	469	1.0	280
Barclays	9	697	630	637	1.3	653
Deutsche Bank	10	142	215	427	1.0	785
Swiss Bank Corp	15	596	459	572	3.0	349
Citicorp	29	747	819	523	7.3	887
Bank of Tokyo	25	849	578	548	3	849
Hongkong Bank	33	112	118	327	4.0	746
JP Morgan	43	147	91	172	1.8	508
SE Banken	58	691	677	490	3.3	492
Toronto Dominion	62	601	339	268	2.2	268
Security Pacific	95	767	858	906	6.8	839
Bayerische Vereinsbank	70	356	388	680	2.0	680
Bankers Trust	88	421	77	206	4.0	623
First Wachovia	102	637	460	393	3.3	249
Texas Commerce	taken over in 1987 by Chemical Bank					
National Westminster	13	729	784	831	2.0	645
PNC Financial[c]	84	3	256	260	4.7	279
SG Warburg[a]	166	213	233	272	5.0	401
CSFB[b]	28	13	342	461	1.3	693

[a]Appear as excellent banks in 1989 but not in 1984 (see below).
[b]The CSFB figures are for CS Holdings Ltd, of which CFSB is a part.
[c]Pittsburgh National Bank.
[d]Capital: total amount of capital in US$.
[e]Performance 1: Real Profits Growth.
[f]Performance 2: Profits on Capital.
[g]Performance 3: Return on Assets.
[h]Credit rating: The Financial Times credit rating: compiled by Financial Times Newsletters with the help of 12 international raters. It is an arithmetical average of numerical scores given to each agency's investment grade ratings for a bank which it reviews. The highest score is 10, the lowest is 1.
[i]Soundness: Capital Assets Ratio: Tier 1 Capital to total unweighted risk assets.
In mid-1991, the following bank mergers were announced: Bank of America and Security Pacific (though these still appear as separate banks in the July 1992 version of *The Banker*); Chemical Bank and Manufacturers Hanover; NCNB and C&S Sovian.
Source: *The Banker*, July 1992.

Davis (1989) looked at how the excellent banks had fared since 1984, using a similar methodology. A panel of 15 experts (roughly the same panel as in 1984) was asked to identify 12 excellent banks. The definition of a bank was broadened to include not only institutions which took deposits and made loans, but all financial institutions engaged in the banking or securities business. Institutions identified as excellent in 1989 were:

The Bankers Trust Company
Citicorp

Credit Suisse First Boston
Deutsche Bank
First Wachovia
HongkongBank
JP Morgan
National Westminster Bank
PNC Financial Corp (Pittsburgh National Bank)
Toronto Dominion Bank
Union Bank of Switzerland
SG Warburg.

Three other financial institutions (two were securities firms) were selected by the panel but declined to participate in the subsequent interviews by Davis.

Some of the 1984 banks are absent from this list. The Bank of Tokyo had problems defending its role as the leading Japanese international bank because of problem overseas loans, and a failure to establish a competitive capability in capital markets. Barclays Bank was overtaken by National Westminster because of its better relative performance using standard measures. Davis claims Anglo-Saxon panellists place a heavy emphasis on performance measures. Panel members agreed that while Bayerische Vereinsbank AG was excellent in its own region, it had failed to expand outside its traditional domestic market, unlike regional banks such as PNC Financial or HongkongBank. The panellists were impressed by Security Pacific Bank's diversification but management's ability to ensure the cohesion of such diverse elements was a source of concern. SE Banken was considered the best international bank in Scandinavia, but on a world scale other banks had done better. Sumitomo Bank had suffered from the acquisition of a non-voting share in Goldman Sachs and the purchase of the retail bank, Heiwa Sogo, which was designed to build market share in the Tokyo region. All panel members felt Swiss Bank Corporation was a domestic leader, but votes went to CSFB because of its international investment banking business. Texas Commerce Bancshares was purchased by Chemical Bank in 1987. Its problems arose from poor asset quality in real estate and energy lending. Six other large Texan banks, including this bank, were under new ownership.

It is notable that by 1989, 50% of the 1984 excellent banks did not appear on the revised list. According to Davis, there were several reasons why these banks were dropped by the panel. First, some failed to penetrate new product and/or geographical markets—examples included SE Banken, Bayerische Vereinsbank, Swiss Bank Corporation, and Barclays. Second, management effectiveness was identified as weak at Sumitomo, Barclays, and Swiss Bank Corporation. Bank of Tokyo and Barclays were overtaken by the competition. There were also examples of ineffective strategy, including Security Pacific because of lack of focus, and Sumitomo because of the terms of acquisition of its minority interest in Goldman Sachs.

Davis admitted that the characteristics which described the excellent banks in 1984 are of marginal value because they identify traits which most banking institutions aspire to. Though they might be used to look at performance, they are not refined enough in a banking environment of rapid change. In 1989, Davis identified four success factors:

- *critical mass*, that is, either the institution has a core business base or it can acquire one by acquisition or organic growth;
- choice of strategic direction;
- the ability to manage diversity through effective management control;
- the creation of a meritocracy, because people will increasingly become the differentiating factor among financial institutions as product differentiation increases.

Based on his 1988 investigation of the excellent banks, Davis concluded:

> The overwhelming challenge for banking leadership will be to achieve a positive balance between entrepreneurship and stability, individual initiative and benefit to the group, and the trade-off between individual and cultural norms within a single organisation.

CONCLUSION: MANAGEMENT CHALLENGES IN BANKING

This chapter has briefly reviewed the meaning of business strategy, and then considered the strategic challenges for banks and the extent to which banks differ from other businesses. Banks do not appear to be any different from other businesses, in the sense that maximising shareholder value added through profitability is their key objective. However, banks do differ from other businesses because their task is to maximise profit through risk management, meaning the maturity structure of their on and off-balance sheet assets and liabilities will be critical to their success. Based on the review of the strategy literature, and its application to banking, most of the business policy models developed to explain and advise on strategy do not appear to be immediately applicable to the banking sector. This comment applies not only to the general strategy models, the most well-known being the Porter framework, but to many of the models developed explicitly for banking. Indeed, as the Davis review of "excellent" banks demonstrates, the central features of excellence can change radically in a period of just five years.

However, aspects of the Kay framework appear to be useful for the banking and financial services sector. His emphasis on the three distinctive capabilities (architecture, reputation, innovation) which allow a firm to create a competitive advantage can be applied in the banking world. Banks need to address the question of what distinctive capabilities they possess, the degree to which they are sustainable and appropriable, and the market structure in which they operate, if a competitive strategy is to be successful in maximising shareholder value added. His advice not to seek a generic strategy for corporate success is sound, because in most markets, but especially in oligopolistic banking markets with relatively few players, differentiation is the key to success. The abandonment of a generic strategic approach by Kay is also consistent with the arguments in Hamel and Prahalad. The MBA group projects and the work by Davis confirm the absence of any generic strategy to explain success—witness the usefulness of the de Carmoy model in explaining Canadian bank strategy, even though there was very little of the model that could be applied to the London-based banks. However, even the Kay model has gaps in the strategic policy it advocates. Kay argued that it is wasteful to allocate resources to create distinctive capabilities, but in banking one can think of many counter-examples. For example, a bank can use resources to improve its reputation, thereby enhancing an important distinctive capability. Also, Kay largely ignored the cost aspect of market structure.

The chapter is concluded with a summary of the management challenges faced by banks, as the 20th century draws to a close. First, competition. International banking markets are characterised by a relatively high degree of competition because of low barriers to entry and largely undifferentiated products. In domestic banking there is less competition, though policy-makers have attempted to deregulate the markets, with varying degrees of success. Thus, both domestically and globally, banks have to improve performance by offering more differentiated products, and/or profit from low-price, high-volume products. Though Davis (1985) argued that all the excellent banks are becoming increasingly dependent on wholesale funding sources, personal depositors should not be ignored—the needs of all customers must be identified and satisfied.

As was noted in Chapter 1, banks have not been very successful in reducing their operating costs. The problem could be most pronounced for multinational banks, as they increase their branch operations in the different countries. Branches are expensive to maintain and a large number of non-revenue-generating personnel must be recruited. This is in contrast to non-MNBs, where wholesale banking operations are confined to a few specialist staff operating from head office. Some banks, following firms in manufacturing, are using active cost management. Using traditional standard costing can sometimes cause costs to be treated as if they were of secondary importance, until the onset of adverse conditions (for example, a plummeting stock market). *Active cost management* is an ongoing, continuous process, designed to maintain effective cost control at all times. It requires managers to seek continuous improvement in products and services on offer, to monitor performance regularly, and to ensure the timely delivery of all the bank's output to a well-defined standard. Advocates of this type of cost control see it to be as crucial to the maintenance of competitive advantage as the choice of products and markets.

Banks must ensure that there is a well-defined method for credit risk assessment, which is used by all staff, and is changed if gaps in the process are made evident from experience with an unanticipated problem loan. The standard techniques for evaluating creditworthiness have limited applicability to many of the new banking products and services they offer. Hence, systems which integrate all aspects of risk management will be critical to the successful operation of any modern bank. *Organisation* of risk management within a bank is just as important as the *development* of risk management techniques and new instruments.

The rapid change in technology in wholesale and retail banking will have a major impact on the competitive structure of banking systems, especially retail banking. Furthermore, new technology will enable banks to introduce cost effective risk management systems, and more generally, to reduce operating costs. The critical question is how banks should choose between alternative forms of new technology.

Until recently, regulation has been largely absent from the international banking markets. But while artificial barriers to competition continue to be reduced, certain types of international bank transactions have become the focus of regulatory control.

Banks also have strategic choices to make. The question is whether banks should diversify to become large financial conglomerates to improve performance and if they choose diversification, whether acquisition of existing firms is the optimal way of diversification. Jackson (1985) identified the options, while Davis (1985) conveyed the impression that diversification is an essential component to future success. But there are many examples of highly profitable niche players in the domestic and global markets.

Davis (1985) noted the "break up of the family" as an important challenge. It includes a movement away from lifetime employment, an improvement in the evaluation of performance at the level of the individual manager and bank level, with a shift away from assessing profitability on a geographic/branch basis to an evaluation of client and product profitability. Employees should be paid for performance rather than adopting some other criterion such as seniority, more outsiders will be recruited, hired in mid-career. Thus, the success of the institution will be dependent on the human capital component of bank management. However, human resources significantly increase the operating costs of banks, as do extensive branch operations. The increasingly specialised nature of banking services, particularly in global markets, combined with the high degree of competitiveness, leads to excess demand for highly skilled but scarce human capital resources.

The important lesson of this chapter is that bankers should not look for a single strategic model to adopt in their quest to create and sustain profitability. The final chapter of this book uses case studies to substantiate this point, and provides students with practical examples of how to apply the important concepts and lessons learned from the various chapters of this book.

9

A Collection of Case Studies

INTRODUCTION

This chapter consists of a collection of case studies that are designed to provide readers with working cases of many of the concepts and ideas presented in the text. Unlike a textbook, case studies do not compartmentalise themselves neatly into an organised set of terms, definitions, and analysis. Each case brings out a number of themes and ideas which are drawn from different parts of the text, providing the reader with an integrated approach to key management issues in modern banking. For example, the case study on Sakura Bank will expose the reader to ideas such as universal banking (Chapter 1), economies of scale and economies of scope (Chapter 4), provide a practical insight into how a bank works in the Japanese financial structure (Chapter 3), and briefly reviews bank regulation in Japan (Chapter 6).

At the beginning of each case, the student is told what chapters are the most relevant for the case. The cases have been ordered so that material covered in later chapters tends to appear in the later cases. However, there is bound to be some overlap, since the nature of case work is that the student is confronted with a wide range of problems and possibilities. One of the purposes of the cases is to test the student's working knowledge of the material covered in the text, and his or her ability to apply the material when required, and not necessarily in sequence. The questions at the end of each case are designed to assist a student's understanding of the key terms, themes, and ideas in the case and the text. Answering the questions will give students experience in applying what they have learned in the book to a series of modern banking issues.* The relevant chapters are noted at the beginning of each case.

As was noted in the acknowledgements, each case originated from New York University Salomon Center (at the Stern School of Business) Case Series in Finance and Economics. The cases have been edited, revised and updated by Shelagh Heffernan, and the questions have been set by Shelagh

---

*Students may also find it helpful to use a banking/finance/business dictionary when asked to explain various concepts.

Heffernan. The contributing authors to the case are noted at the beginning of each case.

1 GOLDMAN SACHS AND LEHMAN BROTHERS*

Relevant parts of text: Chapters 1, 5 (OBS Business) and 8 (architecture).

The investment banking industry has changed dramatically over the past 20 years. The most important manifestation of this change has been a shift from relationship banking to transactional banking. *Relationship banking* exists when a customer of a bank establishes a relationship with a bank that handles most of its business, usually over an extended period of time. In *transactional (or contract) banking*, many banks compete for some of the client's business, and the client may hire several banks to do the business.

For investment banks, the client is a corporation. Transactional or contract banking is evident when one observes investment banks trying to gain the company's business on a deal-by-deal basis. For example, investment banks will be trying to arrange deals between the client and the bank. There will be an exchange of assets and parts or all of companies, between the owners of the assets or firm and the buyers. Investment banks sell the assets on behalf of their owners. The volume of this type of activity increased greatly in the 1980s; deal-making replaced traditional investment banking as the most profitable activity for investment banks.

With an increase in the number and profitability of deals and the greater uncertainty with respect to prices the assets are traded at, the trust between companies and banks became difficult to maintain, thus undermining the foundation for relationship banking. Corporations began to shop around for the best deals, initiating the era of transactional investment banking.

Banks grew more competitive, expanding their products and services through financial innovation. The investment banking industry as a whole became more segmented and specialised. Many bank partners resigned because they feared a drop in the value of their own share in the bank. Some investment banks went public to build up new capital and broaden their financial base.

The rapid growth in investment banking firms increased the demand for skilled human resources to support this growth. These changes required new management techniques, especially in the area of deal-making.

Deals tend to be made quickly, to minimise competition and avoid complications arising from fluctuating asset prices. Each deal is unique, requiring information and assistance from internal and external sources. For example, a deal will require the participation, cooperation and support across several product and service departments (internal sources), and externally from

---

*This case first appeared in the New York University Salomon Center Case Series in Banking and Finance (Case 50). Written by Richard D. Freedman (1991) and Jill Vohr. The case was edited and updated by Shelagh Heffernan; questions set by Shelagh Heffernan.

different industry experts and companies that supply different related services. The flow of information between firms has, as a result, increased, making the boundaries of firms much more porous. Since bank employees are uncertain as to whether their efforts will secure a deal or if they will be compensated for their work, recognition of interdependence and a spirit of sharing and trust is crucial.

Thus, new management techniques should encourage cooperative behaviour and support an organisational structure that is horizontal and flexible, rather than hierarchical and rigid. Top management must oversee the process, making sure employees do not pursue objectives in their individual interest which are at odds with the long-term interests of the firm. Relatively junior employees of a firm are involved in deal-making. To ensure they are operating in the best interests of the firm, tight control systems must be place, including reports on calling activity, customer evaluations, cross-evaluations within and between departments, and measures of financial outcomes. It is the responsibility of management to ensure a balance is struck between a flexible structure that can accommodate each deal, and a management system able to keep this flexibility in check.

Lehman Brothers

In April 1984, Lehman Brothers, one of the longest-surviving investment houses, was sold to Shearson, itself owned by American Express. Only several months before, the company had ranked as one of Wall Street's largest investment banking houses, more profitable than at any other point in its history. Its capital base was about $250 million, and its partners earned incomes of over $2 million. In 1984 the firm was sold after a sudden, unexpected decline in profits.

In 1969, Mr Robert Lehman had died. The loss of a strong leader, who encouraged independence among employees but who also used his authority to ensure a cohesive structure within the bank, provoked the resignation of partners, thereby depleting the firm's capital resources. The firm began to lose money, and turned to another partner, Mr Peter Peterson, to sort out the problems.

As chief executive officer, Mr Peterson reorganised Lehman Brothers. Staff was cut back, and new business brought in to expand its capital resources. He was also responsible for two successful mergers, with Abraham and Company and Kuhn Loeb. His main strength was in the development of external relationships—he had extensive contacts with clients, competitors, governments, the press and the public.

However, Mr Peterson was not considered successful as an inside man—he did not spend much time on partners or employee issues, nor did he play an active role in the management of the business. Though partners respected him, they did not like him—Mr Peterson was criticised for failing to encourage teamwork within the firm.

The partner concerned with the internal operations of Lehman's was Mr Lewis Glucksman, who as a former trader, made the trading floor the centre of Lehman's operations. He used an emotional style of management for employees, expressing disapproval and appreciation in a very public way. Mr Glucksman grew resentful of Mr Peterson, with his banking background and patrician ways. There had always been a conflict between bankers and traders in the investment banking business and at Lehman's there was a war of stereotypes. Traders thought bankers were elitist snobs, Ivy-League types who indulged in long lunches and did not work hard enough. Bankers thought of traders as a group of under-educated, crude robots. The division was manifested by the Peterson–Glucksman relationship. Glucksman thought Mr Peterson distributed Lehman's profits unfairly—60% of the firm's stock was distributed to the banker group, even though they contributed to less than a third of the firm's profits. He also thought Peterson had plans to sell Lehman's before he would be required to start selling his shares back.

Mr Peterson recognised Mr Glucksman as a vital asset to the firm, responsible for much of the firm's success in trading, building commercial paper into a $20 billion business. Peterson promoted Glucksman to co-CEO, giving him greater recognition and managerial freedom to make decisions. Glucksman was insulted by the move—he wanted an announcement from Peterson that he planned to step down. In July 1983, Glucksman used his powers as co-CEO to remove Peterson from the firm. He met with Peterson and suggested he leave by the end of September 1983. Peterson had not expected to leave Lehman so soon, but in July 1983 he announced his resignation to a surprised board—by leaving at this point in time, he would secure excellent financial terms.

Mr Glucksman had planned to re-establish unity and a common purpose at Lehman Brothers, but he quickly ran into internal obstacles. The board believed Mr Peterson's departure had been engineered, and the future of the firm decided without any prior consultation. As soon as Mr Glucksman was in sole charge, he implemented numerous managerial changes. Profits were reallocated, with the traders' bonuses increased at the bankers' expense. He also redistributed the firm's shares. Glucksman was accused of buying off key partners who could have blocked his actions. New partners were brought in, but at incomes which remaining partners resented because, they believed, it undermined their equity positions.

Key partners began to leave and internal turmoil increased. Others criticised the board for being interested only in their shares and bonuses, rather than the long-term future of Lehmans. Business declined in a negative market and the firm began to experience serious capital adequacy problems. Less than a year after Mr Peterson's retirement, Lehmans merged with Shearson, a securities firm owned by American Express.

Goldman Sachs and Company

Goldman Sachs was a New York investment banking firm. In 1984, each of the 75 partners earned $5 million per year. The earnings were largely explained by the firm's corporate culture, which may be summarised as team spirit with a unity of purpose, professional standards, a client service orientation, and a common, accepted set of beliefs, values, and ethics throughout the organisation.

This culture was the long-term result of the joint leadership of Mr John Weinburg and Mr John Whitehead, who had been with the firm since the 1940s and who had succeeded Mr Guy Levy after he died in 1976. Their co-leadership had fostered power-sharing and teamwork for the good of the firm. At all levels of the organisation the emphasis was on entrepreneurial aggressiveness, self-effacing teamwork, a shared knowledge of what the business would and would not do, home-grown talent, and a commitment to serving the customer above all other interests. Employees and partners alike had a reputation for working very hard.

As at other investment banking firms, individual greed was prevalent, but at Goldman Sachs it was channelled in such a way that it worked for and benefited the entire firm. Instead of selfish, back-stabbing behaviour, it was accepted that all had to work toward a single common purpose.

Four factors were important in sustaining this *corporate culture*:

- The firm relied on an entrenched recruitment procedure and in-house training programmes. In a given year, 1500 would apply for 30 places; those hired were the applicants with the brains, humour, motivation, confidence, maturity, and propensity for teamwork. A young graduate, once hired, could expect to spend an entire career in a department. Thus all departments had a wealth of expertise, with departmental staff sharing similar viewpoints.
- The firm was insular—outsiders were rarely brought into the organisation.
- The firm showed little interest in how the competition was doing things.
- Staying power: the great majority of the firm's 75 partners had been with the firm for between 10 and 20 years.

Top priority was given to the customer, but the clients themselves had to meet certain standards if Goldmans was to do business with them. Client operations had to be well-managed, producing only high-quality goods and services, show profits for all their businesses, and benefit the public in some way. Goldman's refused to underwrite any deal involving non-voting stock, because it believed all shareholders should have voting rights. It also refused to participate in unfriendly tender offers.

The management style at Goldmans can be described as "loose tight"—the organisation was rigidly controlled from the top in terms of operational procedures and overhead, but each department was allowed to be entrepreneurial and encouraged to innovate.

The effectiveness of the culture, selection of customers, and management style were reflected in the firm's profit margins, which in 1984 were the widest in the investment banking industry. But changes in the industry itself threatened this apparent recipe for investment banking success. The rapid growth of investment banking firms in the 1980s and the stock market crash of 1987 provoked Goldman Sachs into new forms of behaviour, at odds with its traditional culture.

There were growing concerns about internal tensions and resentments. Eleven current and former partners discussed, among other issues, the threat to the Goldman Sachs culture: ego and greed problems, a rise in the number of staff defections, and a generation gap with respect to values. Increased hiring brought in a large number of young employees with no time to absorb the culture that discouraged egotistical greedy behaviour and rewarded loyalty and teamwork. This problem extended to the higher echelons of the firm as it hired experts to fill senior positions—these senior people tended to have big egos and a need for recognition.

Key threats to the Goldman Sachs culture were identified:

- Hasty hiring, including recruitment at senior levels—unlike "lifetime" employees. For example, by the end of the 1980s, nearly half of Goldman Sachs's employees had been there less than three years. Newcomers joined as partners, rather than starting at the bottom and rising through the ranks. In contrast to long-serving employees, the new partners lacked the background to adopt the firm's entire set of values. Thus the tenets of the Goldman Sachs culture were diluted.
- Hiring and firing of employees. Black Monday (19 October 1987) forced Goldman to make widespread redundancies, an unprecedented move for the company. To keep up with the pace of change in the industry (for example, the growth of the derivatives market), the firm found it had to hire prominent employees from other firms, and bring them into key positions. Home-grown talent and lifetime employment were no longer guaranteed.
- Numerous staff defections and early retirements as employees who, under the traditional regime, could have expected to become partners at Goldman Sachs, saw these positions being filled by newcomers.
- The larger family meant it was difficult to integrate individuals into teams, thereby threatening the team approach.
- It was no longer possible to ignore the competition. For example, in 1989, Mr Weinberg agreed to represent a hostile bidder in a takeover attempt—Goldman Sachs had to enter this business because it was highly profitable, and ignoring it would threaten their competitive position in the increasingly competitive investment banking world.

There was a concern with the rate of growth of the firm and its effect on management style. Growth was recognised as the only means by which their competitive position could be maintained. But it could result in a loss of control. For most firms, the standard solution to growth has been to separate managers from producers, but in investment banking such a move in the investment banking sector was unacceptable because unless managers stayed in touch with the markets, they would lose credibility. Another way to manage growth would be to implement a high degree of formalisation of procedures, but this would be self-defeating because it would discourage entrepreneurial behaviour and decrease flexibility.

Very rapid growth increased capital pressures on the firm, undermining the feasibility of a partnership system. In 1989, it was reported that Goldmans could raise as much as $4 billion on the stock market—the sale of a big minority stake to the public could raise $500 million.* But if it did go public, it was believed the loss of the lure of partnership would undermine the firm's ability to attract top talent.

The integrity of the firm was also called into question:

- A senior stock trader, Robert Freedman, resigned after pleading guilty to insider trading.
- A partner, Lewis Eisenberg, resigned after his secretary filed a sexual harassment suit.
- The firm acknowledged the absence of women and minorities in top management positions. They claimed to have encountered problems with recruitment, and the groups themselves found it difficult to assimilate. In 1990, five women quit the firm to set up a "boutique" investment firm.

But the situation was not all gloom and doom:

- Goldman Sachs hired management consultants to advise them on management techniques. The firm developed programmes to integrate new arrivals into their corporate culture and to generate a sense of involvement. These included management and leadership seminars, and orientation programmes. In role-playing, different teams acted as Goldman competitors and discussed their various strengths and weaknesses, and what they implied for the strategy of the home team—Goldman.
- The problems of growth and control were to be addressed through the application of an old principle at Goldmans: teamwork. Teamwork was encouraged by making the lowliest associate feel a sense of belonging, encouraging staff at all levels to participate in decision-making, and ensuring the developments of the firm were effectively communicated to all levels. Training stressed specialisation, together with a basic understanding of the general issues, so teams could form and disband efficiently and flexibly.
- The recruitment of experts at senior level had caused resentment and a lack of understanding of the culture, but it also supported the company's growth. Given the rapid specialisation of investment banking products, the expertise allowed Goldman Sachs to keep pace with its competitors.

Though the Goldman Sachs' culture had evolved, the company remained in a top position: in the first half of 1990, it earned $29.5 billion in deals and a market share of 14.2%. The firm is cautious about expanding into new areas—as a result they have avoided losses arising from junk bonds and bridge loans, associated with the LBO mania of the 1980s.

In 1993 and 1994, Goldman Sachs showed signs of strain. After a record of $2.3 billion in pre-tax profits in 1993, earnings plummeted, due to huge trading losses and poorly executed overseas expansions. Falling profits explain the ongoing shake-up, and very likely the reason for the numerous partnership defections.

Forbes, 18 September, 1989.

Rising interest rates in 1994 were a large part of the problem, and bedevilled most investment houses on Wall Street. In a period of sustained rising rates, companies are deterred from issuing bonds, and middlemen like Goldmans experienced a big drop in fee income.

Mr Jon Corzine, the firm's current chairman, has admitted that the underlying cause of Goldman's recent setbacks have been managerial problems. There was an overly aggressive foreign expansion programme, which caused an increase in expenses of 40% between 1992 and 1994. Goldman's had targeted China, but fee income was low because of low fees associated with the highly competitive Asian market.

As income was falling, costs increased because of the expansion of staffing levels. Goldman's deteriorating finances prompted a cost-cutting programme, which has included reducing staff by 15%. But defections by key employees is a more serious problem. In September 1994, Mr Stephen Friedman, the firm's former chairman announced that he would be retiring after only four years in the job. Mr Friedman's departure destabilised Goldman's and prompted the resignations of many other partners, roughly 40 by December 1994—because of the prospect of reduced rewards.

Headhunters reported unprecedented interest in career alternatives among Goldman executives. If the number of defections increase, the bank's competitive advantage will be under threat, because human resources has been the main reason for the success of Goldman's. The prospect of partnership has always been central to the bank's ability to attract top talent.

Questions for the Goldman Sachs and Lehman Bros Case Study

1. To what extent does the shift from relationship to transactional investment banking explain the problems which occurred at Lehman Bros and Goldman Sachs?
2. Is transactional or contract banking compatible with a partnership management in an investment bank?
3. Devise a working definition of the term, "corporate culture", using Goldman Sachs as the example.
4. Do you think ignoring the competitor is an acceptable feature of any corporate culture? Does it partly explain some of the problems Goldman subsequently encountered?
5. Sumitomo, a Japanese bank, paid $500 million for a non-voting minority position in Goldman Sachs in 1986. Why would Goldman Sachs and the Japanese bank be interested in such a relationship?
6. Use the Goldman's case to explain how volatile interest rates can affect a bank's fee and trading income.
7. It was reported that Goldman Sachs was in trouble: partnerships were relinquished, and headhunters reported expressions of interest from Goldman employees. Will Goldman Sachs go the same way as Lehman Brothers?

8. Using Kay's definition of architecture (see Chapter 8), briefly summarise the architecture at Lehmans and Goldman Sachs. Was architecture a factor in the problems faced by the firm?

2 AMERICAN EXPRESS*

Relevant parts of text: Chapters 1, 4 (economies of scale and scope, and synergy) and 8 (strategy).

Annie Brownwell was a senior portfolio manager for Diversified Pension Incorporated. Part of her job description was to conduct periodic reviews of companies, to assess whether the pension fund should continue to hold a particular stock.

In this case, the firm in question was American Express (Amex), a key holding in Diversified over the last decade. In January 1990 Annie began a lengthy review, with the objective of advising her board on their future holdings of Amex shares.

Using the 1986 Amex annual report, Annie obtained a list of Amex's strategic objectives

- To sustain Amex's position as a quality leader . . .
- To increase the precision with which Amex segments markets . . .
- To expand Amex's presence in growth markets worldwide . . .
- To remain a leader in the application of new technologies . . .
- To maintain Amex's ability to attract top talent . . .
- Never to lose sight of Amex's principal goal . . . to increase shareholder value.

The report noted that Amex had achieved its distinction in the financial and travel services industries by putting the attributes of strong brand names to use, and by exploiting the multiple distribution channels that comprise the family of Amex companies. However, Amex had been careful to target only those market segments where it had the ability to be a leader in market share and generate a significant financial return. Amex was not trying to be all things to all people.

Chronology of Key Events for Amex, 1979–93

1979

Mr James D. Robinson III became Chairman and CEO at Amex, known as a finance company, and for its charge card and traveller's cheques. Amex had for the past 30 years maintained increased earnings each year. A key task for

---

*These cases first appeared in the New York University Salomon Center Case Series in Banking and Finance (Cases 20 and 49). Written by Roy Smith (C20, 1988; revised, 1992) and Richard D. Freedman and Jill Vohr (1991 C49). The two cases were merged, edited and updated by Shelagh Heffernan; questions set by Shelagh Heffernan.

Robinson was to keep up or improve upon this performance. Yet the firm was threatened because:

- the Travel Related Services (TRS) part of Amex was performing well, but business charge cards and traveller's cheques were seen as a mature business. New competition came from Visa and Mastercharge, not only as credit cards, but because they were entering the business market;
- at this time, the second core business for Amex was American Express International Bank. But in 1977, it experienced a fall in return on assets (ROA), and there was increasing concern about the bank's third world loan exposure;
- Amex owned Fireman's Fund, a property/casualty insurance company. Earnings were volatile.

Robinson decided his key objective was the diversification of the company into a service company, broadly defined. He set up a new department, the Office of Strategic Programme Development, to assist him in his goal. Over time, Robinson redefined the strategy to one of creating a broadly defined financial services company.

1981

In keeping with this strategy, Shearson Loeb Rhodes, a brokerage firm, was acquired by Amex in December 1981. Shearson was made up of seven other securities firms. At the time of acquisition, Shearson had an excellent reputation as a cost-conscious securities firm that was highly profitable. The key advantage would be the cross-marketing of Amex and Shearson's securities products to their respective customer lists.

There were concerns about differences in culture, because Amex was considered a mature, formal, bureaucratic organisation; Shearson was the opposite. Earnings from the brokerage business had a reputation for being volatile, in contrast to the charge card business. Salaries and bonuses at Shearson's far exceeded those at Amex.

However, the strategy of diversifying in the financial services sector, together with an optimistic outlook for the financial sector as a whole, led Amex to purchase Shearson for $930 million.

The CEO of Shearson, Mr Sandy Weill, became President of Amex. Mr Peter Cohen, who had worked for Weill while he was at Shearson, became CEO of Shearson. Cohen's vision was for Shearson to become a powerful investment bank. After an attempt at organic growth which proved unsuccessful, Cohen saw the investment bank, Lehman Brothers Kuen Koeb, as an ideal acquisition opportunity.

1981–84

The acquisition process continued:

1981: Shearson acquired the Boston Company, a regional security firm, and a number of other regional securities firms;

1983: Amex purchased the Swiss-based Trade Development Banks from Mr E Safra for $520 million in cash and stock. Mr Safra became chairman and CEO of Amex International Bank Ltd, and one of Amex's major shareholders. Mr Safra was well known for his personal banking expertise; Robinson was attracted by the wealthy clientele and his international banking connections. It was hoped that both would bolster Amex International Bank and Shearson;

January 1984: Amex acquired a mass market financial planner and manager and distributor of mutual funds, Investors Diversified Services, for $727 million. The plan was for IDS to be used as a key savings outlet for Amex middle income card-holding customers;

May 1984: Shearson merged with Lehman Brothers Kuhn Koeb, an investment bank that was founded in the 1860s. Investment banking trading expertise, together with a list of blue chip clients, were the main attractions of Lehman. However, Lehman had quite a different culture: it used relationship banking to attract and keep clients, with an emphasis on traditions and relatively high operation costs. Shearson, by contrast, was a retail brokerage firm, where the emphasis was placed on aggressive marketing and cost-cutting. Again, however, this acquisition would help bring about the achievement of Robinson's key strategy. Shearson acquired Lehman for $360 million. Within six months, Cohen had Lehman investment bankers aggressively seeking out new business.

At this point, Amex had all the ingredients to become a financial supermarket, offering every type of financial service, with the exception of retail intermediary and payments services. Both Robinson and Cohen thought a global presence was an essential part of the financial supermarket strategy. By the end of 1989, Amex had opened nine branches in Europe, Asia, the Far East, and Australia.

1985

August 1985: Mr Safra bought back certain parts of the Trade Development Bank Business. He resigned as CEO of Amex International Bank and as a director of Amex. Safra resigned because of the poor performance of Fireman's Fund—he felt he had been deceived about the health of this subsidiary, which, in turn, could undermine the value his shareholding.

Safra also disliked the bureaucratic management style of Amex, and did not like leaving Geneva. He agreed not set up a new Swiss bank until March 1988. Amex thought Safra was poaching employees and ideas from Amex in preparation to set up a new Swiss bank, and were concerned his old customers would return to him. Amex made legal attempts to block the setting up of a new bank (citing anti-competitive behaviour) but by the summer of 1988, Safra had established the new, Swiss-based bank. Later that summer, Amex admitted to a smear campaign to undermine Safra's reputation—Robinson made a public apology and $8 million was paid by Amex to Safra charities.

October 1985: Amex sold 58% of Fireman's Fund to the public. Mr Weill, who had been sent to San Francisco to sort out the Fund's problems, resigned (in December 1985) after Amex turned down his bid to buy Fireman's Fund. Mr Gerstner was made Amex President, to replace Mr Weill. He continued to be Chairman of Travel Related Services (TRS) , which had been the most successful arm of Amex.

Amex also repurchased a 25% minority interest in First Data Resources Inc. It had sold these shares in 1983 at $14.00 per share; it bought them back for $38.00 per share.

1986

Two further sales of shares in Fireman's Fund in May and December put an effective end to Amex's involvement in the insurance business.

1987

March 1987: Amex sold 18% of Shearson Lehman Bros to Nippon Life, the largest insurance company in Japan. The deal involved other relationships between Nippon and Amex. In addition, Amex announced a two for one stock split.

April 1987: Amex announced that it owned or managed assets in excess of $200 billion—Shearson accounted for $158 million.

May 1987: Amex sold 18% of Shearson Lehman to the public; Shearson sold additional new shares at the same time. Amex holdings in Shearson dropped to 60%.

June 1987: Amex announced that Amex International Bank had added $600 million to its reserves for loan losses; as a result, Amex had to report an after tax charge of $520 million against its second quarter earnings.

July 1987: Amex announced a further repurchasing of 40 million shares over the next two to three years.

October 1987: stock markets crashed (Black Monday). Shearson experienced large losses, especially because it had been co-managing the US tranche of the British Petroleum stock underwriting. But it still acquired EF Hutton (a retail brokerage chain in financial trouble because of organisational problems) for $1 billion in December.

December 1987: Shearson Lehman announced a fourth quarter loss of $95 million and made 1500 employees redundant. Moody's downgraded its senior subordinated debt from A-2 to A-3. The Standard and Poor's AA rating on this debt remained unchanged.

January 1988: Amex announced that Amex International Bank was adding another $350 million to loan loss reserves and Amex reported losses of $104 million for the fourth quarter of 1987. Net income for 1987 was $533 million, down from $1.1 billion in 1986.

January 1990: Mr Cohen, CEO of Shearson Lehman Bros, is fired by Mr Robinson.

1992–93

In 1992, Amex's profits fell by nearly half to $436 million. This was partly due to a write off of $342 million during the last quarter of 1992, the second write off within 12 months. It was now believed the chairmanship of Mr Robinson was the cause of Amex's poor performance in the 1990s:

- the Amex card business suffered from increasing competition and a poor image;
- lax management of the Optima credit card business cost Amex $112 million;
- TRS was subject to a "re-engineering" programme which proved to be extremely costly. Post-tax profits at TRS slumped in 1992 to $243 million, down from $956 million in 1990;
- after Mr Cohen was fired in January 1990, it soon became evident that Shearson was a poorly integrated set of indifferent investment houses;
- Amex had lost a few key executives, including Mr Sanford Weill, who became CEO of Primerica, and Richard Thoman, a top executive at TRS, who departed because he had lost faith in Robinson's ability to lead a good team.

At a dinner meeting in September 1992, these negative points were put to Robinson. The intention behind the review was to oust Robinson as CEO and appoint a new one by January 1993. However when the board met again on 25 January 1993, it was announced that Robinson was to remain chairman of the travel and financial services group. Mr Harvey Golub, Robinson's protégé, took over as Chairman of Shearson. There were a number of reasons for the board's surprise decision. The board had wanted an outsider to fill the position of CEO. They thought they had found the perfect outsider, rumoured to be Sir Colin Marshall of British Airways. However, his candidacy faded as a row between Virgin Atlantic and British Airways implicated BA in unacceptable practices designed to force Virgin out of business.

The board also realised that if an outsider was appointed, Mr Golub would probably leave. He had an exceptional performance record at Amex. Mr Golub was behind the purchase of IDS Financial Services. He ran it, and IDS turned out to be one of Amex's few successful acquisitions in the 1980s. There were signs Mr Golub was also restoring TRS to profitability. He was considered a valuable asset.

Following the announcement of the continuance of Robinson as CEO, four of the 19 board members dissented. The share price also fell, from $25.63 prior to the decision to $23.88, the day after the announcement. Confidence in AMEX was further undermined.

During the 1980s Mr Robinson had been behind much of the empire-building within the AMEX group, but there were signs he was unloading many acquisitions to raise much-needed capital. The Boston Company was sold to Mellon Bank. There are also plans to spin off Shearson, its investment banking subsidiary. These moves signalled Amex's retreat from investment banking.

The Personalities

Mr James Robinson III

Robinson became CEO of Amex in 1978. His key strategy, to turn Amex into a broadly defined financial services company, had been accomplished on paper, with the acquisitions already noted. But Amex still had to turn this new company into one that maximised shareholder value added. He planned to do this through the development of synergies through the various acquisitions Amex had made.

Robinson implemented a "One Enterprise" synergy plan, whereby Amex was seen as a collection of firms selling different brands to different customers, but sharing a single goal: maximising profits and shareholder value added. Thus, Shearson bankers were encouraged to approach TDB clients for business, TDB bankers to approach Shearson clients for business, Shearson securities were to be sold to investors who were customers in other Amex divisions, and Amex cards and life insurance were to be sold to everyone.

Extra bonuses were awarded to senior and middle managers who identified and developed two to three synergy projects in a year. A monthly report on the One Enterprise strategy was produced.

By the end of 1986, 10% of Amex's net income came from taking advantage of synergistic opportunities. Robinson stressed the need for quality of service, and acceptance and taking advantage of change.

By 1988, Robinson began to concentrate on world policy issues, such as trade and international debt, leaving the operations side of Amex to Mr Gerstner.

Mr Lou Gerstner

Originally an advisor to Mr Robinson (before he became CEO of Amex) Mr Gerstner was placed in charge of TRS in 1978 by Robinson, when Robinson was promoted to CEO of Amex. During Gerstner's tenure at TRS, he implemented the Robinson strategies. The Amex card was combined with Amex's travel agency business (losing money at the time), which allowed companies to monitor and control travel expenses. The Amex card was redefined to include not just business persons, but for personal use as well, thereby attracting new card members and new stores, ranging from high income department stores to petrol stations. Gerstner ensured that the card became associated with a high-quality service.

Under Gerstner, a profitable TRS became even more profitable. Return on equity was 28% in 1988. In 1988, he was made president of Amex after Mr Weill's resignation. He remained chairman of TRS, and was responsible for corporate finance and planning and IDS. Gerstner took responsibility for most of Amex's day-to-day operations, as Robinson increasingly spent time on global trade and debt issues. Gerstner believed that Amex's next major thrust should be in high-priced, high-quality computer services/information management.

Mr Peter Cohen

Cohen's objective (after the acquisition of Lehman Brothers, the investment bank) was to turn Shearson into the most powerful Wall Street financial firm. He was opposed to Robinson's One Enterprise objective, and concentrated on keeping Shearson as a separate entity, but with the financial backing of Amex. Cohen's priorities changed from one of cost control vigilance to a glamorous but high-margin world of investment banking.

Shearson began to take large equity positions in deals such as leveraged buy-outs and bridge loans. It acquired 28% of a life insurance company, First Capital, which had a large junk bond portfolio. It also acquired a primary real estate firm, Balcor, which was moving aggressively into construction lending. The emphasis was on a global presence.

Cohen thought the priorities and strategic planning for Shearson differed from the other firms in Amex—Shearson's goal was to become a giant securities firm, with an extensive retail brokerage network and a global presence in investment banking and capital markets. Thus, while Gerstner was trying to exploit synergies and move into computing services, Cohen was trying to make Shearson a top Wall Street firm, ignoring opportunities for synergy with other Amex operations. Cohen participated in strategic planning sessions at Amex, but continued to emphasise the specialised nature of the securities business.

Cohen considered Shearson critical to making Amex a global financial services industry. He was supported by Robinson—Amex itself had tripled its revenues between 1979 and 1987. Various popular journal publications— *Business Week* (January 1988), *Euromoney* (1987) and *Institutional Investor* (1988)—praised Robinson and Cohen.

Shearson's earnings were volatile, obscuring the results of highly successful TRS. Cohen argued that volatile earnings at Shearson were because it was such a different business from Gerstner's TRS. Earnings of $341 million peaked in 1986, which helped Amex at a difficult time because of the losses at Fireman's Fund.

The October 1987 stock market crash had a severe effect on Shearson's earnings, which dropped off dramatically in 1988. Shearson was criticised for being a broadly based investment house, but one that could not maintain a competitive advantage in anything it offered. Its reputation floundered:

- it had been co-manager of the US British Petroleum flotation, which suffered badly because of the stock market crash;
- in 1988, it was widely criticised in Wall Street circles for backing a hostile bid by Beazer PLC (a British firm) for Koppers, a Pittsburgh firm. Amex customers, especially in Pittsburgh, were infuriated by the role played by Shearson, to the extent that they cut up their Amex cards and sent them to Robinson. Robinson forbade Shearson from backing any more hostile bids;
- Shearson and Cohen's reputations also suffered from their involvement in the RJR Nabisco takeover. Mr Ross Johnson, CEO of RJR Nabisco, attempted to buy out shareholders in late 1988. But Shearson, representing Johnson, put in an extremely low first bid, and was beaten out by Kohlberg

Kravis Roberts and Company. Shearson suffered a further loss in reputation, and more than $200 million in fees. Mr Johnson (a good friend of Robinson) had failed in the takeover bid, largely because the deal was mishandled by Shearson. Robinson was furious. On 20 January 1990 Robinson fired Cohen, and Amex absorbed Shearson, only to discover that it consisted of a number of disparate investment houses, poorly organised.

Question for the American Express Case Study

1. In the context of the case study, explain the meaning of the following terms:
   (a) leveraged buy-out;
   (b) underwriting an issue;
   (c) synergy;
   (d) market segmentation;
   (e) investment bank "reputation".
2. Explain what is meant by each of Amex's long term strategic objectives listed on page 337.
3. To what extent do "personalities" explain the rise and subsequent decline of Amex?
4. Who was responsible for the failure of Robinson's "One Enterprise" scheme?
5. Was Amex's success in the 1980s due to a well-conceived overall strategy, or the result of opportunistic behaviour in a bull market?
6. What is Diversified Pensions Investments Inc, and what are the key objectives of the firm?
7. Annie wants to be sure she does not present *too much* data on Amex when writing her report. She decides no more than four separate pieces of data should be included. Identify the four most important pieces of data Annie might use to report on the performance of Amex, from the following list:
   (a) Amex Company: annual summary of operating results;
   (b) Amex Company: annual summary of balance sheet data;
   (c) Amex Company: annual summary of consolidated balance sheet data;
   (d) Amex Company: a breakdown of annual results for each segment of the company;
   (e) Amex Company: stock price history;
   (f) Amex Company: indexed stock price history relative to the Standard and Poor's 500;
   (g) Amex Company: indexed stock price history relative to a composite of selected companies;
   (h) Amex Company: price/earnings history;
   (i) Amex Company: price/earnings ratios relative to a composite of selected companies;
   (j) Shearson Lehman Bros: indexed stock price history relative to a composite of selected companies.

Justify your selection.

8. What other factors would influence Annie's advice to Diversified Pensions, apart from the performance of Amex?
9. Suppose Annie was asked to advise her board on Diversified's holdings of Amex's stock. What advice would she give in:
   (a) 1988?
   (b) 1990?
   (c) 1992?
   (d) 1995?
Did the advice change, and if so, why?

3 SAKURA BANK*

Relevant parts of text: Chapters 1 (universal banking), 3 (Japanese banking structure), 4 (economies of scale and scope) and 6 (regulation of Japanese banking).

In December 1991 Sakura Bank Ltd was Japan's and the world's second largest bank in terms of assets, valued at $438 billion. It was also one of the largest in terms of capitalisation of common stock ($41.4 billion).

Sakura Bank was formed through the merger of the Mitsui Bank, which dated back to 1683, a distinguished Tokyo bank, with the Taiyo Kobe Bank, a regional, largely retail bank covering the region of Kansai, including Osaka, Kobe, and Kyoto. The Taiyo Kobe Bank was itself the result of an earlier merger between the Taiyo Bank and the Bank of Kobe.

The merger took place in April, 1990—the new bank was to be called the Mitsui Taiyo Kobe Bank until the banks were properly integrated, when it would be renamed the Sakura Bank, after "cherry blossom", a symbol of unity and grace in the Japanese culture. In April 1992, the merged bank became the Sakura Bank.

Japan's Ministry of Finance (MoF) was thought to have played a hand in the merger because, at the time, bank mergers in Japan were rare, and usually occurred between a healthy institution and an unhealthy one. But these two banks were both financially sound. The MoF probably encouraged the merger to increase the consolidation of the banking sector of Japan, thereby making Japanese banks better prepared for financial deregulation, which would increase competition—something, it was believed, which could be better handled by larger sized banks.

---

*This case first appeared in the New York University Salomon Center Case Series in Banking and Finance (Case 25). Written by Roy C. Smith (1992). The case was edited and updated by Shelagh Heffernan; questions set by Shelagh Heffernan.

The newly merged bank had the most extensive retail branch network of any bank in Japan, with 612 offices and 108 international offices. The merger took place for several reasons:

- to allow the newly merged bank to be "universal", providing high-quality management and information systems;
- to achieve greater economies of scale;
- to achieve a greater diversification of credit risk;
- to use the bank's increased size and lending power to increase market share.

Past experience had shown that Japanese bank mergers were rarely successful, because strong cultural links in a particular bank made it difficult to combine staff, clients and facilities. Furthermore, until the mid-1990s there had been a reluctance to make anyone redundant from a Japanese firm, or to shift power away from places that had had it for years. But the announcement in April 1992 that the merged bank was ready to take on its new name, Sakura, suggested these difficulties had been overcome, and well inside the three years management originally announced it would take.

Essential Background

The Japanese banking system was described in Chapter 3 of this book. The system has always been one characterised by functional segmentation and close regulation by the Ministry of Finance and the bank of Japan. During the 1970s Japanese banks experienced a period of steady growth and profitability. The Japanese are known for their high propensity to save, so banks could rely on households and corporations earning revenues from an export boom to ensure a steady supply of relatively cheap funds. The reputation that the Ministry of Finance and Bank of Japan had for casting a 100% safety net around the banking system meant, *ceteris paribus*, the cost of capital for Japanese banks was lower than for major banks headquartered in other industrialised countries.

The global presence of Japanese banks was noticeable by the late 1970s, but in the 1980s their international profile became even more pronounced because of the relatively low cost of deposits, surplus corporate funds, and the increased use of global capital markets. Lending activities increasingly took on a global profile—Japanese banks were sought out for virtually every major international financing deal. For example, in the RJR Nabisco takeover involving a leveraged buy-out of $25 billion, Japanese participation was considered a crucial part of the financing. The combination of rapid asset growth and an appreciating yen meant that by 1991 the top 10 banks, ranked by asset size, were Japanese. By the late 1980s, Japanese banks had a reputation for being safe and relationship-oriented, but nothing special if measured by profit or innovations.

The reputation for "being safe" was explained by the MoF's determination not to allow any banking failures in Japan—there had been no bank failures in the post-war period. It was also known that Japanese banks had substantial hidden reserves. Furthermore, banks held 1% to 5% of the common stock of many of their corporate customers; the customers in turn owned shares in the bank. The cross-shareholding positions had been built up in the early post-war period, before the Japanese stock market had started its 30-year rise. These shareholdings and urban branch real estate were recorded on the books at historic cost, but the market value was far in excess of book value. If one looked at Japanese banks' ratio of capital to assets in the late 1980s, these appeared to be low compared to their US or European counterparts, but such ratios ignored the market value of their stockholdings and real estate.

Japanese banks were less profitable than banks in other countries for three reasons:

- the emphasis on "relationship banking" obliged these banks to offer very low lending rates to their key corporate borrowers;
- operating costs were relatively high;
- the Ministry of Finance discouraged financial innovation because of the concern that it might upset the established financial system.

Japanese banks appeared prepared to accept the relatively low profitability, in exchange for the protective nature of the system.

As Japanese banks became more involved in global activities, either through international lending, through the acquisition of foreign banks, or by multinational branching, Japanese banks became more informed about the financial innovations available by the early 1980s. At the same time, the MoF accepted the reality of *imported deregulation*, that is, the financial sector would have to be deregulated to allow foreign financial firms to enter the Japanese market. The pressure for this change came from the mounting trade surplus Japan had with other countries and a new financial services regime in Europe which would penalise countries that did not offer EU banks equal treatment. As a result, the MoF agreed to the gradual deregulation of domestic financial firms, and to lower entry barriers for foreign banks and securities houses. The MoF lifted the barriers between different types of Japanese banks and between banks and securities firms, and began to allow market access to all qualified issuers or investors. The tight regulation of interest rates was relaxed. Though the full effects of the reforms were not expected to be felt until after 1994, Japanese banks and securities firms realised they would have to adjust to the inevitable effects of deregulation.

Zaitech and the Bubble Economy

As was the case in the west, by the mid-1980s, Japanese corporations realised that issuing their own bonds could be a cheaper alternative to borrowing from Japanese banks. It also became apparent that if a Japanese corporation invested in financial assets rather than Japanese manufacturing businesses they would be more profitable, an investment strategy known as *zaitech*. Early on, these firms borrowed money for simple financial speculation, but over time the process became more sophisticated. The non-financial firm would issue securities with a low cash payout and use the money raised to invest in securities that were appreciating in value, such as real estate or a portfolio of stocks, warrants or options.

The heyday of *zaitech* was between 1984 and 1989—Japanese firms issued a total of about $720 million in securities. More than 80% of these securities were equity securities. Japan's total new equity financing in this period was three times that of the USA, even though the US economy was twice the size of Japan's and it too was experiencing a boom. Just under half of these securities were sold in domestic markets, mainly in the form of *convertible debentures* (a bond issue where the investor has the option of converting the bond into a fixed number of common shares) and new share issues. The rest were sold in the Euromarkets, mainly in the form of low coupon bonds with *stock purchase warrants* attached (a security similar to a convertible debenture but the conversion feature, as a warrant, can be detached and sold separately). The implication of a convertible debenture issue is that one day, new shares will be outstanding, thereby reducing earnings per share. But shareholders did not appear concerned, and share prices rarely declined following an issue.

Japanese banks were also attracted to *zaitech* financing, because:

- they underwrote the new issues, though this was a relatively minor attraction;
- they acted as guarantors of the payment of interest and principal on the bonds being issued;
- they could buy the warrants to replace stock in customer holdings, which allowed profits from a portfolio to be freed up, to be reinvested on a more leveraged basis;
- once the warrants were detached, the bonds could be purchased at a discount of 30% to 40%.

The bonds could then be repackaged with an interest rate swap, and converted into a floating rate asset to be funded on the London deposit market, and held as a profitable international asset.

Zaitech became extremely popular because it offered attractions for banks, corporations and investors alike. The late 1980s came to be known as the "bubble economy" in Japan because of the frequency with which financial market speculation, usually financed by margin loans, occurred. The prices of all financial assets, especially real estate and stocks, rose at rapid rates, encouraging yet more speculative behaviour.

As a result of *zaitech* and the financial surpluses, Japanese companies were no longer dependent on extensive amounts of borrowing. Bank borrowing was not attractive if firms could issue bonds, which would be redeemed by conversion into common stock in the future. The ratios of long-term debt to equity (book value) began to decline for companies listed on the Tokyo Stock Exchange, from more than 50% in 1980 to about 39.6% at the end of 1990. By 1990, only 42% of corporate debt outstanding, or 17% of total capitalisation, was provided by bank loans. Bank loans that were negotiated often supported *zaitech* corporations or investment in bank certificates of deposit, which, because of relationship banking, the borrower could maintain at virtually no cost.

The fall in the leverage or gearing of Japanese firms was far more pronounced if equity was measured in terms of market prices. By 1989, Japanese debt to equity ratios were half those of their US counterparts. But although many companies used surplus cash flow to repay debt, others engaged in *zaitech*—increasing debt to invest in other securities.

Thus the real measure of leverage (gearing) was the ratio of net interest payable to total operating income, where net interest income was defined as interest received minus interest paid. Using this measure, Japanese manufacturing companies, in aggregate, fell from 30% in 1980 to (−)5.3% in 1990. Thus, the manufacturing sector had become *deleveraged* or *degeared*: if *zaitech* holdings (based on December 1989 prices) were sold, they would have no debt at all.

Problem Loans and the Burst of the Bubble

Japanese banks had entered the global lending markets in the early 1980s and, determined to capture market share, competed on interest rates. The competition was not only with foreign banks, but other Japanese banks. Japanese banks became highly exposed in foreign loans, beginning with Latin American debt—they held portfolios of third world loans which they had lent at below market rates. The MoF discouraged banks from writing off this debt after the Mexican crisis of 1982—it wanted the banks to learn from their mistakes and exercise more discipline, and it also wanted to limit tax credits taken by these write-offs. If banks were to write off loans, they had to do it off the books, by using the capital gains from the sale of securities and applying them against bad debt. Thus, the banks' hidden assets became their loan loss reserves.

The Nikkei index peaked in December 1989 having risen sixfold since 1979, and then fell steadily to less than 15 000 in 1992, a 62% drop from its high. The real estate market followed, resulting in large losses for many *zaitech* players. The value of their *zaitech* holdings declined, but there was no change in their loan obligations. By the first half of 1991, bankruptcies in Japan had risen dramatically, with liabilities of $30 billion, six times that of 1989.

As the problems escalated, companies were compelled to sell off relationship shareholdings, which forced down share prices still further and led to expectations of future falls, which, in turn, caused further falls in share prices. Those companies known to be deep into *zaitech* saw their share prices drop even further. Some saw their share prices fall well below the exercise prices of the outstanding warrants and convertible bonds they had issued, which they fully expected to be repaid by the conversion of the securities into common stock. If the conversions did not take place when the bond matured, the companies would have to pay off the bondholders. Over $100 billion of warrants and convertibles maturing in 1992 and 1993 were trading below their conversion prices in late 1991.

With the bursting of the bubble, the number of problem loans to small businesses and individual customers increased dramatically. The *shinkin* banks were the most highly exposed, and it was expected that few would stay independent—the MoF would force troubled banks to merge with healthy ones.

The big banks also suffered, but the degree of their problems was difficult to assess because the banks were not required to declare a problem loan "non-performing" until at least one year after interest payments had ceased. However, it was the long-term banks which were the most affected, because they had been under the greatest pressure to find new business as borrowing by large corporations began to fall. Two key rating agencies downgraded the bond ratings of 10 major Japanese banks in 1990, though most remained in the Aa category. The rating agencies noted Japanese banks were a riskier investment with questionable profitability performance, but were also confident the MoF would intervene to prevent bank failures or defaults on obligations.

Application of the Basle Capital Assets Ratio

International banks headquartered in Japan were required to comply with the risk assets ratio requirements, following the agreement reached in 1988 (see Chapter 6). Banks had to meet these capital adequacy standards by the beginning of 1993.

The interpretation of what counted as tier two capital was partly left to the discretion of regulators in a given country. The MoF allowed Japanese banks to count 45% (the after-tax equivalent amount) of their unrealised gains as tier two capital, because these banks had virtually no loan loss reserves. As share prices escalated in the 1980s, the value of the tier two capital increased, and many banks took advantage of the bubble economy to float new issues of tier one capital. But after December, 1989, stock prices fell, and so did tier two capital, thereby reducing the banks' risk assets ratios. Japanese banks came under increasing pressure to satisfy the minimum requirements.

Sakura Bank in the 1990s

Sakura had shown one of the weakest performances of all the major Japanese city banks in 1991 because of high interest rates, weak net interest margins, and rising overhead costs. The bank's stated risk asset ratios were, in March 1991, 3.67% for tier one, and 7.35% for tiers one and two. The average for Japanese banks was, respectively, 4.35% and 8.35%. Sakura's general expenses as a percentage of ordinary revenues were, on average higher than for other city banks in the period 1988–90. Its net profits per employee were lower. Out of 11 city banks, only three had lower exposures to small business and the retail sector for the year 1990–91.

In its 1991 annual report, Sakura Bank recognised the new pressures of the Basle capital adequacy requirements, and noted that in the current environment it would be difficult to rely on new equity issues to increase the numerator of the risk assets ratio. Sakura intended to raise capital through subordinated debt and other means, and to limit the growth of assets. The strategy of the bank was to focus on improving return on assets and profitability. In anticipation of deregulating markets, Sakura wanted to increase efficiency and risk management techniques.

At this time, analysts believed the positive effects of the merger were just beginning to be felt, with additional benefits coming through over the next three to five years. The benefits would be created through integration of merging branch networks and computer systems, and a reduction in personnel. Though operating profits were recovering, they remained depressed.

Questions for the Sakura Bank Case Study

1. In the context of this case, explain the meaning of:
   (a) imported deregulation;
   (b) deregulation by market forces;
   (c) *zaitech*;
   (d) EU equal treatment and the implications for Japanese banks;
   (e) a firm that is deleveraged/degeared;
   (f) convertible debentures;
   (g) low coupon bonds with stock warrants attached;
   (h) universal banking in Japan.
2. Why has the cost of raising capital on global markets traditionally been lower for Japanese banks than for banks headquartered in western countries?
3. Employing the definition of economies of scale found in Chapter 4, do you agree the merged banks will achieve greater economies of scale?
4. Using the description of the Japanese banking structure found in Chapter 3,
   (a) How will the merger of a regional bank and a city bank achieve a greater diversification of credit risk?
   (b) Did functional segmentation encourage *zaitech*?
   (c) Explain why the long-term credit banks were more heavily exposed in *zaitech* operations than other types of banks in Japan.
   (d) Explain why the Japanese Post Office is one of Sakura's key competitors.
5. Is the bubble economy described in this case the same as Minsky's *financial fragility*, defined in Chapter 6?
6. What has been the role of the MoF in shaping the competitive capabilities of Japanese banks?
7. Using the July issues of *The Banker*, assess the relative performance of Sakura since 1991.

8. Assess Sakura's competitive position. (Hint: to assess competitive position of a firm, one should examine the firm's strengths and weaknesses).

4 NOMURA SECURITIES CO LTD.*

Relevant parts of text: Chapter 3 (Japanese structure); Sakura case.

Organised in its modern form on Christmas Day 1925, Nomura Securities has risen from its modest Osaka roots to become the undisputed leader of the Big Four Japanese securities firms—the other members are Daiwa, Nikko and Yamaichi. The company is believed to account for 20% of the daily stock turnover in Japan and consistently ranks as the nation's leading underwriter of both government bonds and corporate securities. As of 31 March 1993, Nomura reported total assets of $66.5 billion and had shareholders' equity of $17.1 billion, making it the world's largest securities firm in terms of capital. It maintains a retail franchise of 155 branch offices throughout Japan, and employs over 17 000 people worldwide. Through its affiliate Nomura Investment Trust, the firm also manages $82 billion of securities investments for clients.

Nomura also conducts substantial activities outside Japan, mainly for the purposes of attracting foreign investment into Japanese securities, or to invest Japanese funds abroad. Since the mid-1980s, the company has consistently held a top spot in the Eurobond underwriting tables—it was placed second for 1992, lead managing 86 issues worth $19.6 billion. The overwhelming majority of Euro-issues managed by Nomura were for Japanese companies; the securities were in turn sold back into Japan to Japanese investors. During the late 1980s, the heyday of Japanese investment in US securities, Nomura's share of the daily New York Stock Exchange volume sometimes exceeded 5% and its share of US Treasury auctions was as high as 25%.

However, problems developed in the Japanese securities industry in the early 1990s which shattered profits and ushered in great changes. In late 1989 the Japanese stock market began a lengthy decline from record heights. The slide was to last for more than three years and caused prices to drop by more than 60%. Real estate markets collapsed too, and soon Japan was engulfed in the bankruptcies of financial and property market speculators, both corporate and individual. The bankruptcies revealed a seemingly continuous stream of illegal or improper financial behaviour on the part of major banks and brokerages. The public clamoured for reforms, which the Ministry of Finance reluctantly but minimally conceded. Some analysts have compared the period to the early 1930s in the USA, which precipitated a crash of financial markets and far-reaching reforms, such as the separation of commercial and investment

---

*This case first appeared in the New York University Salomon Center Case Series in Banking and Finance (Case 42). Written by Anthony Morris, under the direction of Roy C. Smith (1993). The case was edited and updated by Shelagh Heffernan; questions set by Shelagh Heffernan.

banking. These reforms had a profound effect on the US securities industry for years, and continue to do so.

History of Nomura

The firm was founded in 1904 by Tokushichi Nomura II, grandson of a samurai and his serving girl. It was a broker and dealer in over-the-counter securities. From its beginning, Nomura had shown a special knack for thriving in times of chaos and disaster. The firm profited by going short on stocks during the market crash of 1907, when price levels dropped by nearly 90%. After the great Kanot earthquake of 1923, when 100 000 people died and millions were made homeless, reconstruction bonds were issued in huge quantities and Nomura grew rapidly, broking these issues as the bond market boomed. When the market turned sluggish in the mid-1930s, the company took its cue from a determined salesman Mr Minoru Segawa, and learned to profit from promoting highly speculative stocks to its retail customers. Dishing out hot tips and market rumours to a beholden client base in the port city of Moji, Segawa found he could influence share prices, further adding to his clout and bottom line.

With the onset of the Second World War, Nomura earned big commissions selling Japanese war bonds. The firm realised much earlier than most that Japan faced almost certain defeat, and again, sold stock for its own account before the market collapsed. This prescient step provided Nomura with a cash hoard immediately following the war, when most of Japan lay in ruins and American occupation forces closed the Tokyo Stock Exchange and virtually froze all bank accounts. Minoru Segawa, head of Tokyo's branch office, found innovative ways to earn money for the company in slow times. Dealing in the currency black market, exploiting regulatory loopholes, promoting obscure over the counter securities and directing his sales force to hawk kitchenware and lottery tickets if not stock, he made a fortune for Nomura during Japan's leanest years.

During the war, Nomura introduced the investment trust, or mutual fund, in Japan. This very successful product helped Nomura eclipse Yamaichi, then the largest brokerage in Japan, and assert greater control over the stock market in the post-war years. Nomura's sales force, legendary for its doggedness, was especially adept at pitching investment trusts to retail clients. The resulting inflows of cash grew immense, giving Nomura substantial buying power which it did not hesitate to use.

There is no doubt the investment trust business would have been less successful had it not been for Nomura's powerful post-war political connections. American occupation authorities had banned investment trusts after the war, but Mr Tsunao Okumura, Nomura's president from 1948 to 1959, had gained friends in high places with his social connections and unrivalled ability to raise funds for the newly emerging Liberal Democratic Party (LDP), which dominated Japanese politics for the next 40 years. In 1951 Okumura was given leave to resume investment trust activities. From then on, the relationship between Nomura and top political officials has been carefully maintained, and certain reciprocities observed.

Nomura also benefited from the adoption, at the urging of the US occupation authorities, of the Securities and Exchange Law, passed in 1947. This law was modelled after the Glass-Steagall Act, separating the functions of securities brokerage and underwriting from commercial banking activities. The law prohibited powerful Japanese banks from competing with Nomura over these or any other security.

The Japanese Securities Market

The Japanese securities market differs from the US market in several important respects. In Japan, especially from the 1950s through to the 1970s, financial markets were primarily utilised by the government to issue bonds and other securities. Corporations borrowed almost exclusively from banks with whom they maintained close ties. Corporate bonds were rarely issued—those that were usually in the form of convertible debentures. The stock market, however, became active early in the period of the Japanese economic miracle, mainly as a source of speculative but liquid investment by individuals, who in most cases were exempt from capital gains taxes.

Japanese retail investors have a reputation for possessing a gambler's mentality. Most investments are in small amounts, intended to supplement savings in bank and postal deposits. Few investors ever read a corporate report, relying instead on market rumours, tips, and the latest stock recommendation of their brokers, thought to have superior information. In 1980, personal investors accounted for 59% of trading volume (about 75% of the real market float) but only 29% of the total share ownership.

Institutional investors in Japan, on the other hand, were far less active as equity market investors than institutions in the USA and the UK. Institutions are estimated to own about 42% of all stocks in the US markets but account for 75% of all trading volume. By contrast, Japanese banks, insurance companies, corporations, and other institutions control the majority of Japanese shares—mainly due to their more or less permanent cross-shareholdings arrangements with other companies in their "groups" or *keiretsu*. But they trade relatively little. The float in a typical Japanese stock may be limited to no more than 30%–40% of all shares outstanding. Traditions of cross-shareholdings, the relatively late introduction of pension funds in Japan, a lack of trading skills on the part of portfolio managers, high corporate capital gains taxes, and hefty fixed brokerage commissions made trading less attractive. Thus, trading activity was quite subdued until the middle of the 1980s, after which it began to increase significantly.

By 1990, institutional trading on the Tokyo Stock Exchange had increased to 52% of total transactions. Much of the increased institutional activity is explained by the introduction of special tax advantaged funds used by corporations for stock market investments in the 1980s. This was the time of *zaitech*, when industrial corporations became very active in the market.

Japanese brokerages maintain separate "research institutes" but their output compares poorly with foreign houses' research. The Big Four have resisted making negative assessments, ever-concerned about maintaining good relations with actual or potential clients. Most of the research produced is used by the firms' foreign customers.

Securities Market Regulation

As was observed in Chapter 6, Japan's markets have always been subject to considerable control by the Ministry of Finance (MoF), which governs through "moral suasion". In the absence of specific legislation, the general rule governing financial markets is that every activity is prohibited, unless the MoF decides in favour of a given activity, after informal consultation and discussion with its different regulatory bureaux. The MoF's Securities Bureau is responsible for about 400 securities brokers—it has intervened to rescue troubled firms in the past, tries to ensure an orderly market, and encourages competition, albeit in a limited way. Fixed commission rates still prevail. Foreign firms were not allowed to participate in the Japanese securities and investment advisory businesses until the mid-1980s—this permission was granted because of fears of reprisals if foreign firms did not receive equal treatment.

The Bubble Economy

As was discussed in Chapters 3 and 6 and the Sakura case, the 1980s were boom years for Japan's financial sector, and this period has since become known as the bubble economy, because:

- there was a six-fold increase in stock prices—trading volumes soared as institutions and individuals poured money, in most cases borrowed, into financial markets;
- real estate values kept pace with these developments;
- companies found it possible to raise new capital by issuing shares at 100 or more times earnings;
- most firms borrowed or issued equity securities (often in the Eurobond market) for *zaitech* investments;
- most corporations repaid the debt they owed to banks, reducing the influence of banks on their affairs.

Nomura and the other Big Four securities houses earned enormous profits from stock market activity and underwriting new issues. In 1986, Nomura earned $2.7 billion, making it the most profitable financial services institution in the world. The profits went into retained earnings, increasing Nomura's capital position substantially. The stock prices of the Big Four reflected these developments. In March 1990, Nomura's market capitalisation exceeded $50 billion. By contrast, at the same time, Japan's largest bank, Dai Ichi Kangyo Bank, reported net income of $650 million and a market capitalisation of $30 billion. Merrill Lynch's market capitalisation was less than $5 billion.

Nomura was at the centre of the action in the stock market. Stocks it wished to promote seemed to rocket, and so did investor interest and commissions. The executive managing director, Mr Atsushi Saito, noted Nomura was first in volume, first in customers' accounts, but had no net trading position—retail activity being the key to Nomura's leading position. "Retail is the perfect game",* he was heard to say. Underwritings also surged.

In December 1989 the Nikkei index peaked; by January 1990 the bubble had burst. The Bank of Japan tightened money supply growth rates and forced interest rates sharply upward, to stem the overheating in the financial sector. Retail investors, who had come to think of the stock market as a place of guaranteed profit, fled the market. As the Nikkei tumbled, many lost huge sums—much of it borrowed. Margin loans were called, forcing further sales and price declines. With virtually no buyers, volumes shrank, and so did commissions.

Nomura began to be plagued by scandals. In the summer of 1991, Nomura admitted engaging in a number of controversial (but not illegal) activities. In response to media pressure, Nomura confessed to making more than $1.5 billion of secret payments to clients as compensation for market losses, though other clients received nothing. Other members of the Big Four admitted to additional questionable activities, including large transactions with notorious underworld figures. It was clear from the investigations that the MoF was aware of these activities, but had either refused or was unable to exert control over the giant firm's behaviour.

Though Japanese markets had a reputation for condoning shady activities on a large scale, there was insufficient evidence to make public any allegations. In the early 1990s, however, the evidence was overwhelming, leading many to conclude that these markets resembled the behaviour in the USA in the 1920s. Scandals involved all of the Big Four and some of other leading banks, prompting demands for market reform and precipitating widespread resignations of senior management, including two of the top men at Nomura. The firm was thrown into turmoil, and the MoF expressed extreme displeasure with its behaviour.

By the year ending March 1992, net income at Normura fell to $159 million; by mid-June 1992, it recorded a loss. It managed to sustain yearly profits through the early 1990s, unlike its main Japanese rivals, all of which posted losses in 1992 and 1993. Securities firms also had to confront the diminished values of their share portfolios, losses in their investment trust subsidiaries, and the restructuring of troubled property lending affiliates. Financial statements were not very informative because of lenient Japanese reporting requirements. In Nomura's case, restructuring involved write-offs exceeding $2 billion during fiscal year 1994.

In June 1991 Mr Hideo Sakamaki was appointed the chief executive of Nomura Securities. He likes to think of himself as presiding over a different

---

*The Institutional Investor, January, 1992: p.51.

"New Nomura", where brokerage clients come first. Mr Sakamaki initiated an extensive internal review and consultation process. This concluded that Nomura had to assume a greater responsibility in the market and to society. Nomura centralised its research activities and created a well-defined career path for analysts. Chinese walls were erected between its research and underwriting divisions, to stop underwriters from putting pressure on the researchers into making bullish statements about key markets, even if they were untrue. The firm also switched to a compensation system that gives greater credit for individual performance. Branch offices are no longer given sales targets by head office, a practice that is though to have led to over-aggressive selling in the past.

Nomura's share of turnover increased from 9% to 10%, boosting its commission income. The bank also tried improve its tarnished image. The Nomura sales force have been given incentives to behave more like financial advisors, guiding clients, rather than depending on high commission stock selling. The firm has also been cutting back on staff.

The Foreigners Arise

In the period 1990–93, when Japanese securities firms were having such serious problems, foreign securities firms prospered. They introduced computer-driven program trading (pioneered in the US) to the Tokyo market, primarily to arbitrage between the cash and futures markets on the Nikkei index or in individual stocks. The Big Four lacked the technical capability to compete in this area, and were wary of any disturbance in the markets they controlled. They tried to get program trading disallowed, but though assisted by the market authorities, the effort came to nothing because Nikkei index futures contracts also traded in Singapore, outside the reach of Japanese officials.

The end of easy profits also forced institutional investors in Japan to insist on higher standards of service and performance from their brokers, relationship or no relationship. For example, a money manager at Dai-Ichi Mutual Life Insurance Company announced his intention to use foreign firms for 50% of his trades, up from 30%, because of quality of service and know-how. In the underwriting area, foreign firms, led by Morgan Stanley, Solomon Brothers, and Goldman Sachs, began to challenge the Big Four by introducing more effective practices for securities distribution and pricing from the US and Eurobond markets. Morgan Stanley managed a major offering for the former state telephone monopoly, Nippon Telephone and Telegraph, and co-managed a recent Nissan bond issue—structural changes in the Japanese economy had made these easier. Earnings of the top three US firms far exceeded (by a multiple of nearly eight) those of their Japanese counterparts in the six months to September, 1992. But most of the foreigners' earnings were due to successful and opportunistic trading and a small increase in their share of the underwriting market. Japanese firms continued to have a substantial influence with corporations and investors.

Nomura and Globalisation

Unlike Morgan Stanley, Goldman Sachs, Merrill Lynch and other leading western firms, Nomura earned most of its income from domestic business. It was not a trading firm at a time when most of the Wall Street firms derived between 30% and 90% of their profits from principal trading involving market making and counterparts from all over the world, but especially between institutional investors in the USA, Europe, and Japan. For Nomura, earnings from outside Japan were insignificant.

However, Nomura has tried to establish a global presence, with branches and subsidiaries throughout Europe, Asia and the USA. Nomura Securities International (NSI), the US subsidiary, undertook an aggressive attempt to penetrate US markets, an unusual step. In 1989, NSI shocked its competitors by hiring an ex-president of Kidder Peabody, Mr Max Chapman, to become co-chairman alongside Katsuya Takanashi. He was also appointed to the board of directors, a token gesture because the board met in Tokyo and conducted its deliberations entirely in Japanese. NSI is seen as an Americanised, autonomous unit within Nomura. NSI has built respectable program trading (which Nomura has been unwilling to introduce into Japan), and high-yield, mortgage-backed, and fixed income trading operations in the US, but investment banking remains quite weak. Though NSI is seen as independent, all major decisions must be approved by Head Office in Tokyo, and it is unclear as to whether the Tokyo group regards NSI's activities as relevant to its own. To date, Nomura's profits outside of Japan have been "insignificant", because they have confronted high costs which have hardly been justified by the revenues earned.

Market Reform in Japan

Following the market scandals in the early 1990s, the Japanese government came under considerable pressure to tighten market regulation and create more competition and less concentration in the financial sector. A special commission recommended a series of reforms based on US and European practices. These were thought to weaken the authority of the MoF, and were soon set aside for a MoF-directed "watchdog" authority which would survey markets and recommend to the Ministry appropriate actions, though it is largely considered to be toothless.

In April 1993 the MoF took an early step towards its planned gradual dismantling of Article 65, which separates banking from securities. Banks are to be allowed to underwrite certain types of securities, but not to distribute them. However, investment banking is unlikely to be effective unless underwriting is accompanied by distribution. On the other hand, a commercial paper market has been permitted in Japan, and brokers have been given access to it. It is developing steadily.

Nomura once benefited from the regulations that riddled the Japanese financial system, but the degree of competition has risen with financial market reforms. Foreign firms are trying to penetrate the mutual funds business, but the director of retail banking in Nomura thinks these banks are unlikely to get far, in the absence of a big distribution network. He believes that a more serious threat comes from domestic banks with a huge customer base—they could become strong competitors for Nomura's main businesses. In November 1994 the six big city commercial banks in Japan opened their own securities subsidiaries. They have been granted permission to underwrite and trade bonds, as have the long-term credit banks. The competition unleashed by the banks' new subsidiaries will test the weaker securities houses. The banks' arrival has come at a bad time for the securities firms. Of the Big Four—Yamaichi, Nikko, Daiwa and Nomura—only Nomura did not experience a drop in profits during the first half of 1994.

The broking houses are bound to lose some business to new bank rivals. Until now most could count on underwriting fees from firms within their industrial groups, or *keiretsu*. However it appears the strength of *keiretsu* is weakening, for a number of reasons. Japanese shares only have a ROE of just under 2%, making them less attractive than foreign ones. The appreciation of the yen, especially since March 1995, is squeezing company profits, which in turn is putting pressure on firms to discard mutual shareholdings.

Japanese banks are central to the *keiretsu*, but have not begun to sell their mutual stakes, though they, like industrial firms and life insurers, are under pressure. Over the past three years bad debts have been covered through unrealised gains on their equity portfolios. Any gains are falling rapidly, so an alternative source of funding will have to be found to cover the bad debts. Banks may, in the future, have no choice but to sell off their stakes.

The deregulation of the financial system has also been a contributing factor to the weakening of the *keiretsu*. In the past, banks lent money at rates fixed by the government. By owning shares in a company, the bank would almost certainly secure their custom. With lending rates deregulated, banks have a good reason to sell shares. Some banks have sold shares in *keiretsu* firms and invested in smaller companies which are prepared to reward them with their business.

Yotsu no G (The Four Gs)

In 1993 Mr Sakamaki identified the strategy of the "new" Nomura as "Growth, group, global and glory".* "Growth" refers to an effort by Sakamaki to increase Nomura's ROE, which was 1.6% in 1992; the long-term objective is to raise it to 5%. In terms of profitability, it consistently out-performed its Japanese competitors, Daiwa, Nikko and Yamaichi. "Group" refers to Mr Sakamaki's efforts to stimulate interaction between Nomura's various departments, and to encourage team work among staff. "Global" is an emphasis on action to attract foreign clients. For example, Nomura's European activities had been reorganised along functional lines,

---

*This part of the Nomura case is based on the article by Fingleton (1994).

with equity sales operations in various European cities reporting to a single boss in London. "Glory" means the intention of Mr Sakamaki to improve self-esteem among Nomura's staff, putting the humiliation of the 1991 scandal behind them, and restoring self-confidence with Nomura after many salesmen with the firm suffered from loss of face over their advice to clients when the stock market crashed in 1989.

Questions for Nomura Case Study

1. What is meant by *keiretsu* in Japan? Explain how the following factors might undermine *keiretsu*:
   (a) a falling stock market and poor company results;
   (b) the liberalisation of Japan's financial system: allowing interest rates to be market determined rather than fixed by the government;
   (c) the entry of foreign financial firms;
   (d) the reduced influence of regulatory authorities on financial markets in Japan.
2. Is this case an example of where "relationship" banking can go wrong?
3. From the standpoint of Nomura, do you agree that competition from foreign securities firms is beneficial, as implied by the case study?
4. What factors will enhance or limit Nomura's ability to become a global banking leader in the next decade?
5. Discuss Nomura's competitive position in the global banking market.
6. Has the separation of investment banking from commercial banking in Japan helped or hindered Nomura?
7. How did Nomura fare in 1994 and 1995?
8. Explain *Yotsu no G*. Is it a feasible strategy for Nomura?

5 THE PRIVATISATION OF BANCOMER*

Relevant parts of text: Chapters 3, 4 (economies of scale and scope, and synergy) and 5 (political risk).

In the summer of 1991, Mr Tony Mendez de la Vera was called in to join a meeting with senior executives of the VISA group, a large Mexican industrial holding company involved in beverages, packaging and various other industries. The group of executives was meeting to consider whether or not to bid, and, if so, how much to bid, for one of the large Mexican banks the government had announced it would privatise later in the year. Assuming VISA decided to purchase a bank, one of several banks up for privatisation would

---

*This case first appeared in the New York University Salomon Center Case Series in Banking and Finance (Case 18). Written by Roy C. Smith and Ingo Walter (1992). The case was edited and updated by Shelagh Heffernan; questions set by Shelagh Heffernan.

have to be selected. The VISA group expressed particular interest in Bancomer, the largest and most retail oriented of the Mexican banks.

Background

On 1 September 1982, following a moratorium on the repayment of foreign debt, a balance of payments crisis, the imposition of exchange controls, and a substantial devaluation of the peso, President José Lopez Portillio nationalised Mexico's six commercial banks.

Over the next six years, the government used these depository institutions to channel their resources to finance the national fiscal deficit. Throughout this period, the management teams of banks under state control were given limited discretion over investment and personnel decisions, and there was little scope for strategic planning. Instead, management's focus was on making financial resources available to the government through deposit-gathering, in return for the right to levy fees and other charges on the bank's depositors. Thus, Mexican banks ceased to be the primary provider of market-oriented financial products and services to the Mexican public.

On 28 June 1990 the Mexican Constitution was amended to permit individuals and companies to own controlling interests in commercial banks. The Mexican Banking Law was enacted to regulate the ownership and operation of commercial banks. A privatisation committee was created to oversee the sale of Mexico's banks to private investors.

The Financial Groups Law came into force in 1990, which effectively meant the Mexican government was adopting a system of universal banking,* whereby a range of diverse banking activities would be conducted under a financial services holding company. The plan was to use universal banking to make the Mexican banking system more efficient and competitive, as financial institutions could achieve economies of scale and scope, enter new markets, exploit synergies, and explore new growth and cross-marketing opportunities.

During the decade under state ownership and control, the banking sector in Mexico was noted for its overall stability, sustained growth, and profitability. The banks were well-capitalised and maintained a good asset quality. In the period 1986–91 the Mexican banking sector also underwent significant consolidation and deregulation.

In other Latin American countries, including Argentina, Chile, Brazil and Colombia, banking systems suffered from system-wide asset quality problems because of a high concentration of loans to a few borrowers, extension of credits to affiliated companies, poor auditing and lack of supervision. But Mexican state banks had largely escaped these problems and indeed, experienced fewer problems that many American banks during the 1980s.

---

*Universal banking, as defined under the 1990 Financial Services Group Law, could include commercial banking, stockbroking, investment banking, leasing, factoring, foreign exchange and insurance. The different activities must be conducted under a common financial services holding company.

Overview of Bancomer

Bancomer had undergone significant evolution since 1988. As a result, management believed Bancomer was profitable, well-capitalised, and well-positioned to take advantage of emerging opportunities in the Mexican market.

In December 1988 several senior executives joined Bancomer and began to redirect the operation of the bank. They adopted a strategic goal of re-establishing market leadership in the bank's traditional niches, consumer and middle-market lending. The new management gave managers greater responsibility for business operations in the bank, and emphasised greater investment in new technology and development of an extensive branch network.

In 1989 and 1990 Bancomer further improved its asset quality by absorbing a series of non-recurring charges and creating reserves for loan losses which subsequently exceeded all required regulatory levels. It planned to repeat this exercise in 1991.

Bancomer's profitability during 1989–90 reflected these charges and reserves, as well as the costs of refocusing the business and the impact of recent declines in the Mexican rate of inflation. In 1991, Bancomer's net income was forecast to grow to about $400 million, an increase of over 50% in real terms on 1990, and representing a return on average assets of 1.7% and a return of average equity of about 24%. The net interest margin was expected to increase from 7.22% in 1990 to 7.4% in 1991, despite declining inflation. The improvement in the net interest margin was due to a shift from lower-yielding government securities to higher-yielding private sector loans, the growth of higher-yielding consumer loans as a percentage of the total loan portfolio, and lower cost peso-denominated deposits comprising a larger portion of Bancomer's funding base.

Approaching privatisation, Bancomer thus had a growing, high quality asset base. As of 30 June 1991, assets totalled $24 billion. Asset growth during 1991 reflected, among other things, impressive growth in the Mexican economy, strong demand for credit in pesos and dollars, and Bancomer's increased market share in lending.

Higher-quality credits made up 95% of Bancomer's portfolio as of 30 June 1991. Past-due, lower-quality credits made up 1.78% of the portfolio, compared to 2.79% the year before. Reserve coverage for lower-quality credits improved during the year. A pre-privatisation credit review conducted by independent auditors concluded that Bancomer's portfolio was appropriately classified.

Bancomer was also well-capitalised. At 30 June 1991 the bank's ratio of capital to weighted risk assets was 7.4%, exceeding the 6% minimum requirement for 1991 and the 7% minimum requirement for 1992.

Bancomer's Main Business Activities (year end 1991)

- Ranked first in terms of market share of deposit-gathering, with 23.5% of the market share in 1991. Followed by Banamex and Serfin.
- Regained much of its market share in consumer lending and commercial lending it had lost between 1982 and 1987.

- Outside Mexico City, Bancomer had about a quarter of the deposit market and just under a quarter of the credit market. Enhanced by a branch network and regional boards structure. Bancomer had a network of 750 branches; approximately 115 were in Mexico City. By the end of 1991, it was expected to have more branches than any other commercial bank in Mexico. It controlled 42% of the ATMs operated in Mexico.
- In 1989, Bancomer adopted a strategy of segmenting its markets within a branch: VIP banking (high net worth), personal banking (affluent customers but not VIP), retail banking (for 90% of the customers), and middle market corporate banking.
- Lending is concentrated in the middle market firms (companies with annual sales between $0.7 million and $39.7 million) and retail lending, including consumer, credit card and mortgage loans.
- In 1991, an institutional banking division was created to include international banking, corporate banking, international finance and public finance.
- In 1982, to increase its international presence, Bancomer had acquired Grossmont Bank of San Diego. In 1986, it formed Mercury Bank and Trust Ltd, located in Grand Cayman. It has branches in London and the Cayman Islands, agencies in New York and Los Angeles, and representative offices in Madrid, São Paulo, Buenos Aires, Santiago, Tokyo and Hong Kong. It has correspondent relationships with about 1000 banks.
- Bancomer has specialised in financial services including tourism investment and other equity investments. Its trust division manages assets for clients wanting to take advantage of the Mexican fixed income and equity markets.
- Throughout its 60-year history, Bancomer's owners and management pursued a strategy which focused on growth in the retail and middle market sectors, with a strong marketing orientation, that is, a service orientation with a willingness to respond to customer needs. It operated a decentralised management structure prior to nationalisation, which it argued made the bank highly responsive to community needs. Under nationalisation, decision-making became centralised and bureaucratic, in line with the objective of gathering deposits for investment in Mexican government securities.

With the announcement of pending privatisation, Bancomer reasserted these strategic objectives, that is:

- maintenance of a leading market position in retail banking through a strong consumer and middle market orientation, introduction of new financial products, and distribution of these products through an extensive branch network;
- spreading financial risk through size, industry, and geographic diversification of Bancomer customers and services;
- willingness to hire qualified managers and consultants;

- reinvesting in Bancomer's businesses, especially technology, branch expansion and personnel training;
- maintaining conservative credit standards and diversifying risks, so no single loan affects earnings;
- maintenance of a strong capital base.

At the end of 1991, Bancomer's net worth was projected to be about $2 billion. The Mexican government was expected to be an aggressive seller, and would invite as many potential bidders as it could.

The VISA Group

The Visa Group was a complex of public and private industrial holdings, mainly in the beverages business, operating through a structure designed to ensure an optimum balance between leverage and control.

Through a 60% subsidiary, FEMSA, VISA controlled industrial properties with annual revenues of $1.8 billion. The balance of FEMSA was owned 15% by Citibank, 14% by the Mexican public, and 11% by IFC and other banks.

VISA was 86% owned by a holding company, PROA, controlled by a Mexican family. Eleven per cent of VISA was owned by allied investors and 3% by the Mexican public. PROA also controlled 59% of Valres de Monterrey S.A. (VAMSA), a publicly traded financial services holding company, whose principal subsidiary was Seguros Monterrey, a major insurance company.

The PROA group had extensive experience in banking, and prior to the 1982 nationalisations had controlled Banca Serfin S.A., Mexico's third largest bank. In view of the VISA management group, ties between VAMSA and the Bancomer group could produce substantial synergies and new opportunities, both of which could be realised in the coming years. VAMSA had other financial subsidiaries including financial leasing, factoring, warehouse bonding and the brokerage business.

Combined, Arrendadora Bancomer and VAMSA's Arrendadora Monterrey would become Mexico's market leader in the lease financing business, particularly in the middle market sector, which historically did not have ready access to this type of financing. As of year end 1988, total lease financings were equal to 2.49% of total commercial bank loans in Mexico. By 30 June 1991 they had risen to 16.8% of total commercial bank loans in Mexico.

ABSA, another VAMSA subsidiary, was Mexico's eighth largest brokerage house, measured by trading volume. Management expected the securities brokerage to benefit directly from ABSA's affiliation with Bancomer. Management believed, for example, that many of Bancomer's regional directors would use ABSA for their brokerage services. The bank could use ABSA for its own investment and brokerage needs.

VAMSA's Factor de Capitales would be combined with Factoraje Bancomer. By mid-1991, Factoraje Bancomer and Factor de Capitales together represented the second-largest factoring company in Mexico, with total assets of $379.4 million, and a market share of approximately 11%.

VAMSA's other principal non-bank subsidiary was Almacenadora Monterrey, Mexico's largest warehouse bonding company, with 23% of the market. Almacenadora Monterrey issued negotiable warehouse bills of lading and certificates of deposit representing warehoused goods. These could be used as collateral to obtain financing. Management believed that Almacenadora Monterrey would be able to strengthen its business and increase its market share as a result of cross-selling opportunities with Bancomer's client base.

Structuring A Bid

Tony's assignment was to coordinate the structuring of a bid for Bancomer and its subsidiaries. The bid would have to include a viable financing plan, and would have to meet the hidden and stated objectives of the Mexican government, given the importance of Bancomer to the Mexican financial system.

These objectives included:

- price;
- a concern for transparency;
- the preservation of benefits to be obtained by free market competition in the financial sector;
- the optimal amount of foreign participation, where "optimal" meant the minimum foreign participation needed to satisfy all the other objectives.

Tony concluded that foreign banks would not be aggressive bidders. Many were constrained by capital considerations, and the maximum foreign ownership percentage was strictly limited by government rules. On the other hand, the Mexican securities market, reflecting a high degree of confidence in Mexico's economic policies, had been bullish recently and had attracted considerable foreign buying interest.

Tony also had to determine the price range VISA would have to face in bidding for Bancomer, and how to put together a financial package that would beat the competition from other bidders. These were expected to include several Mexican industrial and financial groups, possibly, in some cases, allied with foreign banks. In recent months a number of Mexican banks had been privatised (Mercantile, Banpais, Cremi, Confia, Banorie, Bancreser, and Banamex), at two to three times their book value. This multiple represented the franchise value, the booming economy, rising stock prices, and protection from foreign bank entry (until 1996) under the North American Free Trade Agreement. However, Tony wondered whether Bancomer was worth it with this multiple.

Additionally, Tony considered the question of who should be selected as financial advisor for the task. Should it be a foreign bank with extensive experience in valuation, or should it be a Mexican bank that knew the situation well? American commercial and investment banks had been the most impressive players in the privatisation discussions to date. VISA was close to JP

Morgan, which often acted as banker to the Mexican government. VISA had also done business with, or knew well, Shearson Lehman Brothers, First Boston, Morgan Stanley and Goldman Sachs. In picking an advisor, Tony knew VISA would have to rely upon not only their financial engineering ability but market judgement, and their ability to distribute any securities associated with the transaction.

The 1994–95 Banking Crisis

In 1994, the authorities granted permission for the entry and establishment of 52 foreign banks, brokerage houses and other financial institutions. The foreign banks will be providing services for large businesses and blue chip companies. Mexican banks such as Bancomer will have to fight hard to retain the business of the blue chip companies.

On 20 December 1994, Mexico devalued the peso by 13%, and the stock market collapsed. Mexican bank shares fell drastically, as the cost of repaying dollar-denominated debt soared. Some banks ran into problems when they tried to roll over their dollar certificates of deposit; foreign banks started to call in dollar-denominated credit.

To restore foreign confidence to the Mexican financial market, interest rates were raised, peaking at 59% on 22 February 1995. The fragile banks requested assistance as they struggled to maintain their reserves against bad debts.

High interest rates and the recession have hit many of the smaller businesses hard, just when entry into NAFTA left them exposed to foreign competition. The banks that lent heavily to these small businesses are now feeling the strain of the resulting non-performing loans. In 1994, non-performing loans on their balance sheets rose to over 10%.

To make matters worse, some banks demanded repayment of credit denominated in dollars. In January 1995, credit rating agencies downgraded the deposits and debt of Mexican banks, including that of Bancomer. The downgradings, it was feared, would precipitate a wholesale loss of confidence in Mexican banks and force them into bankruptcy.

The central bank has promised to inject funds into a deposit insurance fund, but it would be better if banks raised their own capital.

Questions for the Privatisation of Bancomer Case Study

1. In the context of the case, explain the meaning of:
   (a) lease financing;
   (b) brokerage services;
   (c) factoring company;
   (d) warehouse bonding company;
   (e) correspondent banking;
   (f) market segmentation within a retail branch;
2. How should the VISA group go about deciding whether to launch a bid for one of the newly privatised major banks in Mexico?

3. Mexico is a developing economy. What factors are unique to this type of economy (as distinct from an industrialised economy) which might influence Tony's advice to senior executives of VISA?

4. Given Bancomer's stated objectives, do you think the bank has a good chance of overcoming the problems normally associated with developing country banking?

5. Explain how the Mexican version of universal banking differs from models applied to the UK, French and German banking sectors.

6. In the context of Mexican universal banking, explain the difference between economies of scale, economies of scope and synergy. Does universal banking necessarily make a system more efficient?

7. Based on the description of Bancomer as a nationalised bank, is nationalisation of the banking system a sound public policy objective? Justify your answer.

8. Using the July edition of *The Banker*, assess Bancomer's relative performance in 1992, 1993, 1994, and 1995.

9. What sort of political interference were nationalised banks subjected to in Mexico? Will privatisation guarantee an end to it?

10. How will NAFTA (the North American Free Trade Agreement) affect Bancomer's competitive position?

11. Why did the macroeconomic crisis of 1994–95 result in a downgrading of Bancomer and other banks' credit ratings by private rating agencies? From Bancomer's position, does it matter?

12. What practical lessons can Bancomer learn from the 1994–95 macroeconomic crisis?

6 KIDDER PEABODY GROUP*

Relevant parts of text: Chapters 4 (synergy), 6 (financial conglomerates) and 8 (strategy).

"But Leo," said Alan Horrvich, a third-year financial analyst at General Electric Capital Corporation (GECC) in September, 1987: "I don't know anything about investment banking. If I walk in there with a lot of amateurish ideas for what he ought to do with Kidder, Cathart will rip me apart. OK, you're the boss, but why me?"

"Look Alan," replied Mr Leo Halaran, Senior Vice-President, Finance of GECC: "we've got ten thousand things going on here right now and Cathart calls up and says, very politely, that he wants somebody very bright to work with him on a strategic review of Kidder Peabody. You're bright, you spent a semester in the specialised finance MBA programme at City University

---

*This case first appeared in the New York University Salomon Center Case Series in Banking and Finance (Case 26). Written by Roy C. Smith (1988). The case was edited and updated by Shelagh Heffernan; questions set by Shelagh Heffernan.

Business School in London, you earned that fancy MBA from New York University down there in Wall Street, and your available right now, so you're our man. Relax, Si isn't all that tough. If you make it through the first few weeks without getting sent back, you've got a friend for life—", he ended with a grin. "Me."

Mr Silas S. Cathart, 61, had retired as Chairman and CEO of Illinois Tool Works in 1986. He had been a director of the General Electric Company for many years and was much admired as a first-rate, tough though diplomatic results-oriented manager. After the resignation of Mr Ralph DeNunzio as Chairman and CEO of Kidder Peabody following the management shake-up in May 1987, Mr Cathart had been asked by Mr Jack Welch, GE's hard-driving, young CEO, to set aside his retirement for a while and take over as CEO of Kidder Peabody, to give it the firm leadership it needed, particularly now. Cathart had not been able to say no. His first few months were spent trying to get a grip on the situation at Kidder, which had been traumatised by the insider trading problems, and by management uncertainty as to what GE and its outside CEO were going to do to Kidder next. After reporting substantial earnings of nearly $100 million in 1986, Kidder was expected to incur a significant loss in 1987.

Technically, Cathart and Kidder reported to Mr Gary Wendt, President and Chief Operating Officer of General Electric Financial Services (GEFC) and CEO of GECC, but Alan understood everyone believed that old Si reported only to himself and Mr Welch. Mr Cathart wasn't going to be in the job for that long and could not care less about company politics. All he had to do was return Kidder to profitability, and set it on the right strategic course—one that made sense to both the Kidder shareholders and the GE crowd. After that, he could go back to his retirement and let someone else take over. Everyone Alan had talked to at GECC felt that the job would be very tough, and that Cathart might be at a big disadvantage because he did not have prior experience in the securities industry.

Alan's plan was to play it dead straight with Mr Cathart, to work most of the night getting the basics under his belt, and to consider Kidder's strategic position, and how to implement any proposed changes. If asked something he did not know, he would simply say he did not know but would try to find out. A chronology of significant events is summarised below.

Chronology of Significant Events, 1986–87

April 1986

General Electric Financial Services agreed to pay $600 million for an 80% interest in Kidder Peabody and Company, leaving the remaining 20% in the hands of the firm's management. GEFS is a wholly owned subsidiary of General Electric Company. The price paid was about three times the book value—each shareholder was to receive a cash payment equal to 50% of the shares being sold, the remainder being paid out over three years. GEFS was to replace the shareholder capital with an initial infusion of $300 million, with more to follow. When the transaction closed in June 1986, GE and Kidder shareholders had invested more equity in the firm than previously announced—Kidder's total capital was boosted to $700 million.

Mr Robert C Wright, head of GEFS, claimed the expansion of investment banking activities would mean GEFS' sophisticated financial products in leasing and lending could be combined with corporate financing, advisory services, and trading capability at Kidders. There was no plan to institute any management changes.

Kidder ranked 15th among investment banks in terms of capital, and had 2000 retail brokers in 68 offices. The view was that it was too small to compete with the giants, but too large to be a niche player, making it an awkward size. Among analysts, it was generally accepted that Kidder had not been purchased for its retail network, but rather, for its institutional and investment banking capabilities.

Kidder initiated the talks with GE. It was believed the firm agreed to give up its independence as a means of using a more aggressive strategy to achieve a better image—there was a general perception that it was being left behind.

October 1986

Mr Ivan Boesky was arrested for insider trading. He implicated Mr Martin A Siegel, a managing director of Drexel Burnham Lambert, who had been head of Kidder Peabody's merger and acquisition department until his departure in February 1986 to join Drexel.

December 1986

Kidder reorganised its investment banking division. Eighty-five professionals were transferred to the merchant banking division, 45 of whom were placed in acquisition advisory, and another 40 in the high-yield junk bond department. The group was headed by Mr Peter Goodson, a Kidder managing director, who at the time, noted the move was a fundamental change in management structure. Mr Goodson did not anticipate any long-term effects from the insider trading scandal.

February 1987

The 1986 Kidder Annual Report emphasised the importance of synergies apparent in the combination of Kidder Peabody and GEFS—it was believed the synergies far exceeded the firm's expectations. A source of new business at Kidder was existing customer relationships with hundreds of middle-sized American firms at GEF. Additional capital from GEFC allowed Kidder to provide direct financing, picking up a sizeable number of new clients.

The Kidder Annual Report also revealed Kidder's core business had been reorganised to reinforce competitive strengths and facilitate future growth. A Global Capital Markets group was formed under Mr Max C. Chapman Jr. (President of Kidder, Peabody and Co, Incorporated), to direct the investment banking, merchant banking, asset finance, fixed income and financial futures operations on a worldwide basis. Mr John T. Roche, President and Chief Operating Officer, Kidder Peabody Group Inc, established an Equity group. Mr William Ferrell headed up a the Municipal Securities group, formed from the merger of the public finance and municipal securities groups.

The CEO, Mr Ralph DeNunzio, claimed these changes were made to ensure the firm was in a position to compete effectively in the global market place.

February 1987

Mr Richard B. Wigton, managing director, was arrested in his office by federal marshalls on charges of insider trading. A former employee, Mr Timothy Tabor, was also arrested. Both arrests were the result of allegations made against them and Mr Robert Freedman of Goldman Sachs and Company by Martin Siegel, who, next day, pleaded guilty to insider trading an other charges brought against him. Kidder's accountants, Deloitte, Haskin and Sells, qualified Kidder's 1986 financial statements because they were unable to evaluate the impact of insider trading charges. Kidder reported earnings of $90 million (compared to $47 million earned in 1985); ROE was 27%.

The New York Stock Exchange fined Kidder Peabody $300 000 for alleged violations of capital and other rules. Two senior officials, including the President, Mr Roche, were fined $25 000 each for their role in these violations.

The *Wall Street Journal* reported that Mr DeNunzio had instructed Martin Siegel to help start a takeover arbitrage department in March 1984; Mr DeNunzio had indicated that the role played by Mr Siegal should not be disclosed publicly—there were inherent conflicts in having the head of mergers and acquisitions directly involved in trading on takeover rumours. A Kidder spokesman said the report was a "misstatement", and denied that Mr DeNunzio had ordered the formation of such a unit.

May 1987

Mr Lawrence Bossidy, Vice-Chairman of GE and head of all financial services, announced a management shake-up at Kidder Peabody: Mr DeNunzio, Mr Roche, and Kidder's General Counsel, Mr Krantz, would be replaced.

Following the arrests, GE sent in a team to assess Kidder. The internal investigation revealed the need for improved procedures and controls. Mr Cathart was to take over as Kidder's CEO. GE men were also brought in to fill the positions of chief financial and chief operating officers, and a senior vice-president's position for business development. The board of directors was also restructured, to ensure GE had a majority of seats on the Kidder board.

In the same month, charges against Messrs Wigton, Tabor and Freedman were dismissed without prejudice, though it was expected they would be charged at some future date.

June 1987

GE required Kidder to settle matters with the Federal Prosecutor and the SEC. In exchange for a $25 million payment and other concessions, including giving up the takeover arbitrage business, the US Attorney agreed not to indict Kidder Peabody on criminal charges related to insider trading. Civil litigation against Kidder was still possible, though it would not have the same stigma as criminal charges and conviction.

GEFS also agreed to provide an additional $100 million of subordinated debt capital to Kidder Peabody.

July 1987

GE announced its first half results. At the time, GE said its financial services were ahead of a year ago because of the strong performance at GECC (GE Capital Corporation) and ERC (Employers Reinsurance Corporation), which more than offset the effects of special provisions at Kidder Peabody for settlements reached with the government. It was estimated that Kidder had lost about $18 million in the second quarter.

September 1987

Mr DeNunzio retired from Kidder Peabody after 34 years of service. For 20 of these years, he had been Kidder's principal executive officer.

The *Wall Street Journal* reported that morale at Kidder Peabody was improving, with GE and Kidder officials conducting a full strategic review of the firm.

It was also announced that Kidder planned to establish a full service foreign exchange operation and would operate trading desks in London and the Far East.

1989–94

Mr Michael Carpenter joined Kidder as "head" in 1989, just as the bank was reeling from the insider trading scandal. In a deal negotiated with the SEC, Kidder was required to close down its successful risk arbitrage department. This was quite a blow to Kidder because its other businesses were only mediocre.

Kidder had an excellent reputation, but was saddled with high expenses and many unproductive brokers. Half of the firm's retail offices produced no profit at all. In 1989, a number of the productive brokers left Kidder because of dissatisfaction with the level of bonuses. These departures, together with the closure of the risk arbitrage department, resulted in a net $53 million loss in 1989, and a loss of $54 million in 1990.

Mr Carpenter's arrival resulted in millions of dollars and a great deal of management time had been spent nursing Kidder back to health. The bank was also building up its investment banking operations. Profits rose in 1991; in 1992 they peaked at $258 million.

Most of Kidder's profits came from its fixed income securities operations, the one area where it had managed to establish a lead over other investment houses. Underwriting and trading mortgage backed securities (MBS) pushed Kidder up the underwriting league tables. During this time, the profits from mortgage-backed securities were said to have accounted for about 70% of total profits.

Unfortunately, the sharp rise in interest rates at the start of 1994 hurt the mortgage-backed business. The consequences of the "go for it strategy" with MBS (mortgage-backed securities) was seen in the first quarter of 1994—Kidder lost more than $25 million.

The same year, Kidder took a loss of around $25 million on margin trades entered into with Askin Capital Management, a hedge fund group which had to seek protection from its creditors, because of trading losses.

Mr Carpenter's attempts to build Kidder's other businesses produced mixed results. By reducing costs and firing unproductive brokers, Carpenter succeeded in turning round the retail brokerage business—it was the most profitable business, after the fixed income department.

But Carpenter's objective of achieving synergy between GE Capital and Kidder Peabody had been far from successful. There was a great degree of animosity between Mr Carpenter and Mr Gary Wendt, the CEO of GE Capital. It was reported that when clients wanted GE Capital to put up money for a deal, they would avoid using Kidder as their investment banker. Mr Welch was reported as saying, "The only synergies that exist between Kidder and GE Capital are Capital's AAA credit rating".

In April 1994 it was revealed that Kidder had reported $350 million in fictitious profits because of an alleged phantom trading scheme. Kidder blamed Mr Joseph Jett, who had been accused of creating the fictitious profits between November 1991 and March 1994. Kidder had to take a $210 million charge against its first quarter earnings in 1994. There was also the question of how a person with so little experience could have been appointed to a position bearing so much responsibility. This fiasco was reminiscent of a deal that went sour for Kidder in autumn 1993, which cost Kidder $1.7 million. The deal was headed by Mr Kaplan, who like Mr Jett, had insufficient experience.

Both the SEC and the New York Stock Exchange (NYSE) launched enquiries into the Jett affair. In a report prepared by Gary Lynch, (who is a lawyer with the law firm that represented Kidder in an arbitration case against Joseph

Jett) it was concluded that there was lax oversight and poor judgement by Mr Jett's superiors, including Mr Cerrullo (former fixed income head) and Mr Mullin (former derivatives boss). The report suspiciously supports Kidder's claim that no other person knowingly acted with Mr Jett. Kidder's top managers should have been suspicious because Mr Jett was producing high profits in government bond trading—never a Kidder strength. Some of the blame can be attributed to the aggressive corporate culture of Kidder. At an internal Kidder conference, Jett was reported to have told 130 of the firm's senior executives "you make money at all costs".

However, from details that have been revealed in the prepared reports, it is evident that there were problems at Kidder long before the Jett affair, indeed, even before Jett arrived. For example, in December 1993 Kidder had the highest gearing ratio of any bank on Wall Street, at 100 to 1.

Mr Jack Welch of GE attempted to restore the reputation of GE by disciplining or dismissing those responsible. Mr Michael Carpenter was pressurised into resigning; both Mr Mullin and Mr Cerrullo were fired.

On 17 October 1994, GE announced GE Capital was to sell Kidder Peabody to Paine Webber, another investment bank. The sale included the parts of Kidder that Paine Webber wished to purchase. GE Capital also transferred $580 million in liquid securities to Paine Webber, part of Kidder's inventory. In return GE Capital received shares in Paine Webber worth $670 million. Thus GE received a net of $90 million for firm that it had purchased for $600 million in 1986, though GE also obtained a 25% stake in Paine Webber.

Questions for the Kidder Peabody Case Study

1. How might a conglomerate go about assessing the real worth of an investment bank when so many of the assets are intangible?
2. Identify the areas of potential synergy for Kidder and GEFS.
3. Was the emphasis on developing investment banking and corporate finance rather than the use of Kidder's retail outlets a wise decision?
4. Given Mr Cathart's mission of restoring Kidder to profitability, what advice might Alan Horrvich give? What are the implications for each strategic alternative?
5. What in fact happened after 1987?
6. Summarise the various scandals associated with Kidder Peabody. What factors made this securities house prone to scandals?
7. In 1994, GE divested itself of Kidder Peabody. The extent of the failure of this "match" is illustrated by the sale of Kidder to Paine Webber for a net of $90 million, compared to the $600 million price tag for Kidder in 1986.
   (a) Did GE pay too much for Kidder in 1986? Why?
   (b) How much is GE to blame for the subsequent problems at Kidder? Could these problems have been avoided?
8. Was GE wise to take a 25% stake in Paine Webber?

7 CONTINENTAL ILLINOIS BANK AND TRUST COMPANY*

Relevant parts of text: Chapters 6 (US regulation) and 7.

The collapse of Continental Illinois was one of the bank failure cases discussed in Chapter 7. This case study provides more detail on the collapse, and asks some broadly based questions which may be answered in conjunction with the reading of Chapter 7.

A Detailed Summary of the Collapse of Continental

31 December 1981

At the end of December 1981, Continental had assets totalling $45.1 billion, making it the sixth largest bank in the USA. It had received favourable assessments from the Office of the Comptroller of the Currency (OCC) between 1974 and 1981. In 1978, *Dun's Review* listed it as one of the five best managed corporations in the USA. Energy loans amounted to 20% of loans and leases.

30 June 1982

Continental was holding $1.1 billion of loans purchased from Penn Square Bank of Oklahoma City, representing 3% of total loans and leases.

5 July 1982

Penn Square Bank failed. Continental placed $20 billion of collateral with the Chicago Federal Reserve, in anticipation of a run. It was not used, but Continental lost access to Federal Reserve (Fed) funds and the domestic certificates of deposits (CD) market. It replaced the lost deposits with Eurodollar borrowing in the interbank market. By the end of July, it was apparent Continental had survived the run in both the US and Euro-market.

31 December 1982–31 March 1984

Non-performing assets more than trebled. The bank had loans outstanding to International Harvester, Massey-Ferguson, Braniff, the Alpha Group of Mexico, Nucorp Energy and Dome Petroleum.

---

*This case first appeared in the New York University Salomon Center Case Series in Banking and Finance (Case 41). Written by Richard Herring (1991). The case was edited and updated by Shelagh Heffernan; questions set by Shelagh Heffernan.

February 1984

To maintain its dividend, Continental sold its credit card business to Chemical Bank.

16 March 1984–4 May 1984

Seven small banks were closed, using a new "payout-cash advance" procedure, giving rise to losses on uninsured creditors.

9 May 1984

Rumours began to circulate in Tokyo that Continental was about to file for protection under Chapter 11 bankruptcy law. A run on deposits began in Tokyo when traders received the news, and the run followed the sun west, as western financial markets began to open.

10 May 1984

The OCC issued a special news release that it was not aware of any significant changes in the operations of Continental, as reflected in published financial statements. The OCC said Continental's ratios compared favourably with those of other key multinational banks. The statement was an attempt to quash the rumours which had initiated the run.

11 May 1984

Continental borrowed about $3.6 billion (later rising to $4 billion) from the Chicago Fed, almost half the daily funding requirement.

14 May 1984

It was announced that a consortium of 16 major US banks would provide Continental with a 30 day $4.5 billion line of credit. During the week, the spread between CDs and T-bills widened from 40 basis points to 130 basis points.

17 May 1984

The Federal Deposit Insurance Corporation (FDIC) with the Fed and OCC guaranteed *all* depositors and general creditors of the bank. The guarantee was accompanied by a capital infusion of $2 billion (from the FDIC and a group of commercial banks) and a credit line from 28 banks of $5.5 billion. The Fed announced it was prepared to meet any extraordinary liquidity demands.

Mid-May 1984

There was a further run on deposits, amounting to $20 billion, less $5 billion in asset sales. It was covered by borrowing $5 billion from the Fed, $2 billion in subordinated notes placed with the FDIC and domestic banks, and $4.1 billion from another 28 banks in the safety net arrangement. An additional $4 billion came from some banks in the safety net.

1 July 1984

Officials admitted the run had continued, forcing the bank to sell another $5 billion in assets.

The Resolution

- Continental was divided into a "good" bank and a "bad" bank.
- The FDIC paid $2 billion for problem loans with a face value of $3 billion. The "bad" bank was to be managed for the FDIC by a newly formed service subsidiary of Continental. Any loans to sovereigns or guaranteed to sovereigns were exempted. The FDIC committed itself to assume as much as $1.5 billion in other troubled loans over a three-year period. The purchases would take place at book value.
- The FDIC assumed Continental's $3.5 billion debt to the Chicago Fed rather than paying cash. The FDIC was to repay the Fed over five years.
- The FDIC was to provide a $1 billion capital infusion in return for preferred stock, convertible into 80% of Continental's common stock.
- The FDIC replaced the Continental board and management team.

A Review of How the Problems at Continental Arose

Between 1974 and 1981, Continental grew rapidly, acquiring many loans that ultimately resulted in losses. The period 1982–84 was the aftermath of what happened once significant loan problems had been uncovered. The discussion is largely with reference to the bank, not the bank holding company.

Mr Roger E. Anderson became Chairman and Chief Executive Officer in 1973. He and a management team set strategic goals, the objective of which was to transform Continental from a midwestern country bank to a world class bank.

Between 1974 and 1981, Continental's assets grew by an average of over 13% per year. In 1984 it had $45.1 billion in total assets, making it the sixth largest bank in the US, up from the eighth largest in 1974. Continental grew faster than any other wholesale bank in this period. In 1973, Continental had launched an aggressive campaign on segments of the banking market to increase market share. It rapidly built up its consumer loan portfolio.

A private placement unit was created that secured a foothold in the market by arranging placements of debt for small companies. It expanded globally by structuring syndicated Eurodollar loans, making advances in direct lending to European multinational companies, and becoming active in project financing.

Like most banks, Continental suffered during the collapse of the real estate investment trust industry in the mid-1970s. Continental's management, however, handled the problem well—its recovery from the real estate problems was more successful than most other large banks with similar problems. As a result, Continental remained active in property lending throughout the period.

The recession of 1974–75 saw Continental emerge with one of the best loan loss records of its peer group, suggesting management knew how to deal with economic downturns. Some of Continental's main competitors had suffered financial problems, which enabled the bank to take advantage of a competitive opportunity and become the premier bank in the Midwest.

The Office of Comptroller of the Currency conducted eight examinations of the bank during the period 1974–81, all of which were favourable. The bank's handling of its problem loans following the 1974–75 recession was considered superior to most other wholesale money centre banks.

In 1972 the bank had expanded the individual lending officers' authority and removed the loan approval process from a committee framework. In 1976 the bank reorganised itself, eliminating "red-tape" from its lending procedures. Major responsibility was delegated to lending officers in the field, resulting in fewer controls and levels of review. The idea was to provide lending officers with the flexibility to quickly take advantage of lending opportunities as they arose. While decentralised lending operations were common among money centre and large regional banks, Continental was a leader in this approach. Management believed such an organisational structure would allow Continental to expand market share and become one of the top three banks lending to corporations in the USA.

In light of this rapid growth, the OCC examiners stressed the importance of adequate controls, especially in the loan area. The examiners noted certain internal control problems, especially the exceptions to the timing of putting problem loans on the bank's internal watch list. However, given the bank's historical loan loss experience and proven ability to deal with problem situations, supervisors were not seriously concerned about the weaknesses they had reported.

Management implemented new internal controls, in response to the OCC report, including computer-generated past due reports and a system to track exceptions in the internal rating process.

In the period 1974–81 Continental sought to increase loan growth by courting companies in profitable, though in some cases, high-risk businesses. Lending officers were encouraged to move fast, offer more innovative packages, and take on more loans. This aggressive lending strategy worked well for the bank: its commercial and industrial loan portfolio grew from $4.9 billion in 1974 to $14.3 billion in 1981. It expanded its market share in the late 1970s (rising from 3.9% at the end of 1974 to 4.4% at year-end 1981), when many other money centre banks were losing out to foreign banks, the growing commercial paper market, and other non-traditional lenders.

As part of its corporate expansion, Continental was very aggressive in the energy area. In the early 1950s it had created an oil-lending unit and was, reportedly, the first major bank to have petroleum engineers and other energy specialists on its staff. The economic consequences of the 1973 oil embargo and the resulting fourfold increase in world oil prices meant energy self-sufficiency became a top priority on the national political agenda. Various administrations and Congress launched initiatives to increase domestic production and reduce energy consumption. Continental, having cultivated this niche from the 1950s, became a key energy sector lending bank.

The commercial and industrial loan portfolio (including its energy loans) produced high returns for Continental—average returns were consistently higher than those of other wholesale money centre banks. The financial markets reacted favourably to the aggressive loan strategy adopted by Continental. Analysts noted its stable assets and earnings growth, its excellent loan loss record, and its expertise in energy sector lending. In 1976, Continental Illinois Corporation's ratio of market price to book value began to rise—up to this date, it had lagged behind other money centre banks.

The rapid growth in its assets was funded by the purchase of wholesale money, including federal funds, negotiable certificates of deposit, and deposits from the interbank market. It had limited access to retail banking markets and core deposit funding because of state regulations in Illinois which effectively restricted the bank to unit bank status. Purchased funds made up 70% of the bank's total liabilities, substantially higher than the peer group average.

In the 1976 inspection by the OCC, examiners expressed concern about the bank's liquidity and its reliance on Fed funds, foreign deposits, and negotiable CDs. By the summer of 1977, the bank had improved its liquidity and enhanced its monitoring systems. OCC examiners concluded that the bank was adequately monitoring its funding, and maintaining control. However, the bank was requested to submit quarterly status reports on classified assets over $4 million, and also to submit monthly status reports.

Continental's heavy reliance over this period on purchased money, which had a higher interest cost on retail deposits, offset much of the gain that accrued from the higher loan yields. Higher funding costs reduced Continental's net interest margin to a level well below its peer group. However, the bank was able to maintain its superior earnings growth because of low overheads (due to the absence of domestic branches and few foreign branches compared to its peer group) and non-interest expenses. Continental's ratio of non-interest expenses to average assets was far below its peer group average.

Throughout the late 1970s the OCC expressed concern not only about asset quality, but about capital adequacy as well. During the 1976 examination, the OCC pointed out the absence of a capital growth plan by Continental, which was unlike most other large national banks. In response, the bank prepared a three-year capital plan and took immediate measures to increase capital, including cutting the size of its 1976 dividends to the holding company by

$15 million. The bank holding company issued debt and used the proceeds to inject $62 million into the bank's surplus account. However, asset growth outpaced capital growth, and capital declined throughout 1980.

The 1979 OCC examination noted the continued improvement in Continental's asset quality. Classified assets had declined from 86% to 80% of gross capital funds. Liquidity was also considered adequate. The OCC did note some problems in the bank's internal credit review system—deficiencies were cited in the identification and rating of problem loans and in the completeness of credit files. OCC examiners also stressed the importance of a strong capital base, in light of Continental's rapid asset growth rate.

The 1980 examination drew similar conclusions. Liquidity was considered acceptable. Asset quality continued to improve—classified assets as a percentage of gross capital funds declined to 61%. This figure was lower than the average for other money centre banks. Management was encouraged to organise an on-site review of information submitted to the loan review committee, such as periodic visits to foreign offices and other loan origination sites. Capital was considered adequate, even though it was not keeping pace with asset growth. It was thought Continental had sufficient capacity to meet external pressures and to fund projected growth.

In response to the 1980 examiners' report, Continental's management indicated that although they believed the existing internal credit review system was adequate, they were exploring ways of conducting on-site examinations in a cost effective way. An experimental field review was subsequently conducted.

Historically, Continental had made loans to energy producers that were secured by proven reserves or by properties surrounded by producing wells that were guaranteed to produce oil and gas. As part of management's intensified commitment to energy lending in the late 1970s, the bank had begun expanding its energy loan portfolio, including making loans secured by leases on underdeveloped properties with uncertain production potential. This change occurred at a time when energy prices were increasing rapidly and drilling and exploration activity booming. The bank also became particularly aggressive in expanding loans to small independent drillers and refiners.

By 1981, Continental's exposure to the energy sector was very pronounced. Management was unconcerned because it was confident about the strength of the sector and its knowledge of specific oil fields and companies. It was believed the bank had found a good way to leverage (gear) its expertise in the oil industry.

During the 1981 examination, the OCC placed special emphasis on the review of Continental's energy and real estate loan portfolio. The bank's energy portfolio was 20% of its total loans and leases and 47% of all its commercial and industrial loans. The energy portfolio nearly doubled from 1979 to 1980, and increased by 50% in 1981. Losses from Continental's energy loans consistently averaged less than half the net loan losses from non-energy loans.

The 1981 OCC examination relied on information as of April that year. The examiners noted a significant level of participations from Penn Square that were backed up by letters of credit. Extra time was spent examining these loans because they were large relative to Penn Square's size. The OCC concluded the standby letters of credit were issued by banks other than Penn Square, including several money centre banks, alleviating the OCC's concerns. Only two of Continental's oil and gas loans had been classified, and neither loan had been purchased by Penn Square.

In the 1981 examination, the OCC continued to look at the quality of the credit rating system. Classified assets as a percentage of gross capital increased from 61% to 67%. This trend was common to other large banks and the OCC judged it to be due to declining macroeconomic conditions rather than a worsening of credit standards. The internal loan review system of the bank was also reviewed. It was noted that about 375 loans (totalling $2.4 billion) had not been reviewed by the rating committee within one year; 55 of these had not been reviewed over two years. Management admitted to being aware of these exceptions and noted it was in the process of reassessing its loan review system.

At the 1981 examination, the OCC was satisfied with Continental's quality and consistency of earnings. Though holding down dividends had resulted in a steady source of capital augmentation, capital still needed to be brought in line with asset growth. Liquidity was considered adequate to meet any external pressures. The OCC reported that suitable systems of managing funding and rate sensitivity were in place.

In response to the 1981 examination, the management at Continental denied that there was a problem with the quality of the loan portfolio, given the state of the economy at the time, especially record high interest rates. But they stated that close, continued attention would be provided to the quality of the loan portfolio. Improvements were to be made to ensure loans were reviewed on schedule.

Throughout 1981, financial analysts believed that Continental would continue to exhibit superior growth because of its position as prime lender to the energy industry, its potential for an improved return on assets, and its record of loan losses. Continental was complimented for its choice of energy lending as a niche market.

The Demise of Continental: January 1982–July 1984

To fully understand Continental's demise, it is necessary to review the history of Penn Square Bank's involvement. Penn Square was one of the most aggressive lenders in a very active drilling part of the country—Oklahoma City. Its loan-generating ability exceeded its legal lending limit as well as its funding ability, so Penn Square originated energy loans and sold them to other banks, including Continental and Seattle First National Bank.

Although Continental began purchasing loans from Penn Square as early as 1978, significant growth in loan purchases did not occur until 1981. At the end of the 1981 OCC examination, Penn Square loan purchases were in excess of $500 million; at the start of the 1982 examination, they had risen to a total value of $1.1 billion. At their peak in the spring of 1982, loans that originated at Penn square represented 17% of Continental's entire oil and gas portfolio.

The OCC made a quarterly visit to Continental in March 1982, ahead of their main examination. The energy sector was in decline, but even so, bank officials said they were comfortable with their expertise in the area. In the May 1982 examination, the OCC planned to focus on the energy portfolio— a specialist was assigned to the OCC to assist in the examination. OCC's concerns heightened when it was found, at the OCC examination of Penn Square, that Continental had purchased a significant quantity of bad loans from Penn Square. The OCC informed Continental of the serious situation at Penn Square and extended their examination to November, working closely with internal auditors at Penn Square and independent accountants to assess the damage.

On 5 July 1982, Penn Square failed. Continental was directed by the OCC to implement a number of corrective measures; the bank complied. In August, the OCC informed management of its intention to formalise these directives by placing the bank under a Formal Agreement: the Comptroller and OCC staff met with senior management at Continental to discuss the bank's condition and the impending agreement.

Continental moved quickly to determine the extent of its exposure in loans originated by Penn Square, to assess the amount of loan loss provision necessary for the second quarter, and to stabilise funding. The OCC also scrutinised the Penn Square loan purchases carefully, assessing the effect on Continental's loan portfolio and the provision for loan losses.

The 1982 OCC examination determined that many of the purchases from Penn Square, especially in the months just prior to Penn Square's failure, had failed to meet Continental's typical energy lending standards. Many were also poorly documented and were, therefore, not being internally rated in a timely manner. Thus, an increasing number of these loans appeared on Continental's late rating reports. Also, numerous loans had appeared on the bank's internally generated collateral exception report. Recall that, in previous years, the reliability of Continental's internal reporting systems had been questioned. As a consequence, officers from the Special Industries division who were purchasing the loans from Penn Square were able to persuade senior officers to disregard the internal reports. As a result, any internal warning signals were either missed or ignored.

During the OCC's 1982 inspection, the examiners learned that a team of internal auditors had been sent twice in 1981 by Executive Vice-President Bergman, head of Continental's Special Industries group, to review the Penn Square loans being purchased by Continental. The internal auditors singled out several items for special attention, including incomplete and inaccurate records, questionable security interests, and the high level of loans to parties related to Penn Square. However, the Special Litigation report issued by Continental's board of directors in 1984 concluded that his audit report, although submitted to Mr Bergman, had not been seen by senior management at Continental prior to the collapse of Penn Square.

In December 1981, Continental's bank auditors submitted a written report of their findings of a second visit to Penn Square. They expressed concern about:

- loans secured by Penn Square, consisting of stand-by letters of credit, representing one third of Penn Square's equity;
- questionable lien positions (arrangements whereby collateral is held until a debt is paid);
- several loans in which Continental had purchased more than Penn Square's current outstanding balance;
- $565 000 in personal loans from Penn Square to Mr John R Lytle, manager of Continental's Mid-Continent Division of the Oil and Gas group, and the officer responsible for acquiring Penn Square loans;
- the Special Litigation Report indicated that while senior Continental management did receive news of these loans to Mr Lytle, they had not received the full auditors' report from the December review of the Penn Square lending operations. No action was taken by Continental to remove or discipline Mr Lytle until May 1982.

After the collapse of Penn Square in July 1982, Continental sent a staff of experienced energy lenders to Oklahoma City to review Penn Square's records and assess the dimensions of the problem. Each of the loans purchased from Penn Square was reviewed during the first two weeks of July. After analysing the probable risk associated with each credit, senior Continental officers recommended an addition to loan loss reserves of $220 million. The OCC and Continental's accountants, after a review, accepted this figure as realistic. It was published on 21 July along with a full statement of Continental's second quarter results.

Continental's auditors, supported by accountants from Ernst and Whinney, remained in Oklahoma City reconciling Continental's records with Penn Square data, assisting in the Penn Square portfolio assessment programme and preparing loan workouts. In late August and early September, each loan purchased from Penn Square was reviewed by OCC examiners, who discussed their findings with the senior management at Continental before the third quarter results were released. The review resulted in $81 million being added to the bank's provision for loan losses in the third quarter, as reported in Continental Illinois Corporation's 14 October, 1982 press release. It also indicated that non-performing assets had risen to $2 billion, up $700 million from the previous quarter.

Simultaneous with the credit review, Continental undertook an extensive review of the people involved in the Penn Square relationship and lending policies, procedures and practices. Based on the recommendations of an independent review committee appointed by Continental's board of directors, Mr Lytle, Mr Bergman, and his superior, Mr Baker either were fired, took early retirement, or resigned. Other bank personnel were reassigned.

The internal review committee, in the second phase, recommended:

- codification of bank lending policies and procedures;
- enhancement of secured lending and related support systems;
- improvement in cooperation between loan operations and the line;
- revision of loan operations activity to improve its reliability and productivity;

- formulation of a credit risk evaluation division, as had been recommended by the OCC, to strengthen the bank's credit rating system and enhance credit risk identification, evaluation, reporting and monitoring.

Following the Penn Square collapse, the domestic money market's confidence in Continental was seriously weakened. The bank's access to the Fed Funds and domestic CD markets was severely restricted— Continental lost 40% of its purchased domestic funding in 1982.

Continental moved quickly to stabilise and restore its funding. Meetings were held with major funds providers, ratings agencies and members of the financial community. Public disclosures were periodically issued to correct misinformation. In the autumn of 1982, liquid assets were sold or allowed to mature. As the domestic markets for funds dried up, Continental shifted to the European interbank market. Foreign liabilities began to approach 50% of the bank's total liability structure.

Continental's parent holding company maintained its 50¢ per share dividend in August, 1982. The earnings level did not warrant a dividend of this size, but the holding company management felt it was a necessary step to restore confidence and to raise capital in the market place.

Despite these actions, Continental's condition deteriorated throughout 1982. Many of its energy loans that had performed well and had been extremely profitable in the 1970s until well into 1981 were now seriously underperforming or non-performing.

At the holding company level, non-performing assets grew to $844 million at the end of the first quarter of 1982. While most of these had been concentrated in real estate loans and non-energy-related corporate loans through the first quarter of 1982, in the following quarters, a large number of energy loans became non-performing. By the end of 1982, close to half (over $900 million) of Continental's non-performing assets were energy-related. Net loan losses reached $371 million by December 1982, a near fivefold increase over losses for the previous year. Though the economy improved in 1983, losses at Continental remained high.

While oil and gas loans made up about 20% of Continental's average total loan portfolio in 1982 and 1983, they represented about 67% of its June 1982–84 losses. Most of these losses were a direct result of its purchase of loans from Penn Square. Although loans purchased from Penn Square averaged less than 3% of total loans over the past 2.5 years, they accounted for 41% of the bank's losses between June 1982 and June 1984. Penn Square loans had resulted in nearly $500 million in loan losses for Continental. Most of the loan losses originated in 1980 and 1981.

The loan quality problems caused Continental's earnings to collapse. The bank's provision for loan losses consumed 93% of its 1982 operating income, reaching $476.8 million. Net income fell from $236 million in 1981 to $72 million at year end.

The collapse of Penn Square and the energy industry forced Continental's management to reassess the bank's overall direction. Continental's Credit Risk

Evaluation division, which had been created in the autumn of 1982 on the OCC's urging, was strengthened in early 1983 to provide improved risk evaluation and report regularly to senior management and the board of directors. The division also monitored the effectiveness of Continental's early warning credit quality system and provided an important check on corporate lending activities.

The Formal Agreement, signed on 14 March 1983, covered asset and liability management, loan administration, and funding. It required the bank to continue to implement and maintain policies and procedures designed to improve performance. In addition to quarterly progress reports on how the bank was complying with the terms of the Agreement, Continental was also required to make periodic reports to the OCC on its criticised assets, funding, and earnings.

Continental submitted the first quarterly compliance report required by the Formal Agreement to the OCC in March 1983. It indicated that appropriate actions required by the Agreement were being taken by the bank.

In April 1983, OCC examiners visited Continental to review the first quarter financial results. Non-performing assets, at \$2.02 billion, were higher than anticipated by the bank, but market acceptance had improved and premium on funding instruments had declined.

Continental's 1983 recovery plan called for a reduction in assets and staff and a more conservative lending policy. Two executive officers, Mr David Taylor and Mr Edward Bottum, were appointed to Continental's board of directors in August 1983. Immediately after their appointment they instituted key management and organisational changes to aid in the bank's recovery. External market conditions during the second half of 1983, however, slowed Continental's recovery. Increasing interest rates squeezed net interest margins, loan demand was weak, and non-performing energy loans rose further as the energy industry continued to decline.

The general sentiment of bank analysts toward Continental was negative after Penn Square. It had become apparent to bank analysts by early 1983 that Penn Square wasn't Continental's only problem. Most analysts believed that Continental's stock would not recover in the short-term.

At the time of the 1983 examination, the condition of Continental had further deteriorated since the 1982 examination. Asset quality and earnings remained poor. Capital was adequate on a ratio basis, but under pressure due to asset and earnings problems. Funding had improved, but was still highly sensitive to poor performance and other negative developments. The bank was found to be in compliance with the terms of the Formal Agreement. In December 1983, the OCC examination was completed and the Comptroller and senior OCC staff met Continental's board of directors to discuss the findings.

A revised recovery plan for 1984 called for a further reduction in assets, enhanced capital-raising efforts, and a reduction in non-interest expenses and staff. Non-essential businesses, such as real estate and the bank's credit card operation, were to be sold to improve capital and refocus the bank on wholesale banking. Merger alternatives would be pursued with the assistance of

Goldman Sachs, which had been retained in September 1983. Plans were also accelerated to transfer additional responsibilities to Taylor and Bottum.

In February 1984, Mr Taylor replaced Mr Roger Anderson as Continental's CEO; Mr Bottum was elected President. External events in the first quarter of 1984 produced further problems for the new management team. Asset quality continued to deteriorate and Continental recorded an operating loss for the first quarter of 1984.

Continental's condition as of 31 March 1984 remained poor. An OCC examination began on 19 March and targeted asset quality and funding. It concluded that continued operating losses and funding problems could be anticipated unless the bank's contingency plan to sell non-performing assets was successful. But details of this plan were not available at the completion of the examination on 20 April.

The Comptroller and his staff met with Continental's Chairman, CEO and President on 2 May to discuss the bank's dividend policy and contingency plan for selling non-performing assets. Following the meeting, the Comptroller concluded that the OCC's approval of the payment of the second quarter dividend to the holding company in part depended on the successful implementation of provisions contained in the contingency plan, specifically, the sale of non-performing assets.

Later that month, market confidence in Continental deteriorated still further—rumours of the bank's impending bankruptcy were fuelled by two erroneous press reports on 8 May that concerned the purchase of or investment in the bank. From that point on, the OCC was in continual contact with the bank and other bank regulatory agencies, especially the FDIC. On 10 May the OCC took the unusual step of issuing a news release stating that its office had not requested assistance for or even discussed Continental with any bank or securities firm. Additionally, it was noted, the OCC could find no basis for the rumours concerning the bank's fate.

On 10 May 1984, OCC examiners established an on-site presence in Continental's trading rooms in Chicago and London so they could closely monitor the bank's rapidly deteriorating funding situation. Initial reports from OCC examiners indicated that major providers of overnight and term funds were failing to renew their holdings of the liabilities of the bank and the bank holding company, Continental Illinois Corporation. The bank was forced to repay the deposits in Eurodollar and domestic markets. In the absence of other funding sources, Continental was forced to approach the Federal Reserve Bank of Chicago.

From 12 to 14 May, a safety net of 16 banks put together a $4.5 billion line of credit for Continental. By 15 May, the safety net began to unwind because of a lack of confidence. On 16 and 17 May, the Comptroller and staff held meetings with Continental, other money centre banks, and regulatory agencies in Chicago, New York and Washington to consider alternatives. A temporary assistance package was drawn up.

Under the temporary assistance plan (announced on 17 May), Continental received a $2 billion subordinated loan for the period necessary to develop permanent sources of funds. The loan was evidenced by a demand subordinated note: $1.5 billion was provided by the FDIC, with the balance supplied by seven major US banks. In addition, a consortium of 28 banks provided Continental with a $5.5 billion standby line of credit. By virtue of the capital injection, the FDIC in effect provided an assurance that the bank's problems would not be resolved though a pay-off of insured depositors. Effectively, this meant the FDIC would protect all depositors, not just uninsured depositors.

Over the next two months, the regulators held meetings with both domestic and foreign financial institutions and other parties interested in merging with or investing in Continental. Early on, it was apparent that it would be difficult to achieve a private sector solution. But any private sector/government-assisted transactions were likely to be too costly for the FDIC.

Continental's financial situation was stable for the most of June 1984, but began to deteriorate again in July. Despite FDIC guarantees, there was unease about just how the FDIC "assurances" would be honoured if Continental failed. As a result, many large depositors began to withdraw their deposits as they matured.

During the 60 days after the false press reports, Continental's deposits, Fed Funds, and repos had fallen by nearly $10 billion. By July, Continental had borrowed $4 billion from 28 banks, another $3.55 billion from the Federal Reserve Bank of Chicago, and an additional $2 billion from the FDIC and seven banks holding the subordinated notes.

Throughout this period, the OCC held several meetings with senior bank management and various members of the bank's board of directors. There were also numerous internal planning sessions. Intensive monitoring of the bank's funding continued and a joint OCC/FDIC review of the loan portfolio was conducted.

On 26 July the long-term solution was announced, subject to shareholder approval on 26 September. It was intended to restore Continental to health and to allow it to continue to operate without interruption. Two key elements made up the plan: changes in top management, and substantial assistance. The solution resulted in the creation of a smaller and more viable bank. Management was removed, and shareholders incurred substantial losses, but all depositors were protected. Major disruption to the financial system was avoided. Upon implementation of the long-term solution, Continental would be well-capitalised, with stronger assets and management. It was to be returned to private ownership at the earliest possible date.

In 1995, it was reported that a study by Profesor G. Kaufman* has questioned whether Continental's rescue was in fact necessary. At the time, regulators were assuming that 97% of Continental's assets would be recovered; the actual rate came very close to this figure. With a 97% recovery rate, only two creditor banks would have lost all their capital. Altogether, 65 banks had the potential of losing all their capital; another 101 banks could have lost 50% to

---

*As reported in *The Economist*, 25 March 1995: p.116.

100% of their capital. Thus, the bail-out was only justified if regulators thought virtually no assets would be recovered.

Questions for the Continental Bank Case Study

1. In the context of this case, explain the meaning of:
   (a) "an aggressive lending strategy";
   (b) safety net;
   (c) lifeboat rescue operation;
   (d) the case for 100% deposit insurance;
   (e) a policy of "too big to fail";
   (f) regulatory forbearance, with reference to the OCC.
2. Do you agree that a bank should exploit a situation where its competitors are suffering from financial distress?
3. Why was Continental's ratio of non-interest expenses to average assets and net interest margin below that of its peer group average?
4. Does the Continental case demonstrate there is no place for niche markets in banking?
5. List the (a) managerial factors (b) macroeconomic factors and (c) other factors which contributed to the collapse of Continental. Rank these factors in order of importance and give reasons for your ranking.
6. With respect to the various runs on Continental:
   (a) Why did the bank experience a run in 1982 and how did it manage to survive without recourse to official assistance?
   (b) Why was the run in 1984 more devastating, ultimately leading to the demise of Continental as it was known?
7. After the break-up of Continental, the Bank of America became the subject of market rumours reminiscent of the Continental case. Why was the Bank of America able to withstand these rumours but not Continental?
8. Explain how the following recent regulatory changes might have prevented the collapse of Continental:
   (a) the Federal Deposit Insurance Corporation Act, 1991;
   (b) the Riegle–Neale Interstate Banking and Branch Efficiency Act, 1994.
9. Summarise Continental's position today.

8 CRÉDIT LYONNAIS*

Relevant parts of text: Chapters 3 and 6 (EU), 5 (political risk), 7 and 8 (strategy).

On the last working day of 1992, M. Jean-Yves Harberer, Chairman of Crédit Lyonnais (CL), once again reaffirmed his aim to transform CL from a staid,

---

*This case first appeared in the New York University Salomon Center Case Series in Banking and Finance (Case 40). Written by Roy C. Smith and Ingo Walter (1993). The case was edited and updated by Shelagh Heffernan; questions set by Shelagh Heffernan.

state-controlled French bank into a high-performance pan-European universal bank, a key player in both commercial and investment banking markets and a cornerstone of European finance by the turn of the century. On the eve of the EU's single market, in January 1993, Mr Harberer could cite an important milestone in the road to this goal, achieving a DM 1.9 million controlling interest in Bank für Gemeinwirtschaft, giving CL a major stake in Europe's largest and toughest financial services market, Germany.

According to Harberer, the banks likely to be the future leaders in Europe were Deutsche Bank (Germany), Barclays Bank (Great Britain), Istituto Bancaira San Paolo di Torino (Italy), and Crédit Lyonnais of France. These leading banks would come to dominate the pan-European banking markets. It was these banks that would have the capital strength, the domestic market share, and the intra-European networks to intimidate rivals and repel competitive threats from all sources. Few others, in the opinion of Harberer, had much of a chance.

Harberer had chosen the grandest strategy of all. it was a strategy that would have enormous appeal to CL's sole stockholder, the French government, in its proclaimed vision that a few Euro-champions needed to be nurtured in each important industry through an aggressive "industrial policy" of protection, subsidisation, ministerial guidance and selective capital infusions. Each Euro-champion (as many as possible French) must be capable of conducting commercial warfare on the global battlefield. In financial services, according to Harberer, CL would be France's chosen instrument.

To achieve this objective, Harberer had three goals:

- To make CL very, very large, capturing 1 to 2% of all bank deposits in the 12 (now 15) European Community countries. This meant capturing significant market share in multiple areas of banking and securities activities at once, and doing so quickly. Given the competitive dynamics of the financial services sector, speed was of the essence. Acquisitions of existing businesses would be made in various countries on several fronts, simultaneously.
- CL had to become very European. This meant going up against entrenched domestic competition in most of the national EU markets simultaneously, either via aggressive expansion, strategic alliances and networks, or local acquisitions. The strategy was clear, but no one tactic would be enough. Opportunism and flexibility were essential to success.
- Crédit Lyonnais had to exert significant control over its corporate banking customers, using deep lending and investment banking relationships with major non-financial firms and important ownership stakes in many of these same firms. Only in this way, he felt, could CL exert sufficient influence over their financial and business affairs to direct large and profitable businesses his way. Harberer called this *banque industrie*, a French version of the classic German *Hausbank* relationship.

Crédit Lyonnais had to retain the confidence of the French government, because the state owned the bank. The government would have to inject a great deal of capital, and clear the way for CL's acquisitions and ownership stakes. It would also have to look beyond the inevitable accidents that occur on the road to greater glory. Crédit Lyonnais would have to become an indispensable instrument of French and European industrial policy. The special relationship between the government and CL would have to transcend all political changes in France, even changes leading to CL's privatisation.

Crédit Lyonnais and Le Dirigisme Français

Crédit Lyonnais first opened for business in Lyons in 1863 as a *banque de dépôts*, which collected deposits, made loans, and underwrote new issues of debt and equity for its corporate clients. The bank extended its operations to London during the Franco-Prussian war, and, in the 1870s, expanded throughout France and to the major foreign business centres. By 1900, it was the largest French bank, measured by assets.

During the First World War, many of the personnel from the large French banks were conscripted, and competition in French banking increased. Smaller banks took advantage of larger banks' staffing difficulties and expanded rapidly. From 1917, the *Crédits Populaires*, a new form of banking establishment, were permitted, adding to domestic competition. With the 1917 Russian revolution, sizeable deposits were withdrawn as their owners demanded that CL restitute assets confiscated by the Bolsheviks. Though it was profitable in the 1920s, CL was not making nearly the profits it had enjoyed before the Great War.

During the Great Depression, CL adopted a cautious approach, closing about 100 offices in France and abroad. With the onset of the Second World War, CL remained essentially apolitical, continuing the majority of its banking activities, although some of the foreign offices fell out of the control of Head Office during the German occupation. With the restoration of peace in 1945, there were a number of events central to determining CL's future course.

1945

The French government nationalised the *banques de dépôts*—Crédit Lyonnais, Société Générale, Comptoir National d'Escomptes de Paris (CNEP), and Banque Nationale de Commerce et d'Industrie (BNCI). In 1966, the government merged the two smaller banks, CNEP and BNCI into Banque Nationale de Paris (BNP).

1970

The president of CL, François Bloch-Lainé, adopted a strategy of partnerships with other banks in the form of a Union des Banques Arabes et Françaises (UBAF) and Europartners.

1973

A law was passed allowing the distribution of shares to the employees of nationalised banks and insurance companies such as Crédit Lyonnais.

Election victory of the Gaullists, led by Valéry Giscard d'Estaing, and appointment of Jacques Chaine to replace François Bloch-Lainé as chief executive of CL.

1981

The election victory of the Socialists, under President François Mitterand. Jean Deflassieux, financial advisor to the Socialist party, was appointed to replace Jacques Chaine at CL.

1982

The ruling Socialists nationalised all the major French banks not already owned by the state. The declared objective of the government was to influence the functioning of banks in a direction more favourable to small and middle-sized businesses, as well as to help define and implement a new and more interventionist industrial and monetary policy. For Crédit Lyonnais, the only effect was the renationalisation of shares sold to employees in 1973.

1986

The Gaullists took control of the French Legislative Assembly, and Jacques Chirac was appointed as Prime Minister. There was a period of "cohabitation" with President Mitterand. Jean Deflassieux was replaced as CL chief executive by Jean-Maxime Lévêque, known for his advocacy of privatisation. A privatisation law authorised the public sale of 65 large industrial companies, though CL was not targeted in the first round. Groupe Financière de Paribas and the Société Générale were both successfully privatised.

1988

The socialists regained power in the assembly. Privatisations were immediately suspended. Jean Yves Harberer replaced Jean-Maxime Lévêque as president of Crédit Lyonnais.

1992

The socialists were locked in an election battle with a conservative and neo-Gaullist coalition led by Edward Balladur and Valéry Giscard d'Estaing. This led to another period of cohabitation—election prospects looked bleak for the socialists and French presidential elections were not due until 1995. The conservative party platform promised a resumption of the privatisation programme, to include a broad range of state-owned enterprises. Crédit Lyonnais was thought to be on the list.

The successive changes in chief executives at CL and other nationalised firms by incoming governments illustrated the persistent intervention of the state in the running of companies, commonly known as *dirigisme*. After nationalisation in 1945, CL had had relative independence (most of the CL board remained intact) but the government became increasingly interventionist, defining the bank's strategic direction and the structure of its leadership, with a view to using the nationalised banks as an important tool of industrial policy.

Regardless of the political situation, the French financial system underwent substantial structural change and deregulation in the 1970s and 1980s. It was transformed from being highly concentrated and compartmentalised into an open, well developed domestic capital market. The deregulation was a partial response to London's financial reforms, which the Paris financial markets had to keep up with; it was also due to changing political fashion. In particular, the financial reforms under the Chirac administration helped shift French corporate finance toward open capital markets and away from bank lending.

The major French banks and industrial enterprises remained tied together by strong, informal relationships, a cohesion that had its roots in the Grandes Écoles, attended both by leading government officials and by senior managers of state-owned and private companies and banks. The best graduates became Inspecteurs des Finances, a special appointment for the brightest graduates of the elite École Nationale d'Administration. This virtually ensured for an individual instant prestige, lifelong admiration, and responsible employment in the French government or in government-controlled entities.

Jean Yves Harberer was a paragon of this system. He graduated first in his class at the École Nationale d'Administration and quickly joined the French Treasury as an Inspecteur Général des Finances. He rose rapidly, becoming head of the French Treasury while still in his forties. In 1982 President Mitterand moved him from the Treasury to run the newly nationalised Paribas (Compagnie Financière de Paris et des Pays-Bas). Harberer was widely resented at Paribas, and was seen as the instrument of its nationalisation. During his leadership, Paribas suffered its worst fiasco—it acquired the New York stockbroker AG Becker, which it sold at a $70 million loss a few years later. When Paribas was reprivatised in 1986, Harberer was removed from office, but was subsequently appointed chief executive at Crédit Lyonnais.

Harberer was described as authoritarian, brilliant, and intimidating. He was virtually friendless but was the Socialists' favourite banker, with long-standing ties to Pierre Bérégovoy (Minister of Finance, later Prime Minister) and Jacques Delors, President of the European Commission until 1994.

On his appointment to CL in 1988, Harberer soon made it clear that he wanted to implement grandiose schemes that would never have survived board scrutiny or shareholder reactions in privately owned financial institutions. He was not popular in the banking world, where he was thought of as a gambler, who adopted "go for broke" tactics. It was thought that in the event of a Conservative victory in March 1993 he would be replaced—he was still disliked by the Right, for serving as a tool of the Left at Paribas in 1982.

The Launching Pad

By the early 1990s, Crédit Lyonnais had become a highly diversified bank, offering a complete range of financial services to most client segments throughout most of Europe. CL had holdings in Asia and North America under its own name. In South America and Africa it generally operated under the name of either partially or wholly owned subsidiaries.

In its drive to be a universal bank, CL offered a broad spectrum of financial services. At the end of 1992, it had 2639 retail banking outlets in France, as well as an array of specialised financial affiliates such as the Paris stockbroker Cholet-Dupont Michaux, money management affiliates, and niche-type businesses such as leasing. It also offered a range of insurance services, and was notable for its life insurance. It maintained a large portfolio of holdings in different French and European companies.

For operational purposes, Crédit Lyonnais was divided into six units:

- The *banque des entreprises* (business bank), which catered to the financial requirements of a broad spectrum of business and industry. The core function was commercial lending. For small and medium-sized businesses, Crédit Lyonnais also offered risk management products, including financial and foreign exchange options, other derivatives, asset management services covering a broad range of investments, and international development assistance, such as helping to initiate cross-border partnerships and alliances. For large companies, CL services extended from fund raising through to syndicated lending, Euro-note and Eurocommercial paper, distribution to large and complex financing arrangements such as projects and acquisitions financing, mergers and acquisitions advisory activities and real estate financing. It also maintained leasing subsidiaries—Slibail, Slificom, Slifergie in France, Woodchester in Ireland and the UK, and Leasimpresa in Italy.
- The *banque des particuliers et des professionels* (retail bank) serviced private individuals and professional clients, and carried out basic banking services such as deposits, payments services, and personal loans. There had been a significant decline in demand deposit account balances in favour of interest-bearing chequing accounts, but with intensified competition and changes in legislation, clients were increasingly opting for *SICAVs*—open-ended unit trusts, and especially money market funds or *SICAVs monétaires*. To attract and maintain retail clients, CL was forced to innovate and enhance retail banking services. Debit cards, ATMs and home banking through Minitel (the French interactive phone system) were introduced. CL used its Lion Assurances subsidiary to market personal lines of insurance (for example, automobile insurance), in addition to life assurance.

  For large individual and professional clients, CL provided private banking services and tailored insurance plans, as well as special financing arrangements, such as Inter-Fimo and Crédit Médical de France, which financed the purchase and installation of medical equipment.
- The *banque des marchés capitaux* (investment bank) was responsible for underwriting and distributing bonds and new equity issues. In global

markets, Crédit Lyonnais Capital Markets International units (for example, Crédit Lyonnais Securities in London) assured the bank's presence in foreign financial centres, while the French markets were covered by affiliates such as Cholet-Dupont. In 1991, CL was ranked first in placing domestic and Euro-franc bonds. In the derivatives sector, it accounted for about 10% of the volume on the MATIF, France's futures and options exchange.

- Altus Finance, a finance company was the former finance subsidiary of Thomson, in which the CL acquired a 66% interest in 1991. During that year, Altus bought a large portfolio of high-yield junk bonds from the failed American insurance company, Executive Life, a position which amounted to one-third of CL's tier one capital.

- The *gestionnaire pour compte de tiers* (fund management group) was responsible for the management of private portfolios as well as the SICAVs in which private individuals held shares. CL had enhanced its offerings to include those guaranteeing capital, yield, and global diversification.

- As *actionnaire des entreprises*, Crédit Lyonnais had been increasing its shareholdings in other companies to further the concept of a universal bank. The notion was that, by holding substantial shares, especially in non-financial companies, CL would be able to develop a much better understanding of these companies' financial needs and influence its financial decisions. Its holding structures included:

  —Clinvest: CL's *banque d'affaires*, with a diversified holding of French companies, which had been a highly profitable part of the bank;

  —Euro-Clinvest: a Clinvest subsidiary, with a portfolio of shares of companies in eight European countries;

  —Clindus, established in 1991, had strategic and statutory holdings, principally in Rhône-Poulenc and Usinor-Sacilor, that were added to CL's balance sheet with the "assistance" of the government;

  —Innolion: a high technology start-up venture capital fund operating in France;

  —Compagnie Financière d'Investissement Rhône-Alpes, which invested in the Rhône-Alpes region of France;

  —Lion Expansion: a development capital fund for small and medium businesses and industries.

Harberer considered CL's existing structure to be an ideal basis upon which to build his *banque industrie* concept of a pan-European universal financial institution, with enough capacity to launch a simultaneous multi-pronged attack on an array of national markets, financial services, and client segments, and to do so rapidly.

The Pan-European Building Blocks

By late 1992, Harberer had already developed the beginnings of a pan-European bank in the retail sector via an extensive cross-border branch network. He had been making systematic moves toward this goal since 1988. This was needed to meet his target of capturing between 1% and 2% of total retail deposits in Europe, which in turn was intended to provide the "bulk" funding CL required and the basis for all the other growth initiatives.

Several acquisitions and purchases of stakes in other banks had been undertaken in quick succession as CL bought local medium-sized financial institutions in Belgium, Spain, Italy and Germany. Between 1987 and 1992, the number of branches in Europe had increased threefold. In 1991, 47% of the bank's profits came from outside France, compared to 30% in 1987.

- In Belgium, CL had rapidly expanded its local presence via aggressive branching. It tripled the number of retail and private banking clients in 18 months with a new higher yield account called *Rendement Plus*. This offered 9% on savings deposits, compared to 3–4% offered by local banks. These rates were possible mainly because CL did not have the cumbersome and expensive infrastructure of Belgian banks—it had just 960 employees for 32 branches in the country, three per branch. The three big Belgian banks had at least 10 employees per branch in over 1000 branches.
- In the Netherlands, CL had raised its stake in Slavenburgs Bank (renamed Crédit Lyonnais Bank Nederland NV) from 78% to 100%. In 1987, it had acquired Nederlandse Credietbank, a former subsidiary of Chase Manhattan Bank in the USA.
- In Ireland, CL held a 48% stake in Woodchester, renamed Woodchester Crédit Lyonnais Bank, a leasing and financing company which intended to acquire a total of 40 to 50 retail banking outlets.
- CL reinforced its position in the London market by buying the firm of Alexanders, Laing and Cruickshank after Big Bang in 1986, renamed Crédit Lyonnais Capital Markets in 1989.
- In Spain, CL's branches had been merged with Banco Commercial Español, and renamed Crédit Lyonnais España SA, complemented by the acquisition of the medium-sized Banca-Jover in 1991.
- In Germany, CL completed a deal in 1992 to purchase 50% of the bank für Gemeinwirtschaft (BfG), thereby ending a five-year search for a viable presence in the most important European market outside France.

The acquisition of BfG was a key achievement, in Harberer's view. Not only was Germany the largest European banking market, it was also the most difficult to penetrate. Others had tried, and many had failed. Those who succeeded had done so by buying niche-type businesses, often with indifferent results. None was taken seriously as major contenders alongside the three *Grossbanken*, the large regional and state-affiliated banks, and the cooperative and savings bank networks. With the acquisition of the BfG, Crédit Lyonnais expected to break the mould.

In 1990, the second largest German insurance group, AMB (Aachener and Münchener Beteiligungs GmbH) had negotiated with the state-owned French insurer AGF (Assurance Générales de France) about a partnership arrangement. Besides the attractiveness of the German market, AGF was watching strategic moves by its arch-rival, the state-owned insurer UAP, whose expansion into Germany had come by way of the acquisition from Banque Indosuez of a 34% stake in Groupe Victoire, a major French insurer which had earlier purchased a German insurer, Colonia Versicherungs AG.

AGF had bought 25% of AMB stock, but it was limited to only 9% of the voting rights by the AMB board, using a special class of vinculated shares. It was clearly concerned that a French company, twice its size, was out to control and eventually swallow it. Alongside the AGF acquisition of AMB stock, Crédit Lyonnais had bought a 1.8% stake in AMB as well. As part of its defensive tactics, AMB arranged for an Italian insurer, La Fondaria, to acquire a friendly stake, amounting to 20% of AMB shares. AGF then fought a historic shareholders' rights battle in German courts against the AMB board and a German industrial establishment instinctively distrustful of hostile changes in corporate control. The defence was further bolstered by the fact that 11% of AMB stock was held by Dresdner Bank, and 6% by Munich Re. Allianz, the largest German insurer, was a major shareholder in both Dresdner Bank and Munich Re. Harberer took it as a sign of the times that AGF had prevailed in the German courts and, with the help of CL's AMB shares, was able to obtain AGF recognition of its voting rights—no doubt the basis for future AGF share acquisitions, possibly the La Fondaria stake.

The AGF–AMB battle provided Harberer with the opening he was looking for. AGF proposed that Crédit Lyonnais buy AMB's bank, the Bank für Gemeinwirtshaft, which AMB was keen to dispose of and which had been up for sale for some period. BfG had been the bank of the German labour movement, plagued by poor management, periodic large losses and scandals, and a down-market client base. Nevertheless, BfG had some 200 well-situated branches throughout the country and appeared to present a rare opportunity to buy a major German bank. AMB had already made great strides in turning BfG around, but a loss of DM 400 million in 1990 and a meagre profit of only DM 120 million in 1991 indicated that a major capital infusion would be required in 1993. AMB was hardly interested in supplying it, and a takeover by Crédit Lyonnais was seen by AMB as a welcome opportunity to divest itself of an albatross. CL valued BfG at DM 1.8 billion; AMB valued it at DM 2.6 billion. AMB suggested part of the deal could be the 1.8% AGF stock held by CL. In November 1992, it was agreed that CL would buy 50.1% of BfG for DM 1.9 billion, effective at year end.

Of course, acquisition battles like BfG were only the first and perhaps the easiest part of the building process. Certainly not all of CL's acquisitions had been easy to digest. Its purchase of the Slavenburgs Bank in the Netherlands, for example, had been the source of many headaches. Beyond a troublesome clash of corporate cultures, there had been a serious problem in maintaining supervision. Slavenburgs Bank (or CL Nederland) was responsible for large loans to Giancarlo Parretti for the purchase of MGM shares in the USA (see below)—loans which CL's Paris head office indicated it was not aware of until it was too late.

Besides outright acquisitions and aggressive expansion in the important European markets, CL also employed a strategy of engaging in strategic alliances and networks. One of the older of these, Europartners, was set up as a loose association between Crédit Lyonnais, Commerzbank, Banco di Roma, and Banco Hispaño Americano (BHA), based on the idea of extending banking networks into neighbouring countries and setting up new joint operations. The idea was to provide a cheap way of allowing each of the partners' customers access to basic banking services in other countries.

But it was not long before strains began to appear in Europartners. Over the years, Commerzbank had tightened its relations with its Spanish partner, and in 1989, BHA agreed to swap an 11% interest in its shares for a 5% stake in Commerzbank. The 1991 merger of BHA and Banco Central into Banco Central-Hispaño diluted Commerzbank's share in the merged bank to 4.5%. At the same time, there was a dispute over CL's expansion into Spain with the purchase of Banca Jover in the summer of 1991. A year earlier, Crédit Lyonnais had tried to purchase a 20% stake in Banco Hispaño Americano and was flatly rejected. BHA perceived the new action as a threat of direct competition in its home market, and suspended its relationship with CL.

Rebuffed in Spain, CL had also been thwarted in its attempt to deepen the Franco-German part of the Europartners, agreement. In 1991, CL discussed swapping shares with Commerzbank, the smallest of the three German *Grossbanken*, thought to have involved 10% of Commerzbank's equity for 7% of CL's equity. Discussions broke down over German fears that the French bank had more in mind than cementing the Europartners, alliance. Commerzbank clearly did not want to be the German arm of a French bank. There was also the matter of price. Based on comparative figures, Commerzbank wanted a 10% for 10% share swap, even though the French bank was twice its size, because it considered itself to have a much better future in terms of earnings and market potential.

By the end of 1991, Europartners was effectively dead, though this did not preclude other strategic alliances as a future option for Crédit Lyonnais. Other partnerships had been more stable, including:

- the Banco Santander–Royal Bank of Scotland agreement, cemented by a share swap, to create a link-up through which clients could conduct cross-border transactions at terminals located at either bank's branches. Crédit Commerciale de France had signed up to join this alliance;
- there was the proposed BNP–Dresdner deal, a cooperative agreement that involved 10% cross-shareholdings and each bank continuing to run its existing operations, with reciprocal access to branch networks but with a programme of opening joint offices elsewhere, including Switzerland, Turkey, Japan, and Hungary.

The Government Link

The French economic and financial policy environment over the years has been rather unstable. When François Mitterand was elected President in 1981, his approach was to reflate the economy by increasing the size of the public sector, reducing the number of hours in the working week, and nationalising 49 key industrial and financial firms. These policies led to increased imports and a deterioration of both the trade balance and international capital flows. Under these conditions, the possible solutions were either to devalue the franc and take it out of the European Monetary System's Exchange Rate Mechanism, or to seriously reduce monetary expansion, reduce the fiscal deficit (which would involve cuts in spending), and stimulate the private sector.

The latter option was chosen. Taxes were cut, capital markets deregulated, and the French economy boomed throughout the 1980s. The finance minister, Pierre Bérégovoy, the driving force of fiscal prudence, maintained a *franc fort*, low inflation policy throughout the period and committed the country to partial privatisation, starting with the sale of minority stakes in Elf Aquitaine, Total, and Crédit Locale de France in 1991.

On the other hand, the Socialists had not only nationalised the big banks in 1981 when they came to power, but had continued to influence their activities since then. For example, in 1992, BNP had been asked to acquire an equity stake in Air France, and Crédit Lyonnais had been "encouraged" to buy into the large integrated steelmaker Usinor-Sacilor, both of them inefficient state-owned firms making large losses. By linking together the state-owned equity portfolio and the equity holdings of state-owned banks, such deals, could, in the future, allow the government to maintain control despite partial privatisation of non-financial companies. There was considerable debate whether any new government that might take office in 1993 would have a programme of aggressive privatisation with non-intervention in the strategic direction of the operations of banks and industry—that is, whether the micro-intervention of the past was a "socialist" or "French" attribute.

In addition to its direct and indirect equity holdings, the French government had a strong control lever through "moral suasion", a tradition of political meddling by bureaucrats who considered themselves able to come up with better economic solutions to national needs than the interplay of market forces. On a European level, beyond the tampering with free competition of the past and a highly protectionist stance within the EU decision process on matters of industrial and trade policy, there was concern that the French government would continue its *dirigiste* role and even try to extend it to the cross-border relationships of French firms and banks.

Harberer considered the role of the state in France to be a two-edged sword. At times, it could thwart the achievement of his objectives, but the backing of the state could provide the deep pockets and political support to overcome obstacles and setbacks that would stop ordinary banks in their tracks. To maximise the advantages and minimise the disadvantages, strong backing by key government mandarins was crucial.

The value of the government link became obvious in several accidents that befell CL in its drive for growth. Specifically in wholesale lending; balance sheet expansion could be achieved rapidly but growth meant narrower lending margins. As the European recession began to bite during 1990 and 1991, most banks retrenched to weather the storm. Crédit Lyonnais, on the other hand, announced that it would maintain its set course and "buy" its way out of the recession. The bank had taken on much riskier projects than many of its competitors, and the list of CL's lending problems in the early 1990s included:

- Robert Maxwell—credit losses were significant;
- Hachette, the French publisher, whose television channel, La Cinq, went bankrupt;
- Olympia and York, the Canadian real estate developer, which failed. CL was the second largest European creditor of the firm's Canary Wharf project in London;
- loans of over $1 billion to Giancarlo Parretti, an Italian financier (later accused of fraud) for his purchase of the Hollywood film studio, MGM/ UA Communications.

CL's rapid expansion in 1991 and 1992 did provide a significant increase in CL's net banking income. In 1990, it achieved a net profit of FF 3.7 billion, a 20% increase over 1989, although a major proportion of this increase was attributable to Altus Finance. However, there was an equally large increase in provisions because of the long list of bad debts. By the end of 1991, CL's profits fell to FF 3.16 billion, and provisions increased from FF 4.2 billion to FF 9.6 billion.

At 1.6% of total loans, CL's provisions were precarious when compared to those of other French banks. They were three times those of its main French competitors, but still better than most UK banks. However, Moody's Investor Services downgraded CL's bond rating from Aa1 to Aa2 because of the MGM/ UA controversy and CL's increasing exposure to risky loans, even though the French government, which owned the bank, had an Aa rating.

CL's interest margins continued to decline as competition for deposits increased. At the same time, costs were rising as investment in technologies became increasingly necessary to keep pace with competition, and difficulties were encountered in curbing escalating personnel costs. Assuming that margins were unlikely to improve and cost pressures would be difficult to reverse, CL would have to rely far more heavily on commission income in the future than it had in the past.

In September 1992, Crédit Lyonnais announced its group profits had fallen by 92% to FF 119 million in the first half, compared to FF 1.6 billion the year before. Once again, this dramatic fall in profits was due to an increase in provisions for bad debts, from FF 3.4 billion for the first half of 1991 to FF 6.3 billion for the first half of 1992, even as net banking income grew by 16% and gross operating profit before provisions increased by 33% in the same period. Forty per cent of the bad debt provisions were attributed to CL Bank Nederland, the Dutch subsidiary, in connection with the MGM/UA Communications loans. In December 1992, Moody's downgraded CL debt again, to Aa3, citing "higher risk in both the loan portfolio and the bank's strategy" (*Euromoney*, March 1993).

All of these problems notwithstanding, CL's performance was considered acceptable by its owner, the French government, with growth evidently deemed more important than profits. But the issue of capital adequacy could not be avoided, either under the Basle risk assets ratio or the EC Capital Adequacy and Own Funds directives. As a state-owned bank, Crédit Lyonnais had not been allowed to raise equity capital independently. Only 5% of CL's capital was owned by shareholders, in the form of non-voting *certificats d'investissement*. The rest belonged either to the government or to government-controlled companies. As such, new capital infusions would have to come from the state.

From 1989–91, complicated arrangements had been made under French government sponsorship with five state-controlled companies to bolster CL's capital base and at the same time, solve certain industrial problems. In November 1989, CL raised FF 1.5 billion by selling shares to the Caisse de Dépôts et Consignations. In February and December 1990, share swaps with Thomson brought in FF 6.4 billion. A deal with Rhône-Poulenc raised another FF 1.7 billion in 1990.

In 1991, at the request of Prime Minister Edith Cresson, Crédit Lyonnais invested FF 2.5 billion in Usinor-Sacilor, and gained a 10% stake. The bank also swapped 10% of Usinor's shares for 10% of new Crédit Lyonnais shares, thereby boosting CL's shareholder equity by about FF 3 billion. This allowed Crédit Lyonnais to consolidate its share of Usinor-Sacilor's profit and losses. It diluted CL's earnings but provided a temporary solution to the problems of the troubled steelmaker.

By late 1992, about 28% of CL's capital base consisted of shares in state-owned firms. In all of the share-swaps, other parties paid much higher than book value. These agreements had the effect of linking the fate of the bank to the success of the companies concerned, and also represented a powerful incentive to support these same companies in the future in the face of uncertain profitability. In any case, the resulting capital infusions were insufficient to meet the bank's needs, and the question remained what implications these crossholding arrangements would have if and when some of these firms were privatised, especially Thomson and Rhône-Poulenc. The rest of the badly needed equity would have to be injected by the government.

The Grand Design

Harberer's mosaic seemed to be coming together much faster than anyone could have predicted when he took control in 1988. The key achievements were:

- the Bank's balance sheet had grown enormously under his leadership;
- CL had penetrated all of the European markets in significant ways, including the most difficult of all, Germany;
- CL had maintained its close relationship to its shareholder, the French government, which had shown its willingness to inject capital and to tolerate even serious setbacks on the road to greater financial prominence. The bank's rapid growth and European cross-border market penetration was well suited to the French government's industrial policy objective of having one large French firm as a leader in every major sector of the European economy;

- CL's shareholdings in industrial companies had grown from FF 10 billion in September 1988 to FF 45 billion in early 1992, and it accumulated significant equity stakes in key French industrial companies. This meant CL was in a position to influence strategies and financing activities of these corporations. At the same time, it had provided the government with a durable industrial influence, even if the affected firms were to be privatised.

According to Harberer,* the CL strategy was to build a large, profitable, European banking group. He treated western Europe as the domestic market of EU banks for the next decade. The bank was looking beyond the 1993 single market, to the market as it would be by the turn of the century. He accepted that CL location in key financial centres did not matter for major corporate clients, but it was important for small and medium-sized corporations and individuals, which required a local presence.

However, the strategy was considered highly controversial, and various commentators identified a number of weaknesses in the strategy:

- Harberer had ignored the possibility that EU partners would object to the French government tampering with market competition in their countries by using CL to acquire local banks.
- Harberer had not adequately addressed the problem of how to expand rapidly without buying excessive quantities of low-grade paper. He could create such a weak loan portfolio that even the government would blow the whistle.
- Harberer and his strategy were on everyone's casualty list for the political infighting that would follow the French presidential election in 1995. Time was running short for Harberer to accomplish all he was hoping for.
- Harberer had neglected the investment banking and capital markets side of the business. Indeed, even some companies in which CL had holdings, assuming a sufficiently high credit rating, would prefer to use the capital markets rather than bank borrowing for their financing requirements.

Some critics combined all of these points to form a gloomy picture of CL in the late 1990s:

- It was viewed as a bank with impotent industrial shareholdings in companies that were concentrating their financing on the capital markets. CL also had numerous acquisitions and alliances with foreign banks whose clients were likewise defecting to the capital markets.
- In its quest for rapid growth, CL had accumulated many bad loans, leaving the bank with a weak loan portfolio, and vulnerable to recession. By early 1994, the sluggish French economy, together with high interest rates, caused a marked deterioration in the French property market, and the bankruptcy of many small and medium-sized firms.

---

*As reported in *Euromoney* Supplement, March 1991.

- In 1993, Mr Harberer was dismissed, and Mr Jean Peyrelevade took over as CEO. Harberer became the head of Crédit National, but under public pressure was sacked from this post after CL's 1993 results were made public.

The State Rescue of Crédit Lyonnais

The losses at CL reported in 1992 escalated. In March 1994, CL reported a 1993 loss of FF 6.9 billion ($1.2 billion), compared with FF 1.8 billion in 1992. The government rescue plan was announced in late March 1994:

- FF 4.9 billion in new capital was injected into CL;
- a separate "bad bank", called OIG, was established—it meant CL could remove a sizeable proportion (FF 40 billion) of bad property loans from its balance sheet;
- the French government guaranteed any losses from these loans for a period of five years.

After the 1994 bail out, a French parliamentary commission investigated and reported on CL's affairs on 12 July 1994. The Commission concluded CL had lacked a risk management system capable of controlling the risks it took. Many of the problems originated with one or another of its four subsidiaries: Crédit Lyonnais Bank Nederland (CLBN), Altus Finance, Société de Banque Occidentale (SDBO) and International Bankers. One of SDBP's clients was Bernard Tapie, a heavily indebted left-wing businessman, convicted in 1994 of rigging a crucial football game. CLBN had helped an Italian, Sgr. Parretti, to buy MGM. After Sgr. Parretti was ousted, the bank pumped large amounts of money into MGM, hoping to find a buyer and to recoup some of the funds invested in the venture. American banking rules require CL to find a buyer by mid-1997. In early 1995, CL asked S.G. Warburg to sell 500 European cinemas.

CL had been slow to put its affairs in order. Administration costs fell by 3% in the first half of 1994, due mainly to staff cuts, but little progress was made on the sale of assets. CL chose to dispose of non-core activities, i.e.:

- the bank's stake in the FNAC retailing chain;
- the Meridian hotel chain;
- TFI, a television channel;
- Adidas, the German shoe company.

The bank raised about FF 20 billion from these disposals. In late 1994, CL sold a 57% stake in Banca Lombarda, an Italian Bank, but still owns another sizeable bank in Italy and a majority stake in the loss-making German bank, BfG. Mr Peyrelevade is aiming to sell an additional $20 billion in assets to shed troubled businesses and boost the bank's efficiency. It is expected that unprofitable banking enterprises in Spain and Portugal will be sold. There are no plans to sell CL's stake in BfG, and it was announced that future growth will come from CL's remaining retail banking operations in Europe. Little has been done to reduce the bank's expanding pan-European banking network. In December 1994, CL refused to sell the core components of its European network.

CL's 1994 losses rose to FF 12.1 billion, from FF 6.9 billion in 1993, mainly because of a decline in the domestic retail banking business. New account openings were down by 20% in 1994.

A second rescue plan was announced on 17 March 1995, amounting to $27 billion, to counter mounting losses. CL was to transfer $27 billion in troubled assets to OIG, including:

- $8.5 billion in problem real estate loans;
- a $4 billion exposure from the ownership of MGM studios;
- $9 billion in equity holdings.

Under the agreement, CL will make concessional loans to finance the government's purchase of CL's bad assets. The government will be repaid between 34% and 60% of CL's profits. In May 1995 it was announced that details of a further rescue plan would soon be released. It was reported in *The Banker* (May 1995: p.22) that CL is effectively bankrupt, because losses (equal to FF 50 billion) exceed its capital base.

The nationalised status of CL has contributed toward CL's inefficiency, as reflected by it inability to reduce costs and improve performance. For example, when the French economy went into recession, the government pressured CL to keep lending to prevent bankruptcies and therefore loss of jobs, thereby aggravating the bad debt problem. Publicly, the bank has always denied it is subject to interference by the state, but the former CEO, M. Harberer, claimed that CL was frequently pressed to support key industrial companies in an attempt to boost economic growth and reduce the unemployment rate.

Being state-owned makes it unlikely the necessary job-cutting and branch closure strategies will be undertaken at CL, in contrast to any private sector banks which found themselves in a similar position. Staff morale is low.

The EU is investigating the French government's plan to rescue the ailing bank. French and EU rival banks argue the rescue plan for CL gives CL an unfair competitive advantage. Furthermore, CL cross-shareholdings with troubled state-owned industrial firms, such as the steel producer Usinor-Sacilor, also distorts competition. The European Commission is investigating these allegations. At the time of writing, the latest rescue plans had not been approved by either the newly elected President of France or the European Commission.

Appendix 1: The French Banking Scene

The French domestic market for financial services in the 1990s had been a highly competitive one, characterised by both compartmentalised universal as well as specialised institutions, each targeting different financial activities, despite the fact that deregulation had removed many of the legal barriers. The French banking structure consisted of:

- the *caisses d'epargne*, which dominated the liquid savings deposit market, accounting for over 30% of this type of deposit;
- the *banques cooperatives*: these have dominated the agricultural sector, especially Crédit Agricole;
- the *banques de dépôts*: these banks were active in short-term industrial finance, notably BNP and Société Générale. Crédit National was involved in longer-term loans, and Crédit Foncier in mortgage credit. In March, 1989, BNP and UAP had sealed a *bancassurance* alliance, including a 10% share swap, which gave BNP a FF5.3 billion capital infusion and UAP 2000 French banking outlets from which to sell insurance;
- the *banques d'affaires*: these banks dominated corporate finance, and were both aggressive and competent, Paribas being a good example. They have more in common with large financial conglomerates than with traditional British merchant banks or US investment banks;
- the *banques étrangers*: These banks were mounting fairly effective challenges in specific niches. Barclays Bank had moved into private banking; JP Morgan into the wholesale sector. Numerous foreign firms, including Deutsche Bank and Union Bank of Switzerland, were attracted to dynamic French markets;
- *non-bank competitors*: the French postal savings systems, finance companies such as Compagnie Bancaire (an affiliate of Paribas) and the large insurance companies fall into this category. They were stepping up their challenges to the large universal banks.

The most intense battle Crédit Lyonnais faced at home was to attract retail deposits. Interest-earning chequing accounts had been prohibited since 1967, so *SICAVs monétaires* were used as instruments to attract savings—French banks had been pushing this form of investment aggressively. However, the result was that the cost of funds had approached the money market rate, severely penalising those banks which had lived off cheap, unremunerated accounts. This was especially difficult, given the rising cost of technology as banks competed to develop computerised networks offering more electronic services such as ATMs and direct telephone transactions through the domestic Minitel network.

Appendix 2: The Pan-European Playing Field

The EU directives for achieving a single financial market were outlined in Chapters 3 and 6. An important point is that once the minimum requirements of the EU passport are met, conduct of business rules will vary in each EU country. Financial firms which locate in other states will have to comply with the rules imposed by the host country. It will mean firms will have to deal with 16 different sets of rules (the 15 EU countries plus the Euromarkets). This could raise costs of compliance to regulations for pan-European firms, and leaves open the possibility that host country regulations will be used to favour domestic financial firms over firms from other EU states. However, the general view is that these rules will converge over time, creating a level playing field throughout Europe, and creating the competition necessary to make Europe a key world financial market.

It is expected that the regulatory regime will evolve along the lines of a universal banking model. All types of financial institutions will compete in each others' financial markets geographically, cross-client, and cross-product, including insurance, real estate and various areas of commerce. This environment could, in turn, provide a platform for European institutions to mount serious challenges in North American and Asian financial markets.

Indeed, some observers considered financial services one of the few sectors of the European economy where the regulatory bodies were sometimes well ahead of business in promoting competitive change. Though often resisted by market participants themselves, financial services deregulation in Europe, by the early 1990s, had produced intense competition and pricing rivalry in many markets, an erosion of boundaries between types of financial establishments, a proliferation of new technologies, and improved access to capital markets, which shifted the balance of power away from banks in favour of their customers.

Appendix 3: Rivals for Pan-European Stature

CL's strategy, particularly the goal of achieving critical mass by capturing between 1 and 2% of total European bank deposits, is bound to face stiff competition in the evolving EU environment.

Challenges could be expected from several classes of competitors. There were plenty of entrenched competitors in all the national markets in Europe that CL had to target if the bank was to achieve its goal. Despite the EU regulations, many of the national markets were strongly controlled and relatively closed to outsiders. In some cases, these markets were dominated by cartels, interest-rate agreements and other price-fixing arrangements that bred over-capacity. Local savings banks networks, urban and rural cooperative networks, state-run savings institutions, and very large local banks like ABM-AMRO and ING Groep in the Netherlands would be hard to encroach upon.

The most direct competitors, which had declared pan-European aspirations, were Barclays Bank in the UK and Germany's Deutsche Bank. The other British banks had been focusing on the domestic market, although there was always the possibility that National Westminster or Midland Bank (owned by Hong Kong and Shanghai Banking Corporation) might, at some point in the future, attempt a foray into European banking. The Dutch banks, ABN-AMRO and ING Groep, might begin to look toward Europe for new markets. Italy was in such a state of chaos, it was unlikely any of their banks could mount a serious competitive challenge, while the Spanish banks lack critical mass. The Swiss banks, which have the potential to enter Europe, are semi-detached from the EU, and have strategies focused on global capital markets and private banking activities. There was also Citibank of the USA, which had rebranded subsidiaries under its own logo in Germany, Belgium, France, Spain and Greece, and had emerged from recent domestic troubles as a powerful retail player in Europe.

The other French banks did not appear to by vying for the same pan-European position as Crédit Lyonnais. BNP seemed to think that to develop a 1% deposit market share by acquisition was too expensive, although its strategic alliance with Dresdner Bank AG, including a possible 10% share swap, had been given a great deal of publicity and needed to be monitored. Société Générale has no obvious interest in developing retail banks beyond the French border, after an abortive attempt to forge a strategic alliance with Commerzbank AG of Germany.

In view of the domestic conditions in most European countries, CL's retail expansion could be difficult. It is more likely to benefit from the flexibility it could achieve in servicing larger, wholesale clients. Retail banking appears to depend on maintaining a viable branch network. The alternatives include:

- building up the necessary networks, which could be both expensive and risky;
- buying into local retail networks, which could also be expensive and risky;
- strategic alliances formed with local banks or other financial services firms on a mutually beneficial basis.

Whatever the delivery, CL could only succeed if it established a competitive advantage over local banks.

Questions for Crédit Lyonnais Case Study

1. Using the case, explain the meaning of:
   (a) *banque industrie*;
   (b) German *hausbank*;
   (c) *dirigisme*;
   (d) *SICAVs monétaires*;
   (e) moral suasion, in the British and French contexts;
   (f) French universal banking, as compared to German or British universal banking;
   (g) a pan-European bank.
2. What is the principal difference between state-owned (nationalised) public and shareholder-owned public banks?
3. What should be the criteria for taking a decision to become a pan-European bank? Was this the criteria used at CL?
4. (a) Do you agree that capturing 1% to 2% of European deposits is the key to becoming a pan-European bank?
   (b) What is meant by pan-European retail banking? Is it a feasible strategy?
5. In Chapter 3, it was noted that there are obstacles that may inhibit the completion of the single banking market. In this regard, what problems does the CL case highlight?
6. Was Harberer qualified to run Crédit Lyonnais?

7. Is an industrial policy of protection, subsidisation, ministerial guidance, and selective capital infusions the optimal way of ensuring certain domestic firms are able to compete on global markets?
8. What are the conditions under which a state-owned nationalised bank will be an efficient competitor, able to penetrate foreign markets?
9. To what extent did the changing political environment affect CL decision-making? Is this ever a problem for private or shareholder-owned public banks?
10. To what extent did poor risk management contribute to the near collapse of CL?
11. In the context of the CL case, discuss the extent to which a trade-off exists between balance sheet growth and profitability?
12. What factors caused the "failure" of Crédit Lyonnais in 1994, and the need for a second (and possibly third) rescue package in 1995? Could a privately owned bank ever get into a situation like this?
13. Critically analyse the rescue plans for Crédit Lyonnais.

9 SCHWEIZER UNIVERSAL BANK—PLAN 2001*

Relevant parts of text: Chapters 3 and 6 (EU) and 8 (strategy).

Dr Urs Baltenswiler was general manager in charge of global wholesale banking at Schweizer Universalbank, fourth ranked among the large universal credit institutions that had dominated financial transactions in Switzerland for decades. Dr Baltenswiler was one of the bank's most senior general managers and had been asked by the chief executive, Dr Hans-Ulrich Lamprecht, to head a strategic review committee of the Management Board to look into the bank's efforts to realise its widely publicised "Plan 2001". Summarising the bank's strategy, it was announced in 1991, aimed at securing and improving the bank's global competitive in response to the structural changes occurring in Swiss banking and a debate over the universal banking concept. The details of Plan 2001 are summarised below.

Summary of Key Points of Plan 2001—25 March 1990

The objective is to preserve the bank's current position as one of the top 20 most profitable and respected banks in the world, at the end of the decade and throughout the next century.

The strategy for the coming decade must be to emphasise our competitive advantages, and the bank's inherent strengths and capabilities. These include:

---

*This case first appeared in the New York University Salomon Center Case Series in Banking and Finance (Case 38). Written by Ingo Walter and Roy C. Smith. The case was edited and updated by Shelagh Heffernan; questions set by Shelagh Heffernan.

- The bank's unique franchise as one of the most important banks in Switzerland, a country much respected around the world for its banking safety, integrity and privacy.
- The bank's substantial private banking business, which enables the bank to attract and retain clients from all over the world, because of:
   —the bank's skill in trading securities and foreign exchange;
   —the bank's global expertise and extensive financial experience in Europe, North America, and the Far East;
   —the Bank's substantial investment and expertise in information technology.

The bank's global strategy will have the following elements:

- To preserve and increase market share and the profitability of the bank's domestic banking business, though in general this business is in decline, due to deregulation and increasing competition.
- To preserve and increase market share in the bank's private banking business. These services need to be marketed more effectively in the Far East and North America.
- To increase the bank's market position, penetration, and the profitability of the bank's international banking activities, especially those that are capital market oriented. This has been the most rapidly growing segment of the bank's financial services activities over the past decade, and should continue to be so over the next decade. The bank recognises its historical strength in the capital markets, but accepts the need to spread its expertise into new regions and product areas.

At the time Plan 2001 was announced, Dr Lamprecht stated that the bank's single overriding objective was to rank as one of the top 20 banks in the world in terms of reputation, quality, and profitability, although not necessarily in terms of total balance sheet size. With such rankings likely to be dominated by banks such as Deutsche Bank, Union Bank of Switzerland, JP Morgan, and Industrial Bank of Japan, Dr Lamprecht recognised the challenge that lay ahead. He also knew that some of the top 20 nominees of only a few years ago were struggling for survival as independent firms, while new challengers were rising to prominence all the time. Often these were specialist firms, and often, firms that could not even be called banks.

Schweizer Universalbank Strategic Review

SU was no more or less subject to the dynamics of the domestic banking business than its big Swiss competitors, although it had successfully avoided most of the pitfalls encountered by its rivals in the international arena. However, over the last few years, like the other Swiss banks, SU had experienced a number of strategic and tactical problems and difficulties that raised questions as to whether the Plan 2001 goals could in fact be achieved, and indeed, whether the goals themselves were sound.

There were a number of worrying problems. SU's stock price was no better than it had been in 1990, when its bearer* shares traded at around SF 300, down from a peak of nearly SF 700 at the end of 1985. In 1992, Moody's and Standard and Poor's had downgraded the bank's AAA bond rating.

Dr Lamprecht was under increasing pressure, rare in Switzerland, to demonstrate significant progress toward the realisation of goals specified by him and the management board, or to think seriously about giving up his role as chief executive. The members of SU's supervisory board had not expressed themselves publicly in this regard, but the bank's major clients and shareholders knew they were following the situation very closely.

The supervisory board of SU had also expressed concern about recent changes in Swiss corporate law on foreign ownership of public companies, which in effect gave non-Swiss investors access to the bank's registered shares. The bank's statutes would have to be changed and various measures taken without delay to avoid unwarranted foreign shareholdings and the possibility of a hostile takeover.

Herr Ruedi Eppler, principal deputy to Dr Baltenswiler, thought Dr Baltenswiler was either a brilliant or foolish choice to head the Strategic Review Committee. Dr Baltenswiler had, at one point, left the bank for six years to work for Merrill Lynch in New York and Tokyo, before being recruited back to take charge of the division responsible for the International Banking Team (IBT). The team covered all wholesale banking and capital markets worldwide, including those located in Switzerland. IBT was to play a critical role in Plan 2001, providing the growth, global market penetration, and profitability necessary to achieve the desired market standing by early in the next decade.

Apart from IBT, the bank had two other strategic divisions. The Swiss Banking Team (SBT) consisted of domestic deposit taking, consumer finance, mortgage finance, transactional banking,and middle market lending. The Private Banking Team (PBT) was responsible for money management for wealthy clients, mainly residing outside Switzerland. Both SBT and PBT were expected to grow slowly because of increased competition in these areas. Short-term growth was expected for PBT because of recent international political turmoil and tax hikes around the world.

Swiss domestic lending comprised about 60% of SU's consolidated loan book, two-thirds of which were mortgages. It contributed about half the bank's profits. The International Banking Team was responsible for 40% of SU's total loans outstanding, but for the last few years IBT had contributed nothing to profits. The Private Banking Team, which booked no loans at all, provided the other half of the bank's profits.

---

*In Switzerland, there are three main classes of shares. Bearer shares carry a vote, but the holder of these shares can remain anonymous, since it is not required that he/she declares the holding. Registered shares also have a vote, but the names of shareholders are entered into the company's share register; participation certificates do not convey voting rights to holders.

Dr Baltenswiler's division of the bank was to carry much of the weight of the strategic plan, but so far IBT had contributed little if anything to the bottom line. This fact created a number of doubts among the management board members as to whether IBT was capable of achieving the results assigned to it. Dr Baltenswiler and Herr Eppler had looked over the composite international league table as a rough guide to international market standing, and knew it would be extremely tough for SU to achieve the kind of positioning that was a necessary part of Plan 2001. It would be particularly difficult to break into US domestic leagues, a virtual necessity if IBT's contribution to Plan 2001 was to be achieved.

Dr Baltenswiler's report was being awaited with great interest by the other general managers, all of whom were known to be people of strong opinions, with a willingness to express them. He was due to present it to the management board on the following weekend at a three day *Klausur* meeting, so they had just a week to prepare the final presentation.

As Dr Baltenswiler's principal deputy, Herr Eppler waited in Zurich for his boss to return from briefing with Dr Lamprecht on the initial conclusions of the report. He wondered how the meeting was going. Lamprecht had instructed Baltenswiler to conduct his review without taking for granted the initial strategic assumptions made when Plan 2001 was conceived in 1990 (the so-called zero-based approach). He wanted a fresh, objective appraisal of market trends and conditions, the changing competitive structure, with objectives not just tailored to goals but to the bank's capabilities as well.

Herr Eppler knew that several board members would be questioning the fundamental capability of Baltenswiler's division to carry out part of its plan, especially in view of the several major setbacks that had befallen the big Swiss banks in international lending and capital market activity since 1987. However, he also knew that Baltenswiler would be discussing the sharp decline in the bank's net interest income and the greatly increased loan loss provisions associated with Swiss domestic lending activities, as well as the expected increase in competition for domestic retail and international private banking business that the past few years of deregulation and restructuring had assured.

Dr Baltenswiler had asked Eppler to compile a summary of the pros and cons of universal banking as a viable organisational form in international competition, as well as the major problem areas confronting the bank over the past few years. Herr Eppler had passed on these tasks to the Group Planning Department, and had already received their report. This report is reproduced below.

SU's Report on Universal Banking in Switzerland by SU's Group Planning Department

Universal Banking

The different types of universal banking are discussed in detail in Chapter 1. The Swiss banks probably come closest to the German model, but differ in two important respects. First, large Swiss companies are comparatively few in number and are publicly owned. Their connections with the large banks is close but not as tight or as exclusive as in the German case. Nor do Swiss banks, with the exception of Crédit Suisse, take substantial shareholdings in non-financial firms. Second, domestic corporate banking has not been as important for Swiss banks because, traditionally, most of their business comes from international funds management and overseas lending. For generations, Switzerland has provided a politically stable, neutral, safe, confidential and trustworthy haven for foreign capital. For this reason, foreign funds have flowed into Switzerland in far larger amounts than could reasonably be expected to be invested in the country. Thus, the Swiss became adept at global lending and investing. For example, at the end of 1989, foreign assets represented 29% of total assets of Swiss banks, compared to 16% for German banks, 12.8% for Japanese banks, and 10% for American banks.

Traditionally, banking in Switzerland has been quite profitable for the universals. Profits are derived from roughly three equal parts: interest income, commissions from managed funds, and trading, custody and other fee-based income. About 64% of total income comes from non-interest sources. In 1992, it was estimated that about half the total profits for Swiss universal banks came from domestic business, the other half from private banking and funds management. Virtually nothing came from foreign business—the banks' extensive international lending and capital markets activities have operated on average, on a break-even business.

Switzerland also boasts a growing domestic capital market, which is used by Swiss and non-Swiss participants alike. Bonds denominated in Swiss francs are periodically issued by Japanese, US, and European companies in the domestic market, Swiss francs being the only major currency in which no Eurobonds are issued. With Swiss franc denominated issues confined to the domestic market, the major banks, for many years, operated an effective cartel arrangement on bond distribution, which limited competition and kept profits unusually high until the Swiss National Bank, to promote greater competition, deregulated underwriting practices during the late 1980s.

In early 1990, Swiss stock exchange commissions became negotiable. The electronic Swiss Options and Financial Futures Exchange (SOFFEX) was successfully launched in 1989. Switzerland also hopes to be able to consolidate   a national stock market from the fragmented regional exchanges that have traditionally existed. A further objective is to use the highly efficient domestic securities clearance and settlement system (SEGA) to develop an international central securities depository (ICSD) called Intersettle, to compete with the established ICSDs, Euroclear and Cedel, assuming the big Swiss banks support this effort by re-routing cross-border bond and equity issues through Intersettle.

Problem Areas Facing Swiss Banks

The Swiss banking sector appears to be facing challenges from a number of quarters—these could lead to far-reaching structural changes.

Swiss mortgage loans and funding
All the major Swiss banks have large exposures to mortgage loans. SU's mortgage loans made up about 40% of total loans in 1992. The ratios for other large Swiss banks ranged from 32% to 56%. In the past, mortgages have been funded by savings accounts and personal accounts. The balance was made up from capital market issues.

During the 1980s, Swiss savers gradually shifted into higher-yielding time deposits, so that by 1991, only 48% of mortgages were funded by savings and personal accounts. As a result, an increasing amount of short-term time deposits were sold by the banks to fund the mortgage portfolio. One estimate was that 21% to 34% of the mortgages of the big three banks were financed short-term. However, as short-term interest rates doubled between 1988 and 1990, the cost of funding the mortgage portfolios increased dramatically, exceeding the interest income from fixed rate mortgages.

Though the banks made some effort to adjust new mortgage rates to funding rates, mismatched mortgage funding accounted for a substantial erosion of interest income to the big Swiss banks from 1988 to 1992. This erosion largely explains the decline in the compound annual growth rate of net interest income at the three largest Swiss banks, from 12% during 1981–86, to 7% during 1987–91.

Sharp increase in loan loss provisions
Adverse economic conditions in Switzerland and other parts of the world increased the loan loss exposures of the major Swiss banks over the period 1987–92. Approximately 64% of the bad debt charges for the three largest Swiss banks were for Swiss loans, most of them property related. The economists at SU Bank expected a significant amount of provisioning to continue through 1993 and 1994.

International mishaps and bad investments
During the five years to 1992, the three largest Swiss banks (Crédit Suisse, Swiss Bank Corporation and Union Bank of Switzerland) booked substantial losses from bad investments, trading errors or mistakes related to international capital market activity, some of which were not only costly but embarrassing. The Union Bank of Switzerland reported unusual foreign exchange losses and was forced to write off much of its investment in the UK broker Phillips and Drew. Phillips and Drew was also involved in the Blue Arrow case in London, which led to criminal proceedings involving the market equity of a new issue (see Chapter 6 for a complete account of the affair). The Swiss Bank Corporation had to write off most of its investment in another UK broker, Savory Milln, and a French bank, Banque Stern. It also experienced large losses on loans to Robert Maxwell and a German retailing company, Co-Op, with disastrous underwritings of common stock issue for British Petroleum and Co-Op. Crédit Suisse had to bail out a US investment bank, First Boston, which lost hundreds of millions of dollars on bridge loans to leveraged buy-out companies. First Boston ultimately had to be acquired and

recapitalised by Crédit Suisse in order to save it. Both Crédit Suisse and Swiss Bank Corporation sustained losses in the Werner K. Rey affair.

Increasing importance of highly volatile trading income
The large banks have always been major market makers in Switzerland for foreign exchange, metals, and Swiss bonds and notes. However, these activities have declined to half the total trading activities as market-making requirements and exposures in key financial centres such as London, Tokyo, and New York and Chicago have increased sharply from the late 1980s onward. Trading income amounted to about 29% of total income for the largest three Swiss banks in 1992. Many of the new instruments, such as first and second generation derivatives, were also introduced, but most Swiss banks were unprepared. Swiss Bank Corporation addressed the problem through the acquisition of the Chicago derivatives firm, O'Connor and Partners. But none of the large Swiss banks was especially effective in market-making activities outside of the Swiss markets.

Wide-ranging deregulation
Swiss banks, in common with their counterparts throughout the world, have had to confront the effects of changes in regulations. The changes include:

- *Domestic deregulation*: bank cartel agreements were abolished and there were pressures for convergence and equal treatment with the EU, the US, and Japan. The result was increased competition in the wholesale markets.
- *Changes in bank secrecy rules*: Swiss bank secrecy laws and blocking statutes helped to build up enormous accumulations of foreign assets that are managed in Switzerland. Private banking in Switzerland is centred on 22 smaller, older, and usually privately owned institutions in Geneva, Lugano, and Zurich, running a specialised business of managing investments for overseas clients. Quiet, discreet, and efficient, these banks are attempting to add institutional clients to their lists by offering global Swiss investment management skills to predominantly domestically orientated pension funds and other institutional investors in the USA, Japan, and Europe.

External private assets handled by Swiss banks were estimated in 1992 at approximately $1.5 trillion, of which half are thought to be managed by the three large banks. These large sums available for fund management have given the Swiss banks significant placing power with which to compete in the global new issues markets.

However, concerns have been expressed about the likelihood of the erosion of bank secrecy laws in Switzerland after a new law was introduced to discourage the use of Switzerland for money laundering. But the new law is directed at criminal abuse, and should not threaten the principle of bank secrecy.

In common with other financial centres, Switzerland has experienced problems with insider dealing, and has served as a haven for profits from such transactions undertaken elsewhere. To align itself with evolving international standards of conduct, and to compete effectively as a financial centre, Switzerland has imposed measures to combat insider dealing, impose criminal penalties, and introduce effective enforcement of these laws. The action in question must be illegal under Swiss law, and complete privacy is guaranteed if the offence is civil but not criminal. Tax evasion is not a criminal offence under Swiss law, though tax fraud is. Swiss bankers have a greater responsibility to show due diligence and know their client.

The funds under Swiss bank management are very large, the service reliable and efficient, and secrecy still assured with regard to tax matters and capital flight. The foreign clients are unlikely to move banks, because the money held by these banks is considered to be safe from taxation, seizure, or corruption. No other international centre can offer these features. The Gulf War, the unification of Germany, the disintegration of the Soviet Union and the economic reforms in Eastern Europe have all triggered flows of new funds into Switzerland.

BIS and EU capital adequacy rules
Compliance with BIS and EU rules is easy for Swiss banks because Swiss domestic capital adequacy rules are more stringent. However, there is cause for concern over the introduction of capital adequacy rules that cover positioning (as opposed to credit) risks and derivatives exposures. Swiss banks are also worried by the increasing popularity of mark to market accounting by banks.

Swiss bank holding company structure
Although Swiss universal banks are permitted to own non-banking affiliates, the Union Bank of Switzerland and Swiss Bank Corporation have stuck closely to bank related activities. Crédit Suisse has drifted into some other businesses, and formed a holding company to separate its various banking and non-anking activities, called CS Holding. Its investments are separately incorporated in a bank (Crédit Suisse); and Investment Bank (CS First Boston), a private bank (Leu Holdings Ltd), a 45% investment in a major Swiss electric power company (Electrowatt AG), and a life insurance affiliate (CS Life). In 1993, Swiss Volksbank, the fourth largest bank, suffering from poor results and a weak capital position, was acquired by Crédit Suisse Holding, making CS Holding the largest bank in Switzerland. There was some concern that the deal was not a very good one for CS shareholders, unless management could force through a massive cost cutting and staff reduction exercise.

CS Holding organised itself in this way to exclude non-banking investments from the capital adequacy requirements of Swiss banking laws. But the Swiss Banking Commission (the federal banking regulator) rejected the concept and was supported by the Swiss Federal Court, which ruled that under the law governing universal banks, all the holding company entities had to be considered part of the bank. Thus, CS Holding assets must be covered by bank capital requirements. The bank found it had to raise new capital to finance losses at First Boston in 1990.

Transparency of accounting statements and convergence with international standards

A new law has been passed to compel companies to adopt a transparent financial accounting and reporting system. A pending stock exchange law could make it necessary for listed companies to maintain a true and fair view of accounting to remain listed on the exchange—this is likely to become the norm for Swiss corporations, through market pressure.

Relations with the EU

In December 1992 the Swiss voted, by a large majority, against Switzerland's alignment, as a European Free Trade Area (EFTA) country, to the EU through the European Economic Association (EEA). But there is little doubt that some form of association with the EU will come about. Some Swiss bank analysts have expressed concerns that this could increase competition in the Swiss domestic banking market, though banking in Switzerland has already been open to foreigners for many years. Additionally, banks trying to penetrate retail markets in foreign countries have not been very successful. Furthermore, the rejection of the EEA could help the Swiss banks to maintain a competitive advantage in private banking.

Domestic competitive structure

All of these pressures on the Swiss banking industry are set against an "overbanked" domestic financial system. The industry appears to be ripe for a major shake-out and consolidation, especially among the regional and cantonal banks, as well as the private banks, which have found it difficult to contain costs or to benefit from economies of scale and scope. More than 70 bank acquisitions occurred between 1975 and 1992—a third of these involved smaller banks being absorbed by larger Swiss universal, cantonal, or regional banks. By the end of 1991, there were still some 457 banks in Switzerland, with a total of 4191 branches. Population per branch and per bank employee were 1300 and 67, respectively, in 1991, compared with 2283 and 102, respectively, in the UK. Some experts have suggested that the number of surviving banks will fall to around 200 within a decade, depending on the degree to which the cantons* are prepared to subsidise their banks to keep them "independent".

Though there is no regulation of lending or deposit rates and no branching restrictions, there are stamp duties and a 35% withholding tax on interest income. These taxes have discouraged the development of a domestic money market, a Eurobond market and market making activities.

---

*In addition to the four large universal banks (Credit Suisse, Swiss Bank Corporation, and Union Bank of Switzerland plus Swiss Volksbank), there are 29 cantonal banks, owned and guaranteed by various cantons, and usually limited to their region by statute. They are an important part of the domestic retail market. In addition, there are many small regional and savings banks. The private banks make up another important group in the Swiss banking system—most of their business comes from foreign clients.

The prospect of a more competitive environment at home and abroad has caused some analysts to suggest that the Swiss banking industry has been somewhat destabilised by these events. Crédit Suisse was downgraded by Moody's from AAA to AA-1 in January 1992; and again after the acquisition of Swiss Volksbank. The same fate befell Swiss Bank Corporation and, a few months later, Crédit Suisse was downgraded again. Only Union Bank of Switzerland remained AAA rated by both Moody's and Standard and Poor's, along with Deutsche Bank, Morgan Guaranty Trust Company, and Rabobank of the Netherlands. These downgradings suggest that the perception of Swiss banks changed from extraordinary to ordinary in the world of global banking and finance.

Schweizer Universalbank, like UBS, has been able to avoid the various problems encountered by Crédit Suisse and Swiss Bank Corporation. Also, it is unlikely the Swiss authorities would allow the reputation of the Swiss banks for safety, quality and stability among international investors, to be eroded, because it is such an important source of export revenue.

Dr Baltenswiler planned to conclude his presentation with several sharply focused questions to be discussed over the Klauser weekend, after the report had been presented. The questions were:

1. Do the assumptions made about domestic and international market environments in March 1990, which formed the basis for Plan 2001, still apply?
2. Are the strategic moves identified in 1990 the right ones? What unexpected competitive elements could impede the bank in the pursuit of these goals?
3. Is SU capable of implementing these strategic moves in the way that was originally envisaged?
4. Is the traditional universal bank organisational structure the most appropriate one for the competitive environment that lies ahead?
5. On balance, should SU make the adaptions and necessary adjustments to pursue the original goals, as laid out in Plan 2001, or should these goals be changed, along with the bank's operating policies, to reflect a better understanding of market realities?

Questions for Schweizer Universalbank Case Study

1. In Plan 2001, the joint objectives of increasing market share and profitability are to be applied in SU's Swiss domestic banking, private banking, and international banking divisions.
   (a) Under what conditions are these two objectives compatible?
   (b) Can these objectives be achieved in each of the three sections of SU?
   (c) Is increasing market share in the private banking business a sound objective?
   (d) Is the bank correct in not being concerned about balance sheet size, and instead focusing on reputation, profitability, and quality?
   (e) Is concern about the bank's domestic banking business unwarranted?

2. How does the Swiss universal banking model differ from universal banking in:
   (a) Japan?
   (b) the USA?
   (c) the UK?
   (d) France?
3. Is it possible for SU to alter the type of universal banking model to which it conforms, even if it decided it was in the bank's best interest so to do?
4. The Swiss Banking Commission has required bank holding companies to provide capital to cover all their subsidiaries, even those not related to banking. Discuss the pros and cons of this regulation.
5. Why is the supervisory board of SU concerned about foreigners holding registered shares? Is the concern warranted?
6. Why did Moody's and Standard and Poor's downgrade Swiss Banking Corporation and Crédit Suisse? How can SU avoid the same fate?
7. Discuss the extent to which SU's Plan 2001 strategy conforms to the following models, described in Chapter 8 of the text:
   (a) de Carmoy;
   (b) Kay;
   (c) Kenyon and Mathur.
8. Should Plan 2001 be abandoned?

10 BANKERS TRUST*

Relevant parts of text: Chapters 5 and 8.

By the end of 1987, when Mr Alfred Britain III retired after 12 years as CEO of Bankers Trust, his successor, Mr Charles S. Sanford Jr, believed, based on results, that the bank had fully completed the transition from a money centre commercial bank to a global wholesale financial services company, able to compete with the best of the international merchant and investment banks. The stock yielded a 41% return on equity before extraordinary allowance for credit losses, up from 34% in 1984, which, at the time, was already the highest of all money centre banks.

In the late 1980s, media and analyst attention was fixed on BT's remarkable performance, focusing on how a mediocre money centre bank could transgress commercial banking standards to earn such extraordinary returns. Most of the financial press and Wall Street believed that BT had done a wonderful thing. To cite a few examples:

---

*This case first appeared in the New York University Salomon Center Case Series in Banking and Finance (Case 07). Written by Anthony Sinclair, Roy Smith, and Ingo Walter (1991). The case was edited and updated by Shelagh Heffernan; questions set by Shelagh Heffernan.

- Salomon Brothers characterised BT as the most sophisticated US merchant bank, claiming the bank "epitomizes the dedication to merchant banking that its peers and competitors will have to strive to attain".
- An analyst at Kidder Peabody proclaimed: "Bankers Trust is positioning itself to be a true investment bank."
- The *United States Banker*: "Bankers Trust Co has one of the most clear cut images in banking—a big time, self-created international merchant bank, financier of leveraged buy-outs, underwriter of corporate bonds, invader of Wall St turf."
- The *Financial Times* described BT as "a concern which uniquely straddles commercial and investment banking."

These remarks were consistent with Mr Sanford's beliefs. But like any other successful institution, BT was not without its critics. BT's reputation for being one of the most aggressive financiers of leveraged deals (about $3 billion in LBO debt), and having a substantial portfolio of real estate and LDC loans triggered many arguments that its real credit exposure had been masked by exceptional, yet possibly tenuous trading profits. Some of this cynicism was related to actions taken in the second quarter of 1987 when, in line with other New York banks that wrote their Latin American exposure down to 75% of book, BT increased its allowance for credit losses by $700 million. However, it still earned an overall profit, because of trading.

The critic's fears were heightened in 1987, following an earnings announcement, when BT's stock dropped $1.25 to close at $30.00 on the NYSE. Concerns were again raised in 1989, when profits of 1988 were overshadowed by a $980 million loss, resulting from an additional $1.6 billion provision against third world debt and $150 million charge for bad credits. But based on 1989 earnings, and its competitive bearing in investment banking, some critics contended that BT had made insignificant progress since 1984 on its declared road to becoming a global merchant bank.

There is little doubt that BT had established itself as a visionary in the field of banking, but its aggressiveness in volatile high margin businesses, coupled with its decentralised structure, left BT vulnerable. Notwithstanding the protests of BT's management, who insisted they "never bet the bank", not all observers believed the BT strategy had maximised shareholder value added. Thus, the jury was still out on whether BT had achieved its goal of becoming a global merchant bank. It would be important to observe BT's performance when the chips were down: it had not yet been tested in a recession.

The Evolution of Bankers Trust

In the late 1970s, BT was a typical money centre bank, strapped with credit losses arising from recession and the Real Estate Investment Trust crisis. It continued to operate a progressive retail and commercial domestic banking business, with an international focus. But capital requirements, together with provisioning for bad debt, meant the bank would be constrained in any attempt to operate in all markets. BT emerged from the 1970s wounded but still viable, and this position had a profound effect on its strategic focus. BT was placed fifth in the New York market. It had a 200-plus retail bank network, but it was widely accepted that to remain competitive over the next decade, BT would require a substantial investment in new technology, such as ATMs and information systems, and human resources. On the other hand, a retail banking network would be a source of low-cost funding for the bank though Regulation Q and other ceilings on deposits rates were being lifted. For these reasons, BT decided to focus on wholesale and corporate banking.

To disengage from retail banking, between 1980 and 1984, BT sold off its metropolitan retail branches, its credit card business, and four upstate New York commercial banking subsidiaries. These operations represented $1.8 billion in assets and were profitable at the time they were sold. BT earned $155.3 million, which it invested in its merchant banking business.

BT was reorganised around four core businesses:

- commercial banking;
- corporate finance;
- trust services;
- resource management.

Each of these new business was headed by an executive vice-president, who reported to a new "Office of the Chairman", shared by Mr Sanford (president), Mr Al Brittain (chairman), and Mr Carl Mueller (vice-chairman). BT itself was divided into two principal units, Financial Services and ProfitCo (see below).

The shift from money centre commercial banking to international merchant banking prompted changes in the way BT approached its business, especially in terms of management of the balance sheet, funding, costs, and investment philosophy.

In the middle was the merchant bank—its balance sheet relationship is shared with commercial banking, but whose origination and distribution functions are more common to investment banking. The model adopted by BT was to combine deposit-taking and lending functions and the broad relationship list of a commercial bank with the origination and distribution functions of an investment bank.

BT implemented several changes to achieve this objective.

- Marketing efforts were targeted at the institutional sector, redirecting resources to large and middle market corporations, financial institutions, and governments.
- BT initiated an aggressive commercial origination and loan-sale programme to control balance sheet growth, emphasise fee-driven business, and to distribute risk.
- An investment banking emphasis was placed on corporate finance activities.

- A target of 20% return on equity was established as a benchmark to monitor corporate performance and measure risk-adjusted return in all business segments.
- A new incentive compensation scheme was developed to motivate employees to seek out new businesses and profit opportunities in line with corporate goals.
- Organisational changes relating to client and inter-departmental relationships, risk-taking, management hierarchy, and business development were implemented.

The Organisational Framework

In 1984, BT was divided into two main units—Financial Services and ProfitCo.

Financial Services

The merchant bank, with about 5500 employees was headed by Mr Ralph MacDonald. It consisted mainly of three functional units:

- Corporate Finance: headed by Mr David Beim, it provided merchant banking services to clients in the USA and western Europe.
- Emerging Markets: headed by Mr George Vojta, it provided merchant banking services in Latin America, Eastern Europe, Africa, and the Middle East.
- Global Markets: headed by Mr Eugene Shanks, it had worldwide responsibility for capital market based businesses and products. Securities dealing, foreign exchange, interest rate protection, and similar areas all came under Global Markets, as did merchant banking in Asia/Pacific and Canadian markets.

Some interdisciplinary functions, such as loan distribution, reported jointly to Corporate Finance and Global Markets. Financial services did not handle either deposits or operating services, which were dealt with by ProfitCo.

Another 1000 staff were attached to the corporate staff; 3000 employees were based outside the US. The corporate level was responsible for:

- treasury: BT's own funding and risk management;
- credit policy: controlled credit risk in all business lines, and provided some administrative support activities.

ProfitCo

ProfitCo offered transaction processing, fiduciary and securities services, investment management and private banking. About half of BT's staff (6500) worked for ProfitCo.

BT's Fiduciary Services Department was reorganised into ProfitCo in 1984, as part of BT's decentralisation plan. Staff functions were shifted to line functions, with responsibility for earning profit. This elicited a process which effectively created many separate and divisible business segments; for each segment, it was possible to measure profitability against some external measure. It was believed this "profit centre" approach would improve the competitiveness of the service business by allowing BT to attract and motivate high-quality personnel. The entrepreneurial structure was suppose to encourage staff to achieve management responsibility, though it did put pressure on line management personnel to support their existence.

ProfitCo consisted of four departments.

FastCo

FastCo offered institutional fiduciary and securities servicing to both domestic and overseas clients. Within FastCo, there existed several groups which engaged in traditional trust business:

- Investment Management Group: managed several billion dollars in pension, thrift, and employee-benefit plan assets. It ranked as one of the top US firms in custody and clearing.
- Employee Benefit Group: the largest provider of non-investment services, such as administrative and record-keeping services for pension and employee benefit plans.
- The Trust and Agency Group: served as a trustee for public bond issues, and offered other services. Operation of the Securities Processing Group was a marked departure from customary trust activities.

Investment management

This department was concerned with institutional money management, especially in the passive investment area. There was a considerable advantage for clients in having both corporate trust and investment management centralised with the same provider. It made BT one of the largest US institutional money managers.

Private banking

This department targeted high net worth individuals, offering traditional trust services and other commercial banking services. The objective was to offer banking services to upscale customers, cross-marketing a range of fiduciary, banking, and investment services. It had a strong service orientation, and offered high-quality investment-related products. It had six New York City branches, one upstate New York branch, and one branch in Florida.

Global Operations and Information Services (GOIS)

GOIS offered funds transfer, cash management, trade payments and related informational services to worldwide institutional clients. It was extensively involved in dollar-related clearing services, and in trade-related and securities-related payments. As part of its strategy to encourage entrepreneurship, GOIS was treated as a separate business with a separate sales force, product management capabilities, and guidelines for profit. GOIS effectively centralised BT's transactions processing, and was kept separate from the commercial banking function.

Each business within ProfitCo was characterised by a strong level of recurring income. They were similarly organised with a sales/relationship manager, product managers who were involved in marketing, and an attendant product delivery function. The banking segment was a good source of business—products and services were cross-marketed to institutions and clients who were being serviced by other parts of BT.

Though each business was operated independently within BT, ProfitCo operated the bank's back office systems, especially global market activities. ProfitCo provided the data centre for most of BT's business segments.

Bankers Trust Activities

Resource Management (RMD)

Located on Wall Street, RMD can be traced back to 1919, when BT was successful in the bond business. The Glass-Steagall Act largely put an end to BT's underwriting business. The bank was limited to underwriting and dealing in US government securities and general obligation bonds issued by state and local governments.

BT continued to underwrite allowable securities and manage its own portfolio of government securities. The portfolio of government securities had made up a large part of BT's asset base, and was a major source of liquidity. However, in the 1960s, BT, like many commercial banks, began to rely on short-term borrowed funds such as negotiable CDs, bankers acceptances, and commercial paper as a source of funds and liquidity.

Short-term funding was handled within the global markets group. The corporate treasurer managed aggregated risks involving both interest-rate sensitivity and liquidity on a global basis. Capital budgeting decisions were reviewed at the highest level and ALM conducted on an aggregate basis, bringing people from each business segment together to communicate actual and prospective trends in the corporate risk profile. Often, however, the aggregate risk profile was very different from the individual parts because some risk was diversified away through position taking within each business. The emphasis was on slow balance sheet growth, encouraging an integrated approach to balance sheet funding.

Preceding organisational changes within the fiduciary function, RMD was preparing to compete with investment banking firms for both business (trading securities and underwriting) and people. Mr Charlie Sanford was placed in charge of the Department and created a plan to compete on a par with investment banking firms. Traders and other professionals were hired and by 1980, Mr Sanford believed he had a top-rated trading capacity.

Trading

Proprietary trading was the key capital market activity which helped BT sustain a record of positive profits for nearly two decades without a single quarterly loss in the foreign exchange or securities trading markets. By the end of the 1980s, management estimated that 60% of the bank's assets were liquid. The objective was to raise that figure to 80%.

Proprietary trading, and trading on behalf of BT customers, added a new dimension to the challenge facing management regarding long-term profitability and success. Consistent with its organisational layout, the trading function was operated very much like a business. Each trading division was structured to promote profitable activities and was supported by sophisticated information systems, large geographically dispersed staffs, and an emphasis on communication.

Management believed constant communication provided the opportunity for new avenues of profit, with risk diversification the underlying objective. Additionally, the goal of consistent profitability was to generate asymmetric profit and losses. The management directive was twofold: (i) losses should be taken early—as soon as they were evident and (ii) when gains were made, they should be protected.

At the same time, management gave traders who proved themselves full rein to play their positions. In theory, no trader could commit more than a predetermined level of capital, but once that capital was earned back, the trader could play his/her position to amounts limited by accumulated profits. This meant there were single positions which exceeded a billion dollars. BT's reputation for taking the right positions encouraged herd instinct behaviour: traders at rival firms would take the same positions, which would magnify the extent BT moved the market.

Commercial paper

Mr Sanford believed part of the BT strategy should be to offer a wide range of institutional financial services on a global basis. The execution of this strategy involved BT's participation in the domestic commercial paper market, an area normally reserved for investment banks. In 1978, BT began to act as an agent for corporations issuing commercial paper, thereby challenging Glass-Steagall—it convinced the Federal Reserve that commercial paper was a short-term loan, not a security.

Derivatives and risk management

In 1978, BT improved on its internal risk management by establishing the BT Futures Corporation. It operated on the emerging futures and options markets, to provide innovative hedging programmes to customers. It was the second subsidiary of a US banking company to receive full certification as a futures commission merchant.

Mr Sanford introduced *RAROC*, or *risk-adjusted return on capital*, defined as total risk-adjusted returns divided by total capital, a risk measurement system. The idea was to have a common measure of risk for all BT operations, thereby ensuring an efficient allocation of capital. A risk factor was assigned to each category of assets based on the volatility of the asset's market price. For example, a CD trader who ended the day with a long position in 60-day paper would be assigned a risk-adjusted amount of capital based on the risk factor for this maturity.

Performance was assessed by dividing the trader's profit by the amount of capital allocated. An example of the distribution of capital appears below.

Division	Amount (millions of US $)	% of total
Global markets (credit)	$211	4.9
Global markets (market)	$206	4.8
Other (credit)	$2811	65.3
Other (non-credit)	$1080	24.1

Source: Salomon Brothers, as cited in Sinclair, Smith and Walter (1991).

In addition to being the centre of a framework for risk management, RAROC is also used for:

- performance measurement: to allow comparison of the performance of different parts of the BT business;
- Portfolio management for determining areas that appeared most appropriate for investment or divestment.

Corporate finance

BT had shifted its focus to wholesale corporate banking and the institutional market, and needed to develop a competitive corporate finance capability that would make up the core of the merchant bank. The corporate finance department's reorganisation began in 1977. Two individuals with extensive Wall Street experience were hired, Mr Carl Mueller and Mr David Beim.

The Corporate Finance division had five lines of business.

- The Capital Market Group: this acted as financial advisor or agent for corporations in the private placement of their securities with insurance companies, pension funds, and other financial institutions. The group was strongly affiliated with Global Markets and BT's London merchant bank, Bankers Trust International. It maintained a role in Eurosecurities offerings and dealt extensively with interest rate and currency swaps.
- The Lease Financing Group arranged large leases, and placing the assets with other institutions and within BT. It served as an advisor to the lessor and/or lessee in transactions.
- The Venture Capital Group: this group made equity and other investments for the holding company (Bankers Trust New York Corporation). Most of the transactions were part of the leveraged buy-outs and expansion financing, rather than *de novo* financing of companies. BT developed a special product niche in structuring leveraged buy-outs.

- The Public Finance Group: this group acts as a financial advisor, underwriter, or sales agent of tax-exempt financing for public and corporate issuers.
- Loan Sales: BT began a large-scale loan programme, believed to be essential to achieve the goal of stabilising balance sheet growth, maintaining high liquidity levels, and ensuring a superior return on equity.

In 1984, as part of its merchant banking strategy, BT expanded its loan sales programme. The bank believed that in some cases, it could achieve higher returns by originating and selling loans, rather than holding them on its own books. In addition, the ability to originate and sell large loans allowed the bank to provide more services to major corporations. The timing of this effort was coincidental with BT's emphasis on the build up of mergers and acquisitions advisory capacity, which in turn related very well to the growing LBO phenomenon.

Mr Beim followed an employment policy of hiring the best and paying accordingly. Traditional domestic corporate lending was de-emphasised in favour of initiating and completing highly leveraged deals and other specialised lending operations.

By early 1985, BT had placed several groups of asset product managers and sales officers in New York, Tokyo, London and Hong Kong. The asset product management group worked with account officers to design the loan sale structure and related documentation. Most of the business was directed at large companies seeking substantial funding and broad access to the financial markets. The group could recommend financing programmes to improve market access of such companies. Corporate finance product specialists might also be involved, so the bank provides credit knowledge, technical advice, and sales knowledge when working with customers.

Sales officers targeted investors as potential purchasers of the loans, and kept in close contact with them. Loans were sold to foreign banks, pension funds, and insurance firms. Sales officers would have to spend weeks educating potential investors. The whole process ensured that a high proportion of the BT loan portfolio was in liquid form.

The "tactical asset and liability committee" was BT's policy-making body for loan sales. It met on a weekly basis to decide on the quarterly pricing of loan sales. The Committee focused on credit risk, market conditions, and liquidity needs; it also sought out new opportunities for the loan origination function.

Credit Policy

In line with the greater emphasis on merchant banking and the loan sale programme, credit management procedures at BT were also tightened. The old credit review system had required loan approval by at least two account officers. The new process required at least one signature to be from a credit officer. Thus, credit officers became lending officers.

Line management was responsible for the credit approval process. Each department had to write a credit policy statement and specify lending authority for its line and credit officers. For example, division managers would be given a credit approval limit. Loan amounts within this limit can be approved with the signature of an account officer and the division manager. Larger loans would require the signature of the group credit head and the loan officer. Loans larger than the group head's credit limit would go to the department credit officer.

Loans in excess of $200 million required the signature of the department head or the chief credit officer.

Using RAROC, management could assess the amount of credit risk embedded in all areas of the bank. Risks were placed into 60 industry categories, which were graded according to expected performance. The ranking was based on variables such as technical change, regulatory issues, capacity constraints, business cycle sensitivity, ability to protect pricing and margins, and structural stress. These variables were considered important because of their effect on growth and cash flow variability over both near and intermediate term horizons.

Global Markets

Global Markets were considered to be of increasing importance. For example, foreign exchange facilities were expanded to provide 24 hour market-making capacity with 10 geographic locations. The bank was actively involved in the global syndicated loan Euronote market and equity-linked derivatives.

Global Markets was a functional division under the Financial Services side of BT. It had seven divisions. Half dealt with market-related activities, such as short-term funding and foreign exchange). The rest were concerned with financing activities, such as public fixed income markets, private placements, commodities, short-term and variable rate finance, and multiple currency derivatives. The objective was to assist clients in the management of their own risk positions and to establish product areas whose profitability was uncorrelated, to achieve a natural diversification and sustain profitability, no matter what the market situation.

The seven divisions had 60 profit centres, globally organised across time zones, which helped interaction. Customer, product, and geographic variables were connected through a process of synergy. Employees of Global Markets numbered about 2200 and made up about 20% of the BT payroll. They were located in seven countries and 10 cities, including all the major world financial centres.

The nature of the divisional organisation emphasised a global product focus across time zones, at the expense of a more client-oriented regional focus. The system did appeal to large corporate clients who need to structure multi-market financing for a cross-border acquisition. However, the organisational structure would discourage the development of local client relationships—BT acknowledged that the local clients had to be sold the approach by being shown the superiority of the product. There was an ongoing debate about whether the lack of strong client relationships would undermine the attempt to establish a leadership position BT had in financial engineering, deal making and trading.

BT had very little in the way of a distribution and sales network typical of most Euromarkets and Wall Street houses. To maintain a competitive edge, BT had to focus on financial engineering or structured finance, inventing complex and often lucrative products for specific clients. BT normally relied upon other firms to provide the distribution and sales functions it needed.

Management Style

The organisational changes at BT were designed to promote cooperation among BT business units, so as to provide a high quality, innovative service to its clients. For this reason, it moved from a hierarchical structure typical of a commercial bank to the horizontal structure of most investment banks. However, there was hostility to the change among long-time BT employees, who were concerned with the stress on entrepreneurial initiative.

BT modified relationship banking by requiring staff to delve into product specialities and relate these to business lines required by each customer. Staff moved between the main centres loosely assigned to institutional clients, encouraging, it was hoped, organisational agility and fostering innovation. It was also hoped that the high staff mobility would encourage innovation and creativity, and sustain enough flexibility in the organisation to allow BT to take advantage of new market opportunities immediately, whether this was in the form of a long-term relationship or a one-off profit-making opportunity. Though all staff were encouraged to foster relationships with clients, they were also advised to look for opportunities to assist with an individual transaction.

Thus, the BT banking style differed from that of investment banks, where employees were rigidly assigned to either corporate or institutional customers, and from commercial banking, which tended to rely on "hands off" relationships to generate spread income.

To attract the top people into the organisation, BT dispensed with the standard commercial bank compensation scheme. Incentive compensation was introduced in the resource management department (RMD), then extended to other parts of BT. Traders were paid according to their performance, as measured by a high risk-adjusted rate of return on capital, as opposed to limits. The top performers received bonuses of 100% or more. In the Corporate Finance Department, BT also linked compensation to performance, but, unlike RMD, bonuses were based both on the profitability of a new business and the degree to which the officer cooperated with others in the organisation to foster "excellence through common purpose". For example, in commercial banking, bonuses could now exceed 100% of salary (compared to a previous limit of 50%).

The size of the bonus pool was a function of a department's profitability, but, in addition, these bonuses depended on total profits generated throughout BT.

Bankers Trust, 1993–95

In 1993, net profits at BT were $1.07 billion, $596 million of which came from proprietary trading. At the time, the bank congratulated itself for being a model modern investment bank with a performance-driven culture and innovative trading strategies which used derivatives to manage risk.

In April 1994 two of its customers, Procter and Gamble and Gibson Greetings, attacked the bank for selling them high-risk leveraged derivatives, which by their vary nature, can cause profits or losses to undergo sharp changes. The details of the complaint are covered in Chapter 5. The P and G case remains in the courts, but the greeting card company settled out of court in January 1995, after tape recordings showed that a managing director of the bank had misled Gibsons about the size of its losses. BT had to pay a $10 million fine to the Federal Reserve Bank of New York, and agreed to permit the regulator to closely supervise its leveraged derivatives business. BT itself sacked one manager, reorganised the leveraged derivatives unit and reassigned staff to other jobs.

However, from April 1994 up to the time of writing, BT has suffered from a tarnished reputation, with a sudden collapse in the demand for its highly profitable, most sophisticated derivatives products. At the end of 1994, BT had made a $423 million provision for derivatives contracts that might prove unenforceable; $72 million was written off immediately. There has also been a steep decline in profits from proprietary trading. For 1994, BT's net profit was $615 million.

To avoid future law suits, BT is sending product contracts to several members of a client firm, not just the finance officers. In February 1995, a senior committee was formed to look at ways of improving BT customer relations, including compensation schemes will emphasise the importance of teamwork and longer-term client relationships, not just high sales. New information systems will also be introduced. In May 1995, Mr Sanford announced his resignation as chairman, effective in 1996.

Questions for Bankers Trust Case Study

1. In the USA, what is the difference between a money centre commercial bank and a global investment bank or global wholesale financial services company?
2. In the context of this case, explain:
   (a) The traditional difference between merchant and investment banking. Is there any difference in the 1990s?
   (b) The meaning of "the broad relationship list of a commercial bank".
   (c) Corporate finance activities as the main focus of attention among BT's investment banking activities.
   (d) The meaning of the initiation of a large-scale loan sale programme to control and stabilise balance sheet growth.
   (e) Regulation Q.

(f) Why "herd instinct" behaviour tends to be prevalent in financial markets.

3. In the first paragraph of the case, it was noted that in 1987 "the stock yielded a 41% return on equity before extraordinary allowance for credit losses . . ."

   (a) Do you agree with the statement that this figure is an indication of the success of the new strategy at Bankers Trust?

   (b) Identify other ways of measuring the success (or otherwise) of this bank.

4. What is the difference between a staff function and line function in an organisation? Use the case to provide an example of where BT changed the typical organisational structure to suit its strategy.

5. The case revealed, either directly or indirectly, the multifaceted nature of BT's strategy. Answer the following questions:

   (a) Why was one of the objectives of BT to make 80% of its assets liquid?

   (b) Why did BT sell its retail banking network? Given that retail banking was one of the most profitable areas of banking in the 1980s, do you think it was the right decision?

   (c) Explain the meaning and consequences of a global product focus at the expense of a regional client focus.

   (d) What effect would the absence of a distribution and sales network have on BT operations?

   (e) What is RAROC? Identify the key problem associated with RAROC.

6. To fulfil the objectives of its new strategy, BT had to change its management style and employee compensation. Explain the meaning of the following terms, and discuss how they might encourage BT staff to achieve BT's strategic goals.

   (a) A horizontal management structure, and how it differed from management style at commercial banks.

   (b) "Excellence through common purpose".

   (c) Incentive compensation.

   (d) The bonus system.

7. Identify the key advantages and disadvantages of the BT strategy.

8. As noted in the case, Bankers Trust is faced with a number of lawsuits. Identify the weak points of BT's managerial and organisational structure which left it vulnerable to the problems highlighted in the lawsuits.

9. Where do you see BT in the year 2000?

References and Bibliography

Abassi, B. and Taffler, R.J. (1982), "Country Risk: A Model of Economic Performance Related to Debt Servicing Capacity", The City University Business School, Working Papers Series No.36.

Adams, J.R. (1991), "The Big Fix: Inside the S & L Scandal; How an Unholy Alliance of Politics and Money Destroyed America's Banking System", *Journal of Finance* (March), 457–459.

Aharony, J., A. Saunders, and I. Swary (1985), "The Effects of the International Banking Act on Domestic Bank Profitability and Risk", *Journal of Money Credit and Banking*, 17, 4 (November, part 1), 493–511.

Akerlof, G. (1970), "The Market for 'Lemons'", *Quarterly Journal of Economics*, 84, 3, 488–500.

Akerlof, G. and P. Romer (1993), "Looting: The Economic Underworld of Bankruptcy for Profit", *Brookings Papers on Economic Activity*, 2, 1–73.

Alchian, A. and H. Demsetz (1972), "Production, Information Costs and Economic Organisation", *American Economic Review*, 62, 777–795.

Aliber, A.Z. (ed.) (1989), *Handbook of International Financial Management*, New York: Dow Jones-Irwin Publishers.

Aliber, R.Z. (1984), "International Banking: A Survey" *Journal of Money, Credit, and Banking*, 16, 4, Part 2. (November), 661–695.

Altman, E.I. (1968) "Financial Ratios, Discriminant Analysis, and the Prediction of Corporate Bankruptcy", *Journal of Monetary Finance*, 23, 4, 589–609.

Altman, E.I. (1977), "Predicting Performance in the Savings and Loan Association Industry", *Journal of Economics*, October, 443–466.

Altman, E.I. (1983), *Corporate Financial Distress: A Complete Guide to Predicting Avoiding and Dealing with Bankruptcy*, New York: John Wiley and Sons.

Altunbas, Y. and P. Molyneux (1993), "Scale and Scope Economies in European Banking", University of College of North Wales, Bangor, School of Accounting, Banking, and Economics, and Institute of European Finance, Research Paper No. 93/11.

Anderson, P. (1994), "Economic Growth and Financial Markets", in R. O'Brien (ed.), *Finance and The International Economy*, 7, Oxford: Oxford University Press.

Andrews, D. (1985), *Real Banking Profitability*, London: IBCA.

Ardnt, H.W. (1988), "Comparative Advantage in Trade in Financial Services", *Banca Nationale Del Lavoro*, 164, March, 61–78.

Argy, V. (1987), "International Financial Liberalisation: The Australian and Japanese Experiences Compared", *Bank of Japan Journal of Monetary and Economic Studies*, 5, 1, 105–67.

Arshadi, N. and E.C. Lawrence (1987), "An Empirical Investigation of New Bank Performance", *Journal of Banking & Finance*, 11, 33–48.

Ausubel, L.M. (1991), "The Failure of Competition in the Credit Card Market", *American Economic Review*, 81, 1, March, 50–76.

Avery, R.B. and A.N. Berger (1991), "Risk-based capital and Deposit Insurance Reform", *Journal of Banking and Finance*, 15, 4/5, September, 847–874.

Avery, R.B. and G.A. Hanweck (1984), "A Dynamic Analysis of Bank Failures", in *Bank Structure and Competition Conference Proceedings*, Chicago: Federal Reserve Bank of Chicago.

Baer, H.L. and L.R. Mote (1991), "The United States Financial System" in G.G. Kaufman (ed.) *Banking Structures in Major Countries*, Dordrecht: Kluwer Academic Publishers, 1991.

Balkan, E.M. (1992),"Political Instability, Country Risk, and the Probability of Default", *Applied Economics*, 24, 999–1008.

Baltensperger, E. (1980), "Alternative Approaches to the Theory of the Banking Firm", *Journal of Monetary Economics*, 6, 1–37.

Bank for International Settlements (1990), *The Lamfalussy Report*, Basle: Bank for International Settlements.

Bank for International Settlements (1993), *Payments Systems in the Group of Ten Countries* (Red Book), Basle: BIS.

Bank for International Settlements (1994), *64th Annual Report*, Basle: Bank for International Settlements.

Bank of England (1978), "The Secondary Banking Crisis and the Bank of England Support Operations", *Bank of England Quarterly Bulletin*, 18, 2, June, 230–239.

Bank of England (1980), "Measurement of Capital" *Bank of England Quarterly Bulletin*, Sept., 20, 3, 324–330.

Bank of England (1983), "The International Banking Scene: A Supervisory Perspective", *Bank of England Quarterly Bulletin*, 23, 2, March, 61–65.

Bank of England (1984) "International Debt—Thinking About the Longer Term", *Bank of England Quarterly Bulletin*, March, 24, 51–53.

Bank of England (1984), "The Business of Financial Supervision", *Bank of England Quarterly Bulletin*, March, 24, 46–50.

Bank of England (1985), "Change in the Stock Exchange and Regulation of the City", *Bank of England Quarterly Bulletin*, 25, 4, 544–550.

Bank of England (1985), "Managing Change in International Banking", *Bank of England Quarterly Bulletin*, 25, 4, 551–558.

Bank of England (1986), "Developments in International Banking and Capital Markets", *Bank of England Quarterly Bulletin*, 27, 2, May, 234–236.

Bank of England (1987), "Japanese Banks in London", *Bank of England Quarterly Bulletin*, November, 1987, 518–524.

Bank of England (1987) "Supervision and Central Banking", *Bank of England Quarterly Bulletin*, 27, 3, 380–385.

Bank of England (1987), "The Financial Behaviour of the UK Personal Sector, 1976–1985", *Bank of England Quarterly Bulletin*, 27, 2, May, 223–233.

Bank of England (1988), "International Financial Developments", *Bank of England Quarterly Bulletin*, 28, 4, November, 498–507.

Bank of England (1992), "Financial Regulation, What are We Trying to Do?", *Bank of England Quarterly Bulletin*, 32, 3, August, 322–324.

Bank of England (1992), "Major International Banks' Performance", *Bank of England Quarterly Bulletin*, 32, 3, August, 288–297.

Bank of England (1993), "The Bank of England's Role in Prudential Supervision", *Bank of England Quarterly Bulletin*, 33, 2, May, 260–264.

Bank of England (1993), "The EC Single Market in Financial Services", *Bank of England Quarterly Bulletin*, 3, 1, 92–97.

Bank of England (1994), "The Pursuit of Financial Stability", *Bank of England Quarterly Bulletin*, 34, 1, February, 60–66.

Bank of England (1994), "The Development of a UK Real-Time Gross Settlement System", *Bank of England Quarterly Bulletin*, 34, 2, May, 163–171.

The Banker (July 1987), "Top 100 By Size: Importance of Capital", *The Banker*, 153–172.

The Banker (July 1994), "Top 1000 Banks", *The Banker*, 102–207.

Barina, M. and S. Caretti (1986), Changes in the Degree of Concentration in the Italian Banking System: An International Comparison, *Banca Nazionale Del Lavoro*, November.

Barnes, P. (1987), "The Analysis and Use of Financial Ratios: A Review Article", *Journal of Business Finance and Accounting*, 14, 4, 449–461.

Barth, J.R., R.D. Brumbaugh, D. Sauerhaft, and G.H.K. Wang (1985), "Thrift Institution Failures: Causes and Policy Issues", in *Bank Structure and Competition Conference Proceedings*, Chicago: Federal Reserve Bank of Chicago.

Basle Committee on Banking Supervison (1988), *International Convergence of Capital Measurement and Capital Standards*, Basle.

Basle Committee on Banking Supervision (1993), "The Prudential Supervision of Netting, Market Risks and Interest Rate Risks", (Consultative Proposal by the Basle Committee on Banking Supervision), Basle.

Batchelor, R.A. (1986), "The Avoidance of Catastrophe: Two Nineteenth-century Banking Crises", in F. Capie, and G.E. Wood (eds) *Financial Crises and the World Banking System*, London: Macmillan.

Baxter, W.F., P.H. Cootner, and K.E. Scott (1976), *Retail Banking in the Electronic Age: The Law and Economics of Electronic Funds Transfer*, Montclair: Allenheld, Osmun and Co.

Beaver, W.H. (1966), "Financial Ratios as Predictors of Failure", Empirical Research in Accounting: Selected Studies, Supplement to *Journal of Accounting Research*, 71–111.

Bennett, R. (1993), "The Six Men Who Rule World Derivatives", *Euromoney*, August, 45–49.

Benston, G.J. (1965), "Branch Banking and Economies of Scale", *Journal of Finance*, 20, 312–31.

Benston, G.J. (1985), "An Analysis of the Causes of Savings and Loans Association Failures", *Monograph Series in Finance and Economics*, New York University.

Benston, G.J. (1988), "The Problems of Future Commercial Banks", *Midland Corporate Finance Journal*, 5, 4, Winter, 6–13.

Benston, G.J. (1990), *The Separation of Commercial and Investment Banking, The Glass–Steagall Act Revisited and Reconsidered*, New York: Oxford University Press.

Benston, G.J. (1990), "US Banking in an Increasingly Integrated and Competitive World Economy", *Journal of Financial Services Research*, 4, 311–339.

Benston, G.J. (1992), "International Regulatory Coordination of Banking", in J. Fingleton (ed.), *The Internationalisation of Capital Markets and the Regulatory Response*, London: Graham and Trotman, pp. 197–209.

Bentley, R.J. (1987), "Debt Conversion in Latin America", *Columbia Journal of World Business*, Fall, 37–49.

Berger, A.N. and T.H. Hannan (1989), "The Price–Concentration Relationship in Banking", *Review of Economics and Statistics*, 74 (May), 291–299: also, their "Reply" to a "Comment" by W.E. Jackson (1992), *Review of Economics and Statistics* (May), 373–376.

Berlin, M., A. Saunders, and G.F. Udell (eds) (1991), "Deposit Insurance Reform", special issue, *Journal of Banking and Finance* 15, 4/5, September, 733–1040.

Bernanke, B. and M. Gertler (1990),"Financial Fragility and Economic Performance", *Quarterly Journal of Economics*, 105, 1, 87–114.

Bhattacharya, S. and P. Pfleiderer (1985), "Delegated Portfolio Management", *Journal of Economic Theory*, 36, 1, 1–25.

Bisignano, J. (1992), "Banking in the European Community: Structure, Competition and Public Policy", in G.G. Kaufman (ed.), *Banking Structures in Major Countries*, Dordrecht: Kluwer Academic Publishers.

Black, F. (1975), "Bank Funds Management in an Efficient Market", *Journal of Financial Economics*, 2 September, 323–339.

Blake, D. (1985), "Financial Innovations and the Characteristics Model of Portfolio Behaviour", *Centre for International Banking and Finance*, Discussion Paper # 44, City University Business School, London: August.

Blake, D. and M. Pradhan (1991), "Debt Equity Swaps as Bond Conversions: Implications for Pricing", *Journal of Banking and Finance*, 15, 1, 29–42.

Bovenzi, J.F., J.A. Marino, and F.E. McFadden (1983), "Commercial Bank Failure Prediction Models", *Federal Reserve Bank of Atlanta Economic Review*, November, 14–26.

Boyd, G.H. and M. Gertler (1994), "Are Banks Dead? Or are the Reports Greatly Exaggerated?" *In Federal Reserve Bank of Chicago, Conference Proceedings on 'The Declining Role of Banking'*, 30th Annual Conference on Bank Structure and Competition, Chicago, Federal Reserve Bank of Chicago, May, pp. 85–117.

Boyd, G.H. and M. Gertler (1994), "The Role of Large Banks in US Banking Crisis", *Federal Reserve Bank of Minneapolis Quarterly Review*, 18, 1, Winter, 2–21.

Boyd, J.H. and S.L. Graham (1991), "Investigating the Banking Consolidation Trend", *Federal Reserve Bank of Minneapolis Quarterly Review*, Spring, 15, 2, 3–15.

Brainard, L.J. (1991), "Reform in Eastern Europe: Creating a Capital Market", in R. O'Brien and S. Hewin (eds), *Finance and the International Economy: 4 The Amex Bank Review Essays*, Oxford: Oxford University Press, 8–22.

Brewer, T.L. and P. Rivoli (1990), "Politics and Perceived Country Creditworthiness in International Banking", *Journal of Money, Credit and Banking*, 22, 3, 357–369.

Brozen, Y. (1982), *Concentration, Mergers, and Public Policy*, New York: Macmillan.

Burton, F.N. and H. Inoue (1987), "A Country Risk Appraisal Model of Foreign Asset Expropriation in Developing Countries", *Applied Economics*, 19, 1009–1048.

Burton, F.N. and F.H. Saelens (1986), "The European Investments of Japanese Financial Institutions, *Columbia Journal of World Business*, 21, 4, Winter, 27–33.

Business Week (1974), "Franklin Faces a Long Summer", *Business Week*, May 25, 53–54.

Business Week (1974), "Money and Credit: What Went Wrong at Herstatt", *Business Week*, August 3, 13–14.

Butt–Philips, A., (1988), "Implementing the European Internal Market: Problems and Prospects", Royal Institute of International Affairs, Discussion Paper 5, London.

Cagan, P. (1965), *Determinants and Effects of Changes in the Stock of Money 1875–1960*, Washington: National Bureau of Economic Research.

Calverley, J. (1990), *Country Risk Analysis*, London: Butterworths.

Cameron, R. (1967), *Banking in the Early Stages of Industrialization*, New York: Oxford University Press.

Cameron, R.(ed) (1972), *Banking and Economic Development: Some Lessons of History*, New York: Oxford University Press.

Capie, F.H., T.C. Mills, and G.E. Wood (1994), "Central Bank Dependence and Inflation Performance: An Exploratory Data Analysis", Department of Banking and Finance, Centre for the Study of Monetary History, Discussion Paper No.34, City University Business School.

de Carmoy, Herve (1990), *Global Banking Strategy*, Oxford: Basil Blackwell.

Caves, R. (1974), "Causes of Direct Investment: Foreign Firms Shares in Canadian and UK Manufacturing Industries", *Review of Economics and Statistics*, 56, 279–93.

Caves, R. (1982), *The Multinational Enterprise and Economic Analysis*, London: Cambridge University Press.

Cecchini, P. (1988), *The European Challenge: 1992*, London: Wildwood House.

Chamberlain, G. (1980), "Analysis of Covariance with Qualitative Data", *Review of Economic Studies*, 47, 225–238.

Cheng, H.S. (ed.) (1986), *Financial Policy and Reform in Pacific Basin Countries*, New York: Lexington Books.

Chew, D. (ed.) (1991), *New Developments in Commercial Banking*, Oxford: Basil Blackwell.

Chakravarty, S.P., E.P.M. Gardener and J. Teppett (1995), "Gains from a Single European market in financial Services", *Current Politics and Economics of Europe*, 5.1, 1–14.

Chong, B.S. (1991), "The Effects of Interstate Banking on Commercial Banks' Risk and Profitability", *Review of Economics and Statistics*, 73, 1, 78–84.

Clark, J. (1988), "Economies of Scale and Scope at Depository Financial Institutions: A Review of the Literature", *Federal Reserve Bank of Kansas City Economic Review*, September/October, 16–33.

Cleghorn, J.E. (1985), "Strategic Management in International Banking" in D.B. Zenoff (ed.), *International Banking Management and Strategies*, London: Euromoney Publications.

Coase, R.H. (1937), "The Nature of the Firm", *Economica*, 4, 386–405.

Compton, E. (1981), *Inside Commercial Banking*, London: Wiley.

Cooke, W.P. (1983), "The International Banking Scene: A Supervisory Perspective", *Bank of England Quarterly Bulletin*, 23, 1, 61–65.

Cooke, W.P. (1985), "Some Current Concerns of an International Banking Supervisor", *Bank of England Quarterly Bulletin*, 25, 2, 219–223.

Cooper, J. (1984), *The Management and Regulation of Banks*, London: Macmillan.

Cooperman, E.S., W.B. Lee, and G.A. Wolfe (July 1992), "The 1985 Ohio Thrift Crisis, the FSLIC's Solvency and Rate Contagion for Retail CDs", *The Journal of Finance*, 47, 3, 119–942.

Corrigan, G. (1990),"The Role of Central Banks and the Financial System in Emerging Market Economies", *Federal Reserve Bank of New York Review*, 15, 2–17.

Coulbeck, N. (1984), *The Multinational Banking Industry*, London: Croom Helm.

Crouchy, M. and D. Gali (1986), "An Economic Assessment of Capital Adequacy Requirements in the Banking Industry", *Journal of Banking and Finance*, 10, 231–241.

Cumming, C. (1987), "The Economics of Securitization", *Federal Reserve Bank of New York Quarterly Review*, Autumn, 11–23.

Cumming, C. and L.M. Sweet (1988), "Financial Structure of G10 Countries: How Does the United States Compare?", *Federal Reserve Bank of New York Quarterly Review*, 12, (4), Winter, 14–25.

Dale, R. (1992), *International Banking Deregulation*, Oxford: Basil Blackwell.

Damanpour, F. (1986), "A Survey of Market Structure and Activities of Foreign Banking in the US", *Columbia Journal of World Business*, 21, 4, Winter, 35-45.

Darby, M.R. (1986), "The Internationalisation of American Banking and Finance: Structure, Risk and World Interest Rates", *Journal of International Money and Finance*, December, 5, 4, 403–428.

Davidson, J., D.G. Hendry, F. Srba, and S. Yeo (1978), "Econometric Modelling of the Aggregate Time-Series Relationship Between Consumers Expenditures and Income in the United Kingdom", *Economic Journal*, 88, 661–692.

Davis, E.P. (1992), *Debt, Financial Fragility and Systemic Risk*, Oxford: Oxford University Press.

Davis, E.P. (December 1993), "Problems of Banking Regulation — An EC Perspective", London School of Economics Financial Markets Group, Special Paper Series, No. 59.

Davis, E.P. and R.J.Colwell (1992), "Output, Productivity and Externalities: The Case of Banking", Bank of England Working Paper, 3, August.

Davis, S. (1983), *The Management of International Banks*, London: Macmillan.

Davis, S. (1985), *Excellence in Banking*, London: Macmillan.

Davis, S. (1989), *Managing Change in the Excellent Banks*, London: Macmillan.

Demirguc-Kunt, A. (1988), "Deposit-Institution Failures: A Review of Empirical Literature", *Economic Review — Federal Reserve Bank of Cleveland* (4th Quarter).

Department of Finance (Canada), (1985), "The Regulation of Canadian Financial Institutions: Proposals for Discussion", Ottawa.

Dermine, J. (ed.) (1993), *European Banking in the 1990's*, 2nd edn, Oxford: Basil Blackwell.

Dewatripont, M. and J. Tirole (1993), *The Prudential Regulation of Banks*, London. MIT Press.

Diamond, D.W. (1984), "Financial Intermediation and Delegated Monitoring", *Review of Economic Studies*, 51: 393–414.

Diamond, D.W. (1991), "Monitoring and Reputation: The Choice Between Bank Loans and Directly Placed Debt", *Journal of Political Economy*, 99, 4, 689–721.

Diamond, D. and P. Dybvig (1983), "Bank Runs, Deposit Insurance, and Liquidity", *Journal of Political Economy*, 91, 401–419.

Diebold, F.X. and S.A. Sharpe (1990), "Post Deregulation Bank-Deposit-Rate Pricing: The Multivariate Dynamics", *Journal of Business and Economic Statistics*, 8, July, 3, 281–291.

Dimson, E. and P. Marsh, (1993), "The Debate on International Capital Requirements: Evidence on Equity Position Risk for UK Securities Firms", London Business School, June.

Dirienzo, T. and K. Hanson (1994), "Global Cash Management Security", in Brian Welch (ed.), *Electronic Banking and Security: A Guide For Corporate and Financial Managers*, Oxford: Blackwell Business.

Dotsey, M. and A. Kuprianov (1990), "Reforming Deposit Insurance: Lessons from the Savings and Loan Crisis, *Federal Reserve Bank of Richmond Economic Review*, 76, 12, 3–28.

Drake, L. (1992), "Economies of Scale and Scope in UK Building Societies: An Application of the Translog Multiproduct Cost Function", *Applied Financial Economics*, 2, 211–219.

Dufey, G. and I.H. Giddy (1992), *Cases in International Finance* 2nd edn, Wokingham: Addison-Wesley Publishing Company.

Dunn, I. and R. Sime (1991), "Active Cost Management — a Route to Better Results", *Banker's Digest*, August 1991, 29–31.

Dunning, J. (1985), "The United Kingdom", in J. Dunning (ed.), *Multinational Enterprises, International Competitiveness*, New York: Wiley 13–56.

Eaton, J. and M. Gersovitz (1979), "LDC Participation in International Financial Markets: Debt and Reserves", *Journal of Development Economics*, 7 (1980), 3–21.

Eaton, J. and M. Gersovitz (1981), "Debt With Potential Repudiation: Theoretical and Empirical Analysis", *Review of Economic Studies*, 48, 289–309.

Eaton, J. and M. Gersovitz (1981), Poor Country Borrowing in Private Financial Markets and the Repudiation Issue", *Princeton Studies in International Finance*, 47, June.

Eaton, J., M. Gersovitz and J.E. Stiglitz (1986), "The Pure Theory of Country Risk", *European Economic Review*, 30, 481–513.

The Economist (1988), "French Bank Deregulation: Telling Tales from the Wrong Bank", 24 September, 122–125.

The Economist (1992) "Wish You Hadn't Asked?", 8 August, 77–78.

The Economist (1993), "New Rules For Banks: Keep Them Minimal", 8 May, 20–21.

The Economist (1993), "The Sum, Not The Parts", 11 December, 97–98.

The Economist (1994), "Japanese Banks Tough on the Tax Payer", 26 February, 96–97.

The Economist (1994), "American Banking Regulation: Four Into One Can Go", 5 March, 104–107.

The Economist (1994), "Indigestion Strikes Europe", 12 March, 38–39.

The Economist (1995), "Other People's Money, A Survey of Wall Street", 15 April.

Eichberger, J. and I.R. Harper, (1989), "On Deposit Interest Rate Regulation and Deregulation", *Journal of Industrial Economics*, 38, 1, 19–30.

Eichengreen, B. and P.H. Lindert (eds), *The International Debt Crisis in Historical Perspective*, Cambridge, Mass.: MIT Press.

Eichgreen, B. and R. Portes (1986), "The Anatomy of Financial Crises", Centre For Economic Policy Research, Discussion Paper Series, No. 130, London: CEPR.

Eichgreen, B. and R. Portes (1988), "Foreign Lending in the Interwar Years: The Bondholders' Perspective", Centre For Economic Policy Research, Discussion Paper Series, No. 273, London: CEPR.

Eichgreen, B. and R. Portes (1988), "Settling Defaults in the Era of Bond Finance", Centre For Economic Policy Research, Discussion Paper Series, No. 272, London: CEPR.

Eichgreen, B. and R. Portes, R. (1989), "Dealing With Debt: The 1930's and the 1980's", Centre For Economic Policy Research, Discussion Paper Series No. 300, London: CEPR.

Elliehausen, G.E. and J.D. Wolken (1990), "Market Definition and Product Segmentation for Household Credit", *Journal of Financial Services Research*, 4: 21–35.

Ellis, D.M. and M.J. Flannery (1992), "Does the Debt Market Assess Large Banks' Risk? Time Series Evidence From Money Centre CDs", *Journal of Economics*, 30, 3.

Emerson, M., M. Aujean, M. Catinal, P. Goybet, and A. Jacquemin (1989), *The Economics of 1992: The EC Commission's Assessment of the Economic Effects of Completing the Internal Market*, Oxford: Oxford University Press.

Espahbodi, P. (1991), "Identification of Problem Banks and Binary Choice Models", *Journal of Banking and Finance*, 15, 53–71.

Estrin, S., P. Hare, and M. Suranyi (1992), "Banking in Transition: Development and Current Problems in Hungary", Centre for Economic Performance Discussion Paper No. 68, London: CEPR.

Euromoney Bondware (1994), *Euromoney*, September.

European Monetary Institute (1994), *Blue Book Addendum*, Basle: EMI.

Evanoff, D.D. and D.L. Fortier (1988), "Re-evaluation of the Structure-Conduct-Performance Paradigm in Banking", *Journal of Financial Services Research*, 1, 3 (June), 375–390.

Evanoff, D.D. and P.R. Israilevich (1991), "Productive Efficiency in Banking", *Economic Perspectives* 15, 4, July–August, 11–32.

Fama, E.F. (1980), "Banking in the Theory of Finance", *Journal of Economics*, 6, 39–57.

Fama, E.F. (1985), "What's Different About Banks?", *Journal of Economics*, 15, 29–39.

Federal Reserve (1988), "The Profitability of Insured Commercial Banks in 1987", *Federal Reserve Bulletin* 74, 7, July 403–418.

Federal Reserve (1993), "Interstate Banking: A Status Report", *Federal Reserve Bulletin* 79, 12, December, 1075–1089.

Federal Reserve Bank of Chicago (1980), "The Depository Institutions Deregulation and Monetary Control Act of 1980: Landmark Financial Legislation for the Eighties", *Economic Perspectives, Federal Reserve Bank of Chicago*, September/October, 3–23.

Federal Reserve Bank of Minneapolis (1986), "Risk Regulation and Bank Holding Company Expansion into Nonbanking", *Federal Reserve Bank of Minneapolis Quarterly Review*, Spring 1986.

Federal Reserve Bank of New York (1986), "The Recent Performance of the Commercial Banking Industry", *Federal Reserve Bank of New York Quarterly Review*, 11, 2, 1–11.

Federal Reserve Bank of New York (1987), "Capital Requirements of Commercial and Investment Banks: Contrasts in Regulation", *Federal Reserve Bank of New York Quarterly Review*, Autumn, 1–10.

Field, K. (1990), "Production Efficiency of British Building Societies", *Applied Economics*, March, 22, 3, 415–426.

Fingleton, E. (1994), "Nomura Aims To Please", *Institutional Investor*, October, 99–102.

Fisher A. (1987), "Banks Facing up to Foreign Competition", *The Banker*, January 1987.

Fisher, I. (1932), *Booms and Depressions*, New York: Adelphi.

Fisher, I. (1933), "Debt Deflation Theory of the Great Depression", *Econometrica*, 337–57.

Fisk, C. and F. Rimlinger (1979), "Non-Parametric Estimates of LDC Repayment Prospects", *Journal of Finance* 34, 2, March, 429–438.

Flannery, M.J. (1982), Retail Bank Deposits as Quasi-Fixed Factors of Production", *American Economic Review*, 72, June, 527–536.

Flood, M.D. (1992), "Two Faces of Financial Innovation", *Federal Reserve Bank of St Louis Review*, 74, 5, 3–17.

Fordyce, J.E. and M.L. Nickerson, (1991) "An Overview of Legal Developments in the Banking and Financial Services Industry in Canada", *The International Lawyer*, 25, 2, 351–369.

Folkerts Landau, D. and A. Steinherr (1994), "The Wild Beast of Derivatives: To be Chained up, Fenced in or Tamed?", in R. O'Brien (ed.), *Finance and the International Economy*, 8, Oxford: Oxford University Press, 8–27.

Frank, C.R. and W.R. Cline (1971), "Measurement of Debt Servicing Capacity: An Application of Discriminant Analysis", *Journal of International Economics* 1, 327–344.

Frankel, A.B. and J.D. Montgomery (1991), "Financial Structure, An International Perspective", *Brookings Papers on Economic Activity*, 1, 257–310.

Frankel, A.B. and P.B. Morgan (1992), "Deregulation and Competition in Japanese Banking", *Federal Reserve Bulletin*, 78, 8, 579–593.

Freedman, C. (1987), "Shifting Frontiers in Financial Markets", Bank of Canada, Ottawa, March 28–30, 1985 (unpublished conference paper).

Freedman, R.D. and J. Vohr (1991), "American Express", Case Series in Finance and Economics, C49, New York University Salomon Center, Leonard N. Stern School of Business.

Freedman, R.D. and J. Vohr (1991), "Goldman Sachs/ Lehman Brothers", Case Series in Finance and Economics, C50, New York University Salomon Center, Leonard N. Stern School of Business.

Friedman, M. and A. Schwartz (1963), *A Monetary History of the United States, 1867–1960*, Princeton, N.J.: Princeton University Press.

Fry, M. (1988), *Money, Interest and Banking in Economic Development*, Baltimore, MD.: The Johns Hopkins University Press.

Gasktil, R. (1987), *Freedom in the World*, Westport, Conn: Greenwood Press.

Gennotte, G. and D. Pyle (1991), "Capital Controls and Bank Risk", *Journal of Banking and Finance*, 15, 4/5, September, 805–824.

Germany, J.D. and J.E. Morton (1985), "Financial Innovation and Deregulation in Foreign Industrial Countries", *Federal Reserve Bulletin*, 7, 10, October, 743–753.

Gilbert, R.A. (1984), "Bank Market Structure and Competition: A Survey", *Journal of Money, Credit and Banking*, 4, 21–36.

Gilbert, R.A. (1991), "Do Bank Holding Companies Act as Sources of Strength for Their Bank Subsidiaries?", *Federal Reserve Bank of St Louis Review*, 73, 1, 3–18.

Gilbert, R.A. (1991), "Market Discipline and Bank Risk: Theory and Evidence", *Federal Reserve Bank of St Louis Review*, 72, 1, 1–18.

Gilbert, R.A. (1991), "Supervision of Undercapitalised Banks: Is There a Case For Change?", *Federal Reserve Bank of St Louis Review*, 73, 3, 16–30.

Gilligan, T. and M.L. Smirlock (1984), "An Empirical Study of Joint Production and Scale Economies in Commercial Banking", *Journal of Banking and Finance*, 8, 67–78.

Glascock, J.L. (1985), "The Effect of Bond Deratings on Bank Stock Returns", *Journal of Bank Research*, 16, 3, Autumn, 121–127.

Goldberg, L.G. and G.A. Hanweck (1991), "The Growth of the World's 300 Largest Banking Organizations by Country", *Journal of Banking and Finance*, 15, 207–223.

Goodhart, C. and D. Schoenmaker (1995), "Should the Functions of Monetary Policy and Banking supervision be Separated?", *Oxford Economic Papers*, 47, 539–560.

Gowland, D.H. (1991), "Financial Innovation in Theory and Practice", in C.J. Green and D.T. Llewellyn (eds), *Surveys in Monetary Economics*, vol 2, Oxford: Basil Blackwell, 79–115.

Gowland, P. (1994), *The Economics of Modern Banking*, Aldershot: Edward Elgar.

Greenbaum, S.I. (1967), "Competition and Efficiency in the Banking System–Empirical Research and its Policy Implications", *Journal of Political Economy*, 75, 461–481.

Greenspan, A. (1994), "Optimal Bank Supervision in a Changing World" in *Federal Reserve Bank of Chicago, Conference Proceedings on The Declining (?) Role of Banking*, The 30th Annual Conference on Bank Structure and Competition, May, 1–8.

Griffiths, B. (1970), "Competition in Banking", Hobart Paper, No.5, London: Institute of Economic Affairs.

Group of Thirty (1993), *Derivatives: Practices and Principles – Special Report by the Global Derivatives Study Group*, Washington: Group of Thirty.

Group of Thirty (1994), *Derivatives: Practices and Principles: Follow Up Surveys of Industry Practice*, Washington: Group of Thirty.

Gual, J. and D. Neven (1992), "Deregulation of the European Banking Industry (1980–1991), Centre for Economic Policy Research Discussion Paper No 703, London: CEPR.

Gup, B.E. and J.R. Walter (1991), "Profitable Large Banks: the Key to Their Success", in D. Chew (ed.), *New Developments in Commercial Banking*, Oxford: Basil Blackwell, 37-42.

Guttentag, J. and R. Herring (1983), "The Lender of Last Resort Function in an International Context", *Essays in International Finance*, No. 151, International Finance Section, Department of Economics, Princeton University.

Guttentag J. and R. Herring (1985), "Funding Risk in the International Interbank Market" *Princeton Essays in International Finance*, No. 157, Finance Section, Department of Economics, Princeton University.

Guttentag, J. and R. Herring (1986), "Disaster Myopia in International Banking", *Essays in International Finance*, No. 164, International Finance Section, Department of Economics, Princeton University.

Hall, M.J.B., (1985), "UK Banking Supervision and the Johnson Matthey Affair", Loughborough University Banking Centre, Research Paper Series, No. 8, May.

Hall, M.J.B. (1987), *Financial Deregulation: A Comparative Study of Australia and The United Kingdom*, London: Macmillan Press.

Hall, M.J.B. (1991), "Financial Regulation in the UK: Deregulation or Reregulation?", in C.J. Green and D.T. Llewellyn (eds), *Surveys in Monetary Economics*, vol. 2, Oxford: Basil Blackwell.

Hall, M.J.B. (1993), *Banking Regulation and Supervision*, Aldershot: Edward Elgar.

Hamel, G. and C.K. Prahalad (1993), "Strategy as Stretch and Leverage", *Harvard Business Review*, 71, March/April, 75–85.

Hannan, T.H. (1979), "The Theory of Limit Pricing: Some Applications to the Banking Industry", *Journal of Banking and Finance*, 3, 221–234.

Hannan, T.H. (1991), "Foundations of the Structure-Conduct-Performance Paradigm in Banking", *Journal of Money, Credit and Banking*, 23, 1, 68–84.

Hannan, T.H. (1991), "The Bank Commercial Loan Markets and the Role of Market Structure: Evidence from Surveys of Commercial Lending", *Journal of Banking and Finance*, 15, 133–149.

Hanson, J.A. and R. Rocha (1986), "High Interest Rates, Spreads and the Costs of Intermediation: Two Studies", *World Bank Industry and Finance Series*, No 18, September.

Hardwick, P. (1989), "Economies of Scale in Building Societies", *Applied Economics*, 21, 1291–1304.

Hardwick, P. (1990), "Multi-Product Cost Attributes: A Study of UK Building Societies", *Oxford Economic Papers*, 42, 446–461.

Hay, D.A. and D.J. Morris (1991), *Industrial Economics and Organization: Theory and Evidence*, 2nd edn, Oxford: Oxford University Press.

Hector, G. (1985), "Management Challenges Face Bank America", in D.B. Zenoff (ed.), *International Banking Management and Strategies*, London: Euromoney Publications.

Heffernan, S.A. (1984), "Reflections on the Case For an International Central Bank", *Greek Economic Review*, 6, 1, 99–120.

Heffernan, S.A. (1986), "Determinants of Optimal Foreign Leverage Ratios in Developing Countries", *Journal of Banking and Finance*, supplement, 3, 97–115.

Heffernan, S.A. (1986), *Sovereign Risk Analysis*, London: Unwin Hyman .

Heffernan, S.A. (1987), "The Costs and Benefits of International Banking", in Z. Res & S. Motamen (eds) *International Debt and Central Banking in the 1980s*, London: Macmillan, 113–140.

Heffernan, S.A. (1990), "A Characteristics Definition of Financial Markets", *Journal of Banking and Finance*, 14, 583–609.

Heffernan, S.A. (1991), "1992: Financial Markets and Implications", in D. Purvis, *Europe 1992 and the Implications of Canada*, Kingston, Canada: John Deutsch Institute for the Study of Economic Policy.

Heffernan, S.A. (1992), "A Competition of Interest Equivalences for Non-Price Features of Bank Products, *Journal of Money, Credit and Banking*, 24, May, 162–172.

Heffernan, S.A. (1993), "Competition in British Retail Banking", *Journal of Financial Services Research* 7, 3, December, 309–332.

Heffernan, S.A. (1994), "Competition in the Canadian Personal Finance Sector", *International Journal of the Economics of Business*, 1, 3, 323–342.

Heffernan, S.A. (1995), "An Econometric Model of Bank Failure", *Economic and Financial Modelling*, Summer, 49–83.

Heffernan, S.A. and P. Sinclair (1990), *Modern International Economics*, Oxford: Basil Blackwell.

Heggestad, A.A. (1979), "A Survey of Studies on Banking Competition and Performance; Market Structure, Competition, and Performance", in F.R. Edwards (ed.), *Issues in Financial Reguation*, Maidenhead: McGraw Hill, 449–490.

Heggestad, A.A. and J.J. Mingo (1976), "Prices, Nonprices, and Concentration In Commercial Banking", *Journal of Money Credit and Banking*, 8, 107–117.

Heggestad, A.A. and J.J.Mingo (1977), "The Competitive Condition of U.S. Banking Markets and the Impact of Structural Reform", *Journal of Finance*, 32, 3, June, 649–661.

Herring, R. (1984), "Continental Illinois", Case Series in Finance and Economics, C41, New York University Salomon Center, Leonard N. Stern School of Business.

Hey, J.D. (1989), "Introduction: Recent Developments in Microeconomics", *Recent Issues in Microeconomics*, London: Macmillan.

Hirtle, B. (1991), "Factors Affecting the Competitiveness of Internationally Active Financial Institutions", *Federal Reserve Bank of New York Quarterly Review*, Spring, 38–51.

Humpage, O.F. (1990), "A Hitchhiker's Guide to International Macroeconomic Policy Coordination", *Federal Reserve Bank of Cleveland*, 26, 1, 2–14.

Humphrey, D.B. (1987), "Cost Dispersion and the Measurement of Economies in Banking", *Federal Reserve Bank of Richmond Economic Review*, May/ June.

Humphrey, D. (1992), "Flow Versus Stock Indicators of Bank Output: Effects on Productivity and Scale Economy Measurement", *Journal of Financial Services Research*, 6, 2, 115–135.

Hunter, W.C. and S.G. Timme (1986) "Technical Change, Organisational Form, and the Structure of Bank Production", *Journal of Money Credit and Banking*, 18, 2–66.

Hunter, W.C., S.G. Timme and W.K. Yang (1990), "An Examination of Cost Subadditivity and Multiproduct Production in Large US Commercial Banks", *Journal of Money, Credit and Banking*, 22, 504–525.

International Monetary Fund (1986), "The Debt Situation: Prospects and Policy Issues", *World Economic Outlook*, April, Washington: IMF.

Ismail, A.G. (1993), "Profit Sharing in the Modelling of Islamic Banks", *Discussion Papers in Economics and Econometrics*, Department of Economics, University of Southampton.

Jackson W.E. (1992), "The Price–Concentration Relationship in Banking: A Comment", *Review of Economics and Statistics*, 74, 291–299, and "Reply" by Berger and Hannan, 373–76.

Jaffee, P., and T. Russell (1976), "Imperfect Information, Uncertainty and Credit Rationing", *Quarterly Journal of Economics*, 90, 651–66.

Jagtiani, J., A. Saunders and G. Udell (1993), "Bank Off-Balance Sheet Financial Innovations", New York University Salomon Centre (Stern School of Business), Working Paper S-93-50.

John, K., T.A. John, and L.W. Senbet, (1991), "Risk Shifting Incentives of Depository Institutions: A New Perspective on Federal Deposit Insurance Reform", *Journal of Banking and Finance*, 15, 4/5, September, 895–916.

Johnston, R.B. (1983), *The Economics of the Euromarket*, London: Macmillan.

JP Morgan (1994), *Riskmetrics—Technical Document*, 2nd edn, November, New York: JP Morgan.

Kane, E.J. (1984), "Technology and Regulatory Forces in the Developing Fusion of Financial Services Competition", *Journal of Finance*, 39, 3, July, 759–72.

Kane, E.J. and M.T. Yu (1994), "How Much Did Capital Forbearance Add To The Tab For The FSLIC Mess?" in *Federal Reserve Bank of Chicago, Conference Proceedings on The Declining Role of Banking*, The 30th Annual Conference on Bank Structure and Competition May 1994.

Kaufman, G.G. (1988), "Securities Activities of Commercial Banks: Recent Changes in the Economic and Legal Environments", *Midland Corporate Finance Journal* 5, 4, Winter, 14–21.

Kaufman, G.G. (ed.) (1992), *Banking Structures in Major Countries*, The Netherlands: Kluwer Academic Publishers.

Kay, J.A. (1991), "Economics and Business", *The Economic Journal*, 101, January, 57–73.

Kay, J.A. (1993), *Foundations of Corporate Success*, New York: Oxford University Press.

Kay, J. (1993), "The Structure of Strategy", *Business Strategy Review*, 4, 2, Summer, 17–37.

Kay, J. and J. Vickers (1988),"Regulatory Reform In Britain", *Economic Policy*, 7, October, 286–351.

Keehn, S. (1994), "Has Banking Declined?" in *Federal Reserve Bank of Chicago, Conference Proceedings on The Declining Role of Banking*, The 30th Annual Conference on Bank Structure and Competition May 1994, 13–16.

Keeley, M.C. (1990), "Deposit Insurance, Risk, and Market Power in Banking", *American Economic Review*, 80, 5, December, 1183–1200.

Kendall, S.B. and M.E. Levonian (1991), "A Simple Approach to Better Deposit Insurance Pricing", *Journal of Banking and Finance*, 15, 4/5, September, 999–1018.

Kenyon, A. (1981), *Currency Risk Management*, London: Wiley.

Kenyon, A. (1990), *Currency Risk and Business Management*, Oxford: Basil Blackwell.

Kenyon, A. and S. Mathur (1987), "The Development of Strategies by International Commercial Banks", *Journal of General Management*, 13, 2, 56–73.

Key, S.J. and H.S. Scott (1991), "International Trade in Banking Services: A Conceptual Framework", Occasional Papers No. 35, Washington: Group of Thirty.

Khoury, S.J. and K. Hung Chan (1988), "Hedging Foreign Risk: Selecting the Optimal Tool", *Midland Corporate Finance Journal* 5, 4, Winter 40–53.

Khan, M.S. (1987), "Islamic Interest-Free Banking: A Theoretical Analysis in Khan S. and A. Mirakhor (eds), Theoretical Studies in Islamic Banking and Finance, Houston: The Institute for Research and Islamic Studies, 15–35.

Khan, M.S. and A. Mirakhor (1987), "The Framework and Practice of Islamic Banking" in Khan, S. and A. Mirakhor (eds), Theoretical Studies in Islamic Banking and Finance, Houston: The Institute for Research and Islamic Studies, 1–14.

Kim, H.Y. (1987), "Economies of Scale in Multi Product Firms: an Empirical Analysis", *Economica*, 54, 185–206.

Kim, M. (1986), "Banking Technology and the Existence of a Consistent Output Aggregate", *Journal of Economics*, 18, 181–195.

Kindleberger, C.P. (1978), "Debt situation of Developing Countries in Historical Perspective", in S. H. Goodman (ed.), *Financing and Risk in Developing Countries*, London: Praeger.

Kindleberger, C.P. (1984), *A Financial History of Western Europe*, London: George Allen and Unwin Publishers Ltd.

Kindleberger, C.P. and J.P. Laffargue (eds) (1982), *Finanical Crisis: Theory History and Policy*, New York: Cambridge University Press.

King, K.K. and J.M. O'Brien (1991), "Market Based Risk Adjusted Examination Schedules for Depository Institutions", *Journal of Banking and Finance*, 15, 4/5, September, 955–974.

Klein, B. (1974), "Competitive Interest Payments on Bank Deposits and the Long Run Demand For Money", *American Economic Review*, 64, 6, December, 931–949.

Klein, M.A. (1971), "A Theory of the Banking Firm", *Journal of Money, Credit and Banking*, 3, 205–218.

Klein, M.A. and N.B. Murphy, (1971), "The Pricing of Bank Deposits: A Theoretical and Empirical Analysis", *Journal of Financial and Quantitative Analysis*, 6, 747–761.

Kolb, R. W. (1993), *Financial Derivatives*, London: Prentice Hall.

Korobow, L. and D. Stuhr (1985), "Performance Measurement of Early Warning Models: Comments on West and other Weakness / Failure Prediction Models", *Journal of Banking and Finance*, June, 267–273.

Kryzanowski, L. and G.S. Roberts (1992), "Bank Structure in Canada", in G.G. Kaufman (ed.) *Banking Structures in Major Countries*, London: Kluwer.

Laderman, E.S. and R.J.Pozdena (1991), "Interstate Banking and Competition: Evidence From the Behaviour of Stock Returns," *Federal Reserve Bank of San Francisco Economic Review*, 2, 32–47.

Lawrence, C. (1989), "Banking Costs, Generalised Functional Forms, and Estimation of Economies of Scale and Scope", *Journal of Money, Credit and Banking*, 21, 368–379.

Leach, J.A., W.J. McDonough, D.W. Mullins, and B. Quinn (1993), *Global Derivatives: Public Sector Responses*, Washington: Group of Thirty, Occasional Paper 44.

Leland, H. and D. Pyle (1977), "Information Asymmetries, Financial Structures and Financial intermediaries", *Journal of Finance*, 32: 511–13.

Lessard, D.R. (1987), "Recapitalizing Third World Debt: Toward a New Vision of Commercial Financing for Less Developed Countries", *Midland Corporate Finance Journal*, 5, 3, Fall, 6–21.

Levonian, M.E. (1994), " Beyond Traditional Credit Risk: Capital Standards For Market Risks" in *Federal Reserve Bank of Chicago, Conference Proceedings on The Declining (?) Role of Banking*, The 30th Annual Conference on Bank Structure and Competition, May, 381–399.

Levonian, M.E. (1994), "Will Banking Be Profitable In The Long Run" in *The Declining (?) Role of Banking*, The 30th Annual Conference on Bank Structure and Competition, May, 118–129.

Lewis, M.K. (1991), "Theory and Practice of the Banking Firm", in Green, C. and D. Llewellyn (eds), *Surveys in Monetary Economics*, Vol. 2, Oxford: Basil Blackwell, 116–159.

Lewis, M.K. and K.T. Davis (1987), *Domestic and International Banking*, Oxford: Philip Alan.

Llewellyn, D.T. (1985), "The Evolution of the British Financial System", *Gilbart Lectures on Banking*, London: The Institute of Bankers.

Llewellyn, D.T. (1986), "The Regulation and Supervision of Financial Institutions", *Gilbart Lectures on Banking*, London: The Institute of Bankers.

Llewellyn, D.T. (1991), "Structural Change in the British Financial System", in Green, C. and D. Llewellyn (eds), *Surveys in Monetary Economics*, Vol. 2, Oxford: Basil Blackwell, 210–259.

Llewellyn, D.T. (1992), "Competition, Diversification, and Structural Change in the British Financial System", in G.G. Kaufman (ed.), *Banking Structures in Major Countries*, Dordrecht: Kluwer Academic Publishers, 429–468.

Ludwig, E.A. (1994), "Supervising an Evolving Industry" in *Federal Reserve Bank of Chicago, Conference Proceedings on The Declining (?) Role of Banking*, The 30th Annual Conference on Bank Structure and Competition, May, 9–12.

McCormick, J.M. (1987), "The Role of Securitization in Transforming Banks into More Efficient Financial Intermediaries", *Midland Corporate Finance Journal*, 5, 3, Fall, 50–63.

McDonough, W.J. (1993), "The Global Derivatives Market", *Federal Reserve Bank of New York Quarterly Review*, Autumn, 18, 3, 1–5.

McFadden, D. (1974), "The Measurement of Urban Travel Demand", *Journal of Public Economics*, 3, 303–328.

Martin, D. (1977), "Early Warning of Bank Failure: A Logit Regression Approach", *Journal of Banking and Finance*, 15, 53–71.

Mathur, S. (1992), "Talking Straight About Competitive Strategy", *Journal of Marketing Management*, 8, 3, July, 199–218.

Merton, R.C. (1990), "The Financial System and Economic Performance", *Journal of Financial Services Research*, 4, 4, December, 263–300.

Mester, L. (1987), "Efficient Production of Financial Services: Scale and Scope Economies", *Federal Reserve Bank of Philadelphia Business Review*, 15–25 (Jan/Feb), 83–86.

Meyer, P.A. and H.W. Pifer (1970), "Prediction of Bank Failures", *The Journal of Finance*, September, 853–868.

Micossi, S. (1988), "The Single European Market: Finance", *Banca Nazionale Del Lavoro*, 165, June, 217–235.

Miller, M.H. (1986), "Financial Innovation: The Last Twenty Years and the Next", *Journal of Financial and Quantitative Analysis*, 21, 4, December, 459–471.

Minsky, H.P. (1977), "Theory of Systemic Fragility", in Altman E.I. and A. W. Sametz, *Financial Crises: Institutions and Markets in a Fragile Environment*, New York: Wiley, 138–152.

Minsky, H.P. (1982), "The Financial Instability Hypothesis: A Capitalist Process and the Behaviour of the World Economy", in Kindleberger and Laffargue (eds), *Financial Crisis Theory History and Policy*, New York: Cambridge, University Press, 13–41.

Misback, A.E. (1993), "The Foreign Bank Supervision Enhancement Act of 1991", *Federal Reserve Bulletin*, January, 79, 1, 1–10.

Mitchell, D.W. (1979), "Explicit and Implicit Demand Deposit Insurance: Substitutes or Complements From the Banks Point of View?", *Journal of Money Credit and Banking*, 11, 182–191.

Molyneux, P. (1993), "Market Structure and Profitability in European Banking", University College of North Wales, Bangor, School of Accounting, Banking, and Economics, and Institute of European Finance, Research Paper No. 93/9.

Molyneux, P. and W. Forbes (1993), "Market Structure and Performance in European Banking", University College of North Wales, Bangor, School of Accounting, Banking, and Economics, and Institute of European Finance, Research Paper No. 34780/93/5.

Molyneux, P., P.M. Lloyd-Williams and J. Thornton (1994), "European Banking: An Analysis of Competitive Conditions", in J. Revell (ed.), *The Changing Face of European Banks and Securities Markets*, New York: St Martins Press.

Morishima, M. (1993), "Banking and Industry in Japan", London School of Economics Financial Markets Group, Special Paper No. 51, January.

Morris, A. (1993), "The Nomura Securities Co., Ltd", Case Series in Finance and Economics, C42, New York University Salomon Center, Leonard N. Stern School of Business.

Morris, S. (1987), "The Financial Services Act: What it Means for Banks", *Journal of International Banking Law*, 3, 147–158.

Muldur, U. (1993), "Foreign Competition in the French Banking System", University College of North Wales, Bangor. School of Accounting, Banking and Economics, Institute of European Finance, Paper in Banking and Finance, No. 34775/RP93/4.

Mullineaux, A.W. (1993), "Privatisation and Banking Sector Reform: Lessons from Poland", The University of Birmingham, Department of Economics Discussion Paper No. 93–07.

Nathan, A. (1991), "A Simultaneous Analysis of Efficiency and Competitiveness of Financial Intermediaries: The Case of Canadian Commercial Banks", *Administration Sciences of Canada*, Gordon Clark (ed.) 12, 1, 190–199.

Nathan, A. and E.H. Neave, (1989), "Competition and Contestability on Canada's Financial System", *Canadian Journal of Economics*, 22, 3, 576–594.

Nathan, A. and E.H. Neave (1991), "Reply to Perrakis", *Canadian Journal of Economics*, 24, 733–5.

Nellis, J. (1993), "The Changing Structure and Role of Building Societies in the UK Financial Services Sector", Cranfield Institute of Technology, Cranfield School of Management, No 06070 / 28 / 93.

Newman, J.H. (1986), "LDC Debt: The Secondary Market, The Banks and New Investment in Developing Countries, *Columbia Jounral of World Business*, Fall, 69–72.

Nigh, D., K.R. Cho and S. Krishnan (1986), "The Role of Location Related Factors in US Banking Involvement Abroad: An Empirical Examination", *Journal of International Business Studies*, 17, 3, 59–72.

OECD (1987), *Prudential Supervision in Banking*, Paris: OECD.

OECD (1991), *Bank Profitability and Statistical Supplement*, OECD Paris.

OECD (1992), *Economies of Scale and Scope in the Financial Services Industry: A Review of the Recent Literature*, Paris: OECD.

OECD (1994), *Labour Force Statistics*, Paris: OECD.

O'Hara, M. and W. Shaw (1990),"Deposit Insurance and Wealth Effects: The Value of Being Too Big to Fail", *Journal of Finance*, 45, 5, 1587–1600.

Osterberg, W.P. and J.P. Thompson (1991), "The Effect of Subordinated Debt and Surety Bonds on the Cost of Capital for Banks and the Value of Federal Deposit Insurance", *Journal of Banking and Finance*, 15, 4/5, September, 939–954.

Pastena, V. and W. Rutland (1986), "The Merger/Bankruptcy Alternative", *Accounting Review*, 61, 288–301.

Perrakis, S. (1991), "Assessing Competition in Canada's Financial System: A Note", *Canadian Journal of Economics*, 24, 3, 727–732.

Peter, T. (1982), *In Search of Excellence*, New York: Harper and Row.

Picker, I. (1990), "Nomura Takes it to the Max", *Institutional Investor*, July, 107–119.

Porter, M. (1979), "How Competitive Forces Shape Strategy", *Harvard Business Review*, March–April, 137–47.

Porter, M. (1987), "From Competitive Advantage to Corporate Strategy", *Harvard Business Review*, 4 (July–Aug), 43–59.

Porter, M. (1990), *The Competitive Advantage of Nations*, London: Macmillan.

Porter, M. (1991), "Towards a Dynamic Theory of Strategy", Strategic Management Journal, 12, 95–117.

Poulsen, A.B. (1986), "Japanese Bank Regulation and the Activities of US Offices of Japanese Banks", *Journal of Money, Credit and Banking*, 18, 3, 366–73.

Pozdena, R.J. (1992), "Danish Banking: Lessons for Deposit Insurance Reform", *Journal of Financial Services Research*, 5, 3, 289–298.

Pozdena, R.J. and V. Alexander (1991), "Bank Structure in West Germany" in G.G. Kaufman (ed.), *Banking Structures in Major Countries*, Dordrecht: Kluwer Academic Publishers.

Price Waterhouse (1988), "The Cost of Non Europe in Financial Services", in *Research of the Cost of Non Europe*, 19, Brussels: Commission of the European Communities.

Prindl, A.R. (ed.) (1992), *Banking and Finance in Eastern Europe*, New York, London: Woodhead-Faulkner.

Quinn, B. (1993), "Derivatives—Where Next for Supervisors?", *Bank of England Quarterly Bulletin*, 33, 4, November, 535–538.

Rangan, N., R. Grabowski, H. Aly, and C. Pasurka (1988), "The Technical Efficiency of US Banks", *Economic Letters*, 28, 169–75.

Rangan, N., R. Grabowski, C. Pasurka, and H. Aly (1990), "Technical Scale and Allocative Efficiencies in US Banking: an Empirical Investigation", *Review of Economics and Statistics*, 52, 211–18.

Rees, R. (1985), "The Theory of Principle and Agent Parts 1 and 2", *Bulletin of Economic Research*, 1/2, 3–95.

Reid, M. (1982), *Secondary Banking Crisis in the UK*, London: Macmillan.

Remolona, E.M. (1993), "The Resent Growth of Financial Derivative Markets", *Federal Reserve Bank of New York Quarterly Review*, Winter, 17, 4, 1–27.

Revell, J. (1980), *Costs and Margins in Banking: An International Survey*, Paris: OECD.

Revell, J. (ed.) (1994), *The Changing Face of European Banks and Securities Markets*, Basingstoke: Macmillan Press.

Rogers, R.C. (1985), "Financial Innovation, Balance Sheet Cosmetics and Market Response: The Case of Equity-for-Debt Exchanges in Banking", *Journal of Bank Research*, 16, 3, Autumn 1985, 145–149.

Rogowski, R. (1986), "The New Competitive Environment of Investment Banking: Transactional Finance and Consessional Pricing of New Issues", *Midland Corporate Finance Journal*, 4, 1, Spring, 64–71.

Rosse, P.S. and J.C. Panzar (1977), "Chamberlain vs Robinson: An Empirical Test for Monopoly Rents", Bell Laboratories, EDP No. 90.

Rumelt, R.P., D. Schendel, and D.J. Teece (1991), "Strategic Management and Economics", *Strategic Management Journal*, 12, 5–29.

Rummel, R.J. and D.A. Heenan (1978), "How Multinationals Analyse Political Risk", *Harvard Business Review*, January–February, 67–76.

Sachs, J.D. (1986) "A New Approach to Managing the Debt Crisis", *Columbia Journal of World Business*, Fall, 41–49.

Sachs, J.D. (1986), "Managing the LDC Debt Crisis", *Brookings Papers on Economic Activity*, 2, 397–440.

Sachs, J. and Woo, W. T. (1994), "Structural Factors in the Economic Reforms of China, Eastern Europe and the Former Soviet Union", *Economic Policy*, 18, April 101–146.

Salop, S. and J. Stiglitz (1977), "Bargains and Ripoffs: A Model of Monopolistically Competitive Price Disperson", *Review of Economic Studies*, 4, 493–510.

Santomero, A. (1979), "The Role of Transaction Costs and Rates of Return on the Demand Deposit Decision", *Journal of Economics*, 5, 343–364.

Santomero, A. (1984), "Modelling the Banking Firm", *Journal of Money, Credit and Banking*, 16, 4, 576–602.

Santomero, A. and J.D. Vinso, J.D. (1977), "Estimating the Probability of Failure for Commercial Banks and the Banking System", *Journal of Banking and Finance*, September, 185–205.

Saunders, A. (1994), *Financial Institutions Management*, Burr Ridge, Ill.: Irwin.

Saunders, A. (1994), "Universal Banking and The Separation of Banking and Commerce", Special Issue, *Journal of Banking and Finance*, 18, 2, 229–420.

Saunders, A. and I. Walters (1993), *Universal Banking in America—What Can We Gain? What Can We Lose?* New York: Oxford University Press.

Savage, D.T. (1993), "Interstate Banking: A Status Report", *Federal Reserve Bulletin*, 79, 12, 1075–1089.

Schwartz, A.J. (1986), "Real and Pseudo-Financial Crises", in F. Capie and G.E. Wood (eds), *Financial Crises and the World Banking System*, London: Macmillan.

Schwartz, A. (1991), "Indonesia's Economic Boom: How Banks Paved the Way" in R. O'Brien and S. Hewin (eds), *Finance and the International Economy*, 4, 188–207.

Scott, D.H. (1992), "Revising Financial Sector Policy in Transitional Socialist Economies", *World Bank Policy Research Working Papers*, WPS No. 1034, November.

Scott, H.S. (1992), "Supervision of International Banking Post—BCCI", *Georgia State University Law Review*, 8, 3, 487–509.

Scott, H.S. and S. Iwahara (1994), *In Search of a Level Playing Field: The Implementation of the Basle Capital Accord in Japan and the United States*, Washington: Group of Thirty.

Shaffer, S. (1982), "A Non-structural Test for Competition in Financial Markets", in Federal Reserve Bank of Chicago, *Bank Structure and Competition—Conference Proceedings*, 225–243.

Shaffer, S. (1990), "A Test of Competition in Canadian Banking", Federal Reserve Bank of Philadelphia, Working Paper No. 90–18, July.

Shaffer, S. (1991), "Aggregate Deposit Insurance Funding and Taxpayer Bailouts", *Journal of Banking and Finance*, 15, 4/5, 1019–1038.

Shaffer, S. and E. David (1991), "Economies of Superscale in Commercial Banking", *Applied Economics*, 23, 283–293.

Shapiro, A.C. (1988), *Multinational Financial Management*, Boston: Allyn and Bacon.

Shea, T. (1993), "Reforms to Banking Regulation in Eastern Europe and the CIS" (unpublished mimeo, November).

Sherwood, D. (1992), "Process Re-engineering in the Banks", *Banker's Digest*, 12–13.

Shigehara, K (1991), "Japan's Experience with use of Monetary Policy and the Process of Liberalization, *Bank of Japan Monetary and Economic Studies*, 9, 1, 1–21.

Silber, W. (1975), "Towards a Theory of Financial Innovation. in W. Silber (ed.), *Financial Innovation*, Lexington: Heath.

Silber, W.L. (1983), "Recent Structural Change in the Capital Markets: The Process of Financial Innovation", *Annual Economic Review (Papers and Proceedings)*, May 73, 2, 89–95.

Simon, J.D. (1982), "Political Risk Assessment: Past Trends and Future Prospects", *Columbia Journal of World Business*, Fall 1982, 62–71.

Simons, K. (1992), "Mutual-to-Stock Conversions by New England Savings Banks: Where Has all the Money Gone?", *New England Economic Review: Federal Reserve Bank of Boston*, March/April, 43–53.

Simons, K. (1993) "Why Do Banks Syndicate Loans?", *New England Economic Review, Federal Reserve Bank of Boston*, January/ February, 45–52.

Simons, K. (1993), "Interest Rate Structure and the Credit Risk of Swaps", *New England Quarterly Review, Federal Reserve Bank of Boston*, July/ August, 23–34.

Sinclair, A., R. Smith, and I. Walter (1991), "Bankers Trust", Case Series in Finance and Economics, C07, New York University Salomon Center, Leonard N. Stern School of Business.

Sinkey, J. (1975), "A Multivariate Statistical Analysis of the Characteristics of Problem Banks", *Journal of Finance*, March, 30, 21–36.

Sinkey, J. and D.A. Carter (1994), "The Derivatives Activities of U.S. Commercial Banks", in Federal Reserve Bank of Chicago (ed.) *The Declining (?) Role of Banking, Proceedings of The 30th Annual Conference on Bank Structure and Competition*, 165–185. (Updated unpublished version, 1995).

Smirlock, M. (1985), "Evidence of the (Non) Relationship Between Concentration and Profitability in Banking", *Journal of Money, Credit and Banking*, 17, 69–83.

Smith, R.C. (1988), "American Express and Shearson Lehman Brothers", Case Series in Finance and Economics, C20, New York University Salomon Center, Leonard N. Stern School of Business.

Smith, R.C. (1988), "The Kidder Peabody Group", Case Studies in Finance and Economics, C26 New York University Salomon Center, Leonard N. Stern School of Business.

Smith, R.C. (1992), "Sakura Bank Ltd.", Case Series in Finance and Economics, C25, New York University Salomon Center, Leonard N. Stern School of Business.

Smith, R.C. (1994), "Schweizer Universal Bank", Case Series in Finance and Economics, C38, New York University, Leonard N. Stern School of Business.

Smith, R.C. and I. Walter (1991), "Reconfiguration of Global Financial Markets in the 1990s" in R. O'Brien and S. Hewin (eds), *Finance and the International Economy*, Vol. 4, Oxford: Oxford University Press, 142–168.

Smith, R.C. and I. Walter (1992), "The Privatisation of Bancomer", Case Series in Finance and Economics, C18, New York University, Salomon Center, Leonard N. Stern School of Business.

Smith, R.C. and I. Walter (1993), "Crédit Lyonnais", Case Series in Finance and Economics, C40, New York University, Salomon Center Leonard N. Stern School of Business.

Solow, R.M. (1982), "On the Lender of Last Resort", in Kindleberger, C.P. and Laffargue, J.P. (eds) *Financial Crises: Theory History and Policy*, New York: Cambridge University Press, 1982, 237–255.

Somerville, A.A. and R.J. Taffler (1993), "Banker Judgement Versus Formal Forcasting Models: The Case of Country Risk Assessment", *City University Business School Working Paper Series*, Centre for Empirical Research in Finance and Accounting, 93/4.

Spady, R. and A. Friedlaender (1978), "Hedonic cost functions for the regulated trucking industry", *Bell Journal of Economics*, 5, 9, 159–79 .

Startz, R. (1979), "Implicit Interest on Demand Deposits", *Journal of Monetary Economics*, 5, 515–536.

Startz, R. (1983), "Competition and Interest Rate Ceilings in Commercial Banking", *Quarterly Journal of Economics*, 98, May, 255–265.

Stiglitz, J.E. and A. Weiss (1981), "Credit Rating in Markets with Imperfect Information", *American Economic Review*, 71, June: 393–410.

Stiglitz, J.E. and A. Weiss (1988), "Banks as Social Accountants and Screening Devices for the Allocation of Credit", National Bureau of Economic Research Working Paper No. 2710.

Suzuki, Y. (1987), "Financial Reform in Japan: Developments and Prospects", *Bank of Japan Monetary and Economic Studies*, 5, 3, 33–47.

Szoke, M (1991), "Some Aspects of Building Up New Financial Structures: Reflections About the Hungarian Way", in R. O'Brien and S. Hewin (eds), *Finance and the International Economy*, Vol. 4, Oxford: Oxford University Press, 25–38.

Taffler, R.J. (1983), "The Assessment of Company Solvency and Performance Using a Statistical Model", *Accounting and Business Research*, Autumn 1983.

Taffler, R.J. (1984), "Empirical Models for the Monitoring of UK Corporations", *Journal of Banking and Finance*, 8, 199–227.

Terrell, H.S. (1986), "The Role of Foreign Banks in Domestic Banking Markets" in H.S. Cheng (ed.) *Financial Policy and Reform in Pacific Basin Countries*, New York: Lexington Books.

Terrell, H.S. (1990), "The Activities of Japanese Banks in the United Kingdom and the United States, 1980–88", *Federal Reserve Bulletin*, 76, 39–49.

Thompson, J.B. (1992), "Modelling the Bank Regulators' Closure Option: A Two-Step Logit Regression Approach", *Journal of Financial Services Research*, 6, 1, May, 5–23.

Tonks, I. and D. Webb (1989), "The Reorganisation of the London Stock Market: The Causes and Consequences of 'Big Bang'", London School of Economics Financial Markets Group Special Paper Series, Special Paper No. 20.

Tucker, A.L., J. Madura and T.C. Chiang (1991), *International Financial Markets*, New York: West Publishing Company.

Twinn, C. (1994), "Asset Backed Securitisation in the United Kingdom", *Bank of England Quarterly Bulletin*, 34, 2, May, 134–142.

Uyemura, D.G. and D.R. Van Deventer (1993), *Financial Risk Management in Banking: The Theory and Application of Asset Liability Management*, Cambridge: Bankers Publishing Company.

Viner, A. (1987), *Inside Japan's Financial Markets*, London: The Economist Publications Ltd., ch. 7, 8.

Vittas, D. and C. Neal (1992), "Competition and Efficiency in Hungarian Banking", Country Economics Department, *The World Bank, Policy Research Working Papers*, Financial Policy and Systems, October.

Walter, I. (ed.) (1985), *Deregulating Wall Street: Commercial Bank Penetration of the Corporate Securities Market*, New York: John Wiley and Sons.

Walter, I. and R. Smith (1989), *Investment Banking in Europe*, Oxford: Basil Blackwell.

Weatherstone, D. (1994), "Major Themes in Changing Banking and Financial Markets", in Federal Reserve, *Symposium Proceedings: International Symposium on Banking and Payment Services*, Washington: Federal Reserve System, 7–14.

White, E.N. (1986), "Before the Glass–Steagall Act: An Analysis of the Investment Banking Activities of National Banks", *Explorations in Economic History*, 23, 33–55.

White, L.J. (1991), *The S&L Debacle: Public Policy Lessons for Bank and Thrift Regulation*, New York: Oxford University Press.

White, L.J. (1992), "Change and Turmoil in US Banking: Causes, Consequences, and Lessons", Working Paper Series S-92-23 New York University Salomon Center, Stern School of Business, May.

Williams, M.L. (1975), "The Extent and Significance of the Nationalisation of Foreign Owned Assets in Developing Countries, 1956–1972", *Oxford Economic Papers*, 27, 260–73.

Williamson, O. (1981), "The Modern Corporation: Origins, Evolution, Attributes", *Journal of Economic Literature*, 19, 1537–68.

World Bank (1989), *World Development Report*, Oxford: Oxford University Press.

World Bank (Annual), *World Development Report*, Washington: World Bank.

World Bank (1993), *Global Economic Prospects and the Developing Countries*, Washington: World Bank.

World Bank (1994), *World Bank Debt Tables 1993–94*, Washington: World Bank.

Zenoff, D.B. (ed.) (1985), *International Banking Management and Strategies*, London: Euromoney Pubications.

Zimmer, S.A. and R.N. McCauley, (1991), "Bank Cost of Capital and International Competition", *Federal Reserve Bank of New York Quarterly Review*, 15, 3–4, 33–59.

Index